Musicians
& Composers
of the 20th Century

Musicians & Composers
of the 20th Century

Volume 2
Paul Desmond—Joan Jett

Editor
Alfred W. Cramer
Pomona College

SALEM PRESS
Pasadena, California   Hackensack, New Jersey

Editorial Director: Christina J. Moose
Developmental Editor: Jeffry Jensen
Acquisitions Editor: Mark Rehn
Manuscript Editor: Constance Pollock
Research Assistant: Keli Trousdale

Photograph Editor: Cynthia Breslin Beres
Production Editor: Andrea E. Miller
Page Design: James Hutson
Layout: William Zimmerman

Cover photo: Bob Dylan (Steve Morley/Redferns/Getty Images)

Library of Congress Cataloging-in-Publication Data

Musicians and composers of the 20th century / editor Alfred W. Cramer.
    p. cm.
Includes bibliographical references and index.
    ISBN 978-1-58765-512-8 (set : alk. paper) — ISBN 978-1-58765-513-5 (vol. 1 : alk. paper) —
ISBN 978-1-58765-514-2 (vol. 2 : alk. paper) — ISBN 978-1-58765-515-9 (vol. 3 : alk. paper) —
ISBN 978-1-58765-516-6 (vol. 4 : alk. paper) — ISBN 978-1-58765-517-3 (vol. 5 : alk. paper) —
1. Music—20th century—Bio-bibliography—Dictionaries. I. Cramer, Alfred William.
  ML105.M883 2009
  780.92'2—dc22
  [B]

2009002980

First Printing

Contents

Key to Pronunciation

Many of the names of personages covered in *Musicians and Composers of the 20th Century* may be unfamiliar to students and general readers. For these unfamiliar names, guides to pronunciation have been provided upon first mention of the names in the text. These guidelines do not purport to achieve the subtleties of the languages in question but will offer readers a rough equivalent of how English speakers may approximate the proper pronunciation.

Vowel Sounds

Symbol	Spelled (Pronounced)
a	answer (AN-suhr), laugh (laf), sample (SAM-puhl), that (that)
ah	father (FAH-thur), hospital (HAHS-pih-tuhl)
aw	awful (AW-fuhl), caught (kawt)
ay	blaze (blayz), fade (fayd), waiter (WAYT-ur), weigh (way)
eh	bed (behd), head (hehd), said (sehd)
ee	believe (bee-LEEV), cedar (SEE-dur), leader (LEED-ur), liter (LEE-tur)
ew	boot (bewt), lose (lewz)
i	buy (bi), height (hit), lie (li), surprise (sur-PRIZ)
ih	bitter (BIH-tur), pill (pihl)
o	cotton (KO-tuhn), hot (hot)
oh	below (bee-LOH), coat (koht), note (noht), wholesome (HOHL-suhm)
oo	good (good), look (look)
ow	couch (kowch), how (how)
oy	boy (boy), coin (koyn)
uh	about (uh-BOWT), butter (BUH-tuhr), enough (ee-NUHF), other (UH-thur)

Consonant Sounds

Symbol	Spelled (Pronounced)
ch	beach (beech), chimp (chihmp)
g	beg (behg), disguise (dihs-GIZ), get (geht)
j	digit (DIH-juht), edge (ehj), jet (jeht)
k	cat (kat), kitten (KIH-tuhn), hex (hehks)
s	cellar (SEHL-ur), save (sayv), scent (sehnt)
sh	champagne (sham-PAYN), issue (IH-shew), shop (shop)
ur	birth (burth), disturb (dihs-TURB), earth (urth), letter (LEH-tur)
y	useful (YEWS-fuhl), young (yuhng)
z	business (BIHZ-nehs), zest (zehst)
zh	vision (VIH-zhuhn)

Complete List of Contents

Volume 1

Volume 2

Volume 3

Volume 4

Volume 5

Contents lxxxix
Key to Pronunciation xci
Complete List of Contents xciii

Musicians
& Composers
of the 20th Century

Paul Desmond

American jazz saxophonist and composer

As the frantic tempi and technical virtuosity of bebop faded, Desmond emerged as a leading proponent of the new era of cool jazz. Paired with the flamboyant Dave Brubeck, Desmond produced an intimate, warm tone and innovative improvisations.

Born: November 25, 1924; San Francisco, California
Died: May 30, 1977; New York, New York
Also known as: Paul Emil Breitenfeld (birth name); the Stork

Principal recordings

ALBUMS: *Quartet*, 1952 (with Gerry Mulligan); *The Paul Desmond Quartet with Don Elliott*, 1956; *Blues in Time*, 1957 (with Mulligan); *First Place Again*, 1959 (with Jim Hall); *Paul Desmond and Friends*, 1959; *Desmond Blue*, 1961 (with Hall); *Late Lament*, 1962; *Two of a Mind*, 1962 (with Mulligan); *Glad to Be Unhappy*, 1963; *Take Ten*, 1963 (with Hall); *Bossa Antigua*, 1964; *Easy Living*, 1966; *Summertime*, 1968; *Bridge over Troubled Water*, 1969; *From the Hot Afternoon*, 1969; *Skylark*, 1973; *The Duets*, 1975 (with Dave Brubeck); *Like Someone in Love*, 1975; *Pure Desmond*, 1975; *The Only Recorded Performance*, 1982 (with the Modern Jazz Quartet).

The Life

Born Paul Emil Breitenfeld in San Francisco, Paul Desmond legally changed his name in 1946 after supposedly choosing Desmond out of a phone book. His father, an organist, accompanied silent films in theaters. His mother suffered from severe emotional problems. As a result, Desmond spent part of his childhood with relatives in New York. Desmond attended Polytechnic High School in San Francisco, and he began playing the clarinet during his freshman year at San Francisco State College. During World War II, Desmond enlisted in the Army in 1943 to play in the band as a saxophonist. He was stationed in San Francisco, where he was introduced to pianist Dave Brubeck. They went their separate ways following their discharge from the Army, but they reunited in 1951 in forming the Dave Brubeck Quartet. The quartet experienced a few personnel changes on bass and drums before finally settling on bassist Eugene Wright and drummer Joe Morello. "Take Five," from the 1959 landmark album *Time Out*, introduced unusual time signatures to the jazz world. After the quartet disbanded in 1967, Desmond continued to perform as a freelance saxophonist.

Residing in a New York penthouse, Desmond lived comfortably among friends, writers, and fellow musicians. His royalty earnings from "Take Five" alone allowed him to indulge his fondness for Scotch and cigarettes. Eventually, he was weakened to the point that his once-notorious ability to sustain a long phrase on a single breath became impossible. His final concert with Brubeck, in February, 1977, was witnessed by a full house of appreciative fans. However, Desmond was physically unable to perform an encore. Having developed lung cancer from a lifetime of heavy smoking, he died in New York on May 30, 1977.

The Music

The hot jazz of the 1920's, the danceable swing tempi of the 1930's, and the blistering tempi and complex harmonies of the bebop era set the stage for a decidedly different approach to jazz known as cool jazz. The cool jazz period of the late 1940's and 1950's utilized subdued volume, understated textures, improvisational economy, avoidance of dissonance, and little or no vibrato.

On Desmond's first encounter with Brubeck, the saxophonist took note of Brubeck's unusual, almost avant-garde style of piano playing, individualistic for the time. Their paths crossed again after World War II, when Desmond was a civilian and Brubeck was playing at the Geary Cellar with the Darryl Cutler trio. Desmond hired Brubeck and bassist Norman Bates from the trio to form his own jazz group. The role of leader did not appeal to Desmond, however, so he enrolled in San Francisco State College to become a writer. In the late 1940's, he joined Brubeck's octet.

The Dave Brubeck Quartet. In 1950 Desmond went on tour with the Jack Fina band, ending the tour in New York. Just one year later, Desmond was

Paul Desmond. (Library of Congress)

back in San Francisco to become a member of the legendary Dave Brubeck Quartet. A series of recorded concerts followed at universities. Jazz at Oberlin and Jazz at the College of the Pacific led to a recording contract with Columbia Records. Appropriately, the Dave Brubeck Quartet's first recording was *Jazz Goes to College* in 1954. Critics and fans took notice of Desmond's elegant tone and remarkable lyricism in improvised solos. Critics described Desmond's tone as a "dry martini."

The addition of drummer Morello in 1956 and bassist Wright in 1958 solidified the quartet's personnel until 1967, when the group disbanded. Morello's competence with unusual time signatures allowed the quartet to experiment with the 5/4 time signature.

"Take Five." "Take Five," the group's signature composition on the 1959 album *Time Out*, sold more than one million copies. Brubeck's thick chord voicings and Desmond's light, airy tone complemented each other effectively. Completely at ease together, Brubeck and Desmond quoted popular songs in their musical interplay, and they could change moods simultaneously. In a sense, they engaged in musical conversations. The quartet toured the world, performing three hundred concerts a year and recording numerous albums.

After the Quartet. The breakup of the Dave Brubeck Quartet in 1967 gave Desmond a second chance at becoming a writer. He abandoned his saxophone for about three years, and he completed his memoirs about his time with the quartet with an essay titled *How Many of You Are There in the Quartet?*—a question purportedly asked by an airline flight attendant. The memoirs were never released as a book, but a chapter was published in the British magazine *Punch*.

In semiretirement, Desmond performed concerts with baritone saxophonist Gerry Mulligan, guitarists Jim Hall and Ed Bickert, and with the Modern Jazz Quartet. A silver anniversary reunion tour with the Dave Brubeck Quartet in 1976 hastened the end of his career. In 1977 Desmond performed a farewell concert with Brubeck at New York's Lincoln Center.

Musical Legacy

Desmond personified cool jazz with his lyrical and wispy tone quality. Although more introspective than extroverted, he interacted with other musicians on a personal level with a wit and charm that also reached audiences. His audiences rewarded him by voting him to the top of the jazz polls year after year. The success and musical worth of the Dave Brubeck Quartet will be forever linked to Desmond's distinctive sound and style.

Part of Desmond's estate was bequeathed to the American Red Cross, and after his death the proceeds from his recording royalties were donated to the American Red Cross. The Paul Desmond papers are housed in the Holt-Atherton Special Collections at the University of the Pacific, the site of an early Dave Brubeck Quartet concert.

Douglas D. Skinner

Further Reading

Feather, Leonard. *The New Encyclopedia of Jazz.* Oxford, England: Oxford University Press, 1999. Short biographical entries of more than three thousand jazz musicians and their discographies include one devoted to Desmond.

Hall, Fred M. *It's About Time: The Dave Brubeck Story.* Fayetteville: University of Arkansas Press, 1996. This covers Desmond's life and career with the Dave Brubeck Quartet, and it includes discussions of experimentation with polytonality and unusual time signatures.

McPartland, Marion. *All in Good Time.* Oxford, England: Oxford University Press, 1987. One of the few women to succeed in jazz performance, McPartland writes about her experiences with various jazz musicians, including Desmond.

Ramsey, Doug. *Take Five: The Public and Private Lives of Paul Desmond.* Seattle, Wash.: Parkside, 2005. This biography was written by a jazz musician who was a friend of Desmond, and it includes commentary from other jazz musicians, two hundred photographs, and transcriptions of his improvised solos.

Tirro, Frank. *Living with Jazz.* Orlando, Fla.: Harcourt Brace, 1996. A jazz history textbook, with a focus on developing an appreciation for jazz, makes references to Desmond.

See also: Brubeck, Dave; McPartland, Marian; Parker, Charlie.

Neil Diamond

American rock singer, guitarist, and songwriter

With his steady output of albums and relentless worldwide touring, Diamond is one of most successful adult contemporary performers in the world. As a songwriter, he produces tunes with catchy hooks and simple, unforgettable melodies.

Born: January 24, 1941; Brooklyn, New York
Also known as: Neil Leslie Diamond (full name)

Principal recordings

ALBUMS: *Just for You*, 1967; *Velvet Gloves and Spit*, 1968; *Brother Love's Traveling Salvation Show*, 1969; *Touching You, Touching Me*, 1969; *Tap Root Manuscript*, 1970; *Stones*, 1971; *Moods*, 1972; *Serenade*, 1974; *Beautiful Noise*, 1976; *I'm Glad You're Here with Me Tonight*, 1977; *Carmelita's Eyes*, 1978; *You Don't Bring Me Flowers*, 1978; *September Morn*, 1979; *The Jazz Singer*, 1980; *On the Way to the Sky*, 1981; *Heartlight*, 1982; *Primitive*, 1984; *Headed for the Future*, 1986; *The Best Years of Our Lives*, 1988; *Lovescape*, 1991; *The Christmas Album*, 1992; *Up on the Roof: Songs from the Brill Building*, 1993; *The Christmas Album, Vol. 2*, 1994; *Tennessee Moon*, 1996; *The Movie Album: As Time Goes By*, 1998 (with Elmer Bernstein); *Three Chord Opera*, 2001; *Twelve Songs*, 2005.

The Life

Neil Leslie Diamond was born in Brooklyn, New York, to Jewish parents who had emigrated from Russia and Poland. An erstwhile shopkeeper, Diamond's father kept the family on the move around Brooklyn's neighborhoods with a series of stores before attaining middle-class prosperity during Diamond's teenage years. Diamond attended Erasmus Hall High School, the alma mater of other stars, such as Paul Anka and Barbra Streisand. Dropping out of New York University, Diamond sought his fortune writing pop songs. His most famous song of this era is the Monkees' version of "I'm a Believer."

The business of popular music was changing, however, and soon Diamond began performing his own songs rather than selling them to other acts. He had a number of hits, including two gold records, and he was a soothing alternative to the more anarchic rock and roll of the Woodstock era. Diamond reached a pinnacle of success in 1972 with ten sold-out shows at the Greek Theater in Los Angeles. His 1978 duet with Streisand, "You Don't Bring Me Flowers," went platinum. Though Diamond's album sales began to drop off in the mid 1980's, his tours remained highly successful. In 2005 he grossed seventy-one million dollars, the third highest earner on tour that year.

The Music

Diamond's work embodies the pop genre. He began his career in New York City's Brill Building, writing songs alongside such legends as Carole King, Jerry Leiber and Mike Stoller, and Ellie Greenwich and Jeff Barry. (Greenwich and Barry later produced Diamond's first solo albums on the Bang Records label.) Diamond's songs follow a traditional pop structure of verse-chorus-verse, relying on romantic themes and memorable melodies. From the 1970's through the 1990's, these songs were elaborately arranged and performed with embellishments, such as brass and rhythm sections and back-up singers.

Brother Love's Traveling Salvation Show. One of Diamond's best-known hits, "Sweet Caroline," was recorded a few months after *Brother Love's Traveling Salvation Show* was released in 1969. This was his first album with Uni, the label he signed with after leaving Bang. "Sweet Caroline" hit number four and was included on the second release of *Brother Love's Traveling Salvation Show.* The title track, which tells the tale of an itinerant preacher, hit number twenty-two. Diamond originally intended *Brother Love's Traveling Salvation Show* as a concept album, exploring revival meetings, but many of the songs stray from this theme back to Diamond's common subjects of love found and thwarted and of memories of home and youth. Late in 2007, Diamond admitted in an interview that "Sweet Caroline" was inspired by a picture in a magazine of the young Caroline Kennedy, President John F. Kennedy's daughter.

Hot August Night. This live double album was recorded on August 24, 1972, during a ten-day gig at the Greek Theater, and it solidified Diamond's renown for his live performances. Legendary rock critic Lester Bangs reviewed it favorably in *Rolling Stone,* and it went gold less than a month after it was released. The line-up of songs included early classic hits, such as "Solitary Man" and "Cherry, Cherry," and more recent fare from *Stones* and *Moods.* Diamond was at the height of his career during these performances in Los Angeles, and the recording captures his passion and his energy, as well as his characteristic mix of orchestration and spontaneity.

Beautiful Noise. *Beautiful Noise,* another platinum record, was notable for being produced by the Band's Robbie Robertson. The single "If You Know What I Mean" peaked at number eleven on the *Billboard* charts. Known for making hard-driving Dixie-influenced American rock and roll with his bandmates, Robertson seemed like an odd fit for Diamond's sometimes corny mainstream pop music. A connoisseur of songwriting, however, Robertson was able to help Diamond hone his lyrics and his arrangements into perfectly crafted pop-

ular songs. This was Diamond's third album for Columbia Records, and the company spent an unheard-of sum of $450,000 on the production of *Beautiful Noise.*

Twelve Songs. Though Diamond recorded many albums in the 1980's and 1990's and continued to reap gigantic profits from his tours, he was often written off as an oldies act or consigned to middle-of-the-road status. After 2001's *Three Chord Opera,* he began working on the songs that would eventually form *Twelve Songs.* He met Rick Rubin, whose career spans cofounding Def Jam Records, deejaying for the Beastie Boys, and cochairing Columbia Records. Diamond teamed with Rubin to produce an album that harked back to the rawness and energy of his earliest recordings. Diamond played guitar in the studio for the first time since the era of *Hot August Night.* The album debuted at number four, and it received widespread critical acclaim.

Musical Legacy

Diamond's impact on popular music is significant. His songs have been covered by artists as diverse as Johnny Cash, Elvis Presley, Deep Purple, and Urge Overkill, and he has inspired legions of impersonators and cover bands, such as the steadily popular San Francisco-based Super Diamond. His greatest accomplishment is transcending genres and time periods to appeal to a fan base made up of all ages. Simple lyrics and common themes sung with sincerity appealed to generations of Americans, and his worldwide fans are no less enthusiastic. Diamond took elements of the music he liked, ranging from the political folk music of Pete Seeger to the pop stylings of his compatriots in the Brill Building, and mixed in elements of other famous songwriters, such as Joni Mitchell and Leonard Cohen, to create a recognizable sound that has endured for decades.

Lacy Schutz

Further Reading

Blackwell, Roger, and Tina Stephan. "Madonna and Neil Diamond: Sex in Branding" In *Brands That Rock: What Business Leaders Can Learn from the World of Rock and Roll.* Hoboken, N.J.: John Wiley & Sons, 2004. A close look at Diamond's appeal as a branded product.

Jackson, Laura. *Neil Diamond: His Life, His Music, His Passion*. Toronto, Ont.: ECW Press, 2005. This biography recounts Diamond's life from his childhood in Brooklyn to international stardom.

Karanikas Harvey, Diana, and Jackson Harvey. *Neil Diamond*. New York: MetroBooks, 1996. This biography is heavily illustrated with photographs of Diamond.

Wiseman, Rich. *Neil Diamond: Solitary Star*. Toronto, Ont.: PaperJacks, 1988. A popular early biography, Wiseman provides a detailed picture, especially of early recording sessions.

See also: Bacharach, Burt; Cohen, Leonard; King, Carole; Leiber, Jerry; Newman, Randy; Robertson, Robbie; Sainte-Marie, Buffy; Stoller, Mike; Streisand, Barbra; Valens, Ritchie.

Bo Diddley

American rock and rhythm-and-blues singer, songwriter, and guitarist

Diddley—singer, guitarist, and songwriter—was a pivotal transition figure between blues and rock and roll. He is credited with popularizing the Latin-tinged Diddley beat and the rectangular Gretsch guitar.

Born: December 30, 1928; McComb, Mississippi
Died: June 2, 2008; Archer, Florida
Also known as: Ellas Otha Bates (birth name)

Principal recordings

ALBUMS: *Bo Diddley*, 1957; *Go Bo Diddley*, 1959; *Have Guitar, Will Travel*, 1959; *Bo Diddley in the Spotlight*, 1960; *Bo Diddley Is a Gunslinger*, 1961; *Bo Diddley Is a Lover*, 1961; *Bo Diddley*, 1962; *Bo Diddley and Company*, 1962 (with Norma-Jean Wofford); *Bo Diddley's a Twister*, 1962; *Hey! Bo Diddley*, 1962; *Bo Diddley's Beach Party*, 1963; *Surfin' with Bo Diddley*, 1963; *Two Great Guitars*, 1964 (with Chuck Berry); *500% More Man*, 1965; *Hey, Good Lookin'*, 1965; *Let Me Pass*, 1965; *The Originator*, 1966; *Boss Man*, 1967; *Road Runner*, 1967; *Super Blues*, 1968 (with Muddy Waters and Little Walter); *The Black Gladiator*, 1970; *Another Dimension*, 1971; *Where It All Began*, 1972; *The London Bo Diddley Sessions*, 1973; *Big Bad Bo*, 1974; *Pay Bo Diddley*, 1989; *Bo's Guitar*, 1992; *This Should Not Be*, 1992; *Who Do You Love*, 1992; *Promises*, 1994; *The Mighty Bo Diddley*, 1995; *A Man Amongst Men*, 1996; *Mona*, 1996.

The Life

Rock-and-roll pioneer Bo Diddley (DIHD-lee) was born Ellas Otha Bates in McComb, Mississippi. He was subsequently adopted by his mother's first cousin, Gussie McDaniel, with whom he moved to Chicago at age seven. The family settled on the city's south side, where Diddley studied violin and trombone before turning to the electric guitar as a teenager. During his youth, he experimented with instrument construction and sound modification, creating distorted amps through which he filtered his self-made rectangular guitars.

Diddley's musical career began on the corners of Chicago's famous Maxwell Street with his band, the Hipsters. By 1951 their repertoire, inspired by Louis Jordan and John Lee Hooker, helped them become regulars at the 708 Club. Diddley's flamboyant performing style and his idiosyncratic, clave-style rhythm attracted the attention of Chess Records, with which he had his first chart hit with the double-sided "Bo Diddley" and "I'm a Man" in 1955. A series of musical successes continued into the early 1960's. Although his popularity flagged during mid-decade, Diddley's stature as a rock-and-roll innovator was enhanced as popular British bands, such as the Rolling Stones, the Yardbirds, and the Animals, covered his songs.

Diddley subsequently established himself as a prolific touring musician; his frequent European appearances were documented in the 1973 documentary *Let the Good Times Roll*. From the late 1970's through the 1990's, he made brief appearances in Hollywood films (*Trading Spaces* in 2000 and *Blues Brothers 2000* in 1998), music videos (George Thorogood's 1982 "Bad to the Bone"), and ad campaigns (Nike's "Bo Don't Know Diddley" with Bo Jackson). He was inducted into the Rock and Roll Hall of Fame in 1987, and he was the recipient of the National Recording Arts and Sciences Lifetime Achievement Award and the Rhythm and Blues Foundation Lifetime Achievement Award. In 2008

Diddley died of heart failure at seventy-nine; fans sent to his funeral a floral tribute in the shape of his trademark rectangular guitar.

The Music

"I'm a Man" *and* **"Bo Diddley."** The original demo of these two songs, featuring Clifton James on drums, Billy Boy Arnold on harmonica, and Hipster Roosevelt Jackson on bass, caught producer Leonard Chess's attention in 1954. He signed Diddley and rerecorded with session musicians Lester Davenport (harmonica), Frank Kirkland (drums), Otis Spann (piano), and Jerome Green (maracas). This double-sided disc featured Diddley's distorted, tremolo-laden guitar sound; the faster, driving beat of jump blues; and the signature Diddley beat. This rhythm is alternately described as hambone rhythm or Latin three-two clave; coupled with Diddley's playing style, it formed the basis of rock and roll that relied on short, recogniz-

Bo Diddley. (AP/Wide World Photos)

able, syncopated rhythmic and melodic riffs. Of note is the guitar tremolo, a Diddley innovation he achieved by creating his own guitar effects processor. The album's eponymous A side reached number two on the rhythm-and-blues charts in 1955, while side B became a featured single for Muddy Waters, Jimi Hendrix, the Yardbirds, and the Who.

"Who Do You Love." The title of this 1956 Chess release offers a play on words: "Who do" is the unlucky "hoodoo" of African American folk practices. The song was not as successful as his hit, "Diddley Daddy," released that same year, yet it is notable for its virtual absence of melodic line and the complete dominance of the Diddley beat and rhythmic tension. Diddley's playing style here draws upon his early experience as a violinist, as he offers brash, scratched rhythms on a few strings at a time without offering complete chords. It, too, became a popular cover for artists such as the Rolling Stones and the Yardbirds, although Thorogood's 1978 version achieved the greatest commercial success.

"Say Man." Diddley's only *Billboard* Top 20 success came in 1959 with "Say Man," the humorous result of recorded studio banter between Diddley and percussionist Jerome Green. It is in line with the African American oral tradition of "playing the dozens," in which participants verbally contest their wit and mental acumen. The entertaining track presaged the commercial success of novelty songs throughout the 1960's and 1970's.

A Man Amongst Men. As the United States moved away from rock and roll to embrace newer popular music trends in the 1970's and 1980's, Diddley's recording career diminished and he had to carve out a living as a traveling performer. He did not enter the studio for a serious recording effort until 1996. *A Man Amongst Men* featured the Shirelles, Richie Sambora, Ron Wood, and Keith Richards, and it was nominated for a 1997 Grammy Award in the Best Contemporary Blues Album category. It was a departure from his late Chess recordings in its simplicity, offering pared-down arrangements and straightforward, driving beats rather than thick orchestration. The variety of beats and musical styles, including an attempt at hip-hop on "Kids Don't Do It," showcased Diddley's musical evolution and his reluctance to rely on older formulas.

Musical Legacy

Diddley was a key innovator in the development of rock and roll. His signature Latin-tinged beat and rhythmic innovations, his use of special effects such as reverb and tremolo, and his preference for distorted guitar sounds signaled the advent of a new popular music. As his career faltered in the United States, Diddley was lionized by a generation of 1960's British blues-influenced rockers, whose covers of Diddley's original material far outpaced the commercial success of his own. Over the years he fostered a group of young female guitarists in his bands, including Norma Jean "The Duchess" Wofford, Peggy "Lady Bo" Jones, and Cookie Redmond, at a time when women guitarists were an anomaly. His instrument and amplification adaptations expanded the power and range of the guitar and secured its role as the anchor of the rock ensemble. Diddley was the progenitor of 1970's funk, early hip-hop, and the late twentieth century blues revival.

Margaret R. Jackson

Further Reading

Gates, Henry Louis, Jr., ed. *African American Lives.* New York: Oxford University Press, 2004. This effort of the W. E. B. Du Bois Institute for African and African American Research at Harvard University includes a biographical sketch of Diddley and contextualizes him among key African American historical figures.

Kiersh, Edward. *Where Are You Now, Bo Diddley? The Stars Who Made Us Rock and Where They Are Now.* Garden City, N.Y.: Doubleday, 1986. Kiersch examines the fate of forty-seven early rock-and-roll figures. Short chapters combine interviews, photographs, and career synopses.

Lydon, Michael. *Boogie Lightning: How Music Became Electric.* New York: Dial Press, 1974. Lydon offers critical insight into Diddley's musical innovations and the role humor played in his music's success.

Traum, Artie, and Arti Funaro. *The Legends of Rock Guitar.* New York: Oak, 1986. This source includes a biography of Diddley and chronicles his influence on notable guitarists Keith Richards and Jeff Beck.

White, George R. *Bo Diddley, Living Legend.* Surrey, England: Castle Communications, 1995. This biography of Diddley includes extensive interviews with the artist and photographs spanning the breadth of his career. Includes a list of Diddley's recordings (with U.S. and U.K. releases), a list of recordings released on compact disc, a list of recordings of associates with whom Diddley appeared, a list of Diddley songs that made the *Billboard* rhythm and blues, Top 100, and British Record Retailer charts, and a compilation of Diddley's television and film appearances.

See also: Beck, Jeff; Berry, Chuck; Dixon, Willie; Domino, Fats; Eddy, Duane; Hendrix, Jimi; Howlin' Wolf; Jagger, Sir Mick; Jordan, Louis; Otis, Johnny; Paderewski, Ignace Jan; Waters, Muddy.

Marlene Dietrich

German pop and cabaret singer

Dietrich began entertaining as a singer in cabarets and in musical theater, and she later enjoyed a successful film career. When she appeared on concert stages toward the end of her life, her signature smoky voice and nostalgic songs enchanted audiences.

Born: December 27, 1901; Schöenberg, Germany
Died: May 6, 1992; Paris, France
Also known as: Marie Magdalene Dietrich (full name)

Principal recordings

ALBUMS: *Souvenir Album,* 1950; *American Songs in German for the OSS,* 1952; *Dietrich in Rio,* 1953; *Lili Marlene,* 1959; *Marlene,* 1965; *The Magic of Marlene,* 1969; *Marlene Dietrich's Berlin,* 1974.

The Life

Marie Magdalene Dietrich, who would take the stage name Marlene Dietrich (mahr-LEEN-eh DEE-trihk) was born Marie Magdalene Dietrich in Schöenberg, near Berlin. At age eleven she contracted her names into the shorter Marlene. In 1921 Dietrich began working as a chorus girl in theaters, and in 1922 she did a bit part in a film. Soon after, she met and married Rudolf Sieber, a minor film director, and had a daughter, Maria Sieber. In 1929 she performed the breakthrough role of Lola Lola in Josef von Sternberg's film *The Blue Angel* (1930). With a contract from Paramount Pictures, Dietrich and Sternberg moved to Hollywood, where they did six films from 1930 to 1935. Sternberg then left the United States, and Dietrich did not have an important film until *Destry Rides Again* (1939).

Germany's leader Adolf Hitler pleaded with Dietrich to return to Germany, but she refused. She became an American citizen and worked on raising money for war bonds that would help fund U.S. military efforts during World War II. She traveled to the front lines to entertain U.S. troops and to record anti-Nazi songs in German. She was awarded the Medal of Freedom by the United States and the Légion d'Honneur by France.

After the war, Dietrich performed worldwide as a concert singer. During a 1975 performance in Australia, she broke her leg and never fully recovered. Her husband died in 1976, but she was estranged from him and had numerous love affairs with well-known personalities. Mostly bedridden during her last decade, Dietrich died of kidney failure.

The Music

Dietrich presented her songs in a low, sensual, smoky, and world-weary voice, with a slight German accent that made the lyrics more intriguing. Her singing style is described as speak-sing, that is, speaking the lines of a song with a musical note in her voice. Her special vocal quality was reinforced by film directors who presented her visual image in strongly contrasting light and shadow, often emerging from clouds of cigarette smoke. Dietrich's unique musical personality was further enhanced by her androgynous look. From the time of her first major film, her upper body often was costumed in a coat and tie or bow tie and tuxedo, capped by a bowler or a top hat, and her long, beautiful, shapely legs were exposed in silk stockings held up by garters.

Signature Songs. Dietrich began singing professionally in cabarets and musical-theater productions when she was twenty years old, and in 1929 she played Lola Lola in the first German talkie film, *Der Blaue Engel*, released in the United States as *The*

Blue Angel. In it, Dietrich sang "Falling in Love Again," which became one of her signature songs. In the film *Destry Rides Again*, Dietrich sang "See What the Boys in the Back Room Will Have," in a scene where she turns a chair backward, sits down, brazenly raises her leg, and directs her attention to her costar, James Stewart, seated in the audience. Throughout the song, cigarette smoke from the audience passes between Dietrich and the camera, making visual her smoky vocal quality. The song's jaunty rendition runs counter to the morbid lyrics.

During World War II, while entertaining American troops on the front lines, Dietrich became associated with the nostalgic ballad "Lili Marlene," from which she took her nickname in later life. A German-language song that she performed throughout her career was "Du, Du Liebst Mir in Herzen."

After the war, Dietrich appeared in the 1947 film *Golden Earrings*, singing the title song, which became a popular hit. In the 1950 film *Stage Fright*, she sang "La Vie en rose" and the Cole Porter composition "The Laziest Gal in Town."

Cabarets and Concerts. During the late 1950's Dietrich gave up her film career and traveled the world as a cabaret singer and a major concert star. She also affected a more feminine image, her usual costume being a long white silk dress decorated with sequins. She sang all the songs associated with her past, and she sang new works, such as the powerful ballad "Where Have All the Flowers Gone?" Wistful songs such as this, presented in her nostalgic speak-sing style, moved Dietrich's audience.

Musical Legacy

Dietrich transformed the image of a vampish cabaret singer into the ideal of a Hollywood star. She appeared in almost sixty films, and her sensuality, expressed through her dark, moody songs, would be emulated by such stars as Sophia Loren and Elizabeth Taylor. In 1950 Dietrich signed with Columbia Records to record most of her well-known works. In the 1960's she joined with composer-conductor Burt Bacharach in recording her important performances. In 1964 she parted with Bacharach, but in 1967 and 1968 she appeared on Broadway, and for those performances she won a special Tony Award. In 1992 a plaque was unveiled in Berlin at the site of her birth, and in 1997 a stamp bearing her portrait was issued in Germany.

August W. Staub

Further Reading

Dietrich, Marlene, and Salvator Attanasio. *Marlene*. New York: Grove Press, 1989. Dietrich's autobiography, with a co-author, covers her life until three years before her death.

McLellan, Dianna. *The Girls: Sappho Goes to Hollywood*. New York: St. Martin's Press, 2001. A study of possible bisexual relationships between important film stars, including Dietrich.

Pascall, Jeremy. *Hollywood and the Great Stars*. New York: Crescent Books, 1976. A detailed discussion of Dietrich's career, along with impressive images from many of her films.

Riva, J. David. *A Woman at War: Marlene Dietrich Remembered*. Detroit, Mich.: Wayne State University Press, 2006. By her grandson, a presentation of Dietrich's contributions to the American World War II effort.

Riva, Maria. *Marlene Dietrich by Her Daughter*. New York: Random House, 1993. In a book published a year after her mother's death, Dietrich's daughter presents a touching story of her mother's life and accomplishments, with information gleaned from her mother's papers.

See also: Bacharach, Burt; Brel, Jacques; Piaf, Édith; Porter, Cole; Seeger, Pete.

Willie Dixon

American blues singer, bassist, and songwriter

Dixon was an indispensable "behind-the-scenes" musician in the postwar Chicago blues scene. He was a notable songwriter, and his compositions for Muddy Waters, Howlin' Wolf, Little Walter, Koko Taylor, and Otis Rush became part of their signature repertoires.

Born: July 1, 1915; Vicksburg, Mississippi
Died: January 29, 1992; Burbank, California
Also known as: Willie James Dixon (full name)

Principal recordings

ALBUMS: *Memphis Slim and Willie Dixon*, 1959 (with Memphis Slim); *Willie's Blues*, 1959; *The Blues Every Which Way*, 1960 (with Slim); *I Am the Blues*, 1970; *Peace*, 1971; *Catalyst*, 1973; *Maestro Willie Dixon and His Chicago Blues Band*, 1973; *What's Happened to My Blues?*, 1976; *Mighty Earthquake and Hurricane*, 1983; *Hidden Charms*, 1988; *Ginger Ale Afternoon*, 1989.

WRITINGS OF INTEREST: *I Am the Blues: The Willie Dixon Story*, 1989 (with Don Snowden; autobiography).

The Life

Willie James Dixon was born in Vicksburg, Mississippi, in 1915, and as a child he learned from his mother how to rhyme, which became an important tool for his songwriting. His earliest intensive contact with music was with barrelhouse pianist Little Brother Montgomery, and Dixon started writing songs as a teenager. In 1936 he moved to Chicago, where he became a boxer. In 1940 he and his friend Leonard "Baby Doo" Caston formed the Five Breezes with three other musicians, and Dixon learned to play bass. In 1941 and 1942 he was involved in a dispute over his refusal to serve in the military, and after the war he resumed musical activity with the Four Jumps of Jive. He reunited with Caston, and they formed the Big Three Trio with Bernardo Dennis (later replaced by Ollie Crawford). Dixon developed his compositional techniques and record production with this group.

In 1948, Dixon began his relationship with Aristocrat Records (later Chess Records) as a sideman. After the Big Three Trio broke up in 1953, Dixon became a staff member at Chess Records and also signed a contract as a recording artist for the Chess subsidiary Checker. In 1954 his composition for Muddy Waters, "Hoochie Coochie Man," became a big hit. As a vocalist, Dixon had his own hit, "Walking Blues." In 1956, because of a financial disagreement with the label owners, Dixon left for the newly founded Cobra Records, but in 1958 he returned to Chess and worked for there until 1971. In 1977 he sued Arc Music, the publishing company that belonged to Chess Records, to retrieve royalties from and copyrights of his compositions. In 1985 he sued Led Zeppelin for copyright infringement over "Whole Lotta Love," a reworking of his

Willie Dixon. (Hulton Archive/Getty Images)

song "You Need Love." In 1989 Dixon published his autobiography *I Am the Blues*. After a period of declining health, complicated by diabetes, Dixon died in 1992.

The Music

Dixon is best known as a blues songwriter, but he consciously departed from conventional blues. He claimed that Montgomery's ability to use a variety of musical styles was his most important musical inspiration.

Early Works. Montgomery's influence is seen in Dixon's compositions for the Big Three Trio. "Signifying Monkey" is a mixture of folk ballad and jive music, while "My Love Will Never Die" is in a melodramatic style. Other musical styles Dixon used for compositions for his early groups include country and western, novelty, Tin Pan Alley pop, slow blues, and fast boogie-woogie.

Compositions for Chess Artists. When composing, Dixon did not always follow the simple twelve-bar blues pattern. "Hoochie Coochie Man" is in a

sixteen-bar form, and "I Just Want to Make Love to You" is a mixture of the eight-bar form and *aaba* thirty-two-bar pop-song form.

Dixon had a characteristic way of constructing music and words, often using repetition of simple but memorable riffs consisting of two or three pitches as a support for vocal melodies. This musical device sounds similar to the structure of work songs that he would have heard as a youngster in the Mississippi Delta. He also had a characteristic way of writing lyrics—that is, listing or cataloging concepts or words that could be similar or opposite in meaning. This can be heard in his songs for Chess artists: "Hoochie Coochie Man," "I Just Want to Make Love to You," "I'm Ready," "Spoonful," "Twenty-nine Ways," "You Can't Judge a Book by Its Cover," and "Wang Dang Doodle."

Dixon had a remarkable ability to compose songs that effectively capitalized on the assigned artist's public image. His first experiment was "Third Degree" for Eddie Boyd in 1953. Then came the 1954 hit "Hoochie Coochie Man" for Waters, which linked the singer's machismo with a series of stop-time riffs. In "Back Door Man" for Wolf, Dixon added riffs in Wolf's distinctive style to a story about a man who meets secretly with other men's wives.

Dixon's work shows that his development of the performing personalities of Waters, Wolf, and Taylor was highly relevant to the tradition of the blues as a secular religion. In one analysis, blues performers are considered preachers of an alternative African American religion, one that philosophically opposed organized religious institutions. Dixon defined his blues as an expression of "the true facts of life," and he claimed his artistic goal was to express real-life wisdom through his music.

Musical Legacy

Dixon's songs were not only Chicago blues classics but also important in the repertoires of such rock artists as the Rolling Stones, Led Zeppelin, Cream, the Jeff Beck Group (with Rod Stewart), and the Doors. Dixon's work as a sideman, producer, and talent scout should not be underrated. Dixon played bass for many recording sessions of Chess artists, including Chuck Berry and Bo Diddley. As a producer, he (as well as the label owners) required Berry to revise his debut song, "Maybellene." As a talent scout, Dixon organized debut sessions for Albert King, Junior Wells, and Taylor. Dixon worked as an organizer of the American Folk Blues Festival in 1960 in Europe, which introduced blues to European audiences. In 1982 Dixon established the Blues Heaven Foundation to help musicians retrieve their copyrights, promote an ongoing blues tradition, and educate children. In 1994 his achievements were honored with his induction into the "early influence" category of the Rock and Roll Hall of Fame.

Mitsutoshi Inaba

Further Reading

Dixon, Willie. *Willie Dixon: The Master Blues Composer.* Milwaukee, Wis.: Hal Leonard, 1992. A collection of representative works. Along with transcriptions in guitar tablature, Dixon's explanation accompanies each song.

Dixon, Willie, with Don Snowden. *I Am the Blues: The Willie Dixon Story.* New York: Da Capo Press, 1989. Dixon's memories, including discussions of his childhood and youth, relationships with musicians and record-company owners, and stories behind his compositions.

See also: Berry, Chuck; Diddley, Bo; Howlin' Wolf; James, Etta; Morrison, Jim; Rush, Otis; Stewart, Rod; Terry, Sonny; Waters, Muddy; Williamson, Sonny Boy, I; Williamson, Sonny Boy, II.

Dr. Dre

American rapper

Dr. Dre was instrumental in the development of gangsta rap in the late 1980's and early 1990's, and he expanded his involvement in music by producing numerous successful rap albums.

Born: February 18, 1965; Los Angeles, California
Also known as: André Romelle Young (birth name)
Member of: World Class Wreckin' Cru; N. W. A.

Principal recordings

ALBUMS (as producer or coproducer): *Eazy-Duz-It,* 1988 (by Eazy-E); *Doggystyle,* 1993 (by Snoop Dogg); *No Limit Top Dogg,* 1999 (by Snoop Dogg); *The Slim Shady LP,* 1999 (by Eminem); *The Last Meal,* 2000 (by Snoop Dogg); *The Marshall Mathers LP,* 2000 (by Eminem); *The Eminem Show,* 2002 (by Eminem); *Get Rich or Die Tryin',* 2003 (by 50 Cent); *Encore,* 2004 (by Eminem); *The Massacre,* 2005 (by 50 Cent); *Tha Blue Carpet Treatment,* 2006 (by Snoop Dogg); *Curtis,* 2007 (by 50 Cent).

ALBUMS (solo): *The Chronic,* 1992; *Dr. Dre Presents . . . the Aftermath,* 1996 (with others); *2001,* 1999.

ALBUMS (with N. W. A.): *N. W. A. and the Posse,* 1987; *Straight Outta Compton,* 1989; *Efil4zaggin,* 1991.

The Life

Dr. Dre (dray) began his music career in the mid-1980's as a deejay at the Los Angeles dance club Eve After Dark. There he met other deejays and rappers active in the Los Angeles area, and in 1984 he joined the electro-hop group World Class Wreckin' Cru. In 1986 Dr. Dre met the rapper Ice Cube, and they started collaborating on songs for Ruthless Records, a label run by local rapper Eazy-E. Dr. Dre ultimately left the World Class Wreckin' Cru to join a rap group on the Ruthless Record label, N. W. A. (Niggaz With Attitude). The group—which utilized explicit lyrics that depicted life on the streets and originally consisted of Dr. Dre, Ice Cube, Eazy-E, DJ Yella, and electro artist the Arabian Prince—was instrumental in the development of gangsta rap. Easy-E was the leader of the group, but it was Dr. Dre and DJ Yella who handled the production duties. In addition to his duties with N. W. A., Dr. Dre produced albums for other artists, including solo albums by rapper D.O.C. and rhythm-and-blues singer Michel'le.

In 1991 Dr. Dre left N. W. A. and Ruthless Records to found Death Row Records with former bodyguard Suge Knight. In 1992 Dr. Dre released his first single, the title track to the film *Deep Cover* (1992), on the label, and later that same year he released his first solo album, *The Chronic.* The album, which prominently featured protégé Snoop Doggy Dogg, was extremely successful, and it was followed by *Doggystyle*, Dogg's debut album produced by Dr. Dre, the following year. *The Chronic* and *Doggystyle* were the only two albums fully produced by Dr. Dre while he was at Death Row Records, though he did produce a number of songs for other Death Row artists and for film sound tracks. While at Death Row, Dr. Dre did not play a prominent role in the developing feud between Death Row and New York record label Bad Boy Entertainment, nor was he consulted about signing new artists such as M. C. Hammer and Tupac Shakur. These activities and tensions with Knight, along with concerns over the direction of the label, resulted in Dr. Dre leaving Death Row Records in 1996.

After leaving Death Row Records, Dr. Dre formed his record label, Aftermath Entertainment. Most of the albums initially issued by the label, including the compilation album *Dr. Dre Presents . . . the Aftermath*, did not reach commercial expectations. The label had its first big success with Eminem's album, *The Slim Shady LP*, in 1999. Dr. Dre was the executive producer, and it included three tracks produced by Dr. Dre, including "Guilty Conscience," with Dr. Dre as a rapper. That same year Dr. Dre issued his second solo album, *2001*, and after its release he refocused on his activities as a producer.

The Music

More gifted as a producer than as a rapper, Dr. Dre has always been more active behind the scenes than in front of the microphone. Through his signature G-Funk (gangsta funk) beats, Dr. Dre shaped the sound of West Coast rap, and gangsta rap in particular. Derived from the funk music of George Clinton and the Parliament Funkadelic (P-Funk), G-Funk, utilized slowed-down P-Funk beats along with slow-rolling melodies, prominent bass lines, and heavy synthesizers. The smooth, multilayered G-Funk sound that became synonymous with West

Dr. Dre. (Gary Hershorn/Reuters/Landov)

Coast rap contrasted with the more punctuated rhythms and sparser soundscape of East Coast rap, and it helped fuel the rivalry between the two coasts. The G-Funk sound was first hinted at on N. W. A.'s *Efil4zaggin*, but it came to fruition with the release of *The Chronic*. In addition, Dr. Dre generally utilized live musicians instead of samples to interpolate rhythms and melodies throughout his songs.

As a rapper, Dr. Dre's music presents the typical themes of gangsta rap that glorify criminal activities and extravagant lifestyles and support sexual promiscuity and the use of drugs and alcohol. Not a gifted lyricist, Dr. Dre frequently enlisted outside help for his songs.

Straight Outta Compton. N. W. A.'s second album, *Straight Outta Compton*, helped define the gangsta rap genre and established Los Angeles as a center for rap music. It was also the first gangsta rap album to find a large audience, even without any airplay on radio or television. Lyrically, *Straight Outta Compton* explicitly addresses violent criminal behavior and is musically sparser than later Dr. Dre-produced albums. The most controversial song on the album, "Fuck tha Police," is an indictment of the police's brutal treatment of young African American males, drawing attention to racial profiling in the inner city. The song centers on a mock courtroom skit with each of the rapping members of N. W. A. taking a verse. "Fuck tha Police" contributed to N. W. A.'s notoriety as the world's most dangerous group and resulted in a letter of warning being sent to their record label by the Federal Bureau of Investigation.

The Chronic. *The Chronic* helped establish the West Coast rap style, including Dr. Dre's signature G-Funk sound, and it challenged the control New York rappers had of the industry. The album also popularized the newly founded Death Row record label, and it increased the appeal of gangsta rap for mainstream suburban audiences. Lyrically, songs on *The Chronic* address inner-city crime, express misogynist themes, and direct insults at former N. W. A. bandmate Easy-E. In addition to Dr. Dre, *The Chronic* features a number of guest artists, including rapper Dogg, who appears on twelve of the album's sixteen tracks. Dogg also appears on all three of the album's singles, and he wrote much of the album's lyrics. The first, and most successful, of the album's singles was "Nuthin' but a 'G' Thang," which contains several references to Long Beach, Dogg's hometown, and Compton. The second single, "Fuk wit Dre Day," is one of the songs on *The Chronic* that attacks Easy-E, along with East Coast rapper Tim Dog and Luke Campbell of the rap group 2 Live Crew. "Let Me Ride," the final single, while the least successful commercially, won Dr. Dre the 1994 Grammy Award for Best Rap Solo Performance. After the release of *The Chronic*, Dr. Dre focused his attention on producing, and he did not release another full solo album for seven years.

2001. Commonly referred to as *The Chronic 2* or *The Chronic 2001*, Dr. Dre released the album *2001* in 1999. It marks a return by Dr. Dre to some of the same subject matter addressed on his first album, *The Chronic*. Most of the songs on *2001* contain the stereotypical explicit lyrics and criminal themes of gangsta rap, but the album is still sonically innovative. Produced by Dr. Dre and fellow Aftermath producer Mel-Man, *2001* expands on the G-Funk sound of *The Chronic* by adding strings and other elements while still sounding leaner. Dr. Dre enlists the help of several guest artists to augment his own rapping, and they figure prominently in the singles released from the album. The first single, "Still

D.R.E.," announces Dr. Dre's return as a solo artist, and it features guest artist Dogg and lyrics cowritten by Jay-Z. "Forgot About Dre," the next single, features Eminem and samples from "Vela, Together We Await the Storm," by the Human Abstracts. The song won several awards, including the 2001 Grammy Award for Best Rap Performance by a Duo or Group and the 2000 MTV Video Music Award for Best Rap Video. The final single, "The Next Episode," features rappers Snoop Dogg, Nate Dogg, and Kurupt, and it samples David McCallum's "The Edge." "The Next Episode" was later sampled by the hip-hop group City High for its successful 2001 single "What Would You Do."

Musical Legacy

Through his early work with N. W. A., Dr. Dre was instrumental in the creation of gangsta rap, the dominant genre of rap through the mid-1990's. As a producer at Death Row Records, his slow, synthesizer-based G-Funk beats became the sound of West Coast, and some East Coast, rap, and it helped rap become more than just party music. His sound was frequently emulated by other producers and used by Dr. Dre in the albums and songs that he produced for others. His influence continued to be felt throughout the 1990's and 2000's, as he produced and discovered new talent at both Death Row and Aftermath. Protégés Dogg, Eminem, and 50 Cent have all drawn upon Dr. Dre's credibility and resources in order to find their success in the music industry. Dr. Dre remains one of the most influential figures in hip-hop, helping to produce the next generation of rappers that now dominate the industry.

Throughout his career Dr. Dre has received a number of Grammy Awards. In addition to the ones he received for "Let Me Ride" and "Forgot About Dre," he, along with BLACKstreet and Queen Pen, received the 1998 Grammy Award for Best Rhythm and Blues Performance by a Duo or Group for "No Diggity," and, along with Eminem, he received the 2001 Grammy Award for Best Rap Album for Eminem's *The Marshall Mathers LP*.

Matthew Mihalka

Further Reading

Borgmeyer, John, and Holly Lang. *Dr. Dre: A Biography*. London: Greenwood Press, 2007. This biography focuses on the early portion of Dr. Dre's career with N. W. A. and as a solo artist on Death Row Records, though it also includes a short chapter on his activities since leaving Death Row Records.

Brown, Jake. *Dr. Dre in the Studio: From Compton, Death Row, Snoop Dogg, Eminem, 50 Cent, the Game, and Mad Money, the Life, Times, and Aftermath of the Notorious Record Producer, Dr. Dre.* New York: Colossus Books, 2006. This book is a chronological exploration of Dr. Dre's activities as a record producer. Includes numerous black-and-white photographs and a partial discography presented as a timeline.

Oliver, Richard, and Tim Leffel. *Hip-Hop, Inc.: Success Strategies of the Rap Moguls.* New York: Thunder's Mouth Press, 2006. A chapter in this book chronicles the history of gangsta rap, focusing primarily on the rise of Death Row Records and its eventual fall, when Dr. Dre left the label in 1996.

Quinn, Eithne. *Nuthin' But a "G" Thang: The Culture and Commerce of Gangsta Rap.* New York: Columbia University Press, 2005. This book focuses on the emergence of gangsta rap and describes Dr. Dre's involvement in its development.

Ro, Ronin. *Dr. Dre: The Biography.* New York: Thunder's Mouth Press, 2007. This book covers the life of Dr. Dre, with a significant amount of information about his career since leaving Death Row Records. Included is a discography and a filmography.

_____. *Have Gun Will Travel: The Spectacular Rise and Violent Fall of Death Row Records.* New York: Doubleday, 1998. This book recounts the history of Death Row Records, the label Dr. Dre co-founded. Includes several black-and-white photographs.

Wang, Oliver, ed. *Classic Material: The Hip-Hop Album Guide.* Toronto, Ont.: ECW Press, 2003. This book contains a section that analyzes Dr. Dre's *The Chronic*, and other sections investigate the Dr. Dre-produced albums *Doggystyle* by Snoop Doggy Dogg and *The Slim Shady LP* by Eminiem.

See also: Eminem; 50 Cent; Ice Cube; Jay-Z; Salt and Pepa; Shakur, Tupac; Snoop Dogg.

Charles Dodge
American classical composer

Dodge is best known for his work with synthesized voice sounds, with fractal geometry, and with combining computer music with live performers.

Born: June 5, 1942; Ames, Iowa
Also known as: Charles Malcolm Dodge (full name)

Principal works
ELECTRONIC WORKS: *Cascando*, 1978; *Profile*, 1990; *Any Resemblance Is Purely Coincidental*, 1994; *Extensions*, 1994; *Speech Songs*, 1994; *Changes*, 1998; *Earth's Magnetic Field*, 1998.
ORCHESTRAL WORK: *Composition in Five Parts*, 1982.

The Life
While pursuing a bachelor of arts degree in composition at the University of Iowa, Charles Malcolm Dodge attended Vermont's Bennington Composers Conference in 1963. There he met James Tenney, Edgard Varèse, and Vladimir Ussachevsky, which led to his interest in computer music. He finished his undergraduate studies in 1964, and then he earned at Columbia University a master of arts in 1966 and a doctorate of musical arts in 1970. Among his teachers were Richard Hervig, Otto Luening, and Chou Wen-chung. He also studied electronic music with Ussachevsky and computer music with Godfrey Winham at Princeton University from 1969 to 1970.

Between 1971 and 1977, Dodge worked at Bell Telephone Laboratories, and he taught in the music department at Columbia University from 1970 to 1980. Subsequently, he founded the Center for Computer Music at Brooklyn College of the City University of New York, and he taught at the City University Graduate Center. In the mid-1990's he became visiting professor at Dartmouth College in Hanover, New Hampshire.

The Music
Dodge's early instrumental works, such as *Folia* (1965), project different tempi simultaneously,

showing the influence of composers such as Elliott Carter. Works from his graduate-school period exhibit serial principles of musical organization, a reflection of the dominant compositional philosophies at Columbia and Princeton at the time. The influence of Milton Babbitt, in particular his *Ensembles for Synthesizer*, can be seen in Dodge's twelve-tone work for computer *Changes*.

While Dodge was investigating at Bell Telephone Laboratories the feasibility of using computers to make vocal music, he traveled to Stockholm, where he encountered the music of text-sound composers, among them Lars-Gunnar Bodin and Bengt-Emil Johnson. Their works made an especially strong impression, leading Dodge to compose works featuring synthesized voice sounds. Dodge expanded the range of media utilized, including works for tape alone, for tape with musical instruments, for tape with voice, for radio plays, and for musical theater. In addition, Dodge incorporated algorithmic compositional techniques to further unify his musical material.

Earth's Magnetic Field. While an instructor at Princeton in 1969-1970, Dodge received a telephone call from the Goddard Institute for Space Studies. Geophysicists there had a way of recording the effects of the radiation of the sun on Earth's magnetic field, that resembled, in its notation, music (sometimes referred to as a Bartels musical diagram). For his computer-derived tape piece *Earth's Magnetic Field*, Dodge interpreted measurements from January 1 to March 4, 1961, to determine the pitch, duration, tempo, and register of the piece. Although the work makes extensive use of reverberation and location techniques to enhance the simple timbre created through subtractive synthesis, these were determined independently of the other musical elements.

Speech Songs. In 1972 Dodge began composing his first work for synthesized voice, *Speech Songs*, a group of four short songs based on texts by poet Mark Strand. They were realized at Bell Telephone Laboratories in late 1972 and early 1973. First, Dodge recorded himself reading the texts on tape, and then he entered the sound into the computer through an analog-to-digital converter. The computer analyzed the voice sound and resynthesized it, based on that analysis, allowing him to edit the analysis to produce altered vocal effects.

The four songs trace a change in speech synthesis techniques. The first three songs, "A Man Sitting in the Cafeteria," "He Destroyed Her Image," and "When I Am With You," were made with a formant tracking system and present monophonic settings in which the original voice recording is not drastically altered in the process of synthesis. The fourth song, "The Days Are Ahead," was realized with the recently invented linear predictive coding technique, and it presents a polyphonic setting of the text with extensive alteration of the pitch material.

Any Resemblance Is Purely Coincidental. Commissioned by the Arts Council of Great Britain in 1980, this work for piano and tape marks an interesting new direction in Dodge's use of processed voice sounds. According to the composer, the title of the work recalls the standard disclaimer from television crime dramas of the 1950's. The tape part is constructed from a digitized version of the 1907 recording of tenor Enrico Caruso singing "Vesti la giubba" from Ruggero Leoncavallo's opera *I Pagliacci* (1892). In the course of the work, the voice searches for an accompaniment, and it is heard at different times with electronic sounds, with copies of itself, with the live piano, and with combinations of them all. The work's initial efforts are humorous, with the piano set on center stage as if Caruso were somehow present; as the work progresses other emotions come into play.

Musical Legacy

Dodge's *Speech Songs* was one of the first pieces in a new genre: music compositions based on the computer analysis of recordings of a wide variety of material, including speech, song, and musical instruments. The work of Dodge, and others associated with speech synthesis, such as Paul Lansky, influenced such popular bands as the Electric Light Orchestra, Kraftwerk, and Styx.

Dodge's numerous honors include the Bearns Prize, Woodrow Wilson National Fellowship, and two Guggenheim Fellowships. He has received commissions from the Fromm Music Foundation, the Koussevitzky Music Foundation, Swedish National Radio, Groupe de Musique Experimentale de Bourges, the Los Angeles Philharmonic's New Music Group, and the American Guild of Organists.

Philip D. Nauman

369

Further Reading

Dodge, Charles. "*In Celebration*: The Composition and Its Realization in Synthetic Speech." In *Composers and the Computer*. Los Altos, Calif.: William Kaufmann, 1985. The composer's description of the methodology behind his composition *In Celebration*, including a copy of the poem and the score.

_____. "On *Speech Songs*." In *Current Directions in Computer Music Research*. Cambridge, Mass.: MIT Press, 1989. The composer revisits the musical and technological ideas that contributed to the genesis of his work *Speech Songs*.

_____. "*Profile*: A Musical Fractal." *Computer Music Journal* 12 (1988): 10-14. The composer's explanation of how fractal geometry played a central role in the method for choosing the elements and the structure of his composition *Profile*.

Dodge, Charles, and Thomas Jerse. *Computer Music: Synthesis, Composition, and Performance*. 2d ed. New York: Schirmer Books, 1997. A survey and explanation of the fundamental techniques of computer audio.

Thieberger, Ed M. "An Interview with Charles Dodge." *Computer Music Journal* 19 (1995): 11-24. Details Dodge's experiences at the University of Iowa, Bell Telephone Laboratories, IBM, Princeton University, and Columbia University in the late 1960's and early 1970's. Includes a significant section on *Earth's Magnetic Field*.

See also: Babbitt, Milton; Caruso, Enrico; Varèse, Edgard.

Arnold Dolmetsch

French classical pianist, violinist, viol player, lute player, and harpsichord player

Dolmetsch was a performer, instrument maker, and musicologist, and one of the first advocates of the early music revival. Performers who use period instruments are indebted to Dolmetsch's pioneering work in the restoration and reproduction of those artifacts.

Born: February 24, 1858; Le Mans, France
Died: February 28, 1940; Haslemere, Surrey, England
Also known as: Eugène Arnold Dolmetsch (full name)

Principal recordings

ALBUMS: *Domenico Scarlatti: Pastorale from Sonata in D Minor No. 9*, 1920 (harpsichord); *G. F. Handel: The Harmonious Blacksmith*, 1920 (harpsichord); *J. S. Bach: Toccata in G Major*, 1920 (harpsichord); *Nowell's Galliard/Tower Hill*, 1920 (lute); *Rameau: Fugue "La Forqueray" from the 5ième Concert/Le Cupis*, 1921 (violin); *Thomas Tompkins: Pavan in F for Five Violins*, 1921 (violin); *Columbia History of Music by Eye and Ear: Vol. 1, Part 10; Weelkes, Fantasy for a Chest of Six Viols*, 1929 (viol); *Columbia History of Music by Eye and Ear: Vol. 1, Part 11; Dowland, Awake Sweet Love*, 1929 (lute); *Columbia History of Music by Eye and Ear: Vol. 1, Part 12; Bach, Prelude and Fugue in B Flat*, 1933 (piano); *Columbia History of Music by Eye and Ear: Vol. 2, Part 11; Bach, Prelude and Fugue in C*, 1933 (piano).

WRITINGS OF INTEREST: *The Interpretation of the Music of the Seventeenth and Eighteenth Centuries Revealed by Contemporary Evidence*, 1915.

The Life

Eugène Arnold Dolmetsch (DOHL-mehtch) was born in Le Mans, France, to a family of instrument-builders, and as a child he was trained first as a pianist, then as a violinist. He was a violin student at the Brussels Conservatory from 1881 to 1883 under Henri Vieuxtemps, and he later continued his studies at the newly founded Royal College of Music in London. He taught violin at Dulwich College from 1885 to 1889. Dolmetsch spent most of his life in England, though he worked as an instrument maker in Boston from 1905 to 1911 and in Paris from 1911 to 1914. After his stay in Paris, he returned to England. In 1917 he moved to Haslemere, Surrey, where, in 1920, he established an instrument workshop. In 1925 he and his family held the first Haslemere Festival, which lasted two weeks. Dolmetsch was married three times: to Marie Morel, then to Élodie Dolmetsch (his former sister-in-law), and finally to Mabel Johnston.

The Music

Dolmetsch's career involved three interrelated projects: restoration and reproduction of old instruments; scholarship concerning music from the Renaissance and Baroque eras; and the performance of that music using the instruments he helped to revive.

Instrument Making. Dolmetsch first became interested in historical instruments while living in Brussels, where he attempted his earliest restorations, first of an old square piano and then of a viola d'amore. He later acquired and restored such instruments as a lute, a harpsichord, a clavichord, a recorder, a viola da gamba, and a violone, teaching himself (as well as his family members and students) to play the instruments. By 1893 he moved from restoring antique instruments to building reproductions. His activities and success as an instrument-builder coincided with the Arts and Crafts movement in England, a reaction against the factory- and machine-oriented products of the Industrial Revolution. The Arts and Crafts Exhibition Society had mounted exhibitions in London beginning in 1888, and it was at that event in 1896 that Dolmetsch displayed his first handmade harpsichord. He continued his instrument-making while employed by Chickering and Sons, the piano firm based in Boston, where he ran his own department dedicated to the reproduction of early instruments, and later by the Parisian firm of Gaveau, maker of pianos.

Scholarship. By the time Dolmetsch began his studies in London, the field of musicology had entered its nascent stages; indeed, Dolmetsch's mentor at the Royal College, Sir George Grove, was among the most ambitious and prominent scholars of music, publishing the first edition of his dictionary of music in 1879. Early in his career Dolmetsch produced editions of trio sonatas by George Frideric Handel and Arcangelo Corelli, in which he realized the figured bass. In 1904 he published a series of articles in the art journal *The Connoisseur:* two on the lute and one on viols. Though not without inaccuracies, these articles were based on the author's own research into and experience with early instruments, and they demonstrated a knowledge of historical treatises on the instruments and questions of performance. Dolmetsch's most substantial scholarly publication, *The Interpretation of the Music of the Seventeenth and Eighteenth Centuries Revealed by Contemporary Evidence*, appeared in 1915, and it was reprinted twice later in the century. The volume was among the first to offer evidence from primary sources regarding performance practices of the Baroque era. The book treats the topic of ornamentation at great length, and it also contains sections on tempo, rhythmic alteration, figured bass, fingering, and historical instruments. Though Dolmetsch's study is allied to the scholarly work of the period, its conclusion disdains impractical musicology, so wholly disconnected from performance, while simultaneously stating the author's views on the necessity of reviving older performance traditions.

Performance. While a student in London, Dolmetsch began to explore the musical holdings of the British Museum and other libraries, where he discovered long-forgotten manuscripts and prints of Renaissance and Baroque sheet music. He frequently performed these works at gatherings in his home, and, starting in 1890, in public concerts; in these concerts he and his fellow performers used the period instruments he had restored or built. However, his most important performances were at the Haslemere Festival, where he, his family members, and his students presented concerts each evening; the daytime was taken up with displays and demonstrations of historical instruments. Because of the novelty of Dolmetsch's undertakings, his performances displayed problems, especially imperfection of the instruments and playing techniques. Indeed, for Dolmetsch imperfect performances were no sign of musical weakness; most of the music he played was intended to be played by amateurs in private circles, and these were precisely the circumstances he tried to reproduce.

Musical Legacy

Dolmetsch's impact has been felt more keenly since his death than it was during his life. Most performers and critics of his day exhibited little sympathy for his work in the fields of historical instruments and music. Dolmetsch was partly responsible for his rift with the musical mainstream, since he seems to have taken a somewhat accusatory stance toward the performers of his day. Nevertheless, after the first festivals at Haslemere, and especially in the 1930's, musicians and the musical public were increasingly accepting of Dolmetsch's ideas. In 1933 the composer Percy Grainger published an article commending Dolmetsch for his steady adherence to the British musical tradition, and an obituary in the *Musical Times* praised him as a "creative genius."

The Haslemere Festival and the workshop there continued under the guidance of Dolmetsch's descendants and the Dolmetsch Foundation, established in 1929. In the late 1930's Dolmetsch was honored by both the British government and the French government; the former granted him a civil list pension in 1937, and the latter made him Chevalier de la Légion d'Honneur in 1939.

Rebecca Cypess

Further Reading

Campbell, Margaret. "Arnold Dolmetsch." In *The New Grove Dictionary of Music and Musicians*, edited by S. Sadie and J. Tyrrell. London: Macmillan, 2001. A concise and readable summary of Dolmetsch's life and work.

_____. *Dolmetsch: The Man and His Work*. Seattle: University of Washington Press, 1975. An extensive biography of Dolmetsch, from the perspective of an approving author.

Dolmetsch, Arnold. *The Interpretation of the Music of the Seventeenth and Eighteenth Centuries Revealed by Contemporary Evidence*. London: Novello, 1969. Dolmetsch's most important contribution to musical scholarship. Though many of his conclusions have been modified or corrected by later scholars, the work was pioneering in its attempt to understand the performance conventions of the Baroque era.

Grainger, Percy. "Arnold Dolmetsch: Musical Confucius." *Musical Quarterly* 19 (1933): 187-98. This important twentieth century composer praises Dolmetsch for his advocacy of the British musical tradition.

Haskell, Harry. *The Early Music Revival: A History*. Mineola, N.Y.: Dover, 1996. An entertaining evaluation of the early music movement, with an informative chapter on Dolmetsch.

See also: Grainger, Percy Aldridge.

Eric Dolphy

American jazz composer, flutist, clarinetist, and saxophonist

A jazz reedist, Dolphy was a major figure in the free jazz and Third Stream musical movements of the 1960's.

Born: June 20, 1928; Los Angeles, California
Died: June 29, 1964; Berlin, Germany
Also known as: Eric Allan Dolphy (full name)

Principal recordings

ALBUMS: *Hot and Cool Latin*, 1959; *Truth*, 1959; *Wherever I Go*, 1959; *Candid Dolphy*, 1960; *Dash One*, 1960; *Erich Dolphy*, 1960; *Far Cry*, 1960 (with Booker Little); *Fire Waltz*, 1960; *Here and There*, 1960; *Looking Ahead*, 1960; *Other Aspects*, 1960; *Out There*, 1960; *Outward Bound*, 1960 (with the Eric Dolphy Quintet); *Status*, 1960; *Latin Jazz Quintet*, 1961; *Quartet 1961*, 1961; *The Quest*, 1961 (with others); *Softly, as in a Morning Sunrise*, 1961; *Vintage Dolphy*, 1962; *Conversations*, 1963; *Iron Man*, 1963; *Last Date*, 1964; *Naima*, 1964; *Out to Lunch*, 1964; *Unrealized Tapes*, 1964.

The Life

Eric Allan Dolphy (DOHL-fee) was born in Los Angeles, California, to Sadie and Eric Dolphy, Sr., who were of West Indian descent. He took up clarinet while in elementary school, and he eventually started playing alto saxophone at local dances. Dolphy practiced avidly, starting in the hours before school and playing late into the night. He studied music at Los Angeles City College, and after serving two years in the Army, he resumed his studies at the U.S. Naval School of Music. He returned to Los Angeles in 1953, and he began his performing career in earnest, meeting jazz luminaries such as Max Roach and Ornette Coleman, with whom he would later perform and record. Dolphy's first major break came as a member of the drummer Chico Hamilton's band. The film *Jazz on a Summer's Day* (1960) captured the group's performance at the 1958 Newport Jazz Festival, which was Dolphy's first broad exposure. Shortly thereafter, he moved to New York City, where he recorded and performed with Coleman, Charles Mingus, John Coltrane, Gunther Schuller, and Oliver Nelson. After his initial successes in the early 1960's, his increasingly experimental music began to lose face, and in 1964 he decided to settle in Europe where he found audiences less averse to his challenging music. He died in a Berlin hospital of diabetes-related heart failure.

The Music

Dolphy made major contributions to the emergent fields of free jazz and Third Stream music. His training in the swing and bebop traditions is reflected in all of his work, but his ability to move back and forth between tonally grounded harmonies and highly dissonant, nearly atonal frameworks distinguished his improvisational voice. Broadly speaking, his compositional approach begins with a stylistically idiomatic jazz melody, or "head," which sets the parameters for the harmonies and rhythms of his solos. This avant-garde approach to jazz composition and performance set Dolphy on a course that often overlapped with the European art music tradition, as evident in his performance of Edgard Varèse's *Density 21.5* (1936) for flute at the 1962 Ojai Music Festival and his collaborations with Gunther Schuller's Third Stream projects, most notably the album *Jazz Abstractions* (1960).

Early Works. Dolphy's first year in New York resulted in an unprecedented outpouring of creative activity from the artist. He was a notable sideman on a number of important recordings, including *Charles Mingus Presents Charles Mingus* (1960), which features Dolphy's technique of "conversational" improvisation. On the recording, Mingus and Dolphy use their instruments to emulate the inquiring inflections, stuttered pacing, and expressive intonations of human speech—in effect, holding a wordless yet still meaningful conversation. Another important early effort as a sideman came with Dolphy's participation in Coleman's groundbreaking 1960 album *Free Jazz: A Collective Improvisation*, a recording that ostensibly coined the name for a whole genre. In this, Dolphy played the counterpart to the saxophonist Coleman in the double quartet comprising two saxophonists, two trumpeters, two bassists, and two drummers. Exhibiting

his abilities in the mainstream jazz tradition, Dolphy also appeared on Nelson's *Blues and the Abstract Truth* (1961), widely considered that artist's best effort and a classic jazz album.

Out There. In addition to his considerable early body of creative work as a sideman, Dolphy recorded three albums as a bandleader in 1960: *Outward Bound*, *Out There*, and *Far Cry!* Of these, *Out There* remains one of his finest. His performances on the album establish his ability to work both in and outside the jazz tradition, hence the term "out" in the titles, with which various record labels sought to promote his music. The album, with Ron Carter on cello, George Duvivier on bass, and Roy Haynes on drums, featured Dolphy on clarinet, bass clarinet, and flute as well as on saxophone. On the title track, Dolphy on alto sax plays a frenetic bop-inspired head doubled by Carter on cello. The piece then moves into improvised solos that maintain traditional stylistic phrasing, although wandering in and out of tonal coherence. Dolphy's alto saxophone solo on the track displays his technical mastery of the instrument, winding through three-octave scale figures in split seconds and creating spirals of sound that are so artistically attractive that their outright dissonance and their lack of clear tonality become secondary considerations. The recording of Mingus's "Eclipse" on the album is representative of Dolphy's interest in Third Stream music. The vocal piece is arranged for clarinet and cello moving through a highly chromatic two-voice melody. Eschewing the rhythmic pulse of much free jazz, Dolphy's performance on this track moves at a halting rubato pace indicative of its avant-garde classical inspirations.

Out to Lunch. *Out to Lunch* is widely considered Dolphy's masterwork. A number of tracks from the album have achieved the status of standards, forming part of an established musical repertory among free jazz musicians. Dolphy's piece "Gazzellioni," named after an Italian classical flutist, is one such tune—a bop-inspired composition that Dolphy performs on flute. "Hat and Beard" is another musical portrait of sorts—here a tribute to Thelonious Monk. Unlike "Gazzellioni," the piece directly emulates the compositions and improvisatory style of the jazz pianist, albeit in an abstract fashion. The piece features a bass ostinato joined by sporadic and angular interjections on trumpet, alto saxophone (and bass clarinet), and vibraphone, which eventually all join the ostinato. Dolphy's bass clarinet solo on the track is noteworthy for both its growling, squealing, and wailing timbres and its multiphonics—a technique of reed playing that produces two pitches simultaneously. Dolphy's work on the bass clarinet here and elsewhere established the instrument commonly relegated to a supporting role as a viable jazz solo instrument.

Musical Legacy

Dolphy's major historical contributions stem from his foundational involvement in the free jazz and the Third Stream movements. Though many musicians around New York's improvised music scene in the early 1960's performed in both jazz and classical settings, it was the work of Dolphy and a few others that established a space for this music between artistic genres and at the edges of popular taste. His interest in avant-garde classical music inspired Dolphy to perform on nontraditional jazz instruments, such as the bass clarinet, oboe, and flute. His experiments with alternative instrumentations and with crossing stylistic boundaries resulted in the many nontraditional instruments commonly found in jazz settings and the expansion of improvised music beyond the label of jazz.

J. Griffith Rollefson

Further Reading

Horricks, Raymond. *The Importance of Being Eric Dolphy*. Tunbridge Wells, England: DJ Costello, 1988. This is a loving tribute to the artist, with a few transcriptions and analyses of some performances.

Simosko, Vladimir, and Barry Tepperman. *Eric Dolphy: A Musical Biography and Discography*. Cambridge, Mass.: Da Capo, 1996. This excellent overview of Dolphy's life and work places him in context with other innovative jazz artists, including Coltrane, Mingus, and Coleman, and it describes the unique voice of his music, which could mimic speech.

See also: Coleman, Ornette; Coltrane, John; Kirk, Rahsaan Roland; Lewis, John; Monk, Thelonious; Powell, Bud; Roach, Max; Varèse, Edgard.

Plácido Domingo
Spanish-Mexican classical and opera singer

A great lyrical tenor, Domingo is a superb actor on the operatic stage. He is noted for his versatility, not only in the variety of roles he mastered but also in his activities as a director, an arts administrator, and a popularizer of classical music.

Born: January 21, 1941; Madrid, Spain
Also known as: José Plácido Domingo Embil (full name)
Member of: The Three Tenors

Principal works

OPERATIC ROLES: Borsa in Giuseppe Verdi's *Rigoletto*, 1959; Danilo Danilowitsch in Franz Lehár's *The Merry Widow*, 1960; Alfredo in Giuseppe Verdi's *La Traviata*, 1961; Arturo in Gaetano Donizetti's *Lucia di Lammermoor*, 1961; Turiddu in Pietro Mascagni's *Cavalleria rusticana*, 1965; Pinkerton in Giacomo Puccini's *Madama Butterfly*, 1965; Hoffman in Jacques Offenbach's *Tales of Hoffman*, 1965; Don Rodrigo in Alberto Ginastera's *Don Rodrigo*, 1966; Canio in Ruggero Leoncavallo's *Pagliacci*, 1966; Maurice de Saxe in Francesco Cilea's *Adriana Lecouvreur*, 1968; Lohengrin in Richard Wagner's *Lohengrin*, 1968; Ernani in Giuseppe Verdi's *Ernani*, 1969; Don Alvaro in Giuseppe Verdi's *La forza del destino*, 1969; Mario Cavaradossi in Giacomo Puccini's *Tosca*, 1971; Vasco da Gama in Giacomo Meyerbeer's *L'Africaine*, 1972; Paolo in Ricardo Zandonai's *Francesca da Rimini*, 1973; Arrigo in Giuseppe Verdi's *Les Vêpres siciliennes*, 1974; Don Carlo in Giuseppe Verdi's *Don Carlo*, 1975; Otello in Giuseppe Verdi's *Otello*, 1975; Aeneas in Hector Berlioz's *Les Troyens*, 1983; Parsifal in Richard Wagner's *Parsifal*, 1991; Siegmund in Richard Wagner's *Die Walküre*, 1992; Idomeneo in Wolfgang Amadeus Mozart's *Idomeneo*, 1994; Adorno in Giuseppe Verdi's *Simon Boccanegra*, 1996; Hermann in Peter Ilich Tchaikovsky's *The Queen of Spades*, 1999; Rasputin in Deborah Drattell's *Nicholas and*

Alexandra, 2003; Oreste in Christopher Gluck's *Iphigénie en Tauride*, 2007.

Principal recordings

ALBUMS (solo): *Mefistofele*, 1974; *Christmas with Plácido Domingo: Vienna Symphony Orchestra*, 1981; *Always in My Heart (Songs of Ernesto Lecuona)*, 1984; *Domingo at the Philharmonic*, 1989; *Goya: A Life in Song*, 1989; *Great Love Scenes*, 1990; *The Domingo Songbook*, 1992; *Plácido Domingo Sings Caruso*, 1992; *The Great Plácido Domingo*, 1995; *The Young Domingo*, 1999; *Essential Plácido Domingo*, 2004; *Vienna: City of My Dreams*, 2004; *Moments of Passion*, 2006.

ALBUMS (with the Three Tenors): *Carreras, Domingo, Pavarotti: The Three Tenors in Concert*, 1990; *The Three Tenors*, 1997; *The Three Tenors Christmas*, 2000; *Romantic Arias*, 2002; *Romantic Tenors*, 2002.

The Life

Plácido Domingo (PLA-sih-doh doh-MIHN-goh) was born José Plácido Domingo Embil in Madrid, Spain, on January 21, 1941. A sister, Mari Pepa, was born the following year. Their parents were professional performers in the Spanish musical-comedy genre called the zarzuela. In 1950 the parents decided to relocate the family to Mexico City, where they eventually formed their own zarzuela company. Domingo often appeared in their productions, thus developing the acting skill and the stage presence that would be much admired when he became an opera star. He also continued with the piano lessons he had begun as a child in Madrid.

When Domingo was fourteen, his piano teacher died, and his parents enrolled him in the National Conservatory of Music. At that time, he had two great passions: piano and soccer. A talented goalie, he could have become a professional soccer player. However, he also loved piano. At the conservatory, his range of interests broadened. He liked literature and mathematics; he enjoyed composition and observing conducting classes; and he was fascinated by opera.

Domingo was also interested in girls. At sixteen, he left home to live with another piano student, and they were secretly married. The following year,

they had a son, José (Pepe), but soon thereafter they separated and divorced. Because he now had a child to support, Domingo left the conservatory to earn his living as a singer.

While he was at the conservatory, Domingo had met Marta Ornelas, a student taking voice lessons. After a year of courtship, which included his serenading Marta at the apartment building where her family lived and which culminated in her parents giving consent, Domingo and Marta were married on June 15, 1961. By December, 1962, they were living in Tel Aviv, Israel, where for the next two and a half years they sang major roles with the Israel National Opera Company. In 1965 they moved to the United States. A son, Plácido (Placi), was born on October 21, 1965, and another son, Alvaro Maurizio, was born on October 11, 1968. After the birth of the children, Marta abandoned her operatic career. However, she remained her husband's closest friend and his most trusted adviser.

Domingo soon became one of the most highly regarded tenors in the world and one of the busiest. He traveled all over the world, sometimes with Marta and the children, sometimes without them. During the summer he scheduled a vacation, at the family home in Barcelona or at their villa in Acapulco, Mexico. Though he was an international star, Domingo never forgot his roots. After the devastating earthquake in 1985, Domingo flew to Mexico City and joined rescuers working in the rubble. He later gave a series of concerts to benefit the victims. Domingo also retained his love of soccer. In June, 1972, before a performance of *Cavalleria rusticana* and *I Pagliacci* in Hamburg, Germany, he joined the stage crew in a soccer game, he hurt his back, and he had to sing the two operas without moving on stage. It was their shared love of the sport that prompted Domingo and two other famous tenors, Luciano Pavarotti and José Carreras, to plan a joint performance at the 1990 World Cup soccer championship in Rome, Italy, thus starting the tradition of the Three Tenors concerts.

The Music

Though Domingo sang baritone roles in his father's productions and in musical comedies, at his audition for Mexico's National Opera in 1959 he was told that he was a tenor. He was accepted by the company, and he made his operatic debut by singing in its production of Giuseppe Verdi's *Rigoletto*. After returning from Tel Aviv, Domingo joined the New York City Opera, and in 1968 he made his debut with the Metropolitan Opera. Appearances at major European opera houses followed, and he was soon considered one of the world's greatest operatic tenors. However, Domingo also ventured into other areas. He recorded duets with the popular music stars John Denver and Jennifer Rush. He promoted his Hispanic heritage, and he won a Grammy Award for Best Latin Pop Performance for "Siempre en mi corazón," from the album *Always in My Heart*. He was the star of filmed versions of the operas *Otello, La Traviata*, and *Carmen*. In the early 1970's, he began conducting orchestral performances and operas. In 1996 he became creative director of the Washington National Opera in the District of Columbia, and in 2000 he began serving as artistic director of the Los Angeles Opera. Meanwhile, his voice showed no signs of aging and his energy no signs of flagging.

Tosca. Giacomo Puccini's *Tosca* (1900) takes place in Rome in June, 1800. Cesare Angelotti, a former consul, has escaped from prison and fled from the villainous Baron Scarpia, the Roman police chief. The painter Mario Cavaradossi aids Angelotti. Scarpia tricks Cavaradossi's mistress, Floria Tosca, into revealing where Angelotti is hiding. After obtaining what she believes to be a safe-conduct from Scarpia that will enable the lovers to escape, Tosca kills Scarpia. However, Scarpia has betrayed her again. Cavaradossi is executed, and Tosca leaps to her death.

Domingo first sang in *Tosca* in August, 1961, when he was cast in the minor role of Spoletta in a production in Mexico's National Opera. On September 30, when *Tosca* was again performed in Mexico City, Domingo played Cavaradossi. The role became a permanent part of Domingo's repertoire. By the time he appeared in *Tosca* in New York's Central Park on June 16, 1981, opening the Metropolitan Opera's summer season, Domingo had played Cavaradossi some 150 times. These outdoor productions in Central Park were presented in concert style. The singers wore evening dress and stood on a raised platform. Most of the crowd of some two hundred thousand could not see them but merely listened to the performance, projected by loudspeakers. Nevertheless, the crowd roared its approval after Domingo's showcase arias. More typical in format were the three performances of *Tosca* in late May, 1983, during the Opera Festival at the Liceo in Barcelona, Spain. The audience there was as enthusiastic as the New Yorkers had been. Domingo's aria "E lucevan le stelle" in act 3 produced such extended applause that the conductor had to have it repeated.

Otello. Based on William Shakespeare's play *Othello* (1604), Verdi's *Otello* (1887) involves the machinations of Jago, an ensign, as he works to destroy the Moorish general, Otello, along with his bride Desdemona, and his second-in-command Cassio, by persuading Otello that his wife and Cassio are having an affair. Jago succeeds, and Otello kills Desdemona. After Jago is exposed, Otello stabs himself.

Plácido Domingo. (Keith Bedford/Reuters/Landov)

In his memoir *My First Forty Years* (1983), Domingo calls September 28, 1975, one of the major milestones in his life. That was the night he first performed the title role in *Otello*. Though he had been warned that the role would ruin his voice, Domingo found that its challenges helped him to improve his technique. His dramatic interpretation of the role changed markedly in December, 1976, when he played the part at La Scala in Milan, with Franco Zeffirelli as director. Domingo notes how changes in staging suggested by Zeffirelli made Otello's credulity more believable. He also explains that while earlier he had thought of Otello as a Moor, he now saw him as a black man and an outsider among the white Venetians. It is significant that Domingo's most difficult role, that of Otello, is the one for which he is best known.

Tales of Hoffmann. When he died in 1880, Jacques Offenbach left his comic opera *Tales of Hoffmann* unfinished. As a result, each director makes a number of decisions about the text, even the order in which the three tales are presented. In the prologue, the poet Hoffmann talks about his three loves, and in each of the three acts that follows, one of the romances is portrayed. One of his loves, Olympia, proves to be a mechanical doll; another, Antonia, is so frail that Hoffmann cannot save her from death; the third, the courtesan Giuletta, takes Hoffmann's shadow from him and then sails away with another man. In an epilogue, Hoffmann is told that his present love, Stella, combines the qualities of all the others, and she, too, abandons him for another, leaving Hoffmann alone with his Muse.

In *My First Forty Years*, Domingo explains that the role of Hoffmann is very difficult for a tenor because he must sing so many extended passages in a high register. Though he first sang in the opera in 1965, as his vocal technique developed and as he came to understand the character he played, he found himself much more at ease in the role. Between 1980 and 1982, when four opera houses observed the centenary of Offenbach's death and of the first performance of *Tales of Hoffmann*, Domingo sang the title role in thirty-nine productions. He continued to enjoy performing in the opera, both because he felt he had mastered a difficult role and because he found the approaches of the various directors so interesting.

Musical Legacy

Domingo, a superb tenor, triumphed in roles ranging from comic opera to dark tragedy. He appeared in opera houses throughout the world, and he made more than one hundred recordings. He ventured into other kinds of entertainment as well, recording Latin popular music and duets with popular artists and acting in three filmed versions of operas. The first Three Tenors performance, featuring Domingo, Pavarotti, and Carreras, reached some eight hundred million people on television, thus introducing classical music to many who had never been exposed to it. The album sold more copies than any other classical album in recording history.

Part of Domingo's legacy includes his founding a vocal competition for young singers, as well as his work as a director and as an arts administrator. He won numerous awards, including France's Légion d'Honneur and the 2000 Kennedy Center Honors.

Rosemary M. Canfield Reisman

Further Reading

Domingo, Plácido. *My First Forty Years*. New York: Alfred A. Knopf, 1983. Covers his personal life and professional works in detail. Of particular interest are the author's comments about opera houses, audiences, and conductors. Includes a list of performances, discography, photographs, and index.

Franchi, Cristina, ed. *Plácido Domingo and the Royal Opera*. London: Oberon Books, 2006. Focuses on Domingo's relationship with the Royal Opera House and its company. Includes several photographs, some provided by the Domingo family.

Lewis, Marcia. *The Private Lives of the Three Tenors: Behind the Scenes with Plácido Domingo, Luciano Pavarotti, and José Carreras*. New York: Birch Lane Press, 1996. The author pays special attention to the three musicians' connections with pop culture and Hollywood and to rumors of extramarital relationships. Includes source notes, bibliography, and index.

Matheopoulos, Helena. *Plácido Domingo: My Operatic Roles*. Fort Worth, Tex.: Baskerville, 2003. This important work, which might be considered the second volume of Domingo's autobiography, is the result of a collaboration between the famous tenor and a journalist who knows opera well. Much of the volume consists of Domingo's account of his experiences, which Matheopoulos supplements with factual material. Includes glossary, three appendixes, an index of names, and numerous illustrations.

Schnauber, Cornelius. *Plácido Domingo*. Translated by Susan H. Ray. Boston: Northeastern University Press, 1997. Though this volume is presented as a biographical study of Domingo during the 1980's and early 1990's, it deals primarily with the singer's vocal technique and his acting skills. Includes illustrations, glossary, discography, bibliography, and index.

Snowman, Daniel. *The World of Plácido Domingo*. London: Bodley Head, 1985. A well-researched study by a BBC producer who is a longtime friend of Domingo. Snowman provides the backdrops for Domingo's performances by describing various locations and providing character sketches of friends and colleagues. Includes chronology and index.

See also: Aznavour, Charles; Denver, John; Pavarotti, Luciano; Piaf, Édith; Puccini, Giacomo; Ross, Diana; Santana, Carlos; Warwick, Dionne.

Fats Domino

American rock and rhythm-and-blues singer, songwriter, and pianist

A pioneer of rock and roll, Domino is noted for his energetic piano playing and his smoky voice with its New Orleans accent.

Born: February 26, 1928; New Orleans, Louisiana
Also known as: Antoine Domino, Jr. (full name)

Principal recordings

ALBUMS: *Carry on Rockin'*, 1955; *Fats Domino Rock and Rollin'*, 1956; *Rock and Rollin' with Fats Domino*, 1956; *This Is Fats Domino*, 1957; *Here Stands Fats Domino*, 1958; *The Fabulous Mr. D.*, 1958; *This Is Fats*, 1958; *Let's Play Fats Domino*, 1959; *A Lot of Dominos*, 1960; *Fats Domino*, 1960; *I Miss You So*, 1961; *Let the Four Winds Blow*, 1961; *Twistin' the Stomp*, 1962; *What a Party*, 1962; *Here Comes Fats*, 1963; *Here He Comes Again*, 1963; *Just Domino*, 1963; *Let's Dance with Domino*, 1963; *Fantastic Fats*, 1964; *Fats Domino '65*, 1965; *Trouble in Mind*, 1965; *Getaway with Fats Domino*, 1966; *Southland U. S. A.*, 1966; *Fats Domino Swings*, 1967; *Stompin'*, 1967; *Fats Is Back*, 1968; *Ain't That a Shame*, 1970; *Fats*, 1970; *Cookin' with Fats*, 1971; *Big Rock Sounds*, 1974; *Fats Domino 1980*, 1980; *Jambalaya*, 1984; *Easy Riding*, 1988; *Christmas Gumbo*, 1993; *Happy Days of Rock 'n' Roll*, 1995; *The Fats Man*, 1995.

SINGLES: "The Fat Man," 1949; "Every Night About This Time," 1950; "Rockin' Chair," 1951; "Goin' Home," 1952; "Going to the River," 1953; "Please Don't Leave Me," 1953; "Something's Wrong," 1953; "You Done Me Wrong," 1954; "Ain't That a Shame," 1955; "Don't You Know," 1955.

The Life

Antoine Domino, Jr., was born in New Orleans on February 26, 1928, the last of eight children of Antoine and Donatile Gros Domino. His father was an amateur violinist, and his uncle played with several New Orleans jazz bands. Domino's brother-in-law, Harrison Verrett, who performed in New Orleans clubs, taught the five-year-old Domino to play piano. By the time he was ten, Domino played blues and ragtime at roadhouses and honky-tonks. Domino could not be deterred from a musical career, even after severely injuring his fingers while working in a bed-spring factory.

Domino married Rosemary Hall on August 6, 1947, and they had eight children. While performing at the Hideaway Club, Domino was signed for Imperial Records by Dave Bartholomew, a bandleader and producer. Domino's first hit was "The Fat Man," a title referring to the 250-pound singer's nickname, Fats. It reached number twenty-six on the rhythm-and-blues charts, and later it earned Domino the first of his twenty-three gold records, a total surpassed at the time by only Bing Crosby and Elvis Presley.

Domino formed his own band in 1951, and a string of rhythm-and-blues hits, written alone or in collaboration with Bartholomew, followed: "Rockin' Chair," "Goin' Home," "Going to the River," "Please Don't Leave Me," "You Done Me

Wrong," and "Don't You Know." *Billboard* chose Domino as favorite rhythm-and-blues artist in 1955 and 1956. He has been widely acknowledged as one of the first rhythm-and-blues performers to become popular with both black and white audiences.

The success of such songs as "Ain't That a Shame" in 1955 led to his being considered a pioneer of rock and roll, along with Bill Haley and the Comets, Bo Diddley, Chuck Berry, Little Richard, Jerry Lee Lewis, and Presley. Domino was more visible than most black rockers, singing in such films as *Shake, Rattle, and Rock!* (1956), *The Girl Can't Help It* (1956), *Jamboree* (1957), and *The Big Beat* (1958), which takes its title from a Domino song.

When Domino's sales declined during the 1960's, his contract with Imperial Records was not renewed. He began drifting from label to label, with his music seeming old-fashioned in the era of the Beatles, Otis Redding, and Jimi Hendrix. With help from Bartholomew, Domino unsuccessfully tried to launch his own label, Broadmoor.

In 2005 Domino made international news because of Hurricane Katrina. While others fled New Orleans, Domino stayed at the insistence of his wife Rosemary, a semi-invalid. Domino survived Katrina, but he lost most of his memorabilia and the home in the working-class neighborhood where he had lived all his life. He eventually moved to a gated community across the Mississippi River in Harvey, Louisiana.

Fats Domino. (AP/Wide World Photos)

The Music

Domino's voice is soothing and friendly, in contrast to the louder, more aggressive voices of many of his contemporaries.

"The Fat Man." Like much of Domino's early music, "The Fat Man" is a blend of blues, ragtime, and boogie-woogie. Domino learned eight-bar riffs as a young man by listening to Clarence "Frogman" Henry, Professor Longhair, and Huey Smith perform in clubs, and his music rarely strayed from this New Orleans style. His heavy beat on the piano works in counterpoint to his high, nasal, slightly raspy voice. His emphasis on the beat helped make his music popular during an era when rock and roll was essentially dance music. His relaxed yet energetic piano style caused everyone listening to keep the beat.

"Ain't That a Shame." In 1955 Domino's "Ain't That a Shame" became his first crossover hit, earning the tenth spot on the pop charts. A subsequent version by Pat Boone, as "Ain't That a Shame," reached number one. To make certain songs more palatable to young white record buyers in the 1950's, it was common for white singers such as Boone, Presley, and Ricky Nelson, whose first single was Domino's "I'm Walkin'," to have hit versions of songs originally recorded by black singers.

More Hits. Domino had more Top 40 hits during the 1950's than all other rock performers except Presley. In addition to "Ain't It a Shame," his other Top 10 pop hits were "I'm in Love Again," "Blueberry Hill," "Blue Monday," "I'm Walkin'," "Valley of Tears," "Whole Lotta Lovin'," "I Want to Walk You Home," "Be My Guest," and "Walking to New Orleans," the last in 1960. While many of his contemporaries, such as Berry and Lewis, favored raw, suggestive lyrics, Domino's style was always mellower and more nonchalant. His simple, repetitive, easy-to-remember lyrics were inspired by his everyday experiences and chance remarks he overheard.

"Blueberry Hill." In 1956 Domino took the 1940 pop standard "Blueberry Hill" (previously recorded by Sammy Kaye, Gene Autry, Glenn Miller, Louis Armstrong, and many others), added his gliding, syncopated rhythms, and remade it into a rock classic. It remains the song with which he is most identified. He also adapted other Tin Pan Alley songs, such as "My Blue Heaven," "When My Dreamboat Comes Home," and "Red Sails in the Sunset," his final Top 40 hit in 1963, to rock rhythms, his driving piano accompanied by wailing saxophones, making the songs his own.

"Lady Madonna." Domino's last single to reach the pop charts was his 1968 rendition of the Beatles' "Lady Madonna." Ironically, Paul McCartney wrote the song as a tribute to Domino's smoothly flowing sound. In *Christmas Gumbo*, he brought his bouncy rhythms to "Silent Night," making the familiar holiday favorite sound brand new.

Musical Legacy

The debt the musical industry felt it owed Domino became clear after the Hurricane Katrina disaster. Dr. John, Ben Harper, Norah Jones, B. B. King, Lenny Kravitz, Los Lobos, Paul McCartney, Willie Nelson, Tom Petty, Robert Plant, Bonnie Raitt, Lucinda Williams, Neil Young, and others perform his songs on *Goin' Home: A Tribute to Fats Domino* to raise money for the Tipitina's Foundation, a nonprofit musicians-aid organization in New Orleans. The rendition of "My Girl Josephine" by Taj Mahal and the New Orleans Social Club demonstrates how Domino and the New Orleans sound are inseparable.

Domino was one of the first ten inductees into the Rock and Roll Hall of Fame in 1986, and he was honored with a Lifetime Achievement Award at the Grammy Awards show the following year. In 1995 he received a Rhythm and Blues Foundation Pioneer Award and in 1998 the National Medal of Arts. By 2007 he had sold 110 million records, second only to Presley among rockers.

Michael Adams

Further Reading

Berry, Jason. "Fats Domino." *New Orleans Magazine* 42 (October, 2007): 80-83. Details the effects of Hurricane Katrina on Domino's life and the creation of the tribute album.

Coleman, Rick. *Blue Monday: Fats Domino and the Lost Dawn of Rock 'n' Roll.* Cambridge, Mass.: Da Capo Press, 2006. This is a thoroughly researched biography. Includes photographs.

Lichtenstein, Grace, and Laura Dankner. *Musical Gumbo: The Music of New Orleans.* New York: Norton, 1993. This resource places Domino's music in cultural context.

Miller, James. *Flowers in the Dustbin: The Rise of Rock and Roll, 1947-1977.* New York: Simon & Schuster, 1999. Looks at the contribution of "Ain't That a Shame" to rock history.

See also: Berry, Chuck; Crosby, Bing; Diddley, Bo; Hendrix, Jimi; Lewis, Jerry Lee; Little Richard; Nelson, Ricky; Presley, Elvis; Professor Longhair; Redding, Otis.

Thomas A. Dorsey

American gospel songwriter and pianist

Dorsey transformed the character, performance, and distribution of gospel music, bringing it out of the realm of church choirs and into the popular music arena.

Born: July 1, 1899; Villa Rica, Georgia
Died: January 23, 1993; Chicago, Illinois
Also known as: Thomas Andrew Dorsey (full name); Barrel House Tome; the Reverend Thomas A. Dorsey; Georgia Tom
Member of: Famous Hokum Boys

Principal recordings

ALBUMS: *Precious Lord: The Great Gospel Songs of Thomas A. Dorsey,* 1973; *Thomas Andrew Dorsey,* 1990.

SINGLES: "It's Tight Like That," 1928 (with Tampa Red Whittaker); "How About You," 1932; "If You See My Savior," 1932; "Peace in the Valley," 1939 (recorded by Mahalia Jackson);

"Take My Hand, Precious Lord," 1967
(recorded by Jackson; written in 1932).

The Life

Thomas Andrew Dorsey was the son of Thomas Madison Dorsey, an itinerant minister and sharecropper, and Etta Plant Spencer, a church organist and piano teacher. His early musical experience was piano lessons from his mother and the shapenote hymns and spirituals of the church. The Dorsey family moved to Atlanta in 1908, and Dorsey began working in the Eighty-One Theater, selling concessions and doing other odd jobs. There he was exposed to the music of Ma Rainey and Bessie Smith, and he was captivated by the blues. He began learning to play the blues from several pianists in the city, including Ed Butler, James Henningway, and Eddie Heywood. By age twelve he was known around Atlanta for playing house parties under the name Barrel House Tom.

In 1916 Dorsey moved with his family to Chicago, Illinois, where he studied music formally at the Chicago School of Composition and Arranging. He began working as an agent for Paramount Records, writing songs for a Chicago publishing house, and playing in clubs under the name Georgia Tom. While Dorsey made a name for himself as a jazz and blues performer, sacred music was still important to him. After hearing W. M. Nix sing at the 1921 National Baptist Convention, Dorsey began writing sacred songs. His first sacred composition, "If I Don't Get There," was published in the second edition of *Gospel Pearls* (1921), alongside the works of Ira Sankey, Homer Rodeheaver, Isaac Watts, Fanny Crosby, and Charles Wesley. In 1922 he became the director of music for the New Hope Baptist Church in Chicago, where he began to incorporate his blues-playing techniques with sacred music in earnest.

Financial issues forced Dorsey to continue playing in clubs. In 1923 Dorsey became the pianist for Will Walker's Whispering Syncopators, where he worked alongside Lionel Hampton and met W. C. Handy. Meanwhile, his compositions were attracting the attention of other performers, including Joe "King" Oliver, whose Creole Jazz Band recorded Dorsey's "Riverside Blues." These successes caught the attention of Rainey, who chose Dorsey to organize and lead her Wild Cats Jazz Band. In 1928

Dorsey had his biggest blues hit, with Wild Cats Jazz Band guitarist Tampa Red Whittaker. It was called "It's Tight Like That," and the two would record several times together as the Famous Hokum Boys.

Dorsey was at the height of his blues career when personal tragedy caused him to change direction. In 1932 his wife, Nettie Harper, died in childbirth, and his son died the next day. In the wake of this loss, Dorsey renounced the blues and turned his attention to religious music full time. His sacred music had already garnered him some level of fame after Willie Mae Ford Smith performed his "If You See My Savior" at the 1930 National Baptist Convention. In 1932 Dorsey organized a performance of the three church choirs with which he was involved, and that led to the development of the National Convention of Gospel Choirs and Choruses (with Smith). Dorsey was elected president of the organization, over his objections, and he held the title until he stepped down in 1983. He also founded the first independent publishing house for black gospel music, the Dorsey House of Music, in Chicago.

In the late 1930's and early 1940's, Dorsey turned his focus away from gospel choirs and toward individual singers, including Mahalia Jackson, Roberta Walker, Clara Ward, and Della Reese. Dorsey's work with these singers transformed gospel music into a popular musical genre, with many of the solo gospel singers performing in clubs beside Billie Holiday and Ella Fitzgerald as well as in churches. He toured with these artists, playing piano and selling the sheet music for the songs they sang, a Dorsey innovation. Before Dorsey, gospel-music composers published their songs in songbooks or song collections by a variety of composers, such as *Gospel Pearls*. Dorsey published his songs individually as sheet music, like the blues and Tin Pan Alley songs.

Dorsey continued composing and working with gospel choirs and singers throughout the rest of his life. In 1979 he was elected to the Nashville Songwriters International Hall of Fame, becoming the first African American to receive that honor. Three years later he became the first African American elected to the Gospel Music Association's Living Hall of Fame. In 1981 his home state honored Dorsey by enshrining him in the Georgia Music

Hall of Fame. In August, 1982, the Thomas A. Dorsey Archives were opened at Fisk University in Nashville, Tennessee, where his papers reside next to those of W. C. Handy and George Gershwin. Dorsey died in 1993 in Chicago of complications from Alzheimer's disease. He is buried in the Oak Woods Cemetery in Chicago.

The Music

"It's Tight Like That." Dorsey's first hit was "It's Tight Like That," a duet with guitarist Tampa Red Whittaker. Whittaker approached Dorsey with the lyrics, and he composed the music. The song is an example of hokum, which combines urban sophistication with rural, lowbrow humor by using euphemisms and sexual innuendo to produce a bawdy song that could work in proper society. The simple musical accompaniment provides a bouncy, lighthearted rhythmic backing to the lyrics. Whittaker is the guitarist and primary vocalist, while Dorsey plays piano and sings harmony on the chorus. Since its release in 1928, "It's Tight Like That" has sold more than seven million copies.

"If You See My Savior." Dorsey's first gospel hit was "If You See My Savior," which he wrote in 1926 after the death of a friend. Its first major performance was at the National Baptist Convention, after which Dorsey sold four thousand copies of the sheet music. The song's lyrics tie in with the tradition of spirituals, particularly in their use of the "crossing Jordan" allusion, in this case to reference dying and going to heaven. The lyrics are written from the perspective of someone sending a message to Jesus through a dying friend that the singer is on his way.

"Take My Hand, Precious Lord." Dorsey wrote his best-known song, "Take My Hand, Precious Lord" in August, 1932, after the death of his wife, Nettie, and his newborn son. After the tragedy, which occurred while Dorsey was in St. Louis playing at a revival, he felt wronged by God. He said he did not want to write gospel songs any longer. A friend arranged for Dorsey to be left alone in a room with a piano, and while he was playing around on the keys, the tune and lyrics came to him. The song is linked to the blues in the same way that the spirituals were linked to the slaves: It is a song crying out for God's help through the hardships of life. The melody was adapted from the hymn "Mait-

land," composed in 1844 by George N. Allen, although it is often attributed to Dorsey. (The same tune was used for Thomas Shepherd's "Must Jesus Bear the Cross Alone.") The first recording of "Take My Hand, Precious Lord" was made by Emory Johnson in 1938, and since then it has been recorded by numerous performers from diverse backgrounds, including Elvis Presley, Mahalia Jackson, Lawrence Welk, Pat Boone, Nina Simone, Chaka Kahn, Little Richard, and Faith Hill. The lyrics have appeared in forty different languages. In 2001 it was listed as one of the top 365 songs of the twentieth century by the Recording Industry Association of America, and it was inducted into the Christian Music Hall of Fame in 2007. The song was also a favorite of Dr. Martin Luther King, Jr.

"Peace in the Valley." In 1939 Dorsey wrote "Peace in the Valley" for his protégé Jackson. It is a song of hope and longing, akin to many spirituals and other gospel songs with the same theme. Unlike other songs in this tradition, which speak of heaven as a place of rest from the toils and labors of life, "Peace in the Valley" focuses on the glory of heaven. Dorsey describes "the valley" as a place free from sorrow, sadness, and trouble, where the flowers are always in bloom and the sun always shines. "Peace in the Valley" has been recorded by numerous other artists, including Hill, Johnny Cash, Loretta Lynn, and Red Foley. Foley's 1951 recording, with the Sunshine Boys, was the first gospel recording to sell one million copies, and in 2006 it was selected by the Library of Congress to be one of the entries in the National Recording Registry, which preserves recordings deemed to be important for historical, cultural, or aesthetical reasons.

Musical Legacy

Dorsey transformed the performance, dissemination, and the character of gospel music. He transformed the gospel blues of the street evangelists into the music of the church, writing and arranging songs for a choral setting and for solo singers. He published his compositions in sheet-music format rather than in songbooks, which allowed for greater distribution and caused them to be treated like popular songs rather than church songs. He was the first African American elected to the Nashville Songwriters Hall of Fame as well as the Gospel Music Association's Living Hall of Fame. His songs have been recorded by numerous artists, including Jackson, Clara Ward, Aretha Franklin, Elvis Presley, Tennessee Ernie Ford, and Johnny Cash. In addition, they have been praised by U.S. Presidents, civil rights leaders, and music historians.

Eric S. Strother

Further Reading

Boyer, Horace Clarence. *How Sweet the Sound: The Golden Age of Gospel.* Washington, D.C.: Elliott and Clark, 1995. A well-researched history of gospel music, defining it as an American art form. It describes the lives of some of the most prominent artists of the genre, including Dorsey. Illustrated with photographs.

Harris, Michael W. *The Rise of Gospel Blues: The Music of Thomas Andrew Dorsey in the Urban Church.* New York: Oxford University Press, 1992. This resource focuses on Dorsey, who wrote two thousand blues songs before he turned to writing the hybrid sacred and profane songs that worked in both the church and the nightclub. His work forms the foundation for gospel repertoire.

See also: Cleveland, James; Fitzgerald, Ella; Hampton, Lionel; Handy, W. C.; Holiday, Billie; Jackson, Mahalia; Presley, Elvis; Rainey, Ma; Simone, Nina; Smith, Bessie.

Lamont Dozier

American rhythm-and-blues
singer-songwriter

During the 1960's, the songwriting and production team of Brian Holland, Dozier, and Eddie Holland (better known as Holland-Dozier-Holland, or H-D-H) produced some of the most memorable "Motown sound" hits in the history of popular music.

Born: June 16, 1941; Detroit, Michigan
Also known as: Lamont Anthony
Member of: The Romeos; the Voice Masters

Principal works

SONGS (with Eddie and Brian Holland): "Can I Get a Witness," 1963 (performed by Marvin Gaye); "Heat Wave," 1963 (performed by Martha and the Vandellas); "Mickey's Monkey," 1963 (performed by the Miracles); "Baby I Need Your Loving," 1964 (performed by the Four Tops); "Baby Love," 1964 (performed by the Supremes); "Come See About Me," 1964 (performed by the Supremes); "How Sweet It Is (to Be Loved by You)," 1964 (performed by Gaye); "Where Did Our Love Go?," 1964 (performed by the Supremes); "Back in My Arms Again," 1965 (performed by the Supremes); "I Can't Help Myself (Sugar Pie, Honey Bunch)," 1965 (performed by the Four Tops); "(It's the) Same Old Song," 1965 (performed by the Four Tops); "Nowhere to Run," 1965 (performed by Martha and the Vandellas); "Stop! In the Name of Love," 1965 (performed by the Supremes); "Take Me in Your Arms (Rock Me a Little While)," 1965 (performed by Kim Weston); "Little Darling (I Need You)," 1966 (performed by Gaye); "Reach out I'll Be There," 1966 (performed by the Four Tops); "This Old Heart of Mine (Is Weak for You)," 1966 (performed by the Isley Brothers); "You Can't Hurry Love," 1966 (performed by the Supremes); "You Keep Me Hangin' On," 1966 (performed by the Supremes); "Bernadette," 1967 (performed by the Four Tops); "The Happening," 1967 (performed by the Supremes); "Jimmy Mack," 1967 (performed by Martha and the Vandellas); "Love Is Here and Now You're Gone," 1967 (performed by the Supremes); "Reflections," 1967 (performed by Diana Ross and the Supremes); "Give Me Just a Little More Time," 1970 (performed by Chairmen of the Board).

Principal recordings

ALBUMS (solo, as songwriter and performer): *Out Here on My Own,* 1974; *Black Bach,* 1975; *Love and Beauty,* 1975; *Right There,* 1976; *Peddlin' Music on the Side,* 1977; *Bittersweet,* 1979; *Lamont,* 1981; *Working on You,* 1981; *Bigger than Life,* 1983; *Inside Seduction,* 1991; *Reflections Of,* 2004.
SINGLES (solo, as songwriter and performer): "Let's Talk It Over," 1960 (as Lamont

Anthony); "Benny the Skinny Man," 1961 (as Anthony); "Just to Be Loved," 1961 (as Anthony); "Dearest One," 1962; "Jamie," 1962; "Two Hearts," 1988 (written with Phil Collins; performed by Collins).

SINGLES (with the Voice Masters): "Hope and Pray," 1959; "Needed," 1959; "Oops, I'm Sorry," 1959; "Everytime," 1960; "Free," 1960; "In Love in Vain," 1960; "Orphan Boy," 1960.

The Life

Lamont Dozier (lah-MONT DOH-zyur) was born on June 16, 1941, in Detroit, Michigan. At a young age, he learned to appreciate both gospel and classical music. Dozier sang in a Baptist church choir. Out of this experience, he learned to appreciate the impact that music could have on people. His aunt played classical music on the family piano, and Dozier was taken by the beauty of the melodies. In addition, he loved to listen to his father's record collection. By the time Dozier was ten years old, he had begun to collect his own records. He liked to listen to such popular singers as Johnny Mathis and Frankie Lymon. He began composing his own songs and envisioned himself becoming a recording star. By the late 1950's, Dozier had become a member of the Romeos. They released the singles "Gone, Gone, Get Away" and "Moments to Remember You By" in 1957. With the breakup of the Romeos, he joined the Voice Masters and left Northwestern High School before graduation. This group was short lived and Dozier decided to record as Lamont Anthony in 1961. Dozier married Barbara Ullman, with whom he had three children.

The Music

In 1959, a youthful Berry Gordy, Jr., established Motown Record Corporation in Detroit, Michigan. Dozier had first met Gordy in the late 1950's. Recording as Lamont Anthony, he released a couple of singles on the label Anna Records in 1961. Anna Records had been named after one of Gordy's sisters, Anna Gordy, who was a part owner in the company. In the following year, Dozier recorded under his own name for Mel-o-dy, which was a subsidiary of Motown Records. Eddie and Brian Holland had had a working relationship with Berry Gordy since the late 1950's. Dozier's 1962 single

"Dearest One" for Mel-o-dy brought the Holland brothers and Dozier together for the first time. While "Dearest One" was not a hit single, the three eventually decided that it was in their best interests to form a partnership and to concentrate their efforts on writing songs for other performers. Brian focused on writing the music, while Eddie worked on the lyrics and Dozier contributed to both the music and the lyrics. The trio would come to be known as Holland-Dozier-Holland (H-D-H).

Holland-Dozier-Holland helped to shape the Motown sound. While the Memphis soul sound was hard-edged and choppy, the Motown sound was full and much smoother. It had a straightforward and danceable rhythm that became known as the "Motown backbeat." The tempo for the Motown sound ranges from 80 beats per minute (bpm) to 100 bpm, and the time signature is 4/4. Within this 4/4 time, the snare drum is hit on beats 2 and 4.

Gordy demanded the highest of technical standards, and he was able to count on Holland-Dozier-Holland to deliver the very best. The trio's songs came to be known as the "Sound of Young America." These up-tempo tunes combined elements of gospel, rhythm and blues, and pop. Brian focused on the structure of the song and Dozier worked on the melody. Eddie's catchy lyrics were taken from real-life experiences. Once the key and chords were determined, someone on the Motown staff would transcribe the piece, since none of the three songwriters could write music. After the composition was finished, Eddie would concentrate on getting the lead vocal right, Brian would take control of the sound board and work on the keyboard and guitar parts of the song, and Dozier turned his attention to the rhythm section and the background vocals. They had a wonderful working relationship that allowed for each of their creative and technical strengths to be used to best advantage.

Early Hits. H-D-H began having success in 1963 working for Gordy's Motown Records. During the year, they wrote such memorable songs as "Come and Get These Memories," "Heat Wave," and "Quicksand" for Martha and the Vandellas; "Locking up My Heart" for the Marvelettes; "Mickey's Monkey" for the Miracles; and "Can I Get a Witness" for Marvin Gaye. All of these singles charted on the pop charts, with "Heat Wave" rising to number four and "Quicksand" rising to number eight. Martha and the Vandellas would have four more hit singles between 1963 and 1967. The single "Nowhere to Run" would rise to number eight on the pop singles chart in 1965, while "I'm Ready for Love" would rise to number nine in 1966 and "Jimmy Mack" would rise to number ten in 1967. During this same period, the H-D-H team would write the number six hit in 1964 "How Sweet It Is to Be Loved by You" for Gaye and the number twelve hit in 1965 "This Old Heart of Mine" for the Isley Brothers. The up-tempo hit songs that they were writing for the Motown stable of artists established H-D-H as one of the premier songwriting teams in America.

The Supremes and the Four Tops. While H-D-H continued to write quality songs for other groups, the team produced an amazing string of hits for the Supremes and the Four Tops. The first single they wrote for the Supremes, "When the Lovelight Starts Shining Through His Eyes," only went to number twenty-three on the pop singles chart, but the songs to come would make music history. The group would have three number-one hits in 1964: "Where Did Our Love Go," "Baby Love," and "Come See About Me." In the next three years, the Supremes would have seven number-one hits, including the extraordinary songs "Stop! In the Name of Love," "Back in My Arms Again," "You Can't Hurry Love," "You Keep Me Hanging On," and "The Happening." With the help of Holland-Dozier-Holland, Diana Ross and the Supremes became superstars.

The team also was writing memorable hits for the Four Tops during these years, including "Baby I Need Your Loving," "It's the Same Old Song," "Reach Out and I'll Be There," "Standing in the Shadows of Love," and "Bernadette."

Solo Career. By 1968, Holland-Dozier-Holland were not happy with the royalty arrangement that they had with Motown. They left Motown and started Hot Wax and Invictus Records. Starting in 1974, Dozier would release several solo albums, including *Out Here on My Own*, *Peddlin' Music on the Side*, *Bigger than Life*, and *Reflections Of*. He also has worked with other artists, including Phil Collins on the 1988 hit single "Two Hearts," which won a 1989 Grammy Award for Best Song Written Specifically for a Motion Picture or Television for both Dozier and Collins.

Musical Legacy

During the 1960's, the Motown songwriting and production team of Holland-Dozier-Holland created hit single after hit single for such illustrious recording artists as the Supremes, the Four Tops, the Marvelettes, the Miracles, Martha and the Vandellas, and Marvin Gaye. Their songs epitomized what came to be known as the Motown sound. From 1963 to 1967, they wrote more than twenty Top 10 hits, and twelve of these songs went to number one on the pop singles chart. They also wrote twelve other songs that made it to the Top 10 on the rhythm-and-blues singles charts. Their songs appealed to a vast listening audience because of the team's ability to combine the best elements of pop, soul, country, and rhythm and blues.

In 1988, Lamont Dozier, Brian Holland, and Eddie Holland were inducted into the Songwriters Hall of Fame. They were inducted into the Rock and Roll Hall of Fame in 1990.

Jeffry Jensen

Further Reading

Bianco, David. *Heat Wave: The Motown Fact Book.* Ann Arbor, Mich.: Pieran Press, 1988. A wonderful overview of Motown Records, including a portrait of Holland-Dozier-Holland.

Egan, Sean. *The Guys Who Wrote 'Em: Songwriting Geniuses of Rock and Pop.* London: Askill, 2004. Includes a fine chapter on Holland-Dozier-Holland.

George, Nelson. *Where Did Our Love Go? The Rise and Fall of the Motown Sound.* New York: St. Martin's Press, 1985. Takes a hard look at the rise and fall of Motown Records.

Posner, Gerald. *Motown: Music, Money, Sex, and Power.* New York: Random House, 2002. While the music put Motown on top, money, sex, and power tore at its very foundation.

Smith, Suzanne E. *Dancing in the Street: Motown and the Cultural Politics of Detroit.* Cambridge, Mass.: Harvard University Press, 1999. Reveals the crucial role Motown played in the socially charged African American community.

Waller, Don. *The Motown Story.* New York: Charles Scribner's Sons, 1985. Gives the reader an inside look at how Motown produced such extraordinarily popular music.

See also: Cooke, Sam; Costello, Elvis; Fogerty, John; Gabriel, Peter; Gaye, Marvin; Holland, Eddie and Brian; Jackson, Janet; Jackson, Michael; Jamerson, James; Latifah, Queen; Odetta; Pickett, Wilson; Plant, Robert; Robinson, Smokey; Ross, Diana; Seger, Bob; Taylor, James; Van Halen, Eddie; Webb, Jimmy; Wilson, Jackie; Wonder, Stevie.

Jacqueline du Pré

English classical cellist

Du Pré's heartfelt cello performances and recordings charmed audiences and influenced other cellists. Suffering from multiple sclerosis, du Pré impressed the world with her courage, and she heightened public awareness of the autoimmune disease that cut short her career and her life.

Born: January 26, 1945; Oxford, England
Died: October 19, 1987; London, England
Also known as: Jacqueline Mary du Pré (full name)

Principal recordings

ALBUMS: *A Jacqueline du Pré Recital*, 1962; *Elgar: Concerto in E Minor, Op. 85; Sea Pictures, Op. 37*, 1965; *Delius: Concerto for Cello and Orchestra*, 1966; *Beethoven: Sonata No. 3 in A Major, Op. 69; Sonata No. 5 in D Major, Op. 102, No. 2*, 1967; *Haydn: Concerto in D Major, Op. 101*, 1969; *Brahms: Sonatas for Cello and Piano*, 1968; *Schumann: Concerto in A Minor, Op. 129*, 1970; *Dvořák: Cello Concerto in B Minor, Op. 104; Silent Woods: Adagio for Cello and Orchestra, Op. 68*, 1971; *Impressions*, 1988.

The Life

Jacqueline Mary du Pré (zhahk-LEEN doo-PRAY) was the second child born to Derek and Iris du Pré. At age four, she asked to play the cello, and she began private study with Alison Dalrymple. In 1955 du Pré began studying with William Pleeth, and while under his tutelage, she was awarded the Suggia Gift, a scholarship for young cellists. Although du Pré was extremely gifted, she did not

like school, and her parents frequently allowed her to miss classes in order to practice.

In 1960 du Pré won the prestigious Queen's Prize, and she participated in master classes with Pablo Casals. She made her professional debut at Wigmore Hall in 1961, and in 1962 she made her orchestral debut, playing Edward Elgar's Cello Concerto with the BBC Symphony Orchestra. In that same year she began recording with EMI Records. During these early years of her career, besides playing solo and chamber-music recitals, du Pré studied for brief periods with Paul Tortelier and Mstislav Rostropovich.

Du Pré met pianist and conductor Daniel Barenboim in 1966, and the two musicians were married in Israel in 1967. For the next few years, they performed around the world and recorded together. In 1971 du Pré began to experience bewildering physical symptoms, including numbness and extreme fatigue, that forced her to curtail her performance schedule. Finally, in 1973, she was diagnosed with multiple sclerosis. Du Pré's condition rapidly deteriorated, and by 1975 she was bound to a wheelchair, remaining musically active by giving lessons and master classes. Tragically, at just forty-two years old, du Pré lost her battle with multiple sclerosis on October 19, 1987.

The Music

Despite the brevity of her playing career, du Pré performed and recorded the majority of the standard cello repertoire along with select contemporary works. In addition to Elgar's work, du Pré frequently performed the cello concerti of Johannes Brahms, Robert Schumann, Antonìn Dvořák, Franz Joseph Haydn, and Camille Saint-Saëns. She recorded all of these concerti (among others) for EMI Records.

Du Pré also enjoyed playing chamber music. In 1964 she formed a successful duo with pianist Stephen Bishop; critics especially admired the duo's interpretation of the Beethoven cello sonatas. Once she met Barenboim, however, du Pré preferred to play chamber music with him. For nearly five years, Barenboim and du Pré regularly performed together, often as a duo, but also as a trio with violinist Pinchas Zukerman.

Elgar's Cello Concerto in E Minor, Op. 85. Over the course of her career, du Pré performed Elgar's

Cello Concerto more than any other. She first became acquainted with the concerto in her lessons with Pleeth when she was thirteen years old. The teenage cellist was so taken with the work, she purportedly memorized the first movement and half of the second movement in just two days. When du Pré performed this concerto in her orchestral debut concert, critics and audience members alike were stunned by her mature interpretation. Elgar composed his Cello Concerto at the end of World War I. Perhaps not surprisingly, the concerto evokes a sense of poignant tragedy, which du Pré, despite her tender age, was able to vividly capture in her playing.

Du Pré first recorded this concerto with Sir John Barbirolli and the London Symphony Orchestra in 1965. This legendary recording offers a spectacular demonstration of her daring and uninhibited style. Du Pré rerecorded the concerto with Barenboim and the Philadelphia Orchestra in 1971. This later recording, spliced from two live performances in Philadelphia, reveals even further self-indulgence

Jacqueline du Pré. (Hulton Archive/Getty Images)

on du Pré's part, especially in terms of rubato. Yet this extraordinary sense of freedom is grounded by solid technique, a combination that made du Pré's performances of the concerto awe-inspiring.

Schumann's Cello Concerto in A Minor, Op. 129. Du Pré was also admired for her interpretation of the Schumann Cello Concerto. She first performed this concerto with the BBC Symphony Orchestra in 1962. Composed after Schumann had begun to suffer from mental illness, this concerto is, like Elgar's, a rather somber work. In her 1968 recording with Barenboim and the New Philharmonia Orchestra, du Pré's playing is more disciplined and structured than was typical of her live performances of the work. Nonetheless, the performance is full of emotional intensity.

Brahms's Sonatas for Cello and Piano. In her chamber-music recitals with Bishop and Barenboim, du Pré frequently performed the two Brahms cello sonatas. She and Barenboim recorded both sonatas in 1968, and this recording offers a glimpse into the couple's passionate musical relationship. In the first sonata, which Brahms composed in 1866 and which shows the clear influence of Ludwig van Beethoven, du Pré and Barenboim are flexible with their tempi, yet they are always perfectly synchronized. The duo aptly expresses both the somber and heroic sides of the E minor sonata. The second sonata, in F major and composed in 1886, has a more tempestuous character and is more technically demanding, but both players are up to the challenge. Du Pré and Barenboim create a convincing and expressive dialogue between their instruments, perfect for such intimate chamber pieces.

Musical Legacy

Du Pré's inspiring performances and recordings of the Elgar concerto are largely responsible for the integration of this piece into the mainstream cello repertoire. Her free and innovative technique (including her frequent slides and unconventional fingerings) also opened up new possibilities for different playing styles. Such world-renowned cellists as Steven Isserlis and Yo-Yo Ma have acknowledged her influence. While some critics found her rather physical approach to performance excessively mannered and distracting, none could deny her innate musical genius. In recognition of the honor and distinction she brought England through her music, du Pré was made an Officer of the Most Excellent Order of the British Empire (OBE) in 1976.

Jennifer L. Smull

Further Reading

Du Pré, Hilary, and Piers du Pré. *A Genius in the Family: An Intimate Memoir of Jacqueline du Pré.* London: Chatto & Windus, 1997. These memoirs, written by du Pré's siblings, were used as the basis for the 1998 film *Hilary and Jackie.*

Easton, Carol. *Jacqueline du Pré: A Biography.* Cambridge, Mass.: Da Capo Press, 2000. This biography emphasizes du Pré's private life more than her public musical life.

Keener, Andrew. "The Cello Concerto: Jacqueline du Pré's Recordings." In *Elgar: An Anniversary Portrait.* London: Continuum, 2007. In this chapter, Keener discusses du Pré's special relationship with Elgar's Cello Concerto, and he compares her eight extant recordings.

Wilson, Elizabeth. *Jacqueline du Pré.* London: Weidenfeld & Nicolson, 1998. This thorough biography emphasizes du Pré's musical achievements. The author is a cellist and was personally acquainted with du Pré.

Wordsworth, William, ed. *Jacqueline du Pré: Impressions.* London: Grenada, 1983. Contains tributes to du Pré by friends and colleagues. Includes photographs and reviews of her performances.

See also: Barenboim, Daniel; Casals, Pablo; Elgar, Sir Edward; Ma, Yo-Yo; Rostropovich, Mstislav.

Bob Dylan

American folk and rock singer-songwriter

Dylan spearheaded the folk revival of the early 1960's and forged a new genre of music called folk-rock. His major talent as the most significant song-poet of the twentieth century lies in his extraordinary ability to synchronize profound poetry with simple yet infectious musical composition.

Born: May 24, 1941; Duluth, Minnesota

Also known as: Robert Allen Zimmerman (birth name); Blind Boy Grunt; Jack Frost; Elston Gunn; Sergei Petrov

Member of: The Traveling Wilburys

Principal recordings

ALBUMS: *Bob Dylan*, 1962; *The Freewheelin' Bob Dylan*, 1963; *Another Side of Bob Dylan*, 1964; *The Times They Are A-Changin'*, 1964; *Bringing It All Back Home*, 1965; *Highway 61 Revisited*, 1965; *Blonde on Blonde*, 1966; *John Wesley Harding*, 1967; *Nashville Skyline*, 1969; *New Morning*, 1970; *Self Portrait*, 1970; *Dylan*, 1973; *Pat Garrett and Billy the Kid*, 1973; *Planet Waves*, 1974; *The Basement Tapes*, 1975 (with the Band); *Blood on the Tracks*, 1975; *Desire*, 1976; *Street Legal*, 1978; *Slow Train Coming*, 1979; *Saved*, 1980; *Shot of Love*, 1981; *Infidels*, 1983; *Empire Burlesque*, 1985; *Knocked out Loaded*, 1986; *Hearts of Fire*, 1987; *Down in the Groove*, 1988; *Emotionally Yours*, 1988; *The Traveling Wilburys, Vol. 1*, 1988; *Oh Mercy*, 1989; *The Traveling Wilburys, Vol. 3*, 1990; *Under the Red Sky*, 1990; *Good as I Been to You*, 1992; *World Gone Wrong*, 1993; *Bob Dylan and Johnny Cash*, 1994; *Time out of Mind*, 1997; *Love and Theft*, 2001; *Masked and Anonymous*, 2003; *Modern Times*, 2006; *Tell Tale Signs: Rare and Unreleased, 1989-2006*, 2008; *Together Through Life*, 2009.

The Life

Robert Allen Zimmerman was born to Abram and Beatrice Zimmerman, descendants, respectively, of Russian- and Lithuanian-Jewish immigrants. He changed his name legally to Bob Dylan (DIH-luhn) in 1962, but he adopted the name as early as 1959. Dylan began to play piano around the age of ten, though according to his uncle Lewis Stone he was not a particularly gifted musician as a child. In fact, his family considered his younger brother David the more musically precocious. Dylan was notably perturbed by his family's misgivings; as a result, he gave up his cousin Harriet Rutstein's piano lessons and taught himself music.

As a young teen growing up in 1950's America, Dylan was keenly interested in rock-and-roll music and Hollywood films. He had a natural affinity for Elvis Presley, Buddy Holly, and James Dean; Dylan, like Elvis, Holly, and Dean, was a rebel at heart. His individuality is a trait no less significant to his success as an artist than is his talent for music and his gift with words. At Hibbing High, Dylan joined a number of rock-and-roll bands, including the Golden Chords and Elston Gunn and the Rock Boppers. With the Boppers he became for the first time a band's front man. Dylan was not much of a singer or instrumentalist at this time. He was just beginning to learn his trade and, like many other teenagers at the time, emulated the fashions and trends of his rock-and-roll heroes.

Dylan's discovery of the world of folk music did not occur until he graduated from high school and moved to "Dinky-town," a small beatnik community in the downtown core of Minneapolis. He briefly attended the University of Minnesota, where he enrolled in the liberal arts program as a music major. Dylan was never too interested in institutionalized education; while he was supposed to be attending classes, he spent most of his daytime hours sleeping and his nighttime hours playing music and fraternizing with musicians and fellow poets. Dylan was by no means uneducated, however; he was at this time and throughout his life a voracious reader and a keen self-learner. By early adulthood he already had a solid grounding in the Bible and had read much canonical literature.

In Dinkytown Dylan was introduced to the music and writings of Woody Guthrie and to Harry Smith's six-album "folk-Bible," *The Anthology of American Folk Music* (1952). Dylan's previous preference for rock and roll was soon displaced by an obsessive passion for folk music. For the next few years he learned primarily Guthrie songs and imitated his mentor's vocal stylings and performance techniques. When Dylan had heard that Guthrie was bedridden in a New Jersey hospital, he hitchhiked to New York to meet his hero and to live out the life of the hobo-songster that he had read about in Guthrie's 1943 autobiography *Bound for Glory*.

Dylan arrived in New York in January, 1961, and over the course of two years his life changed dramatically. He went from a Guthrie imitator, playing songs from a modest repertoire of folk standards, to

Bob Dylan. (AP/Wide World Photos)

a legitimate folk star, having signed a major record deal with Columbia Records and having written some of his most famous and anthemic songs, such as "Blowin' in the Wind" and "The Times They Are A-Changin'."

In 1961, to the surprise of many in the folk community, John Hammond, Sr., the highly touted record executive for Columbia Records, signed Dylan to a five-year album contract. Dylan's first album, self-titled *Bob Dylan*, was relatively unsuccessful, selling only five thousand copies in its debut year. The letdown of the album precipitated scathing commentary from the press—for a short spell Dylan was blacklisted as "Hammond's Folly."

Dylan's second album, *The Freewheelin' Bob Dylan*, stocked with Dylan originals, quickly changed people's minds about the songwriter's ability and Hammond's vision. Songs like "Blowin' in the Wind," "Girl from the North Country," and "Don't

Think Twice" seized the media's attention and soon drew the eye of Albert B. Grossman, a shrewd businessman from Chicago who would eventually become Dylan's most important promoter and manager. Grossman would turn the young twenty-year-old folksinger into an American icon and a multimillionaire.

Dylan's performances at the Newport Folk Festival in 1963 and 1965 catapulted him into the public mainstream and became the breakout performances of his career. At Newport he emerged as the artist who many believed captured in song the zeitgeist of the 1960's. Newport ignited a chain of important events and honors for Dylan. One month after the festival, on August 28, 1963, Dylan performed at the March on Washington, where Martin Luther King, Jr., gave his "I Have a Dream" speech. Shortly thereafter, the Emergency Civil Liberties Committee presented Dylan with its prestigious Tom Payne Award for outstanding social activism.

Dylan's return to Newport in 1965 accrued as much media attention for the rising star as had his appearance in 1963, though for different reasons. Until this point, Dylan had epitomized for many traditionalists the authentic folksinger. So far he had maintained an unamplified acoustic sound and had become for many folk gurus the Left's most important political spokesperson, but this changed at Newport in 1965. To the chagrin of many in attendance, Dylan performed on the Newport stage with a blues band and played an electrified version of "Maggie's Farm." Together, the amplified sound and the song's nonconformist lyrics struck the likes of folk icon Pete Seeger and others as a direct affront to folk music and to folk politics.

Dylan was at his most creative and productive during the mid-1960's. From 1965 to 1966, he recorded his famous "rock cycle": *Bringing It All Back Home*, *Highway 61 Revisited*, and *Blonde on Blonde*. His mysterious motorcycle accident on July 29, 1966, closed a decisive chapter in his life and ended a two-and-a-half-year stint of almost continuous touring. Speaking only in terms of his career, the accident proved timely; although it may well have cut short Dylan's creative output, it nipped in the bud a life-threatening touring schedule and concomitant drug addiction. Prior to the accident Dylan had been excessively taking pills and hallucinogens in order to uphold the contractual expectations of his indefatigable and money-hungry manager. The accident allowed the exhausted songwriter to recalibrate his decentered life and to reconnect with his newly acquired family. Less than a year before, on November 22, 1965, Dylan had married Sara Lownds and had taken on the role of stepfather to her daughter Maria. In the near future, Dylan and Lownds would have four children together: Jesse, Anna, Samuel, and Jakob.

After the accident, Dylan remained close to his home in Woodstock, New York, and out of the public limelight. Domestic life for the next few years changed Dylan considerably and deeply affected his songwriting. The calm, meditative sounds of his 1967 album *John Wesley Harding* reflect a time in Dylan's life when he was relatively happy and at ease with his surroundings. For a short time, then, between the late 1960's and the early 1970's, Dylan regained his equilibrium. Still, temptation lingered and his relationship with Lownds soon deteriorated. For much of his life, Dylan was drawn to women like he was drawn to perform, and the combination of these appetites ultimately destroyed his marriage and pulled him back onto the stage.

The years between 1975 and 1978 held their ups and downs for Dylan, yet more downs than ups. His Rolling Thunder Revue tour (1975-1976) outstripped any of the musician's expectations and produced some the most revolutionary live performances in music history. Like a traveling circus in a Shakespearean play, the Rolling Thunder Revue was a peripatetic band of likeminded musicians and poets that performed in costume and played for small stages across the United States. Unlike the Revue tour, which was a generally positive experience for Dylan, his world tour of 1978 was an exercise in commercialism and hedonism. The 1978 tour, which grossed an estimated twenty million dollars and had Dylan performing for more than two million people across Japan, Europe, and the United States, witnessed Dylan toying with promiscuity and sacrificing his musical integrity for fame and fortune.

Dylan converted to Christianity in 1978 and released in succession his "born-again" albums: *Slow Train Coming*, *Saved*, and *Shot of Love*. To say the least, Dylan's conversion shocked his community of family, friends, and fans, though his move to Christianity was not entirely unforeseeable. While some still consider his "religious" music of the late 1970's and early 1980's a radical departure from his earlier work, Dylan had been moving in a spiritual direction as least since *John Wesley Harding*, if not before. At any rate, his Christian albums significantly altered people's perceptions of his music and would negatively affect his future record sales and even his reputation.

Dylan reached the nadir of his career in the 1980's. Musically speaking, the climate did not bode well for Dylan. Rock music was the fashion, with its predominant focus on technical virtuosity, synthesized reproduction, and a kind of headbanger mentality—all things un-Dylan. Emotionally, Dylan was being torn apart by custody and settlement battles. As late as 1987, he was still entangled in a legal case with Grossman's estate, an affair that had begun as far back as 1970, when Dylan's contract with Grossman first expired. Also, Dylan was in anguish over the legal fallout from a divorce from his second wife, Carolyn Dennis, with whom he had fathered a child. It was during this period that Dylan had serious bouts of depression and alcohol abuse and contemplated early retirement.

In the early 1990's, Dylan began to reroot himself. His albums *Time out of Mind*, *Love and Theft*, and *Modern Times* constitute the fruition of everything that the now elder statesman had gathered and digested about traditional roots music. Dylan had managed to emerge as the last of America's late, great bluesmen; he now symbolized a walking, talking reservoir of American history whose sorrow-filled lyrics corresponded with his sorrow-filled life.

The early years of the twenty-first century were accompanied by a loss of distinction for Dylan. He faced the hardships of growing old with the passing of many friends and the death of his beloved mother on January 25, 2000. Nevertheless, these years also brought recognition on a new scale: a Nobel Prize nomination, a Kennedy Center medal, Sweden's prestigious Polar Music Prize, multiple Grammy Awards, and honorary induction into the Rock and Roll Hall of Fame.

The Music

Early Music. Dylan began his career as a traditional folksinger, playing for small clubs and cafés in and around the city of New York. Dylan's first album, *Bob Dylan*, showcases his clever knack for songwriting with two originals, "Talkin' New York Blues" and "Song to Woody" (Guthrie), and demonstrates his consummate understanding of and appreciation for the blues and folk traditions. While this debut was by no means a full exposition of Dylan's creativity—most of the songs are country-blues standards—the album does reveal the musical foundations upon which Dylan's music rests.

"Blowin' in the Wind." "Blowin' in the Wind" tops the list of classics on Dylan's second album *The Freewheelin' Bob Dylan*. Within only two years of its release on May 27, 1963, the song had been covered and recorded by at least eighty different musical acts. By 2002, an estimated 375 recordings of the song had been recorded worldwide, including renditions by Elvis Presley, Neil Young, and Sam Cooke.

"Like a Rolling Stone." Finally recorded on June 16, 1965, after fifteen takes and released four days later on *Highway 61 Revisited*, "Like a Rolling Stone" is Dylan's "Mona Lisa." This masterpiece defies the disjunction of language and thought, and like other great works of art it attains a certain degree of attunement between words and feeling. "How does it feel?," the song's driving line and repeated rhetorical question, does not dissociate the statement—how does it feel?—from the feeling about which it asks, but the expression is caught up *in* the feeling. Dylan's best songs often come closest to accomplishing what poet T. S. Eliot describes as "the [artist's] task of trying to find the verbal equivalent for states of mind and feeling." "Like a Rolling Stone" is Dylan's greatest attempt at pinpointing this equivalency. Because of the song's unprecedented length of six minutes and five seconds, it was originally divided between two sides of a 45-rpm record and was, consequently, either shelved by radio stations or played only in part. Eventually the entire song was reissued on one side because of the demands of disgruntled radio listeners.

Later Music. For sheer musicality, *Time out of Mind*, *Love and Theft*, and *Modern Times* are as layered and as complete as anything Dylan ever produced. To listen to *Love and Theft*, for example, is to rediscover the history of America through music, as many of the album's songs enact both instrumentally and lyrically the different times, places, and people of America's past. Each song on that album plays like a mini-musical short story and can be as imaginatively engaging as an audio-play. These last three albums are now being compared to Dylan's almighty rock-trilogy of the mid-1960's and have reclaimed Dylan's eminence in the twenty-first century world of popular music.

Musical Legacy

Dylan's influence in the evolution of popular music is unprecedented and reaches into a multitude of genres and subgenres. Beginning in the early 1960's, he had his creative finger on nearly every offshoot of American music, from folk to country to blues to rock and roll to early forms of rap.

Dylan's folk music of the early 1960's nuanced and revitalized traditional music with sophisticated poetry and political subject matter. His mid-1960's folk-rock trilogy intellectualized the visceral sounds of rock and roll with raplike rhyme schemes and surrealistic imagery, reminiscent of the imagery of poets William Blake and Arthur Rimbaud. Dylan's folk-country albums of the late 1970's and early 1980's helped resuscitate country and gospel in a time when they were considered dying musical forms. With *Nashville Skyline*, for example, a bona fide country album, Dylan put the "hip" back into "twang" and paved the way for new collaborations between folk, rock, and country. With his Christian rock albums of the same period, Dylan instigated a radical shift in Christian music. Although he was certainly not the first to move gospel music from the church to the street, he was one of the first to incorporate rock into gospel and to present popular music as a suitable medium for the expounding of faith and religious sentiment.

Jason Salter

Further Reading

Dylan, Bob. *Chronicles*. New York: Simon & Schuster, 2004. Dylan's autobiography provides a critical backdrop to the man behind the music and the touchstones of inspiration that contributed to the creation of his art.

Gray, Michael. *The Bob Dylan Encyclopedia*. New York: Continuum, 2006. This massive (736-page), A-Z compilation of facts about Dylan—from "All Along the Watch Tower" to Zigman Zimmerman—covers all things Dylan. Illustrations, bibliography, index.

Ricks, Christopher. *Dylan's Visions of Sin*. New York: Penguin, 2004. Ricks's challenging read offers a close look at Dylan as a poet. The book is designed for scholars and academics with a strong knowledge base in canonical literature.

Shelton, Robert. *No Direction Home: The Life and Music of Bob Dylan*. New York: Da Capo Press, 1986. *No Direction Home* is an indispensable biography of Dylan written from the perspective of a New York journalist who was actually close friends with the songwriter during the heyday of the 1960's.

Sounes, Howard. *Down the Highway: The Life of Bob Dylan*. New York: Grove Press, 2001. Without being sinister or sycophantic, Sounes's biography is a biting yet realistic account of the all-too-human sides of Bob Dylan.

See also: Babyface; Baez, Joan; Blow, Kurtis; Brel, Jacques; Burke, Solomon; Butterfield, Paul; Cash, Johnny; Cliff, Jimmy; Collins, Judy; Costello, Elvis; Crosby, David; Denny, Sandy; Earle, Steve; Fuller, Blind Boy; Garfunkel, Art; Guthrie, Arlo; Guthrie, Woody; Harris, Emmylou; Harrison, George; Hendrix, Jimi; Jagger, Sir Mick; Jansch, Bert; Jefferson, Blind Lemon; Kristofferson, Kris; Lomax, Alan; McGuinn, Roger; Martin, Sir George; Matthews, Dave; Mayfield, Curtis; Memphis Minnie; Morrison, Van; Nelson, Ricky; Neville, Aaron; Odetta; Oldfield, Mike; Orbison, Roy; Patton, Charley; Paxton, Tom; Petty, Tom; Prine, John; Raitt, Bonnie; Reed, Jimmy; Robertson, Robbie; Robinson, Smokey; Rush, Tom; Scruggs, Earl; Seeger, Pete; Smith, Patti; Springsteen, Bruce; Staples, Pops; Sting; Tweedy, Jeff; Van Ronk, Dave; Van Zandt, Townes; Vincent, Gene; Waits, Tom; Waters, Roger; Watson, Doc; Webb, Jimmy.

E

Steve Earle

American country singer, songwriter, and guitarist

Earle was an early member of the "alt-country" movement based in Austin, Texas, which opposed the rigidity of the Nashville country-music industry. His experimentation with a variety of musical styles and with left-wing politics brought diversity to country music.

Born: January 17, 1955; Fort Monroe, Virginia
Also known as: Stephen Fain Earle (full name)
Member of: Steve Earle and the Dukes

Principal recordings

ALBUMS (solo): *Pink and Black*, 1982; *Guitar Town*, 1986; *Early Tracks*, 1987; *Copperhead Road*, 1988; *The Hard Way*, 1990; *Train a Comin'*, 1995; *I Feel Alright*, 1996; *El Corazón*, 1997; *The Mountain*, 1999; *Transcendental Blues*, 2000; *Jerusalem*, 2002; *The Revolution Starts . . . Now*, 2004; *Washington Square Serenade*, 2007.

ALBUMS (with Steve Earle and the Dukes): *Exit Zero*, 1987; *The Hard Way*, 1990.

The Life

Stephen Fain Earle was born to Barbara Thomas and Jack Earle in Fort Monroe, Virginia. His father, an air traffic controller, was stationed in various parts of the United States, and most of Earle's childhood was spent in Schertz, Texas, north of San Antonio. Earle dropped out of school in the eighth grade to join his uncle, Nick Fain, in Houston. While there, he met outlaw country singer Townes Van Zandt, who inspired him to move to Nashville, Tennessee, to work in the country-music industry.

Earle arrived in Nashville in 1975. He worked as a backup singer and songwriter for the Sunbury Dunbar division of RCA, meeting other up-and-coming performers, such as Guy Clark and Emmylou Harris. Earle had his first major song-writing success in 1981 with "When You Fall in Love" (recorded by Johnny Lee). In 1986 his album, *Guitar Town*, was released to critical success and gold-record sales. *Exit Zero* followed in 1987, and 1990's *Copperhead Road* also generated successful singles.

Earle's longtime heroin addiction led to multiple arrests throughout the 1980's and 1990's, and in 1994 he was sentenced to eighteen months in prison for drug possession. After regaining his sobriety in prison, Earle was paroled later that year. His comeback album, *Train a-Comin'*, was released on an independent label, marking Earle's reemergence in the "alt-country" movement.

After he left prison, Earle turned to protest music. He became an anticapital-punishment activist, and he contributed to the sound track of the antideath-penalty film *Dead Man Walking* (1995). The invasion of Iraq in 2003 reawakened Earle's Vietnam-era antiwar sentiments, as heard on *Jerusalem* and *The Revolution Starts . . . Now*. Earle's political views led to controversy among usually conservative country-music fans. From 2004 until 2007, Earle hosted a program on the liberal talk-radio network Air America. Earle has been married seven times (twice to the same woman), and he settled in New York City with his wife, Alison Moorer, whom he married in 2005.

The Music

Earle's musical output can be divided into two parts: his preprison work (from *Guitar Town* through *The Hard Way*) and his post-1994 albums. Although his prison term lasted slightly over a year, the experience changed and informed his songwriting. Earle's pre-1991 output reflects rockabilly and rock styles, while later albums utilize a variety of musical traditions. Earle's first major success came with *Guitar Town*, and subsequent albums were critically successful, if not easily categorized into standard genres. Earle's drug abuse and legal troubles forced a recording hiatus until 1994, when *Train a-Comin'* was released. Earle's post-1994 output is notable for its political content and its debt to protest music singers, such as Bob Dylan and Bruce Springsteen.

Guitar Town. Earle's first major success as a performer, *Guitar Town* showcases his songwriting abilities. The album's ten tracks are a fusion of country, folk, and rock-and-roll influences. Widely credited with reviving a dormant Texas-based rockabilly sound, *Guitar Town* was ranked 489 on *Rolling Stone*'s 500 Greatest Albums of All Time in 2003.

Copperhead Road. This album veered toward a harder sound, reminiscent of 1970's Southern rock. While singles from *Guitar Town* received airplay on both rock and country radio, *Copperhead Road* was marketed primarily to rock audiences. The title track, "Copperhead Road," became Earle's best-known song in mainstream popular music.

Jerusalem. This was the first of Earle's explicitly political albums, a meditation on the attacks of September 11, 2001, and the U.S. government's response to them. "John Walker's Blues," a song written from the point of view of American Taliban fighter John Walker Lindh, caused an uproar in conservative circles for seeming to humanize Lindh and condone his actions.

The Revolution Starts . . . Now. Earle's Grammy Award-winning album of protest music was one of the first full albums about the Iraq War by a major artist. It is notable for its radical eclecticism, with musical gestures from rock, folk, reggae, and spoken-word. Explicitly topical in nature, the album was a centerpiece in the 2004 Rock Against Bush movement attached to John Kerry's presidential campaign.

Musical Legacy

Earle's career as both a songwriter and a performer has been extremely important for Texas-based "alt-country" music. The respect he earned from both the Nashville and the Austin music establishments has paved the way for crossover influence between the two, and his left-wing political views have brought political diversity into country music. Earle's work has been nominated for thirteen Grammy Awards, and *The Revolution Starts . . . Now* and *Washington Square Serenade* were named Best Contemporary Folk/Americana Album in 2005 and 2008, respectively.

Earle's most important musical works, however, remain the albums *Guitar Town* and *Copperhead Road*. The former revitalized country music's take on the rockabilly sound (undergoing a revival in popular music in the 1980's), while the latter brought Southern rock-influenced country music to mainstream attention. His recent works of protest music will also be remembered as a consistent dissenting voice to country music's conservative politics of the late 1990's and early 2000's.

Marcus Desmond Harmon

Further Reading

Blackstock, Peter. "Steve Earle: Can't Keep a Good Man Down." *No Depression* 1, no. 3 (Spring, 1996): 33-37. A profile of the singer in the wake of his 1994 imprisonment and release.

Earle, Steve. "The Politics of Retribution." In *It's a Free Country: Personal Freedom in America After September 11*, edited by Danny Goldberg, Victor Goldberg, and Robert Greenwald. New York: RDV/Akashic Books, 2000. This well-known essay by the singer discusses his views of the September 11 attacks and their effect on his musical and political development.

Lewis, George H. "Transcendental Blues." *Popular Music and Society* 26 (October, 2003). Review of Earle's 2000 album *Transcendental Blues*, which includes discussion of Earle's musical styles and influences.

McGee, David, and Steve Earle. *Steve Earle: Fearless Heart: Outlaw Poet*. San Francisco: Backbeat Books, 2005. An authorized biography of Earle, produced with the singer's cooperation. Includes extensive bibliography.

St. John, Lauren. *Hardcore Troubadour: The Life and Near-Death of Steve Earle*. New York: Harper-Collins, 2002. An extensive biography of Earle from his birth in 1955 through 2002.

See also: Dylan, Bob; Harris, Emmylou; Springsteen, Bruce; Van Zandt, Townes; Williams, Lucinda.

Fred Ebb

American musical-theater lyricist

Ebb collaborated with composer John Kander to write some of the most controversial and memorable musical-theater pieces of the twentieth century, including Cabaret *and* Chicago. *Ebb's lyrics are some of the most sardonic, wittiest, sharpest, and creative phrases in the Broadway canon, instrumental in developing character as well as moving the plot forward.*

Born: April 8, 1933; New York, New York
Died: September 11, 2004; New York, New York

Principal works

MUSICAL THEATER (lyrics; music by John Kander): *Flora, the Red Menace*, 1965 (libretto by George Abbott and Robert Russell; based on Lester Atwell's novel *Love Is Just Around the Corner*); *Cabaret*, 1966 (libretto by Joe Masteroff; based on John van Druten's play *I Am a Camera*); *The Happy Time*, 1968 (libretto by N. Richard Nash); *Zorba*, 1968 (libretto by Joseph Stein; based on Nikos Kazantzakis's novel *Zorba the Greek*); *Seventy, Girls, Seventy*, 1971 (libretto by David Thompson and Norman L. Martin; based on Peter Coke's play *Breath of Spring*); *Chicago*, 1975 (libretto by Ebb and Bob Fosse; based on Maurine Dallas Watkins's play); *The Act*, 1978 (libretto by George Furth); *Woman of the Year*, 1981 (libretto by Peter Stone); *The Rink*, 1984 (libretto by Terrence McNally); *And the World Goes 'Round*, 1991 (libretto by Thompson); *Kiss of the Spider Woman*, 1993 (libretto by McNally); *Steel Pier*, 1997 (libretto by Thompson); *All About Us*, 1999 (libretto by Stein; based on Thornton Wilder's play *The Skin of Our Teeth*); *The Visit*, 2001 (libretto by McNally; based on Friedrich Dürrenmatt's play); *Curtains*, 2006 (libretto by Rupert Holmes).
SONGS (lyrics): "Heartbroken," 1953 (music by Phil Springer); "I Never Loved Him Anyhow," 1956 (music by Springer); "My Coloring Book," 1962 (music by John Kander); "Say Liza (Liza with a 'Z')," 1972 (music by Kander); "New York, New York," 1977 (music by Kander).

The Life

Born of Jewish parents, Fred Ebb grew up in a house without music. He worked in his family's dry-goods business until he graduated as valedictorian from high school. Although his mother hoped he would pursue a more stable path, Ebb had fallen in love with theater after seeing an Al Jolson show and decided to become a writer. He worked in a variety of odd jobs while in school but managed to earn his bachelor of arts from New York University and a master's degree from Columbia University in English literature. He lived in New York City, decorating his apartment with Expressionist and other avant-garde artwork. Shortly before his death, Ebb was awarded two honorary doctorate of fine arts degrees, from Boston University and St. John's University. Ebb never married. His work monopolized his life until he died of a heart attack in September, 2004. The lights on Broadway were dimmed in his honor.

The Music

Ebb began work as a songwriter with Paul Klein and Phil Springer (whom he credits as his mentor) in the 1950's. Although he enjoyed modest success with a few hits recorded by Judy Garland and Eartha Kitt, it was not until his music producer and friend Tommy Valando introduced him to composer and pianist John Kander that his legacy as one of the great Broadway lyricists became a certainty. Once they met, Kander and Ebb began writing together almost immediately. Their early work impressed director-producer Harold Prince enough to hire them to write the songs for his Broadway musical *Flora, the Red Menace*. The show closed after only eighty-seven performances but netted the star, Liza Minnelli, a Tony Award and catapulted Kander, Ebb, and Prince to national theatrical prominence. Prince immediately hired them to begin work on his next major project, *Cabaret*.

Cabaret. Adapted from a 1951 play by John van Druten, *I Am a Camera*, which was based on short stories from the 1930's by Christopher Isherwood, *Cabaret* tells the story of an English nightclub singer, Sally Bowles, living in pre-Nazi Germany, who falls in love with an American writer, becomes pregnant, and has an abortion. Book writer Joe Masteroff revised the play to focus on the anti-Semitic sentiments of the time and added the devilishly delicious emcee. Bowles's love story is developed before the backdrop of the Kit Kat Club and political turmoil, which is explored through the characters of the German landlady, Fraulein Schneider, and her Jewish boyfriend, Herr Schultz. When *Cabaret* opened on Broadway in 1966, it became a huge success, enjoying a run of 1,166 performances and winning the Drama Critics' Circle Award for Best Musical and eight Tony Awards, including Best Composer and Lyricist and Best Musical. *Cabaret* helped establish the new form of "concept musical," one that has a nonrealistic, episodic plotline with a mixture of scenes and songs. Jay Presson Allen's book for the 1972 film adaptation made a few changes, and the film won eight Academy Awards. A Broadway revival ran for six years.

Chicago. Kander and Ebb's next big hit, *Chicago*, enjoyed 923 performances. The plot revolves around a starstruck murderess, Roxie Hart, who kills her

Fred Ebb (standing) with John Kander. (AP/Wide World Photos)

lover to get publicity, and a slimy attorney who manipulates the public's heartstrings to get her acquitted. The musical is based on a play by Maurine Watkins, *Chicago* (1926), which was inspired by an event she covered as a reporter. Bob Fosse adapted the play, calling it *Chicago: A Musical Vaudeville*. True to its name, the musical features scenes and songs announced as in a vaudeville show, and it contains rhythm numbers, a ventriloquist, strippers, a female impersonator, musical soliloquies, soft-shoe dance numbers, and comic duets. Beneath the glitz, however, is a serious satire on the way media attention makes celebrities of criminals. Ebb cowrote the book with Fosse. When it was revived in 1996, *Chicago* received an even greater reception and became one of the longest-running revivals in Broadway history. The film version in 2002 was nominated for thirteen Academy Awards, winning six, including Best Picture.

Later Work. In 1993 *Kiss of the Spider Woman*, based on Manuel Puig's novel about two criminals in a Latin American prison, had 907 performances and won seven Tony Awards, including Best Musical. Of the Kander and Ebb shows that followed, many received high critical praise, especially *Steel Pier* (1997), which was nominated for eleven Tony Awards, winning for Best Original Score, even though it closed after only two months. *Curtains* (2006), nominated for eight Tonys, was in development when Ebb died. Kander worked with others to finish it and made plans to complete three other unfinished Ebb works: *The Visit*, *All About Us*, and *The Minstrel Show*.

Unlike many musical collaborators, Kander and Ebb worked together in the same room. They always wrote the opening number first to give them a sense of style for the show. Besides collaborating on Broadway musicals, they wrote songs for television and film. "New York, New York," from *New York, New York* (1977), became New York's official anthem. Although Ebb and Kander sometimes worked independently, nothing equaled the success they had together in their musical-theater efforts.

Musical Legacy

Ebb was the recipient of four Tony Awards (twelve nominations), one Grammy Award, and four Emmy Awards as well as the prestigious Kennedy Center Lifetime Achievement Award, Dramatists Guild of America Lifetime Achievement Award, and the Laurence Olivier Award. With Kander, he was inducted into the Songwriters Hall of Fame and the New York Theater Hall of Fame and won numerous other special awards.

Ebb gave Broadway some of the greatest lyrics ever written, and through his forty-two-year collaboration with Kander, he helped develop a new style of musical theater that raised the standards for excellence in the genre. Their impact on musical-theater writers and performers of today and tomorrow is immeasurable.

Jill Stapleton-Bergeron

Further Reading

Kander, John, Greg Lawrence, and Fred Ebb. *Colored Lights: Forty Years of Words and Music, Show Biz, Collaboration, and All That Jazz.* New York: Faber & Faber, 2004. Firsthand accounts by Kander and Ebb about their lives, collaboration, and musical-theater experiences.

Kasha, Al, and Joel Hirschhorn. *Notes on Broadway: Conversations with the Great Songwriters.* Chicago: Contemporary Books, 1985. Contains a chapter for each major Broadway songwriter, including Ebb.

Lewis, David H. *Broadway Musicals: A Hundred Year History.* Jefferson, N.C.: McFarland, 2002. Overview of the important musicals that shaped the development of the genre, including a solid section on the work of Kander and Ebb.

Mordden, Ethan. *The Happiest Corpse I've Ever Seen: The Last Twenty-five Years of the Broadway Musical.* New York: Palgrave Macmillan, 2004. Evolution of the Broadway musical from 1979 to 2004.

Suskin, Steven. *More Opening Nights on Broadway: A Critical Quotebook of the Musical Theatre 1965 Through 1981.* New York: Schirmer Books, 1997. A valuable collection of opening-night reviews for Broadway musicals from 1965 to 1981 that encompasses Kander and Ebb's Broadway offerings from *Flora, the Red Menace* to *Woman of the Year.*

See also: Fields, Dorothy; Hart, Lorenz; Kander, John; Rodgers, Richard; Sondheim, Stephen.

Duane Eddy
American rock songwriter and guitarist

During the 1950's, Eddy established himself as one of the most influential guitarists in the history of rock music. His guitar sound became known as "twang." This unique sound was created through the use of tremolo and reverb on the guitar. Through the efforts of Eddy, the guitar became the most important instrument in rock music.

Born: April 26, 1938; Corning, New York
Also known as: Mr. Twang

Principal recordings

ALBUMS: *Especially for You,* 1959; *Have Twangy Guitar—Will Travel,* 1959; *The Twang's the Thang,* 1960; *$1,000,000 Worth of Twang,* 1960; *Songs of Our Heritage,* 1960; *Girls! Girls! Girls!,* 1961; *Twangy Guitar—Silky Strings,* 1962; *Twistin' and Twangin',* 1962; *Twistin' with Duane Eddy,* 1962; *Duane Eddy in Person,* 1963; *Twang a Country Song,* 1963; *Twangin' up a Storm,* 1963; *Surfin',* 1963; *Lonely Guitar,* 1964; *Water Skiing,* 1964; *Duane a-Go-Go,* 1965; *Duane Does Dylan,* 1965; *Twangin' the Golden Hits,* 1965; *Twangsville,* 1965; *The Biggest Twang of Them All,* 1966; *The Roaring Twangies,* 1967; *Duane Eddy,* 1979; *Star Power,* 2002.

The Life

Duane Eddy was born on April 26, 1938, in Corning, New York. At the age of five, he was given his first guitar and his father taught him some basic chords. He loved to listen to the cowboy singers Gene Autry and Roy Rogers on the radio. The family moved to Phoenix, Arizona, when he was a teenager. At the age of sixteen, he decided to quit school and began playing his guitar at local clubs. A local disc jockey, Lee Hazlewood, met the young Eddy in 1957 and was impressed by his guitar work. Although Hazlewood worked as a disc jockey, he became Eddy's record producer and songwriting partner. This partnership would become extraordinarily successful.

In 1958, Eddy signed a recording contract with Jamie Records after the company had reviewed a demo tape of the song "Movin' 'n' Groovin'." Through the support of Hazlewood, Eddy was inspired to create a sound that blended rock, country, jazz, and soul music. In 1962, Eddy married singer-songwriter Jessi Colter (born Miriam Johnson). The marriage lasted until 1968. Colter would marry legendary country singer Waylon Jennings in 1969.

During the 1960's, Eddy began an acting career. He appeared in such films as *A Thunder of Drums* (1961), *The Wild Westerners* (1962), *Kona Coast* (1968), and *The Savage Seven* (1968). He also appeared in a 1961 episode of the television series *Have Gun, Will Travel*, which starred Richard Boone.

The Music

With the help of Hazlewood, Eddy created the "twang" sound that would make him famous. The sound was produced on his Chet Atkins-model Gretsch 6120 hollow-body guitar by picking on the low strings and manipulating the guitar's tremolo and reverb. In 1958, Eddy released his first hit single, "Rebel Rouser." The single went to number six on the *Billboard* pop singles chart, making it one of the most popular rock instrumental hits of the decade. He would have two more hits in 1958 with "Ramrod" and "Cannonball."

Eddy recorded these hits with his backing band the Rebels. The Rebels included Steve Douglas on saxophone, Larry Knechtel on piano, and Al Casey on guitar. These musicians would become some of the most respected session musicians in the history of popular music. From 1958 to 1963, Eddy was the premier instrumentalist in popular music. During this period, he released more than twenty singles that would make the pop singles charts.

Have "Twangy" Guitar—Will Travel. Recorded in 1958 and released on January 9, 1959, this debut album was very successful for Eddy. It would remain on the *Billboard* pop albums charts for eighty-two weeks and rise as high as number five. The album included most of Eddy's early hits, including "Rebel Rouser," "Ramrod," "Cannonball," "Movin' 'n' Groovin'," and "Three-30-Blues." In

Duane Eddy. (Hulton Archive/Getty Images)

1999, the album was reissued on compact disc (CD) and included some extra B-side songs from 1958. His second album, *Especially for You*, was released in 1959 and would reach number twenty-four on the pop albums charts.

That year was very productive for Eddy. In addition to the albums, he released such successful singles as "Yep!," "Forty Miles of Bad Road," "The Lonely One," and "Some Kind-a Earthquake." The single "Forty Miles of Bad Road" would rise to number nine on the *Billboard* pop singles chart, making it the second single for Eddy to reach the Top 10.

Twangy Guitar—Silky Strings. This 1962 album emphasized a more romantic tone. The lushness found on this album was a welcome change in approach for Eddy. The album went to number seventy-two on the pop albums charts and included such songs as Henry Mancini's "Moon River," Dimitri Tiomkin's "High Noon," and Elvis Presley's "Love Me Tender." The combination of twangy guitar and strings made this album a bona fide success. In 1962 Eddy also released the albums *Twistin' and Twangin'* and *Twistin' with Duane Eddy.*

Hit Singles. At the same time that he was releasing albums during the early 1960's, Eddy was releasing memorable hit singles. In 1960, he released such important singles as "Because They're Young," "Bonnie Came Back," "Shazam!" and "Peter Gunn." "Because They're Young" went to number four on the pop singles chart and was the title song of the film of the same name. The theme song "Peter Gunn" had been written by Mancini for the television program of the same name. Eddy's single would go to number twenty-seven on the same charts. In the busy album year of 1962, Eddy found the energy to release the singles "Dance with the Guitar Man," "Deep in the Heart of Texas," and "The Ballad of Paladin." Although all three of these singles did well, it was "Dance with the Guitar Man" that reached number twelve on the pop singles chart. In 1963, Eddy released "Boss Guitar." This single would climb to number twenty-eight and became his last major hit.

Eddy continued to tour, do session work, and occasionally record a new album. He was in demand in England and Europe. In 1986, he teamed with the Art of Noise in order to do a new version of his 1960 hit "Peter Gunn." This new version became a huge hit around the world and garnered for Eddy a Grammy Award for Best Rock Instrumental. Rhino Records released an extraordinary two-CD anthology *Twang Thang: Anthology* in 1993, which reintroduced Eddy to a generation of young listeners who had not been exposed to his music.

Musical Legacy

Before Eddy, guitarists were not considered stars or centers of attention. Rock stars of the 1950's were not loved because of what they played on guitar. Even such important guitarists as Bo Diddley and Chuck Berry were stars in the public's eye more for their singing, songwriting, and onstage style than for their guitar playing. Eddy completely changed this attitude. Idolized for his guitar work alone, he made the guitar the focal point of the popular music band and helped launch the birth of the "guitar god" in rock music.

During the late 1950's and the early 1960's, Eddy had fifteen Top 40 singles. Over his career, he sold more than a hundred million records and became one of the most successful instrumentalists in the history of rock music. In addition to paving the way for future guitar heroes like Eric Clapton, Jimi Hendrix, and Jimmy Page, Eddy inspired such rock luminaries as George Harrison of the Beatles, John Fogerty of Creedence Clearwater Revival, and Bruce Springsteen. In 1994, Eddy was inducted into the Rock and Roll Hall of Fame.

Jeffry Jensen

Further Reading

Escott, Colin, ed. *All Roots Lead to Rock: Legends of Early Rock 'n' Roll.* New York: Schirmer Books, 1999. Includes a penetrating portrait of Eddy by Rob Finnis entitled "Boy and His Guitar: Twangin' from Phoenix to Los Angeles, Duane Eddy."

Kienzle, Richard. *Great Guitarists.* New York: Facts On File, 1985. Along with such guitar gods as Elmore James, Robert Johnson, Les Paul, Jeff Beck, Jimi Hendrix, Eric Clapton, and Jimmy Page, Eddy is discussed as one of the most influential guitarists in the history of rock music.

Sumrall, Harry. *Pioneers of Rock and Roll: One Hundred Artists Who Changed the Face of Rock.* New York: Billboard Books, 1994. Eddy is credited as the first guitar hero of rock music.

See also: Jennings, Waylon; Presley, Elvis; Scruggs, Earl.

Danny Elfman

American singer, songwriter, and film-score composer

A rock musician for two decades, Elfman became one of the most sought-after composers of film scores in Hollywood.

Born: May 29, 1953; Amarillo, Texas
Member of: Oingo Boingo

Principal works

FILM SCORES: *Forbidden Zone,* 1980; *Pee-wee's Big Adventure,* 1985; *Back to School,* 1986; *Wisdom,*

1986; *Summer School*, 1987; *Beetlejuice*, 1988; *Big Top Pee-wee*, 1988; *Hot to Trot*, 1988; *Midnight Run*, 1988; *Scrooged*, 1988; *Batman*, 1989; *Darkman*, 1990; *Dick Tracy*, 1990; *Edward Scissorhands*, 1990; *Nightbreed*, 1990; *Pure Luck*, 1990 (with Jonathan Sheffer); *Article Ninety-Nine*, 1992; *Batman Returns*, 1992; *Army of Darkness*, 1993; *Sommersby*, 1993; *Tim Burton's Nightmare Before Christmas*, 1993; *Black Beauty*, 1994; *Shrunken Heads*, 1994; *Dead Presidents*, 1995; *Dolores Claiborne*, 1995; *To Die For*, 1995; *Freeway*, 1996; *The Frighteners*, 1996; *Mars Attacks!*, 1996; *Mission: Impossible*, 1996; *Flubber*, 1997; *Good Will Hunting*, 1997; *Men in Black*, 1997; *A Civil Action*, 1998; *Psycho*, 1998; *A Simple Plan*, 1998; *Anywhere but Here*, 1999; *Instinct*, 1999; *Sleepy Hollow*, 1999; *Proof of Life*, 2000; *Planet of the Apes*, 2001; *Chicago*, 2002 (with John Kander); *Men in Black II*, 2002; *Spider-Man*, 2002; *Big Fish*, 2003; *The Hulk*, 2003; *Spider-Man 2*, 2004; *Charlie and the Chocolate Factory*, 2005; *The Corpse Bride*, 2005; *Serenada Schizophrana*, 2005; *Charlotte's Web*, 2006; *Nacho Libre*, 2006.

TELEVISION THEMES: *Pee-wee's Playhouse*, 1986; *Sledge Hammer!*, 1986; *The Simpsons*, 1989; *Beetlejuice*, 1989; *The Flash*, 1990 (with Shirley Walker); *Tales from the Crypt*, 1990 (main theme); *Batman*, 1992; *Desperate Housewives*, 2004.

Principal recordings

ALBUMS (with Oingo Boingo): *Oingo Boingo*, 1980; *Only a Lad*, 1981; *Nothing to Fear*, 1982; *Good for Your Soul*, 1984; *So-Lo*, 1984; *Dead Man's Party*, 1986; *Boi-ngo*, 1987; *Boingo Alive*, 1988; *Dark at the End of the Tunnel*, 1990.

The Life

Danny Elfman was born in Texas in 1953, though the family moved to Los Angeles in his childhood. His father Milton was a teacher, and his mother Blossom wrote children's books and television scripts. The Elfmans' children followed the family's artistic bent, Danny playing the violin and his older brother Richard turning to cinematography. When Richard moved to France, Danny dropped out of high school and followed him, acting in a theater troupe and supporting himself as a street musician.

When the brothers returned to the United States in 1972, Richard formed a musical-theater group billed as the Mystic Knights of Oingo Boingo. The interests of the other musicians soon turned the group into a rock band, and as Oingo Boingo they became a force in pop music from 1976 until disbanding in 1995. Danny wrote and Oingo Boingo performed the music for Richard's 1980 film *Forbidden Zone*, but Danny did not consider himself a film scorer until director Tim Burton asked him to score *Pee-wee's Big Adventure* in 1985. For the next several decades, Danny scored two or three films a year. In 2007 he was awarded an honorary doctorate from the North Carolina School of the Arts.

The Music

As a new wave rock songwriter, Danny Elfman found his success to be largely a cult phenomenon. He did chart twice on the *Billboard* Hot 100 with "Weird Science" (1985) and "Just Another Day" (1986). By that time, however, he had already been identified as a film composer. This second career should not have come as a surprise, since even as a youth Elfman had been conscious of film music as an influence on his own style, particularly the work of Bernard Herrmann and Franz Waxman.

Pee-wee's Big Adventure. Elfman's first orchestral film score was Burton's first feature film, based on comedian Paul Reubens's character Pee-wee Herman. To match the character's frenetic adolescent energy, Elfman wrote a manic, staccato main theme, reminiscent of Aram Khachaturian's *Saber Dance* (though influenced, according to Elfman, by Nino Rota's scores for motion-picture director Federico Fellini and *The Godfather* films). Although an accomplished violinist, Elfman had never attempted a full orchestration, having worked only in the rock idiom. With the help of Oingo Boingo's arranger Steve Bartek, however, Elfman soon gained confidence and came to appreciate the fuller range of a symphonic orchestra.

Batman. For his sixth film score, and his third for Burton, Elfman wanted to capture in musical style the retro Art Deco style of the film's sets, as well as the romantic flavor of the first *Batman* comic books. To do so he imitated the lush, neo-Romantic film scores of Erich Wolfgang Korngold, particularly the adventure themes for Erroll Flynn vehicles *Captain Blood* (1935) and *The Adventures of Robin Hood*

(1938). The fourth bar of the title music introduces a five-note "bat theme" that continues throughout the film, identified with the title character. Alternating with this theme is Elfman's experiment with whole-tone music, which in film scores is traditionally associated with dream sequences—appropriate for a fantasy film.

Edward Scissorhands. Elfman has said that this score, his fourth for Burton and seventh overall, was his favorite. It is easy to see why. Like many of his predecessors in film music, Elfman imitates Richard Wagner in interweaving a musical theme, or leitmotif, for each major character or setting. There is a delicate music-box chime for the flashback scenes of the title character's creation by his inventor; an awed chorus of female voices singing cascades of random vowels in the style of Carl Orff whenever Edward's love interest, Kim, appears; and a frenetic, jerky pastiche of ostinatos (short, repeated musical phrases reminiscent of *The Simpsons*, which Elfman had composed the previous year) during the suburban scenes. Elfman even combined motifs: When Edward carves an ice sculpture of Kim, the chimes of the inventor motif merge with the chorus of the Kim motif. This score was nominated for both an Emmy and a Saturn award (the latter given for science fiction, fantasy, or horror films). It debuted as a ballet in London in November, 2005.

Serenada Schizophrana. Elfman's symphonic debut in 2005 at Carnegie Hall in New York was a twenty-minute piece in six movements for full orchestra and female chorus. The enthusiastic reviews put to rest the suspicion that Elfman was nothing more than a pop musician dependent on the army of orchestrators and copyists provided by film studios or on a music sequencer (composition software).

Musical Legacy

Elfman's reputation was troubled in the 1990's by accusations, particularly in a series of letters in *Keyboard* magazine, that he was a "hummer" who hummed his melodies into a tape recorder and turned them over to others to transcribe into musical notation. This myth is handily refuted by a glance at archival scores in Elfman's handwriting in studio files. Although Elfman did not have conservatory training in composition, working out his

Danny Elfman. (AP/Wide World Photos)

early scores with Bartek provided him a thorough, if informal, education in scoring and orchestration from studio professionals. The concern that Elfman's self-taught status would tempt would-be composers to avoid music theory and composition classes is no longer given much credence, since many composers are now in conservatories precisely because of Elfman's example. Three of Elfman's film scores have been nominated for Oscars; his score for Burton's *Batman* won a Grammy Award for best sound track; his theme song for *The Simpsons* was nominated for an Emmy in 1989; and his theme for *Desperate Housewives* won an Emmy in 2004.

John R. Holmes

Further Reading

Breese, Keith T. *Clowns of Death: A History of Oingo Boingo*. Philadelphia: Xlibris, 2001. An account of Elfman's music before he became a film composer.

Donnelly, K. J. "*Batman, Batman Returns*, and Post-Classical Film Music." In *Contemporary Holly-*

wood Cinema, edited by Steve Neale and Murray Smith. London: Routledge, 1998. A study of Elfman's scores for two Burton films.

Halfyard, Janet K. *Danny Elfman's Batman: A Film Score Guide*. Lanham, Md.: Scarecrow Press, 2004. A thorough study of the music with liberal reproductions of cues and musical passages from the score.

McMahan, Alison. *The Films of Tim Burton*. New York: Continuum, 2005. A comprehensive study of Burton's films that contains an analysis of Elfman's scores.

Russell, Mark, and James Young. *Film Music*. Boston: Focal Press, 2000. This lavishly illustrated book of interviews with thirteen twentieth century film composers includes a section on Elfman and reproduces the first two pages of the orchestral score for *Batman* and the first three for *Edward Scissorhands*.

See also: Herrmann, Bernard; Kander, John; Korngold, Erich Wolfgang; Orff, Carl; Rota, Nino; Waxman, Franz.

Sir Edward Elgar

English classical composer

A composer in all genres, Elgar brought the English musical renaissance to its peak, earning new respect for the English symphony. His first march from Pomp and Circumstance *is widely recognized, often played at school graduations.*

Born: June 2, 1857; Broadheath, England
Died: February 23, 1934; Worcester, England
Also known as: Edward William Elgar (full name)

Principal works

CHAMBER WORKS: Piano Quintet in A Minor, 1919; Sonata in E Minor, 1919 (for violin); String Quartet in E Minor, 1919.

OPERAS (music): *The Crown of India*, 1912 (libretto by Henry Hamilton); *The Starlight Express*, 1915 (libretto by Violet Pearn, based on Algernon Blackwood's novel *A Prisoner in Fairyland*); *The*

Fringes of the Fleet, 1917 (based on the novella by Rudyard Kipling); *The Pageant of Empire*, 1924 (libretto by Alfred Noyes); *The Spanish Lady*, 1994 (libretto by Barry Johnson, based on Ben Johnson's *The Devil Is an Ass*).

ORCHESTRAL WORKS: *The Black Knight*, 1893; *The Banner of St. George*, 1897; *Imperial March*, 1897; *Caractacus*, 1898; *Enigma*, 1899; *The Dream of Gerontius*, 1900 (oratorio; libretto by Elgar; based on a poem by Cardinal John Henry Newman); *Cockaigne (In London Town)*, 1901; *Pomp and Circumstance*, 1901; *Enfants d'un rêve*, 1902 (Dream Children); *In the South (Alassio)*, 1904; *The Wand of Youth*, 1907; Symphony No. 1 in A-flat Major, 1908; *Elegy*, 1909; Violin Concerto in B Minor, 1910; Symphony No. 2 in E-flat Major, 1911; *Falstaff*, 1913; *Sospiri*, 1914; Cello Concerto in E Minor, 1919; *Nursery Suite*, 1931; *The Spanish Lady*, 1986.

PIANO WORKS: Sonata in G Major, 1895; *Concert Allegro*, 1901.

The Life

Edward William Elgar (EHL-gahr) was born to William, a piano tuner, and Ann Elgar, the well-read daughter of a Herefordshire farmer. Elgar was the only one of their seven children born in the family's Broadheath cottage, just outside the busy city of Worcester, which perhaps explains Elgar's musical connection to the English countryside.

In 1872, still only fourteen, Elgar left school. His dreams of studying composition in Leipzig were never realized; he had no way to finance such a project. Elgar's lack of a higher education and his lower-class background combined to cause a nagging self-doubt that plagued his career.

Elgar met Caroline Alice Roberts in 1886, when she came to Elgar for piano accompaniment lessons. On May 8, 1889, they were married. Her death in 1920 is often cited as one of the many reasons that Elgar stopped composing in the last fifteen years of his life.

Even though he was already famous by 1904, the year was notable for Elgar. In March there was a three-day festival of his music in Covent Garden, the first of its sort mounted for a living composer. Later that month, he was invited to join the Athenaeum, an exclusive gentlemen's club that usually conferred membership based on wealth or

Sir Edward Elgar. (Library of Congress)

descent. In June, King Edward VII bestowed knighthood on Elgar in the Birthday Honors list. In November, Elgar was invited to become the Peyton Professor of Music at Birmingham University, a newly created chair that he was the first to hold.

World War I had a deep impact on Elgar. As a figurehead of English composition who had taken inspiration from Germanic composers, he found his loyalties torn. Like many in England, Elgar was initially confident about the prospect of battle and victory, but he did not foresee the full extent of the devastation that the war would cause. Elgar lived until 1934, but the Cello Concerto in E Minor, which premiered in 1919, was his last major work.

The Music

Elgar composed in a number of genres, and broad characteristics can be identified across his oeuvre. His musical language was always Romantic and largely Austro-Germanic inspired; he particularly admired the composer Richard Strauss. In spite of Elgar's continental inspiration, his music is often described as quintessentially English, with his adroitness for tapping the musical tastes of the British public, around which he crafted the ideas that he adopted from others. In many ways, Elgar took the stylistic traits of the older school of English composers (Charles Hubert Hastings Parry, Charles Villiers Stanford, and more) and raised them to a more sophisticated level. The British public demanded choral-orchestral works and symphonies, and Elgar responded.

The Dream of Gerontius. Elgar's oratorio *The Dream of Gerontius* secured his fame. It belongs to the corpus of English choral-orchestral compositions written at the turn of the twentieth century, especially for the amateur choral societies that were the lifeblood of English music at the time. The compositional mastery that Elgar exhibits in *The Dream of Gerontius*, however, distinguishes it from others. Elgar selected for the libretto a poem by Cardinal John Henry Newman, the title of which is shared by the oratorio. It is deeply Roman Catholic in nature. The work centers on the death of a man who is reborn in the afterlife. It is largely through-composed, with only two parts. It is often associated with Richard Wagner's opera *Parsifal*. Among the shared characteristics of *The Dream of Gerontius* and *Parsifal* are chromatic harmonies and an extensive network of leitmotifs.

The Dream of Gerontius premiered at the Birmingham Festival in 1900. Hans Johann Richter, with whom Elgar would forge a lasting friendship, conducted the performance, although it was a disastrous rendition. Richter saw the score for the first time just ten days before the performance, and the work had to be accommodated in a crowded program. In spite of the premiere's poor quality, *The Dream of Gerontius* received great acclaim, with music critics recognizing that Elgar had produced a masterpiece.

Pomp and Circumstance. No work better exemplifies Elgar's ability to satisfy popular tastes than the first of his *Pomp and Circumstance* marches, written in 1901. Beginning with an invigorating march and culminating in the famous *nobilmente* melody, this work exerted wide appeal. In 1902 Arthur Christopher Benson set the big tune of the march to poetry ("Land of Hope and Glory"). While not lacking in artistic construction, this march is part of a body of English art from the turn of the twentieth century that celebrated and glorified imperialism.

Elgar eventually turned his back on this nationalist style of composition, and his feelings toward the imperial past were seemingly given voice in the laments of the Cello Concerto.

Symphony No. 1 in A-flat Major. Throughout his career, even when his output consisted almost entirely of choral-orchestral works, Elgar believed the symphony to be the most distinguished form of composition. He realized that the musical achievements possible in the choral-orchestral medium were finite, and he finally turned to composing a symphony.

Elgar dedicated the work to Richter, who conducted its first performance on December 3, 1908. The symphony is in four movements, and it is without a program. Like many of Elgar's works, the piece is characterized by its adventurous harmonic language and concertic treatment of the thematic material. Elgar uses classical forms as templates, but he often diverges from structural norms exemplified in, for example, the symphonies of Johannes Brahms.

Cello Concerto in E Minor. This was Elgar's last major original composition, and it can be considered the closest he came to writing a requiem. It is a nostalgic and introspective lament, expressing the many sorrows that Elgar had experienced by his sixties. The work premiered on October 27, 1919, in the inaugural concert of the London Symphony Orchestra's first season after the World War I. Elgar was the conductor, and Felix Salmond was the soloist.

The concerto is famous for its opening: four solo fortissimo cello chords so wide that they must be spread, followed by the haunting violin melody with a 9/8 lilt. The declamatory chords return as a ghostly pizzicato at the second movement's opening. The third movement is, like the first, defined by a poignant melody. During the fourth movement's coda, the opening cello chords return, as if the work has gone full circle.

Musical Legacy

Although, unlike his colleagues Parry and Stanford, Elgar never taught composition at a music college, the impact of his works on the next generation of musicians was substantial. He contributed to ev-

ery major genre, and he left indelible marks on the forms of symphony and oratorio. His contribution to the symphony brought the English musical renaissance to its peak, and the English symphony was finally accorded respect at home, in Europe, and in America, on a par with the repertoire of the Viennese tradition. Elgar opened the way for composers such as Ralph Vaughan-Williams and Benjamin Britten to become established on the international stage. Composers such as Anthony Payne and Robert Walker have reconstructed a number of pieces from Elgar's sketches. Elgar's first march from *Pomp and Circumstance* is played every year at the last night of the BBC Proms, a series of summertime concerts, in London, and its famous *nobilmente* melody is played frequently at graduation ceremonies.

Luke Berryman

Further Reading

Elgar, Edward, and Jerrold Northrop Moore. *Letters of a Lifetime*. Oxford, England: Oxford University Press, 1990. Selected by Moore, this collection of Elgar's letters covers the breadth of his career and provides valuable insight into the composer's state of mind and his personal relationships.

Grimley, Daniel M., and Julian Rushton, eds. *The Cambridge Companion to Elgar*. Cambridge, England: Cambridge University Press, 2004. This collection of essays by leading Elgar scholars covers a diverse range of topics based on Elgar's life and works.

Harper-Scott, J. P. E. *Edward Elgar, Modernist*. Cambridge, England: Cambridge University Press, 2006. This analytical inquiry into Elgar's output paints a portrait of him as a modernist composer. Much of his music, argues Harper-Scott, is a pessimistic commentary on the nature of human existence.

Kennedy, Michael. *The Life of Elgar*. Cambridge, England: Cambridge University Press, 2004. A compact biography of Elgar, in which a number of Elgar's letters are cited. Kennedy neatly aligns key events in Elgar's life with his compositions.

Moore, Jerrold Northrop. *Edward Elgar: A Creative Life*. Oxford, England: Oxford University Press, 1984. An indispensable, extremely detailed biography of Elgar, with a wealth of firsthand material from letters, diaries, memoirs, and so on. Includes photographs and copies of scores.

Riley, Matthew. *Edward Elgar and the Nostalgic Imagination.* Cambridge, England: Cambridge University Press, 2007. A careful examination of nostalgic sentiment in Elgar's music. Includes excerpts from scores.

See also: Britten, Benjamin; Casals, Pablo; du Pré, Jacqueline; Hogwood, Christopher; Kreisler, Fritz; Menuhin, Sir Yehudi; Perlman, Itzhak; Previn, Sir André; Strauss, Richard; Vaughan Williams, Ralph; Walton, Sir William.

Duke Ellington

American jazz pianist and composer

Ellington's inexhaustible explorations of timbre, texture, and musical color in his compositions and arrangements gave jazz music an enduring refinement and elegance.

Born: April 29, 1899; Washington, D.C.
Died: May 24, 1974; New York, New York
Also known as: Edward Kennedy Ellington (full name)
Member of: Jungle Band; the Harlem Footwarmers

Principal works

FILM SCORES: *Anatomy of a Murder*, 1959; *Paris Blues*, 1961; *Assault on a Queen*, 1966; *Change of Mind*, 1969.

Principal recordings

ALBUMS (solo): *Daybreak Express*, 1947; *Masterpieces by Ellington*, 1950; *Hi-Fi Ellington Uptown*, 1951; *Duke Ellington Plays the Blues*, 1953; *The Duke Plays Ellington*, 1953; *Ellington '55*, 1953; *Ellington Showcase*, 1953; *Ellington Uptown*, 1953; *Premiered by Ellington*, 1953; *Dance to the Duke!*, 1954; *Duke Ellington Plays*, 1954; *The Duke and His Men*, 1955; *Duke's Mixture*, 1955; *Al Hibbler with the Duke*, 1956 (with Al Hibbler); *A Drum Is a Woman*, 1956; *Historically Speaking: The Duke*, 1956; *Ella Fitzgerald/The Duke Ellington Songbook*, 1957; *Indigos*, 1957; *Such Sweet Thunder*, 1957; *Black, Brown, and Beige*, 1958; *Blues in Orbit*, 1958; *Blues Summit*, 1958; *Cosmic Scene: Duke Ellington's Spacemen*, 1958; *Side by Side*, 1958 (with Johnny Hodges); *The Ellington Suites*, 1959; *Jazz Party*, 1959; *Piano in the Background*, 1960; *Three Suites*, 1960; *First Time! The Count Meets the Duke*, 1961 (with Count Basie); *Piano in the Foreground*, 1961; *Afro-Bossa*, 1962; *All American*, 1962; *Duke Ellington and John Coltrane*, 1962; *Duke Ellington Meets Coleman Hawkins*, 1962 (with Coleman Hawkins); *Featuring Paul Gonsalves*, 1962 (with Paul Gonsalves); *Midnight in Paris*, 1962; *Money Jungle*, 1962 (with Charles Mingus and Max Roach); *Will Big Bands Ever Come Back?*, 1962; *Duke Ellington's Jazz Violin Session*, 1963; *The Symphonic Ellington*, 1963; *Duke Ellington Plays Mary Poppins*, 1964; *Ellington '65*, 1964; *Hits of the Sixties: This Time by Ellington*, 1964; *Jumpin' Punkins*, 1965; *Duke Ellington*, 1966; *Orchestral Works*, 1966 (with Cincinnati Symphony Orchestra); *The Pianist*, 1966; *Sacred Music*, 1966; *Soul Call*, 1966; *. . . and His Mother Called Him Bill*, 1967; *The Intimacy of the Blues*, 1967 (with various backing bands); *Johnny Come Lately*, 1967; *North of the Border in Canada*, 1967; *The Popular Duke Ellington*, 1967; *Latin American Suite*, 1968; *Second Sacred Concert*, 1968; *The Intimate Ellington*, 1969; *Pretty Woman*, 1969; *Up in Duke's Workshop*, 1969; *New Orleans Suite*, 1970; *The Afro-Eurasian Eclipse*, 1971; *Togo Brava*, 1971; *Collages*, 1973; *Third Sacred Concert*, 1973.

SINGLES (solo): "Limehouse Blues," 1931; "Mood Indigo," 1931; "It Don't Mean a Thing (If It Ain't Got That Swing)," 1932; "Sophisticated Lady," 1932; "Cotton," 1935; "Love Is Like a Cigarette," 1935; "Saddest Tale," 1935; "Caravan," 1937; "Lambeth Walk," 1938; "I Got It Bad (And That Ain't Good)," 1941; "Take the 'A' Train," 1941.

SINGLES (with Harlem Footwarmers): "Diga Diga Doo," 1928; "Doin' the New Lowdown," 1928.

SINGLES (with Jungle Band): "Creole Rhapsody," 1931; "Rockin' in Rhythm," 1931.

The Life

Edward Kennedy Ellington was born in Washington, D.C., to a middle-class African American family. Though modest in income, the family members presented a sense of pride in the way they dressed and behaved. By the age of eight, Ellington had earned his nickname Duke because of the impeccable and distinguished manner in which his mother dressed him. Ellington's parents shielded him from most of the racial problems of the time, teaching him to overlook "unpleasantness." This developed a sense of self-esteem in Ellington that helped him throughout his life, and it contributed to his elegant and polished appearance.

Ellington began piano lessons at an early age, and he began composing in 1913 with the piece "Soda Fountain Rag," named after his job as a soda jerk at the Poodle Dog Café. While hanging out at a local pool hall, Ellington heard several ragtime piano players, and he was influenced particularly by Oliver "Doc" Perry.

Offered an art scholarship to the Pratt Institute in 1916, Ellington declined because he had already been successful as a working musician. In 1918 he married Edna Thompson, and he also formed his first band, the Washingtonians. His son Mercer was born a year later.

Duke Ellington. (AP/Wide World Photos)

Ellington moved to New York City in 1923 (after a previously failed attempt in 1922) on the advice of Fats Waller. With the addition of trumpeter Bubber Miley and baritone saxophonist Harry Carney, Ellington's band landed a long-running gig at Harlem's famous Cotton Club in 1927. Alto saxophonist Johnny Hodges joined in 1928, and by 1932 the band had increased to fourteen members. They began touring the United States in 1931, and in 1933 they toured Europe. This was just the beginning of extensive touring for Ellington, who was now an international attraction.

Ellington fell naturally into the role of bandleader. He had a good sense of business, and he had a great rapport with audiences. His talent for arranging and composing for the band also solidified his leading role. Ellington continued to add significant personnel to his orchestra, including tenor saxophonist Ben Webster, bassist Jimmy Blanton, and trombonist Juan Tizol. In 1938 Ellington formed one of his most significant musical relationships when Billy Strayhorn joined the band as a fellow composer, arranger, and second pianist.

Throughout the 1940's and 1950's, Ellington continued to tour, despite the band's struggle to survive as new jazz styles were emerging. Ellington remained true to his own work, and he carefully avoided commercialization. He explored longer compositions, and he even composed for the film *Anatomy of a Murder* in 1959. Toward the end of his career he turned his attention toward liturgical music, and he considered his sacred concerts to be his most important works.

Ellington was diagnosed with lung cancer in 1972. Shortly afterward, in 1973, he published his memoir, *Music Is My Mistress*. He died at age seventy-five in New York, and his son, Mercer Ellington, took over the direction of the band.

The Music

While Ellington certainly showed mastery of the piano, many would say that his true instrument was his orchestra. Ellington's compositional genius lay in his ability to explore the different timbres possible in a larger group, while also tapping into the strengths of his band members. He welcomed their input, and he considered any limitations a problem to solve. For Ellington, it was the challenge that made the musical results special.

Ellington's refined outward appearance reflected his inner perfectionist attitude. In his process of composition, he constantly revised his work, not being satisfied until every note fit flawlessly. He composed tirelessly, often staying at the piano until the tour manager made him get on the bus. His favorite songs were always the next ones being written. As his music and compositional style progressed, he employed an extended harmonic vocabulary that subsequently guided many jazz artists in their harmonic thinking.

Early Works. Ellington's early works presage the five pervasive styles around which his repertoire is built. The "jungle" style features raucous and growling sounds in the brass instruments, especially in the trumpet playing of Miley. Songs such as "East St. Louis Toodle-loo" were staples during the band's stint at the Cotton Club, where the exotic floor shows reflected the primitive feel of Ellington's music. "Mood" pieces were another style of Ellington's works. Early versions of the popular "Mood Indigo" feature a reduced instrumentation and Bigard on clarinet. Soft and lyrical ballads such as "Solitude" and "Prelude to a Kiss" often featured Hodges on saxophone.

Ellington's "concerto" style included pieces written specifically for individuals. Some examples of this style are "Clarinet Lament," written for Bigard in 1936, and "Concerto for Cootie," written for trumpeter Cootie Williams in 1939. The "standard" was a style of song written for dancing, similar to the popular songs written for other large bands of the time. However, Ellington's songs had a certain sound that no one else could duplicate. With all the styles, Ellington often worked with his band and the soloists in rehearsal to achieve the sound effects he desired. Many times these could not be notated, and therefore other bands were unable to copy the style.

A fifth style of music emerged as Ellington began to explore more abstract music. "Creole Rhapsody," written in 1931, was the first piece of music Ellington wrote that was not for dancing or social entertainment. It was solely for listening.

"Reminiscing in Tempo." This work was written in 1935 after the death of Ellington's mother, and it is one of his first attempts to raise jazz music to the status of art. At the time, this work was a departure from his popular compositions, reflecting his more experimental side. The piece comprised a theme with thirteen variations, and it employed strong melodic and harmonic material. Longer than any of his previous compositions, the work lasted thirteen minutes (four sides of a record).

"Caravan." Created in collaboration with trombonist Tizol, the song was so popular that it was often the second song on the band's set list. Many consider this to be the first jazz song with Latin influences in rhythm, although it also includes Middle Eastern influences in melody and harmony. Numerous jazz artists over the years have had great success covering the tune, including Billy Eckstine, who sold more than a million copies of his 1949 version of the song.

Black, Brown, and Beige. This extended work, subtitled *A Tone Parallel to the History of the American Negro*, was written in 1943, and it was performed at Ellington's Carnegie Hall debut. Fifty minutes in length, this was intended to represent the musical evolution of the African American race. Scored for jazz band and voice, the three-part work was essential in establishing the validity of large-scale works in the jazz repertoire. Although Ellington was disappointed in the critical response it received, and he never performed the entire work in public again, he did go on to create other jazz suites in this style. "Harlem," "Far-East Suite," and "New Orleans Suite" were all works that explored the same type of thematic and harmonic development.

The Sacred Concerts. Ellington was a spiritual man, and he claimed to have read the Bible four times (three times after his mother's death). However, it was not until much later in his life that he explored this side of himself musically. Beginning in 1965 he gave three different sacred concerts in churches and cathedrals around the world: in San Francisco, in London, and in New York City. Combining the elements of jazz, classical, choral, blues, gospel, and dance, these concerts require a large number of performers. Because of this complexity, they have not been performed regularly since Ellington's death in 1974. Highlights from these concerts include his musical version of the Twenty-third Psalm and a reprise of "Come Sunday" from his suite *Black, Brown, and Beige*. Especially poignant is his musical composition based on the spoken rhythms of the Lord's Prayer.

Musical Legacy

Ellington earned nineteen honorary doctorates from institutions such as Yale and the New England Conservatory, eleven Grammy Awards, a Pulitzer Prize nomination, a Presidential Medal of Freedom, and a Legion of Honor from France. More than a thousand works are attributed to Ellington, either wholly his own composition or collaborations. His music has been a powerful influence on generations of jazz musicians, and his songs and melodies remain part of the standard jazz repertoire.

Staci A. Spring

Further Reading

Ellington, Edward K. *Music Is My Mistress*. New York: Doubleday, 1973. An autobiography tells Ellington's story and pays tribute to the important people in his life. Includes photographs.

Ellington, Mercer K. *Duke Ellington in Person: An Intimate Memoir*. New York: Da Capo Press, 1979. Ellington's son's memoir gives a detailed look at his complex relationship with his father, as they interacted in a personal and a professional capacity.

Hasse, John Edward. *Beyond Category: The Life and Genius of Duke Ellington*. New York: Simon & Schuster, 1993. Written by the curator of American music at the Smithsonian Institution, this biography uses thousands of previously unavailable pages from the Ellington archives to give a complete and in-depth view of Ellington's life and compositional process. Includes references to musical manuscripts, scrapbooks, letters, and business papers.

Lambert, Eddie. *Duke Ellington: A Listener's Guide*. Lanham, Md.: Scarecrow Press, 1999. Offers critical commentary on recordings from 1924 to 1974. Includes a bibliography, an extensive discography, and a list of band members and their dates of membership.

Lawrence, A. H. *Duke Ellington and His World: A Biography*. New York: Routledge, 2001. The author examines the sociopolitical culture surrounding Ellington's career, and he provides interviews with several band members, friends, and family. Includes illustrations.

Tucker, Mark, ed. *The Duke Ellington Reader*. New York: Oxford University Press, 1993. An anthology of writings about the life and music of Ellington. Includes profiles of Ellington and band members, interviews with Ellington, musical analysis, remembrances by prominent authors in the jazz world, and some of Ellington's own writings.

See also: Armstrong, Louis; Basie, Count; Bechet, Sidney; Blades, Rubén; Burton, Gary; Coltrane, John; Crosby, Bing; Fitzgerald, Ella; Gillespie, Dizzy; Goodman, Benny; Grusin, Dave; Hampton, Lionel; Hawkins, Coleman; Horne, Lena; King, B. B.; Makeba, Miriam; Mingus, Charles; Monk, Thelonious; Otis, Johnny; Peterson, Oscar; Roach, Max; Shorter, Wayne; Strayhorn, Billy; Tatum, Art; Tormé, Mel; Tyner, McCoy; Vaughan, Sarah; Waller, Fats; Webster, Ben; Whiteman, Paul; Williams, Mary Lou; Wonder, Stevie.

Cass Elliot

American rock singer and songwriter

Renowned for her powerful, clear contralto voice and dynamic stage presence, Elliot achieved popularity as a member of the 1960's group the Mamas and the Papas. She was the only member of the group to have a successful solo career.

Born: September 19, 1941; Baltimore, Maryland
Died: July 29, 1974; London, England
Also known as: Ellen Naomi Cohen (birth name); Mama Cass
Member of: Triumvirate; the Big Three; the Mugwumps; the Mamas and the Papas

Principal recordings

ALBUMS (solo): *Dream a Little Dream of Me*, 1968; *Bubble Gum, Lemonade, and Something for Mama*, 1969; *Make Your Own Kind of Music*, 1969; *Cass*

Elliot, 1971; *Road Is No Place for a Lady*, 1972; *Don't Call Me Mama Anymore*, 1973.

ALBUMS (with the Big Three): *The Big Three*, 1963.

ALBUMS (with the Mamas and the Papas): *If You Can Believe Your Eyes and Ears*, 1966; *The Mamas and the Papas*, 1966; *Deliver*, 1967; *The Papas and the Mamas*, 1968; *People Like Us*, 1971; *Elliot, Phillips, Gilliam, Doherty*, 1988.

ALBUMS (with the Mugwumps): *The Mugwumps*, 1967.

SINGLES (with the Mamas and the Papas): "California Dreamin'," 1965.

The Life

"Mama Cass" Elliot was born Ellen Naomi Cohen to Philip Cohen and Beth Levine, who were in the restaurant business. Both parents were musical: Her father loved opera, and her mother played the piano. As a child, Elliot listened to singers; her favorites were Ella Fitzgerald, Judy Garland, and Blossom Dearie. She took piano lessons in grade school, and later, her enthusiasm growing for folk music, she switched to the guitar. At Forest Park High School in Baltimore, she sang in the choir, and she acted in school plays. By age seventeen she had adopted the name Cassandra Elliot. Nicknamed Cass by her father, for the prophetess Cassandra of Greek mythology, she added Elliot in honor of a friend who had been killed in an automobile accident.

During the summer between her junior and senior years in high school, she filled in for a cast member at the Owings Mills Playhouse, playing the role of the French maid in Sandy Wilson's musical *The Boy Friend* (1954). This was her theatrical debut, and after her success, high school was less interesting. Elliot dropped out and took a part-time job at the *Jewish Times*, but she still yearned for a singing career.

Although her parents wanted her to finish high school and enroll at Goucher College to become a teacher, Elliot chose to start her performing career by moving to New York City, where she made the rounds of auditions, singing "Glitter and Be Gay" from Leonard Bernstein's *Candide* (1956). Although she came close to getting the part of Miss Marmelstein in Harold Rome's *I Can Get It for You Wholesale* (1962), the part went to another unknown: Barbra Streisand. After completing a tour with Meredith

Willson's *The Music Man* (1957), Elliot decided to enroll in college to get a foundation in drama. She went to American University in Washington, D.C., but she spent a lot of time at the university's theater, anxious to return to performing. When a fellow student who appreciated her voice asked her to relocate to Chicago to join a singing group, she jumped at the chance. She started her professional singing career in Chicago with the folk-singing group the Triumvirate. When the group relocated to Omaha, Nebraska, Jim Hendricks replaced one of the male singers. Elliot married Hendricks in 1963, so he could avoid being drafted for the Army. They divorced in 1969. When that group broke up, Elliot joined another group with Hendricks, Zalman Yanovsky, and Denny Doherty, billed as Cass Elliot and the Big Three. In 1964, after a drummer was added to the group, the name was changed to the Mugwumps. The group lasted about a year. In 1965 Elliot joined the Mamas and the Papas and became a star. She gave birth to a daughter, Owen Vanessa Elliot, in April, 1967.

Although Elliot enjoyed success as a group member, she wanted a solo career. When the Mamas and Papas disbanded in 1968, Elliot gained acclaim as a soloist. She recorded six albums, and she sang in nightclubs. She appeared on a number of television variety shows, and she had two prime-time television specials of her own in 1969 and 1973. She married Baron Donald von Weidenman in 1971, but the marriage was annulled shortly thereafter. In 1974, following a successful two-week run at the London Palladium, she died of a heart attack.

The Music

The Mamas and the Papas. In 1965 Elliot joined friends in the Virgin Islands, and there she met John Phillips, who was forming a group with his wife Michelle and Doherty. Initially, Phillips rejected Elliot because her vocal range was too low to complement the harmonies he was developing. However, as the story goes, Elliot was felled by a steel pipe at a construction site, she suffered a concussion, and after that she found she could sing the higher notes. Phillips immediately hired her. After working months to perfect a distinctive sound, the group moved to Los Angeles, where it was discovered by producer Lou Adler, who had formed the Dunhill Records label.

The music generated by the Mamas and the Papas was a mix of folk and rock, characterized by intricate harmonies. What supported the sound was Elliot's strong contralto, which she had to keep under control, so she did not overwhelm the light soprano of Michelle Phillips. In 1965 Dunhill Records released the group's first record, the single "California Dreamin'." It climbed to number four on the charts, and it sold more than a million copies. A second hit, "Monday, Monday," sold 160,000 copies the first day, and it won a Grammy Award in March, 1967, in the Best Group Performance category. Critics noted that the Mamas and the Papas were the right group for the time, with their flower-child appeal and innocence.

Although constantly fighting a battle with her weight, Elliot, with her wisecracking sense of humor, was a crowd pleaser. Her fans were enthralled by her rich voice, and they enjoyed her unpretentious manner.

Solo Career. When the Mamas and Papas broke up in 1968, Elliot started her solo career in earnest. In 1969 her signature song, "Dream a Little Dream of Me," launched her career, becoming her biggest hit. Other best-selling singles included "It's Getting Better," "Make Your Own Kind of Music," and "New World Coming."

Musical Legacy

Elliot's voice, with its warmth and power, contributed significantly to the success of the Mamas and the Papas. In 1998 Elliot, as a member of the Mamas and the Papas, was inducted into the Rock and Roll Hall of Fame. With the Mamas and Papas and as a solo act, Elliot was known as the queen of pop music. She was generous with her friends, and she hosted many aspiring artists in her home. Elliot introduced Graham Nash to David Crosby and Stephen Stills, who later formed the group Crosby, Stills, and Nash. Elliot demonstrated that a large woman could be a commercial success, with her fans focusing on her voice. A 1996 British film, *Beautiful Thing*, featured many of Elliot's songs. In the second-season opener of the television show *Lost*, Elliot's song "Make Your Own Kind of Music" introduced another generation to her distinctive voice.

Marcia B. Dinneen

Further Reading

Haag, John. "Elliot, Cass." In *Women in World History*, edited by Anne Commire. Waterford, Conn.: Yorkin, 2002. Includes biographical material and an overview of Elliot's career.

Kloman, William. "Sing Along with Mama Cass." *Esquire* (June, 1969): 102-104. Good background on Elliot's childhood and her Las Vegas solo debut.

Phillips, John, with Jim Jerome. *Papa John, an Autobiography*. Garden City, N.Y.: Doubleday, 1986. Includes information on Elliot's involvement with the Mama and the Papas.

Phillips, Michelle. *"California Dreamin'": The True Story of the Mamas and the Papas*. New York: Warner, 1986. Dedicated to Mama Cass, the book includes background information about the group and about Elliot.

See also: David, Hal; Fitzgerald, Ella; Garland, Judy; Stills, Stephen; Streisand, Barbra; Willson, Meredith.

Missy Elliott

American rap singer and songwriter

In her redefinition of rap and hip-hop, Elliott created a musical collage of near and nonsense rhyme, street language, comic profanity, offbeat rhythms, unique instrumentation, sound effects, and vocalizations. Elliott raised the profile of women in rap, first as a lyric writer and a producer and later as the owner of a record label and a singer.

Born: July 1, 1971; Portsmouth, Virginia
Also known as: Melissa Arnette Elliott (full name); Missy "Misdemeanor" Elliott
Member of: Sista

Principal recordings

ALBUMS (solo): *Supa Dupa Fly*, 1997; *Da Real World*, 1999; *Miss E . . . So Addictive*, 2001; *Under Construction*, 2002; *This Is Not a Test!*, 2003; *The Cookbook*, 2005.
ALBUMS (with Sista): *4 All the Sistas Around da World*, 1994.

The Life

Born to Ronnie and Pat Elliott in 1971, in Portsmouth, Virginia, Melissa Arnette Elliott was a church choir member who repeatedly told her mother that she would someday be a star, often singing to an audience of her dolls. She began writing songs, singing them to her family and even to passing cars from atop overturned trash cans. She created her own musical breakthrough in 1991, taking the members of her first group, Sista, to a Portsmouth hotel where Devante Swing of Jodeci was staying. Swing was impressed by the performance of Elliott's original songs. He signed the group, which cut an album in 1995 for Elektra Records; however, the work was never released.

Undaunted, Elliott formed her own production team, working with MC Timothy Z. "Timbaland" Moseley, now a producer, and she began penning tunes for Jodeci and others. After some success writing and producing, she launched a string of platinum albums and lost seventy pounds between 2001 and 2002. She is known for her humility and for her kindness to fans, signing autographs for those who recognize her on the streets. Elliott went public about her father's physical abuse of her mother, leading her to donate her time to the organization Break the Cycle, helping youth to end domestic violence.

The Music

Elliott and Moseley produced four hits from Aaliyah's *One in a Million* (1996), and at age twenty-two Elliott had her own label (The Gold Mind, Inc.) with Elektra Records. Thus began the dual careers of one of the most influential female performers in hip-hop and rap music. As producer, Elliott worked with such artists as Mary J. Blige, Whitney Houston, Mariah Carey, and Janet Jackson. Her albums are known for staccato dance rhythms, sound effects (cartoons), comic profanity, raw sexuality, blunt treatment of violence, inclusion of spoken-word interludes, and underlying lyrical sarcasm. *Rolling Stone* compared an Elliott album with a Beatles album in conception and reception, each redefining the singer and the genre itself.

Early Works. As Missy "Misdemeanor" Elliott, she released *Supa Dupa Fly* in 1997, and it went platinum. Her first hit, "The Rain," was an adaptation of an Ann Peebles hit. The album was praised as

Missy Elliott. (AP/Wide World Photos)

forging a new direction in hip-hop, eschewing gangsta imagery for rhythm and blues, and for it Elliott received her first Grammy Award nomination. The more streetwise and angry *Da Real World* was musically experimental and futuristic, and it featured collaborations with Aaliyah, Beyoncé, Lil' Kim, and Big Boi. The rhythm-and-blues hits "All N My Grill" and "Hot Boyz," as well as "She's a Bitch" and "Beat Biters," exemplified the beat-rhyme partnership she would perfect with Timbaland. "Hot Boyz" spent eighteen consecutive weeks at the top of the *Billboard* rap charts and six weeks at number one on the rhythm-and-blues/hip-hop chart. In June, 1999, Elliott was named by *Ebony* magazine as one of the Ten at the Top of Hip-Hop.

Missy E . . . So Addictive. This 2001 platinum album garnered Elliott recognition with mainstream listeners, and it is noted for its Top 10 hits "One

Minute Man" and "Get Ur Freak On," frenetic club favorites "Scream aka Itchin" and "4 My People," as well as for collaborations with Jay-Z, Ludacris, Redman, Method Man, and Eve. The singles enjoyed heavy rotation on radio stations and MTV. "Get Ur Freak On" was a genre-defying experiment, and for it Elliott won her first Grammy Award and a Soul Train Award.

Under Construction. Dropping "Misdemeanor" from her name for *Under Construction,* Elliott became with this album the best-selling female hip-hop artist. Collaborating with Ludacris, Jay-Z, Beyoncé, and TLC, she showcased old school hip-hop, tinged with rhythm and blues, bookended by spoken-word interludes and sound bites. The Grammy Award-winning "Work It" featured a staccato dance beat juxtaposed with a variable sine wave, comic sound effects, and lines rapped forward and backward. It stayed at the top of the *Billboard* rhythm-and-blues/hip-hop chart for five weeks, and it won a Soul Train Award. "Gossip Folks" featured the sound of real background gossip, and "Back in the Day" was a straightforward rhythm-and-blues tribute.

This Is Not a Test! Showing Elliott at the apex of experimentation, *This Is Not a Test!* spawned the single "Pass That Dutch," and it featured R. Kelly, Nelly, and Jay-Z. It contained a love ballad for a vibrator ("Toyz"), a send-up of classic 1980's rap ("Let It Bump"), and sound effects such as car alarms, whistles, horses, and heavy breathing.

The Cookbook. *The Cookbook* marked a change, as Elliott began using producers other than Timbaland. The single "Lose Control" peaked at number three on the *Billboard* Hot 100. The video garnered six MTV nominations, winning two. Elliott was also nominated for three Grammy Awards, two for "Lose Control" (with one win) and one for *The Cookbook*. In 2006 she was nominated for Best International Female Artist at the BRIT Awards, the British music industry award.

Musical Legacy

Elliott has been successful as a producer, songwriter, rapper, singer, and video presence. Her phenomenal achievements include releasing critically acclaimed albums; winning Grammy, BET, Soul Train, MTV, and American Music Awards; achieving two *Billboard* dance and rhythm-and-blues/hip-hop chart number ones; performing on the Lilith Fair tour; changing the look of rap and hip-hop videos; and composing a song for the film *Stick It* (2006). Along with Timbaland, she popularized a new hip-hop sound, featuring variable syncopated musical phrasing, accentuated by snare and high hat drums rather than bass. This beat is typically juxtaposed with sound effects and comic vocalizations.

Anthony J. Fonseca

Further Reading

Diehl, Matt. "Missy Elliott." *Interview* 35, no. 8 (2005): 152. An interview with Elliott discusses her experience with early rejection.

Emerson, Rana A. "'Where My Girls At?' Negotiating Black Womanhood in Music Videos." *Gender and Society* 16, no. 1 (February, 2002): 115-135. The article analyzes women in rap and hip-hop videos, including Elliott's "Beep Me 911" and "Sock It to Me."

Hirshey, Gerri. *We Gotta Get Out of This Place: The True, Tough Story of Women in Rock*. New York: Grove Press, 2001. Contains an extended biographical discussion of Elliott, including little-known information, in the "Riot Grrls" chapter.

Kimpel, Dan. *How They Made It: True Stories of How Music's Biggest Stars Went from Start to Stardom*. Milwaukee, Wis.: Hal Leonard, 2006. A chapter on Elliott offers biographical information and brief quotes.

Rohm, Andy, Fareena Sultan, and David T. A. Wesley. *Brand in the Hand: Mobile Marketing at Adidas*. London: Richard Ivey School of Business Case Collection, 2005. Briefly chronicles Adidas's marketing strategy for Elliott's Respect M.E. sportswear line.

Vibe Magazine. *Hip-Hop Divas*. New York: Three Rivers Press, 2001. *Vibe* staffer Karen Renee Good focuses on Elliott's life and musical contributions.

See also: Blige, Mary J.; Carey, Mariah; Grant, Amy; Jay-Z.

Eminem

American rap singer and songwriter

A controversial rap artist, Eminem is noted for his high-energy, witty, and offensive lyrics. As a white musician performing in a genre dominated by black artists, Eminem is often compared to Elvis Presley.

Born: October 17, 1972; St. Joseph, Missouri
Also known as: Marshall Bruce Mathers (birth name); M&M; Slim Shady
Member of: D12

Principal recordings

ALBUMS (solo): *Infinite*, 1996; *The Slim Shady EP*, 1997; *The Slim Shady LP*, 1999; *The Marshall Mathers LP*, 2000; *The Eminem Show*, 2002; *Encore*, 2004; *Eminem Presents: The Re-Up*, 2006; *So U Wanna Freestyle?*, 2008.

ALBUMS (with D12): *Devil's Night*, 2001; *D12 World*, 2004.

The Life

Marshall Mathers, who later took the name Eminem (ehm-ih-NEHM), had an unstable childhood, moving repeatedly between Missouri and Michigan. His father left the family shortly after he was born, and his mother, Deborah "Debbie" Mathers, raised him. Eminem had a close relationship with his uncle, Ronald "Ronnie" Polkinghorn, who was only a few months older. One of Eminem's tattoos and the military identification tags he wears commemorate Polkinghorn's 1991 suicide.

At school Eminem was the victim of bullying, and one beating left him in a coma for five days. After repeating ninth grade three times, he dropped out of high school, and he held various unfulfilling jobs until his music career became profitable. He maintained a turbulent relationship with Kimberly "Kim" Scott, and they had a daughter, Hailie Jade, in 1995. Many of Eminem's lyrics refer to the people closest to him: Debbie, Kim, Hailie, and Ronnie.

Eminem spent his teenage years around Detroit, where he began performing hip-hop music with Bassmint Productions, Soul Intent, Royce da 5'9",

and D12. D12, also known as the Dirty Dozen or Detroit 12, comprised six Detroit rappers, with two distinct rap personalities. In this context, Eminem rapped as M&M, for Marshall Mathers (which became Eminem), and Slim Shady. Both names stuck. Eminem's earliest musical success came in improvisational-rap competitions, called battles, in Detroit, and later Eminem finished second in the 1997 Rap Olympics MC Battle in Los Angeles. Around that time a promotional tape of his performance reached Dr. Dre.

Dr. Dre signed Eminem to his Aftermath record label, and in 1999 he produced Eminem's first studio album, *The Slim Shady LP*. The album was an international success. That year Eminem married Kim; they were married for two years before divorcing in 2001, remarrying in 2006, and redivorcing later that year.

Eminem's subsequent albums were successful, making him one of rap's best-selling artists. His performance as the lead character in the 2002 film *8 Mile* earned some critical acclaim and an Academy Award for Best Song. During his career he served two years of probation, stemming from assault charges, and his mother and his ex-wife, among others, have sued him.

The Music

Eminem developed his signature dense rhyming patterns, frequent use of homonyms, and intricate rhythms through improvised rap battles. An improvisational sound and self-deprecating lyrics were characteristic of his work. While still young he performed on various albums, including the solo *Infinite*, although these are generally omitted from discussions of his music. His musical reputation rests primarily on the four studio albums he had completed by 2004.

Eminem's music has been the source of considerable controversy, earning him accusations of misogyny and homophobia as well as rallying cries of artistic freedom. Various works of his have been banned on the radio, MTV, and the Black Entertainment Television (BET), and he appeared before a congressional hearing on violence in the media.

The Slim Shady LP. Produced by Dr. Dre in 1999 and dedicated to Eminem's daughter Hailie, *The Slim Shady LP* was Eminem's first studio album and winner of the Grammy Award for Best Rap Album.

Rappers as role models and the struggles of drug users and poor people are among the main themes of the album. While many of the songs depict scenes that seem real and even autobiographical, one of the last tracks on the album, "I'm Shady," explains that not all of Eminem's lyrics are to be taken literally.

"My Name Is" is the hit single from *The Slim Shady LP*, and this introduced Eminem to a wider audience. "Rock Bottom" is set against a hymnlike musical background, but it is about the willingness to commit crimes when there is no hope of a better life. Eminem attempted suicide around the time he recorded this track. The cover art of *The Slim Shady LP* depicts the haunting fantasy that Eminem describes in "'97 Bonnie & Clyde": a man and his young daughter disposing of her mother's body. Distant, minor melodies and the use of a harp create a mysterious, ethereal background while the sounds of waves and of Eminem's daughter, Hailie, add realism. Tori Amos released a cover of this piece in 2001.

The Marshall Mathers LP. In 2000 Eminem released his second studio album, *The Marshall Mathers LP*, which debuted at number one on the *Billboard* charts and earned Eminem his second consecutive Grammy for Best Rap Album. Eminem raps in a more aggressive and angry style on this album. The topic of rappers as role models reemerges, along with songs about Eminem's rise to fame. Eminem dedicated the album to daughter Hailie, Polkinghorn, and Cornell Pitts, better known as Bugz, a former D12 rap associate.

The first single released from *The Marshall Mathers LP*, "The Real Slim Shady," is a catchy, memorable tune that emphasizes the rapper's name. "Stan" is one of Eminem's most critically acclaimed raps: The music samples Dido's "Thank You," combined with thunder, rain, and the sound of writing on paper, the story unfolding in the form of three letters from an unstable fan named Stan. At the end of the third verse, Stan performs reckless actions described in "My Name Is," and he ultimately kills himself and his pregnant girlfriend in a scenario similar to the one described in "'97 Bonnie & Clyde." The last verse is Eminem's concerned response that comes too late.

"Lose Yourself." In 2002 Eminem starred in the motion picture *8 Mile*, which at the time had the largest opening weekend for an R-rated motion picture. Eminem played a white Detroit rapper, Jimmy "B-Rabbit" Smith, although the plot is not strictly autobiographical. The song "Lose Yourself," which is about Smith's struggle to become a successful musician, is heard as a work in progress throughout the film, and by the end Smith finishes it. This was Eminem's first number-one *Billboard* single, holding that position longer than any other song by a rap artist. It was also the first rap song to win an Academy Award for Best Original Song.

The Eminem Show. *The Eminem Show* earned the artist his third Grammy Award for Best Rap Album; he was the first person to win the award three times. The album has a more mature sound, with less distortion and more layering, and some of the lyrics (especially in "White America" and "Square Dance") are more political than in previous albums. However, there is still a personal side: "Hailie's Song" is about Eminem's daughter, and "My Dad's Gone Crazy" features her singing throughout the track. "Cleanin' Out My Closet" is mostly about Eminem's mother, but it also contains references to Eminem's father and uncle.

"Without Me," a high-energy hit, could be likened to "My Name Is" and "The Real Slim Shady" from previous albums. "Without Me" contains one of the best examples of Eminem's lyrical virtuosity. After a rapid-fire succession of rhymes woven into a complex pattern, he concludes the second verse with the sound being sent with five different meanings. Rappers as role models is a central theme in "When the Music Stops" and "Sing for the Moment." The latter rap samples "Dream On" by Aerosmith, and it features Steven Tyler and Joe Perry. Here Eminem offers a coherent defense against the accusations that his music is dangerous for children, and, further, he argues that his music could be beneficial to them and that those who censor his lyrics could be harming children by limiting their artistic outlets.

Encore. Dr. Dre served as executive producer for *Encore*, which Eminem released in 2004. Critics attacked *Encore* for being more heavy-handed and less clever than his previous albums. Nevertheless, "Mockingbird" is perhaps Eminem's most personal and touching rap. While previous albums included a catchy single from the perspective of Slim Shady, *Encore* contains "My First Single," a blatant mockery of that formula. Like *The Eminem Show*, *Encore* features some political content. "Mosh," for instance, is a harsh, detailed criticism of the George W. Bush presidency, and it encourages political activism. The video was released shortly before the 2004 U.S. presidential election as a way to recruit young voters. "Like Toy Soldiers" is a call for an end to violence among rappers. The music is characterized by its persistent, militant snare drum and its sample of "Toy Soldiers" performed by Martika. The music video concludes with images of rappers who had been killed recently: Tupac Shakur, the Notorious B.I.G., Big L, and Bugz, formerly of D12. The video also includes images of the fictional killing of Proof, a member of D12 and the best man in Eminem's second wedding. In 2006 Proof would, in fact, be shot and killed in a Detroit nightclub.

Musical Legacy

Eminem was the first rap artist to win an Academy Award for best song, and he won several Grammy Awards. He is known for his sometimes witty, sometimes tragic lyrics, which feature dense and intricate rhyming patterns. Eminem expanded the traditional topics of rap music to include personal, psychological, and political content rather than the more typical focus on drugs, violence, and women. He responded to critics who accused him of homophobia by performing live with Elton John on "Stan" on numerous occasions. In addition to his musical legacy, Eminem challenged censorship in America and violence among rappers. He was one of the factors in a cultural shift that has turned away from judging rappers by their skin color or violent reputation, paving the way for white rappers such as Paul Wall and Bubba Sparxxx as well as black rappers with nontraditional backgrounds such as Kanye West. Often praised and often attacked, Eminem has been one of the most significant figures in rap music.

Joseph R. Matson

Further Reading

Als, Hilton, and Darryl A. Turner, eds. *White Noise: The Eminem Collection*. New York: Thunder's Mouth Press, 2003. An excellent collection of essays on Eminem, covering a wide range of topics.

Bozza, Anthony. *Whatever You Say I Am: The Life and Times of Eminem*. New York: Three Rivers Press, 2003. A detailed biography by an author who has done numerous interviews with and written several articles about Eminem. Includes photographs and a lengthy bibliography.

Doggett, Peter. *Eminem: The Complete Guide to His Music*. London: Omnibus, 2005. A valuable reference tool that includes brief but thorough descriptions of all the music written or cowritten by Eminem until 2005. Includes photographs and index.

Friskics-Warren, Bill. "License to Ill: The Stooges, the Sex Pistols, PiL, and Eminem." In *I'll Take You There: Pop Music and the Urge for Transcendence*. New York: Continuum, 2005. A provocative analysis emphasizes the philosophical undertones of Eminem's lyrics.

Green, Jared, ed. "Case Study in Controversy: Eminem and Gay Bashing." In *Rap and Hip-Hop: Examining Pop Culture*. San Diego: Greenhaven Press, 2003. Articles present contrasting opinions on Eminem's controversial lyrics, not limited to homophobia.

Hasted, Nick. *The Dark Story of Eminem*. London: Omnibus, 2003. A thorough biography of Eminem contains photographs and discography.

Kitwana, Bakari. "Fear of a Culture Bandit." In *Why White Kids Love Hip-Hop: Wankstas, Wiggers, Wannabes, and the New Reality of Race in America*. New York: Basic Civitas Books: 2005. An analysis of the racial issues surrounding Eminem and his music.

Tsiopos-Wills, Katherine V. "Eminem." In *Icons of Hip-Hop: An Encyclopedia of the Movement, Music, and Culture*, edited by Mickey Hess. Westport, Conn.: Greenwood Press, 2007. A practical guide to understanding Eminem and the culture of hip-hop. Includes bibliography and discography.

See also: D. M. C.; Dr. Dre; 50 Cent; Hammer, M. C.; Jay-Z; John, Sir Elton; Shakur, Tupac; Simmons, Joseph "Run."

Brian Eno

English rock singer, songwriter, and keyboard player

Eno achieved early fame playing synthesizers with the pioneering British glam rock band, Roxy Music. He went on to define the ambient music genre, and he brought his distinctive sound to the production of hit albums for other artists, such as U2, the Talking Heads, and Devo.

Born: May 15, 1948; Woodbridge, Suffolk, England
Also known as: Brian Peter George St. John le Baptiste de la Salle Eno (full name)
Member of: Roxy Music; Fripp and Eno; Portsmouth Sinfonia; Cluster; Harmonia 76; 801

Principal recordings

ALBUMS (solo): *Here Come the Warm Jets*, 1974; *Taking Tiger Mountain (By Strategy)*, 1974; *Another Green World*, 1975; *Discreet Music*, 1975; *Before and After Science*, 1977; *After the Heat*, 1978 (with Dieter Moebius and Hans-Joachim Roedelius); *Ambient 1: Music for Airports*, 1978; *Music for Films*, 1978; *Empty Landscapes*, 1981; *My Life in the Bush of Ghosts*, 1981 (with David Byrne); *Ambient 4: On Land*, 1982; *Apollo: Atmospheres and Soundtracks*, 1983; *Music for Films, Vol. 2*, 1983 (with Daniel Lanois); *Thursday Afternoon*, 1985; *Music for Films, Vol. 3*, 1988; *Wrong Way Up*, 1990 (with John Cale); *Nerve Net*, 1992; *The Shutov Assembly*, 1992; *Neroli*, 1993; *Robert Sheckley's In a Land of Clear Colours*, 1993 (with Peter Sinfield); *Headcandy*, 1994; *Spinner*, 1995 (with Jah Wobble); *Generative Music 1*, 1996; *The Drop*, 1997; *Extracts from Music for White Cube*, 1997; *Lightness: Music for the Marble Palace*, 1998; *I Dormienti*, 1999; *Kite Stories*, 1999; *Music for Civic Recovery Center*, 2000; *Music for Onmyo-Ji*, 2000 (with D. J. Jan Peter Schwalm); *Drawn from Life*, 2001 (with Schwalm); *January 07003: Bell Studies for the Clock of the Long Now*, 2003; *Another Day on Earth*, 2005; *The Pearl*, 2005 (with Harold Budd); *Everything That Happens Will Happen Today*, 2008 (with Byrne).

ALBUMS (with Cluster): *Cluster and Eno*, 1977.
ALBUMS (with Fripp and Eno): *No Pussyfooting*, 1973; *Evening Star*, 1975; *The Equatorial Stars*, 2005; *Beyond Even (1992-2006)*, 2007.
ALBUMS (with Harmonia 76): *Tracks and Traces*, 1997.
ALBUMS (with Portsmouth Sinfonia): *Plays the Popular Classics*, 1974; *Hallelujah*, 1976.
ALBUMS (with Roxy Music): *Roxy Music*, 1972; *For Your Pleasure*, 1973.

The Life

Born in England in 1948, Brian Peter George St. John le Baptiste de la Salle Eno (EE-noh) grew up near a U.S. Air Force base. The sounds of early rock-and-roll and rhythm-and-blues music, with the tight harmonies and nonsense words of doo-wop, coming from Armed Forces Radio provided early inspiration to Eno. He attended the Winchester School of Art at the University of Southampton, where he encountered the music of contemporary composers, including minimalists such as John Cage, Steve Reich, and La Monte Young. He studied avant-garde subjects such as conceptual painting and sound sculpture. In 1967 Eno married Sarah Grenville, and their daughter, Hannah, was born later that year. Eno graduated from college in 1969.

After finishing school, he moved to London, where he cofounded Roxy Music. At first his role was offstage, mixing the band members' instruments and voices through synthesizers and other electronic devices, occasionally creating loops for live playback on tape recorders. He later joined his bandmates on the stage, where his outrageous make-up and drag costumes helped define the band's aesthetic. After Roxy Music's second album, *For Your Pleasure*, came out in 1973, Eno left the band, citing creative differences with the lead singer, Bryan Ferry, and general boredom with the rock-and-roll lifestyle.

Eno immediately embarked on a number of projects, beginning with a collaboration with King Crimson cofounder Robert Fripp. A series of health problems changed Eno's course, starting with a collapsed lung that forced him to abandon a British tour as front man of a band called the Winkies. A year later, in 1975, Eno was in a car accident, and his injuries left him bedridden. His immobility allowed time for contemplation of the environmental sounds around him, and in this situation Eno's concept of ambient music was born.

In addition to recording ambient music's seminal early albums, Eno was collaborating with musicians such as David Bowie, John Cale, and David Byrne. In 1988, after the demise of his first marriage, Eno married his manager, Anthea Norman-Taylor, with whom he had two daughters, Irial and Darla. Solo albums and collaborations continued, and at the same time Eno found success as an installation artist and a video artist. In 1975 Eno published, in conjunction with artist Peter Schmidt, Oblique Strategies, a deck of cards that offers solutions for overcoming creative block. In 1996 Eno founded the Long Now Foundation, which encourages public consideration of the long-term future of society and culture.

The Music

As a teenager, Eno made his first recording: the sound of a pen tapping a tin lampshade. He slowed it down and played it back, and in this way the foundation for his experimental, electronic, and ambient music was laid. For Eno, the tape recorder became an instrument. He was inspired by twentieth century minimalist composers' reliance on chance, and he used tape-delay feedback systems, synthesizers, and computer-generated compositions. Though his earliest solo albums were oriented toward the pop sound, in the 1970's Eno created and coined ambient music, that is, music played at a low volume, that alters the experience of the surrounding environment. Eno brought his distinctive, eclectic, and sought-after sound to the production of hit albums by Paul Simon, U2, and Coldplay.

Roxy Music. Roxy Music's eponymous first album was released in 1972. The band's music was an amalgamation of postmodernist, art-school, and glam rock. The album contained a variety of cultural references, including to Humphrey Bogart, to the Beatles, and to Richard Wagner's *Ride of the Valkyries* (1870). It was recorded in one week's time, before the band signed a contract with Island Records. Eno sang back-up vocals, and he played the synthesizer, creating weird, atonal noise using tape recorders. With this debut album Roxy Music joined the ranks of the significantly influential

avant-garde bands of the era, such as the Velvet Underground and Captain Beefheart, paving the way for subsequent groups that relied on electronics to define their sound, such as the Cars and Devo. When Eno departed Roxy Music after its second album, the remaining band members pursued a raucous, less-cutting-edge sound, becoming known for the polished music of their hit 1982 album, *Avalon*.

Another Green World. Eno released this solo album in 1975, following two other successful solo albums: *Taking Tiger Mountain (By Strategy)* and *Here Come the Warm Jets*. *Another Green World* was a bridge between the experimental pop that came before it and the ambient music that followed. Nine of the fourteen songs were instrumental, and those that were not contained strange, unconventional lyrics. Though many found the album less accessible than Eno's prior work, critics and fans praised it. Fripp played guitar, and Eno mixed and distorted that sound with keyboards and complex rhythms.

Brian Eno. (Tobias Schwarz/Reuters/Landov)

Genesis member and future solo artist Phil Collins played drums on three tracks, and Velvet Underground cofounder Cale played viola. The textures of the sounds on *Another Green World* create a haunting, lovely album that is widely considered to be one of Eno's masterpieces.

My Life in the Bush of Ghosts. Eno's long-term collaboration with the Talking Heads, a new wave band made up of art students inspired by Roxy Music, began with their second album, 1978's *More Songs About Buildings and Food*. Eno produced two more albums for the Talking Heads, most notably *Remain in Light* in 1982. Later, however, his relationship with the band soured, although he remained friends with Talking Heads front man Byrne. In 1981 Byrne and Eno released *My Life in the Bush of Ghosts*, an album comprising recordings of radio broadcasts and other found recordings, sounds made with random objects such as frying pans and cardboard boxes, and complex African and South American rhythms that would later be termed world music beats. Solidly within Eno's oeuvre, the album was an early indication of the direction in which Byrne's solo career would proceed.

Apollo: Atmospheres and Soundtracks. This 1983 album is one of Eno's best-known ambient recordings. His younger brother, Roger Eno, and the producer, musician, and composer Daniel Lanois collaborated on the writing, production, and music. It was originally composed to accompany a filmed collage of footage from the U.S. Apollo space program called *For All Mankind*. However, the film was not released until 1990, when National Geographic issued one nonnarrative version with Eno's music and the National Aeronautics and Space Administration (NASA) released another version, replacing the sound track with interviews and commentary. The music evokes both the Western frontier and the final frontier of space. Lanois's performance adds a flavor of country music to the recording, and the combination of acoustic and electronic sounds has a complex, mesmerizing quality. A seminal album of the genre, it may be considered a primer on ambient music.

Nerve Net. In 1992 Eno returned to a more rock-inflected sound with this album. Several guests, including Tom Petty and the Heartbreakers' drummer Benmont Tench, guitarist Robert Quine, and Led Zeppelin multi-instrumentalist John Paul Jones,

contributed to the tracks. "My Squelchy Life," a song Eno had recorded earlier for a more pop-oriented album he never released, made it onto *Nerve Net*. The album received mixed reviews, but it was notable for foreshadowing the wave of techno rock that soon became popular.

Musical Legacy

A founder of ambient music and a pioneering electronic musician, Eno has recorded a large number of albums since the early 1970's, ranging from solo pop efforts, to ambient recordings, to collaborations with some of the most influential and respected artists in rock. His production work, or what his management company calls sound landscaping, is recognizable on the recordings of musicians as diverse as Jane Siberry and U2. Eno's creative drive led him to a variety of endeavors. He composed the six-second set of notes that accompanied the start-up of Microsoft's Windows 95 operating system. In the mid-1990's he collaborated with software engineers to create a computer program that would compose music; his software album *Generative Music 1* was a product of it. His video artwork and installations have been displayed around the world, and his theories about creativity and the artistic process have reverberated not only with musicians but also with visual artists and writers.

Lacy Schutz

Further Reading

Bracewell, Michael. *Re-make Re-model: Becoming Roxy Music*. New York: Da Capo Press, 2008. Written with the cooperation of all the members of Roxy Music, this book examines the evolution of the band and the culture in which the band existed.

Dayal, Geeta. *Brian Eno's Another Green World*. London: Continuum, 2007. This slender volume is one of a series in which authors take an in-depth look at a particular album.

Eno, Brian. *A Year with Swollen Appendices: The Diary of Brian Eno*. London: Faber and Faber, 1996. This diary, written by Eno during 1995, traces his music and ideas, with a few details on his personal life.

Eno, Brian, Russell Mills, and Rick Poyner. *More Dark than Shark*. London: Faber and Faber, 1986. This book contains Eno's lyrics accompanied by

Mills's visual interpretations, and the essays by Poyner examine the artistic process.

Prendergast, Mark, and Brian Eno. *The Ambient Century: From Mahler to Trance, the Evolution of Sound in the Electronic Age.* New York: Blooms-bury USA, 2001. This history of sound and elec-tronic music from classical music through rock and roll includes a foreword by Eno.

Stump, Paul. *Unknown Pleasures: A Cultural Biogra-phy of Roxy Music.* New York: Thunder's Mouth Press, 1999. A music journalist examines the his-tory of Roxy Music in the context of 1970's music and culture.

Tamm, Eric. *Brian Eno: His Music and the Vertical Color of Sound.* New York: Da Capo Press, 1995. A scholarly look at Eno, his music, and his influ-ence.

Toop, David. *Ocean of Sound: Aether Talk, Ambient Sound, and Imaginary Worlds.* London: Serpent's Tail, 1995. This book offers a history of ambient music, from Javanese gamelan to Eno's cre-ations.

See also: Bono; Bowie, David; Byrne, David; Cage, John; Collins, Phil; Gabriel, Peter; Petty, Tom; Reich, Steve; Satie, Erik; Simon, Paul.

Enya

Irish New Age and Celtic singer and songwriter

Enya's musical style seamlessly blends the emo-tional lyricism of New Age music with classical and Celtic folk forms.

Born: May 17, 1961; Gweedore, Donegal, Ireland
Also known as: Eithne Patricia Ní Bhraonáin (birth name); Eithne Brennan
Member of: Clannad

Principal recordings

ALBUMS (solo): *The Celts*, 1987; *Enya*, 1987; *Watermark*, 1988; *Shepherd Moons*, 1991; *The Frog Prince*, 1995; *The Memory of Trees*, 1995; *A Day Without Rain*, 2000; *Amarantine*, 2005; *Sounds of the Season with Enya*, 2006.

ALBUMS (with Clannad): *Fuaim*, 1982; *Pretty Maid*, 1982.

The Life

Eithne Patricia Ní Bhraonáin, known as Enya (EHN-yah), was born into a large musical family in County Donegal, Ireland. Her grandparents and fa-ther performed in Irish folk music bands, and her mother was a music teacher at an Irish-speaking school. After studying piano and classical music, Enya began her career in the early 1980's as a keyboardist and background vocalist in her fam-ily's popular Irish band, Clannad. Leaving the group after only two years to pursue a solo career, Enya participated in several minor projects before being commissioned to score a 1986 BBC documen-tary, *The Celts*.

Though the sound track for *The Celts* was re-leased in 1987, Enya did not gain major attention until the release of *Watermark* in 1988. After that, her career and international reputation climbed, pri-marily through the release of several Grammy Award-winning solo albums and through the use of her music in television shows and films. In 1996 Enya moved into Manderley Castle in County Dub-lin, Ireland.

The Music

Enya's music is often categorized as New Age for its emotionally lyrical and ethereal quality. However, it also exhibits the characteristics of clas-sical music and of traditional Celtic folk tunes, spe-cifically the Irish sean nós (old style). Equally im-portant is her signature method of combining multiple layers of recorded instruments (primarily keyboards) with those of her voice (both as soloist and as choir), a process that results in richly col-ored, lavish orchestrations and dense vocal tex-tures. As a consequence of this process, live perfor-mances of her music are virtually impossible. This, coupled with her private nature, explains why Enya rarely appears in public as a performer.

Although considered a solo artist, Enya owes much of her success to longtime friends Nicky Ryan (producer) and his wife Roma Ryan (lyricist), the three having worked closely on nearly all aspects of Enya's career since her departure from Clannad. In particular, Roma Ryan's highly poetic and some-times elusive lyrics—in such languages as English,

Gaelic, Latin, Welsh, French, and Spanish, as well as those created by J. R. R. Tolkien and Ryan herself—play a significant role in Enya's music.

Early Works. Though written as the sound track to the BBC documentary *The Celts*, the self-titled *Enya* is generally regarded as the artist's first solo album. It includes such popular tracks as "The Celts," "I Want Tomorrow," and "Boadicea." The release of her second album, *Watermark*, brought Enya international fame. Featuring such hits as "Storms in Africa" and "Orinoco Flow," *Watermark* established the artist's successful formula of including both instrumental and vocal numbers on every album.

Shepherd Moons. In addition to placing at the top of European and American music charts, *Shepherd Moons* won the Grammy Award for Best New Age Album. The influence of traditional Irish music is more prominent on *Shepherd Moons* than on *Watermark*, particularly on such tracks as "Ebudae" and "Smaointe. . . ." Notable are the songs "Caribbean Blue" and "Book of Days" and Enya's arrangements of the traditional hymn tune "How Can I Keep From Singing?" and the aria "Marble Halls" from the nineteenth century operetta *The Bohemian Girl* (1843) by Michael Balfe and Alfred Bunn. *Shepherd Moons* has guest musicians, including Steve Sidwell on cornet and Liam O'Flynn on uilleann pipes (Irish bagpipes).

The Memory of Trees *and* A Day Without Rain. Garnering Grammy Awards for Best New Age Album, these albums contained little new in terms of musical vocabulary, but they were immensely successful commercially. Both albums feature entirely original music, with *The Memory of Trees* including such popular tracks as "Anywhere Is," "Hope Has a Place," "Once You Had Gold," and "On My Way Home." The individual offerings on *A Day Without Rain* are overall not as noteworthy, the entire album instead creating a singular mood, with the exception of the hits "Wild Child" and "Only Time." The latter song became especially popular following the

Enya. (AP/Wide World Photos)

attacks in New York City and Washington, D.C., on September 11, 2001.

Amarantine. *Amarantine*, which won a Grammy Award for Best New Age Album in 2007, is derived from the Greek word *amarantos*, referring to a flower that never fades. Enya charts no new musical territory, this album being slightly more sedate than her previous releases. Notable, however, is the use of Japanese lyrics in the song "Sumiregusa (Wild Violet)" and lyrics in Loxian—a language invented by Roma Ryan—in such tracks as the upbeat "The River Sings." *Amarantine* is Enya's first album not to include any lyrics in her native Gaelic. All of the remaining songs are in English, including the title track and "It's in the Rain," and the album features the moody instrumental "Drifting."

Musical Legacy

Enya is often considered a popular Celtic musician, although her composing and singing style is closer to New Age music. Working slowly, she meticulously crafts each of her compositions to be immediately appealing and emotionally satisfying, even after repeated hearings. She has garnered numerous honors, not only for her solo albums but also for such projects as her Academy Award-nominated song "May It Be," written for director Peter Jackson's motion picture *The Lord of the Rings: The Fellowship of the Ring* (2001). Though rarely appearing in public as a performer, and despite her somewhat static development as a composer, Enya has attracted a large, loyal fan base, and she has built an outstanding international reputation.

Frederick Key Smith

Further Reading

Duffy, Tom. "Ireland's Enya Strikes a Universal Chord." *Billboard* (July 23, 1994): 11-12. The article discusses the success of Enya's album *Shepherd Moons*.

Forbes, Michelle. "Enya at Ease." *World of Hibernia* 6, no. 3 (2000): 74. This interview with Enya, which takes place in her castle, covers her career and her music.

Ritchie, Fiona. *The NPR Curious Listener's Guide to Celtic Music*. New York: Berkley, 2004. This guide provides a general overview of the artist's musical career.

Wallis, Geoff, and Sue Wilson. *The Rough Guide to Irish Music*. London: Rough Guides, 2001. A brief biography and other references to Enya.

White, Timothy. "Enya: 'Memory,' Myth and Melody (Music to My Ears)." *Billboard* (November 25, 1995): 5. Though focused on her album *The Memory of Trees*, the article provides insight into the connection between Enya's music and her Celtic heritage.

See also: Kitarō; Vangelis; Yanni.

Melissa Etheridge

American rock and country singer, songwriter, and guitarist

Etheridge is a rock singer-songwriter known for her raspy renditions of songs with soul-baring, passionate lyrics.

Born: May 29, 1961; Leavenworth, Kansas
Also known as: Melissa Lou Etheridge (full name); Missy Etheridge

Principal recordings

ALBUMS: *Melissa Etheridge*, 1988; *Brave and Crazy*, 1989; *Never Enough*, 1992; *Yes I Am*, 1993; *Your Little Secret*, 1995; *Breakdown*, 1999; *Skin*, 2001;

Lucky, 2004; *The Awakening*, 2007; *Greatest Hits: The Road Less Traveled*, 2007.

The Life

Melissa Lou Etheridge (ETH-rihj) was born to schoolteacher John Etheridge and his wife Elizabeth in Leavenworth, Kansas, in 1961. She describes her family as supportive but not warm or loving. As a teenager, she performed with various cover bands in Kansas, often in bars, chaperoned by her father. After high school she enrolled at Berklee College of Music in Boston, but she soon returned home to earn enough money to move to Los Angeles. She headed to Southern California in 1982, and over the next several years she developed a following by playing at women's bars. Longtime manager Bill Leopold discovered Etheridge at Vermie's bar in Pasadena, and after Island Records owner Chris Blackwell heard her sing at Que Sera in Long Beach, Etheridge signed a contract with the label.

Etheridge publicly came out as a lesbian at the Triangle Ball following President Bill Clinton's inauguration in 1993. Her public announcement brought her relationship with longtime partner Julie Cypher to the forefront. The pair met in 1988, when Cypher was the assistant director for Etheridge's first music video and still married to actor Lou Diamond Phillips. Cypher and Etheridge split in 2000, but they had two children (daughter Bailey, born in 1997, and son Beckett, born in 1998), fathered by singer David Crosby through artificial insemination. In 2001 Etheridge became romantically involved with actress Tammy Lynn Michaels, who gave birth to twins in 2006 (son Miller Steven and daughter Johnnie Rose), fathered by an anonymous sperm donor through artificial insemination. In October, 2004, Etheridge was diagnosed with breast cancer, which she successfully battled with chemotherapy, and she began performing again in 2005.

The Music

Etheridge's personal life is tied inextricably to her music, which has often—but not always—worked to her benefit. From an early age she used music as an emotional outlet from her stifled family life, retreating to the basement to write songs. As Etheridge says in her autobiography, "a string of nonmonogamous relationships" led to a "bunch of really good songs." Etheridge's first five albums—

Melissa Etheridge, Brave and Crazy, Never Enough, Yes I Am, and *Your Little Secret*—went platinum or multiplatinum. Her later albums—*Breakdown, Skin*, and *Lucky*—never reached that success. She came back, however, to win the Academy Award for Best Original Song in 2007 for the rock anthem "I Need to Wake Up," written for Al Gore's documentary about global warming, *An Inconvenient Truth* (2006). The Oscar-winning song is included on a 2007 rerelease of Etheridge's 2005 album *Greatest Hits: The Road Less Traveled*. Later, *The Awakening*, recorded after her recovery from breast cancer, showed Etheridge at a creative peak, exploring life from a new, hard-won perspective. Although *The Awakening* is a more relaxed, mature effort than her earlier work, she delivers it with her trademark passion, conviction, and humor.

Melissa Etheridge. Etheridge's self-titled debut album featured the singles "Like the Way I Do," "Similar Features," and the Grammy Award–nominated hit "Bring Me Some Water." The last song centers on an infectious, bluesy guitar riff, with Etheridge singing that she is "burning alive" with jealousy. Although the Grammy Award went to Tina Turner, Etheridge's live performance at the awards show led to a huge increase in her visibility and her record sales, and her follow-up album, *Brave and Crazy*, was also well received.

Never Enough. The cover photograph for Etheridge's 1992 album *Never Enough* featured the singer topless with her back to the camera, receiving almost as much attention as the music. The album incorporated some dance music, and in general it was more tightly produced than its somewhat raw predecessors. The techno sound of "2001" and the mellow pop of "Dance Without Sleeping" offer glimpses of these new sounds, and Etheridge won her first Grammy Award for "Ain't It Heavy," an empowering, guitar-driven rock anthem more true to her roots.

Yes I Am. Although the title track to Etheridge's wildly popular 1993 album is not specifically about her sexuality, the bold statement became synonymous with her coming out as a lesbian earlier that year. The album featured songs that became huge hits: "If I Wanted To," "I'm the Only One," and "Come to My Window," the last of which earned a Grammy Award and catapulted her into superstardom. "Come to My Window" is a haunting rock ballad about a woman desperately trying to reach her lover. Although Etheridge's autobiography indicates that the song relates to a difficult time in her relationship with Cypher, the universal theme mirrors many listeners' experiences. Etheridge's follow-up album, *Your Little Secret*, was also a hit, but *Yes I Am* stood as a definitive statement.

Musical Legacy

While rarely described as musically innovative, Etheridge made music that exemplifies her rock-and-roll roots, and she remained committed to it in the face of divergent popular trends. Her willingness to bare her soul and share her personal journey makes her compelling to her fans. In addition to her music, Etheridge supports many causes—human rights and environmental issues in particular—making her an important role model.

Gretchen Rowe Clements

Further Reading

Dunn, Jancee. "Melissa Etheridge Takes the Long Hard Road from the Heartland to Hollywood." *Rolling Stone* 709 (1995): 38-45. This article describes Etheridge's rise to stardom, with details on her music and her personal life.

_____. "Melissa's Secret." *Rolling Stone* 833 (2002): 40-45. This attention-getting article reveals singer Crosby to be the father of Etheridge and Cypher's child, and it explores the relationships involved.

Etheridge, Melissa, with Laura Morton. *The Truth Is . . .: My Life in Love and Music*. New York: Random House, 2001. This is Etheridge's refreshingly candid and modest account of the events that shaped her life and her music. Includes numerous family and personal photographs.

Luck, Joyce. *Melissa Etheridge: Our Little Secret*. Toronto, Ont.: ECW Press, 1997. This unauthorized but carefully researched biography chronicles Etheridge's rise to stardom. Includes bibliography and discography.

Udovitch, Mim. "How Do You Mend a Broken Heart?" *Rolling Stone* 872 (2001): 62-64. This interview discusses Etheridge's autobiography, her personal life, her latest album, and the music industry.

See also: Crosby, David; Lang, K. D.

Bill Evans

American jazz pianist and composer

A major contributor to the development of modern jazz, Evans is noted for his harmonic inventions in the context of jazz piano. He recorded more than fifty albums as a leader and received five Grammy Awards.

Born: August 16, 1929; Plainfield, New Jersey
Died: September 15, 1980; New York, New York
Also known as: William John Evans (full name)
Member of: The Bill Evans Trio

Principal recordings

ALBUMS: *New Jazz Conceptions*, 1956; *Everybody Digs Bill Evans*, 1958; *Kind of Blue*, 1959 (with Miles Davis and others); *On Green Dolphin Street*, 1959; *Portrait in Jazz*, 1959 (with the Bill Evans Trio); *Explorations*, 1961; *Sunday at the Village Vanguard*, 1961; *The Village Vanguard Sessions*, 1961; *Waltz for Debby*, 1961; *Empathy*, 1962; *How My Heart Sings!*, 1962; *Interplay*, 1962; *Loose Blues*, 1962; *Moon Beams*, 1962; *At Shelly's Manne-Hole*, 1963 (with the Bill Evans Trio); *Conversations with Myself*, 1963; *The Solo Sessions, Vol. 1*, 1963; *The Solo Sessions, Vol. 2*, 1963; *Time Remembered*, 1963; *Undercurrent*, 1963 (with Jim Hall); *Trio '64*, 1964; *Bill Evans Trio with Symphony Orchestra*, 1965; *Trio '65*, 1965; *Bill Evans at Town Hall*, 1966; *Intermodulation*, 1966 (with Hall); *A Simple Matter of Conviction*, 1966; *California, Here I Come*, 1967; *Further Conversations with Myself*, 1967; *Alone*, 1968; *What's New*, 1969; *From Left to Right*, 1970; *Quiet Now*, 1970; *The Bill Evans Album*, 1971; *Living Time*, 1972; *Serenity*, 1972; *Eloquence*, 1973; *My Foolish Heart*, 1973; *Blue in Green*, 1974; *But Beautiful*, 1974; *Intuition*, 1974; *Re: Person I Knew*, 1974; *Since We Met*, 1974; *Symbiosis*, 1974; *Alone (Again)*, 1975; *The Tony Bennett/Bill Evans Album*, 1975; *Quintessence*, 1976; *Cross-Currents*, 1977; *I Will Say Goodbye*, 1977; *You Must Believe in Spring*, 1977; *Affinity*, 1978; *New Conversations*, 1978; *We Will Meet Again*, 1979; *Turn Out the Stars: Final Village Vanguard Recordings*, 1980; *Alternative Man*, 1987; *The Last Waltz*, 2000.

The Life

William John Evans was born to Harry and Mary Evans in the middle-class suburban setting of Plainfield, New Jersey. His musical interests began at the age of three while listening to his older brother Harry's piano lessons. Before he reached the age of seven, Evans had started lessons of his own, later recalling, "From the age of six to thirteen, I acquired the ability to sight-read and to play classical music."

By the time he attended North Plainfield High School, Evans had established an unrivaled thirst for the contemporary Western European repertoire, namely the works of Darius Milhaud, Claude Debussy, and Maurice Ravel. Around the same time, Evans was introduced to the big band recordings of Tommy Dorsey and Harry James. The freedom to improvise, as found in the jazz idiom, excited Evans; consequently, he turned his attention to performing in the technically complex piano style of boogie-woogie. His sight-reading skills led to his first professional performing opportunities. He began playing at weddings and dances while still in high school.

In September, 1946, Evans accepted a scholarship to Southeastern Louisiana University at Hammond, located fifty miles from the birthplace of jazz, New Orleans. In 1950 Evans graduated with bachelor's degrees in piano performance and music education and moved to New York City to pursue a performance career. One of his earliest experiences was with a trio led by guitarist Mundell Lowe, who subsequently brought Evans's playing to the attention of Orrin Keepnews of Riverside Records.

New Jazz Conceptions, Evans's first recording under his own name, was made on September 27, 1956. He was accompanied by Teddy Kotick on bass and Paul Motian on drums; this trio format of piano, bass, and drums would be one in which Evans would musically thrive. His later trios, especially with bassist Scott LaFaro and Motian, would ultimately transcend the prescribed role of merely keeping time to establish polyphonic, contrapuntal textures.

In April, 1958, Evans joined the sextet led by trumpeter Miles Davis. This experience provided great exposure for the young pianist and consequently augmented his professional viability. The following year, while still with Davis, Evans participated in the seminal recording of Davis's *Kind of Blue*, one of the best selling jazz albums of all time. Exhausted from the Davis association, Evans left the band to launch his career as a leader.

Evans found in LaFaro and Motian musical companions who subscribed to his conception of a three-way musical dialogue. In 1959 they began their exploration in earnest. Sadly, this kinship would be torn by the accidental death of LaFaro in July, 1961 (just days after their groundbreaking live recording at the Village Vanguard).

The remainder of the 1960's consisted of triumphs and struggles for Evans. He managed to reform his trio with a new bassist, continued to record and compose original compositions, won the critics' poll in *Down Beat* magazine for pianist of the year, toured the world, and sank into heroin addiction.

In the 1970's Evans secured a recording contract with Columbia Records and, later, Fantasy Records. He continued to tour and seemed to be in something of a musical revival, invigorated by his musical companionship with such artists as bassist Marc Johnson and drummer Joe La Barbera, along with his newest addiction, cocaine. In 1980 his health rapidly declined, and in September Evans passed away, his death hastened by an unattended bleeding ulcer and acute liver disease.

The Music

Perhaps one of Evans's greatest contributions to the tradition of jazz was his unique approach to the conventional trio of piano, bass, and drums: He encouraged his accompanists to maintain a musical dialogue rather than simply propel the rhythm. Understanding Evans's trios leads to a true appreciation of his musical contribution.

Portrait in Jazz. Evans's first trio consisted of himself, bassist LaFaro, and drummer Motian. In their first recording, *Portrait in Jazz*, Evans approached the piano in an uncharacteristically percussive fashion with florid melodic lines, complex harmonies, and a tense, swinging rhythm; LaFaro and Motian offset Evans's intensity with a combined pensiveness. This was most evident in the album's first track, "Come Rain or Come Shine." The record also featured two original compositions by Evans, "Blue in Green" (often wrongly attributed to Miles Davis) and "Peri's Scope," named after Evans's girlfriend Peri Cousins.

Sunday at the Village Vanguard. On June 25, 1961, the trio performed at the famed Village Vanguard and the material would be subsequently released as the album, *Sunday at the Village Vanguard*. This recording illustrated the trio's maturity and the increased freedom given to LaFaro. The performance, which opened with his composition "Gloria's Step," displayed the bassist's vast

Bill Evans. (AP/Wide World Photos)

creativity and command of his instrument as he juxtaposed melodic lines with Evans. The intense interplay continued throughout the set and perhaps reached its apex on the George Gershwin tune "My Man's Gone Now." An additional album of material from the Vanguard performance would be released as *Waltz for Debby*.

After the death of LaFaro, Evans faced the challenge of replicating the spontaneous collaboration with a new trio. Although he would find a competent instrumentalist in bassist Chuck Israels, a true sense of cohesion was not secured until the connection with bassist Eddie Gomez. This association would last from 1966 through 1977.

Conversations with Myself. Among the most innovative of Evans's career, this album found the pianist employing the technical advances of multi-track recording. The repertory was typical Evans fare, including the jazz standard "Stella by Starlight" and the Thelonious Monk composition "'Round Midnight." The unconventional treatment of each tune was the ingenuity: Evans overdubbed himself three times, each take separated to a different channel—left, right, and center. This gave the pianist the opportunity to have a conversation with himself. His efforts were rewarded with a 1963 Grammy Award.

The Bill Evans Album. During the spring of 1971, Evans's second recording date under the Columbia Records label spawned *The Bill Evans Album*. Music mogul Clive Davis insisted that his jazz artists incorporate electric instruments into their playing, an attempt to make jazz more accessible and commercially viable. Although Evans would go on to suggest that the electric pianos, such as the Fender Rhodes, could never capture the nuance of an acoustic piano, the effort was not fruitless. The album went on to win two Grammy Awards and allowed Evans to experiment with the new timbres of the instrument. Additionally, Evans had the opportunity to augment his trio setting with string and woodwind sections.

The Tony Bennett/Bill Evans Album. It was a rare occasion when Evans broke from the comfortable environment of the trio. During the summer of 1975, he joined vocalist Tony Bennett for their first duet recording. This album illustrates the pianist's tremendous versatility in artistically supporting the vocalist while remaining true to his creative vi-

sion. The set consisted of the likely ballads "My Foolish Heart" and "But Beautiful," along with the midtempo tune "When in Rome." Evans's "Waltz for Debby," traditionally an instrumental, was performed by Bennett with lyrics by Gene Lees.

Turn Out the Stars. Evans's last appearances at the Village Vanguard in June, 1980, and his penultimate recording date resulted in *Turn Out the Stars: Final Village Vanguard Recordings*, with Evans accompanied by the members of his final trio, Johnson and La Barbera. This unrivaled cohesive unit articulated a barrage of moods and textures and was the most uniquely collaborative since the trio of Evans, LaFaro, and Motian. On the album, Evans exudes a youthfully powerful approach on up-tempo tunes and his characteristically introspective playing on ballads such as "Polka Dots and Moon-beams."

The Last Waltz. Evans's final recordings were made from August 31 through September 7, 1980, just days before his death. Todd Barkan, the owner of Keystone Korner (the San Francisco jazz club that hosted Evans's last appearance), recorded on tape the weeklong engagement. Each set was a well-balanced collection of jazz standards and original Evans tunes. On many of the songs, there exists a sense of urgency—perhaps because of the pianist's comprehension of his physical deterioration. His left-hand passages are more florid and rhythmically complex than his earlier approach, yet he maintains a three-way dialogue with Johnson and La Barbera. The trio, acting as a single entity, displays great contrast during the slower jazz waltz "Gary's Theme."

Musical Legacy

Evans was one of the most influential jazz musicians of the post-bebop era. His exceptionally refined touch, advanced harmonic conception, and insistence on the equally expressive roles of his accompanists left an indelible mark on subsequent generations. Pianists such as Chick Corea, Herbie Hancock, Keith Jarrett, Fred Hersch, and Brad Mehldau exhibit the influence of Evans in their playing. Like many jazz artists before him, Evans succumbed to a horrific struggle with drug addiction—cutting short his life and robbing the public of brilliance yet to come.

Michael Conklin

Further Reading

Larson, Thomas. *Fragmentation: The Piano Trio in History and Tradition of Jazz.* Dubuque, Iowa: Kendall/Hunt, 2005. Larson's text on the history of jazz is a concise, well-organized, and well-researched effort. Includes photographs and listening examples.

Lees, Gene. *Meet Me at Jim and Andy's.* New York: Oxford University Press, 1988. An insightful look at the life and personality of Evans, as told by a close friend and collaborator.

Pettinger, Peter. *Bill Evans: How My Heart Sings.* New Haven, Conn.: Yale University Press, 1998. Perhaps the most well-organized document on Evans's life, with a wonderfully diachronic approach to the development and ultimate demise of the jazz icon. Photographs, discography, and musical examples.

Porter, Lewis, and Michael Ullman."Bill Evans and Modern Jazz Piano." In *Jazz, from Its Origins to the Present.* Englewood Cliffs, N.J.: Prentice Hall, 1993. Porter, a leader in jazz scholarship and a jazz pianist, devotes a chapter to Evans and subsequent generations of modern jazz piano. Photographs, musical examples, and thorough musical analysis.

Reilly, Jack. *The Harmony of Bill Evans.* Milwaukee, Wis.: Hal Leonard, 1993. An in-depth analysis of Evans's piano style and compositional techniques by a jazz pianist.

Shadwick, Keith. *Bill Evans: Everything Happens to Me—A Musical Biography.* San Francisco: Backbeat Books, 2002. A detailed examination of one of jazz's great innovative forces. The book traces the musical life of Evans from his first trio in the 1950's to his tragic death in 1980. Photographs and selected discography.

See also: Bennett, Tony; Corea, Chick; Davis, Miles; Debussy, Claude; Getz, Stan; Hancock, Herbie; Jarrett, Keith; Legrand, Michel; Ligeti, György; McPartland, Marian; Powell, Bud; Ravel, Maurice.

Don and Phil Everly

American rock and country singers, songwriters, and guitarists

With their two-part harmony singing style and their open G-string guitar tuning, the Everly Brothers introduced Appalachian music, rockabilly, and blues into rock music.

Don Everly
Born: February 1, 1937; Brownie, Kentucky
Also known as: Isaac Donald Everly (full name)

Phil Everly
Born: January 19, 1939; Chicago, Illinois
Also known as: Phillip Everly (full name)
Members of: The Everly Brothers

Principal recordings

ALBUMS (as the Everly Brothers): *The Everly Brothers,* 1958; *The Real Everly Brothers,* 1958; *Songs Our Daddy Taught Us,* 1958; *The Fabulous Style of the Everly Brothers,* 1960; *It's Everly Time,* 1960; *Rockin' with the Everly Brothers,* 1960; *Both Sides of an Evening,* 1961; *A Date with the Everly Brothers,* 1961; *Souvenir Sampler,* 1961; *Christmas with the Everly Brothers,* 1962; *Folk Songs of the Everly Brothers,* 1962; *Instant Party!,* 1962; *The Everly Brothers Sing Great Country Hits,* 1963; *Gone, Gone, Gone,* 1964; *Beat and Soul,* 1965; *Price of Love,* 1965; *Rock 'n' Soul,* 1965; *In Our Image,* 1966; *Two Yanks in England,* 1966; *The Everly Brothers Sing,* 1967; *The Hit Sound of the Everly Brothers,* 1967; *Roots,* 1968; *Chained to a Memory,* 1970; *Stories We Could Tell,* 1972; *Don't Worry Baby,* 1973; *Pass the Chicken and Listen,* 1973; *Everlys,* 1975; *The New Album: Previously Unreleased Songs from the Early Sixties,* 1977; *EB '84,* 1984; *All They Had to Do Was Dream,* 1985; *Home Again,* 1985; *Born Yesterday,* 1986; *Some Hearts,* 1989; *Thirty-one Unforgettable Memories,* 1997; *Christmas with the Everly Brothers and the Boys Town Choir,* 2005; *Give Me a Future,* 2005; *Too Good to Be True,* 2005.

ALBUMS (Don, solo): *Don Everly,* 1970; *Sunset Towers,* 1974; *Brother Juke Box,* 1977.

ALBUMS (Phil, solo): *Star Spangled Springer,* 1973; *Phil's Diner,* 1974; *Mystic Line,* 1975; *Living*

Alone, 1979; *Phil Everly*, 1983; *Louise*, 1987; *A Portrait of Phil Everly*, 1994.

The Lives

Isaac Donald and Phillip Everly (EH-vur-lee) were born into an accomplished and established musical family. Don, the older brother, was born in Kentucky on February 1, 1937; Phil was born in Chicago on January 19, 1939. Ike Everly, their father, and his brothers, Charles and Leonard, were singers and musicians who moved from the coal-mining community of Muhlenberg, Kentucky, to Chicago in order to make a living as a country-blues group. Although they were successful, Ike decided he did not want to raise his sons in Chicago, and so in 1944 he moved his family to rural Iowa.

In Iowa, Ike hosted a live radio show that featured Little Donnie, age eight, and Baby Boy Phil, age six, singing and playing guitar. Many famous musicians played on the show, and the boys sang and performed with them live. They became the special favorites of Chet Atkins, already a major figure of the Nashville music community. He was instrumental in getting them established in Nashville, and he arranged their Grand Ole Opry debut in 1954.

In 1954 Don got his first break as a songwriter, with "Thou Shalt Not Steal," recorded by Kitty Wells. In 1955 Don and Phil signed their first recording contract, but they had little success until 1957, when they signed with Cadence Records. Again, Atkins proved indispensable to their career, by insisting that Cadence allow the brothers to record a demo, despite the failure of their first album. From 1957 until 1961, the Everly Brothers could be heard on pop, country, and rock-and-roll radio stations, turning out multiple million-selling hits for Cadence Records.

In 1961 the brothers split from their longtime manager, Wesley Rose, and Cadence Records, and this started a decade-long slump during which their five-year history of producing Top 20 hits ended. They joined the U.S. Marines for a year, and when they were discharged in 1962, they found their music no longer relevant because of the rising influence of the folk revival and the coming British Invasion, when rock-and-roll and pop performers from England, among them the Beatles, gained popularity in the United States.

In 1966 the Everlys went to England, where they had always enjoyed success, and they recorded an album featuring the Hollies as back-up, with Jimmy Page and John Paul Jones, soon to form Led Zeppelin, appearing as studio musicians.

The Everlys' last album of new material appeared in 1973. During the tour to promote this album, long-simmering tensions boiled over, and during a concert Phil smashed his guitar and stormed off the stage, leaving Don to finish solo. Because of Don's drug addiction and alcoholism, and their unresolved feud, they stopped performing together until 1983. The Reunion Concert at the Royal Albert Hall, a great success, was made into an HBO film special. In 1984 they were back on the charts, singing a song written by Paul McCartney.

The Everlys perform occasionally, and Don continues to write music. They try to appear at the annual Muhlenberg Agricultural Fair. Phil started the Everly Music Company, designing and producing quality guitar and banjo strings. They appear as guests on many country and rock albums, notably singing back up for Paul Simon's *Graceland* (1986). In 2005 they had a successful tour in England.

The Music

The Everlys grew up singing gospel, country, and Appalachian folk music along with their father and his brothers. The Everly Brothers became famous for their beautiful harmonies, with Don singing lead and Phil taking high harmony. Don began writing music, selling songs as a teenager to famous Nashville singers such as Patsy Cline, but the brothers got their big break with "Bye Bye Love," written by Felice and Boudleaux Bryant. They continued to record the Bryants' songs as well as write their own. For five years they dominated the charts. In the mid-1960's, as they were losing favor in America because of the British Invasion, they continued to chart in England, and they produced some of their most sophisticated work, such as "Gone, Gone, Gone" and "The Price of Love." Their songs are characterized by perfect harmonies, country roots-inspired guitar playing, and intricate chord patterns, all of which helped bridge the gap between country and pop and led the way for rock and roll.

"Bye Bye Love." This was the Everly Brothers' first hit. The song, written by the Bryants, was turned down by thirty singers before the Everlys

427

Don (right) and Phil Everly. (AP/Wide World Photos)

decided to record it. Atkins worked a deal with Cadence Records owner Archie Bleyer, who allowed the brothers to record "Bye Bye Love" as an audition demo. An expert at open G-string tuning, Don composed a six-second guitar introduction, and the song became a legend. It became the signature format for the Everly Brothers: guitar introduction by Don; two-part harmonies, with Phil taking the high parts; and solos in the middle taken by Don. "Bye Bye Love" was their first million seller.

"Wake Up, Little Susie." This follow-up to "Bye Bye Love," also by the Bryants, was the Everly Brothers' second million seller. The harmonies combined close-third intervals with country-inspired fifths and sixths, making the song more musically sophisticated than "Bye Bye Love." It was a hit on several charts, and its focus on teenage problems made it an undeniable success with young listeners. Although banned in Boston for suggestive lyrics, the song was a number-one hit in America and overseas.

Songs Our Daddy Taught Us. This album, rereleased many times since 1958, featured the Everlys singing traditional country and Appalachian music, playing a stand-up bass and an acoustic guitar. It was a departure from the teen-angst pop songs that had made them famous and a return to their roots. *Rolling Stone* awarded it four out of five stars for its faithful interpretation of important roots music.

"Let It Be Me." This was the Everlys' first non-Nashville recording. Don had heard the melody of this French song played by Atkins, and the brothers recorded this version with English lyrics in 1960. This was one of the first pop songs to use a string section, and it was the final record produced before their break with Rose-Acuff music. "Let It Be Me" proved to be one of their most enduring hits.

"Cathy's Clown." The split from Rose-Acuff music meant that the Everlys could no longer record songs by the Bryants, who had written almost all of their hits. "Cathy's Clown," written by Don with help from Phil, was the first single produced while under contract with Warner Bros. It included a sixth level of harmony, Phil's new addition to the Everly Brothers' style. It was the biggest single of their career.

All They Had to Do Was Dream. All the tracks on this album are alternate versions of songs recorded between 1957 and 1960 for Cadence Records. This is an interesting album because it comprised all the songs that became big hits for the Everlys, but with different arrangements.

Later Music. The Everlys have recorded almost thirty albums, none of which was a big seller in America despite receiving good reviews and containing both originals and covers. *Rock 'n' Soul* and *Gone, Gone, Gone* were both popular in England. *Two Yanks in England* and *In Our Image* also did very well in England, and they featured British musicians such as the Hollies and Page. These were not nostalgic or old fashioned; they were sophisticated and imbued with rock sensibilities. Nevertheless, they did not promote the duo's image back in the United States. *Pass the Chicken and Listen* was the last album of new material for a decade. After their feud and reunion, the Everlys produced three albums containing new material: *EB '84, Born Yesterday*, and *Some Hearts. Too Good to Be True* and *Give Me a Future* contain previously unreleased songs from their early career in the 1950's and 1960's.

Musical Legacy

The Everlys' primary contribution to rock and roll is their country-music style harmony singing. Rock singers coming after the Everlys owe them a debt of gratitude. John Lennon and Paul McCartney once billed themselves as the Foreverly Brothers. Listed at number thirty-three in *Rolling Stone*'s Top Immortals of All Time, the Everlys were called the greatest rock duo of all time. Their singing has influenced and has been openly acknowledged as influential by Paul Simon and Art Garfunkel, Dave Edmonds, Gram Parsons, Linda Ronstadt, and others. This influence can be heard in many American groups, such as the Flying Burrito Brothers, the Byrds, Buffalo Springfield, Poco, and the Eagles, as well as in British groups such as the Hollies, Nick Lowe, the Buckinghams, and the Bee Gees.

Equally important is Don's impact on rock guitar playing. The introduction to "Bye Bye Love," played using open G-string tuning, changed the way rock and roll sounded. Although played on an acoustic guitar, the large-bodied Gibson created a powerful sound and became the foundation for rock power chords. Keith Richards of the Rolling Stones credits Don Everly with creating the rock guitar sound, and Richards, as do most rock guitarists, uses the same tuning for many of his songs.

As testament to their lasting influence on rock and roll, the Everly Brothers received a Lifetime Achievement Award from the Recording Academy, and they were inducted into the Rock and Roll Hall of Fame; the Country Music Hall of Fame; the Nashville Songwriters Hall of Fame; the Iowa Rock 'n' Roll Music Association's Hall of Fame; and the Vocal Group Hall of Fame.

Leslie Neilan

Further Reading

Hosum, John. *Legends: The Everly Brothers, the History of the Everly Brothers on Record, an Illustrated Discography*. Seattle, Wash.: Foreverly Music, 1985. This provides stories about the Cadence Records years, but very little about any of their other recording history.

Karpp, Phyllis. *Ike's Boys: The Story of the Everly Brothers*. Ann Arbor, Mich.: Popular Culture Ink, 1990. This book provides a history of the Everly family and the brothers' early years.

Kosser, Michael. *How Nashville Became Music City, U.S.A.: Fifty Years of Music Row*. Milwaukee, Wis.: Hal Leonard, 2006. This book contains a chapter devoted to the collaboration between the Everly Brothers and the Bryants.

Rachlis, Kit. "The Everly Brothers." In *The Rolling Stone Illustrated History of Rock and Roll*, edited by Anthony DeCurtis and James Henke. New York: Random House, 1992. This rock-and-roll history has a chapter devoted to the Everly Brothers and their influence on pop music.

White, Roger. *The Everly Brothers: Walk Right Back*. 2d ed. London: Plexus, 1998. This is a revised version of a 1984 book, providing updated information on the Everly Brothers. It includes interviews, photographs, and commentary on their lives and music.

See also: Atkins, Chet; Garfunkel, Art; Lennon, John; McCartney, Sir Paul; Page, Jimmy; Richards, Keith; Simon, Paul; Travis, Merle.

F

Sammy Fain

American singer, songwriter, lyricist, and film-score composer

In a polished Tin Pan Alley style, Fain wrote senti-mental, funny, and whimsical songs that en-chanted listeners and influenced composers and songwriters for the stage and the screen.

Born: June 17, 1902; New York, New York
Died: December 6, 1989; Los Angeles, California
Also known as: Samuel Feinberg (birth name)

Principal works

FILM SCORES: *Roadhouse Nights*, 1930; *Young Man of Manhattan*, 1930; *Moonlight and Pretzels*, 1933; *The Road Is Open Again*, 1933; *Harold Teen*, 1934; *Goin' to Town*, 1935; *Tarnished Angel*, 1938; *Hellzapoppin'*, 1941; *Three Sailors and a Girl*, 1953; *April Love*, 1957; *A Certain Smile*, 1958; *Calamity Jane*, 1963; *Half a House*, 1979; *Halloween Treat*, 1982.

MUSICAL THEATER (music and lyrics unless listed otherwise): *Everybody's Welcome*, 1931 (lyrics by Irving Kahal; libretto by Lambert Carroll); *Hellzapoppin*, 1938 (with Charles Tobias; libretto by Chic Johnson and John Olsen); *George White's Scandals*, 1939 (lyrics by Jack Yellen; libretto by Matt Brooks, Eddie Davis, and George White); *Boys and Girls Together*, 1940 (lyrics by Yellen and Kahal; libretto by Ed Wynn and Pat C. Flick); *Sons o' Fun*, 1941 (with Yellen; libretto by Johnson, Olsen, and Hal Block); *Toplitzky of Notre Dame*, 1946 (lyrics and libretto by George Marion, Jr.); *Flahooley*, 1951 (lyrics by E. Y. Harburg; libretto by Harburg and Fred Saidy); *Ankles Aweigh*, 1955 (lyrics by Dan Shapiro; libretto by Guy Bolton and Davis); *Catch a Star*, 1955 (with Philip Charig; lyrics by Paul Francis Webster and Ray Golden; libretto by Danny Simon and Neil Simon); *Christine*, 1960 (lyrics by Webster; libretto by Pearl S. Buck and Charles K. Peck,

Jr.; based on the novel *My Indian Family* by Hilda Wernher); *Around the World in Eighty Days*, 1962 (lyrics by Harold Adamson); *Something More!*, 1964 (lyrics by Marilyn Bergman and Alan Bergman; libretto by Nate Monaster; based on the novel *Portofino P.T.A.* by Gerald Green).

Principal recordings

SINGLES: "Nobody Knows What a Red Head Mama Can Do," 1924; "Let a Smile Be Your Umbrella," 1927; "You Brought Me a New Kind of Love," 1930; "When I Take My Sugar to Tea," 1931; "By a Waterfall," 1933; "That Old Feeling," 1937; "I Can Dream, Can't I?," 1938; "I'll Be Seeing You," 1938; "I'm Late," 1951; "Second Star to the Right," 1953; "Secret Love," 1953; "Love Is a Many Splendored Thing," 1955; "April Love," 1957; "Black Hills of Dakota," 1958; "The Deadwood Stage," 1958; "Mardi Gras," 1958; "A Very Precious Love," 1958; "Once Upon a Dream," 1959; "Tender Is the Night," 1961; "Strange Are the Ways of Love," 1972; "A World That Never Was," 1976; "Someone's Waiting for You," 1977.

The Life

Samuel Feinberg, who took the professional name Sammy Fain (fayn), grew up in the Catskill Mountains of New York surrounded by music: His father was a cantor, and his brother was a violinist. His cousins Willie and Eugene Howard became a famous musical-comedy team, working in vaude-ville. Fain believed this musical environment con-tributed to his writing style, which he described as a process of "writing with a tear." Fain taught him-self to play piano and to write music. By the time he went to high school, he had written two songs, "When the Boys Come Marching Home" and "Bound for the Bronx." These songs did not catch the attention of the Tin Pan Alley publishers, but by the time Fain finished high school, he was working in the stockroom at an esteemed New York publish-ing company, Shapiro-Bernstein. When the boss,

Louis Bernstein, heard Fain play piano, he immediately moved Fain to work in the music department. Fain's job was to present new songs to the artists and the vaudeville musicians. During this time Fain meet Artie Dunn, with whom he formed a singing duo that became popular in vaudeville and on radio.

In 1925 Fain left the duo to devote himself completely to composing. Two years later he started a partnership with lyricist Irving Kahal, which lasted for seventeen years, until Kahal's death. After the success Fain and Kahal had with the song "By a Waterfall" (for the 1933 film *Footlight Parade*), Warner Bros. immediately signed them to a contract, and they continued writing for Hollywood motion pictures until 1938. When the film studios stopped making musical extravaganzas, Fain went back to New York City, and from 1938 through 1941 he wrote six Broadway musicals. Two major hits—"I'll Be Seeing You" and "I Can Dream Can't I?"—were featured in *Right This Way* (1938). The musical was unsuccessful, but "I'll Be Seeing You" became a theme for a film with the same title in 1943. At the invitation of Metro-Goldwyn-Mayer, Fain went back to Hollywood, and from that point on his music was featured in films released by almost every motion-picture studio.

Fain was elected to the Songwriters Hall of Fame in 1972. In 1989 he was honored by the American Society of Composers, Authors, and Publishers (ASCAP) on its seventy-fifth anniversary; he had been a member since 1926. Fain died of a heart attack in Los Angeles at the end of 1989.

The Music

Fain's first hit was a tune called "Nobody Knows What a Red Head Mama Can Do," with lyrics by Irving Mills and Al Dubin. Once Fain started working with Kahal, they almost immediately had a hit with a song "Let a Smile Be Your Umbrella." Introduced by Maurice Chevalier in *The Big Pond* (1930), a romantic comedy by Paramount Pictures, Fain's next big hit was

"You Brought Me a New Kind of Love." While he worked in Hollywood, Fain wrote "That Old Feeling" (for the film *Vogues of 1938*). The song was written in collaboration with Lew Brown, and it was nominated for an Academy Award for Best Song.

For "Secret Love" (from the film *Calamity Jane*, 1953), Fain received a second nomination for Best Song, and this time he and Paul Francis Webster took home the Oscar. They received another Academy Award for "Love Is a Many Splendored Thing." "April Love" was nominated in 1957, and in 1958 there were nominations for "A Very Precious Love" (from the film *Marjorie Morningstar*) and the title song from *A Certain Smile*. The nominations continued for "Tender Is the Night," "Strange Are the Ways of Love," "A World That Never Was," and "Someone's Waiting for You." Between these films Fain wrote another show with lyricist Harold Adamson, *Around the World in Eighty Days*, which debuted in St. Louis in 1962, and it was performed at Jones Beach in 1964 during the World's Fair.

Hellzapoppin'. *Hellzapoppin'* was a show by Fain and lyricist Charlie Tobias, a Broadway vaudeville extravaganza that ran for 1,404 performances. Despite the negative reviews from critics, it was the longest-running show at that time.

"Let a Smile Be Your Umbrella." This typical Tin Pan Alley song—joyful, with an uplifting text—

Sammy Fain. (Hulton Archive/Getty Images)

is composed of a simple melody accompanied by the main harmonies, tonic, subdominant, and dominant. The melody is built from a broken arpeggio, and the verse is divided in two eight-measure phrases. The form of the chorus is *a* (sixteen bars), *b* (eight bars), *a'* (eight bars). The *a* section opens on a tonic harmony, and the melody revolves around the tonic chord, ending the phrase on a dominant. The next eight measures are a sequence and lead into the middle section, *b*, which is based on dominant chords (D7 and G7) and presents a rhythmic variation of the *a* section. The last section, *a'*, repeats the first eight measures with a small melodic variation at the end.

"I'll Be Seeing You." This song was introduced in the show *Right This Way* (1938), which closed after fourteen performances. In the second measure of the verse there is a harmonic shift from E-flat major (the key of the piece) to E major, which provides instability. In the refrain melody (*abac*; each section has eight measures) the third and fourth measures are repeated and the downbeat of the phrase switches. Fain used syncopation and dotted rhythms throughout the song, giving it a complex texture. During World War II this song became a nostalgic favorite, and it remains one of the most emotionally moving songs ever written.

Musical Legacy

Jule Styne described Fain as one of the great popular songwriters, one who helped Tin Pan Alley flourish at its highest level. Fain's music shows a development from a simple tune to a picturesque song complex enough to be labeled a short character piece. Every song provides different contours and shapes in the melody and in the advanced harmonies. Through this writing style, which went beyond the simplicity of Tin Pan Alley, Fain influenced the generations of songwriters and film composers that followed.

Daniela Candillari

Further Reading

Furia, Philip, and Michael Lasser. *America's Songs. The Stories Behind the Songs of Broadway, Hollywood, and Tin Pan Alley.* New York: Routledge, 2006. Chronologically ordered and spanning the years 1910 to 1977, this book presents the songs and their stories, covering Fain's major hits.

Green, Stanley. *Broadway Musicals, Show by Show*. Milwaukee, Wis.: Hal Leonard, 1985. Fain's works are represented in this book, which gives a short performance history. The musicals are set chronologically, from 1866 to 1985.

Hischak, Thomas S. *The Tin Pan Alley Song Encyclopedia*. Westport, Conn.: Greenwood Press, 2002. The author discusses important songs from the pre-Civil War years to the end of the 1950's, covering major songwriters (among them Fain), performers, musical styles, and time periods.

Jasen, David A. *Tin Pan Alley. An Encyclopedia of the Golden Age of American Song*. New York: Routledge, 2003. The author discusses the history of Tin Pan Alley, and he includes short biographies of the main composers of the style and their biggest successes, with an entry on Fain.

See also: Bergman, Alan; Cahn, Sammy; Chevalier, Maurice; Styne, Jule.

Morton Feldman

American classical composer

Part of the New York School, a circle of composers associated with John Cage, Feldman was a pioneer in indeterminism and graphic notation. His music is known for its static quality and soft dynamics.

Born: January 12, 1926; New York, New York
Died: September 3, 1987; Buffalo, New York

Principal works

CHAMBER WORKS: *The Straits of Magellan*, 1961; *The King of Denmark*, 1964; *The Viola in My Life*, 1970; *Madame Press Died Last Week at Ninety*, 1971; *The Viola in My Life 4*, 1971; *For Frank O'Hara*, 1973; *Routine Investigations*, 1976; *Ixion*, 1977; *Why Patterns?*, 1978; String Quartet, 1980; String Quartet 2, 1983; *For Philip Guston*, 1984.

CHORAL WORKS: *Rothko Chapel*, 1972.

ORCHESTRAL WORKS: *Intersection*, 1953; *Atlantis*, 1960.

PIANO WORKS: *Extensions 3*, 1952; *Extensions 4*, 1954; *Vertical Thoughts*, 1963; *Vertical Thoughts 4*, 1964; *Triadic Memories*, 1981; *Palais de Mari*, 1986.

The Life

Morton Feldman was born in 1926 in New York City. At the age of twelve, he began piano lessons with Vera Maurina Press, a student of Ferruccio Busoni. While in high school, Feldman studied composition with Wallingford Riegger, and later he became a student of Stefan Wolpe.

Meeting the composer John Cage in 1950 was a turning point for Feldman. Cage had little direct influence on Feldman's music, but his openness to new ideas gave Feldman the confidence to pursue an iconoclastic path. Cage also introduced Feldman to other musicians and artists. Meeting a group of Abstract Expressionist artists that included Jackson Pollock, Mark Rothko, and Philip Guston was especially important to Feldman. He was fascinated by their art and by their ways of working. While many composers were occupied with such compositional systems as serialism, Feldman, like the painters he had met, relied on intuition; he worked deliberately, letting the music come to him sound by sound.

Feldman worked in his family's clothing business until he was forty-four. In 1974 he accepted the Edgard Varèse professorship at the State University of New York at Buffalo, becoming a dynamic and unorthodox teacher. He developed an interest in Turkish rugs, which influenced and inspired his later music, just as painting had earlier. Feldman died of pancreatic cancer in 1987.

The Music

Although Feldman's music evolved throughout his career, the unique aspects of his compositional style remained remarkably consistent. His music is abstract with little sense of a narrative or dramatic structure. Extended melodies are rare; his thought was predominantly harmonic. He favored dissonant chords, but the bite of the dissonances is moderated by his use of extremely soft dynamics. His music tends to move slowly and deliberately, dwelling on the sensuality of pure sound.

The King of Denmark. *The King of Denmark* for a solo percussionist uses graphic notation. The score consists of three rows of boxes, specifying high, middle-range, and low sounds, and each column is a unit of time. Numbers in the boxes specify how many sounds are to be played, but the precise patterns are left to the performer's discretion. All sounds are to be extremely soft and equal in vol-

ume. To this end, the instruments (drums, cymbals, bell gongs, vibraphone) are played only with the fingers. This is exceedingly delicate music, as barely audible sounds emerge from silence and then return.

Rothko Chapel. The Rothko Chapel in Houston, Texas, is a nonsectarian chapel designed by Rothko. Fourteen Rothko paintings surround the octagonal space. When Rothko committed suicide in 1970, Feldman was commissioned to write a piece in his memory. This is one of Feldman's most well-known and emotionally expressive works.

Rothko Chapel is scored for viola, percussion, celesta, vocal soloists, and chorus. At one point, the chorus softly sustains slowly changing chords for three full minutes. Time seems to stand still, perhaps reflecting the sense of immobility represented in Rothko's large canvases. Near the end, Feldman uncharacteristically uses an expressive tonal melody. The melody, which he had written when he was fifteen, is reminiscent of music he heard in synagogue.

Why Patterns? Scored for the unusual combination of flute, glockenspiel, and piano, *Why Patterns?* reflects Feldman's interest in handmade Turkish rugs. He was fascinated by the intricate woven patterns and the subtle changes of color in the dyed yarn. *Why Patterns?* is a musical analogue to the patterns of the rugs. The individual parts are notated with exactitude, but they do not coordinate precisely, so that the instruments seem to proceed independently of one another. A quiet and slowly unfolding piece, it creates a calm, mesmerizing atmosphere as disparate melodic patterns undergo subtle variation as they are woven together.

Palais de Mari. Some of Feldman's late works are exceedingly long. (String Quartet 2 lasts more than five hours.) *Palais de Mari*, one of Feldman's final works, is similar in concept to the lengthy works, but it is compressed into a shorter span of time. The piano work lasts about twenty minutes. *Palais de Mari* is soft and slow moving, with pauses of varying lengths. The sustaining pedal is kept down nearly throughout, causing the notes of one gesture to blur into the next (reminiscent of the way Rothko's rectangles bleed into the background color rather than have a sharp edge). Feldman dwells on the opening four-note motive throughout. Other ideas displace it temporarily, but the undulating motive continually returns, varied and presented in different contexts. This is intimate music addressed to the inner self.

Musical Legacy

In an age when compositional experimentalism often resulted in chaotic and unstructured music, Feldman pursued his singular vision with great effort and discipline, drawing as much inspiration from visual artists as from other musicians. Although stunningly original, Feldman's music challenges his audience to learn to listen in new ways. Most works have a dramatic structure, with one event leading to another; Feldman's music, in contrast, is fragmentary and static. For some, it is simply boring; others find that the slow, quiet music encourages them to listen more closely and with greater awareness of the pure sensuousness of the sounds. For these listeners, Feldman's music possesses unique and extraordinary beauty.

Brian G. Campbell

Further Reading

DeLio, Thomas, ed. *The Music of Morton Feldman.* New York: Excelsior, 1996. This collection of essays includes a discussion of Feldman's aesthetic, musical analyses, and three essays by Feldman. The music analyses require an understanding of music theory, but the other essays are approachable by the general reader.

Feldman, Morton. *Give My Regards to Eighth Street: Collected Writings of Morton Feldman.* Edited by B. H. Friedman. Cambridge, Mass.: Exact Change, 2000. Feldman writes about his music, his artistic ideas, his career, and many of the musicians and artists he knew.

_____. *Morton Feldman Says: Selected Interviews and Lectures, 1964-1987.* Edited by Chris Villars. London: Hyphen Press, 2006. Interviews and lectures, most of which have been previously published in various journals, are brought together under a single cover. Includes examples of pages from Feldman's scores and a chronological outline of his life.

Gann, Kyle. "Painter Envy: Morton Feldman Ascends His Pedestal as Softly as Possible." *The Village Voice* (July, 23, 1996). A short but substantive summary of and a subjective evaluation of Feldman's work.

Johnson, Steven, ed. *The New York Schools of Music and Visual Arts.* London: Taylor & Francis, 2001. A superb collection of essays about the interactions among the musicians of the New York School (Cage, Feldman, Earle Brown, and Christian Wolff) and their counterparts in the visual arts, the Abstract Expressionists (Pollock, Rothko, Willem de Kooning, Robert Motherwell, and more). Several essays focus on Feldman in particular.

See also: Busoni, Ferruccio; Cage, John; Lucier, Alvin; Schaeffer, Pierre; Seeger, Ruth Crawford; Takemitsu, Tōru; Varèse, Edgard.

Freddy Fender

American Latin and rock singer, songwriter, and guitarist

Combining elements of 1950's rock, Tejano, Louisiana swamp pop, and country music in his exuberant style, Fender paved the way for Latin American performers in country and popular music.

Born: June 4, 1937; San Benito, Texas
Died: October 14, 2006; Corpus Christi, Texas
Also known as: Baldemar Garza Huerta (birth name); El Bebop Kid; Eddie Con Los Shades
Member of: The Texas Tornados; Los Super Seven

Principal recordings

ALBUMS (solo): *Before the Next Teardrop Falls*, 1974; *Are You Ready for Freddy?*, 1975; *Before the Next Teardrop Falls*, 1975 (alternate tracks); *Since I Met You Baby*, 1975; *If You're Ever in Texas*, 1976; *Rock 'n' Country*, 1976; *If You Don't Love Me*, 1977; *Swamp Gold*, 1978; *Christmas Time in the Valley*, 1991; *Los Super Seven*, 1998 (with Los Super Seven); *Canto*, 2001 (with Los Super Seven); *New Orleans Sessions*, 2001; *La musica de Baldemar Huerta*, 2002; *Back to Back*, 2003 (with Johnny Rodriguez); *Eddie con los Shades: Rock 'n Roll*, 2003 (with the Shades); *Interpreta el rock*, 2003; *Heard It on the X*, 2005 (with Los Super Seven).

ALBUMS (with the Texas Tornados): *Texas Tornados*, 1990; *Zone of Our Own*, 1991; *Hangin' on by a Thread*, 1992; *Four Aces*, 1996.

The Life

Freddy Fender was born Baldemar Garza Huerta to migrant workers Serapio and Margarita Huerta in 1937. At ten, he entered and won a radio contest. At sixteen, he joined the U.S. Marines. By 1957, using the names El Bebop Kid and Eddie Con Los Shades, he had recorded Spanish versions of rock hits for distribution in the United States, Mexico, and South America. He married Evangelina "Vangie" Muniz in 1957, and they had four children. In 1959, after he signed a contract with Imperial Records, he became Freddy Fender (in honor of his guitar). Arrested in 1960 in Louisiana for possession of marijuana, he served three years in the Angola prison system, and he was released by Louisiana Governor Jimmie Davis. While in Louisiana, Fender worked with swamp pop musicians, resulting in the Gulf Coast influence heard on his early hits. In 1969 he returned to Texas, working as a mechanic and attending junior-college classes. He had a string of country and pop hits in the 1970's, and he tried acting in the 1980's. After a decade of battling substance abuse, Fender joined the groups Texas Tornados and Los Super Seven. Surviving both a kidney and liver transplant, he succumbed to lung cancer on October 14, 2006, in Corpus Christi, and he was buried in his hometown.

The Music

Introduced to various musical influences as a child migrant worker among Latinos and African Americans (conjunto, Tejano, and blues) and later as an adult living in Texas and Louisiana (country, Cajun, zydeco, swamp pop), Fender was a bilingual crossover musician, with an appeal to Latino as well as to gringo audiences. His fingerpicking guitar style was accentuated by his distinctive voice: a gentle tenor with a signature tremolo that could switch keys with ease.

El Bebop Kid. As El Bebop Kid, Fender was the first American to reach number one in Mexico and South America, with Spanish versions of Elvis Pres-

Freddy Fender. (AP/Wide World Photos)

ley's "Don't Be Cruel" and Harry Belafonte's "Jamaica Farewell." These and other Spanish remakes led to "Wasted Days and Wasted Nights" and "Holy One," two singles in English. After prison, Fender worked in New Orleans, where he was introduced to swamp pop musicians Joe Barry and Rod Bernard, as well as two of the Neville brothers, Art and Aaron. Fender returned to Texas, and, at fellow musician Doug Sahm's suggestion, he visited Huey Meaux, owner of Crazy Cajun records, in Houston. Meaux persuaded the singer to release a remake of Charley Pride's "Before the Next Teardrop Falls" in 1974.

"Before the Next Teardrop Falls." A number-one country song that went as well to number one on the pop charts in 1975, the title song from Fender's 1974 album won the Single of the Year Award, given by the Country Music Association (CMA); the song achieved gold certification. Fender won CMA's Vocalist of the Year, and the album won Album of the Year. The album contained standards such as "Roses Are Red," "Please Don't Tell Me How the Story Ends," and Fender's second *Billboard* hot country number one, a revamping of "Wasted Days and Wasted Nights," which crossed over to become a *Billboard* Top 10 rock hit.

Are You Ready for Freddy? *Are You Ready for Freddy?* was a collection of Cajun dance tunes, childhood favorites ("How Much Is That Doggy in the Window?"), and a number-one country hit, a bilingual remake of "Secret Love." The song also became Fender's third consecutive release to make it on the *Billboard* rock chart, peaking at number twenty.

Since I Met You Baby *and* Rock 'n' Country. *Since I Met You Baby* and *Rock 'n' Country* contained Fender's next three country hit remakes: "You'll Lose a Good Thing" (his fourth number one), "Vaya Con Dios," and "Since I Met You Baby." Fender met with only marginal success after the release of *Rock 'n' Country*, never again reaching the top spot on the *Billboard* hot country chart. His life and music took a downward spiral as he struggled with drugs and alcohol.

Texas Tornados *and* Los Super Seven. In 1989 Fender joined the first Tejano Grammy Award-winning supergroup, working with Sahm, Flaco Jimenez, and Augie Myers. Texas Tornados was a band that fused conjunto (Mexican polka), Tejano, rhythm and blues, and country. Its music was well received in the United States, Australia, and the Netherlands, and the first album, *Texas Tornados*, did well on the *Billboard* charts, reaching number twenty-one in rock and number twenty-nine in Latin. The group released three studio albums and two live albums, and *Zone of Our Own* was a huge critical success.

Fender later helped create a second Grammy Award-winning group, Los Super Seven. This group included Fender, Jiminez, Joe Ely, Rick Trevino, Ruben Ramos, Joel José Guzman, and Los Lobos' David Hidalgo and Cesar Rosas.

La musica de Baldemar Huerta. This represents Fender's return to his roots. He paid homage to the songs he heard while growing up in the Rio Grande Valley—boleros from the 1940's and 1950's—and he sings bolero versions of "Secret Love" and "Before the Next Teardrop Falls." In a *Texas Monthly* interview in 2001, Fender called this recording a hybrid, which he termed mariachi country. The album earned Fender his last Grammy Award.

Musical Legacy

Fender performed for three presidents of the United States, and he was given a star on the Hollywood Walk of Fame. He reached the top spot on the *Billboard* country and pop charts, and he had nine Top 10 country hits. He was the first rock singer to receive airplay in both Mexico and Latin America. Along with his Grammy Awards and his CMA Awards, Fender received a Golden Eagle Award, given by an organization of Chicano entertainers. His success helped set the stage for Los Lobos, David Garza, and El Vez.

Anthony J. Fonseca

Further Reading

Cocoran, Michael. *All Over the Map: True Heroes of Texas Music*. Austin: University of Texas Press, 2005. The chapter on Sahm chronicles Fender's meeting with Meaux.

Fender, Freddy. "A Few Words with Freddy Fender." *Texas Monthly* (December, 2001): 56. Transcription of an interview with Fender concerning *La musica de Baldemar Huerta*.

Marez, Curtis. "Brown: The Politics of Working-Class Chicano Style." *Social Text* 48 (Autumn, 1996): 109-132. This article discusses Fender's music in the film *Rush* (1991), and it describes his musical and personal assimilation—as an impoverished Chicano moving into an Anglo culture.

San Miguel, Guadalupe, Jr. *Tejano Proud: Tex-Mex Music in the Twentieth Century*. College Station: Texas A&M University Press, 2002. Provides context for Fender within the Tejano tradition.

Stambler, Irwin, and Grelun Landon. *Country Music: The Encyclopedia*. New York: St. Martin's Press, 1997. Includes a detailed entry on Fender's life and work.

See also: Belafonte, Harry; Neville, Aaron; Presley, Elvis; Pride, Charley; Valens, Ritchie.

Arthur Fiedler

American classical conductor

Known as "Mr. Pops," Fiedler is distinguished for bringing classical and light classical music to the general public. He accomplished this as the conductor of the Boston Pops orchestra for nearly fifty years, founder of the open-air Esplanade concerts in Boston, and performer on recordings and television programs.

Born: December 17, 1894; Boston, Massachusetts
Died: July 10, 1979; Brookline, Massachusetts
Member of: Boston Sinfonietta

Principal recordings

ALBUMS: *Tchaikovsky: The Nutcracker*, 1956; *Pops Christmas Party*, 1959; *Christmas Festival*, 1970; *Arthur Fiedler and the Boston Pops Plays the Beatles*, 1971; *Arthur Fiedler with the Boston Pops: Fiedler's Favorite Overtures*, 1971; *Fiedler's Favorite Marches*, 1971; *Opera's Greatest Hits: Arthur Fiedler Conducts Boston Pops*, 1971; *I Got Rhythm: Fiedler Conducts Gershwin*, 1979; *Saturday Night Fiedler*, 1979.

The Life

Arthur Fiedler (FEED-lur) was born to Emanuel and Johanna Fiedler, Austrian immigrants. Emanuel was a violinist in the Boston Symphony Orchestra (BSO), and Fiedler followed in his father's footsteps. After studying at the Royal Academy of Music in Berlin, Fiedler became a second violinist with the BSO in 1915.

Fiedler also had an interest in conducting. He started conducting on a regular basis in 1921, and in 1924 he formed his own group, which he called the Boston Sinfonietta. Its success led to his founding of the outdoor Esplanade concerts, free concerts held next to the Charles River, that have remained popular for decades. In 1930 Fiedler became conductor of the Boston Pops Orchestra (called simply the Pops), a position that he held until his death in 1979. During his tenure, the Pops became internationally famous, and his approach became the model for pops orchestras around the globe. He also conducted the San Francisco Pops from 1951 to 1978.

Considered to be quite the ladies' man, Fiedler did not get married until the age of forty-six, marrying Ellen Bottomley, who was twenty years younger. Fiedler did not appear to participate much in family life, and he was often distant with his closest friends. However, he could be quite demonstrative, and his effusive character on the podium helped make him a well-known figure in the United States. Fiedler was passionate about fires and firefighting, and he often conducted to raise money for charities. Fiedler, in failing health for several years, died at the age of eighty-four.

The Music

As well as conductor, Fiedler was the music director for the Boston Pops Orchestra, meaning that he chose the program for each concert. In contrast to his predecessor, Alfredo Casella, Fiedler selected music he believed would be popular with the general public. This included classical works, such as Maurice Ravel's *Boléro* (1928); light classical fare, such as Johann Strauss's waltzes; and arrangements of musical-theater and popular tunes, such as selections from *Oklahoma!* (1943) by Richard Rodgers and Oscar Hammerstein II.

"The Stars and Stripes Forever." "The Stars and Stripes Forever," written by John Philip Sousa in 1897, has been a favorite for the Pops since the beginning of Fiedler's reign. Fiedler usually used the work to close a concert, although he would occasionally open the concert with it or present it as an encore. It may be seen as exemplifying the patriotic flavor that the Boston Pops holds in the public eye. It also acts as a showcase for the flutes and the brass section: The work opens with a virtuosic melody on piccolo accompanied by the entire flute section; the second part allows the brass to shine, with the main melody in the trumpets and a countermelody in the trombones. In a concert performance, the featured groups usually stand, adding to the enthusiastic atmosphere and leading to a rousing finale.

Sleigh Ride. Fiedler helped Leroy Anderson come into prominence as an arranger and composer of light classical music. After Anderson arranged some Harvard songs for a Pops concert, Fiedler encouraged him to arrange and compose other works for the Pops. One of these works was "Sleigh Ride" (1948). Its sprightly melody and its clever sound effects, used to imitate sounds heard

Arthur Fiedler. (Hulton Archive/Getty Images)

on a sleigh ride (such as the trumpet imitating a horse neigh), contribute to its popularity not only with Boston Pops audiences but also with audiences around the world. In addition, it exemplifies the types of works that appeared on holiday Pops concert programs.

"Jalousie." "Jalousie" (1925), by Danish composer Jacob Gade, is one of the Boston Pops' greatest hits, among the most popular orchestral recordings of all time. According to Robin Moore, Fiedler discovered the sheet music in a music store in 1935, found it interesting, arranged it for orchestra, and started performing it that year. It seemed to be popular with audiences, so Fiedler convinced RCA to record it. The recording became the first orchestral recording to sell more than a million copies. The work is a lush, romantic tango. It features a solo violin at the beginning, and its tango rhythms and use of tambourine give it an exotic flavor.

Musical Legacy

Through his concerts around the globe, his television specials, and his recordings, Fiedler brought classical music to millions of people who might not otherwise have heard it. Under his direction, the Boston Pops Orchestra became the standard for pops orchestras, and he conducted it for fifty years. Fiedler started the extremely popular outdoor Esplanade concerts, which became a model for other outdoor concerts, particularly Fourth of July celebrations. In fact, Fiedler and the Pops set a record for concert attendance at the July 4, 1976, Esplanade concert: approximately four hundred thousand people attended. The television show *Evening at Pops* started with Fiedler, and it combined the Boston Pops with popular guest artists such as Roberta Flack. Fiedler helped to launch the careers of composers and arrangers, such as Anderson and Richard Hayman.

Elizabeth Scoggin

Further Reading

Dickson, Harry Ellis. *Arthur Fiedler and the Boston Pops: An Irreverent Memoir.* Boston: Houghton Mifflin, 1981. Written by the assistant conductor of the Boston Pops, this offers an objective look at Fiedler. Includes illustrations.

Fiedler, Johanna. *Arthur Fiedler: Papa, the Pops, and Me.* New York: Doubleday, 1994. Fiedler's daughter's account takes a sometimes dark view of her father's life. Includes notes and selected discography.

Holland, James. *Mr. Pops.* Barre, Mass.: Barre, 1972. A photographic essay with a brief biography is suitable for young readers.

Moore, Robin. *Fiedler: The Colorful Mr. Pops, the Man, and His Music.* Boston: Little, Brown, 1968. Well-written and complimentary account of Fiedler's life. Includes illustrations and extensive discography.

Wilson, Carol Green. *Arthur Fiedler: Music for the Millions, the Story of the Conductor of the Boston Pops Orchestra.* New York: Evans, 1968. Written by a friend of the family, this book is an affectionate biography. Includes illustrations.

See also: Anderson, Leroy; Gershwin, George; Hammerstein, Oscar, II; Ravel, Maurice; Rodgers, Richard; Sousa, John Philip; Williams, John.

Dorothy Fields

American popular music and musical-theater composer, lyricist, and librettist

In a career that spanned the 1920's to the 1960's, Fields wrote intelligent and witty lyrics for the Broadway stage and for films.

Born: July 15, 1905; Allenhurst, New Jersey
Died: May 28, 1974; New York, New York

Principal works

MUSICAL THEATER (lyrics and libretto unless listed otherwise): *Blackbirds of 1928*, 1928 (music by Jimmy McHugh); *Hello, Daddy*, 1928 (libretto by Herbert Fields; music by McHugh); *Ziegfeld Midnight Frolic*, 1929 (music by McHugh); *The International Review*, 1930 (libretto by Nat N. Dorfman and Lew Leslie; music with McHugh); *The Vanderbilt Revue*, 1930 (libretto by Lew M. Fields with others; lyrics and music with others); *Shoot the Works*, 1931 (libretto by Heywood Broun with others; lyrics with others; music by Michael H. Cleary with others); *Singin' the Blues*, 1931 (libretto by John McGowan; lyrics with Harold Adamson; music by McHugh and Burton Lane); *Stars in Your Eyes*, 1939 (libretto by J. P. McEvoy; music by Arthur Schwartz); *Let's Face It!*, 1941 (libretto with Herbert Fields; lyrics and music by Cole Porter); *Something for the Boys*, 1943 (libretto with Herbert Fields; lyrics and music by Porter); *Mexican Hayride*, 1944 (libretto with Herbert Fields; lyrics and music by Porter); *Up in Central Park*, 1945 (libretto with Herbert Fields; music by Sigmund Romberg); *Annie Get Your Gun*, 1946 (libretto with Herbert Fields; lyrics and music by Irving Berlin); *Arms and the Girl*, 1950 (libretto with Herbert Fields and Rouben Mamoulian; music by Morton Gould); *A Tree Grows in Brooklyn*, 1951 (libretto by Betty Smith and George Abbott; music by Schwartz); *By the Beautiful Sea*, 1954 (libretto with Herbert Fields; music by Schwartz); *Redhead*, 1959 (libretto with others; music by Albert Hague); *Annie Get Your Gun*, 1966 (libretto with Herbert Fields; lyrics and music by Berlin); *Sweet Charity*, 1966 (libretto by Neil Simon; music by Cy Coleman); *Seesaw*, 1973 (libretto by Michael Bennett; music by Coleman); *Shirley MacLaine*, 1976 (libretto by Fred Ebb; music by Coleman); *Sugar Babies*, 1979 (libretto by Ralph G. Allen and Harry Rigby; lyrics with Al Dubin; music by McHugh).

The Life

Dorothy Fields was born as the youngest of the four children of vaudeville star Lew Fields and his wife Rose. After high school, Fields wanted to go into show business, but her father did not allow it. Without the endorsement of her father or his influential theatrical organization, she had to prove that she could write lyrics and succeed on her own. Despite these obstacles, she teamed with songwriter Jimmy McHugh on such hits as "I Can't Give You Anything But Love, Baby" from 1928. She and McHugh became a successful team, and over the next seven years they produced other enduring standards, including "On the Sunny Side of the Street" and "I'm in the Mood for Love."

In 1925 Fields married surgeon J. J. Werner; they divorced in 1932. In 1938 she married Eli Lahm, with whom she had a son and a daughter. For the next thirty-five years, Fields was one of the most productive lyricists in the songwriting world. She died of a heart attack in the spring of 1974.

The Music

Fields in Hollywood. In the 1930's, Fields worked in Hollywood, most notably with composer Jerome Kern. The pair reached their artistic peak in the film *Swing Time* from 1936. A vehicle for Fred Astaire and Ginger Rogers, the film featured such hits as "Pick Yourself Up," "A Fine Romance," and "Bojangles of Harlem." They also wrote for this film "The Way You Look Tonight," which won the Academy Award for Best Song in 1936. When Astaire sang the song to Rogers, it was clear that the combination of Kern's compelling melody and Fields's elegant rhymes was magical. Kern and Fields collaborated for another four years without ever again attaining the artistic heights of *Swing Time*.

Fields on Broadway. Fields worked with her brother Herbert writing the libretto for several Broadway shows. Their most successful and important collaboration was on *Annie Get Your Gun* (1946), based on the life of sharpshooter Annie Oakley. While talking with a World War II Marine, Fields got the idea for a musical about Oakley with Ethel Merman in the lead. The music was written by Irving Berlin, who drew on the Fieldses' dialogue for much of his inspiration. The musical, *Annie Get Your Gun*, produced by Richard Rodgers and Oscar Hammerstein, was a great hit, and it represented one of Fields's high points as a contributor to the evolution of the art form of the Broadway musical.

Fields returned to lyric writing for *A Tree Grows in Brooklyn*, based on the Betty Smith novel and popular film. The show, for which Arthur Schwartz furnished the music, featured one of her best lyrics. Though the show closed after 270 performances, the songs such as "I'll Buy You a Star" and "Make the Man Love Me" have endured as standards.

Collaborating with Coleman. Fields continued to write musicals during the 1950's and 1960's. She won a Tony Award for her work on *Redhead*, starring Gwen Verdon, in 1959. She and songwriter Cy Coleman had an even greater success in 1964 with *Sweet Charity* and the hit "Big Spender." Finally, she and Coleman wrote a musical version of the William Gibson play *Two for the Seesaw* (1958), called *Seesaw*, which opened in 1973. Her talent showed no signs of flagging as she kept turning out hits into the 1970's and as audiences responded to her work with the same enthusiasm they had shown three decades earlier.

Musical Legacy

Although her work was never judged on the basis of her gender, Fields was one of the most important females in the coterie of songwriters and lyricists who worked during the Golden Age of American popular song between 1925 and 1955. She was a superb writer of romantic and poignant lyrics, who brought out the best in her partners, Kern, McHugh, Romberg, and Coleman. Several decades after it first appeared, "The Way You Look

Dorothy Fields and Arthur Schwartz. (Library of Congress)

Tonight" endures as a rare example of the exceptional fusion between words and music that makes a love song a standard. Fields had a wide-ranging talent that enabled her to move from the ribaldry of the 1920's to the more cynical expressions of the 1960's with equal deftness. Her contributions to the literature of the musical theater are also impressive. *Annie Get Your Gun* is frequently revived as an artful blend of the plot that Fields and her brother conceived and the music of Berlin. With the wit and the sophistication of her lyrics, Fields made a memorable contribution to musical theater and film.

Lewis L. Gould

Further Reading

Furia, Philip. *Poets of Tin Pan Alley: A History of America's Great Lyricists.* New York: Oxford University Press, 1990. This source includes an incisive analysis of Fields and her work.

Sheed, Wilfred. *The House That George Built with a Little Help from Irving, Cole, and a Crew of About Fifty.* New York: Random House, 2007. A deft survey of popular songs that places Fields in the context of other songwriters of the period in which she enjoyed her greatest hits.

Wilk, Max. *They're Playing Our Song: The Truth Behind the Words and Music of Three Generations.* New York: Moyer and Bell, 1991. This collection contains an informative interview with Fields that sheds light on her working habits.

Winer, Deborah Grace. *On the Sunny Side of the Street: The Life and Lyrics of Dorothy Fields*. New York: Schirmer Books, 1997. An anecdotal biography of Fields.

See also: Arlen, Harold; Berlin, Irving; Coleman, Cy; Ebb, Fred; Hammerstein, Oscar, II; Kern, Jerome; Merman, Ethel; Porter, Cole; Rodgers, Richard; Romberg, Sigmund.

---

50 Cent

American rapper

With his explicit lyrics and driving beats, 50 Cent made a major contribution to the development of gangsta rap.

Born: July 6, 1975; Queens, New York
Also known as: Curtis James Jackson III (birth name)
Member of: G-Unit

Principal recordings

ALBUMS (solo): *Power of the Dollar*, 2000; *Guess Who's Back?*, 2001; *Get Rich or Die Tryin'*, 2003; *The Massacre*, 2005; *Before I Self-Destruct*, 2007; *Curtis*, 2007; *Superstar*, 2008.

ALBUMS (with G-Unit): *Beg for Mercy*, 2003; *G-Unit Radio, Pt. 10: 2050 Before the Massacre*, 2007; *Sight of Blood*, 2007.

The Life

Curtis James Jackson III was born on July 6, 1975, in South Jamaica, Queens, a suburb of New York City. After his mother, Sabrina, was murdered, Jackson went to live with his grandparents. At age twelve, he began selling crack cocaine, and in 1994 he was arrested twice on drug charges.

In 1996 Jackson began to focus on a music career, working with Jam Master Jay of Run-D.M.C. He chose the stage name 50 Cent (FIHF-tee sehnt), the name of a 1980's Brooklyn robber. In 1997 he left Jam Master Jay to sign a contract with Columbia Records. In the same year his son, Marquise Jackson, was born to his girlfriend, Shanequa Tompkins. A well-publicized dispute between Ja Rule

and 50 Cent started in 1999, which resulted in an altercation at the Hit Factory, a recording studio, in 2000.

On May 24, 2000, 50 Cent was shot nine times in front of his home in Queens. After he recovered, he was dropped from Columbia Records, and his album was canceled. He moved to Canada to work with Sha Money XL. At the time, 50 Cent made mixtapes that were later rereleased on the album, *Guess Who's Back?* (2001). On New Year's Eve in New York City, he was arrested and cited for possession of two loaded firearms. In 2002 50 Cent was signed to Eminem's label, Interscope Records, which released *Get Rich or Die Tryin'* in 2003 to huge success.

After the debut of his first album, 50 Cent started his own label, G-Unit Records. He appeared in an episode of the animated television series *The Simpsons* and in the motion pictures *Get Rich or Die Tryin'* (2005), loosely based on his life, and *Home of the Brave* (2006).

The Music

Excelling in the pop genre of gangsta rap, 50 Cent derives many of his lyrics from his life as a drug dealer in the inner city. His frequent use of rap beefs (feuds) with fellow rap artists brings him attention in the media and in the musical world. Underlying his graphic lyrics are dark, driving grooves and dance beats. Because of the 2000 shooting, which affected his jaw, he has developed a mumbling quality in his singing.

"How to Rob." This single came from 50 Cent's unreleased and incomplete album, *Power of the Dollar*, and it is an example of 50 Cent's use of beefs against other rap artists. In the song 50 Cent explicitly details how he would rob rappers such as Jay-Z and Will Smith of their jewelry. The single evoked numerous responses from the artists mentioned. However, it was the response 50 Cent wanted, as the reaction brought him much-needed attention in the rap community.

Get Rich or Die Tryin'. 50 Cent's debut album was released to huge critical and market success. Throughout the album, 50 Cent bases his lyrics on his experience in selling drugs, on such tracks as "What Up Gangsta" and "High All the Time." He recounts his near-fatal shooting, accentuated by musical samples of gunshots, in "Patiently Waiting" (featuring Eminem) and "Many Men

(Wish Death)." "In da Club" is an appealing single for the dance club that samples heavy dance beats with forceful string punctuations.

The Massacre. The 2005 follow-up album continues in the genre of gangsta rap. Choosing a mellow tone on some of the songs, 50 Cent samples instrumental melodies that soften the accompanying drumbeat. Additionally, he creates more singles for the dance floor, such as "Disco Inferno" and "Outta Control." He returns to the theme of gangsta violence and drug use in the single "Gunz Come Out." Perhaps the most inventive single is "A Baltimore Love Thing," in which the narrator directs his statements toward a female heroine addict, whom he loves, and tries to persuade her to stop using. There are also collaborative singles with vocalists Jamie Foxx ("Build You Up"), Olivia ("So Amazing" and "Candy Shop"), and Eminem ("GATman and Robin").

Curtis. In *Curtis*, 50 Cent returns to a hard sound, and he reemphasizes his gangsta background, especially on the opening track, "My Gun Go Off." A soft sound emerges, however, in his collaboration with Robin Thicke on "Follow My Lead," which samples sensual, lyrical piano melodies and harmonies. There are also collaborative singles on this album, with Justin Timberlake ("Ayo Technology"), P'Diddy and Jay-Z ("I Get Money"), and Mary J. Blige ("All of Me"). Though *Curtis* was a commercial success, critics found the album to be unoriginal and the lyrics to be at times incoherent and silly.

Musical Legacy

In the genre of gangsta rap, 50 Cent is a huge commercial and critical success. Through his record label G-Unit, 50 Cent helps young rap artists, such as Young Back, Lloyd Banks, and Tony Yayo. With the release of *Get Rich or Die Tryin'*, 50 Cent was nominated for a Grammy Award for Best New Artist, and he won ASCAP Songwriter of the Year and Album of the Year from *Billboard*. *The Massacre* was nominated for a Grammy Award in the Best Rap Album category. Throughout his career he has won and has been nominated for various awards, including the World Music Awards, Rhythm and Soul Music Award, Black Entertainment Television (BET) Awards, Music of Black Origins (MOBO) Awards, Source Awards, and MTV Music Video Awards.

Eric Olds Schneeman

50 Cent. (AP/Wide World Photos)

Further Reading

Brown, Ethan. *Queens Reigns Supreme: Fat Cat, 50 Cent, and the Rise of the Hip-Hop Hustler*. New York: Anchor Books, 2005. Brown provides a cultural and historical account of the gangs and drug lords of Queens and the impact they would have on 50 Cent and other rap artists. Includes bibliography.

Brown, Jake. *50 Cent: No Holds Barred*. Phoenix: Colossus Books, 2005. A brief biography of 50 Cent, mainly derived from interviews the artist has given to magazines. Includes discography.

Callahan-Bever, Noah, and 50 Cent. *50 × 50: 50 Cent in His Own Words*. New York: Pocket Books, 2007. Updated autobiography includes pictures, handwritten lyrics, other memorabilia, and a compact disc of unreleased material. Includes illustrations.

Ex, Kris, and 50 Cent. *From Pieces to Weight: Once upon a Time in Southside Queens*. New York: MTV

Books and Pocket Books, 2005. In this book, 50 Cent recounts his journey from drug dealer to rap artist.

See also: Blige, Mary J.; D. M. C.; Dr. Dre; Eminem; Jay-Z; Simmons, Joseph "Run"; Snoop Dogg.

Dietrich Fischer-Dieskau

German classical and opera singer

Fischer-Dieskau is a consummate interpreter of classical song, opera, and oratorio, and his recordings spread his fame worldwide. He is noted for his virtuosic interpretations of lieder and of Franz Schubert's vocal works.

Born: May 28, 1925; Berlin, Germany

Principal works

OPERATIC ROLES: Marquis of Posa in Giuseppe Verdi's *Don Carlos*, 1948; Wolfram in Richard Wagner's *Tannhäuser*, 1949; John the Baptist in Richard Strauss's *Salome*, 1952; Don Giovanni in Wolfgang Amadeus Mozart's *Don Giovanni*, 1953; Busoni in Charles Gounod's *Faust*, 1955; Amfortas in Wagner's *Parsifal*, 1955; Count Almaviva in Mozart's *Le nozze di Figaro*, 1956; Renato in Verdi's *Un ballo in maschera*, 1957; Falstaff in Verdi's *Henry V*, 1959; Mathis in Paul Hindemith's *Mathis der Maler*, 1959; Wozzeck in Alban Berg's *Wozzeck*, 1960; Yevgeny Onyegin in Peter Ilich Tchaikovsky's *Eugene Onegin*, 1961; Barak in Strauss's *Die Frau ohne Schatten*, 1963; Macbeth in Verdi's *Macbeth*, 1963; Don Alfonso in Mozart's *Così fan tutte*, 1972; King Lear in Aribert Reimann's *Lear*, 1978.

Principal recordings

ALBUMS: *Schubert: Die Winterreise*, 1952; *The Magic Flute—Die Zauberflöte*, 1956; *Arabella*, 1957; *Capriccio*, 1958; *Wagner: Die Fliegende Holländer*, 1960; *Brahms: Ein Deutsches Requiem*, 1961; *Schubert: Die Schöne Müllerin*, 1961; *Lohengrin: Romantic Opera in Three Acts*, 1962; *Britten: War Requiem*, 1963; *Don Carlos*, 1965; *Tosca*

Highlights, 1967; *Elektra*, 1961; *Wozzeck*, 1962; *Doktor Faust*, 1969; *Handel: Giulio Cesare in Egitto*, 1969; *Salome*, 1971; *Palestrina*, 1972; *Il Matrimonio Segreto*, 1975; *Béatrice et Bénédict Opéra-comique en Due Actes*, 1982; *Hänsel und Gretel*, 1985; *Jessonda*, 1991.

The Life

Dietrich Fischer-Dieskau (DEE-trihk FEE-shur DEE-skow) was born into a middle-class family in Berlin. His parents, both educators, shared with their son a love of literature and music. Fischer-Dieskau's paternal ancestors were mostly Protestant clergymen, and one of his maternal ancestors is memorialized in a Berlin monument depicting Frederick the Great and General Baron von Dieskau, an artillery expert and inventor of a light cannon depicted on the monument, known as Dieskaus.

Fischer-Dieskau began to sing at an early age, starting formal voice instruction at age sixteen. Upon completion of high school in 1943, he made his first solo appearances in Berlin. Later that year, he was drafted into the German army, and in 1945 he was captured by Allied forces and sent to a prisoner-of-war camp in Italy. While in prison, he presented informal lieder concerts to his fellow German prisoners.

After World War II ended, he returned to Berlin to resume his vocal studies and to begin his singing career. His artistic reputation grew, and he was in great demand in the United States and England. Fischer-Dieskau is one of the few singers who excels at concert performance and at opera singing. He is also a prolific recording artist, who has produced an enormous repertoire of works, ranging from obscure Renaissance pieces to operatic roles to contemporary songs. Throughout his career, he has collaborated with an impressive list of accompanists, conductors, and orchestras.

The Music

Fischer-Dieskau's remarkable professional success may be attributed to his debut at an early age, the reconstruction and subsequent economic boom of West Germany following World War II, and the advent and worldwide distribution of the long-play recording.

Lieder. Fischer-Dieskau began to collaborate with the English pianist Gerald Moore in 1951. For

Dietrich Fischer-Dieskau. (AP/Wide World Photos)

the next two decades, the pair made numerous recital appearances in Europe, Japan, and North America. By 1970 Fischer-Dieskau had recorded with Moore every Franz Schubert song appropriate for male voice, along with most of the songs of Robert Schumann, Ludwig van Beethoven, Johannes Brahms, Hugo Wolf, Franz Liszt, Felix Mendelssohn, and Wolfgang Amadeus Mozart. These recordings in the new long-playing format were sold all over the world, and they introduced the genre of lieder to generations of music lovers and musicians. So impressive were his renditions that Fischer-Dieskau became internationally known as a foremost interpreter of lieder.

His 1952 recording of Schubert's *Die Winterreise* (1827), with Moore at the piano, continues to be the standard against which all other versions are judged. It rates highly with the recording of Schubert's *Die Schöne Müllerin* (1824) as one of the finest recordings of the genre. "Der Neugierige" (The Curious Boy), song number six from *Die Schöne Müllerin*, provides a splendid example of the tre-

mendous range in pitch, dynamics, and tone color Fischer-Dieskau gave this repertoire. His interpretive approach was to start with the poem and analyze Schubert's setting, phrase by phrase, word by word, and note by note.

Oratorio. Fischer-Dieskau's long career as an oratorio soloist began with *Ein deutsches Requiem* (1868) of Brahms. His first performance of this work, which was also his professional debut at the age of twenty-one, was as a last-minute substitute for an ailing colleague in 1947. He performed the work dozens of times throughout his career, and he recorded it several times, under such conductors as Rudolf Kempe and Herbert von Karajan. However, the most popular of those recordings continues to be the one from 1961, which includes Elisabeth Schwartzkopf, soprano, and the New Philharmonia Chorus and Orchestra, conducted by Otto Klemperer.

Ein deutsches Requiem is a masterful expression of the gift of life triumphing over death. In the two solo sections for baritone, Fischer-Dieskau is able to use a variety of vocal color and shading to express the contrite spirit of the third movement. Then, in the sixth-movement solo, his voluminous power creates a contrasting prophetic sense, giving the listener a tremendous emotional impact. A work that has occupied him for his entire career, *Ein deutsches Requiem* was the singer's choice to end his career as an oratorio soloist, in a 1992 performance in Tokyo, Japan.

The British composer Benjamin Britten requested that Fischer-Dieskau sing the premiere performance of *War Requiem* (1962), given in Coventry, England, in 1962. This premiere was part of a series of consecration ceremonies for the rebuilt Coventry Cathedral, which had been destroyed in a German air raid in 1940. Fischer-Dieskau continued to sing performances of the *War Requiem* throughout his career as an oratorio soloist. Soon after the premiere, he recorded it with soprano Galina Vishnievskay, tenor Peter Pears, the Melos Ensemble of London, and the London Symphony Orchestra, with the composer conducting. As is often the case with Fischer-Dieskau's recordings, this effort remains unparalleled in intensity and expression.

The oratorio is an attempt at international reconciliation, with soloists coming from Germany (Fischer-Dieskau), the Soviet Union (Vishnievskay), and England (Pears), all memorializing the great loss of life in World War I and World War II. Although Fischer-Dieskau was not a pacifist (as was Britten), he was not attracted to the social and political goals of the Third Reich, and he resisted his conscription into the German army. Tall and lanky, ill-suited for a combat role, he finally joined as required, and he was quickly captured by Allied forces.

Fischer-Dieskau's war experience certainly colored his singing of this piece, although a more personal experience is at the heart of his relationship with the *War Requiem*. One of the main baritone solos draws its text from Wilfred Owen's sonnet *On Seeing a Piece of Our Artillery Brought into Action*. The segment is set in a highly dramatic musical style, including a fusillade of kettle drums announcing the deployment of the artillery. For Fischer-Dieskau, who grew up in Berlin, admiring the monument that included his ancestor, this combination of words and music must have been shattering. As reported by Michael Steinberg in his book *Choral Masterworks*, tenor Pears recalled that he "could hardly get his colleague (Fischer-Dieskau) to stand and leave the choir stalls at the end of the Coventry performance."

Fischer-Dieskau's ability to take the universality of the war experience, to add his own personal experience, and to sing in English (for him a foreign language) is indicative of the singer's singular power of artistic achievement.

Opera. Fischer-Dieskau's legacy includes more than one hundred operatic roles, spanning the entire history of the genre. His voice, possibly best classified as a lyric bass-baritone, is not well suited for the majority of dramatic baritone or bass roles. However, his overall musicianship did ensure him great success in some roles, notably those created by Mozart, Giuseppe Verdi, and Richard Wagner.

Favoring the smaller opera houses of his native Germany, Fischer-Dieskau seldom performed operas outside of Europe, and he never appeared at the Metropolitan Opera in New York. He did frequently appear at the major opera houses of Europe, such as the Vienna State Opera, the Munich Opera, and London's Covent Garden, as well as in the *Deutsche Oper Berlin*, and at many important festivals, such as the ones at Beyreuth and at Salzburg. These smaller houses allowed Fischer-Dieskau to use his voice in the way he was accustomed, with a wide palette of colors, dynamics, and inflections.

Among the roles that Fischer-Dieskau sang on stage and in the recording studio were a number of title roles: Mozart's Don Giovanni, Verdi's Falstaff, Alban Berg's Wozzeck, Handel's Giulio Cesare, and Wagner's Flying Dutchman. The breadth of his repertoire spans the history of opera.

About half of the opera roles in Fischer-Dieskau's repertoire were never performed on stage but were recorded only. An examination of his discography makes it clear that Fischer-Dieskau made a consistent effort to support contemporary composers, premiering new works such as Heinz Werner Henze's *Elegie für junge Liebende* (1961), Gottfried von Einem's *Danton's Tod* (1943), and Aribert Reimann's *Lear* (1978), which was composed for him.

Musical Legacy

For his pursuit of artistic excellence, Fischer-Dieskau has been awarded honorary degrees from the universities of Oxford, Yale, Heidelberg, and the Sorbonne. He has won multiple Grammy Awards and the Deutsche Schallplatten Preis (the German Recording Prize). He has won the Grand Prix du Disque almost every year between 1955 and the end of his career. He is a member of the American Academy of Arts and Sciences, of the Royal Academy of Music in London, of the Accademia Santa Cecilia in Rome, and of other international music organizations. In 2000 Deutsche Grammaphon issued a commemorative box set of twenty-one compact discs devoted to the entirety of Fischer-Dieskau's singing career. With a discography of more than one thousand recordings, covering the works of more than two hundred composers, Fischer-Dieskau has created an impressive permanent legacy of performances.

Richard Allen Roe

Further Reading

Fischer-Dieskau, Dietrich. *Reverberations: The Memoirs of Dietrich Fischer-Dieskau*. Translated by Ruth Hein. Portland, Oreg.: Froom, 1990. This personal account of the events of Fischer-Dieskau's life and distinguished career contains many anecdotes. Well written, it is for the general audience and cultivated musicians alike.

_____. *Schubert's Songs: A Biographical Study.*

Translated by Kenneth S. Whitton. New York: Alfred A. Knopf, 1978. As in-depth study of Schubert, using the composer's songs as the primary source for assertions on Schubert's personal life and outlook. Written more for cultivated musicians than for general readers, it is rich in detail and presents Fischer-Dieskau's subjective experience of preparation and performance of Schubert's music.

Ivry, Benjamin. "A Voice of the Century Past." *New England Review* 27, no. 1 (2006). An excellent, if not enthusiastic, appraisal of Fischer-Dieskau's singing career.

Moore, Gerald. "Dietrich Fischer-Dieskau." In *Am I Too Loud?* London: Hammish Hamilton, 1961. A testimonial to the relationship between singer and accompanist. Moore, with whom Fischer-Dieskau made the complete Schubert lieder for male voice recordings, presents a singular insight into the artist.

Neunzig, Hans A. *Dietrich Fischer-Dieskau: A Biography*. Translated and annotated by Kenneth S. Whitton. Portland, Oreg.: Amadeus Press, 1998. A thorough biography of Fischer-Dieskau, with rare photographs and examples of the singer's painting and other artwork.

Steinberg, Michael. "Benjamin Britten: *War Requiem*." In *Choral Masterworks: A Listener's Guide*. New York: Oxford University Press, 2005. This chapter on Britten's oratorio contains accounts of Fischer-Dieskau's contribution to the premiere.

See also: Barenboim, Daniel; Britten, Benjamin; Karajan, Herbert von; Klemperer, Otto; Stern, Isaac.

Ella Fitzgerald
American jazz singer

Fitzgerald began her career as a jazz singer but became known all over the world by her first name alone as a popular singer. Her greatest ambition and realized achievement was to entertain audiences by singing songs as she felt them.

Born: April 25, 1917; Newport News, Virginia
Died: June 15, 1996; Beverly Hills, California

Also known as: Ella Jane Fitzgerald (full name); First Lady of Song

Principal recordings
ALBUMS: *Lullabies of Birdland*, 1945; *Miss Ella Fitzgerald and Mr. Nelson Riddle Invite You to Listen and Relax*, 1949; *Ella, Lena, and Billie*, 1950 (with Lena Horne and Billie Holiday); *Ella Sings Gershwin*, 1950; *Souvenir Album*, 1950; *Sweet and Hot*, 1953; *Songs in a Mellow Mood*, 1954; *Pete Kelly's Blues*, 1955 (with Peggy Lee); *Ella Fitzgerald Sings the Cole Porter Song Book*, 1956; *Ella Fitzgerald Sings the Rodgers and Hart Song Book*, 1956; *Ella and Louis*, 1956 (with Louis Armstrong); *Ella and Louis Again*, 1957 (with Armstrong); *Ella Fitzgerald Sings the Duke Ellington Song Book*, 1957; *Like Someone in Love*, 1957; *One O'Clock Jump*, 1957 (with Joe Williams and the Count Basie Orchestra); *Porgy and Bess*, 1957 (with Armstrong); *Ella Fitzgerald Sings the Irving Berlin Song Book*, 1958; *Ella Swings Lightly*, 1958; *Ella Fitzgerald Sings Sweet Songs for Swingers*, 1959; *Ella Fitzgerald Sings the George and Ira Gershwin Song Book*, 1959; *Get Happy!*, 1959; *Hello Love*, 1959; *Ella Fitzgerald Sings Songs from "Let No Man Write My Epitaph,"* 1960; *Ella Fitzgerald Sings the Harold Arlen Song Book, Vol. 1*, 1960; *Ella Fitzgerald Sings the Harold Arlen Song Book, Vol. 2*, 1960; *Ella Fitzgerald Wishes You a Swinging Christmas*, 1960; *Clap Hands, Here Comes Charlie!*, 1961; *Ella Swings Brightly with Nelson*, 1961 (with Nelson Riddle); *Ella Swings Gently with Nelson*, 1962 (with Riddle); *Rhythm Is My Business*, 1962; *Ella and Basie!*, 1963 (with Count Basie's New Testament Band); *Ella Fitzgerald Sings the Jerome Kern Song Book*, 1963; *These Are the Blues*, 1963; *Ella Fitzgerald Sings the Johnny Mercer Song Book*, 1964; *Hello, Dolly!*, 1964; *Ella at Duke's Place*, 1965 (with the Duke Ellington Orchestra); *Whisper Not*, 1966 (with Marty Paich and his Orchestra); *Brighten the Corner*, 1967; *Ella Fitzgerald's Christmas*, 1967; *Misty Blue*, 1968; *Things Ain't What They Used to Be (And You Better Believe It)*, 1970; *Ella Loves Cole*, 1972; *Take Love Easy*, 1973 (with Joe Pass); *Fine and Mellow*, 1974; *Ella and Oscar*, 1975 (with Oscar Peterson); *Fitzgerald and Pass . . . Again*, 1976 (with Pass); *Dream Dancing*, 1978; *Lady Time*,

1978; *A Classy Pair (Ella Fitzgerald Sings, Count Basie Plays)*, 1979 (with the Count Basie Orchestra); *Ella Abraça Jobim*, 1980 (*Ella Fitzgerald Sings the Antonio Carlos Jobim Song Book*); *The Best Is Yet to Come*, 1982; *Let's Call the Whole Thing Off*, 1983; *Nice Work if You Can Get It*, 1983; *Speak Love*, 1983; *Easy Living*, 1986; *All That Jazz*, 1989; *Back on the Block*, 1989 (with others); *Ella Fitzgerald: First Lady of Song*, 1993.

The Life

Although many sources have Ella Jane Fitzgerald born in 1918, the true date is April 25, 1917. In 1920 her unmarried mother, known as Tempie Fitzgerald, moved from Virginia to Yonkers, New York, with a new partner. In 1932 Tempie died, and Ella was taken from her stepfather by Tempie's sister Virginia, who lived in the Harlem section of New York.

The next few years were difficult ones. Ella, formerly a good student, dropped out of school and began to live on the streets of Harlem. She was ambitious, however, and in November, 1934, she entered a talent competition at the Apollo Theater, won first prize, and attracted the attention of Chick Webb, the director of a prominent Harlem jazz band. An immediate sensation as a vocalist with the band, she performed with it until 1939, when Webb died, and she, already labeled "the First Lady of Swing," was chosen to front the band.

In 1941 she married Benny Kornegay, who unknown to her had a criminal record, and the marriage was annulled the following year. Later Fitzgerald denied marrying or even knowing him. In 1942, with many musicians departing for military duty in World War II and orchestras hampered by a ban on recording by the American Federation of Musicians, her orchestra failed. She then began to perform with a singing and instrumental ensemble called the Three Keys. The next few years she toured with the better known group the Ink Spots and then with the orchestra of Dizzy Gillespie, one of the leading exponents of the newly popular version of jazz known as bebop.

Musical tours and hundreds of recordings made her an international favorite. Her association with promoter Norman Granz, who became her personal manager in 1953, made her the star of his recording company, Verve, for which she made her highly successful *Song Books* of the most eminent popular composers of the twentieth century. Nevertheless, she continued to perform in the jazz idiom.

Her personal life remained largely unfulfilled. Fitzgerald married musician Ray Brown in 1947 and, unable to have a child, she and Brown adopted Ray Brown, Jr. The marriage ended in divorce in 1953. In the 1940's she began to support orphaned and disadvantaged children and later made extensive donations of money and service to organizations combating child abuse.

She performed until she was in her seventies, when the breakdown of her health—she suffered from weak eyesight and diabetes—gradually forced her into retirement. In 1993 both her legs were amputated below the knee. She died at her home in Beverly Hills, California, on June 15, 1996.

The Music

Untrained, unsophisticated, and overweight, Fitzgerald did not look like anyone's idea of a band singer, but eighteen-year-old Fitzgerald possessed from the start of her career a keen sense of rhythm and a warm voice. Early in her career she tried to emulate Connee Boswell, a white singer from New Orleans. An immediate sensation with Webb's orchestra, which she joined in 1935, Fitzgerald performed a variety of songs, her first hit being a novelty she helped adapt from a nursery rhyme, "A-Tisket, A-Tasket," in 1938. Always eager to please her audiences, she continued to sing this song for decades thereafter.

Fitzgerald readily made the transition from orchestra singer to soloist in concert halls and exclusive nightclubs and remained an internationally known singing star for decades. Under the management of Granz she recorded hundreds of songs by George Gershwin, Irving Berlin, Cole Porter, and other major songwriters. She also excited audiences with her inimitable scat singing. Only her deteriorating health in her later years slowed her down, and she continued to sing publicly even when she was no longer able to walk or to see very well. Not an egotistic or colorful interpreter of songs, she could, in her prime, range over nearly three octaves and demonstrate a manner of phrasing that revealed the full possibilities of a melody.

Early Career. One of the best drummers and bandleaders of his time, Webb was a hunchbacked victim of spinal tuberculosis with whom Fitzgerald began to develop her natural talent. In his orchestra she learned to do the scat singing that later would enliven her concerts. Although she performed many novelty songs, she displayed a fondness and sensitivity for ballads, some of which she was able to sing with other masters such as Teddy Wilson and Benny Goodman. Her three recorded sides with Goodman in 1936 violated what Decca Records claimed was her exclusive contract and brought on a legal battle. Often performers would adopt pseudonyms to evade this difficulty, but Fitzgerald's voice was already too well known for this kind of duplicity.

In 1939 Webb succumbed to his illness at the age of thirty, and Fitzgerald was chosen to head the band. Ella Fitzgerald and Her Famous Orchestra survived until 1942, when it collapsed from financial distress. A number of her songs of this period,

Ella Fitzgerald. (AP/Wide World Photos)

including "The Starlight Hour," "Sugar Blues," and "Shake Down the Stars," all recorded in 1940, became minor hits. Fitzgerald spent several years singing with small groups, her association with the Ink Spots being the most successful.

Jazz at the Philharmonic. In 1944 jazz promoter Granz initiated a series of concerts at the Los Angeles Philharmonic Auditorium called Jazz at the Philharmonic. The event, often shortened to JATP, blossomed into an annual tour, and in 1948 Granz sought Fitzgerald as one of the stars of the production. Singing with Gillespie's band, Fitzgerald had developed her scat singing in a manner resembling Gillespie's trumpet style. Some of her most popular numbers were the ones she recorded with Gillespie in 1947: "Flying Home," "How High the Moon," and "Lady, Be Good!". Fitzgerald quickly emerged as the most popular performer in JATP productions.

Up to this time most of Fitzgerald's recordings were made for Decca, whose director of artists and repertoire was Milt Gabler. Granz suggested to Fitzgerald that her career had not been properly promoted at Decca, and he wished to become her manager. In fact, Gabler had not neglected her; he had, for instance, brought her and Louis Armstrong together several times. Fitzgerald was also a loyal person, and so it was not until 1953 that Granz would sign her to a contract. Probably the most stirring of Fitzgerald's JATP performances was the one given at the Chicago Civic Opera House in September, 1957, when she sang such ballads as "Bewitched, Bothered, and Bewildered" and "Moonlight in Vermont" and an extended version of "Stompin' at the Savoy," which Granz hailed on the record jacket as "the most incredible, brilliant jazz vocal performance ever put to wax."

The Song Books. In 1950 Gabler produced *Ella Sings Gershwin*, in the very early days of long-playing (LP) records, also issuing it at speeds of 78 and 45 rotations per minute (rpm). When Fitzgerald began to record for Granz's Verve Records, with LP now the standard format, he encouraged her to do a series of what became known as *Song Books*. She recorded two of them in 1956, *Ella Fitzgerald Sings the Cole Porter Song Book* and *Ella Fitzgerald Sings the Rodgers and Hart Song Book*. Of the others that followed, *Ella Fitzgerald Sings the George and Ira Gershwin Song Book* (1959), much more extensive than her earlier Gershwin recording, was ably arranged and conducted by Nelson Riddle. The *Song Books*, containing dozens of memorable songs, have remained among the most popular of all Fitzgerald recordings.

Ella in Rome: The Birthday Concert. Over the decades Fitzgerald gave concerts all over the world. Her tours were so wide ranging and intense that they wore out some of the musical groups with which she performed. A 1958 concert in Rome included much of her best *Song Book* material, her scat songs, and even her popular imitation of Armstrong's singing, which she did with great gusto, although with considerable strain on her vocal cords. None of the musicians who took part in this concert knew that Granz had recorded it, and somehow the recording vanished. Resurfacing in 1987, it appeared the following year to become the leading recording on the *Billboard* charts. In the opinion of many listeners, this album sums up Fitzgerald's artistry.

Musical Legacy

Fitzgerald was not a jazz singer in the manner of Billie Holiday, but in her work with such jazz musicians as Webb, Gillespie, and Armstrong, she absorbed what critics, despite their difficulty in adequately defining the jazz genre, recognize as its materials and forms. She wedded them to songs ranging from ballads to scat songs and carried these features through her career of more than fifty years. For many listeners her crowning achievements are the *Song Books*, which constitute an anthology of the best songs written by distinguished twentieth century songwriters.

Fitzgerald discouraged attempts to theorize about her singing, saying simply that she sang as she felt. She did not impose herself on her material but respected it and concentrated on rendering it superbly well. She left hundreds of performances, recorded in both studios and concert halls, that continue to delight audiences and are likely to do so in the foreseeable future.

She received many accolades, among them the Honors Medal of the Kennedy Center for Performing Arts in Washington, D.C.; the Pied Piper Award of the American Society of Composers, Authors, and Publishers; and honorary doctorates from Dartmouth College and Howard University. Singers from Carmen McRae to Diana Krall have acknowledged her influence, but her greatest contribution has been to the ears of millions of listeners throughout the world.

Robert P. Ellis

Further Reading

Colin, Sid. *Ella: The Life and Times of Ella Fitzgerald*. London: Elm Tree Books, 1987. Written in an engaging style, this short book summarizes her major achievements.

Crowther, Bruce, and Mike Pinfold. *The Jazz Singers: From Ragtime to the New Wave*. New York: Blandford Press, 1986. Authors consider Fitzgerald to be one of the best jazz singers and stress the importance of her live performances as distinct from studio recordings.

David, Norman. *The Ella Fitzgerald Companion*. Westport, Conn.: Praeger, 2004. With its many musical transcriptions, this book exemplifies Fitzgerald's work in a way that will interest professional musicians, but it also can be profitably consulted by the general reader.

Giddins, Gary. "Joy." In *Visions of Jazz: The First Century*. New York: Oxford University Press, 1998. Chapter on Fitzgerald summarizes the author's reaction to her singing.

Nicholson, Stuart. *Ella Fitzgerald: A Biography of the First Lady of Jazz*. New York: Charles Scribner's Sons, 1994. Accurate and well-researched Fitzgerald biography that corrects earlier accounts and offers insights from people who knew her well. Extensive, although incomplete, discography.

Vail, Ken, and Ron Fritts. *Ella Fitzgerald: The Chick Webb Years and Beyond, 1935-1948*. New York: Scarecrow Press, 2003. Authors' interest is Fitzgerald's early development as a singer.

See also: Armstrong, Louis; Basie, Count; Berlin, Irving; Cahn, Sammy; Dorsey, Thomas A.; Ellington, Duke; Elliot, Cass; Gershwin, George; Gershwin, Ira; Hart, Lorenz; Holiday,

Billie; Jobim, Antônio Carlos; Jones, Hank; Jones, Quincy; Jordan, Louis; Lewis, John; Odetta; Peterson, Oscar; Porter, Cole; Previn, Sir André; Robinson, Smokey; Rodgers, Richard; Vaughan, Sarah; Washington, Dinah; Webb, Jimmy.

Kirsten Flagstad

Norwegian classical and opera singer

Possessing a rare combination of heroic vocal strength, faultless intonation, and superlative musicianship, Flagstad was among the finest Wagnerian sopranos of the twentieth century.

Born: July 12, 1895; Hamar, Norway
Died: December 7, 1962; Olso, Norway
Also known as: Kirsten Målfrid Flagstad (full name)

Principal works

OPERATIC ROLES: Nuri in Eugen d'Albert's *Tiefland*, 1913; Aida in Giuseppe Verdi's *Aida*, 1929; Floria Tosca in Giacomo Puccini's *Tosca*, 1929; Elsa in Richard Wagner's *Lohengrin*, 1932; Kundry in Wagner's *Parsifal*, 1932; Rodelinda in George Frideric Handel's *Rodelinda*, 1932; Elisabeth in Wagner's *Tannhäuser*, 1932; Isolde in Wagner's *Tristan and Isolde*, 1932; Gutrune in Wagner's *Götterdämmerung*, 1934; Brünnhilde in Wagner's *Die Walküre*, 1935; Sieglinde in Wagner's *Die Walküre*, 1935; Brünnhilde in Wagner's *Götterdämmerung*, 1935; Leonore in Ludwig van Beethoven's *Fidelio*, 1948; Alceste in Christopher Willibald Gluck's *Alceste*, 1951; Dido in Henry Purcell's *Dido and Aeneas*, 1951.

Principal recordings

ALBUMS: *Snow*, 1929; *Lieder (8), Op. 10: No. 8, Allerseelen*, 1935; *Songs (6), Op. 48: No. 6, Ein traum*, 1936; *Tristan und Isolde: Einsam Wachend . . . Habet Acht!*, 1936; *Die Walküre: Hojo-to-ho!*, 1936; *When I Have Sung My Songs*, 1936; *Songs (9), Op. 63: No. 5, Junge Lieder I: Mein Liebe Ist Grün*, 1937; *Die Walküre: Du Bist der Lenz*, 1937; *Haugtussa, Op. 67: No. 7, Evil*

Day, 1940; *Tristan und Isolde: Wie Lachen Sie Mir: "Narrative and Curse,"* 1947; *Tristan und Isolde: Mild und Leise "Liebestod,"* 1948; *Four Last Songs, AV 150: No. 1, Frühling*, 1950; *Lieder (4), Op. 27: No. 2, Cäcilie*, 1950; *Dido and Aeneas, Z 626: Thy Hand, Belinda . . . When I Am Laid in Earth*, 1951; *Elektra, Op. 58: Orest! Est Rührt Sich Niemand*, 1952; *Die Schöne Magelone, Op. 33: No. 12, Muss Es Eine Trennung Geben*, 1954; *Paskemorgen Slukker Sorgen*, 1956; *Melodies (12), Op. 33: No. 2, Spring*, 1957.

The Life

Kirsten Målfrid Flagstad (KER-stehn MAHL-freed FLAG-stahd) made her operatic debut at the age of eighteen, singing the role of Nuri in Eugen d'Albert's *Tiefland* (1913) at the National Theater in Oslo. In the nearly two decades that followed, she performed exclusively in Scandinavia, with contracts at the Opera Comique in Oslo (1919) and the Storm-Theater in Göteborg (1928). International fame would soon follow. In 1932 a triumphant run as Isolde in Oslo led to engagements at the Bayreuth Festspiele in Germany. After two successful summers at Bayreuth, Flagstad signed with the Metropolitan Opera in New York in 1935. Her American debuts as Sieglinde and Isolde, and shortly thereafter as Brünnhilde, earned her a worldwide reputation as a leading Wagnerian soprano.

World War II temporarily interrupted Flagstad's career, and she faced criticism, especially in the United States, for her decision to return to Nazi-controlled Norway. Following the war, she performed for several seasons at Covent Garden in London to great acclaim, and American audiences gradually re-embraced her. A high point in her career came in May, 1950, when she gave the premiere of Richard Strauss's *Four Last Songs* (1950). Flagstad retired from the operatic stage in 1953, and she later served as general manager of the Norwegian Opera in Oslo for two seasons (1958-1960) before succumbing to bone marrow disease on December 7, 1962.

The Music

Flagstad was virtually unknown outside of Scandinavia until her late thirties, and for the first two decades of her career, she performed mostly light roles. The late 1920's marked a turning point: She began singing heavy roles in the operas of Giuseppe Verdi, Giacomo Puccini, and Richard Wagner. Flagstad gained fame as a dramatic soprano, and her performance background in oratorios, operettas, Baroque opera, and even musical comedy is often overlooked. One of her most performed roles was that of Dido in the seventeenth century opera *Dido and Aeneas* (1689) by Henry Purcell, which she performed first in 1951. Her ability to draw upon both lighter and heavier vocal techniques, to sing with both delicate control and striking power, are hallmarks of a style that exerted wide influence on succeeding generations of sopranos.

Isolde. With her premiere of the role on June 29, 1932, in Oslo, Flagstad quickly established herself as a foremost interpreter of Wagner's Isolde in *Tristan and Isolde* (1865).

The most important recordings include a live performance conducted by Fritz Reiner in 1936 with Lauritz Melchior as Tristan and a 1952 studio recording conducted by Wilhelm Furtwängler with Ludwig Suthaus as Tristan. The pairing of Flagstad and Melchior was definitive. Already in her early forties, Flagstad ascended to Wagner's more demanding roles at a relatively late age, but her patience resulted in powerful performances. The Reiner recording offers a voluptuous and highly passionate sound that seizes upon the dichotomy of Isolde's isolation in act 1 and her tenderness and eroticism in act 2. The 1952 performance is the first complete recording of the opera. Flagstad's nuanced phrasing and perceptive characterization are perhaps at their finest in the act 3 finale, "Isolde's Transfiguration." Her profound understanding of the role is supported by the sensitive pacing of Furtwängler, one of the great interpreters of Wagner's music.

Brünnhilde. Having triumphed in the smaller role of Sieglinde, Flagstad tackled Wagner's great heroine, Brünnhilde. Her premiere at the Metropolitan Opera on February 15, 1935, was one in a string of critically acclaimed performances that cemented her status as a leading Wagnerian soprano. As she had with *Tristan and Isolde*, Flagstad enjoyed a long history of performing Brünnhilde with Furtwängler and Melchior, the latter often singing opposite her as Siegfried.

The only extant, complete recording with Flagstad as Brünnhilde is of a now-legendary live performance at Milan's La Scala in 1950. Notwithstanding the poor audio quality, Flagstad's singing is both powerful and dramatically convincing. Her performance in *Götterdämmerung* (1874), and in particular its concluding "Immolation Scene," is especially memorable and emblematic of her authoritative reading of Brünnhilde.

Four Last Songs. Less than four months before his death, Strauss asked Flagstad to give the premiere of what would be his final orchestral songs. The first performance was given on May 22, 1950— about eight months after the composer's death— at the Albert Hall in London, with Furtwängler conducting the Philharmonia Orchestra. The surviving recording is badly deteriorated, and it is un-

Kirsten Flagstad. (AP/Wide World Photos)

certain whether it documents the May premiere or an earlier rehearsal. Flagstad's performance in "Frühling" suffers from the wide vocal range demanded by Strauss's score, displaying an uncharacteristic weakness in the lower register. The placid contours of "September" better suit her mature voice, for example, in her serene delivery of the line "Summer smiles, astonish and languid in the dying garden dream." However, the second and third verses of "Beim Schlafengehen" are particularly moving as Flagstad captures the sentiment of an impending, yet peaceful end of life as described in Hermann Hesse's poem. "Im Abendrot" stands out among the four songs, in part from Furtwängler's slow pacing, and despite the poor recording, the long melodic lines are sung expressively and with a remarkable naturalness that set the standard for later interpreters of *Four Last Songs*.

Musical Legacy

During the politically tense circumstances of the 1930's and 1940's, when Adolf Hitler was coming to power in Germany, Flagstad's popularity at the Metropolitan Opera was central to the sustained interest in the Wagnerian repertoire in the United States. The arc of her career, dominated by lighter roles until middle life, allowed her to sing professionally well into her fifties, an approach that is now widely endorsed by vocal coaches. Flagstad's influence on the brilliant careers of fellow Scandinavians Birgit Nilsson and Astrid Varnay, who followed in her footsteps, was significant.

Joseph E. Jones

Further Reading

Biancolli, Louis. *The Flagstad Manuscript*. New York: Putnam, 1952. These autobiographical documents were dictated by Flagstad in 1941 and 1950-1952, and included are commentaries on her political controversies. Includes a list of roles and a selection of newspaper reviews.

Hunt, John. *Six Wagnerian Sopranos*. London: John Hunt, 1994. Expansive discography of Flagstad and five of her contemporaries. A short biography is included.

McArthur, Edwin. *Flagstad: A Personal Memoir*. New York: Alfred A. Knopf, 1965. Reflections from Flagstad's accompanist, vocal coach, and longtime friend. Includes photographs, the author's testimony at a 1946 court case in Norway, and an appendix with premiere dates and numbers of performances for each role.

Rasponi, Lanfranco. *The Last Prima Donnas*. New York: Alfred A. Knopf, 1982. Contains a chapter dedicated to Flagstad based on a 1940 interview in New York. Includes insights into her favorite roles.

Vogt, Howard. *Flagstad: Singer of the Century*. London: Secker and Warburg, 1987. Offers especially strong coverage of Flagstad's formative years and a balanced account of her return to Nazi-controlled Norway during World War II.

See also: Melchior, Lauritz; Puccini, Giacomo; Strauss, Richard.

Lester Flatt

American country singer, songwriter, and guitarist

In partnership with Earl Scruggs and other popular musicians, Flatt defined the American bluegrass style of music. A regular performer at the Grand Ole Opry, he was one of the first bluegrass musicians to perform in Carnegie Hall.

Born: June 19, 1914; Overton County, Tennessee
Died: May 11, 1979; Nashville, Tennessee
Also known as: Lester Raymond Flatt (full name)
Member of: Flatt and Scruggs; Foggy Mountain Boys

Principal recordings

ALBUMS (solo): *Flatt on Victor*, 1970; *Flatt Out*, 1970; *Nashville Airplane*, 1970; *The One and Only Lester Flatt*, 1970; *Kentucky Ridge Runner*, 1972; *Foggy Mountain Breakdown*, 1973; *On the South Bound*, 1973; *Before You Go*, 1974; *Over the Hills to the Poorhouse*, 1974; *Flatt Gospel*, 1975; *Lester Raymond Flatt*, 1975; *Tennessee Jubilee*, 1975; *Heaven's Bluegrass Band*, 1977; *Lester Flatt*, 1977; *Foggy Mountain Banjo*, 1978; *Nashville Grass: Fantastic Pickin'*, 1978.

ALBUMS (with Scruggs): *Foggy Mountain Jamboree*, 1957; *Country Music*, 1958; *Lester Flatt and Earl*

Scruggs, 1959; *Flatt and Scruggs with the Foggy Mountain Boys*, 1960; *Songs of Glory*, 1960; *Foggy Mountain Banjo*, 1961; *Songs of the Famous Carter Family*, 1961; *Folk Songs of Our Land*, 1962; *The Ballad of Jed Clampett*, 1963; *The Original Sound of Flatt and Scruggs*, 1963; *The Fabulous Sound of Flatt and Scruggs*, 1964; *Beverly Hillbillies*, 1965; *Town and Country*, 1965; *The Versatile Flatt and Scruggs*, 1965; *Stars of the Grand Ole Opry*, 1966; *When the Saints Go Marching In*, 1966; *Changin' Times*, 1967; *Hear the Whistles Blow*, 1967; *Sacred Songs*, 1967; *Strictly Instrumental*, 1967; *Nashville Airplane*, 1968; *The Original Foggy Mountain Breakdown*, 1968; *Original Theme from Bonnie and Clyde*, 1968; *Songs to Cherish*, 1968; *The Story of Bonnie and Clyde*, 1968; *Detroit City*, 1969; *Breaking Out*, 1970; *Final Fling*, 1970; *Flatt and Scruggs*, 1970; *Foggy Mountain Chimes*, 1970; *Country Boy*, 1972; *A Boy Named Sue*, 1973; *Blue Ridge Cabin Home*, 1979; *You Can Feel It in Your Soul*, 1988; *Father's Table Grace*, 2002; *Foggy Mountain Special*, 2003.

The Life

Lester Raymond Flatt was one of nine children, and he grew up near Sparta, Tennessee. His father taught him to play musical instruments, and, by age seven, Flatt could play the guitar. By age ten, he was singing at school and in church.

While still a teen, he began working at a silk mill in North Carolina. When it shut down, he and his wife Gladys found work at another one, in Johnson City, Tennessee. Later, they moved to Roanoke, Virginia, where Flatt began performing on radio with Charlie Scott's Harmonizers.

Problems with rheumatoid arthritis led Flatt to give up mill work and pursue music. In 1940 he and his wife moved to Burlington, North Carolina, where Flatt worked with a variety of musical groups. He cut his first record with Charlie Monroe's Kentucky Partners at a radio station in Winston-Salem, and the copies sent to other radio stations gave them wider exposure. The increased popularity led to nightly tent performances before audiences of up to two thousand.

Flatt first played at the Grand Ole Opry with Bill Monroe and his Blue Grass Boys sometime in 1945, and he became a lead singer and rhythm guitarist. Earl Scruggs joined the group near the end of 1945.

Unhappy with long periods on the road, Flatt and Scruggs quit the band early in 1948, and they formed a new band, the Foggy Mountain Boys. They performed together for the next twenty-one years, until they split in 1969. Scruggs had been pushing for a more contemporary sound, and Flatt wanted to stay with the traditional bluegrass they had helped create.

The Music

Flatt was not only a vocalist and instrumentalist but also a composer of dozens of popular bluegrass songs, such as "Cabin on the Hill," "Bouquet in Heaven," "I'll Never Shed Another Tear," "Come Back, Darling," and "We'll Meet Again, Sweetheart." It is his performances of pieces written by others that are remembered, both by bluegrass enthusiasts and by the general public.

Martha White. Martha White, a company that made flour, cornmeal, and mixes for cornbread, cakes, and muffins, was a longtime sponsor of the radio program and live show Grand Ole Opry. The company's advertising jingle, written by Pat Twitty in 1953, was introduced by Flatt and Scruggs on the Grand Ole Opry stage. It became a bluegrass standard, and much later it became a signature piece for Rhonda Vincent and the Rage.

"The Ballad of Jed Clampett." Flatt and Scruggs performed this theme song for the comedy television series *The Beverly Hillbillies* (1962-1971), which ran for 274 episodes. The story of a naive backwoods family striking oil and moving to California was reprised as a television movie in 1981 and a theatrical film in 1993, always with the theme made popular by Flatt and Scruggs. The song, written by Paul Henning, reached number forty-four on the music charts in 1962. The two musicians appeared periodically on the television show. They had another *Billboard* country Top 10 hit with "Pearl, Pearl, Pearl," which referred to a character featured in an episode of the series.

The theme song was adapted by "Weird Al" Yankovic for his 1989 record of "Money for Nothing/Beverly Hillbillies," which appeared in his film *UHF*. It was performed in a different arrangement by banjo artist Béla Fleck in concerts, and it was parodied on television's *Saturday Night Live*. It is likely the best-known vocal by Flatt and Scruggs outside of bluegrass circles.

"Foggy Mountain Breakdown." First recorded in 1949, this instrumental was written by Scruggs, and it is probably the most popular instrumental composition performed by Flatt and Scruggs. Many five-string banjo players consider it the fastest and most challenging piece they can perform. In 2004 it was among fifty recordings added to the National Recording Registry by the Library of Congress. It was used to dramatize car chases and other highlights in the 1967 film *Bonnie and Clyde.* Other motion pictures and television shows have used it in a similar manner.

Musical Legacy

Flatt is one of the reasons that bluegrass music remains popular. In conjunction with other artists, such as Scruggs and Monroe, he helped define the sound of bluegrass. Flatt brought his style of bluegrass to the Grand Ole Opry, with its national following, and, with Scruggs, he took it to such performance centers as Carnegie Hall. Bluegrass artists try to emulate his signature sound. In 2003 Country Music Television (CMT) ranked Flatt and Scruggs at number twenty-four among CMT's Forty Greatest Men of Country Music.

Paul Dellinger

Further Reading

Lambert, Jake. *A Biography of Lester Flatt: The Good Things Outweigh the Bad.* Hendersonville, Tenn.: Jay-Lyn, 1982. The book recounts Flatt's life, from his boyhood through the various bands and musicians with whom he worked, and describes his influence on the evolution of country music.

Smith, Richard D. *Bluegrass: An Informal Guide.* Chicago: Chicago Review Press, 1995. Focuses on many aspects of bluegrass in a comprehensible manner, with separate chapters on various musicians and bands, including one on Flatt and Scruggs.

Whitburn, Joel, ed. *The Billboard Book of Top 40 Country Hits.* North Hollywood, Calif.: Billboard Books, 2006. A complete guide to the *Billboard* Top Country Singles, with a history of all the Top 40 hits since 1942 and photographs of the recording artists.

Willis, Barry R., Dick Weissman, Art Menius, and Bob Cherry, eds. *America's Music: Bluegrass—A History of Bluegrass Music in the Words of Its Pioneers.* Franktown, Colo.: Pine Valley Music, 1997. More than six hundred pages of interviews with people in bluegrass music, including biographies, festivals, instruments, record companies, and speculation on the future of bluegrass.

See also: Fleck, Béla; Monroe, Bill; Ritchie, Jean; Scruggs, Earl; Stanley, Ralph; Watson, Doc.

Béla Fleck

American banjoist and composer

Fleck expanded the banjo's role in music, using a conventional instrument in an unconventional way, and his style borrows heavily from bluegrass, fusion, jazz, classical, and progressive rock influences.

Born: July 10, 1958; New York, New York
Member of: Tasty Licks; Spectrum; New Grass Revival; Strength in Numbers; the Flecktones; Aras

Principal recordings

ALBUMS (solo): *Crossing the Tracks,* 1979; *Fiddle Tunes for Banjo,* 1981 (with Tony Trischka and Bill Keith); *Natural Bridge,* 1982; *Double Time,* 1984 (duets with others); *Inroads,* 1986; *Drive,* 1988; *Solo Banjo Works,* 1991 (with Trischka); *Tales from the Acoustic Planet,* 1995; *Tabula Rasa,* 1996; *Uncommon Ritual,* 1997 (with Mike Marshall and Edgar Meyer); *The Bluegrass Sessions: Tales from the Acoustic Planet, Vol. 2,* 1999; *Perpetual Motion,* 2001; *Little Worlds,* 2003.

ALBUMS (with Aras): *Curandero,* 1996.

ALBUMS (with the Dreadful Snakes): *The Dreadful Snakes,* 1983.

ALBUMS (with the Flecktones): *Béla Fleck and the Flecktones,* 1990; *Flight of the Cosmic Hippo,* 1991; *UFO Tofu,* 1992; *Three Flew over the Cuckoo's Nest,* 1993; *Left of Cool,* 1998; *Outbound,* 2000; *The Hidden Land,* 2006.

ALBUMS (with New Grass Revival): *Deviation,* 1984; *On the Boulevard,* 1984; *New Grass Revival,* 1986; *Hold to a Dream,* 1987; *Friday Night in America,* 1989.

ALBUMS (with Spectrum): *Opening Roll*, 1981; *It's Too Hot for Words*, 1982.

ALBUMS (with Strength in Numbers): *The Telluride Sessions*, 1989.

ALBUMS (with Tasty Licks): *Tasty Licks*, 1978; *Anchored to the Shore*, 1979.

The Life

Named after Hungarian composer Béla Bartók, Béla Fleck (BEH-lah flehk) began his interest in music by listening to the bluegrass duo Lester Flatt and Earl Scruggs perform the theme to the television situation comedy *The Beverly Hillbillies*. Fleck recalls that hearing Flatt and Scruggs "was like sparks going off in my head." Another early influence was the instrumental "Dueling Banjos" from the film *Deliverance* (1972).

Fleck started playing banjo at fifteen, and in 1973 his grandfather purchased him an instrument. Enthralled with music, Fleck enrolled in New York's High School of Music and Art. Because banjo lessons were not offered, he studied French horn and switched to chorus, though banjo remained his instrument of choice. Fleck studied with outside instructors Erik Darling, Marc Horowitz, and Tony Trischka, and he began experimenting with bebop (a form of jazz).

After graduating from high school, Fleck went to Boston. His band, the Tasty Licks, recorded two albums with Rounder Records: a self-titled album in 1978 and *Anchored to the Shore* the following year. In 1981—around the time Fleck moved to Kentucky—he joined Sam Bush, a Nashville-based mandolin player, in the band New Grass Revival. With this group, he found success as a musical innovator and a popular artist.

The Music

Early Works. When Fleck joined Bush in New Grass Revival, the band also featured John Cowen on bass and vocals and Pat Flynn on guitar. Their musical influences (mainly rock, country, and bluegrass) made them a nationwide hit, and Fleck benefited from the exposure he gained on New Grass Revival tours. Fleck stayed with the group for nine years, appearing in the albums *Deviation*, *On the Boulevard*, *New Grass Revival*, *Hold to a Dream*, and *Friday Night in America*.

Drive. Even while playing in New Grass Re-

vival, Fleck continued recording the solo albums that he had been making since the beginning of his career, which included *Crossing the Tracks*, his first solo album, and *Inroads*. *Drive* featured a few guest performers, such as New Grass Revival bandmate Bush. The album earned Fleck a Grammy Award nomination for Best Bluegrass Album.

Béla Fleck and the Flecktones. Released in 1990, Fleck's first major project after the demise of New Grass Revival garnered attention from fans and from the music industry. The Flecktones formed when Fleck met harmonica player Howard Levy at the Winnipeg Folk Festival and bassist Victor Wooten. In 1988 public television offered Fleck his own show, and Fleck and Wooten set out to find a drummer to complete the band—which they did in Wooten's brother Roy, who was playing an instrument he had invented called the drumitar, a drumguitar hybrid. Manipulating their music on Fleck's Apple Macintosh, the Flecktones signed a contract with Warner Bros., and soon after they won a Grammy Award for Best Pop Instrumental Performance for "The Sinister Minister." The group's next album, *Flight of the Cosmic Hippo*, also received Grammy Award nominations.

Outbound. Later albums, such as the wide-ranging *Outbound*, evolved beyond the simple, live style of the earlier albums. More sophisticated in production, later studio albums demonstrated Fleck's experimentation, not only with his virtuosic playing but also with classical instruments, such as those found in a symphony, and with whimsical instruments, such as steelpan drums and pennywhistles. The album also featured more than a dozen guest artists, including guitarist Adrian Belew and singers Jon Anderson and Shawn Colvin. The album picked up Best Contemporary Jazz Performance honors at the Grammy Awards that year. With Jeff Coffin eventually replacing Levy, Béla Fleck and the Flecktones has gained in popularity and has performed with such artists as the Dave Matthews Band, Sting, and the Grateful Dead.

Musical Legacy

Fleck revolutionized the sonic and playing possibilities of the banjo, much as Jimi Hendrix did with the guitar in the 1960's. His contributions as a composer and as a stylist revitalized the genres of fusion and bluegrass. Fleck's skill in playing different styles has been rewarded with eight Grammy Awards and twenty nominations. He was the first musician to be nominated for Grammy Awards in jazz, bluegrass, pop, country, spoken word, Christian, composition, and world music. His 2001 classical album, *Perpetual Motion*, in which he collaborates with bassist Edgar Meyer, won two Grammy Awards, including one for Best Classical Crossover.

Louis R. Carlozo, Judy Tsui, and LeeAnn Maton

Further Reading

Fleck, Béla. *Béla Fleck and the Flecktones*. Milwaukee, Wis.: Hal Leonard, 1998. This songbook compiled by Fleck includes twenty-five tunes, including "Blu-Bop" and "Flight of the Cosmic Hippo."

Graham, Jefferson. "Summer Tours Help Bands Pay Bills." *USA Today*, August 5, 2004. This article outlines Fleck's touring strategy, explaining how the multi-Grammy Award winner makes a living on the road, even without the benefit of a Top 10 hit, a gold record, or substantial radio airplay.

See also: Bartók, Béla; Flatt, Lester; Garcia, Jerry; Scruggs, Earl; Sting.

John Fogerty

American singer, songwriter, and guitarist

With his raw voice and bluesy guitar, Fogerty created the signature sound of the Creedence Clearwater Revival.

Born: May 28, 1945; Berkeley, California
Also known as: John Cameron Fogerty (full name)
Member of: Creedence Clearwater Revival

Principal recordings

ALBUMS (solo): *The Blue Ridge Rangers*, 1973; *John Fogerty*, 1975; *Hoodoo*, 1976; *Centerfield*, 1985; *Eye of the Zombie*, 1986; *Blue Moon Swamp*, 1997; *Deja Vu All over Again*, 2004; *Revival*, 2007.

ALBUMS (with Creedence Clearwater Revival): *Creedence Clearwater Revival*, 1968; *Bayou Country*, 1969; *Green River*, 1969; *Willy and the Poor Boys*, 1969; *Cosmo's Factory*, 1970; *Pendulum*, 1970; *Mardi Gras*, 1972.

The Life

John Cameron Fogerty (FOH-gur-tee) was the third of five brothers born to Galen and Lucile Fogerty. Fogerty's parents divorced when he was a child, creating an emotional scar that appears in songs such as "Someday Never Comes" from *Mardi Gras*. On the other hand, positive memories of his childhood are recounted in the classic "Green River" (from the album of the same title), about the Fogerty family's outings to a campground run by the son of Wild Bill Cody. Fogerty attended high school in El Cerrito, a blue-collar suburb of San Francisco, and he formed a rock-and-roll cover band with Stu Cook (bass) and Doug Clifford (drums). Eventually they were joined by Fogerty's older brother Tom as lead singer, and the group called itself the Blue Velvets.

Fogerty married Martha Paiz in 1965, and they had three children before they divorced in the 1970's. He supported his family by playing music and by working for Berkeley's Fantasy Records, an independent jazz label. Saul Zaentz, a producer for the label, wanted to expand its offerings, and he signed a contract with Fogerty's band. After several singles failed to make it to the record charts, Fogerty was drafted into the Army. Ironically, the man who wrote the anti-Vietnam War anthem "Fortunate Son" (from *Willy and the Poor Boys*) avoided combat service in Vietnam by joining the Army Reserve from 1966 to 1967. After his discharge, Fogerty returned to his band and to Fantasy Records, which was now owned by Zaentz.

Dubbed Creedence Clearwater Revival, the band released its self-titled debut in 1968. Though the album was produced by Zaentz, Fogerty was clearly in charge of creating the band's distinctive sound. A cut from the album, a cover version of Dale Hawkins's "Suzie Q" (modified by a jam guitar solo and Gregorian-style chanting), became a Top 40 hit. In 1969 and 1970 Creedence Clearwater Revival entered a period of amazing artistic production amid an almost nonstop touring schedule. In 1969 the band released three Top 10 albums that

John Fogerty. (AP/Wide World Photos)

featured multiple Top 10 singles: *Bayou Country*, featuring the classic "Proud Mary"; *Green River*, with its iconic title song as well as "Bad Moon on the Rise" and "Lodi"; and *Willy and the Poor Boys*, with "Down on the Corner," "Fortunate Son," and the Leadbelly cover "Midnight Special." In the following year the group continued its commercial and critical success with *Cosmo's Factory*, perhaps their finest album, and *Pendulum*.

However, the grueling touring schedule and competition within the band for control undermined its successes. Tom Fogerty, relegated to rhythm guitar player, quit the band in 1971, and bandmates Cook and Clifford demanded more input in the band's recording and finances. In turn, Fogerty demanded that the two remaining bandmates each write and produce a third of the material on their next album, *Mardi Gras*. In a vindictive mood, Fogerty refused to sing or play lead guitar on the other members' songs. The album included Fogerty's hit "Sweet Hitchhiker" and a cover of "Hello, Mary Lou," but Cook's and Clifford's songs were savaged by critics.

The band fell apart after the debacle of *Mardi Gras*. Moreover, Fogerty found himself at odds with Zaentz over the complex contracts and royalty arrangements with Fantasy Records. Zaentz's investment in Creedence Clearwater Revival had turned a respected jazz label into a media giant

loaded with cash. David Geffen reportedly paid Zaentz one million dollars to buy Fogerty out of his contract, but the rock style of *John Fogerty*, released domestically on Geffen's Asylum label, failed to resonate with audiences attuned to dance music and soft rock.

Fogerty spent the next ten years away from the music industry. He returned with *Centerfield*, whose title song became an international hit as well as a mainstay at baseball games. It also included the hit "The Old Man Down the Road," which resulted in one of the most unusual legal cases in music history. Zaentz, who owned publishing rights to Fogerty's 1970 song "Run Through the Jungle," sued Fogerty for copyright infringement, claiming that the chord progression and riffs in the later song plagiarized the earlier song. Fogerty took the stand in his own defense, and with guitar in hand he played the two songs to show their differences. The jury found in Fogerty's favor, which seemed to establish a legal precedent that an artist could not plagiarize himself or herself. Zaentz also sued Fogerty for defamation over the song "Zanz Kant Dance" (a thinly veiled attack on Zaentz's alleged "robbery" of Fogerty's publishing royalties). Fogerty settled out of court, and the song was retitled "Vanz Kant Dance." Fogerty made further legal history by countersuing Fantasy Records for his attorneys' fees arising from the initial lawsuit; the Supreme Court found in Fogerty's favor in a 1994 decision.

The stress of lawsuits and an unsuccessful follow-up album forced Fogerty to retreat again from the music industry. Though he appeared in some live concerts, he refused to play any of his Creedence Clearwater Revival material since Zaentz owned the publishing rights. In Creedence Clearwater Revival's Rock and Roll Hall of Fame induction ceremony in 1993, Fogerty refused to play with ex-bandmates Cook and Clifford. In 1997 he released the Grammy Award-winning rock album *Blue Moon Swamp*, which featured a more upbeat Fogerty, coming to terms with his artistic life and legacy. He also started to play his Creedence

Clearwater Revival songs in concert again. In a final reversal of fortune, Fogerty rejoined the Fantasy label in 2007 with the release of the appropriately titled *Revival*. Fantasy, under new ownership, offered Fogerty a return of his lost publishing rights for his Creedence Clearwater Revival-era songs.

The Music

Fogerty combined a Louisiana "swamp" beat with well-crafted rock songs to create a string of hits and several outstanding album cuts. Creedence Clearwater Revival began as a somewhat typical San Francisco psychedelic guitar-rock band. Like the early Grateful Dead or Quicksilver Messenger Service, they reworked 1950's rock classics into extended jams built around a lead guitar improvisation (as in "Suzie Q").

The Creedence Sound. By 1969 Fogerty had redefined the direction of Creedence Clearwater Revival's music toward three-minute songs built upon simple but memorable guitar riffs and incisive, image-filled lyrics. Already the band's songwriter, singer, and lead guitarist, Fogerty became its producer. A master of a number of other instruments (harmonica, organ, and saxophone), he practically dictated the Creedence Clearwater Revival sound. Later, as a solo artist, he often played every instrument (including bass and drums) on his records. *Centerfield*, perhaps the best example, sounds remarkably close to the Creedence Clearwater Revival sound that he had developed decades earlier.

Guitarist. As a guitarist, Fogerty fuses the riff-based Chicago blues tradition exemplified by Freddy King and Hubert Sumlin with the Bakersfield country crisp guitar-picking of Don Rich (of Buck Owens's Buckaroos). Fogerty's post-1969 work would occasionally include extended jams, such as the masterfully orchestrated buildup of tension and release in Creedence Clearwater Revival's eleven-minute reworking of the Motown hit "I Heard It Through the Grapevine" (from *Cosmo's Factory*) as well as in "Ramble Tamble," the opening song from the same album, which begins as a country romp built around an intricate guitar riff, then transforms into a stately blues-rock guitar anthem similar to Eric Clapton and Duane Allman's work with Derek and the Dominos.

Fogerty's music is best known for deceptively simple blues and country guitar riffs. The classic introduction to "Green River" makes use of a common blues riff in the key of E, which Fogerty adapts with his own rhythmic pauses and accents. The song eschews the classic blues chord progression to incorporate country chord progression of E to C to A, before returning to the E root. Likewise, the power-chord riff of "Proud Mary" uses a relatively simple group of chords (C, A, G, F, and D) in a slightly syncopated beat that accents the chord changes.

Lyricist. While Fogerty is one of rock and roll's premier guitarists, he is also one of its finest lyricists. His blue-collar roots often color the subjects he tackles in song. For example, his famous antiwar song "Fortunate Son" stands apart from many of the antiwar rock songs of the period, which offered simplistic solutions to complex problems of war and peace. Fogerty's speaker in the song is not an antiwar protest marcher so much as an angry blue-collar realist who sees Vietnam as a rich man's war and a poor man's fight. This populist, realist message is also evident in the two-minute gem "Don't Look Now" (an album cut from *Willy and the Poor Boys*). The song's speaker notes that society relies on common laborers to plow fields and mine coal, and it allows them to live in poverty and starvation as long as it does not have to witness the toll those take.

Bayou Country. Another dominant mode in Fogerty's songwriting is his nostalgia for a lost Eden. Rich in music and culture, the Bayou country of Louisiana and Mississippi became Fogerty's personal dreamland. Although he never actually spent much time in the region until the 1980's, during one of his retirements from the music industry, Fogerty took possession of the place in song as early as "Born on the Bayou" (from *Bayou Country*), which refers to a hound dog, hoodoo, and a Cajun queen. Similarly, the hit single "Up Around the Bend" (from *Cosmo's Factory*) promotes a back-to-roots lifestyle that replaces the flashy superficiality of a neon culture with a simple, sustainable culture of wood.

Fogerty's connection to the mythic Bayou carries through to his solo work in classics such as "The Old Man Down the Road" (from *Centerfield*), whose title character has a valise made of rattlesnake hide and who acts as a conjurer or hoodoo-man.

Musical Legacy

Fogerty is a musical individualist. He is a songwriter who is capable of playing every instrument on his albums and of producing the final product. As such, he became a founding father of the Americana or roots music movement that flowered in the 1990's. It sought to celebrate individualism in America as well as its rich musical heritage of popular music genres, ranging from blues, folk, country, and soul. Fogerty may be remembered primarily for the landmark legal decisions regarding an artist's inability to plagiarize himself or herself and the awarding of attorneys' fees to defendants in nonfrivolous lawsuits.

Luke A. Powers

Further Reading

Bordowitz, Hank. *Bad Moon Rising: The Unofficial History of Creedence Clearwater Revival.* New York: Schirmer Books, 2001. Bordowitz chronicles the rise and fall of Creedence Clearwater Revival, emphazising Fogerty's hubris in the tragic demise of the band.

Henke, James. "John Fogerty." *Rolling Stone* (November 5-December 10, 1987): 146-148. In this interview, Fogerty discusses everything from Creedence Clearwater Revival's participation in the original Woodstock Festival to the political apathy of the President Ronald Reagan era.

Perone, James. *Songs of the Vietnam Conflict.* Westport, Conn.: Greenwood, 2001. This work places Fogerty's anti-Vietnam War songs in a music history context. It focuses primarily on three Creedence Clearwater Revival songs: "Fortunate Son," "Run Through the Jungle," and "Who'll Stop the Rain."

Werner, Craig, and Dave Marsh. *Up Around the Bend: The Oral History of Creedence Clearwater Revival.* New York: Harper Perennial, 1999. Werner weaves together new and old interviews to create a coherent chronicle of the band's highs and lows and Fogerty's special role within the group. The group members speak candidly about themselves and their conflicts. Fogerty also provides insight into his songwriting process and his influences (particularly that of blues players).

See also: Clapton, Eric; Eddy, Duane; Leadbelly; Nelson, Ricky.

Aretha Franklin

American rhythm-and-blues singer and songwriter

With her gospel-influenced voice and overpowering performances, Franklin stretched the boundaries of rhythm-and-blues and soul music, becoming known as the Queen of Soul.

Born: March 25, 1942; Memphis, Tennessee
Also known as: Aretha Louise Franklin (full name); Queen of Soul; Sister Ree

Principal recordings

ALBUMS: *The Gospel Soul of Aretha Franklin*, 1956; *Aretha*, 1961; *The Electrifying Aretha Franklin*, 1962; *The Tender, the Moving, the Swinging Aretha Franklin*, 1962; *Laughing on the Outside*, 1963; *Songs of Faith*, 1964; *Unforgettable: A Tribute to Dinah Washington*, 1964; *Once in a Lifetime*, 1965; *Aretha Arrives*, 1967; *I Never Loved a Man the Way I Love You*, 1967; *Aretha Now*, 1968; *Lady Soul*, 1968; *I Say a Little Prayer*, 1969; *Soul '69*, 1969; *Don't Play That Song*, 1970; *Spirit in the Dark*, 1970; *This Girl's in Love with You*, 1970; *Aretha Live at Fillmore West*, 1971; *Young, Gifted, and Black*, 1971; *Amazing Grace*, 1972 (with James Cleveland and the Southern California Community Choir); *Hey Now Hey (The Other Side of the Sky)*, 1973; *Let Me in Your Life*, 1974; *With Everything I Feel in Me*, 1974; *You*, 1975; *Sparkle*, 1976; *Most Beautiful Songs*, 1977; *Satisfaction*, 1977; *Sweet Passion*, 1977; *Almighty Fire*, 1978; *La Diva*, 1979; *Aretha*, 1980; *Aretha Sings the Blues*, 1980; *Love All the Hurt Away*, 1981; *Jump to It*, 1982; *Get It Right*, 1983; *Never Grow Old*, 1984 (with Reverend C. L. Franklin); *First Lady of Soul*, 1985; *Who's Zoomin' Who*, 1985; *Aretha*, 1986; *Soul Survivor*, 1986; *One Lord, One Faith, One Baptism*, 1987; *Through the Storm*, 1989; *What You See Is What You Sweat*, 1991; *What a Difference a Day Makes*, 1997; *A Rose Is Still a Rose*, 1998; *Nobody Like You*, 1999; *Touch My Soul Presents Aretha*, 1999; *Duets*, 2001; *So Damn Happy*, 2003; *Jazz Moods: 'Round Midnight*, 2005.

The Life

Aretha (ah-REE-thah) Louise Franklin was born to the Reverend C. L. Franklin, a Baptist minister and gospel singer, and Barbara Siggers Franklin. When Franklin was six years old, her mother abandoned the family and died a few years later. Franklin and her family moved to Buffalo, New York, and then to Detroit, Michigan, where her father became the pastor of New Bethel Baptist Church, one of the largest churches in Detroit. At age eight, Franklin joined the choir, and at age twelve, she was singing solo. While attending her father's church, Franklin embraced the music around her and molded her style.

Franklin grew up on the east side of Detroit in a large house shaded by trees, but she was shy and isolated as a child. Franklin had several mother surrogates, such as Mahalia Jackson, Marion Williams, and Clara Ward, who were world-renowned gospel singers, and they had a great impact on her career. Franklin took piano lessons as early as age eight, but she was not disciplined enough to study the instrument. She disliked practicing beginner songs, wanting to play more sophisticated songs immediately.

Franklin's father was an emotional gospel singer who befriended popular gospel and soul singers, and his powerful sermons moved large congregations. Franklin had a close relationship with her father, and she had a great desire to please him. At age fourteen, she dropped out of school in order to travel with her father and other performers. Her father preached and sang gospel songs, and she joined him in song. By age fifteen Franklin had her first child, and by age seventeen she had her second child. Her children remained in Detroit while Franklin continued her music career and recorded demo tapes with her father's friends.

In 1961 Franklin married Ted White, who was eleven years her senior. He was involved in real estate, and later he became Franklin's manager. White and Franklin had an abusive marriage, and in 1969 they divorced. Franklin married two more times: to musician Ken Cunningham and to actor Glynn Turman. She bore two more children, one son with White and another son with Cunningham. On June 10, 1979, Franklin's father was shot during a robbery in his Detroit home. This left him in a comatose state for more than five years, until his death on July 7, 1984.

The Music

Franklin's style was largely influenced by her father's and Ward's gospel singing. At eighteen years of age, Franklin decided to focus her career on pop music by signing for the Columbia Records label in 1960. She then signed with Atlantic Records in 1966, and in 1980 she signed with the Arista Records label. Franklin brought her gospel-inspired singing to soul music, and her songs display her exceptional vocal power and nuances of black vocal traditions.

Early Works. Franklin was first recorded at the age of fourteen in a live session by the Checkers label in 1956. The album contains a set of gospel songs, including "Precious Lord." Her album *Aretha* contains twelve songs, and it features Franklin playing the piano. On this album her song "Today I Sing the Blues" reached number ten on the rhythm-and-blues charts. Other songs on this album include "Over the Rainbow" and "Rock-a-Bye Your Baby with a Dixie Melody." In the early 1970's Franklin released several albums geared thematically toward the Black Power social and political movement of the time, which promoted racial pride. *This Girl's in Love with You, Spirit in the Dark*, and *Young, Gifted, and Black* all feature Franklin playing the piano in a gospel style, while *Aretha Live at Fillmore West* showcases Franklin's ability to blend with a dominating rock sound. One of her most successful albums during this time period was *Amazing Grace*, which signaled a return to her roots, gospel music.

"Respect." Franklin premiered "Respect" in the spring of 1967, and she recorded it on her album *I Never Loved a Man the Way I Love You*. Her interpretation of the song was much different from that of its originator, Otis Redding. Franklin approached the song with a full-throated ascending shout of freedom. The song utilizes background singers that provide a response to Franklin's phrases. During the vamp section, Franklin employs lyric improvisation by developing the lyric in a way that meets her personal style. The song reached number one on the pop singles chart.

"Chain of Fools." "Chain of Fools" was first released as a single in 1967. Later, it appeared in several of Franklin's albums. The word chain is emphasized, through repetition and through stressing the syllables "a-ee," scooping from one note to the next. The overall song is in binary form with a verse and choral refrain, and there is an antiphonal texture during the repetitive chorus section. Franklin begins the verses in the upper range and drops her voice down the blues scale. During the a cappella section, hand-claps accompany Franklin and the background singers, reminiscent of early gospel male vocal quartets. During the vamp, the word chain continues to be emphasized, but Franklin adds lyric variation with her unpredictable soaring phrases. The song reached number one on the rhythm-and-blues charts and number two on the pop charts.

"Natural Woman." Franklin recorded "Natural Woman" in 1967. In the beginning of this song, the piano is played in a gospel style at a moderate tempo, and Franklin sings with exquisite expression. Although Franklin was only twenty-five at the time she recorded "Natural Woman," she sounds as if she were a much older woman who had overcome a lifetime of obstacles. The background singers create an antiphonal texture throughout the verses by harmonizing and scooping the syllables "ah-ew." During the chorus, the background singers join Franklin in creating a heterophonic texture, and she utilizes lyric variation during the vamp as the song comes to an end. "Natural Woman" reached number two on the pop charts and number eight on the *Billboard* Hot 100.

"I Never Loved a Man the Way I Love You." "I Never Loved a Man the Way I Love You" was one of Franklin's most popular songs, and it was the title of an album released in 1967. Franklin sings this song with liberty, using a scooping technique, and her soaring voice is similar to a cry of pain. Very little background singing is utilized in the song. At the end of the piece Franklin transitions directly into a lyric variation as she extends the text by embellishing the lyrics. The song reached number one on the rhythm-and-blues charts and number nine on the pop charts.

"Think." "Think" was released in 1968 on *Aretha Now*. The song is an anthem for women, encouraging them to demand the respect and the freedom they deserve. A fast-paced song, it begins with the piano being played in a gospel style and with the background singers creating an antiphonal texture. Between the verses, Franklin adds lyrical variation by filling in musical moments with material (such

as an emotional, soaring wail) based on the lyrics. At the end of the song she employs lyric improvisation during the vamp, similar to many of her songs. "Think" reached number seven on the pop singles chart and number one on the black singles chart.

"Young, Gifted, and Black." "Young, Gifted, and Black" was released in 1971 on Franklin's album *Young, Gifted, and Black*, which won a Grammy Award for Best Female Vocal Performance. The song was originally recorded in 1969 by Nina Simone, a singer, songwriter, pianist, and civil rights activist, under the title "To Be Young, Gifted, and Black." The song celebrates and encourages young blacks during a time of blatant racism. Franklin sings with emotional power, beginning with a call-and-response pattern between Franklin and the piano. Shortly after the introduction, the background singers join her. This song reached number two on the rhythm-and-blues charts and number eleven on the pop charts.

Musical Legacy

At a young age, Franklin captivated the world with her soulful voice, and she remains a dominating figure. Her songs confront her personal life and the political movements of her time. She applied her gospel-inspired voice to soul music as well as to rock and roll. She has been honored with eighteen Grammy Awards, six gold albums, and fourteen gold singles. She was the first female artist to be inducted into the Rock and Roll Hall of Fame in 1987.

Monica T. Tripp

Further Reading

Awkward, Michael. *Soul Covers: Rhythm and Blues Remakes and the Struggle for Artistic Identity (Aretha Franklin, Al Green, and Phoebe Snow)*. Durham, N.C.: Duke University Press, 2007. Close consideration of the lives of three leading contributors to soul music.

Bego, Mark. *Aretha Franklin: The Queen of Soul*. New York: Da Capo Press, 2001. A major biographical study of Franklin, covering her personal life and her career, with an examination of her most popular songs.

Boyer, Horace Clarence. *The Golden Age of Gospel*. Urbana: University of Illinois Press, 1995. Coverage of the early history of gospel music, with a focus on its leading exponents and performers, including Franklin.

Guralnick, Peter. *Sweet Soul Music: Rhythm and Blues and the Southern Dream of Freedom*. New York: Harper and Row, 1986. A discussion of the leading figures of soul music during the 1960's, including Franklin.

Werner, Craig. *A Change Is Gonna Come: Music, Race, and the Soul of America*. Ann Arbor: University of Michigan Press, 2006. A narrative of the growth of soul music over a span of forty years, with mentions of Franklin and her contributions.

See also: Blige, Mary J.; Burke, Solomon; Cleveland, James; Combs, Sean; Dorsey, Thomas A.; Goffin, Gerry; Holiday, Billie; Jackson, Mahalia; Jones, Quincy; King, Carole; Mayfield, Curtis; Pickett, Wilson; Redding, Otis; Reed, Jimmy; Simone, Nina; Smith, Bessie; Ward, Clara; Warwick, Dionne; Washington, Dinah.

Lefty Frizzell

American country guitarist, singer, and songwriter

Frizzell, with his signature vocal style of pitch-bending with muddled word pronunciation, helped bring honky-tonk to maturity.

Born: March 31, 1928; Corsicana, Texas
Died: July 19, 1975; Nashville, Tennessee
Also known as: William Orville Frizzell (full name)

Principal recordings

ALBUMS: *Songs of Jimmie Rodgers*, 1952; *Listen to Lefty*, 1953; *The One and Only Lefty Frizzell*, 1959; *Saginaw, Michigan*, 1964; *The Sad Side of Love*, 1965; *Great Sound*, 1966; *Lefty Frizzell's Country Favorites*, 1966; *Lefty Frizzell Puttin' On*, 1967; *Mom and Dad's Waltz*, 1967; *Signed Sealed and Delivered*, 1968; *Classic Style*, 1975.

SINGLES: "I Love You a Thousand Ways," 1950; "If You've Got the Money (I've Got the Time)," 1950; "Always Late (With Your Kisses)," 1951; "Mom and Dad's Waltz," 1951; "I Love You Mostly," 1954; "Cigarettes and Coffee Blues," 1958; "She's Gone, Gone, Gone," 1965; "Lucky Arms," 1974.

The Life

William Orville "Lefty" Frizzell (frihz-ZEHL) said he was born and raised "in an oil field behind an oil well." His parents, Naamon and A. D., regularly moved the family to follow the changing flow of the oil industry. Frizzell earned his nickname for delivering a left hook to a bully in the schoolyard. Always close to family, Frizzell, as a child, enjoyed visiting his Uncle Lawrence, and there a neighboring farmer introduced him to guitar picking. Within his immediate family, Frizzell's mother enjoyed singing and his father moonlighted in a Western band. After Frizzell began collecting musical repertory from songs he heard on the radio, he was afforded an opportunity to perform on KPLT radio in Paris, Texas.

At this time, Frizzell met Alice Lee Harper; and the teenage couple married in March, 1945. Soon after, the couple moved from town to town and state to state to maintain a living. They eventually settled in New Mexico, where Frizzell performed on KGFL until 1947, when he was put in jail for statutory rape.

After his incarceration, Frizzell and his wife moved back to Texas, where he auditioned for Jim Beck, a liaison for Columbia Records. Beck took great interest in Frizzell's song "If You've Got the Money (I've Got the Time)." However, when Columbia Records executive Don Law heard the singer, he was impressed with Frizzell's distinctive voice. Frizzell signed a recording contract, and soon he had several number-one hits and a spike in popularity. Frizzell went on tour with Hank Williams, and he joined the Grand Ole Opry. By 1953, because of poor contracts, mismanagement, and a growing alcohol addiction, Frizzell found his career floundering. Nevertheless, he remained popular on tour, and he released his last number-one hit in 1964. When Law retired from Columbia Records in 1972, Frizzell was dropped from the label. The singer died of a stroke three years later.

The Music

Although initially he modeled his style on that of Jimmie Rodgers, Ernest Tubb, and Bob Wills, Frizzell eventually found his own voice. Called the "boy with a wave in his hair and a curl in his voice," his vowel-bending, syllable-extending vocal practice entranced countless listeners, making him one of the most mimicked country singers of all time. Frizzell favored ballads and romance-themed lyrics, which showcased his nasal, but warm, voice. Lyrically romantic or otherwise, his reflections on life's trials and tribulations, in his jagged, emotional tone, connected him with a working-class audience. At the same time, his up-tempo tunes were equally admired in the honky-tonk blood buckets (taverns) and on the stage of the Grand Ole Opry.

"If You've Got the Money (I've Got the Time)." Encouraged to perform something upbeat for his audition, Frizzell completed "If You've Got the Money (I've Got the Time)" in Beck's recording studio. Upon hearing his note-bending vocal strains, Law offered Frizzell a two-year contract. The singer's slurred pronunciation and muddied vowels in lines such as "dance, drink beer and wine" captivated the Columbia Records executive. The heavy, offbeat rhythm of Madge Suttee's honky-tonk piano drives throughout most of the song, and it is briefly featured halfway through the song. Her instrumental solo breaks up the repetitive form. Thematically, the lyrics play on the reversal of standard gender roles, and Frizzell makes use of edgy double-entendres.

"I Love You a Thousand Ways." At summer's end in 1950, Frizzell released "I Love You a Thousand Ways" and "If You've Got the Money (I've Got the Time)" on opposite sides of the same record. Both sides eventually hit number one on the charts. The lyrics for this love ballad were composed by Frizzell while he was imprisoned in New Mexico. He was fueled by an intense longing for his wife, and he demonstrated an apologetic sentiment through his words. Again going up and down elongated syllables, Frizzell reveals his heartfelt emotions throughout the song. His regular upward slide and extended tones on "you" in the first verse resemble a child's whining plea.

"Always Late (With Your Kisses)." After Curly Chalker's gently progressing steel guitar riff, Frizzell picks up the vocal line on "Ah-al-waay-yays lay-ee-yay-ate," rolling each syllable through an extensive gamut of tones and glissandos. This may be the primary example of his innovative vocal practice. While Chalker claims no such confronta-

Lefty Frizzell. (Hulton Archive/Getty Images)

tion occurred, he and Frizzell reportedly had a minor physical dispute over the singer's inability to time accurately his entrance. In the song, the steel guitar, piano, and fiddle take turns reproducing the melodic material presented by Frizzell. Chalker's instrumental portion on steel guitar comes close to emulating Frizzell's vocal ornamentations, but it seems less complex without the added encumbrance of words.

"Mom and Dad's Waltz." This was the other side of the hit "Always Late (With Your Kisses)," and the origins of this sentimental ballad are in dispute. While Frizzell maintained he composed it when homesick in Dallas, his sister claimed it was initially penned for their mother, A.D., in Big Spring, Texas. Similar to "Always Late (With Your Kisses)," "Mom and Dad's Waltz" features an instrumental interlude midway through, where the fiddle, guitar, and piano take turns performing the verse and chorus melodic material. The lyrical material highlights Frizzell's dedication and reverence for his parents. Expectedly, the rhythmic meter is 3/4 time.

"Cigarettes and Coffee Blues." Featuring a danceable tempo, strong backbeat, shuffling snare rhythm, walking bass line, and boogie-woogie-style piano, "Cigarettes and Coffee Blues" is, when compared to Frizzell's earlier songs, stylistically closer to rockabilly. This musical change may have been intentional at a time when rock and roll was taking serious command over popular music. Other stylistic changes included clearer word pronunciation and fewer syllabic extensions. However, analogous to Frizzell's earlier works, the lyrical theme is one of lost love. Published in 1958, the song reached number thirteen on the charts.

Musical Legacy

Frizzell's primary musical contribution was, as noted by Law, his voice. He mastered the nuances of the Texan accent and dialect, placing them in song. Instrumentally, his voice paralleled the microtonal ability of the steel guitar. The vowel-bending vocal technique developed by Frizzell focused listeners' attentions on key lyrics, and it brought emotional substance to each extended syllable. These contributions significantly shaped the genre of honky-tonk, influencing Merle Haggard, George Strait, George Jones, Willie Nelson, Randy Travis, and Roy Orbison. Frizzell was one of the few singers to have four songs simultaneously on the country Top 10. In addition, he was the first country act to perform at the Hollywood Bowl in 1955. Frizzell received a star on the Hollywood Walk of Fame, and he was inducted posthumously into the Country Music Hall of Fame in 1982.

Janine Tiffe

Further Reading

Cooper, Daniel. *Lefty Frizzell: The Honky-Tonk Life of Country Music's Greatest Singer*. New York: Little, Brown, 1995. In writing this biography, Cooper conducted detailed interviews with Frizzell's family members, who provided him with primary sources. Includes photographs, discography, and bibliography.

Jensen, Joli. *The Nashville Sound: Authenticity, Commercialization, and Country Music*. Nashville, Tenn.: Country Music Foundation Press and Vanderbilt University Press, 1998. This resource discusses topics such as authenticity and commercialization, within the context of Nashville's country music industry. It includes a center section of photographs.

Kingsbury, Paul, and Alan Axelrod, eds. *Country:*

The Music and the Musicians. New York: Abbeville Press, 1988. Rich with photographs, this book provides topical and chronological information on country music, placing honky-tonk within a larger historical context. Includes selected discography and bibliography.

Tribe, Ivan. *Country: A Regional Exploration*. Westport, Conn: Greenwood Press, 2006. A chronological survey of eighty years of country-music history, including a chapter on honky-tonk and sixty pages of biographical sketches, including one on Frizzell.

See also: Haggard, Merle; Nelson, Willie; Orbison, Roy; Rodgers, Jimmie; Tubb, Ernest; Williams, Hank.

Blind Boy Fuller

American blues singer

Although his recording career lasted a mere six years, Fuller was one of the most recorded blues artists of his time. His eclectic repertoire included blues, ragtime, spirituals, and pop music. He was known for his finger-picking, bottleneck slide playing, and expressive vocal style.

Born: July 10, 1907; Wadesboro, North Carolina
Died: February 13, 1941; Durham, North Carolina
Also known as: Fulton Allen (birth name)

Principal recordings

ALBUMS: *Blind Boy Fuller with Sonny Terry and Bull City Red*, 1966; *Truckin' My Blues Away*, 1978; *Blind Boy Fuller, 1935-1938: Shake That Shimmy*, 1979; *Blue and Worried Man*, 1983 (with Sonny Terry); *Blind Boy Fuller, 1935-1940*, 1990; *East Coast Piedmont Style*, 1991; *Harmonica and Guitar Blues, 1937-1945*, 1996 (with Terry); *Untrue Blues*, 1998; *Rag, Mama, Rag*, 2000; *Get Your Ya Yas Out*, 2007.

SINGLES: "Ain't It a Crying Shame," 1935; "Good Feeling Blues," 1935; "Homesick and Lonesome Blues," 1935; "I'm a Rattlesnakin' Daddy," 1935 (with Gary Davis and George Washington); "Rag, Mama, Rag," 1935 (with Davis and Washington); "Cat Man Blues,"

1936; "Bye Bye Baby Blues," 1937 (with Sonny Terry); "Weeping Willow," 1937; "Big House Bound," 1938 (with Terry); "Pistol Slapper Blues," 1938 (with Terry); "Stop Jivin' Me Mama," 1938; "I Want Some of Your Pie," 1939 (with Terry); "You've Got Something There," 1939 (with Terry and Washington); "Good Feeling Blues," 1940; "Harmonica Stomp," 1940 (with Terry); "Precious Lord," 1940; "Step It Up and Go," 1940.

The Life

Blind Boy Fuller was one of ten children born to Calvin and Mary Jane Allen in Wadesboro, North Carolina. Following the mother's death in the mid-1920's, the family moved to Rockingham, North Carolina, where Fuller met Cora Mae Martin. In 1926 he and Cora Mae married; he was nineteen, she was just fourteen. Also in 1926, Fuller began experiencing problems with his vision. He and his wife moved to Winston-Salem to look for work, and he labored in a coal yard for a short time. Completely blind by 1928, he became largely dependent on his young wife.

With little money and a lack of steady work, Fuller and Cora Mae moved around often, eventually settling in Durham, where they applied for blind assistance from the welfare department. Fuller earned extra money by singing and playing outside tobacco warehouses and for house parties.

In 1934 James Baxter Long, the manager of a local department store and a talent scout for the American Record Corporation (ARC), discovered Fuller performing on the street. Soon Fuller traveled with Long to New York to lay down his first recordings for ARC.

In 1940 Blind Boy Fuller underwent a kidney operation, after which his health continued to decline. He died in February, 1941, of blood poisoning caused by an infection. He was thirty-three.

The Music

Faced with blindness and an inability to work amid the Great Depression, Fuller found music the only viable means of earning money for himself and his wife. While much of the economy was suffering in the early 1930's, the tobacco industry in North Carolina was thriving, and the workers created a demand for recorded and live music.

Fuller largely learned his repertoire by listening to recordings, but he also met two influential musicians in his early days who would accompany him on his first record dates. Gary Davis, a singer and masterful guitar player from South Carolina, was a profound influence on Fuller's guitar technique. Bull City Red, a washboard player and singer, often served as Fuller's guide on the streets.

In July, 1935, Long took Fuller, Davis, and Red to New York for their first recording session. Fuller recorded mostly solo pieces, playing a steel-bodied National Guitar, but on a few sides he was accompanied by Davis on guitar and Red on washboard. The session produced up-tempo dance pieces such as "Rag, Mama, Rag," provocative numbers such as "I'm a Rattlesnakin' Daddy," and slow, mournful blues such as "Ain't It a Crying Shame?"

Fuller's initial recordings were well received, and over the next six and half years Fuller recorded often. Almost all of his recordings were for ARC, but one July, 1937, session for Decca angered Long. Although he did not have an exclusive agreement with Fuller, Long threatened to sue Decca, which withdrew the recordings. Subsequently, Long bullied Fuller into an exclusive lifetime contract.

In 1937 Saunders Terrell, a blind harmonica player better known as Sonny Terry, became a regular recording partner. He is featured on many of Fuller's late-1930's recordings, including "I Want Some of Your Pie," "Stop Jivin' Me Mama," "Pistol Slapper Blues," and "Good Feeling Blues."

Fuller produced some of his finest material in the last two years of his life. The following works recorded during that time demonstrate his broad repertoire of blues, ragtime, and spirituals.

"Step It Up and Go." Recorded in March, 1940, this up-tempo dance piece is an example of Fuller's fine ragtime playing and features Red on washboard. A good-time dance number, "Step It Up and Go" was a big country-blues hit and became a standard among the Piedmont blues artists. Brownie McGhee recorded the tune soon after Fuller's death, and it was later recorded by Bob Dylan, John Hammond, Leon Redbone, and many others.

"I Want Some of Your Pie." Throughout his career, Fuller recorded many blues that contained sexual innuendo. "I Want Some of Your Pie" is a typical example. A common form of blues in the 1920's and 1930, these often humorous songs were known as hokum or party blues. Other examples from Fuller are "I'm a Rattlesnakin' Daddy," "Truckin' My Blues Away," and "Get Your Yas Yas Out."

"Precious Lord." This spiritual features Terry on harmonica. Fuller increasingly recorded gospel numbers late in his career. "Precious Lord" was recorded in his last session, only a few months before his death. Other spirituals recorded were "No Stranger Now," "Jesus Is a Holy Man," and "Must Have Been My Jesus." Although not a deeply religious man, Fuller promised to join the church if he survived his 1941 illness.

"Night Rambling Woman." This slow and devastating song is a plea to an unfaithful woman. Fuller's emotive vocals and adept fingerpicking are reminiscent of Delta bluesman Robert Johnson's style. Perhaps because of his deteriorating health, Fuller's voice is sometimes strained. "Night Rambling Woman" was the last song Fuller ever recorded.

Musical Legacy

Immediately following Fuller's death, Long recorded McGhee and released the record under the pseudonym Blind Boy Fuller, No. 2. McGhee recorded "Death of Blind Boy Fuller" in addition to several of Fuller's biggest hits. Afterward, Terry and McGhee often played together, eventually moving to New York and joining the folk-music scene there.

Fuller's recordings were an important influence on subsequent Piedmont artists. Several of his songs—such as "Step It Up and Go," "Truckin' My Blues Away," and "Rag, Mama, Rag"—were often covered by young artists in the Piedmont region and later by blues revivalists. Although Fuller's music career was short, it was prolific, producing more than 130 sides in less than seven years. Today almost all of Fuller's recordings have been reissued on compact discs, a testament to his continued importance in the blues genre.

Cara Lemon

Further Reading

Bastin, Bruce. "Blind Boy Fuller." In *Red River Blues: The Blues Tradition in the Southeast*. Chicago: University of Illinois Press, 1995. This chapter contains biographical information, as well as a detailed account of Fuller's relationship with Long and his recording sessions.

Blind Boy Fuller. (Hulton Archive/Getty Images)

_____. "Truckin' My Blues Away: East Coast Piedmont Styles." In *Nothing but the Blues*, edited by Lawrence Cohn. New York: Abbeville Press, 1993. Places Fuller in the Piedmont blues tradition. Mostly biographical, it also provides insight into Fuller's influence on the blues genre.

Charters, Samuel B. "Hey, Mama, Hey, Pretty Girl." In *The Country Blues*. New York: Da Capo Press, 1959. This chapter focuses on Fuller's relationship with Terry.

Oliver, Paul. "Piccolo Rag." In *Blues Off the Record: Thirty Years of Blues Commentary*. New York: Da Capo Press, 1984. Analyzes the meaning behind several of Fuller's songs.

Pearson, Barry Lee. "Blind Boy Fuller." In *All Music Guide to the Blues: The Definitive Guide to the Blues*. 3d ed. San Francisco: Backbeat Books, 2003. This guide contains only a short biography but includes reviews of reissues of Fuller's work.

Whirty, Ryan. "Blues Legend Inspires Quest." *News & Observer*, Raleigh, North Carolina, January 22, 2006. New biographical data as well as analysis of Fuller's significance in the blues genre.

See also: Clapton, Eric; Dylan, Bob; Johnson, Robert; Terry, Sonny.

G

Peter Gabriel

English rock singer and songwriter

Initially famous as cofounder, lead singer, and lyricist for the progressive rock band Genesis, Gabriel later forged a reputation as a solo performer noted for his innovative audio and video compositions and for his entrepreneurial spirit. Gabriel is also recognized for his philanthropic efforts to uphold human rights and to promote talented artists from around the world.

Born: February 13, 1950; Woking, Surrey, England
Also known as: Peter Brian Gabriel (full name)
Member of: Genesis

Principal works

FILM SCORES: *Birdy*, 1985; *The Last Temptation of Christ*, 1988; *Rabbit-Proof Fence*, 2002.

Principal recordings

ALBUMS (solo): *Peter Gabriel I (Car)*, 1977; *Peter Gabriel II (Scratch)*, 1978; *Peter Gabriel III (Melt)*, 1980; *Peter Gabriel IV (Security)*, 1982; *So*, 1986; *Us*, 1992; *Ovo: Millennium Show*, 2000; *Up*, 2002; *Big Blue Ball*, 2007 (with others).

ALBUMS (with Genesis): *From Genesis to Revelation*, 1969; *Trespass*, 1970; *Nursery Cryme*, 1971; *Foxtrot*, 1972; *Selling England by the Pound*, 1973; *The Lamb Lies Down on Broadway*, 1974.

The Life

Peter Brian Gabriel was born February 13, 1950, in Woking, Surrey, England. He was the son of Ralph, an electrical engineer and inventor, and Irene, a musician; his parents' vocations would have a powerful influence on Gabriel's career.

A sensitive, precocious child, Gabriel was raised in affluence on a farm in Surrey called Deep Pool. A victim of sexual abuse perpetrated by classmates at school, Gabriel composed his first song at age eleven, a ditty about a slug. He attended Charterhouse, a renowned exclusive boys' school founded in 1611 in Goldalming, Surrey. In the mid-1960's at Charterhouse Gabriel joined two bands comprising fellow Carthusians (classmates at Charterhouse)—Garden Wall and the Spoken Word—as singer, songwriter, flutist, and occasional drummer. By the end of the decade, the bands had metamorphosed into Genesis (featuring Gabriel as lead vocalist and lyricist, keyboardist Tony Banks, guitarist Steve Hackett, bassist Mike Rutherford, and drummer Phil Collins). Like Emerson, Lake, and Palmer, King Crimson, and Yes, Genesis became a leader in the new musical genre of progressive rock. With Gabriel as front man, Genesis released six critically acclaimed albums between 1969 and 1974, beginning with *From Genesis to Revelation* and ending with *The Lamb Lies Down on Broadway*.

Gabriel, who wed childhood sweetheart Jill Moore in 1971 and fathered two girls (Anna, born in 1974, and Melanie, born in 1976), experienced creative differences with the other members of Genesis and left the band in 1975 to go solo. He released his initial self-titled album in 1977, which yielded the first in a succession of hit singles. A number of these spawned the highly creative and award-winning music videos that Gabriel produced. In the mid-1980's, along with live, studio, and compilation albums, he began contributing to several movie sound tracks.

Long an advocate of protecting human rights and promoting world peace and a staunch supporter of global music, Gabriel in 1982 founded the World of Music, Arts, and Dance (WOMAD), an organization that has sponsored ethnically diverse music festivals in more than seventy countries. Since then, Gabriel has also founded Real World Studios, Real World Records, and Real World Multimedia, which are committed to recording and promoting musical artists from everywhere on the planet. Other causes to which Gabriel, a multimillionaire, has lent physical, intellectual, and financial support include Amnesty International, Greenpeace, the Secret World Live tour, the Millennium Dome in Greenwich, England, and Witness. The last of these organizations has provided activists in more than fifty countries with video cameras and computers to document human-rights abuses. Ever the entrepreneur willing to embrace new technology, in 2000 Gabriel cofounded On Demand Distribution, a European online music provider (later sold to a company in Seattle, Washington).

Gabriel and his first wife Jill divorced in 1987. After highly publicized romances with actress Rosanna Arquette and singer Sinead O'Connor during the 1990's, Gabriel wed again in 2002 to a much younger Meabh Flynn, an Irish sound engineer, by whom he had a son, Isaac.

The Music

The Genesis Years. Gabriel first burst onto the musical scene in the 1960's as lead singer-lyricist for the powerhouse progressive art rock band Genesis. Initially an acquired taste in a world where pop was king, Genesis built a fan base for its complicated, classically inspired conceptual compositions. Some fans appreciated the close harmonies, arcane lyrics, complex rhythms, creative orchestrations, and frequent tempo changes that set Genesis apart from its more rock-oriented peers. Much of the band's popularity, however, came from the theatricality of its presentations, led by Gabriel, who, to cope with stage fright, performed in outrageous homemade costumes, masks, and makeup. While the first Genesis album, *From Genesis to Revelation*, sold poorly, each succeeding release—*Trespass, Nursery Cryme, Foxtrot,* and *Selling England by the Pound*—did better than the one before. The final Genesis album on which Gabriel appeared, *The Lamb Lies Down on Broadway*, has been favorably compared with such progressive classics as Pink Floyd's *Dark Side of the Moon* (1973) and Yes's *Tales from Topographic Oceans* (1973).

Solo Start-up. After leaving Genesis, Gabriel released four consecutive albums between 1977 and 1982 that bore only his name as title, because he believed each was a fresh issue of a continuing publication, similar to a magazine. (To differentiate among individual albums, they are typically called *Peter Gabriel I, II, III,* and *IV*, while fans usually refer to them by the cover art as *Car, Scratch, Melt,* and *Security*.)

The debut album, generally well received, reached number seven in England and produced the hit single "Solsbury Hill," Gabriel's wistful reflection about leaving Genesis. The second solo album was an experimental departure from his previous work, a collection of pop ballads and rock tunes containing social commentary that, though it the contained the provocative tracks "On the Air" and "D.I.Y.," produced no major hits.

Peter Gabriel III (Melt). Gabriel's third album represented a major turning point in his musical career. Featuring one of the first uses of cymballess drum machines, *Peter Gabriel III* was praised for its clever if unsettling lyrics (always Gabriel's strength), its social consciousness, and its incorporation of world beat rhythms. It also produced a number of hits, including "Intruder," "Family Snapshot," "And Through the Wire," "Games Without Frontiers," "Not One of Us," and "Biko," the last one of the first musical acknowledgments of South African apartheid.

Peter Gabriel IV (Security). Gabriel's fourth self-titled solo album—grudgingly subtitled *Security* for the American market—continued the experimental and ethnically diverse themes established with his previous effort. An intriguing blend of modern rock and world beat, this album yielded several hits, including "The Rhythm of the Heat," "San Jacinto," "I Have the Touch," and the rollicking "Shock the Monkey," for which Gabriel produced an innovative music video.

Peter Gabriel Plays Live. A set comprising live performances of songs primarily from the third and fourth solo albums—recorded at different venues during a 1982 tour of the United States—*Peter Gabriel Plays Live* captures the fervid audience reception and demonstrates the synergy among a small group of musicians in re-creating onstage some of Gabriel's best-known early studio hits. Included among sixteen songs are stage renditions of "The Rhythm of the Heat," "Not One of Us," "D.I.Y.," "San Jacinto," "Solsbury Hill," "Shock the Monkey," and "Biko."

So. Following extensive tours, during which he continued the dramatic presentations reminiscent of his tenure with Genesis (collected on *Peter Gabriel Plays Live*), the singer-songwriter took time off to compose the sound track for the critically acclaimed film *Birdy*. Returning to the studio, Gabriel in 1986 released his most commercially successful album to date, *So*. Titled for the fifth note on the musical scale, the album was a huge commercial and critical success. It featured a stunning range of songs, from the evocative, image-laden "Red Rain" to the Motown-influenced "Sledgehammer." Other cuts included an inspirational duet with Kate Bush, "Don't Give Up"; a love ballad, "In Your Eyes"; the cynical "Big Time"; and the dark, moody "We Do What We're Told."

Us. Gabriel's return to the studio after a six-year hiatus, *Us* (certified platinum in the United States, England, and Canada) showcased the talents of a large number of musicians: Dozens of individuals—including Sinead O'Connor, Brian Eno, Peter Hammill, John Paul Jones, and little-known ethnic talents—contributed to the album. *Us*, which chronicled the breakup of his first marriage and subsequent romantic entanglements, reached number two on the charts, thanks to such video-backed hits as "Digging in the Dirt," and "Steam."

Later Work. With his increasing involvement in other aspects of a multifaceted career, Gabriel's studio releases grew fewer and farther between after the mid-1980's. The emphasis shifted to his various Real World enterprises, his dedication to the development and promotion of underappreciated musical talent from around the globe, and devotion to charitable causes. These efforts include extensive touring on behalf of both world beat musicians (as documented on *Secret World Live*, 1994) and personal appearances and extensive financial contributions. There has also been a growing demand for Gabriel's compositional skills in other venues. The singer-composer wrote the score for Martin Scorsese's controversial film *The Last Temptation of Christ*; *Ovo: Millennium Show*, the music and video for the Millennium Dome; and the score for the Australian film *Rabbit-Proof Fence*.

Despite his busy schedule, Gabriel manages on occasion to produce new and original additions to his catalog. *Up*, dealing with maturity and the growing awareness of mortality, yielded such tracks as "I Grieve," "More than This," and "Signal to Noise." Sometimes, Gabriel's music touches a particularly sensitive nerve: Following the collapse of New York's World Trade Center in the wake of the attacks on September 11, 2001, America's Clear Channel Communications network included the Gabriel-Afro Celt Sound System collaboration,

"When You're Falling," among a list of 150 songs recommended for banning.

Musical Legacy

A leader in progressive rock since the mid-1960's, Gabriel, both with Genesis and later as a solo artist, has greatly influenced musical showmanship with his elaborate, dramatic live performances. His recorded music—incorporating complex rhythms and textures, motifs from diverse cultures, and subject matter that heightens awareness of important social issues while simultaneously appealing to pop audiences—has garnered both commercial and critical acknowledgment in the form of Grammy nominations and awards and platinum records. His groundbreaking music videos—the multi-Grammy-nominated "Sledgehammer," which earned nine MTV Video Music Awards, as well as "Digging in the Dirt" and "Steam," which were the first to win consecutive short-subject video Grammy Awards—have inspired a creative visual renaissance among other musicians.

As significant as his contributions to popular music are, Gabriel's determination to promote talented worldwide artists is likely to have a more lasting effect. By giving voice to ignored or underrepresented cultures and by drawing attention to their particular needs, Gabriel will be remembered not only for his music but also for his contributions to a more egalitarian and peaceful world.

Jack Ewing

Further Reading

Baehr, Peter R. *Human Rights: Universality in Practice*. Amsterdam, Netherlands: Palgrave Macmillan, 2002. A professor of human rights at the University of Utrecht, Baehr explores the political and legal issues of human rights with an emphasis on supporters such as Gabriel.

Benioff, Marc, and Carlyle Adler. *The Business of Changing the World*. New York: McGraw-Hill, 2006. An intriguing study of philanthropy, this book features profiles of twenty corporate leaders, including Gabriel.

Holm-Hudson, Kevin. *Progressive Rock Reconsidered*. London, England: Routledge, 2001. A professor of popular culture and music discusses the importance of the progressive rock genre through an examination of the music of Yes, Genesis, Pink Floyd, and Procol Harum.

Thompson, Dave. *Turn It On Again: Peter Gabriel, Phil Collins, and Genesis.* San Francisco: Backbeat Books, 2004. Relies heavily on interviews to document the complete history of Genesis, including band members' solo careers.

Welch, Chris. *Genesis: The Complete Guide to Their Music.* London, England: Omnibus Press, 2006. Genesis's complete oeuvre and a section on Gabriel's solo work.

_____. *The Secret Life of Peter Gabriel.* London, England: Omnibus Press, 1998. Biography of the singer-songwriter written by one of England's best-known rock writers.

See also: Collins, Phil; Eno, Brian; Harris, Emmylou; Khan, Nusrat Fateh Ali; Nascimento, Milton; Robertson, Robbie; Sting.

Sir James Galway

Irish classical flutist

Galway's performances and recordings serve as a bridge for his audiences, crossing freely between popular and classical music genres.

Born: December 8, 1939; Belfast, Northern Ireland

Principal recordings

ALBUMS: *The Man with the Golden Flute,* 1976; *Annie's Song and Other Galway Favorites,* 1978; *Pachelbel Canon and Other Favorites,* 1981; *The Wayward Wind,* 1982; *Nocturne,* 1983; *James Galway Plays Mozart,* 1984; *Christmas Carol,* 1986; *Serenade,* 1989; *Over the Sea to Skye: The Celtic Connection,* 1991 (with the Chieftains); *The Wind Beneath My Wings,* 1991; *At the Movies,* 1992; *Bach: Flute Sonatas,* 1995; *Celtic Minstrel,* 1996 (with the Chieftains); *Legends,* 1997 (with Phil Coulter); *Music for My Friends,* 1997; *Meditations,* 1998; *Unbreak My Heart,* 1999; *Wings of Song,* 2004; *My Magic Flute,* 2006.

The Life

James Galway (GAHL-way) was born in Belfast, Northern Ireland. He studied flute at the Royal College of Music under John Francis and at the Guildhall School of Music with Geoffrey Gilbert. Afterward, he went to the Paris Conservatory to become a student of Gaston Crunelle and Jean-Pierre Rampal; he also studied privately with Marcel Moyse.

Thereafter, Galway performed for fifteen years in flute sections of the Philharmonia Orchestra, the London Symphony, and the Royal Philharmonic Orchestra. In 1969 he became principal flute of the Berlin Philharmonic, which he left in 1975 to pursue a solo career.

Galway has performed worldwide as a soloist with renowned orchestras. He also gives master classes, he performs chamber and popular-music concerts, and he makes numerous television appearances. As a recording artist, Galway has sold more than thirty million albums for labels such as Deutsche Grammophon, Sony, and RCA. While Galway's recordings of the classical flute repertoire are definitive, he is also a successful crossover artist, recording pop and Celtic music in addition to film sound tracks. Galway plays Muramatsu and Nagahara flutes. Early in his career he played a solid-gold flute by Cooper, earning him the nickname "the man with the golden flute."

The Music

Galway's voluminous discography reveals a performer who freely crosses boundaries. While some of his albums contain exclusively classical repertoire or popular tunes arranged for flute, he is just as likely to include both on the same album. In addition to recording the standard flute repertoire, Galway commissions and records new works.

The Man with the Golden Flute. Galway's debut album in 1976, *The Man with the Golden Flute,* consisted of short works (or single movements excerpted from larger works) intended to showcase Galway's prowess as a solo flutist. Most were familiar to those with little acquaintance with classical music, including flute arrangements of technical showpieces for violin or piano. The album does contain works originally for or featuring the flute, mostly from the eighteenth and nineteenth centuries.

Sir James Galway. (AP/Wide World Photos)

Annie's Song and Other Galway Favorites. In 1978 Galway released *Annie's Song and Other Galway Favorites.* Like his debut album, this release featured short works from a variety of composers. Some display Galway's technical ability with adaptations of works for other instruments, such as Marin Marais's "Le Basque," Fritz Kreisler's "Love's Joy," and a movement from Wolfgang Amadeus Mozart's Piano Sonata. These and the title work on this album, a charming adaptation of "Annie's Song" by John Denver, are complemented by arrangements of folk songs from Spain and Northern Ireland. In typical Galway style, this album brings together works from wide-ranging musical worlds.

During the 1980's, Galway continued to release albums featuring a mix of classical favorites and adaptations of popular or folk tunes. Examples include *Pachelbel Canon and Other Favorites*, *The Wayward Wind*, *Nocturne*, *Serenade*, and the holiday album *Christmas Carol.*

James Galway Plays Mozart. Recordings of the Mozart concerti are a staple in most flutist's discographies, and in 1984 Galway released the album *James Galway Plays Mozart.* This recording contains the two concerti K. 313 and K. 314, the Andante K. 315, and the Concerto for Flute and Harp, K. 299. In addition, it features the Rondo K. 373, the minuet from the Divertimento K. 334, and an arrangement of *Eine kleine Nachtmusik.*

This was not Galway's first album devoted to the works of a single composer, nor was it the first time he recorded some of the Mozart concerti, but the appearance of these particular works on a single album was important in establishing Galway as a serious flutist, and it contrasted sharply with his previous mixed-genre releases. Galway's renditions of these concerti are lighthearted and appealing, and they showcase his expert control over technical passages.

Music for My Friends. Alongside numerous greatest hits albums, in the 1990's Galway recorded albums of popular appeal and those of the standard flute repertoire. Of the former variety, *The Wind Beneath My Wings*, *At the Movies*, and *Unbreak My Heart* are representative examples, with renditions of songs by Stephen Sondheim, Paul McCartney, and Stevie Wonder.

While Galway's earlier albums tended to be accompanied by full orchestra, he later began to release recital albums, on which Galway collaborated with pianists such as Philip Moll, Christopher O'Reilley, and Martha Argerich. A representative example of this album was 1997's *Music for My Friends*, with his wife Lady Jeanne Galway on flute and Moll on piano. On this recording, Galway tackles some of the difficult recital repertoire for the flute, such as Jules Mouquet's "La Flûte de Pan," Phillipe Gaubert's "Nocturne et Allegro Scherzando," and Georges Hüe's "Fantasie." Galway's renditions of these works are characteristically flamboyant, but at the same time they display keen sensitivity to the contributions of his collaborators.

Musical Legacy

With his tireless performing schedule and his huge number of recordings, Galway has became one of the best-known flutists of his era. His willingness to cut across boundaries of genre has been important as a gateway experience for listeners to explore music they might not otherwise know. Among the early crossover classical artists, Galway paved the way for others to breach the traditional boundaries between popular and classical music.

Galway was knighted by Queen Elizabeth II in 2001, he was named the 1997 Musician of the Year by *Musical America*, and he has received numerous Record of the Year awards from *Billboard* magazine. In 2005 he was given the Outstanding Contribution to Classical Music Award at the Classic Brits Awards. In commemoration of his sixtieth birthday, RCA Victor Red Seal released a fifteen-disc retrospective of Galway's career. Galway has also edited several performing editions.

Carey L. Campbell

Further Reading

Galway, James. *An Autobiography*. New York: St. Martin's Press, 1979. Galway details the successes and trials of his childhood, his training, and his rise to fame. His comments about his teachers are especially enlightening.

_____. *The Flute*. New York: Schirmer Books, 1982. Galway provides a history of the flute, discusses playing techniques, and offers career advice.

Mann, William, with James Galway. *James Galway's Music in Time*. Englewood Cliffs, N.J.: Prentice-Hall, 1982. A music history textbook for nonspecialists that originated as a sixteen-part television series narrated by Galway. The text of Galway's introduction and his participation in this project reflect his concerns about classical music's accessibility.

Skowronek, Felix. *Speaking Out! Interviews With Eminent Flutists*. Seattle, Wash.: Seattle Flute Society, 1982. Interviews with various flutists, with both orchestral and solo artists represented. Galway reflects upon the work behind his accomplishments.

See also: Argerich, Martha; Denver, John; Kreisler, Fritz; Mahler, Gustav; Rampal, Jean-Pierre; Sondheim, Stephen; Wonder, Stevie.

Jerry Garcia
American rock singer, guitarist, and songwriter

A founding member and leader of the iconic band the Grateful Dead, Garcia was a prolific artist on the 1960's psychedelic countercultural scene, creating songs that captivated a legion of devout fans called Deadheads and inspiring artists in a variety of genres, including classical, jazz, folk, rock, and rap.

Born: August 1, 1942; San Francisco, California
Died: August 9, 1995; Forest Knolls, California
Also known as: Jerome John Garcia (full name)
Member of: Mother McCree's Uptown Jug Champions; the Grateful Dead; the Jerry Garcia Band; New Riders of the Purple Sage; Legion of Mary; Old and in the Way

Principal recordings

ALBUMS (solo or with various others): *Hooteroll?*, 1971 (with Howard Wales); *New Riders of the Purple Sage*, 1971; *Garcia*, 1972; *Compliments of Garcia*, 1974; *Old and in the Way*, 1975; *Reflections*, 1976; *Cats Under the Stars*, 1978 (with the Jerry Garcia Band); *Run for the Roses*, 1982; *Mother McCree's Uptown Jug Champions*, 1999.

ALBUMS (with the Grateful Dead): *The Grateful Dead*, 1967; *Anthem of the Sun*, 1968; *Aoxomoxoa*, 1969; *American Beauty*, 1970; *Workingman's Dead*, 1970; *Wake of the Flood*, 1973; *Grateful Dead from the Mars Hotel*, 1974; *Blues for Allah*, 1975; *Terrapin Station*, 1977; *Shakedown Street*, 1978; *Go to Heaven*, 1980; *In the Dark*, 1987; *Built to Last*, 1989.

ALBUMS (with David Grisman): *Garcia/Grisman*, 1991; *Not for Kids Only*, 1993; *Shady Grove*, 1996; *So What*, 1998; *The Pizza Tapes*, 2000 (featuring Tony Rice); *Grateful Dawg*, 2001; *Been All Around This World*, 2004.

WRITINGS OF INTEREST: *Harrington Street*, 1995 (autobiography); *Garcia: A Signpost to New Space*, 2003 (memoir).

The Life

Jerome John Garcia was the second son of Joseph Garcia, a swing band leader turned bar owner, and

Ruth Marie "Bobbie" Clifford, a nurse. Named after his mother's favorite composer, Jerome Kern, Garcia took an early interest in rock and roll, blues, and folk music.

In 1947 Garcia lost the middle finger on his right hand while chopping wood with his brother, Clifford "Tiff" Garcia. Later that summer, his father drowned while fishing on a family vacation in Northern California. Trying to support her family, Garcia's mother spent the majority of her time at the family's tavern, Joe Garcia's, and by the end of the year Jerry and Tiff had moved in with their maternal grandparents, who lived across the street from their home. Garcia viewed this separation as abandonment by his mother, and he developed a feeling of being unloved.

After remarrying for the second time in 1953, Bobbie moved the family twenty-five miles south of San Francisco to suburban Menlo Park. Regarded as highly intellectual, Garcia enrolled in the public school's Fast Learner Program for eighth grade in the fall of 1955, but because of his aversion to test taking, he did not graduate until two years later. While at school, Garcia immersed himself in art, creating murals and sets for school plays, and literature, exploring the works of D. H. Lawrence.

In June, 1957, Garcia moved back to San Francisco to live with his grandparents. That August Bobbie gave him an accordion for his fifteenth birthday, which she allowed him to trade in for an electric guitar. Garcia used the time he spent as a dishwasher at Joe Garcia's to learn, by ear, all the Chuck Berry songs he heard on the jukebox.

By the fall of 1957, when he entered Denman Junior High School in the Outer Mission District, Garcia was smoking cigarettes and marijuana. In 1958 he read Jack Kerouac's beat tale *On the Road* (1957), a book that solidified his connection to the budding alternative beatnik counterculture. By the end of 1960, Garcia, dismissing attempts to conform, joined a band, the Chords, after his mother transferred him to another suburban school.

Later Garcia enlisted in the Army, and he was discharged after a few months. He moved in with friends in Palo Alto, California, near Stanford University. While working the lights for a local theater production of *Damn Yankees* (1955) in March, 1961, he met future songwriting partner Robert Hunter. The two performed at local music spots, such as

Kepler's Books, where Garcia was first introduced to Ronald C. McKernan ("Pigpen") and St. Michael's Alley, where he met Phil Lesh. Garcia also met Sara Ruppenthal, a Stanford sophomore, at Kepler's Books. The two married on April 25, 1963; in December, Ruppenthal gave birth to their daughter, Heather. Ruppenthal and Garcia divorced when Heather was three.

Aside from performing with Hunter, Garcia worked as an acoustic guitar and banjo instructor. On New Year's Eve, 1963, he met Bob Weir. Weir and Pigpen would soon join Garcia in forming the jug band Mother McCree's Uptown Jug Champions.

In 1964, a defining year in Garcia's life, he tried the hallucinogenic drug LSD, legal at the time. In addition, the jug band transformed, with the addition of Lesh and Bill Kreutzmann, into the Warlocks. The Warlocks were aligned socially with Ken Kesey's Merry Band of Pranksters, an antiestablishment group, and often performed at the group's Acid Tests, where partyers knowingly or unknow-

Jerry Garcia. (AP/Wide World Photos)

ingly ingested LSD. In 1965 the Warlocks changed their name to the Grateful Dead, and Garcia's life as a highly successful musician and charismatic counterculture icon began. Garcia also became a father two more times: to Annabelle in 1970 and Theresa ("Trixie") in 1974. Garcia and the girls' mother, Carolyn Adams, nicknamed Mountain Girl by the Merry Pranksters, married in 1981.

Unfortunately, the following decades hosted mental and physical lows for Garcia. His mother, severely injured in an automobile accident in 1970, died a few weeks later. In 1986 Garcia slipped into a diabetic coma that lasted for five days. In 1993 he and Adams divorced; Garcia married Deborah Koons on Valentine's Day, 1994. His involvement with drugs escalated to include opiates as well as cocaine, and his health quickly deteriorated. On August 8, 1995, Garcia admitted himself to Serenity Knolls, a rehabilitation center twenty miles north of San Francisco. On August 9, 1995, at 4:23 in the morning, Garcia died of a heart attack.

The Music

Garcia's music mirrored the collective disenchantment members of the counterculture often found with notions of conformity inherent in American culture. Much more than arbitrary psychedelic experimentation, his songs represented highly constructed spaces where divergent musical techniques and society harmoniously collided. Believing that "art is not only something you do, but something you are as well," Garcia used his own life experiences as a basis for his compositions. Captivated by classical, blues, folk, and rock music, Garcia played eclectic music that crossed racial and socioeconomic boundaries. Blending these styles and sounds into one fluidly composed musical arrangement, Garcia successfully broke established social customs and demonstrated how music and culture could embrace diversity and multiplicity.

"Scarlet Begonias." One of five Garcia songs on the album *Grateful Dead from the Mars Hotel*, "Scarlet Begonias" debuted live on March 23, 1974, at San Francisco's Cow Palace. The song became a fan and band favorite because its complex composition and numerous instrumental solo sections provided for free-flowing improvisation. In live performances, "Scarlet Begonias" was frequently followed by "Fire on the Mountain," and this combination was

referred to as "Scarlet Fire." The lyrics "Strangers stoppin' strangers just to shake their hands" and "Everybody's playin' in the Heart of Gold Band," which appear at the end of "Scarlet Begonias," hold special meaning, affirming the intimate relationship between the fans and the band.

"Shakedown Street." The title song to the Grateful Dead's tenth album, "Shakedown Street," was Garcia's ode to disco. When the album was released in 1978, fans were wary, because disco was a divisive genre. While disco had legions of avid supporters, many others loathed the synthesized, repetitive nature of disco music. However, the band's fans learned through the Grateful Dead's live performances of it that the studio version of "Shakedown Street" was merely a launching pad for extended improvisation. "Shakedown Street" became synonymous with the area outside a performance venue where fans often doubled as vendors and sold an assortment of goods, ranging from T-shirts and food to drugs and drug paraphernalia.

"Touch of Grey." First played live on September 15, 1982, "Touch of Grey" did not appear on an album until five years later, on 1987's *In the Dark*. The lyrics were penned by Hunter, and Garcia composed for them an upbeat arrangement that caught notice. Released at a point when popular hit singles reigned, "Touch of Grey" brought mainstream mass-media attention to the country's most successful and popular touring band. As the refrain's lyrics shift from "I will survive" to "We will survive," the song advocates personal and collective perseverance and triumph. The most successful mainstream Grateful Dead song, it listed on the *Billboard* Top 10. The band produced its only music video for "Touch of Grey," and it aired as the culminating point on what MTV dubbed Day of the Dead. The song, however, divided the band's fan base. Some delighted in the mainstream's sudden interest in the band, while others felt the song paved the way for fair-weather fans who attended shows simply to hear one song, which, in traditional Grateful Dead form, was not played every night.

Musical Legacy

Garcia's music, especially that written and produced for the Grateful Dead, helped many individuals find peace and happiness in an alienating world, giving a voice to and kinship for members of the counterculture. Even after Garcia's death, people of various races, ages, genders, nationalities, and socioeconomic classes identified themselves as his fans. Rock-and-roll artists, rappers, and classical composers cite Garcia as an influential model. On September 29, 2005, ten years after his death, a group of such individuals came together in Berkeley, California, to celebrate Garcia's life, influence, and legacy at the tribute concert, Comes a Time: A Celebration of the Music and Spirit of Jerry Garcia.

Elizabeth Anne Yeager

Further Reading

Dodd, David, and Diana Spaulding. *The Grateful Dead Reader*. London: Oxford University Press, 2001. A vault of Grateful Dead information, with interviews, articles, lyric interpretations, and show reviews.

Gans, David. *Conversations with the Dead*. New York: Routledge, 1991. A collection of interviews with band members, including Garcia. Gans, a musician and self-identified Deadhead, hosted the radio program "The Grateful Dead Hour."

_____. *Not Fade Away*. New York: Avalon, 1995. A collection of fan stories and memories that were posted on the Internet in memory of Garcia immediately following his death. A key tool in examining the cultural impact of Garcia's life as well as his musical legacy.

Garcia, Jerry. *Harrington Street*. New York: Delacorte Press, 1995. This is an autobiographical and anecdotal personal history by Garcia.

Garcia, Jerry, Charles Reich, and Jann Wenner. *Garcia: The Rolling Stone Interview*. San Francisco: Straight Arrow Books, 1972. Detailed interview with Garcia during the Grateful Dead's formative years.

Hunter, Robert. *Box of Rain*. New York: Penguin, 1993. A collection of song lyrics and stories regarding song origins.

Jackson, Blair. *Garcia: An American Life*. New York: Penguin Books, 1999. A detailed biography of Garcia written by an established rock journalist and longtime Grateful Dead reporter. Jackson blends interviews with Garcia that cover a thirty-year span with those of other band members, close friends, family members, and business associates for a humane portrait of Garcia.

McNally, Dennis. *A Long Strange Trip*. New York: Broadway Books, 2002. Historiography of the Grateful Dead and individual members written by the band's official historian and longtime publicist.

See also: Anastasio, Trey; Carter, Maybelle; Dodge, Charles.

Art Garfunkel

American rock and folksinger and songwriter

Garfunkel, who formed a folk-rock duo with Paul Simon, is noted for his haunting and hushed vocal style.

Born: November 5, 1941; Queens, New York
Also known as: Arthur Ira Garfunkel (full name); Artie Garr
Member of: Tom and Jerry; Simon and Garfunkel

Principal recordings

ALBUMS (solo): *Angel Clare*, 1973; *Breakaway*, 1975; *Watermark*, 1977; *Fate for Breakfast*, 1979; *Scissors Cut*, 1981; *The Animals' Christmas*, 1986; *Lefty*, 1988; *Songs from a Parent to a Child*, 1997; *Everything Waits to Be Noticed*, 2002; *Some Enchanted Evening*, 2007.

ALBUMS (with Simon and Garfunkel): *Wednesday Morning, 3 A.M.*, 1964; *Parsley, Sage, Rosemary, and Thyme*, 1966; *The Sounds of Silence*, 1966; *Bookends*, 1968; *The Graduate*, 1968 (with others); *Bridge over Troubled Water*, 1970.

The Life

Arthur Ira Garfunkel (GAHR-fuhn-kuhl) was born in Queens, New York, to parents of Romanian Jewish descent. In sixth grade, Garfunkel met Paul Simon when they both appeared in their school's production of *Alice in Wonderland* (Garfunkel was the Cheshire Cat). As juniors at Forest Hills High School, the duo adopted stage names of Tom and Jerry, and they released a moderate-selling single entitled "Hey Schoolgirl." They also appeared on the televised dance show *American Bandstand*, sharing the bill with Jerry Lee Lewis. Their follow-up single was not successful, so they disbanded and went to college. Garfunkel attended Columbia University to study architecture (later obtaining a degree in art history) and performed occasionally as Artie Garr.

Garfunkel and Simon reunited in 1962, and they began performing in Greenwich Village folk coffeehouses before being signed to CBS Records by Tom Wilson. Their debut album, *Wednesday Morning, 3 A.M.*, sold only a few copies until Wilson had the single "The Sounds of Silence" overdubbed with electric instruments, which transformed it into a huge hit. After years of commercial success, Garfunkel decided to pursue an acting career, and the duo disbanded again. They have reunited for several performances, and both perform and record as solo artists.

The Music

Simon and Garfunkel performed primarily between 1957 and 1970. After being signed to CBS Records by Wilson in 1964, they released their debut album, *Wednesday Morning, 3 A.M.*, which was not a commercial success. The disappointed duo temporarily split, with Simon moving to Europe (and releasing his solo British album, *The Paul Simon Songbook*, in 1965), and Garfunkel pursuing a master's degree in mathematics from Columbia University. A year later, without their knowledge, Wilson used Bob Dylan's studio band to overdub "The Sounds of Silence" with electric guitar, bass, and drums, releasing it as a single and making it a number-one hit. Radio stations across the country began receiving requests for the song, and CBS decided to salvage the album. Simon returned to the United States to regroup with Garfunkel, and the two became stars. Though neither of them initially approved of Wilson's "electrified" version of their music, it was that folk-rock style that made them famous.

Early Works. The Wilson remixed single appeared on the duo's second album, *The Sounds of Silence*, which also featured material taken from *The Paul Simon Songbook*. A surprise success, the album contained the hits "Homeward Bound" and "I Am a Rock." Their next album, *Parsley, Sage, Rosemary, and Thyme*, contained such favorites as

"A Hazy Shade of Winter," "At the Zoo," "The Fifty-ninth Street Bridge Song" ("Feelin' Groovy"), and "Scarborough Fair."

The Graduate. Filmmaker Mike Nichols commissioned the duo to do some songs for the sound track of his 1967 film, *The Graduate*. The sound track was an instant hit, and in 1968 it knocked the Beatles' *White Album* off the top of the record charts. In 1969 the single "Mrs. Robinson" later won the first of several Grammy Awards for Simon and Garfunkel. Initially composed by Simon as a nostalgic salute to Americana, "Mrs. Robinson" began lyrically as "Mrs. Roosevelt." Nichols suggested the name change to relate it to his movie, and with that edge the duo ended up with a huge success. Their follow-up album, *Bookends*, became a number-one *Billboard* hit. The themes on the album were more complex than previously released albums, and it also included an updated version of "Mrs. Robinson."

Bridge over Troubled Water. At the height of their success, Simon and Garfunkel experienced pronounced personal differences. By 1969 Garfunkel was earnestly pursuing a film career, and he was given the role of Nately in Nichols's film adaptation of Joseph Heller's novel *Catch-22* (1961). Simon had also been promised a part in the film, but it was ultimately cut. Garfunkel's filming time conflicted with studio recording time for the duo's next album, *Bridge over Troubled Water*, causing further tension in their relationship. The album, featuring eleven tracks, took two years to complete. Despite the strain between Simon and Garfunkel, the album was one of the best-selling of the entire 1970's, and it won several Grammy Awards in 1971, including Album of the Year and Best Engineered Recording. The title track, featuring Garfunkel's unmistakable tenor, won Record of the Year and Song of the Year. That same year, they also won Best Contemporary Song and Best Arrangement Accompanying Vocalists.

Other highlights from the album include "The Boxer," "Cecilia," and "El Condor Pasa." Despite their overwhelming success, the duo separated in 1970, stating that their intention was not to part permanently, but rather to take a break from each other. Garfunkel divided his time between acting and a small solo career, and the two have occasionally reunited, recording hits and performing for packed venues. They were inducted into the Rock and Roll Hall of Fame in 1990.

Musical Legacy

Influenced by the Everly Brothers and Bob Dylan, Garfunkel and his partner Simon sang songs with themes that appealed to teenagers and adults alike. Their duets married the elements of folk music (sometimes incorporating actual folk songs, such as the traditional English tune "Scarborough Fair") with rock music (drums, electric guitars, bass). That musical coupling, combined with the duo's close vocal harmonies, clean-cut images, and distinct academic backgrounds, made them unique among the folk-rock musicians of the day.

Anastasia Pike

Further Reading

Charlton, Katherine. *Rock Music Styles: A History.* New York: McGraw Hill, 2008. This rock music textbook places Simon and Garfunkel in context with other folk-rock musicians of the day.

Grodin, Charles. *If I Only Knew Then: Learning from Our Mistakes.* New York: Springboard Press, 2007. In this collection, Garfunkel recounts what he learned from his experiences with the *Bookends* album. The essay gives an insight into his personality.

McLeod, Kembrew. "Simon and Garfunkel." In *St. James Encyclopedia of Popular Culture.* Detroit, Mich.: St. James Press, 1999. The entry on the duo provides a brief synopsis of their major works.

Unterberger, Richie. *Eight Miles High: Folk Rock's Flight from Haight-Ashbury to Woodstock.* Milwaukee, Wis.: Backbeat Books, 2003. This documents the evolution of the folk-rock movement from 1966 until the end of the decade, with details about Simon and Garfunkel's musical contributions.

_____. *Turn! Turn! Turn! The '60's Folk-Rock Revolution.* Milwaukee, Wis.: Backbeat Books, 2002. An interesting and resourceful book containing numerous interviews with many of folk-rock's revolutionaries.

See also: David, Hal; Dylan, Bob; Everly, Don and Phil; Iglesias, Julio; Lewis, Jerry Lee; Simon, Paul; Webb, Jimmy.

Judy Garland

American popular music and musical-theater singer

Garland achieved stardom as a childhood singer and actress, appearing in vaudeville, in cabarets, in films, and on stage. She went on to international renown in American films, starring in the 1939 classic The Wizard of Oz.

Born: June 10, 1922; Grand Rapids, Minnesota
Died: June 22, 1969; London, England
Also known as: Frances Ethel Gumm (birth name)

Principal works

MUSICAL THEATER (singer): *Judy Garland at the Palace: Two-a-Day,* 1951; *Judy Garland,* 1956; *Judy Garland: At Home at the Palace,* 1967.

Principal recordings

ALBUMS: *Judy Garland Souvenir Album,* 1940; *The Wizard of Oz,* 1940; *Judy Garland Second Souvenir Album,* 1943; *Judy Garland Third Souvenir Album,* 1949; *Easter Parade,* 1950; *Words and Music,* 1950; *Girl Crazy,* 1953; *Miss Show Business,* 1955; *If You Feel Like Singing,* 1955; *In the Good Old Summertime,* 1955; *Judy Garland with the MGM Orchestra,* 1956; *Alone,* 1957; *Harvey Girls,* 1957; *Meet Me in St. Louis,* 1957; *Judy in Love,* 1958; *The Letter,* 1959; *That's Entertainment,* 1960; *Gay Purr-ee,* 1961; *Judy at Carnegie Hall,* 1961; *The Magic of Judy Garland,* 1961; *The Garland Touch,* 1962; *I Could Go on Singing,* 1963; *Our Love Letter,* 1963; *Just for Openers,* 1964; *"Live" at the London Palladium,* 1965 (with Liza Minnelli).

SINGLES: "(Dear Mr. Gable) You Made Me Love You," 1937; "Oceans Apart," 1939; "How About You," 1941; "Yah-Ta-Ta Yah-Ta-Ta (Talk, Talk, Talk)," 1945; "Changing My Tune," 1946; "Send My Baby Back to Me," 1954; "Swanee," 1961.

The Life

Judy Garland was born Frances Ethel Gumm in Grand Rapids, Minnesota, to Frank and Ethel

Milne Gumm, former vaudevillians. From the age of two, she performed first with her two older sisters, Mary Jane and Virginia, singing "Jingle Bells" in her father's theater, and she was smitten by audience applause. To be closer to Hollywood, the family relocated to Lancaster, California, where her father bought a theater, where the Gumm sisters performed. Ethel Meglin's dance school taught them dancing, and they were showcased in the Kiddies dance troupe. They appeared in short films and with actor George Jessel at Chicago's Oriental Theatre.

Jessel persuaded them to change their name to the Garland Sisters in 1934, and Frances took the name Judy after the Hoagy Carmichael song "Judy." Garland signed with Metro-Goldwyn-Mayer in 1935, and at thirteen she went to school at the studio. With her powerful singing voice and her youthful charm, she won film roles. To support her active filming pace, she was administered drugs, and she then required drugs to sleep, leading to a lifetime of addiction. Garland was competitive, she

Judy Garland. (AP/Wide World Photos)

loved the critical praise, and her acting talents grew as she starred in major films, singing signature songs. Overwork created stress, and she had a breakdown. In 1948 Garland failed to complete several pictures, and she made attempts at suicide.

Garland's will to live and her career were revived on the international stage. Craving the attention and warmth of live audiences, Garland made a concert tour of England in 1951, and audiences were thrilled to hear her sing. The venues, including the London Palladium, were sold out, and her performances received rave reviews.

Garland made her second signature film, *A Star Is Born*, in 1954. She continued to appear in concert and on television specials. After suffering from hepatitis in November, 1959, she recovered fully to play again at the London Palladium. She appeared at Carnegie Hall in 1961, and she aired her own television show in 1962. In November, 1964, she sang again at the London Palladium. Her following concert tour in Australia hit a low point, and she performed for only forty-five minutes in Melbourne, announcing that she suffered from pleurisy. She was contracted for, then let go from, the film *Valley of the Dolls* (1967). Later she recovered sufficiently to perform with her children, Lorna Luft and Joey Luft, at New York's Palace Theatre in July, 1967.

Garland was married to David Rose from 1941 to 1944, to Vincente Minnelli from 1945 to 1951, to Sidney Luft from 1952 to 1965, to Mark Herron from 1965 to 1967, and to Mickey Deans in 1969. Garland died from an accidental drug overdose in 1969 in London.

The Music

Early Works. As part of the Meglin Kiddies, Garland made her film debut in *The Big Revue* (1929), and it was followed by *A Holiday in Storyland* (1930), in which she sang her first solo on screen. In *La Fiesta de Santa Barbara* (1935), filmed in Technicolor, the Gumm sisters trio sang "La Cucaracha." After signing with Metro-Goldwyn-Mayer in 1935, Garland sang "Zing! Went the Strings of My Heart" impressively in a radio performance for the *Shell Chateau Hour*. Showing her powerful adult voice, Garland recorded for Decca Records in June, 1936, "Swing Mr. Charlie" and "Stomping at the Savoy," her debut single with Bing Crosby's Orchestra. She appeared in Twentieth Century-Fox's college musical *Pigskin Parade* in November, 1936, singing "The Balboa," "The Texas Tornado," and "It's Love I'm After." Garland sang "After You've Gone" for the *Shell Chateau Hour*. She won considerable attention singing "You Made Me Love You" honoring Clark Gable at his studio-sponsored birthday party, and she filmed it in *Broadway Melody of 1938* (1937), crooning to his photograph. As a fresh singing duo, the team of Mickey Rooney and Judy Garland were paired in *Love Finds Andy Hardy* in 1937, and its success brought them eight additional musical films together.

"Over the Rainbow." In 1939 Garland played the role for which she would be most recognized, Dorothy in *The Wizard of Oz*, and she sang the song for which she would be most recognized, "Over the Rainbow." At sixteen, Garland was dressed in blue gingham and her hair was plaited in braids, a simple presentation that was designed to focus all the attention on her singing and acting. Producers Arthur Freed and Mervyn LeRoy and an international film audience gave their overwhelming approval of her performance. *The Wizard of Oz* proved a smash hit, and she received a special Juvenile Academy Award for her performance. Her next film was *Babes in Arms* (1939) with Mickey Rooney. Decca Records released her first album, *Judy Garland Souvenir Album*, in three discs.

"For Me and My Gal." Working through a frantic filming schedule in 1940, she starred in *Andy Hardy Meets Debutante*, *Strike Up the Band*, and *Little Nellie Kelly*. In the last film, Garland shared her first grown-up on-screen kiss. and she demonstrated her mature acting style by portraying the roles of both the mother and the daughter. In the Andy Hardy film, she sang "I'm Nobody's Baby," and her record made it to the Top 10. In 1941 Garland appeared in *Ziegfeld Girl*, *Life Begins for Andy Hardy*, and *Babes on Broadway*. In 1942 she starred with Gene Kelly in *For Me and My Gal*, and she received top billing for singing the film's signature song, with the record listing in the Top 10. Garland had reached stardom, propelled largely by her singing ability in film musicals. Beginning in 1941, at age twenty-one, Garland began to portray glamorous roles, and in 1943 she starred in *Presenting Lily Mars* and *Girl Crazy*. Garland made her concert debut with the Philadelphia Orchestra directed by André Kostelanetz on July 1, 1943, at the Robin Hood Dell outdoor theatre. She toured military service camps during World War II.

"The Trolley Song." In 1944 Garland had another big success with Metro-Goldwyn-Mayer's *Meet Me in St. Louis* directed by Vincente Minnelli. Judy sang songs that would prove to be some of her favorites—"The Trolley Song," "The Boy Next Door," and "Have Yourself a Merry Little Christmas"—all romantic and upbeat. "The Trolley Song" hit the Top 10, as did her album of movie songs. Her only dramatic nonsinging role was in 1945 in *The Clock*, with Robert Walker. Garland's first record to hit the Top 10 without first being sung in a film was "Yah-Ta-Ta Yah-Ta-Ta (Talk, Talk, Talk)," sung with Bing Crosby. Recognizing that Garland's fans desired to see her in singing film roles, the studio featured her in *The Harvey Girls* (1946), singing "On the Atchison, Topeka, and the Santa Fe." This was a career high point, which was followed by some low points. In 1947 Garland had difficulty completing *The Pirate*, suffering a mental breakdown and spending time in a private sanatorium. Ever the trouper, she bounced back from overwork to film *The Easter Parade*, costarring Fred Astaire, in 1948, and to film *Words and Music*, which produced a number-one sound track album. *In the Good Old Summertime* (1949) and *Summer Stock* (1950), which produced a Top 10 sound track album, proved to be her last films with Metro-Goldwyn-Mayer.

Going abroad to perform on stage at the London Palladium in April, 1951, she found again the adoration she craved, and she embarked on a major comeback. Applause and appreciation renewed her career aspirations and her vitality. Beginning on October 16, 1951, she played the Palace Theatre in New York, and she was presented a special Tony Award in 1952 for her revival of vaudeville traditions on the Broadway stage.

"Born in a Trunk." Garland and Sidney Luft formed Transcona, a production company that contracted to produce a remake of the musical *A Star Is Born*, a vehicle designed to propel Garland back to her former star status, with Warner Bros. supplying financial support. James Mason and Garland starred; George Cukor directed; Jack Warner supervised. The famous Garland "Born in a Trunk" medley was inserted into the film to showcase her musical performance talents and to help make the film a financial success. Largely because of the film's excessive length, however, it lost money. It did earn wide critical acclaim, and Garland was nominated for an Academy Award for Best Actress, winning a Golden Globe for Best Actress in a Musical Role in 1954. The sound track album released by Columbia Records became a Top 10 hit, and it was coordinated with a Garland television special, *Miss Show Business*, for which she received an Emmy Award nomination for Best Female Singer.

Garland further revived her singing career by appearing on television in the *Ford Star Jubilee* for three years, from 1955 to 1958, and doing a special live concert for *General Electric Theatre* on CBS in 1956. Garland also sang in Las Vegas at the New Frontier Hotel for fifty-five thousand dollars per week. She received the highest salary ever paid a Las Vegas entertainer in 1956. In 1958 Garland made the albums *Judy in Love* and *Judy Garland at the Grove*.

Judy at Carnegie Hall. Garland capitalized on her comeback success with her album *That's Entertainment* in 1960. *Judy at Carnegie Hall* recorded her appearance on April 23, 1961, at Carnegie Hall, which went to gold and number one on the charts. Garland filmed *Judgment at Nuremberg* (1961), for which she was nominated for both a Golden Globe and an Academy Award for Best Supporting Actress.

Many in the industry equated Garland's personal life with her starring role in her final film, *I Could Go on Singing* (1963), the story of an ambitious female singer striving for recognition. The sound track reached the Top 40. She appeared on television in *The Judy Garland Show* special in 1962, with guests Frank Sinatra and Dean Martin, and it was extended to a series in 1963. This series was nominated for an Emmy Award for Outstanding Performance in a Variety or Musical Program or Series. Her album *The Garland Touch*, released in 1962, reached the Top 20, and her album *Just for Openers* showcased songs sung in her television series. With Burt Lancaster, she made the dramatic film *A Child Is Waiting* (1963).

"Live" at the London Palladium. In November, 1964, Garland sang with her eighteen-year-old daughter Liza Minnelli at the London Palladium,

and this performance was filmed and recorded. The film version appeared on British television. The recording was used for the album *"Live" at the London Palladium*, and it was released in 1965 by Capitol Records. This success opened the way for another Garland singing tour of the United States. In 1967 she returned to the Palace Theatre in New York, and she produced a live album, *Judy Garland: At Home at the Palace*, released by ABC Records.

Musical Legacy

Several of Garland's recordings have been inducted into the Grammy Hall of Fame—"Over the Rainbow," "Have Yourself a Merry Little Christmas," "Get Happy," "The Trolley Song," and "The Man That Got Away." When the American Film Institute ranked the top one hundred movie songs over the last one hundred years, "Over the Rainbow" ranked number one, and the other four ranked from number eleven to number seventy-six. Posthumously, Garland was awarded a Grammy Lifetime Achievement Award in 1997, testimony to her musical resilience and her radiant vocal achievements.

Barbara Bennett Peterson

Further Reading

Clark, Gerald. *Get Happy: The Life of Judy Garland*. New York: Random House, 2001. This biography illustrates Garland's drive to succeed in her long-standing and multifaceted career.

Edwards, Anne. *Judy Garland*. New York: Simon & Schuster, 1975. A sympathetic portrayal of the nuanced life of Garland as a singing icon.

Luft, Lorna. *Me and My Shadows: A Family Memoir*. New York: Simon & Schuster, 1999. A laudatory biography, written by her daughter.

Shipman, David. *Judy Garland: The Secret Life of an American Legend*. New York: Hyperion, 1992. Fully illustrated biography relates the personal and professional life of Garland, using information from film institute archives and from an unpublished biography of Vincente Minnelli.

See also: Andrews, Dame Julie; Arlen, Harold; Ebb, Fred; Elliot, Cass; Kern, Jerome; Previn, Sir André; Ronstadt, Linda; Sinatra, Frank; Tormé, Mel.

Erroll Garner

American jazz songwriter and pianist

A self-taught musician of prodigious technique, Garner was known for the rhythmic independence of his left and his right hands. The composer of the standard "Misty," Garner was also known for his original and florid treatments of ballads.

Born: June 15, 1921; Pittsburgh, Pennsylvania
Died: January 7, 1977; Los Angeles, California
Also known as: Erroll Louis Garner (full name)

Principal recordings

ALBUMS: *Overture to Dawn, Vol. 1*, 1944; *Overture to Dawn, Vol. 2*, 1944; *Overture to Dawn, Vol. 3*, 1944; *Overture to Dawn, Vol. 4*, 1944; *Overture to Dawn, Vol. 5*, 1944; *Passport to Fame*, 1944; *Yesterdays*, 1944; *Erroll Garner and Billy Taylor*, 1945 (re-released as *Separate Keyboards*, 1945); *Gone with Garner*, 1945; *Serenade to Laura*, 1945; *Cocktail Time*, 1947; *Erroll Garner at the Piano*, 1949; *Erroll Garner Playing Piano Solos, Vol. 1*, 1949; *Erroll Garner Playing Piano Solos, Vol. 2*, 1949; *Erroll Garner Playing Piano Solos, Vol. 3*, 1949; *Erroll Garner Playing Piano Solos, Vol. 4*, 1949; *Garnering*, 1949; *Rhapsody*, 1949; *Encores*, 1950; *Erroll Garner Plays Gershwin and Kern*, 1950; *Long Ago and Far Away*, 1950; *Piano Moods*, 1950; *Piano Solos, Vol. 1*, 1950; *Piano Solos, Vol. 2*, 1950; *Plays for Dancing*, 1950; *Body and Soul*, 1951; *Garnerland*, 1951; *Gone-Garner-Gonest*, 1951; *Piano Stylist*, 1951; *Piano Variations*, 1951; *The Provocative Erroll Garner*, 1951; *Solo Flight*, 1952; *Contrasts*, 1954; *Erroll!*, 1954; *Erroll Garner Plays Misty*, 1954; *Mambo Moves Garner*, 1954; *The Original Misty*, 1954; *Afternoon of an Elf*, 1955; *Concert by the Sea*, 1955; *Solitaire*, 1955; *Solo*, 1955; *Erroll Garner*, 1956; *He's Here! He's Gone! He's Garner*, 1956; *The Most Happy Piano*, 1956; *Swinging Solos*, 1956; *Another Voice*, 1957; *Soliloquy*, 1957; *Paris Impressions, Vol. 1*, 1958; *Paris Impressions, Vol. 2*, 1958; *Dreamstreet*, 1959; *The One and Only Erroll Garner*, 1960; *Close-up Swing*, 1961; *Easy to Love*, 1961; *You Brought a New Kind of Love*, 1963; *Erroll Garner*, 1964; *Now Playing: A Night at the Movies*, 1964; *That's My Kick*, 1966; *Up in Erroll's Room*, 1968; *Feeling Is Believing*, 1970; *Gemini*, 1971; *Magician*, 1974.

The Life

Erroll Louis Garner was born into a musical family in Pittsburgh, Pennsylvania, in 1921. His father and older brother were professional musicians, and his three sisters were also musically gifted. Though his father encouraged him to take piano lessons, Garner preferred playing baseball. However, the lure of music eventually overcame his interest in sports, and he began learning to play piano by ear. Dodo Marmarosa and Billy Strayhorn, who lived nearby and who later became important jazz pianists, helped the fledgling pianist. Garner was playing professionally in the Pittsburgh area by the time he was twelve.

Garner moved to New York City in 1944, and by the end of the decade he was recording and performing extensively. In 1955 he recorded *Concert by the Sea*, one of the best-selling jazz records of all time. Garner's melodic, hard-swinging playing had tremendous popular appeal, and by the late 1950's he was one of the most well-known figures in jazz. His popularity extended beyond jazz audiences, and he appeared on television many times in the 1950's and 1960's. He toured Europe extensively in the early 1960's. He was also an occasional composer. He wrote his most well-known song, "Misty," in 1954. Garner died of a heart attack in 1977.

The Music

Garner began his career firmly rooted in the stride tradition of Fats Waller and James P. Johnson. His own style evolved quickly, retaining elements of stride and ragtime, but also showing the strong influence of swing pianists such as Teddy Wilson and Earl "Fatha" Hines. His ballad style reflects the influence of Art Tatum, containing florid, right-hand sixteenth- and thirty-second-note passages surrounding statements of the melody. Like Tatum, Garner left few spaces unfilled. His dense, two-hand chordal passages also recall Tatum. His ballad treatments, often containing extended introductions of unrelated material before the beginning of the actual song, are another signature of Garner's style.

Garner's up-tempo playing is often characterized by rhythmically propulsive left-hand quarter notes. This device represents an updated treatment of the left hand common in Scott Joplin's ragtime writing, expanding the voicings to four-note seventh chords in open position, often with a tenth between the outer voices. These left-hand voicings, which come directly from the stride piano style, recall the guitar style made famous by Freddie Green of the Count Basie Band. Over this rock-solid left hand, Garner superimposed melodies and improvised lines in octaves and block chords, a pianistic device often first attributed to Hines. Garner's right-hand lines were often played behind the beat, especially at medium tempi, sometimes lagging behind the left hand as much as an eighth note. This rhythmic independence between right and left hands, technically quite difficult, is one of the most identifiable traits of Garner's playing.

Erroll Garner. (CBS/Landov)

The Dial Sessions. Soon after moving to New York City in 1944, Garner began playing regularly at jazz clubs on Fifty-second Street. In February of 1947, he recorded a session in California with Charlie Parker, along with bassist Red Callender and drummer Doc West. Garner recorded several tunes, including "Bird's Nest" and "Cool Blues," for Dial Records. Although Garner afterward remembered the session as one of the highlights of his career, he was not a bebop player, and he never played with Parker again.

"Laura" *and* "Misty." Garner's first hit was the 1955 recording of the standard "Laura." The clearly stated melody (surrounded by lush block chords and florid right-hand lines) and its brevity (just under three minutes long, it contains a short introduction and coda surrounding a single statement of the song form) made the recording accessible to non-jazz audiences and no doubt account for its popular success. Garner wrote a number of songs, such as "Dreamy," "It Gets Better Every Time," "One Good Turn," and "No More Shadows," but his best-

known composition—and one of the most recorded standards of all time—is the ballad "Misty," written in 1954.

Concert by the Sea. Garner recorded extensively, and his records sold well. He was something of a legend in the music industry for his ability to record a great deal of music in a relatively short period of time: Most of his albums consist of first takes recorded in a single session. On September 19, 1955, he recorded one of the best-selling jazz albums of all time, *Concert by the Sea,* at a live concert in Carmel, California. This record contains the trademark Garner devices. The up-tempo versions of "I'll Remember April," "Red Top," and "It's All Right with Me" feature the now-famous left-hand strumming with right-hand octaves and block chords on the melody. Lush introductions to "Autumn Leaves" and "April in Paris" reveal the influence of Tatum. Medium-tempo versions of "They Can't Take That Away from Me" and "Teach Me Tonight" showcase his legendary dexterity, with the on-top-of-the-beat left-hand pulse supporting the laid-back right-hand line.

Musical Legacy

Garner's playing was highly idiosyncratic. While the particulars of his style were not widely imitated, his heavily orchestrated yet pianistic approach to arrangements of popular songs—with its wide dynamic range and imaginative variety of textures—has influenced generations of pianists. His innate lyricism, coupled with his imaginative yet accessible treatments of well-known melodies, made him immensely popular, and his hard-swinging right-hand lines and his sophisticated harmonic approach rooted him in the jazz tradition. One of the most impressive qualities of his playing is its sheer joy and ebullience.

Matthew Nicholl

Further Reading

Collier, James Lincoln. *The Making of Jazz: A Comprehensive History*. New York: Dell, 1978. This source covers the development of jazz piano, placing the contributions of the most well-known players in context. Includes numerous references to and biographical information about Garner.

Doerschuk, Robert. *88: The Giants of Jazz Piano*. San Francisco: Backbeat Books, 2001. This historical overview of jazz piano includes short portraits of important pianists, with a chapter on Garner.

Doran, James M. *Erroll Garner: The Most Happy Piano*. Metuchen, N.J.: Scarecrow Press, 1985. This resource contains extensive biographical information on Garner and a discography complete through 1985.

Feather, Leonard. *Encyclopedia of Jazz in the Sixties*. New York: Horizon Press, 1967. Contains photographs, a short discography, and biographical information about Garner.

Rizzo, Gene. *The Fifty Greatest Jazz Piano Players of All Time*. Milwaukee, Wis.: Hal Leonard, 2005. This book contains a chapter about Garner, placing his work and contributions in context with the historical development of jazz piano.

Taylor, Billy. *Jazz Piano: A Jazz History*. Dubuque, Iowa: William C. Brown, 1982. Written by a highly respected jazz pianist, this excellent overview of jazz piano contains numerous references to Garner, his influences, and his contributions.

See also: Blakey, Art; Burke, Johnny; Gershwin, George; Hancock, Herbie; Joplin, Scott; Kern, Jerome; Parker, Charlie; Tatum, Art; Waller, Fats.

Marvin Gaye
American soul singer and songwriter

Possessed of a soulful, passionate voice with great range and versatility, Gaye was a star in the early decades of soul music. Recording solo and duet hits with the 1960's Motown sound, in the 1970's he branched into groove-oriented albums with social and sensual content.

Born: April 2, 1939; Washington, D.C.
Died: April 1, 1984; Los Angeles, California
Also known as: Marvin Pentz Gay, Jr. (birth name)

Principal recordings

ALBUMS: *The Soulful Moods of Marvin Gaye*, 1961; *That Stubborn Kinda Fellow*, 1963; *Hello Broadway*, 1964; *Together*, 1964 (with Mary Wells); *When I'm Alone I Cry*, 1964; *How Sweet It Is to Be Loved by You*, 1965; *A Tribute to the Great Nat King Cole*, 1965; *Moods of Marvin Gaye*, 1966; *Take Two*, 1966 (with Kim Weston); *United*, 1967 (with Tammi Terrell); *I Heard It Through the Grapevine!*, 1968; *In the Groove*, 1968; *You're All I Need*, 1968 (with Terrell); *Easy*, 1969 (with Terrell); *M.P.G.*, 1969; *That's the Way Love Is*, 1970; *What's Going On*, 1971; *Trouble Man*, 1972; *Let's Get It On*, 1973; *Diana and Marvin*, 1974 (with Diana Ross); *I Want You*, 1976; *Here, My Dear*, 1978; *In Our Lifetime*, 1981; *Midnight Love*, 1982; *Dream of a Lifetime*, 1986; *Romantically Yours*, 1989.

The Life

Marvin Pentz Gay, Jr., was born in Washington, D.C., in 1939 to Marvin and Alberta Gay. Marvin, Sr., pastored a church with music-filled services, and Marvin, Jr., began singing in the church at the age of three, later learning piano and drums. Marvin, Sr., was a harsh parent who beat Marvin and his three siblings.

In 1956 Marvin, Jr., left high school to join the Air Force. An uncooperative soldier, he was discharged within a year. Soon after, he helped start the Marquees singing group; however, its single "Wyatt Earp" failed to become a hit. In 1958 he joined Harvey Fuqua's New Moonglows group.

When the Moonglows disbanded in 1960, he signed a contract with Berry Gordy's fledgling Motown Records in Detroit. On January 8, 1961, he married Gordy's sister, Anna, who was eighteen years his senior. He also added an "e" to his last name. Gaye's first hit, "Stubborn Kind of Fellow," came the next year, soon followed by other hits. With his good looks and sensual voice, Gaye was paired with some of Motown's leading female stars, including Mary Wells, Kim Weston, and Tammi Terrell.

On November 12, 1965, Gaye's son, Marvin Pentz Gaye III, was born, although his mother was apparently Anna's teenage niece Denise Gordy, with Anna's consent. Gaye and Anna adopted two more children over the next few years. In 1972 they separated and eventually divorced acrimoniously.

In 1971 Gaye's career took a new turn with the release of his socially conscious *What's Going On* album, reflecting the Vietnam-era turbulence in the United States. With the album's success, Gaye

Marvin Gaye. (AP/Wide World Photos)

moved to Los Angeles, purchased his own recording studio, and immersed himself in popular psychology, meditation, physical fitness, and use of cocaine. In 1977 Marvin married Jan Hunter, with whom he already had two children. With claims against him by his former wife Anna and the Internal Revenue Service, Gaye declared bankruptcy in 1978. Soon thereafter Jan started divorce proceedings. In difficult straits, Gaye embarked on international tours, eventually moving to Europe, where he continued to record successfully. Returning to the United States after a couple of years, he rented a home with his mother, who was recuperating from surgery. His father came to live with them and the two men often quarreled. On April 1, 1984, Marvin Gay, Sr., shot Gaye, killing him. Claiming self-defense, Gay pleaded no contest and was sentenced to five years' probation.

The Music

Singing in church from an early age, Gaye developed a wide range of vocal talents and a spiritual touch that he would never lose. At first Gaye tried for success as a romantic balladeer. Despite his smooth tenor and three-octave range, success would come only with Gaye's embrace of rhythm-and-blues, or, as it came to be known, soul music.

Motown Solo and Duet Hits. Gaye became one of Motown's first solo stars with such hits as "Stubborn Kind of Fellow," "Hitch Hike," "Can I Get a Witness," "I'll Be Doggone," and "How Sweet It Is." These songs epitomize the Motown sound with lush, symphonic instrumentation backing Gaye's energetic singing and gospel-like passion. "Can I Get a Witness" refers to the call-and-response of African American church preaching. Supported by a driving double beat of piano and drum that mimics rhythmic clapping in a church, Gaye sings both sweetly and with a rough edge. His vocals echoed by a male and female chorus, with horns chiming in, "Can I Get a Witness" is Gaye's most successful effort at transplanting the music of a Pentecostal church into the Motown sound.

Gaye's versatility was displayed to good effect in his 1964 duets "Once upon a Time" with Mary Wells and "What Good Am I Without You" with Kim Weston. In his 1966 hit recording "It Takes Two" with Weston, the power of Weston's voice easily matches Gaye's.

The most celebrated of his duets were with the more delicately voiced Tammi Terrell. They recorded a string of hits in 1967 and 1968, including "Your Precious Love," "If I Could Build My Whole World Around You," "Ain't Nothing Like the Real Thing," and "You're All I Need to Get By." Introduced by memorable drum sticking and bass lines, Gaye's and Terrell's yearning for each other on "Ain't No Mountain High Enough" is palpable. Although distraught by Terrell's tragic onstage collapse in October, 1967, and subsequent fatal illness, Gaye made a recording of "I Heard It Through the Grapevine" that hit number one on the pop charts and sold more than four million copies. Backed by ominous instrumentation, Gaye sings with pathos, and sometimes falsetto, of his lover's betrayal, his few tender notes beckoning her return.

What's Going On. Although Gordy resisted Gaye's idea of instilling social relevance into his songs, Gaye's best-selling album *What's Going On* was a milestone in soul music. *What's Going On* reflected the social turbulence in America, as Gaye sang of war and protest on the title track and on "What's Happening Brother"; poverty and civil rights on "Inner City Blues (Make Me Wanna Holler)"; environmental degradation on "Mercy Mercy Me (the Ecology)"; and spiritual themes on "Wholy Holy" and "God Is Love." Gaye was now increasingly producing and writing his own music, embellishing it with a mellow, relaxed sound marked by a funky, percussive beat and vocal overlays. Undergirded by groove-oriented bass and congas, Gaye's singing on *What's Going On* reflects his wide vocal range from soft tenor to angry shouts.

Later Works. *Let's Get It On* represented another departure for Gaye with the open eroticism of its title track. With the advent of disco he recorded the dance-oriented hit "Got to Give It Up" (1977). He expressed his bitterness over his divorce proceedings, as well as a hope for personal peace, in such songs as the rhythmically rich "Anger" from *Here, My Dear*, an album titled for his alimony settlement. It is hard not to hear a confessional element in Gaye's aggressive single "Ego-Tripping Out" (1979), where he brags of his magnetism to women. Gaye's embrace of New Age sexuality reached its height in his last big hit, Grammy Award-winning "Sexual Healing" (1982), which launched him on his troubled Midnight Love tour.

Musical Legacy

Gaye recorded some of the best 1960's Motown-sound songs. Whether joyous, yearning, moody, or plaintive—or anxious and vulnerable, as in his biggest Motown hit, "I Heard It Through the Grapevine"—Gaye sings with gospel-inspired exhilaration. His duets with Motown's female stars, especially Terrell, rank among popular music's finest love songs. In the 1970's and early 1980's, Gaye pioneered a distinctive musical trend, recording albums with songs that reflected social angst, erotic fulfillment, and personal troubles. Taking control of the production and content of his music, Gaye fashioned a relaxed, stylish sound, influenced by funk but tinged with the spiritual passion of his earlier days.

Howard Bromberg

Further Reading

Dahl, Bill. *Motown: The Golden Years*. Iola, Wis.: Krause, 2001. With more than one hundred rare photographs, the book focuses on twelve Motown superstars, including Gaye. Extensive quotes from Gaye's Motown writers and producers.

Dyson, Michael Eric. *Mercy, Mercy Me: The Art, Loves, and Demons of Marvin Gaye*. New York: Basic Civitas, 2004. Assesses Gaye's life and music in a cultural context.

Gaye, Frankie and Fred Basten. *Marvin Gaye, My Brother*. San Francisco: Backseat Books, 2003. Firsthand account of Gaye's troubles with his father at the beginning and end of his life.

Posner, Gerald. *Motown: Music, Money, Sex, and Power*. New York: Random House, 2002. Motown history, including founder Berry Gordy's efforts to dissuade Gaye from expanding to socially oriented records such as *What's Going On*.

Ritz, David. *Divided Soul: The Life of Marvin Gaye*. New York: Da Capo Press, 1991. By Gaye's cowriter on "Sexual Healing," based on extensive interviews with Gaye.

Taylor, Marc. *The Original Marvelettes: Motown's Mystery Girl Group*. Jamaica, N.Y.: Aloiv, 2004. History of the group that Gaye backed up with occasional drumming and songwriting.

Turner, Steve. *Trouble Man: The Life and Death of Marvin Gaye*. New York: Ecco Press, 2000. Straightforward biography with a comprehensive listing of Gaye's recordings, tours, and update on the people in his life.

See also: Cole, Nat King; Cooke, Sam; Dozier, Lamont; Holland, Eddie and Brian; Jagger, Sir Mick; Jamerson, James; Kirk, Rahsaan Roland; LaBelle, Patti; Mayfield, Curtis; Robinson, Smokey; Ross, Diana.

George Gershwin

American musical-theater and classical composer

Gershwin's ability to transcend the division between classical and popular music, in his career and individual works, makes him a uniquely American composer. His memorable songs and concert works draw from a variety of influences, including Broadway, African American jazz and blues, and European art music.

Born: September 26, 1898; Brooklyn, New York
Died: July 11, 1937; Beverly Hills, California
Also known as: Jacob Gershvin (birth name); Fred Murtha; Bert Wynn

Principal works

CHAMBER WORKS: *Lullaby*, 1919 (for string quartet); *Short Story*, 1925 (for violin and piano).
MUSICAL THEATER (music): *La La Lucille*, 1919 (lyrics by Arthur J. Jackson, Buddy G. DeSylva, and Irving Caesar; libretto by Fred Jackson); *Morris Gest's Midnight Whirl*, 1919 (revue; lyrics and libretto by DeSylva and John Henry Mears); *George White's Scandals*, 1920-1924 (revue; lyrics by Ira Gershwin; libretto by Andy Rice and George White); *A Dangerous Maid*, 1921 (lyrics by Ira Gershwin; libretto by Charles W. Bell); *The French Doll*, 1922 (lyrics and libretto by A. E. Thomas); *Our Nell*, 1922 (music with William Daly; lyrics by Brian Hooker); *Spice of 1922*, 1922 (revue; lyrics and libretto by Jack Lait); *Little Miss Bluebeard*, 1923 (lyrics by Ira Gershwin and DeSylva); *The Rainbow*, 1923 (lyrics by Clifford Grey and Hooker; libretto by Albert de Courville, Noel Scott, and Edgar Wallace); *Lady, Be Good!*, 1924

(lyrics by Ira Gershwin; libretto by Guy Bolton and Fred Thompson); *Primrose*, 1924 (lyrics by Desmond Carter and Ira Gershwin; libretto by George Grossmith and Bolton); *Sweet Little Devil*, 1924 (lyrics by DeSylva; libretto by Frank Mandel and Laurence Schwab); *Song of the Flame*, 1925 (music with Herbert Stothart; lyrics and libretto by Oscar Hammerstein II and Otto Harbach); *Tell Me More!*, 1925 (lyrics by Ira Gershwin and DeSylva; libretto by Thompson and William K. Wells); *Tip Toes*, 1925 (libretto by Bolton and Thompson); *Oh, Kay!*, 1926 (lyrics by Ira Gershwin and Howard Dietz; libretto by Bolton and P. G. Wodehouse); *Funny Face*, 1927 (libretto by Paul Gerard Smith and Thompson); *Strike Up the Band*, 1927 (libretto by Morrie Ryskind; based on George S. Kaufman's libretto); *Rosalie*, 1928 (music with Sigmund Romberg; lyrics by Ira Gershwin and Wodehouse; libretto by Bolton and William Anthony McGuire); *Treasure Girl*, 1928 (libretto by Thompson and Vincent Lawrence); *Show Girl*, 1929 (lyrics by Ira Gershwin and Gus Kahn; libretto by McGuire and J. P. McEvoy); *Girl Crazy*, 1930 (libretto by Bolton and John McGowan); *Of Thee I Sing*, 1931 (music with Ira Gershwin; libretto by Kaufman and Ryskind); *Let 'Em Eat Cake*, 1933 (libretto by Kaufman and Ryskind); *Pardon My English*, 1933 (libretto by Herbert Fields and Ryskind); *Porgy and Bess*, 1935 (folk opera; lyrics by Ira Gershwin and Dorothy Heyward; based on DuBose Heyward's novel *Porgy*); *The Show Is On*, 1936 (revue; libretto by David Freedman and Moss Hart).
OPERA: *Blue Monday*, 1922 (jazz operetta; libretto by Buddy G. DeSylva; later renamed *135th Street*).
ORCHESTRAL WORKS: *Rhapsody in Blue*, 1924; Piano Concerto in F, 1925; *An American in Paris*, 1928; *Cuban Overture*, 1932; *Second Rhapsody*, 1932 (for piano and orchestra); *Variations on "I Got Rhythm,"* 1934 (for piano and orchestra); *Catfish Row*, 1936 (five-movement suite for orchestra; adapted from *Porgy and Bess*).
PIANO WORKS: *Tango*, 1915; *Three Preludes*, 1926.
SONGS (music; lyrics by Ira Gershwin unless otherwise stated): "When You Want 'Em, You Can't Get 'Em, When You Got 'Em, You Don't

Want 'Em," 1916; "The Real American Folk Song (Is a Rag)," 1918; "Mischa, Jascha, Toscha, Sascha," 1919; "Swanee," 1919 (lyrics by Irving Caesar); "The Man I Love," 1924; "I Got Rhythm," 1930; "Let's Call the Whole Thing Off," 1937; "Nice Work If You Can Get It," 1937; "They Can't Take That Away From Me," 1937; "Our Love Is Here to Stay," 1938.

The Life

George Gershwin (GURSH-wihn) was the second son of Russian Jewish immigrants, Moishe and Rose Gershvin. His parents purchased a piano in 1910 so that George's older brother Ira could learn to play, but George proved to be more musically inclined. In 1914, four years after he began taking piano lessons, he dropped out of school to work for Jerome H. Remick and Company, a Tin Pan Alley music publishing company, as a song plugger, a pianist who demonstrated the company's songs to singers who might choose to perform them onstage. In 1917 Gershwin left his job to pursue a career on Broadway, first as an accompanist for rehearsals and concerts. Soon he was writing songs for Broadway shows and revues, and in 1919 the first musical with a score entirely by Gershwin, *La La Lucille*, enjoyed a moderate run and positive critical reception.

Between 1917 and 1933 Gershwin wrote songs and scores for more than two dozen Broadway musicals and revues, many of which were commercially and critically successful. (Beginning in 1924 the majority of his songs' lyrics were written by his brother Ira, an exceptionally talented and witty wordsmith.) He also composed several works for the concert stage and appeared as a piano soloist and conductor (almost always playing and conducting his own compositions). His celebrity increased steadily from the 1924 premiere of *Rhapsody in Blue* onward; in July, 1925, he was the first composer to have his face on the cover of *Time* magazine; in 1934 and 1935 he hosted a CBS radio show, *Music by Gershwin*.

Although he never married, Gershwin was romantically involved with a number of women, including several stage and screen actresses. Perhaps his most serious relationship was with Kay Swift, a fellow composer whose musical *Fine and Dandy* was a success in 1930. She was Gershwin's musical confidant, particularly on his opera *Porgy and Bess*, and the title of his 1926 musical, *Oh, Kay!*, may have been an homage to her.

In 1936 Gershwin moved to Hollywood with his brother Ira to write songs for Fred Astaire's films at RKO Pictures. During his time there, he became friends with the modernist composer Arnold Schoenberg; the two played tennis and talked about music, each admiring the other's work. Gershwin was unhappy with the constraints of working for the studio, expressing to friends his loneliness and desire to return to New York. His increasingly erratic behavior and worsening headaches were attributed to psychological problems, until on July 9, 1937, he fell into a coma; a spinal tap revealed a brain tumor. Surgery was unsuccessful, and Gershwin died two days later, at age thirty-eight.

The Music

Gershwin's output runs the gamut from seemingly effortless, frothy popular songs to ambitious and groundbreaking opera, but he did not keep the popular and serious sides of his career sealed off

George Gershwin. (Library of Congress)

from each other. The decidedly American nature of his music, which he consciously cultivated, can be seen in the confluence of elements from both sides of the tracks: The concert works include infectious rhythms and memorable melodies, while the popular songs are harmonically complex and ingeniously crafted.

Popular Songs. Gershwin was a veritable American Franz Schubert, composing hundreds of songs over the course of his short life. His songs have proved endlessly adaptable and attractive to singers and jazz musicians. Their style is marked by rhythmic energy, use of repeated notes, and harmonic inventiveness. The majority of Gershwin songs are complemented by his brother Ira's delightfully clever lyrics.

"Swanee," Gershwin's first hit (with lyrics by Irving Caesar), rocketed to best-seller status when entertainer Al Jolson began performing it in 1919. This ironic and rollicking pastiche of tropes from Stephen Foster songs was Gershwin's most profitable song and became Jolson's trademark.

A 1932 collection published by Random House, *George Gershwin Song-Book*, contains piano-vocal scores for eighteen of his popular songs, including "Fascinating Rhythm," "The Man I Love," "'S Wonderful," and "I Got Rhythm." The songs he wrote for films in the last year of his life are among his best loved, such as "Let's Call the Whole Thing Off," "They Can't Take That Away from Me," and "Love Is Here to Stay."

Rhapsody in Blue. Paul Whiteman, the self-proclaimed King of Jazz and director of a popular, all-white jazz band, commissioned Gershwin to compose a jazz piano concerto. The result was *Rhapsody in Blue*, a single-movement work whose 1924 premiere at New York City's Aeolian Hall propelled its composer to the forefront of the debate then raging about the artistic value of the new music called jazz. As orchestrated by Whiteman's staff arranger Ferde Grofé, *Rhapsody in Blue* features instruments that were then associated with jazz (including clarinet and banjo), as well as lively syncopated rhythms, blue notes, a showy part for the piano soloist, and a generous handful of memorable melodies. There are two recordings of *Rhapsody in Blue* with Gershwin at the piano, playing with panache and a remarkable lack of sentimentality; the piece has been performed and recorded count-

less times since, becoming the single most popular concert work by an American composer.

Concerto in F. Impressed by *Rhapsody in Blue*, New York Symphony conductor Walter Damrosch commissioned a piano concerto from Gershwin in 1925. The three-movement piece is in many ways reminiscent of those by Peter Ilich Tchaikovsky and Franz Liszt, with sweeping themes, grand and idiosyncratic orchestration, and a virtuosic part for the soloist. The slow middle movement, inspired by the blues, is especially expressive.

An American in Paris. Gershwin described this 1928 tone poem, inspired by visits to Paris, as "a rhapsodic ballet." (It has been choreographed for dancers several times, most famously by Gene Kelly in the 1951 film *An American in Paris*.) While it is an easy work to enjoy, featuring a number of winning melodies and engagingly innovative orchestration (including the use of taxi horns), it is also a highly complex and sophisticated composition, rewarding careful study.

Of Thee I Sing. A comedy satirizing American politics, *Of Thee I Sing* (1931) was the first musical to be awarded the Pulitzer Prize, in 1932. (The award went to those responsible for the show's book and lyrics: Morrie Ryskind, George S. Kaufman, and Ira Gershwin.) Its music is masterfully ironic and consistently interesting, and the work is a virtual operetta, featuring a structurally cohesive overture, solos, ensemble numbers that advance the plot, and several scenes that contain a steady succession of such numbers without any spoken dialogue.

Porgy and Bess. Gershwin's magnum opus was his American folk opera, with libretto by poet and playwright DuBose Heyward and additional lyrics by Ira Gershwin. The work, which premiered in 1935, tells the story of love and death on Catfish Row, an impoverished African American community in Charleston, South Carolina. Gershwin's score draws upon a wide variety of black musical styles, from spirituals and work songs to ragtime and blues, as well as upon American musical-theater and European operatic tradition. At the insistence of the Gershwin estate, the African American characters in *Porgy and Bess* have been played by black performers in every American production of the work. For decades, some have argued that the opera is marred by the libretto's racial stereotypes and demeaning dialect, while others believe that the humanity and complexity of the characters transcend the libretto's dated elements. While *Porgy and Bess* is the most famous and frequently performed American opera, it is best known for its songs, including "Summertime" and "It Ain't Necessarily So," which have been popular since the opera's premiere.

Musical Legacy

Gershwin's music is almost unrivaled for its ability to conjure the image of an iconic urban America: energetic, optimistic, confident, commercial, and yet sincere. Although he thought of himself as a typical New Yorker, the composer was at home with the heterogeneity of American culture, and he sought to reflect that national character in his work. Those who have criticized his concert music, particularly *Porgy and Bess*, as stylistically inconsistent or tasteless, have often failed to note that inclusiveness was part of a deliberate, nationalistic approach on Gershwin's part.

His ability to write music both instantly popular and enduring and his choice to draw upon a range of musical styles have had a lasting impact on subsequent generations of American composers. Today, much of the music composed for Broadway is deemed worthy of critical respect and scholarly attention, and the idea that serious contemporary art music might draw on elements from jazz and popular song is no longer shocking. Gershwin's groundbreaking output played an important role in shaping those attitudes.

Gwynne Kuhner Brown

Further Reading

Alpert, Hollis. *The Life and Times of Porgy and Bess: The Story of an American Classic*. New York: Alfred A. Knopf, 1990. A fascinating and well-researched history of Gershwin's opera, from the novel that first caught the composer's attention to fifty years of productions.

Carnovale, Norbert. *George Gershwin: A Bio-Bibliography*. Westport, Conn.: Greenwood Press, 2000. An extremely useful resource for researchers, including an extensive annotated bibliography, a list of works and performance dates, the names of performers who first performed songs, a discography, and a filmography.

Jablonski, Edward, and Lawrence D. Stewart. *The Gershwin Years*. Garden City, N.Y.: Doubleday, 1973. A chatty and readable biography of George and Ira Gershwin. Particularly valuable for its wealth of illustrations, including photographs, sketches, reproductions of manuscripts, playbills, letters, and more.

Pollack, Howard. *George Gershwin: His Life and Works*. Berkeley: University of California Press, 2006. Exhaustively researched and meticulously detailed. Particularly noteworthy is its substantial treatment of Gershwin's entire musical output. Illustrations, bibliography.

Rimler, Walter. *A Gershwin Companion: A Critical Inventory and Discography, 1916-1984*. Ann Arbor, Mich.: Popular Culture Ink, 1991. Contains background information, descriptions, and analytical notes on all of Gershwin's published music in chronological order. Numerous unpublished works are cataloged as well. Discography.

Schiff, David. *Gershwin: Rhapsody in Blue*. Cambridge, England: Cambridge University Press, 1997. Concise and useful account of the work, including its history, reception, influence, and musical analysis and insights. Select bibliography.

Schneider, Wayne, ed. *The Gershwin Style: New Looks at the Music of George Gershwin*. New York: Oxford University Press, 1999. New essays by twelve highly regarded scholars are featured, with topics including score analysis, reception history, and performance issues.

Wyatt, Robert, and John Andrew Johnson, eds. *The George Gershwin Reader*. New York: Oxford University Press, 2004. A valuable source of primary documents and selected secondary literature, including letters to and from the composer, newspaper reviews, interviews with original cast members from *Porgy and Bess*, essays by Gershwin, eulogies and reminiscences, and a few scholarly articles. Bibliography.

See also: Arlen, Harold; Bechet, Sidney; Beiderbecke, Bix; Burton, Gary; Carter, Benny; Charles, Ray; Cooke, Sam; Copland, Aaron; Davis, Sammy, Jr.; Dorsey, Thomas A.; Evans, Bill; Gershwin, Ira; Goodman, Benny; Grappelli, Stéphane; Hammerstein, Oscar, II; Heifetz, Jascha; Lewis, John; Merman, Ethel; Nichols, Red; Romberg, Sigmund; Steiner, Max; Stoller, Mike; Strayhorn, Billy; Tatum, Art; Webster, Ben; Whiteman, Paul.

Ira Gershwin

American musical-theater lyricist and composer

Gershwin was a witty, skillful, and musically sensitive lyricist, particularly well attuned to the rhythm and energy of his younger brother George's music. With his gift for ingenious wordplay and delightfully singable word choices, he is widely considered one of the finest lyricists of his era.

Born: December 6, 1896; New York, New York
Died: August 17, 1983; Beverly Hills, California
Also known as: Israel Gershvin (birth name); Arthur Francis

Principal works

MUSICAL THEATER (lyrics; music by George Gershwin unless otherwise stated): *George White's Scandals*, 1920-1924 (revue; libretto by Andy Rice and George White); *A Dangerous Maid*, 1921 (libretto by Charles W. Bell); *Little Miss Bluebeard*, 1923 (lyrics with Buddy G. DeSylva); *Lady, Be Good!*, 1924 (libretto by Guy Bolton and Fred Thompson); *Primrose*, 1924 (lyrics with Desmond Carter; libretto by George Grossmith and Bolton); *Two Little Girls in Blue*, 1924 (music by Vincent Youmans and Paul Lannin; libretto by Fred Jackson); *Tell Me More!*, 1925 (lyrics with DeSylva; libretto by Thompson and William K. Wells); *Tip Toes*, 1925 (libretto by Bolton and Thompson); *Oh, Kay!*, 1926 (lyrics with Howard Dietz; libretto by Bolton and P. G. Wodehouse); *Funny Face*, 1927 (libretto by Paul Gerard Smith and Thompson); *Strike up the Band*, 1927 (libretto by Morrie Ryskind; based on George S. Kaufman's libretto); *Rosalie*, 1928 (music by George Gershwin and Sigmund Romberg; lyrics with Wodehouse; libretto by Bolton and William Anthony McGuire); *Treasure Girl*, 1928 (libretto by Thompson and Vincent Lawrence); *Show Girl*, 1929 (lyrics with Gus Kahn; libretto by McGuire and J. P. McEvoy); *Girl Crazy*, 1930 (libretto by Bolton and John McGowan); *Of Thee I Sing*, 1931 (music with George Gershwin; libretto by Kaufman and Ryskind); *Let 'Em Eat Cake*, 1933 (libretto by Kaufman and Ryskind); *Pardon My English*, 1933 (libretto by Herbert Fields and Ryskind); *Porgy and Bess*, 1935 (folk opera; lyrics with Dorothy Heyward; based on DuBose Heyward's novel *Porgy*); *The Show Is On*, 1936 (revue; libretto by David Freedman and Moss Hart); *Ziegfeld Follies of 1936*, 1936 (revue; music by Vernon Duke); *Lady in the Dark*, 1941 (music by Kurt Weill; libretto by Hart); *The Firebrand of Florence*, 1945 (libretto with Edwin Justus Mayer; music by Weill; based on Mayer's play *The Firebrand*); *Park Avenue*, 1946 (music by Arthur Schwartz; libretto by Nunnally Johnson and Kaufman); *My One and Only*, 1983 (libretto by Peter Stone and Timothy S. Mayer).

SONGS (lyrics; music by George Gershwin unless otherwise stated): "When You Want 'Em, You Can't Get 'Em, When You Got 'Em, You Don't Want 'Em," 1916; "The Real American Folk Song (Is a Rag)," 1918; "Mischa, Jascha, Toscha, Sascha," 1919; "The Man I Love," 1924; "I Got Rhythm," 1930; "Let's Call the Whole Thing Off," 1937; "Nice Work If You Can Get It," 1937; "They Can't Take That Away From Me," 1937; "Our Love Is Here to Stay," 1938; "Long Ago and Far Away," 1944 (music by Jerome Kern); "The Man That Got Away," 1954 (music by Harold Arlen).

The Life

Ira Gershwin (I-ruh GURSH-wihn) was the first child of Russian Jewish immigrants, Moishe and Rose Gershvin. A quiet, studious boy and avid reader of poetry, he developed a particular appreciation for light verse and began writing his own. After dropping out of City College of New York in 1916, he took a variety of jobs, while submitting verse to newspapers and magazines.

In 1917 Ira began providing some lyrics for his brother George, whose career as a songwriter was getting under way. They first published a cowritten song, "Waiting for the Sun to Come Out," in 1920. For this and other early lyrics, Ira used the pseudonym Arthur Francis (based on the names of their younger brother and sister respectively). He collaborated with other composers, as George did with other lyricists, but by the mid-1920's they were a well-established team, and the majority of George's songs until his death in 1937 featured his brother's lyrics. Ira generally wrote lyrics to fit George's music, but there was much give and take between them as they worked to complete a song.

Ira and his wife Leonore moved to Hollywood in 1936, to work in films along with George. They would live there for the rest of their lives. After George's death, Ira worked with other composers on Broadway musicals and films until 1954, at which point he largely retired. He devoted himself to his brother's legacy, donating a wealth of George Gershwin-related material to the Library of Congress. He died in 1983.

The Music

Musical Comedies. From 1924 until 1933 Ira wrote the lyrics for a series of mostly successful musical comedies with music by his brother, beginning with *Lady, Be Good!* and including *Oh, Kay!*, *Funny Face*, *Girl Crazy*, and *Pardon My English*. Each show contains a mixture of comic songs and ballads, the former witty and colloquial, the latter poignant but free of excessive sentimentality. Among the classic songs from these shows are "Fascinating Rhythm" from *Lady, Be Good!*, "Someone to Watch over Me" from *Oh, Kay!*, and "Embraceable You" and "I Got Rhythm" from *Girl Crazy*.

Political Satires. In 1927 Ira and George joined with playwright George S. Kaufman to create *Strike up the Band*, a biting political satire about war profiteering. This operetta offered Ira his first chance at lyrics that were fully integrated into the plot. A revised version in 1930, with libretto improved by Morrie Ryskind and the addition of more love songs, was substantially more successful than the 1927 production.

Two more political operettas followed, created by the same foursome: *Of Thee I Sing* and *Let 'Em Eat Cake*. Ira Gershwin's lyrics for these works rival those of W. S. Gilbert (of Gilbert and Sullivan fame) for ingeniousness. *Of Thee I Sing* was the Gershwins' longest-running show on Broadway and garnered Ira, along with Ryskind and Kaufman, the first Pulitzer Prize ever awarded for a musical.

Porgy and Bess. Ira contributed significantly to the libretto for George's *Porgy and Bess*. He wrote the lyrics for several songs, including "It Ain't Necessarily So" and "There's a Boat Dat's Leavin' Soon for New York," and collaborated with librettist DuBose Heyward on others, such as "I Got Plenty o' Nuttin'" and "I Loves You, Porgy." Gershwin helped Heyward, who was an accomplished novelist and poet but a novice lyricist, to make his lyrics more natural and singable.

Hollywood. The songs that the Gershwin brothers wrote during their brief time together in Hollywood are among their best, such as "They Can't Take That Away from Me" and "Let's Call the Whole Thing Off" from *Shall We Dance?* (1937), and "Love Is Here to Stay" (*The Goldwyn Follies*, 1938), the last song George composed before his death in 1937. Ira's lyrics for these songs, with their wonderfully mundane details and seemingly effortless eloquence, are the perfect complement to some of George's most memorable music.

Lady in the Dark. Of his various collaborations after 1937, perhaps the most significant was *Lady in the Dark*, with the book by Moss Hart and score by Kurt Weill. Gershwin's sophisticated, contemporary, and often hilarious lyrics were an ideal fit for this ambitious musical about a woman's psychoanalysis, with extended dream sequences that Weill called "one-act operas." The show ran for 467 performances, beginning in 1941.

Ira Gershwin. (Library of Congress)

Musical Legacy

Happy throughout his life to take a backseat to his famous brother, Ira's contribution to the golden era of Broadway songwriting has been increasingly appreciated over the years. His musically sensitive, endlessly inventive, and brilliantly witty lyrics have played an important role in the ongoing popularity of dozens of Gershwin songs.

While his best-known work was done in collaboration with his brother, Ira went on to work with several other notable composers, including Weill, Aaron Copland, Jerome Kern, and Harold Arlen. In addition, Ira was a dedicated guardian of his brother's legacy after 1937, working to ensure that his music was preserved at the Library of Congress and protected from infringement.

Gwynne Kuhner Brown

Further Reading

Furia, Philip. *Ira Gershwin: The Art of the Lyricist*. New York: Oxford University Press, 1996. Detailed and illuminating examination of Gershwin's lyrics by an English professor. Illustrated.

Gershwin, Ira. *Lyrics on Several Occasions: A Selection of Stage and Screen Lyrics Written for Sundry Situations; and Now Arranged in Arbitrary Categories. To Which Have Been Added Many Informative Annotations and Disquisitions on Their Why and Wherefore, Their Whom-For, Their How; and Matters Associative*. New York: Limelight Editions, 1997. Anecdotes and witty comments from the lyricist.

Jablonski, Edward. "What About Ira?" In *The Gershwin Style: New Looks at the Music of George Gershwin*, edited by Wayne Schneider. New York: Oxford University Press, 1999. An engaging account of Ira's artistic life after George's death.

Jablonski, Edward, and Lawrence D. Stewart. *The Gershwin Years*. Garden City, N.Y.: Doubleday, 1973. An informative biography of George and Ira Gershwin. Particularly valuable for numerous photographs, sketches, reproductions of manuscripts, playbills, letters, and more.

Kimball, Robert, ed. *The Complete Lyrics of Ira Gershwin*. New York: Alfred A. Knopf, 1993. A mostly chronological collection of more than seven hundred lyrics, many previously unpublished, with information about each. Includes anecdotes from Gershwin's *Lyrics on Several Occasions*. Illustrations.

Kimball, Robert, and Alfred Simon. *The Gershwins*. New York: Atheneum, 1973. A sprawling collection of lyrics, photographs, excerpts from Ira Gershwin's diary, lists of shows and songs, and lore, with an introduction by Richard Rodgers.

McClung, Bruce. *Lady in the Dark: Biography of a Musical*. Oxford, England: Oxford University Press, 2007. A well-researched history and analysis of the Weill musical, from conception to revivals. Bibliography, illustrations, score excerpts.

Rosenberg, Deena. *Fascinating Rhythm: The Collaboration of George and Ira Gershwin*. New York: E. P. Dutton, 1991. Rev. ed. Ann Arbor: University of Michigan Press, 1997. Explores the brothers' working relationship and oeuvre. Includes score excerpts, photographs, bibliography, and discography.

See also: Arlen, Harold; Cohan, George M.; Fitzgerald, Ella; Gershwin, George; Kern, Jerome; Merman, Ethel; Newman, Alfred; Petty, Tom; Romberg, Sigmund; Ronstadt, Linda; Taylor, James; Tormé, Mel; Weill, Kurt.

Stan Getz

American jazz saxophonist and composer

With his signature tone quality on the tenor saxophone, Getz introduced the bossa nova craze of the early 1960's and influenced countless jazz musicians.

Born: February 2, 1927; Philadelphia, Pennsylvania
Died: June 6, 1991; Malibu, California
Also known as: Stanley Gayetzky (birth name)
Member of: Thundering Herd

Principal recordings

ALBUMS: *All Star Series*, 1946; *The Brothers*, 1949; *The New Sounds*, 1949; *Prezervation*, 1949; *Quartets*, 1949; *Stan Getz and Tenor Sax Stars*, 1949; *Getz Age*, 1950; *Modern World*, 1950; *The*

Sounds of Stan Getz, 1950; *Split Kick*, 1950; *Billie and Stan*, 1951; *Chamber Music*, 1951; *The Sound*, 1951; *Moonlight in Vermont*, 1952; *Stan Getz Plays*, 1952; *Diz and Getz*, 1953 (with Dizzy Gillespie); *Interpretations by the Stan Getz Quintet, Vol. 1*, 1953; *Interpretations by the Stan Getz Quintet, Vol. 2*, 1953; *Interpretations by the Stan Getz Quintet, Vol. 3*, 1953; *The Melodic Stan Getz*, 1953; *More West Coast Jazz with Stan Getz*, 1953; *Stan Getz '57*, 1953; *Stan Getz Plays Blues*, 1953; *Another Time, Another Place*, 1954; *Eloquence*, 1954; *Stan Getz and the Cool Sounds*, 1954; *For Musicians Only*, 1956; *Hamp and Getz*, 1955 (with Lionel Hampton); *Stan Getz Quintet*, 1955; *West Coast Jazz*, 1955; *The Steamer*, 1956; *Award Winner: Stan Getz*, 1957; *The Getz/J. J. Set 1957*, 1957 (with J. J. Johnson); *Getz Meets Mulligan in Hi-Fi*, 1957 (with Gerry Mulligan); *The Soft Swing*, 1957; *Stan Getz and Gerry Mulligan/Stan Getz and Oscar Peterson*, 1957 (with Mulligan and Oscar Peterson); *Stan Getz and the Oscar Peterson Trio*, 1957 (with Peterson); *Imported from Europe*, 1958; *Jazz Giants '58*, 1958; *Stan Getz with Cal Tjader*, 1958; *Stan Meets Chet*, 1958 (with Chet Baker); *Cool Velvet*, 1960; *Jazz Jamboree '60*, 1960; *Stan Getz at Large, Vol. 1*, 1960; *Stan Getz at Large, Vol. 2*, 1960; *Focus*, 1961; *Rhythms*, 1961; *Stan Getz and Bobby Brookmeyer*, 1961; *Big Band Bossa Nova*, 1962; *Jazz Samba*, 1962 (with Charlie Byrd); *Getz/Gilberto*, 1963 (with João Gilberto); *Jazz Samba Encore!*, 1963 (with Luiz Bonfa); *Reflections*, 1963; *Stan Getz with Guest Artist Laurindo Almeida*, 1963; *Chick Corea/Bill Evans Sessions*, 1964 (with Chick Corea and Bill Evans); *Stan Getz and Bill Evans*, 1964; *Look at Yesterday*, 1965; *Mickey One*, 1965; *Quartet in Paris*, 1966; *A Song After Sundown*, 1966; *Voices*, 1966; *What the World Needs Now: Stan Getz Plays Bacharach and David*, 1966; *Sweet Rain*, 1967; *Didn't We*, 1969; *Marakesh Express*, 1969; *Change of Scenes*, 1971; *Communications '72*, 1971; *Dynasty*, 1971; *Captain Marvel*, 1972; *But Beautiful*, 1974 (with Evans); *The Best of Two Worlds*, 1975 (with Gilberto); *The Master*, 1975; *The Peacocks*, 1975 (with Jimmy Rowles); *Affinity*, 1977; *Another World*, 1977; *Children of the World*, 1978; *Forest Eyes*, 1979; *Stan Getz*, 1979; *Autumn Leaves*, 1980; *Billy Highstreet Samba*, 1981; *Blue Skies*, 1982; *Pure Getz*, 1982; *Line for Lyons*, 1983 (with Baker); *Poetry*, 1983; *Voyage*, 1986; *The Lyrical Stan Getz*, 1988; *Just Friends*, 1989; *Soul Eyes*, 1989.

The Life

Stanley Getz was born in Philadelphia. Proficient on the harmonica, string bass, and alto saxophone, he decided to pursue a jazz career, declining a bassoon scholarship to Juilliard.

By age fifteen, Getz was playing saxophone at New York City's Roseland Ballroom and touring with trombonist Jack Teagarden. After stints with Stan Kenton and Jimmy Dorsey, Getz recorded with Benny Goodman in 1945, performing his first solo. After Goodman fired him, he joined Woody Herman's band, the Thundering Herd, and he was a charter member of the famous Four Brothers saxophone section.

Getz moved to California, formed his own quintet, and released the successful *Moonlight in Vermont*. During the 1950's he recorded with jazz luminaries Chet Baker, Dizzy Gillespie, Count Basie, and Lionel Hampton. Getz spent the end of the decade in Denmark. In 1961 he collaborated with guitarist Charlie Byrd on *Jazz Samba* and with João Gilberto and Astrud Gilberto on *Getz/Gilberto*, a Grammy Award winner.

During the 1970's Getz joined the jazz fusion movement, but he returned to his traditional bop roots. The 1980's, in part, were spent as an artist-in-residence at Stanford University while he continued to record. In 1988 he was stricken with liver cancer and suffered a hemorrhage. Getz died in June, 1991, at his home in Malibu, California.

The Music

Like many renowned jazz musicians, Getz had a distinctive sound, flawless rhythm and technique, and creativity. From the 1940's through the 1980's, Getz crafted his style on the tenor saxophone with the utmost care. Like many of his jazz compatriots, he was trained in the ballroom dance bands and progressed to sharing the stages and recording studios with jazz giants. The instant popularity of bossa nova propelled him to new heights and opened up opportunities for further musical exploration with voices, string orchestras, and electric-fusion jazz. Later in life, Getz regretted that he had

Stan Getz. (AP/Wide World Photos)

never formally studied the arts of orchestration and composition. Consequently, he worked with composers who knew how he played and could arrange or write music to fit his needs and style. Getz usually studied the prepared score, then he proceeded to play strictly by ear.

"Early Autumn." It was during his time with Herman's band, the Thundering Herd, that Getz launched his solo career and developed his unmistakable tone. He joined the second edition of the Thundering Herd in 1947 as a member of the Four Brothers, along with Serge Chaloff, Zoot Sims, and Herbie Steward. This saxophone section—consisting of three tenor and one baritone—created a sound quite different from the standard two alto, two tenor, and one baritone saxophone configuration of most big bands. Besides the namesake arrangement titled "Four Brothers," the band had a certified hit with "Early Autumn." Getz demonstrated an incomparable ability to romanticize a

melody with his lyrical and mellow tone. His solo on "Early Autumn" established Getz as rising star.

Moonlight in Vermont. When Getz left Herman's orchestra, he moved to New York and formed his own quartet. Guitarist Johnny Smith invited him to a session for a quintet recording on the Roost label, released as *Moonlight in Vermont.* The title-track version of the well-known standard sold not only to jazz aficionados but also to the general public. It was voted Jazz Record of the Year by *Down Beat* magazine. With Smith's simple and supportive chordal guitar and his masterful arrangements, Getz's solos were at times technically incredible and at other times wispy and refined. The quality of performance is even more remarkable considering that Getz was addicted to heroin at the time.

Focus *and* Jazz Samba. Getz's recordings during the 1950's were a mixture of various-size groups, and they included such artists as Gillespie, Horace Silver, Oscar Peterson, and others. Although he was well known and admired, Getz had not yet distinguished himself as an innovator. After he returned from Europe to America in 1961, he recorded the remarkable album *Focus* with strings. *Focus* allowed Getz to improvise over the richly orchestrated string arrangements of Eddie Sauter. The result was sensational. The next year, Getz and guitarist Charlie Byrd recorded the bossa nova-inspired *Jazz Samba.* The album included "Desafinado," which won the Grammy Award for Best Jazz Performance. It was the first jazz album to attain a number-one ranking on the pop charts.

Getz/Gilberto. "The Girl from Ipanema," from the album *Getz/Gilberto*, stayed ninety-six weeks on the charts, with the song and the album winning Grammy Awards. The union of Brazilian samba and American jazz catapulted Getz into the limelight, much to the delight of Verve Records. Bossa nova, like cool jazz, was a blend of colorful timbres, restrained techniques, and mellow tone qualities— with a Brazilian beat. The collaboration of Gilberto and Getz was a great success, both commercially and artistically.

Musical Legacy

As a boy, Getz practiced eight hours a day for two years in order to fulfill his dream of becoming a jazz saxophonist. He became a major figure in the cool jazz era of the 1950's, and he popularized bossa nova-Brazilian jazz in the early 1960's. His lush and romantic tone occupies a singular place in jazz history. Others have tried, without success, to imitate his tone. Unfortunately, his lifelong battle with alcohol and heroin cut his career short. The Berklee School of Music in Boston honors Getz's legacy by housing the Stan Getz Media Center and Library, made possible by a donation from the Herb Alpert Foundation. Eight thousand compact discs, tapes, laser discs, and CD-ROMS are stored there.

Douglas D. Skinner

Further Reading

Budds, Michael J. *Jazz in the Sixties: The Expansion of Musical Resources and Techniques.* Iowa City: University of Iowa Press, 1978. Provides insights into Getz and the jazz samba movement, with information specific to the 1960's.

Churchill, Nicholas. *Stan Getz: An Annotated Bibliography and Filmography, with Song and Session Information for Albums.* Jefferson, N.C.: McFarland Books, 2005. A bibliography with more than two thousand citations, some annotated. Periodicals, articles, dissertations, films, Web sites, and more are included.

Gelly, Dave, and Stan Getz. *Stan Getz: Nobody Else But Me.* Milwaukee, Wis.: Backbeat Books, 2002. Getz's autobiography provides insights into his improvisational style, his unique tone, his substance abuse, and his criminal acts.

Maggin, Donald L. *Stan Getz: A Life in Jazz.* New York: HarperCollins, 1997. Biography with emphasis on Getz's addictions to heroin and alcohol as well as details on his musical career.

Ostransky, Leroy. *Understanding Jazz.* Englewood Cliffs, N.J.: Prentice-Hall, 1977. Ostransky, a jazz educator, presents an overview of jazz history to the 1970's. Includes several references to Getz.

Wein, George. *Myself Among Others: A Life in Music.* New York: Da Capo Press, 2003. Wein led an active life as a club owner and promoter, and he maintained a close relationship with many jazz artists. His reflections on Getz are included.

See also: Alpert, Herb; Bacharach, Burt; Burton, Gary; Corea, Chick; Davis, Miles; Gilberto, João; Gillespie, Dizzy; Hampton, Lionel; Iglesias, Julio; Jobim, Antônio Carlos; Legrand, Michel; Peterson, Oscar; Young, Lester.

Barry, Maurice, and Robin Gibb

English rock and rhythm-and-blues singers, songwriters, and guitarists

Winners of multiple Grammy Awards, the Bee Gees—brothers Barry, Maurice, and Robin Gibb—were successful as a soft-rock act in the late 1960's and early 1970's and as leading superstars of the disco-music era in the late 1970's.

Barry Gibb
Born: September 1, 1946; Isle of Man, England
Also known as: Barry Allan Crompton Gibb (full name)

Maurice Gibb
Born: December 22, 1949; Isle of Man, England
Died: January 12, 2003; Miami, Florida
Also known as: Maurice Ernest Gibb (full name)

Robin Gibb
Born: December 22, 1949; Isle of Man, England
Also known as: Robin Hugh Gibb (full name)
Members of: The Bee Gees

Principal recordings

ALBUMS (as the Bee Gees): *Bee Gees Sing and Play Fourteen Barry Gibb Songs*, 1965; *Spicks and Specks*, 1966; *Bee Gees 1st*, 1967; *Horizontal*, 1968; *Idea*, 1968; *Odessa*, 1969; *Cucumber Castle*, 1970; *Trafalgar*, 1971; *Two Years On*, 1971; *To Whom It May Concern*, 1972; *Life in a Tin Can*, 1973; *Mr. Natural*, 1974; *Main Course*, 1975; *Children of the World*, 1976; *Saturday Night Fever: Original Soundtrack*, 1977 (with others); *Spirits Having Flown*, 1979; *Living Eyes*, 1981; *E. S. P.*, 1987; *One*, 1989; *High Civilization*, 1991; *Size Isn't Everything*, 1993; *Still Waters*, 1997; *This Is Where I Came In*, 2001.

ALBUMS (Barry, solo): *Now, Voyager*, 1984; *Shine, Shine*, 1984.

ALBUMS (Robin, solo): *Robin's Reign*, 1970; *How Old Are You?*, 1983; *Secret Agent*, 1984; *Walls Have Eyes*, 1985; *Magnet*, 2003; *My Favourite Carols*, 2006.

The Lives

Barry Allan Crompton Gibb, born on September 1, 1946, and his fraternal twin brothers Robin Hugh Gibb and Maurice Ernest Gibb, born on December 22, 1949, were three of five children of Hugh Gibb, a bandleader, and Barbara Gibb, a singer. The three Gibb brothers made their first performances at local film theaters in Manchester in 1955, singing between shows. They performed under an assortment of names, including the Blue Cats and the Rattlesnakes.

In 1958 the family moved to Brisbane, Australia. The trio, known as the Brothers Gibb, continued performing at talent shows, and they caught the attention of a local deejay, Bill Gates. They ultimately got their own local television show in Brisbane, and they took the name the Bee Gees (for Brothers Gibb). They secured their first recording contract in 1962 with the Festival Records label in Australia. They were incredibly popular, in the press and on television, and they performed to enthusiastic audiences.

By late 1966, they had made a decision to abandon the Australian music world and return to England, which had launched the British Invasion.

Robin, Barry, and Maurice Gibb (from left). (AP/Wide World Photos)

During their trip back to England, the Gibbs learned that the Bee Gees had at last topped the charts back in Australia with their final release, *Spicks and Specks*. The group had forwarded demo recordings ahead of time to England, and *Spicks and Specks* had attracted the notice of producer Robert Stigwood. Stigwood signed the trio to a five-year contract upon their arrival.

In 1969 the trio got into a disagreement over a double album called *Odessa*. Since the brothers could not agree on which song was to be the single, Robin decided to leave the group. Even Barry and Maurice parted company for a while. In 1970 they resolved their differences and re-formed the group.

In 1977 the group was contacted about contributing to the sound track of a film entitled *Saturday Night Fever*. Their featured songs—"Stayin' Alive," "How Deep Is Your Love," and "Night Fever"—became number-one hits, and the album stayed in the top spot for twenty-four weeks, while the film broke existing box-office records. A fourth Gibb brother, Andy, also had enormous chart success during this same period as a solo singer.

By the end of the 1970's, however, disco had fallen out of favor. The Bee Gees experienced a backlash for their domination of the airwaves, with mass burnings of Bee Gees posters and albums at public forums sponsored by radio deejays. Some radio stations did not play new releases by the group after 1979. The Bee Gees participated (at Stigwood's persistence) in the film *Sgt. Pepper's Lonely Hearts Club Band* (1978), loosely inspired by the Beatles' album and songs. The film was a box-office and critical failure.

Due to their association with the disco era, the successes and opportunities they found in the 1960's and 1970's eluded them in the 1980's. Barry worked as a producer creating hits for artists such as Barbra Streisand and Diana Ross. Even though the older Gibb brothers had struggled with the abuse of alcohol and drugs, the youngest sibling, Andy, died in 1988, five days after his thirtieth birthday, from heart condition complications created by the use of cocaine.

The Bee Gees stayed active in the music industry until the untimely death of Maurice in January, 2003. While getting treatment for an intestinal blockage, he suffered cardiac arrest and died at the age of fifty-three. After his death, Robin and Barry chose to stop performing as the Bee Gees.

The Music

The Bee Gees' records are widely recognized for their gorgeous melodies, tight three-part harmonies, and lush orchestral arrangements (contributed by conductor Bill Shepherd). The lyrics of these songs are romantic yet complex, with a melancholy tinge. Barry and Robin took turns singing lead vocals, harmonizing together and with Maurice. Barry played rhythm guitar, while Maurice, along with singing background vocals, played bass, piano, organ, Mellotron, and other instruments.

In the late 1960's, the Bee Gees began to deconstruct elements in the singing and harmonies of black American music and to rebuild them in their style. After getting back together in the early 1970's, their relationship improved, and they evolved musically out of pop-psychedelia and into pop-progressive rock. In their disco years, the Bee Gees began to use falsetto in their songs. By 1977 the Bee Gees were heard on black radio stations that were usually reluctant to play any white acts. The group managed to merge all their influences—from the Mills Brothers to the Beatles and early 1970's soul—into their signature sound.

"To Love Somebody." "To Love Somebody" is the second single released by the Bee Gees in 1967 from their album *Bee Gees 1st*. The song was originally written by Barry and Robin for soul legend Otis Redding, but the singer died in a plane crash before he could record the song. The Bee Gees decided to record their own version of the song, with Barry taking the lead vocals. It has become one of the most famous Gibb compositions. "To Love Somebody" is a soulful ballad in the style of 1960's rhythm-and-blues and soul groups such as Sam and Dave. The song follows the typical late 1960's soft-rock style, with opulent orchestral arrangements featuring prominent solos by the violin, harp, trumpet, and flute. This soul standard has

been covered by many artists, including Nina Simone, Janis Joplin, and Michael Bolton.

"Nights on Broadway." "Nights on Broadway" is the second single from *Main Course*. "Nights on Broadway" established Barry's falsetto voice in the chorus. While recording, the producer Arif Martin asked if one of the Bee Gees could do some screaming during the main chorus to make the song more exciting. In return, Barry began singing higher and higher, revealing a surprising yet powerful falsetto. It was a defining moment in the Bee Gees' musical style. This legendary falsetto became a hallmark of the Bee Gees sound.

"Stayin' Alive." "Stayin' Alive" was released as a single in 1977, the group's second hit from the album *Saturday Night Fever: Original Soundtrack*, one of the best-selling film sound tracks of all time. Partly because it was played in the opening scene of the tremendously successful disco film, "Stayin' Alive" is one of the Bee Gees' most popular and most identifiable songs. The lyrics and the bouncy backbeat of "Stayin' Alive" mirror the central character (played by John Travolta) as he coolly struts along the streets of New York. The chorus features the famous falsetto vocals and the percussive background track.

"Alone." "Alone" is the opening track and first single on the multiplatinum *Still Waters* album released by the Bee Gees in 1997. The song is a melancholy pop ballad written by Barry, Robin, and Maurice and recorded in 1996. The use of bagpipes and upbeat tempo conflict with the sad lyrics of the song. This highly criticized album was the Bee Gees' attempt to get into the adult contemporary music market. This particular song was considered one of the standout tracks, displaying the Bee Gees' unique blend of soft rock and falsetto.

Musical Legacy

At numerous times throughout their careers, the Gibb brothers endured commercial dry spells and critical backlash. Nonetheless, the legacy of the Bee Gees is marked by the extraordinary success of their *Saturday Night Fever* disco period, their continuing pop appeal, and the contemporary standards they produced ("To Love Somebody," "How Can You Mend a Broken Heart"). Many hit covers of the Bee Gees' songs have been recorded by such artists as Janis Joplin, Al Green, Destiny's Child, and Feist.

The band's music has also been sampled by dozens of hip-hop artists, including Wyclef Jean. The Bee Gees demonstrated a remarkable musical adaptability and an astonishing aptitude for creating hits.

In recognition, the Bee Gees have twice received Britain's Ivor Novello Trust for Outstanding Contribution to British Music (1988, 1997) and the BRIT Award (1997). In 1994 they were placed in the Songwriters Hall of Fame. Their induction into the Rock and Roll Hall of Fame in 1997 led to the release of the album *Still Waters*.

Samantha Ryan Barnsfather

Further Reading

Bebbington, Warren. *The Oxford Companion to Australian Music*. New York: Oxford University Press, 1997. This resource, which contains biographies of chief musical figures and groups and lists of musical organizations and companies, musical works, genres, instruments, and terms, has an extended reference on the Bee Gees.

Bee Gees. *Bee Gees Anthology*. Milwaukee, Wis.: Hal Leonard, 1991. This forty-three-song anthology includes the group's music for piano, vocal, and guitar. It provides a brief discography, bibliography, and song-by-song recollection from each one of the Gibbs.

Bilyeu, Melinda, Hector Cook, and Andrew Mon Hughes. *The Bee Gees: Tales of the Brothers Gibb*. London: Omnibus Press, 2004. With a heavy reliance on press clippings and interviews, this seven-hundred-page book covers the life of the Gibb family members, beginning in the 1940's and ending with the death of Maurice. Includes appendixes, a complete album and singles discography, a cover versions list, and a bibliography with books, magazines, newspapers, and Web sites.

English, David. *The Legend: The Illustrated Story of the Bee Gees*. London: Quartet Books, 1983. Illustrated by Alex Brychta, this cartoon biography of the Bee Gees portrays Barry as "Lionheart," Robin as the "Red Setter," and Maurice as an "Eager Beaver." English was a close friend of Barry Gibb, and his book is a favorite among Bee Gees' fans because it captures the personalities of the Gibb brothers.

Leaf, David. *Bee Gees: The Authorized Biography by Barry Gibb, Robin Gibb, and Maurice Gibb*. London:

Octopus Press, 1979. Although authorized, this book is surprisingly frank about many aspects of their lives and careers. It contains hundreds of black and white photographs, a discography, and a song list until the late 1970's.

See also: Harrison, George; Joplin, Janis; Lennon, John; McCartney, Sir Paul; Ross, Diana; Simone, Nina; Streisand, Barbra.

Gilberto Gil
Brazilian singer, guitarist, and songwriter

A famous artist of the MPB (Música Popular Brasileira) generation, Gil promotes the music and culture of Brazil. The components of compassion and social conscience in his music have made his work popular throughout the world.

Born: June 29, 1942; Salvador, Brazil

Principal recordings

ALBUMS: *Vira mundo*; *Louvação*, 1967; *Frevo rasgado*, 1968; *Cérebro eletrônico*, 1969; *Nega*, 1971; *Expresso 2222*, 1972; *Gil e Jorge*, 1975 (with Jorge Ben); *Refazenda*, 1975; *Refavela*, 1977; *Refestança*, 1978; *Nightingale*, 1979; *Realce*, 1979; *Brasil*, 1981; *Luar (A gente precisa ver o luar)*, 1981; *Um banda um*, 1981; *Extra*, 1983; *Quilombo*, 1984; *Raça humana (Human Race)*, 1984; *Dia dorim noite neon*, 1985; *Personalidade*, 1987; *Soy loco por ti America*, 1987; *Um trem para as estrelas*, 1987; *O eterno deus mu dança*, 1989; *Parabolic*, 1991; *Acoustic*, 1994; *Caetano y Gil: Tropicalia 2*, 1994; *Indigo Blue*, 1997; *Quanta*, 1997; *Copacabana mon amour*, 1998; *O sol de Oslo*, 1998; *Quanta Live*, 1998; *Me You Them*, 2000; *Gilberto Gil and Milton Nascimento*, 2001; *Kaya n'gan daya*, 2002; *Z: 300 anos de Zumbi*, 2002; *Eletracústico*, 2004; *As canções de "Eu tu eles,"* 2005; *Gil luminoso*, 2006; *Rhythms of Bahia*, 2006.

The Life

Gilberto Gil (zhihl-BEHR-toh zhihl) was born in Salvador, the capital of the Brazilian state of Bahia, but he grew up in Ituaçu, a small town in the interior of Bahia. His early musical influences were varied, including the folk music of the sertão (the remote, sparsely populated interior of northeastern Brazil), especially the accordion music of Luiz Gonzaga; European classical music; North American jazz; Afro-Cuban music; and the polkas and waltzes of Europe. Not surprisingly, his first instrument was the accordion, but he switched to guitar after he heard Antônio Carlos Jobim's "Chega de Saudade" (No More Blues) in 1958.

He received a degree in business administration from the federal university in Salvador, and he worked for a year for a São Paulo corporation before becoming a full-time musician. In 1965 he released his first single. The year after, Elis Regina's recording of Gil's "Louvação" (Praise) became a hit, and the same year his song "Ensaio Geral" (General Rehearsal) was awarded a prize at an important MPB (Música Popular Brasileira) festival. Música Popular Brasileira is a form of urban popular music that combines traditional Brazilian music with contemporary influences. In 1967, along with Caetano Veloso (whom he had met at the university), he founded the radical musical movement Tropicalia.

Briefly imprisoned without charges by the ruling military junta in 1969, Gil moved to England, returning to Brazil in 1972. Throughout the late 1980's and 1990's, Gil continued to record and to perform, though at this time he became active in politics. He took time off from his musical career to serve as the secretary of culture for the city of Salvador and as a member of its city council.

Gil has performed all over the world, while releasing a steady stream of both popular and critically acclaimed recordings, including two that won Grammy Awards: *Quanta Live* and *Eletracústico*. Brazilian President Lula da Silva named Gil Minister of Culture in 2003, and Gil served in that post for five years.

The Music

Gil's earliest recordings exhibit the social awareness that has typified his writing throughout his career. His first release contained the protest songs "Roda" (Circle) and "Procissão" (Procession). *Louvação* contained his version of the song made famous by Regina. These early songs shared the theme of the redemption of the common man from oppression.

Gilberto Gil. (AP/Wide World Photos)

Tropicalia. The Tropicalia movement—freely absorbing and transforming any and all musical influences—was effectively launched by Gil and Veloso with their entries in the 1967 TV Record Festival. Gil's entry, "Domingo no Parque" (Sunday in the park), was emblematic of the Tropicalia aesthetic: It mixed a wide and disparate array of musical and cultural elements in a modern and cinematic way. The song, arranged by avant-garde composer-conductor Rogério Duprat, was heavily influenced by the production techniques of the Beatles' song "A Day in the Life," mixing folk rhythms and instruments, electric guitars, and sound effects. While the Tropicalia movement was effectively over by the early 1970's, Gil's music continued to display the eclecticism made possible by the movement's suspension of musical boundaries.

Spirituality. When he returned from England in 1972, Gil was firmly committed to his own spiritual and artistic cultivation. The ideas of rebirth, revival, and growth are common themes in his lyrics. "Oriente," which he wrote that year, contains a subtle wordplay on the idea of the individual orienting himself or herself spiritually in the world and an obvious reference to Eastern philosophy implicit in the song's title. A number of tunes from the same period, such as "Então Vale a Pena" (then it's worth it) and "A Morte" (a death), are meditations on death and the perspective it offers on the nature and value of life.

Gil was deeply affected by his experiences performing in Africa in 1976, and much of his music since then is concerned with exploring his African roots. His 1980 collaboration with Jimmy Cliff, which included the cover of Bob Marley's "No Woman, No Cry," brought reggae to Brazil.

Reaching the Mainstream. In the late 1970's and early 1980's, Gil performed extensively in the United States and Europe. During this period, he released two recordings in the United States, *Nightingale* and *Human Race*. At the same time, he consciously shifted his musical focus from the poetic and artistic concerns of the song to the accessibility of the rhythm. His exploration of the dance rhythms of afoxé, reggae, funk, soul, and rock was a deliberate attempt to make his music more popular and to reach a wider audience. His concern with black culture, personal spiritual growth, and social justice remained, however. He saw the mass-audience appeal of dance music as a vehicle to reach out to a wide international audience.

Quanta. The 1997 album *Quanta*, containing twenty powerful songs, is an example of Gil at his most prolific. Stylistically diverse and with unusually high production values, the album represents Gil at the peak of his abilities. The live version of the materials from the album won a Grammy Award in 1998.

Musical Legacy

Gil's musical career represents the successful resolution of a paradox. At once sacred and profane, his work has mass appeal without sacrificing honesty and integrity. Like the seeming opposites of Gil himself—politician and pop star—his music reconciles the sensuality of dance music with the spirituality of personal and societal salvation. Gil's powerful message of hope and redemption, aligned with the celebration of his African heritage,

is an inspiration to the people of the African diaspora. Nevertheless, his appeal and his message are not exclusive to any one group, no matter what their race, and they embrace all who share the human experience.

Matthew Nicholl

Further Reading

Gil, Gilberto. *Songbook, Vol. 1 and Vol. 2.* Edited by Almir Chediak. Rio de Janeiro: Luniar Editora, 1992. This collection has more than one hundred Gil songs, along with essays about his life and music, in Portuguese with English translation. The lead sheets and essays have been reviewed and approved by Gil.

McGowan, Chris, and Rocardo Pessanha. *The Brazilian Sound.* Philadelphia: Temple University Press, 1998. This well-researched book tells the story of Brazilian popular music, beginning with samba at the beginning of the twentieth century, and covering the development of bossa nova and MPB (Música Popular Brasileira). Excellent photographs, discography, and bibliography.

Murphy, John P. *Music in Brazil: Experiencing Music, Expressing Culture.* New York: Oxford University Press, 2006. This book provides an excellent presentation of the cultural context of contemporary Brazilian popular music, and it contains numerous references to Gil and other MPB musicians. Includes a sampler compact disc.

Perrone, Charles A. *Master of Contemporary Brazilian Song: MPB, 1965-1985.* Austin: University of Texas Press, 1989. Provides cultural and musical context for the songwriting of five important MPB songwriters: Chico Buarque, Veloso, Gil, Milton Nascimento, and João Bosco. Includes biographical detail and translations and analyses of many song lyrics.

Schreiner, Claus. *Música Brasileira: A History of Popular Music and the People of Brazil.* New York: Marion Boyars, 1993. This resource is written by a German radio producer and journalist who has been involved in the Latin music scene since the early 1970's. Includes references to Gil, a bibliography, a glossary, an index, and a list of samba schools in Rio de Janeiro.

See also: Gilberto, João; Jobim, Antônio Carlos; Nascimento, Milton.

João Gilberto

Brazilian Latin guitarist, singer, and songwriter

Gilberto created the subdued, lyrical style of bossa nova by transforming the composition and performance of samba canção (samba song), introducing Brazilian popular music to the world.

Born: June 10, 1931; Salvador, Bahia, Brazil
Also known as: João Gilberto Prado Pereira de Oliveira (birth name)

Principal recordings

ALBUMS: *Chega de saudade*, 1959; *Brazil's Brilliant*, 1960; *Gilberto and Jobim*, 1960 (with Antônio Carlos Jobim); *O amor, o sorriso e a flor*, 1960; *Samba de uma note so*, 1960; *João Gilberto*, 1961; *The Boss of the Bossa Nova*, 1962; *Getz/Gilberto*, 1963 (with Stan Getz); *The Warm World of João Gilberto*, 1964; *João Gilberto en Mexico*, 1974; *Best of Two Worlds*, 1976; *Amoroso*, 1977; *Brasil*, 1981 (with others); *João Gilberto*, 1988; *The Brazilliance Music of Rhythm*, 1990; *Performance*, 1991; *João*, 1992; *Bossa Nova Jubileu, Vol. 1*, 1994; *Bossa Nova Jubileu, Vol. 2*, 1994; *Ela e' carioca*, 1994; *Eu sei que vou te amar*, 1994; *Musica!*, 1998; *Prado Pereira de Oliveira*, 1999; *Besame mucho*, 2000; *João voz e violão*, 2000; *So João*, 2000.

The Life

The youngest of six children of a prosperous businessman who lived in the interior of northeast Brazil, João Gilberto Prado Pereira de Oliveira (zhoo-OW zheel-BEHR-toh) early demonstrated an exceptional affinity for music. Skilled in the guitar and immersed in Brazilian and American popular music, he sought a musical career, moving to Rio de Janeiro in his late teens. Although he was recognized for his musical talent, he was withdrawn and temperamental, unable to hold a steady position with a musical group. He moved to various cities, finally settling again in Rio de Janeiro in 1956.

Throughout these itinerant years, resolutely composing and practicing, he developed the bossa nova (new wave) beat. The composer-lyricist duo Antônio Carlos Jobim and Vinicius de Moraes rec-ognized the resonance of Gilberto's style, and began to record his music in 1958.

Attracting attention in the United States, Gilberto moved to New York in 1962, recorded with Stan Getz, performed at Carnegie Hall, and collaborated with Frank Sinatra. After a two-year period in Mexico, Gilberto returned to New York, settling definitively in Rio de Janeiro in 1980. He married the singer Astrud Weinert in 1960. After their divorce, he married the singer Miúcha Buarque de Holanda in 1968. Their daughter is the singer Bebel Gilberto.

The Music

Gilberto wove the alluring web of bossa nova from numerous strands. Sung slowly and softly, the music achieved a warm intimacy. Its spare simplicity and gliding improvisation achieved a rich lyricism, accentuated by the play of syncopated dissonance against a dominant harmony in the interaction of solo voice and instrument. This interplay was underscored by the so-called stuttering (gago) guitar. The effect was like that of a piano nocturne, one hand playing a slight disrhythm overlaid by a dominant harmonizing hand.

Three phases define Gilberto's musical development. The first was the matured emergence in Brazil of bossa nova, encapsulated principally in three albums: *Chega de saudade*, *O amor, o sorriso e a flor*, and *João Gilberto*. The next phase was the diffusion around the world of bossa nova from the collaborative base Gilberto established with American musicians in the United States from 1962 to 1980. Among the principal albums of this phase are *Getz/Gilberto* and *Best of Two Worlds*, along with the one from his Mexican sojourn, *João Gilberto en Mexico*. The third phase extends over the period since his return to Brazil in 1980, characterized by recordings of works of the historic creators of Brazilian popular music and with the leading contemporary Brazilian artists of that genre. Prominent albums include *Prado Pereira de Oliveira*, *Brasil*, the Montreux Jazz Festival discs, *Eu sei que vou te amar*, and *João voz e violão*.

"Chega de saudade." This vanguard music of bossa nova was the first in which Jobim incorporated Gilberto's distinctive rhythm. With lyrics by de Moraes, this song was first recorded on a single by Elisete Cardoso in 1958. Gilberto's rendition appeared a year later on the *Chega de saudade* album.

"Bim Bom." This onomatopoeic presentation of the swish of female hips expresses the minimalist, soothing quality of bossa nova. In this genre also is "Hó-bá-lá-lá," echoing the Yoruba sounds of the rituals of candomblé (an Afro-Brazilian religion). Experimentally conceived in the early 1950's, the songs first appear as identifiable recordings of Gilberto on *Chega de saudade*.

"The Girl from Ipanema." This Grammy Award-winning signature anthem of bossa nova swept the world in the mid-1960's, and it celebrates the insouciant, hypnotizing beach stroll of a young girl in Ipanema. The original Portuguese lyrics by de Moraes were translated into English by Norman Gimbel in a version sung by Astrud Gilberto on *Getz/Gilberto*. The song reverberated more resonantly when recorded in 1967 by Frank Sinatra.

Musical Legacy

Over the course of his career, Gilberto molded the classic canon of Brazilian popular music, particularly the samba canção. He created a singular style of music that listeners worldwide immediately recognize as Brazilian. Brazilian performers and composers attest to Gilberto's influence on their work, especially the leading figures of the tropicalismo (tropicalism) movement, such as Caetano Veloso and Gilberto Gil. His admirers have imitated the gliding, intimate style with which he imbued samba canção, the signature Brazilian musical genre. Significantly, Gilberto pioneered collaborations with U.S. musicians, composers, and record producers, which helped spread Brazilian popular music throughout the world.

Edward A. Riedinger

Further Reading

Buenosaires, Oscar de. *Bossa Nova and Samba: History, People, Scores, Books, Lyrics, Recordings.* Albuquerque, N.Mex.: FOG, 1999. Bibliographic reference work and critical assessment of the creators and creations of bossa nova.

Castro, Ruy. *Bossa Nova: The Story of the Brazilian Music that Seduced the World.* Chicago: A Capella Books, 2000. A journalist familiar with the important figures of bossa nova details the origins and diffusion of the style.

McGowan, Chris, and Ricardo Pessanha. *The Brazilian Sound: Samba, Bossa Nova, and the Popular Music of Brazil.* 2d ed. Philadelphia, Pa.: Temple University Press, 1998. Standard work introducing Brazilian popular music, placing the work of Gilberto in its national context.

Moreno, Albrecht. "Bossa Nova, Novo Brasil: The Significance of Bossa Nova as a Brazilian Popular Music." *Latin American Research Review* 17, no. 2 (1982): 129-141. The writer discusses the bossa nova as a reflection of Brazil's socioeconomic and political conditions.

Veloso, Caetano. *Tropical Truth: A Story of Music and Revolution in Brazil.* Translated by Isabel de Sena. New York: Alfred A. Knopf, 2002. A leading musician of the tropicalismo movement, the writer expresses his admiration for and his debt to the work of Gilberto.

See also: Getz, Stan; Gil, Gilberto; Jobim, Antônio Carlos; Sinatra, Frank; Tormé, Mel.

Dizzy Gillespie
American jazz trumpeter, singer, and songwriter

Gillespie was a significant contributor to jazz, pioneering bop with Afro-Cuban rhythms, adapting big band orchestration to modern harmonies, teaching and inspiring new generations of musicians, and becoming an international icon of music through his showmanship and good will.

Born: October 21, 1917; Cheraw, South Carolina
Died: January 6, 1993; Englewood, New Jersey
Also known as: John Birks Gillespie (full name)

Principal recordings

ALBUMS: *Dizzy Gillespie with Charlie Christian,* 1941; *Jivin' in Be Bop,* 1947; *Dizzy Gillespie Plays, Johnny Richards Conducts,* 1950; *The Champ,* 1951; *Dizzy Gillespie,* 1951; *School Days,* 1951; *Dizzy Gillespie, Vol. 1,* 1952; *Dizzy Gillespie with Strings,* 1952; *Horn of Plenty,* 1952; *On the Sunny Side of the Street,* 1952; *Diz and Getz,* 1953 (with Stan Getz); *Dizzy Gillespie/Gerry Mulligan,* 1953; *Dizzy Gillespie/Stan Getz Sextet, Vol. 1,* 1953; *Dizzy Gillespie/Stan Getz Sextet, Vol. 2,* 1953; *Hot vs. Cool*, 1953; *Afro*, 1954; *Diz Big Band*, 1954; *Dizzy and Strings*, 1954; *Dizzy Gillespie and His Latin Rhythm: Afro*, 1954; *Dizzy Gillespie and His Orchestra*, 1954; *Dizzy Gillespie and His Original Big Band*, 1954; *Dizzy Gillespie Orchestra*, 1954; *Dizzy Gillespie with Roy Eldridge*, 1954; *Jazz Recital*, 1954; *Trumpet Battle*, 1954; *The Trumpet Kings*, 1954; *The Dizzy Gillespie Big Band*, 1955; *Tour de Force*, 1955; *Dizzy Gillespie Plays*, 1956; *For Musicians Only*, 1956; *The Modern Jazz Sextet*, 1956; *World Statesman*, 1956; *Birk's Works*, 1957; *Dizzy at Home and Abroad*, 1957; *Dizzy Gillespie and Stuff Smith*, 1957; *Dizzy Gillespie Duets*, 1957 (with Sonny Rollins and Sonny Stitt); *Duets: Sonny Rollins and Sonny Stitt*, 1957; *The Greatest Trumpet of Them All*, 1957; *Sittin' In*, 1957; *Sonny Rollins/Sonny Stitt Sessions*, 1957; *Sonny Side Up*, 1957 (with Rollins and Stitt); *Diz and Bird*, 1959 (with Charlie Parker); *The Ebullient Mr. Gillespie*, 1959; *Have Trumpet, Will Excite!*, 1959; *An Electrifying Evening with the Dizzy Gillespie Quintet*, 1961; *Gillespiana*, 1961; *A Musical Safari*, 1961; *Perceptions*, 1961; *Composer's Concepts*, 1962; *Dizzy on the French Riviera*, 1962; *The New Continent*, 1962; *New Wave*, 1962; *Dateline Europe*, 1963; *Dizzy Gillespie Goes Hollywood*, 1963; *Something Old, Something New*, 1963; *The Cool World*, 1964; *Jambo Caribe*, 1964; *Dizzy Gillespie and His Quintet*, 1965; *With Gil Fuller and the Monterey Jazz Festival Orchestra*, 1965; *Soul Mates*, 1966 (with Roy Eldridge); *Jazz for a Sunday Afternoon*, 1967; *Swing Low, Sweet Cadillac*, 1967; *Reunion Big Band*, 1968; *Cornucopia*, 1969; *My Way*, 1969; *Soul and Salvation*, 1969; *Enduring Magic*, 1970; *Blues People*, 1971; *Dizzy Gillespie and the Dwike Mitchell-Willie Ruff Duo*, 1971; *Giants*, 1971 (with others); *The Real Thing*, 1971; *The Giant*, 1973; *Dizzy's Big Four*, 1974 (with others); *Trumpet Kings Meet Joe Turner*, 1974 (with others); *Afro-Cuban Jazz Moods*, 1975; *Bahiana*, 1975; *The Dizzy Gillespie Big Seven*, 1975 (with others); *Dizzy's Party*, 1976; *Free Ride*, 1977; *Gifted Ones*, 1977 (with Count Basie); *Diz*, 1978; *Manteca*, 1979 (with Chano Pozo); *The Trumpet Summit Meets the Oscar Peterson Big Four*, 1980; *Endlessly*, 1981; *To a Finland Station*, 1982 (with Arturo Sandoval); *Closer to the Surface*, 1984;

New Faces, 1984; *Dizzy Gillespie Meets the Phil Woods Quintet*, 1986; *'Round Midnight*, 1986; *Symphony Sessions*, 1989; *The Winter in Lisbon*, 1990; *Bebop and Beyond Plays Dizzy Gillespie*, 1991; *Dizzy Gillespie and Mitchell-Ruff*, 1991; *Rhythmstick*, 1991; *Ruff Duo*, 1993; *To Diz with Love: Diamond Jubilee Recordings*, 1992; *All the Things You Are*, 1994; *Big Bands*, 1994; *Con Alma*, 1994; *Diz Meets Stitt*, 1995 (with Rollins); *Lady Be Good*, 1994; *Strangers in Paradise*, 1994; *Groovin' with Diz*, 1995; *Hot House*, 1995; *No More Blues*, 1995; *Swing Love*, 1995; *Dizzy Gillespie*, 1996; *Dizzy for President*, 1997; *Triple Play*, 1998; *Continental*, 2002; *Portrait*, 2003.

The Life

John Birks Gillespie was born in a small South Carolina town in 1917, the youngest of nine children of James and Lottie Powe Gillespie. James was a bricklayer who played in a local band on weekends. Gillespie began playing the piano at three years old; at twelve he played trumpet in Robert Smalls secondary school band. In 1933 Gillespie received a music scholarship to attend the prestigious Laurinburg Institute in North Carolina. While there he fell under the influence of the music of Louis Armstrong, who had transformed the art of improvised jazz with his Hot Five and Hot Seven recordings. At the end of the 1935 academic year, Gillespie left Laurinburg for Philadelphia, where his family had migrated. Gillespie joined the local black musicians' union and played in local swing bands, earning the nickname Dizzy for his comic stage antics. In 1937 Gillespie moved to Harlem, New York, where he played in the Teddy Hill Orchestra and, starting in 1939, the Cab Calloway Orchestra. On May 9, 1940, Gillespie married Lorraine Willis. On September 21, 1941, the hot-tempered Gillespie stabbed Calloway with a knife in the course of an argument, and he was fired from the band.

Joining the Earl Hines Orchestra, Gillespie collaborated with fellow band member Charlie "Yardbird" Parker to pioneer the bebop (or bop) revolution in jazz. Gillespie was the leader in the bop quintets he played with Parker on New York's Fifty-second Street in 1945 and 1946. From 1946 to 1950 he headed two big bands, introducing Afro-Cuban music to jazz. In the 1950's he began touring internationally, sometimes sponsored by the U.S.

State Department. Although he was celebrated for his contributions to jazz and bop and was a popular performer through the 1960's and 1970's, Gillespie experienced personal difficulties, some brought on by his ingesting too much alcohol. Despite his stable marriage to Lorraine, he was the subject of several paternity suits and acknowledged that Jeanie Bryson was his daughter from a liaison in the 1950's with Connie Bryson. In 1970 Gillespie became an adherent of the Baha'i faith, a conversion that helped stabilize his personal life and spurred his interest in becoming an international spokesperson for unity—in jazz, in music, and among cultures. He formed the United Nations Orchestra (UNO) in 1989. After several years of successful international tours with the UNO, Gillespie died in 1993 of pancreatic cancer.

The Music

As a young trumpet player in leading swing bands of the late 1930's and early 1940's, Gillespie was noted for several talents, all of which played significant roles in his career: his technical virtuosity, his harmonic boldness, and his stage antics. With Gillespie's first big band chair in Philadelphia's Frankie Fairfax Orchestra from 1935 to 1937, he already showed the influence of jazz trumpeter Roy Eldridge. Eldridge was a fiery, upper-register trumpeter, and the early performances of Gillespie reflected the same dazzling use of rapid high notes and powerful attack. Playing with New York's Teddy Hill Orchestra from 1937 to 1939, and with the Cab Calloway Orchestra from 1939 to 1941, Gillespie picked up much of the showmanship and stage presence that earned him his nickname. Gillespie acknowledged that he was influenced by New York's leading jazz showman of the day, Fats Waller.

Gillespie's most important big band apprenticeships were from 1943 to 1944 with the orchestras of Hines, Coleman Hawkins, and Billy Eckstine; he served as the musical director of the Eckstine orchestra. (Gillespie arranged for the brilliant young trumpeter Fats Navarro to take his position as trumpet player when he left.) Gillespie was developing the new harmonic and melodic ideas emerging from the famous after-hours jam sessions at Minton's Playhouse and Monroe's Uptown House. His music already incorporated such elements as

double time playing, new chord variations, substitution chords (such as an A minor chord), offbeat accenting, asymmetrical and jagged melodic lines, and double bass patterns that replaced the swing sound of walking bass lines. Some of these ideas would be displayed in the small combo (bop differed from swing orchestration in its emphasis on the small band), which he formed with bassist Oscar Pettiford in 1944 to play at the Onyx Club on New York's Fifty-second Street. In his recording of "I Can't Get Started" with Pettiford and a septet on January 9, 1945, Gillespie produced a beautifully lyrical solo bursting with his new harmonic ideas.

Gillespie and Parker Quintets. While playing for the Hines band, Gillespie began the collaboration with alto saxophonist Parker that would establish bop. As Gillespie biographer Donald Maggin explains, bop was a multifaceted innovation that greatly expanded the range of possibilities for the improviser. It created irregular rhythmic patterns out of the constant four-beat pattern of swing. Its melodies were linear, were oddly phrased, and, although played by the horns, rested on complex, imaginative rhythms of the drums, piano, and bass. Bop brought a harmonic freshness to jazz, focusing on chromaticism, building chords on all twelve notes of the scale, not just the seven notes that characterized the diatonic harmony of blues and swing. In other words, bop musicians discovered the chords at higher intervals, the ninth, eleventh, and thirteenth, which bop musicians referred to as "flatted" or "flattened" fifths (deriving from the augmented eleventh interval, which is also a flat fifth).

Gillespie's discovery of the flatted fifth, while listening to a Rudy Powell arrangement in 1938, paralleled Parker's famous epiphany in Dan Wall's Chili House in December, 1939, while playing the higher-interval chords of "Cherokee." Parker brought an essentially blues phrasing to bop, which unified bop's rapid rhythms, angular melodies, virtuosic soloing, and innovative note choices. Gillespie was not captivated by jazz's blues roots. Instead, he focused on the development of bop theory in his playing, composition, and arrangements, emphasizing the overall architectural shape and articulating harmonic and rhythmic principles. It was a role that made Gillespie the natural spokesman for and teacher of the bop movement.

Gillespie and Parker exploded on the postwar scene with their famous quintet of 1945 and 1946, headlining the Three Deuces Club on New York's Fifty-second Street and making seminal bop recordings, such as the Gillespie compositions "Salt Peanuts," "Dizzy Atmosphere," "Groovin' High," "Shaw Nuff," "Bebop," "Oop Bop Sh'Bam," "Things to Come," and "Anthropology" (also known as "Thriving from a Riff").

"Groovin' High." "Groovin' High," recorded with Parker in a sextet on February 28, 1945, is emblematic of the new jazz style. Gillespie's careful composition features a jagged two-note phrase throughout that illustrates how bebop derived its onomatopoeic name. "Groovin' High" opens with an infectious melodic theme played in perfect unison by Gillespie and Parker, alternating with bass, drum, and piano patterns, exemplifying the central role the rhythm section assumes in bop. The ensemble playing of Gillespie and Parker is taken at breathless speed, gliding up and down the scale. The soloists improvise complex variations over the underlying chords derived from the popular standard "Whispering," before Gillespie slows the tempo for a bravura high-note trumpet climax.

"Night in Tunisia." Gillespie recorded his most famous composition, "Night in Tunisia," several times with Parker and throughout his career. The song reflects Gillespie's innovative harmonic ideas, his interest in Latin rhythms, and his roots in big band swing. Gillespie derived the basic compositional framework of "Night in Tunisia" from his first major composition, the chromatic and polyrhythmic "Pickin' the Cabbage," recorded by Calloway and his orchestra on March 8, 1940. As Gillespie biographer Alyn Shipton points out, "Night in Tunisia" is built around an A thirteenth chord, which resolves to D minor. Gillespie's interest in Latin music is apparent in the opening ostinato rhythm in the bass line. In his January 26, 1945, recording as a guest soloist with the Boyd Raeburn Orchestra, Gillespie builds a dramatic solo from a series of staccato phrases before resolving the song with a high-note coda. In September, 1946, Gillespie and Parker recorded a sizzling live version at Carnegie Hall.

Perhaps Gillespie's most celebrated recording of "Night in Tunisia" is from the famous performance recorded live in Toronto's Massey Hall in 1953 with other pioneers of bop—Parker, Bud Powell on pi-

Dizzy Gillespie. (AP/Wide World Photos)

ano, Max Roach on drums, and Charles Mingus on bass. After Roach, Mingus, and Powell introduce the tempo and ostinato line in the first twelve bars, Gillespie plays the first theme of the song over Parker's countermotives. Parker replies with a second theme played over Gillespie's perfectly rendered counterpoint. Parker, Gillespie, and Powell follow with three choruses each of beautiful soloing. Gillespie dramatically ends the tune with a retard, free solo, and a high-note cadenza.

Manteca. Gillespie believed that Latin and Cuban rhythms reflected the direct influence of African percussion. In 1947 Gillespie collaborated with Cuban percussionist Chano Pozo to introduce Afro-Cuban polyrhythms to jazz. Their most celebrated recording was *Manteca*, recorded in December of that year. Pozo plays an infectious conga rhythm of eighth notes while Gillespie showcases two exciting eight-bar solos and cries of "Manteca!"

Dizzy Gillespie Big Band. Gillespie maintained a love of big band music throughout his life. Although bop contrasted with swing in its emphasis on smaller bands, as opposed to a dance-oriented orchestra, Gillespie led two big bands in the 1940's and 1950's, until economic realities curtailed both efforts. Gillespie also enjoyed playing with the best orchestras whenever possible. For example, in 1959, Gillespie was a guest soloist with the Duke Ellington Orchestra for a recording of Billy Strayhorn's composition "U.M.M.G." Gillespie plays his first two choruses with a muted horn. (A chorus is a structured sequence that repeats itself in different variations throughout a song. In most jazz and popular songs such as "U.M.M.G." a chorus consists of a thirty-two-bar *aaba* structure.) After several choruses by the Ellington orchestra, Gillespie returns for a blaring open-horn solo before concluding with another brilliant coda. When the State Department financed Gillespie's international touring orchestra in 1956, Gillespie revived his big band arrangements as a goodwill ambassador. It was a natural role for Gillespie, with his innate flair for showmanship reinforced by his trademark goatee and beret, chipmunk-like puffed cheeks, and angled trumpet. Gillespie's love of orchestral play and humor found ample room at the annual Monterey Jazz Festival. Gillespie was the master of ceremonies and star performer who opened the first Monterey Jazz Festival on October 3, 1958, with a performance of the "Star-Spangled Banner." He was a fixture at the festival over the following decades. His orchestral flair was revived again at the end of his career when the United Nations sponsored his international orchestra, which toured twenty-seven countries.

Musical Legacy

Gillespie made numerous contributions to jazz history, any one of which would have been enough to earn him prominence. Foremost was his status as a pioneer of bop. Although bop derived from the ideas of many jazzmen, including such artists of Harlem after-hours jam sessions as Charlie Christian, Kenny Clarke, Thelonious Monk, and Bud Powell, it was Gillespie and Parker who brought bop to fruition and prominence. After Parker's sad demise, Gillespie was bop's living icon for forty years, receiving five Grammy Awards. He

continuously revived the flame of big band jazz, although it was imbued with the complexities of his rhythmic, melodic, and harmonic thoughts. Gillespie introduced Afro-Cuban rhythms to jazz, paving the way for the bossa nova craze that would sweep the nation in the early 1960's. Gillespie mentored numerous young musicians, and he was an instantly recognizable figure with his puffed cheeks, angled horn, and clowning antics. He was the successor to Armstrong as the international goodwill ambassador of jazz.

Howard Bromberg

Further Reading

Gillespie, Dizzy, with Al Fraser. *To Be, or Not—To Bop: Memoirs*. London: W. H. Allen, 1980. Includes interviews with Gillespie's family, friends, and collaborators.

Maggin, Donald. *Dizzy: The Life and Times of John Birks Gillespie*. New York: Harper, 2006. Sympathetic biography organized around extensive quotes, anecdotes, and insightful musical analysis.

Shipton, Alyn. *Groovin' High: The Life of Dizzy Gillespie*. New York: Oxford University Press, 1999. Prolific jazz historian argues that Gillespie's contributions to bop outweighed even those of Parker.

Yanow, Scott. *Afro-Cuban Jazz*. San Francisco: Miller Freeman Books, 2000. A history of Afro-Cuban jazz in which Gillespie plays the critical role, beginning with his collaboration with Pozo in 1947.

See also: Akiyoshi, Toshiko; Armstrong, Louis; Bacharach, Burt; Barretto, Ray; Blades, Rubén; Blakey, Art; Brown, Clifford; Burton, Gary; Carter, Benny; Christian, Charlie; Coltrane, John; Corea, Chick; Fitzgerald, Ella; Getz, Stan; Gordon, Dexter; Hawkins, Coleman; Jones, Quincy; Kirk, Rahsaan Roland; Legrand, Michel; Makeba, Miriam; Masekela, Hugh; Mingus, Charles; Monk, Thelonious; Navarro, Fats; Parker, Charlie; Peterson, Oscar; Powell, Bud; Roach, Max; Rollins, Sonny; Shaw, Artie; Stone, Sly; Vaughan, Sarah; Waller, Fats; Williams, Mary Lou.

Philip Glass

American classical and
film-score composer

A self-characterized theater composer, Glass was a founder of minimalism, a style based on repetitive melodies and rhythms that pleased large audiences and influenced other avant-garde composers.

Born: January 31, 1937; Baltimore, Maryland

Principal works

BALLET: *Glass Pieces*, 1983.

CHAMBER WORKS: String Quartet, 1966; *Music in the Shape of a Square*, 1967 (for two flutes); *Dance No. 2*, 1979 (multimedia work); *Dance No. 4*, 1979 (multimedia work); *Fourth Series, Part III*, 1979 (for violin and clarinet); *Dance No. 1*, 1980 (multimedia work); *Dance No. 3*, 1980 (multimedia work); String Quartet No. 2, 1983; String Quartet No. 3, 1985; String Quartet No. 4, 1989; String Quartet No. 5, 1999.

CHORAL WORKS: *Another Look at Harmony, Part IV*, 1975 (for chorus and organ); *Dressed like an Egg*, 1977 (for chorus and organ); *Fourth Series, Part I*, 1979 (for chorus and organ); *The Photographer*, 1982 (for chorus and mixed media); *The Civil Wars: Cologne*, 1984; *The Civil Wars: Rome*, 1984; *The Olympian*, 1984 (for chorus and orchestra).

FILM SCORES: *Koyaanisqatsi*, 1982; *Mishima*, 1985; *Hamburger Hill*, 1987; *Powaqqatsi*, 1988; *The Thin Blue Line*, 1988; *Mindwalk*, 1990; *A Brief History of Time*, 1991; *Candyman*, 1992; *Orphée*, 1992 (chamber opera; libretto by Glass; based on Jean Cocteau's film); *Candyman II: Farewell to the Flesh*, 1994; *Jenipapo*, 1994 (*The Interview*); *La Belle et la bête*, 1994 (*Beauty and the Beast*; libretto by Glass); *Bent*, 1996; *The Secret Agent*, 1996; *Kundun*, 1997; *The Truman Show*, 1998; *Dracula*, 1999; *The Hours*, 2002; *Naqoyqatsi*, 2002; *The Fog of War: Eleven Lessons from the Life of Robert S. McNamara*, 2003; *Notes on a Scandal*, 2006; *Animals in Love*, 2007; *Cassandra's Dream*, 2007; *Monsters of Grace*, 2007; *New York Nights*, 2007; *No Reservations*, 2007.

INSTRUMENTAL WORKS: *In Again Out Again*, 1967 (for two pianos); *One Plus One*, 1967 (for amplified tabletop); *Gradus*, 1969 (for saxophone); *Strung Out*, 1976 (for amplified violin); *Mad Rush*, 1979 (for solo piano or organ); *Fourth Series, Part II*, 1979 (for solo organ); *Fourth Series, Part IV*, 1979 (for solo organ); *Arabesque in Memoriam*, 1988 (for flute); *Melodies for Saxophone*, 1995; *Études for Piano*, 1999.

OPERAS: *Einstein on the Beach*, 1976 (libretto by Glass and Robert M. Wilson); *Satyagraha*, 1980 (libretto by Glass and Constance DeJong; based on the *Bhagavad-Gita*); *Akhnaten*, 1984 (libretto by Glass); *The Juniper Tree*, 1984 (two-act opera for chamber orchestra, small chorus, and soloists; music with Robert Moran; libretto by Arthur Yorinks; based on a story by J. L. Grimm and W. C. Grimm); *The Making of the Representative for Planet Eight*, 1986 (three-act opera; based on Doris Lessing's novel); *One Thousand Airplanes on the Roof: A Science Fiction Music Drama*, 1987 (libretto by David Henry Hwang); *Hydrogen Jukebox*, 1990 (chamber opera; based on Allen Ginsberg's poetry); *The Voyage*, 1992 (libretto by Hwang); *Les Enfants terribles*, 1996 (libretto by Glass and Susan Marshall; based on the novel by Jean Cocteau); *Waiting for the Barbarians*, 2005 (libretto by Christopher Hampton; based on J. M. Coetzee's novel); *Appomattox*, 2007 (libretto by Hampton).

ORCHESTRAL WORKS: *Two Pages*, 1968; *Music in Contrary Motion*, 1969; *Music in Fifths*, 1969; *Music in Similar Motion*, 1969; *Music with Changing Parts*, 1970; *North Star*, 1977; *Glassworks*, 1982; *A Descent into the Maelstrom*, 1985 (based on Edgar Allan Poe's story); *Songs from Liquid Days*, 1986; Concerto for Violin and Orchestra, 1987; *Dancepieces*, 1987; *The Canyon*, 1988; *The Fall of the House of Usher*, 1988 (two-act opera; based on Poe's story); *Anima Mundi*, 1992; *Glassworks*, 1993; Symphony No. 1, 1993 (also known as *Low Symphony*; based on David Bowie's film *Low*); Symphony No. 2, 1994; Symphony No. 3, 1995; Symphony No. 4, 1996 (also known as *Heroes Symphony*; based on Bowie's album *Heroes*); Symphony No. 5, 2000 (*Requiem, Bardo, Nirmanakaya*); Symphony No. 6, 2001 (*Plutonian Ode*); Symphony No. 7, 2005 (*A Toltec Symphony*); *Book of Longing*, 2007.

VOCAL WORKS: *Music for Voices,* 1970; *Music in Twelve Parts,* 1974 (for voice, winds, and keyboards); *Another Look at Harmony: Part III,* 1976 (for voice, clarinet, and piano).

The Life

Philip Glass was born in Baltimore, the grandson of Lithuanian Jewish immigrants and the son of Benjamin Glass, who ran a radio repair shop that also sold records. The slow-selling records served as Glass's introduction to such composers as Ludwig van Beethoven, Dmitri Shostakovich, and Béla Bartók. He began violin lessons at age six but quickly switched to the flute, and in 1946 he became the youngest student ever admitted to the Peabody Conservatory of Music in Baltimore, Maryland. After only two years of high school he gained admission to the University of Chicago, where he majored in philosophy and mathematics while continuing his musical development by studying the piano. Having decided to become a composer, he left Chicago in 1956 for the Juilliard School in New York, where he studied such genres as concerti and choral works as well as modern film scoring. During a summer in Aspen, Colorado, he was the pupil of French composer Darius Milhaud. After receiving his master's degree from Juilliard, he accepted a Ford Foundation composer-in-residence grant to work in the Pittsburgh public school system.

An early turning point in his career occurred when he accepted a Fulbright scholarship to study with the acclaimed composition teacher Nadia Boulanger at the Paris Conservatory. Boulanger's methods forced him to reevaluate his previous musical education, and his marriage to first wife JoAnne Akalaitis, an actress, playwright, and director, influenced his developing fascination with modern theater. Also felicitous was his encounter with Indian sitarist Ravi Shankar, whose raga improvisations helped to shape Glass's emerging musical style, which increasingly centered on cyclic musical events created through a tension between melody and harmony.

Upon his return to New York in 1967, he formed the Philip Glass Ensemble to perform his new music, which others characterized as minimalist or systematic, while he preferred calling it "music with repetitive structures." Glass's group performed in such unconventional venues as nightclubs, lofts, restaurants, and public parks. Though the ensemble helped to disseminate his new music, he still needed to support himself by such jobs as cabdriving, plumbing, and furniture moving. All this changed with the phenomenal success of his theatrical extravaganza *Einstein on the Beach.* He capitalized on this success with a series of large- and small-scale works, which in turn led to fruitful collaborations with choreographers and filmmakers. During the 1980's, 1990's, and early twenty-first century he expanded and deepened his style by continuing to work on film scores, most notably a trilogy based on the films of Jean Cocteau, but he also collaborated with artists from a wide variety of fields, including such popular singers as Paul Simon and David Byrne and such writers as

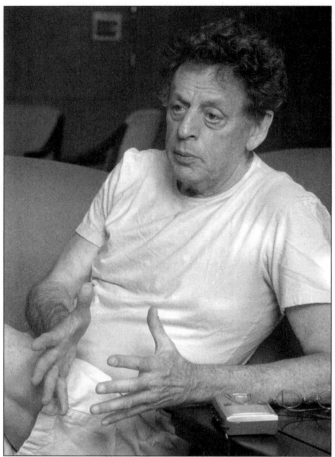

Philip Glass. (AP/Wide World Photos)

Allen Ginsberg, Doris Lessing, and J. M. Coetzee. During this period he also managed to reinvigorate such traditional classical forms as the symphony, concerto, and string quartet.

The Music

Through his early life and education, Glass had become familiar with classical and modern music, but his own style evolved as an esoteric blend of Western and Eastern traditions, established and avant-garde music, as well as various theatrical influences. He learned about modern compositional techniques from his Juilliard teachers, and, while in Paris, he was deeply impressed by new French plays and films. He was so fascinated by Shankar that Glass traveled to India, where he deepened his knowledge of Eastern culture and music. By the time he returned to the United States, the basics of his distinctive minimalist style were already informing his compositions.

Early Works. The first concert of Glass's new music in 1968 contained *Music in the Shape of a Square* for two flutes, composed as an homage to Erik Satie, who had written *Music in the Form of a Pear* (1903). Glass and a fellow flutist performed the piece while walking in opposite directions around a square on the stage. During the early years of the Philip Glass Ensemble, he also wrote *Music in Fifths* as an ironic tribute to Boulanger, who had attempted to wean Glass from using hidden fifths in his compositions. This early phase of Glass's compositional odyssey culminated in *Music in Twelve Parts*, which took three years to write and ran more than four hours in performance. Some saw this composition as an anthology of twelve independent pieces with various rhythmic and harmonic patterns, while others saw it as a unified composition characterized by a progressive movement of greater and greater vertical complexity.

The Portrait Trilogy. *Einstein on the Beach*, which has been called a landmark of twentieth century musical theater, originated in the early 1970's, when Glass met the director Robert M. Wilson. They chose Albert Einstein as their opera's "subject" (a term that Glass was reluctant to use) because this great scientist could symbolize, through music and spectacle, the themes of creativity, space, and time. Organized more like a dream than a conventional narrative, this theater piece was uncon-

ventional in its libretto, singing, and acting. Its premiere occurred at the Avignon Summer Festival in France on July 25, 1976, but it was its American premiere at the Metropolitan Opera in New York that made Glass famous and helped to determine the direction of his subsequent career.

Glass and Wilson collaborated on two other dramatic works, *Satyagraha* and *Akhnaten*, which, like *Einstein on the Beach*, were character operas. *Satyagraha*'s character was Mahatma Ghandi, and *Akhnaten*'s was the pharaoh who introduced monotheism to Egypt. Glass scored *Satyagraha* for a full symphony orchestra, whereas *Akhnaten*, which had been commissioned by the Stuttgart Opera and which was sung in Akkadian, biblical Hebrew, and ancient Egyptian, eventually required a small orchestra, because the premiere in Germany took place in a theater with a small orchestra pit. Glass felt that the chamber-like sound was better suited to the nature of the material.

Works for the Theater, Films, and Special Occasions. Glass was able to adapt his music of repetitive structures to a wide variety of forms. For example, he was able to continue his collaboration with Wilson in *The Civil Wars*, both in its Cologne section and in its Rome section. He collaborated with other artists in *The Juniper Tree* for chamber orchestra, small chorus, and soloists. The American Repertory Theater of Cambridge, Massachusetts, commissioned this work, which was based on a tale by the Brothers Grimm. *One Thousand Airplanes on the Roof* had its premiere in a hangar at the Vienna International Airport. One critic described it as "a light show, a ballet, a spoken opera, an art exhibit, [and] a lesson in Zen."

During the 1980's, 1990's, and the early twenty-first century, Glass composed the scores for a wide variety of films. For example, he created the scores for a trilogy of "cinematic poems" directed by Godfrey Reggio: *Koyaanisqatsi*, *Powaqqatsi*, and *Naqoyqatsi*, whose non-narrative views of the interaction between humans and their environment were well served by Glass's hypnotic music. His scores for the documentaries of Errol Morris—*The Thin Blue Line*, *A Brief History of Time*, and *The Fog of War*—were highly praised for enhancing the themes of these films. Glass also scored such Hollywood narrative films as Paul Schrader's *Mishima*, John Irvin's *Hamburger Hill*, and Stephen Daldry's

The Hours. His score for Martin Scorsese's *Kundun* earned him an Academy Award nomination, and his score for *The Truman Show* won a Golden Globe Award.

Glass's many successes enhanced his reputation as an efficient composer, and he was often invited to create music for special occasions and distinguished musicians. For example, he wrote the music for the torch-lighting ceremony at the 1984 Los Angeles Olympics. In 1987 he created a concerto for violinist Paul Zukovsky, and in 1992 the Metropolitan Opera commissioned him to compose *The Voyage*, a three-act opera to commemorate the five-hundredth anniversary of Columbus's discovery of America.

New Ways of Composing in Traditional Forms. Though he had a penchant for theatrical work, Glass still found time to compose music in such traditional forms as symphonies, concerti, and string quartets. He composed several symphonies that blended his musical style with historical materials from Romantic and polytonal musical approaches. He adjusted his style to the talents of the Kronos Quartet, and his knowledge of Bartók's work informed his piano études composed for Dennis Russell Davies.

A Second Triptych. Glass eliminated the original music from three films of Jean Cocteau and created a new experience for viewers. His treatment of Cocteau's *Orphée* (1949) was emotionally rooted in his personal experience of the untimely death of his third wife, the artist Candy Jernigan. He treated the script of *La Belle et la bête* (1946) as a cinematic libretto to be performed by opera singers accompanied by the Philip Glass Ensemble. He scored *Les Enfants terribles* for voices and three pianos. Glass composed these new scores in the 1990's.

A Composer for All Seasons. In the twenty-first century Glass manifested no signs of slowing down. His operas *Waiting for the Barbarians* and *Appomattox* exhibited his love for experimentation characteristic of his theatrical works throughout his career. He also continued his collaborations with important artists. For example, he wrote a concerto for cello and orchestra for Julian Lloyd Webber's fiftieth birthday. His piano concerto, "After Lewis and Clark," commemorated these explorers' famous trip across the North American continent. His love for Leonard Cohen's poetry resulted in his

Book of Longing for seven instruments and a vocal quartet.

Musical Legacy

Glass is one of the most prolific and influential composers of the twentieth and twenty-first centuries. Through his many compositions and his collaborations with some of the most talented artists in the world, he has exerted an extraordinary influence on the musical and cultural life of his time. His works have been extensively performed and recorded, and to preserve for posterity his entire musical legacy, Glass founded, with some colleagues, the Orange Mountain Music label. His music has not lacked critics, some of whom find his minimalist works lacking in depth and variety, and others have been repelled by what they see as his predilection for self-promotion. Glass has found it easy to ignore his critics since he has acquired the largest audience of any contemporary composer of serious music. What Andy Warhol did for art, Glass accomplished for classical music, which he showed could be commercially successful if it borrowed mass-media methods. His music has certainly given pleasure to many listeners, and as a composer of liberation, he has freed both himself and his audiences to hear new and wonderful sounds.

Robert J. Paradowski

Further Reading

Kostelanz, Richard. *Writings on Glass: Essays, Interviews, Criticism.* New York: Schirmer Books, 1996. Written with Glass's cooperation and with access to his archives, Kostelanz's book contains an analysis of his subject's life and compositions. Includes a bibliography, discography, and a list of works.

Maycock, Robert. *Glass: A Portrait.* London: Faber & and Faber, 2002. Maycock, an English critic, combines biography and musical analysis in his readable account of Glass's evolution from early minimalist works to twenty-first century symphonies and concerti. Contains a concise chronological list of Glass's principal compositions.

Mertens, Wim. *American Minimal Music: La Monte Young, Terry Riley, Steve Reich, and Philip Glass.* Translated by J. Hautekiet. New York: Alexander Broude, 1983. Mertens analyzes Glass's chief works in the context of other minimalist composers, especially their roots in African and Asian music. Illustrated, with a bibliography.

Potter, Keith. *Four Musical Minimalists: La Monte Young, Terry Riley, Steve Reich, Philip Glass*. New York: Cambridge University Press, 2000. Potter emphasizes the early works of these minimalist composers, which he analyzes from a biographical perspective.

Rockwell, John. *All American Music: Composition in the Late Twentieth Century*. New York: Alfred A. Knopf, 1983. Rockwell's chapter on Glass is a critical overview rather than a systematic survey. Includes bibliography, discography, and index.

See also: Bartók, Béla; Boulanger, Nadia; Bowie, David; Carlos, Wendy; Cohen, Leonard; Milhaud, Darius; Reich, Steve; Shankar, Ravi; Shostakovich, Dmitri; Vega, Suzanne.

Gerry Goffin

American rock singer and songwriter

Songwriter Goffin made the transition from the commercial tunes produced in New York's Brill Building in the early 1960's to the introspective style of the Woodstock generation in the 1970's.

Born: February 11, 1939; Queens, New York
Also known as: Gerald Goffin (full name)

Principal recordings

ALBUMS: *It Ain't Exactly Entertainment*, 1973; *Back Room Blood*, 1996.

SONGS: "Will You Still Love Me Tomorrow," 1960 (with Carole King; recorded by the Shirelles); "Run to Him," 1961 (with Jack Keller; recorded by Bobby Vee); "Take Good Care of My Baby," 1961 (with King; recorded by Vee); "Who Put the Bomp (In the Bomp, Bomp, Bomp)," 1961 (with Barry Mann; recorded by Mann); "Go Away Little Girl," 1962 (with King; recorded by Steve Lawrence); "The Loco-Motion," 1962 (with King; recorded by Little Eva); "Don't Say Nothing Bad (About My Baby)," 1963 (with King; recorded by the Cookies); "Hey Girl," 1963 (with King; recorded by Freddie Scott);

"One Fine Day," 1963 (with King; recorded by the Chiffons); "Just Once in My Life," 1965 (with King and Phil Spector; recorded by the Righteous Brothers); "Pleasant Valley Sunday," 1967 (with King; recorded by the Monkees); "(You Make Me Feel Like) A Natural Woman," 1967 (with Aretha Franklin; recorded by Franklin); "I've Got to Use My Imagination," 1973 (with Barry Goldberg; recorded by Gladys Knight and the Pips); "Theme from *Mahogany* (Do You Know Where You're Going To)," 1975 (with Michael Masser; recorded by Diana Ross); "Saving All My Love for You," 1985 (with Masser; recorded by Whitney Houston); "Miss You Like Crazy," 1989 (with Masser; recorded by Natalie Cole).

The Life

Gerald Goffin remembers making up songs as an eight-year-old. Upon graduation from Brooklyn Technical High School, Goffin enlisted in the Marine Corps Reserves, and later he went to the U.S. Naval Academy. Resigning from the Navy in 1958, Goffin enrolled in the chemistry program at Queens College, where he met a musically talented education major named Carole King. They began writing music together, and in 1959 they were married. In 1960 Don Kirschner signed them to the Aldon Music label, where their first hit, "Will You Still Love Me Tomorrow," went to *Billboard*'s number-one spot for the Shirelles later that year. They literally started at the top, and their first hit proved one of the most enduring, recorded by dozens of major artists, including five other *Billboard* Top 100 versions between 1968 and 1978.

Although they divorced in 1968, Goffin and King continued to write together into the 1970's, and Goffin, who had collaborated with other composers even during his string of hits with King, continued to find talented composers with whom to work. With their help, he learned to write his own melodies. Goffin and King's daughter, Louise Lynn Goffin, also became a successful songwriter and singer.

The Music

Goffin and King were among the last of the Brill Building composers, who churned out hits in small offices that had been home to music publishers

511

since the 1930's. Many of the writers working there had been creating songs since the big band era, and they had made the transition to rock and roll only by imitation, trying to guess the tastes of the teen audience that was driving popular music by 1960. Barely out of their teens at that time, Goffin and King were in tune with youthful listeners. Goffin was later critical, though never apologetic, about the commercial nature of his early writing, but the continued rerecording of those hits over five decades is a tribute to their universality.

"Will You Love Me Tomorrow." Although rated by *Rolling Stone* as one of the top five hundred pop-rock songs of all time, this hit was almost discarded. Lead singer Shirley Owens of the Shirelles thought it was too country for her style, but she gave it a second chance when the producers added a string arrangement. Despite being banned by many radio stations for its sexually suggestive lyrics, it succeeded both commercially and artistically. "Will You Love Me Tomorrow" explored the fears and anxieties of the generation's increasing sexual freedom. The question in the title (which is repeated in the chorus) is clearly heartfelt, and it is posed the moment before the singer's decision, creating a certain amount of tension. Cover versions appeared almost immediately: Mike Berry's in 1961; Dusty Springfield's in 1964 in England; Cher's in 1966; and the Four Seasons' in 1968, a rendition that peaked at number twenty-four on the pop charts.

"Who Put the Bomp (In the Bomp, Bomp, Bomp)." While not nearly as successful as Goffin's other hits, this novelty tune, which reached *Billboard*'s number-seven spot for co-author Barry Mann (backed by the Halos), is noteworthy as a mark of Goffin's ability not to take himself or his craft too seriously. Goffin playfully provides lyrics that were merely nonsense doo-wop sounds, such as the "bomp-bomp-ba-bomp" of the Marcels' remake of "Blue Moon" and the title sounds of the Edsels' "Ram-a-lam-a-ding-dong," both of which were still playing on the radio when Mann and Goffin wrote the song. Unfortunately, the irony was lost on some critics. Comedian Steve Allen, who had created a comic sensation on his *Tonight Show* by donning a tuxedo and reciting "Be-Bop-a-Lulu" as if it were a Shakespearean sonnet, gave the Mann-Goffin song the same treatment, without acknowledging the fact that the lyrics were already parodic.

Musical Legacy

Inducted into the Rock and Roll Hall of Fame in 1990, along with his former wife, King, Goffin is assured a prominent place in popular music history. Goffin's Academy Award nomination (with composer Mike Masser) for the theme song to *Mahogany* (1975), also known as "Do You Know Where You're Going To," brought him recognition beyond the world of rock and roll. His knack for finding the top singers in the business continued when he hired Kelly Clarkson to do some demo work a year before her success on the television talent show *American Idol*. His songs continue to be revived by new generations of singers ("Will You Still Love Me Tomorrow" alone was recorded by eleven major artists between 1960 and 1992) and to inspire new generations of songwriters, including Louise Goffin, his daughter by King.

John R. Holmes

Further Reading

Brown, Mick. *Tearing Down the Wall of Sound: The Rise and Fall of Phil Spector*. London: Bloomsbury, 2007. Because Spector was involved with the "Aldon group" of songwriters, to which Goffin belonged, the early part of this biography is rich in references to Goffin.

Friedlander, Paul. *Rock and Roll: A Social History*. 2d ed. Boulder, Colo.: Westview Press, 2006. This general history of rock and roll is designed as a textbook for popular culture courses.

Pollock, Bruce. *In Their Own Words*. New York: Collier Books, 1975. This collection includes a 1974 interview with Goffin at the offices of Screen Gems Music, in which the songwriter talks about his creative process, his musical influences, and changing musical tastes.

Simons, David. *Studio Stories: How the Great New York Records Were Made: From Miles to Madonna, Sinatra to the Ramones*. New York: Backbeat Books, 2004. This general history of the New York recording studios prominently features the songwriters of the Brill Building, including Goffin.

See also: Franklin, Aretha; King, Carole; Ross, Diana; Spector, Phil; Stoller, Mike.

Jerry Goldsmith

American classical and
film-score composer

A prolific composer, beloved especially for his themes for the television series Star Trek, *Goldsmith is a key figure in the development of the language of contemporary film music.*

Born: February 10, 1929; Los Angeles, California
Died: July 21, 2004; Beverly Hills, California
Also known as: Jerrald Goldsmith (full name); J. Michael Hennagin

Principal works

FILM SCORES: *City of Fear*, 1959; *Studs Lonigan*, 1960; *Freud*, 1962; *Lonely Are the Brave*, 1962; *The Spiral Road*, 1962; *A Gathering of Eagles*, 1963; *Lilies of the Field*, 1963; *The Prize*, 1963; *The Stripper*, 1963; *Fate Is the Hunter*, 1964; *Rio Conchos*, 1964; *Shock Treatment*, 1964; *In Harm's Way*, 1965; *Morituri*, 1965; *A Patch of Blue*, 1965; *Von Ryan's Express*, 1965; *The Blue Max*, 1966; *Our Man Flint*, 1966; *The Sand Pebbles*, 1966; *Seconds*, 1966; *Stagecoach*, 1966; *To Trap a Spy*, 1966; *Trouble with Angels*, 1966; *The Flim-Flam Man*, 1967; *Hour of the Gun*, 1967; *In Like Flint*, 1967; *Warning Shot*, 1967; *Bandolero!*, 1968; *The Detective*, 1968; *Planet of the Apes*, 1968; *The Chairman*, 1969; *A Hundred Rifles*, 1969; *The Illustrated Man*, 1969; *Justine*, 1969; *The Ballad of Cable Hogue*, 1970; *Patton*, 1970; *Rio Lobo*, 1970; *Tora! Tora! Tora!*, 1970; *The Travelling Executioner*, 1970; *Escape from the Planet of the Apes*, 1971; *Homecoming: A Christmas Story*, 1971; *The Last Run*, 1971; *The Mephisto Waltz*, 1971; *Ace Eli and Rodger of the Skies*, 1972; *Anna and the King*, 1972; *The Other*, 1972; *Pursuit*, 1972; *The Don Is Dead*, 1973; *Hawkins on Murder*, 1973; *One Little Indian*, 1973; *Papillon*, 1973; *Police Story*, 1973; *Red Pony*, 1973; *Shamus*, 1973; *Winter Kill*, 1973; *Chinatown*, 1974; *High Velocity*, 1974; *QB VII*, 1974; *S*P*Y*S*, 1974; *A Tree Grows in Brooklyn*, 1974; *Babe*, 1975; *Breakout*, 1975; *A Girl Named Sooner*, 1975; *Ransom*, 1975; *The Reincarnation of Peter Proud*, 1975; *Take a Hard Ride*, 1975; *The Wind and the Lion*, 1975; *Breakheart Pass*, 1976; *Logan's Run*, 1976; *The Omen*, 1976; *The Cassandra Crossing*, 1977; *Contract on Cherry Street*, 1977; *Damnation Alley*, 1977; *Islands in the Stream*, 1977; *MacArthur*, 1977; *Twilight's Last Gleaming*, 1977; *The Boys from Brazil*, 1978; *Capricorn One*, 1978; *Coma*, 1978; *Damien: Omen II*, 1978; *Magic*, 1978; *The Swarm*, 1978; *Alien*, 1979; *The Great Train Robbery*, 1979; *Players*, 1979; *Star Trek: The Motion Picture*, 1979; *Caboblanco*, 1980; *The Final Conflict: Omen III*, 1981; *Inchon*, 1981; *Masada*, 1981; *Night Crossing*, 1981; *Outland*, 1981; *Raggedy Man*, 1981; *The Salamander*, 1981; *The Challenge*, 1982; *First Blood*, 1982; *Poltergeist*, 1982; *The Secret of N.I.M.H.*, 1982; *Psycho 2*, 1983; *Twilight Zone: The Movie*, 1983; *Under Fire*, 1983; *Gremlins*, 1984; *Runaway*, 1984; *Supergirl*, 1984; *Baby: Secret of the Lost Legend*, 1985; *Explorers*, 1985; *King Solomon's Mines*, 1985; *Legend*, 1985; *Rambo: First Blood Part II*, 1985; *Amazing Stories*, 1986; *Hoosiers*, 1986; *Link*, 1986; *Poltergeist II*, 1986; *Extreme Prejudice*, 1987; *Innerspace*, 1987; *Lionheart*, 1987; *Alien Nation*, 1988; *Criminal Law*, 1988; *Rambo III*, 1988; *Rent-a-Cop*, 1988; *The 'Burbs*, 1989; *Leviathan*, 1989; *Star Trek V: The Final Frontier*, 1989; *Warlock*, 1989; *Gremlins 2: The New Batch*, 1990; *The Russia House*, 1990; *Total Recall*, 1990; *Help*, 1991; *Love Field*, 1991; *Mom and Dad Save the World*, 1991; *Not Without My Daughter*, 1991; *Sleeping with the Enemy*, 1991; *Basic Instinct*, 1992; *Forever Young*, 1992; *Hollister*, 1992; *Matinee*, 1992; *Mr. Baseball*, 1992; *Dennis the Menace*, 1993; *Malice*, 1993; *Rudy*, 1993; *Six Degrees of Separation*, 1993; *The Vanishing*, 1993; *Bad Girls*, 1994; *The River Wild*, 1994; *The Shadow*, 1994; *City Hall*, 1995; *Congo*, 1995; *First Knight*, 1995; *Powder*, 1995; *Chain Reaction*, 1996; *Executive Decision*, 1996; *Fierce Creatures*, 1996; *The Ghost and the Darkness*, 1996; *Star Trek: First Contact*, 1996; *Two Days in the Valley*, 1996; *Air Force One*, 1997; *The Edge*, 1997; *L.A. Confidential*, 1997; *Deep Rising*, 1998; *Mulan*, 1998; *Small Soldiers*, 1998; *Star Trek: Insurrection*, 1998; *U.S. Marshals*, 1998; *The Haunting*, 1999; *The Mummy*, 1999; *The Thirteenth Warrior*, 1999; *Hollow Man*, 2000; *Along Came a Spider*, 2001; *The Last Castle*, 2001; *Star Trek: Nemesis*, 2002; *The Sum of All Fears*, 2002; *Looney Tunes: Back *in Action*, 2003; *Basic Instinct 2*, 2006; *Inside Man*, 2006.

The Life

Jerrald Goldsmith was born and raised around Los Angeles. His parents encouraged their son's musical talents with lessons in piano, theory, and musicianship under pianist Jakob Gimpel, who later introduced Goldsmith to Miklós Rózsa, composer of the score to *Spellbound* (1945), a movie that had impressed Goldsmith as a teenager. He briefly attended Rózsa's composition class at the University of Southern California and later decided to attend Los Angeles City College, where he studied with the leading composers Mario Castelnuovo-Tedesco and Ernst Krenek.

In 1950 Goldsmith got a job typing scripts at CBS, which had a full music department on staff and had given several composers their start. His first assignments were composing for radio shows and then for live television; by the time he left in 1960, he had scored several series, notably episodes of *The Twilight Zone*, *Climax*, and *Playhouse 90*. Impressed by Goldsmith's television scores, legendary film composer Alfred Newman hired him to do the music for the film *Lonely Are the Brave*, his first major feature film score.

By the late 1960's Goldsmith was one of the most in-demand film composers in Hollywood, with credits such as *Freud*, *A Patch of Blue*, *Planet of the Apes*, and *The Sand Pebbles*, all of which were nominated for Academy Awards. The 1970's brought him even more success with scores for *Patton*, *Star Trek: The Motion Picture*, *Chinatown*, *The Boys from Brazil*, and *The Omen*, which won the Oscar for Best Score in 1977.

Goldsmith went on to bigger-budget movies in the 1980's, mostly a mix of comedy and adventure films, including the box-office hit *Gremlins* and the *Rambo* series, among several other action movies, a genre that he helped redefine musically.

In the 1990's Goldsmith's career continued to flourish through his collaboration with directors Paul Verhoeven (*Total Recall*, *Basic Instinct*) and Fred Schepisi (*The Russia House, Six Degrees of Separation*), more big-budget action movies (*Air Force One*, *The Mummy*), thrillers (*L.A. Confidential*), and *Star Trek* sequels. He continued his successful career into the new millennium, with such projects as

The Sum of All Fears, *Along Came a Spider*, and *Mulan*.

Beyond scoring films, Goldsmith also enjoyed conducting his music all over the world, building a strong relationship with the London Symphony Orchestra. He received an honorary doctorate from the Berklee College of Music in Boston and taught a graduate seminar in film scoring at the University of California, Los Angeles. He died on July 21, 2004, after a long battle with cancer.

The Music

A musical chameleon, Goldsmith came from an era when film composers were well trained in classical and contemporary idioms. Constantly experimenting, Goldsmith expanded the boundaries and scope of film music: *Planet of the Apes* and *The Omen* were essentially avant-garde scores, with textures and extended (or unconventional) techniques new to film music. Extremely sensitive to orchestral timbre, he explored unusual instrumental combinations. He embraced technology and experimented with a wide variety of electronic sounds and instruments as they became available. He also conducted and produced most of his scores.

Beyond his natural sense for melody, Goldsmith was inventive with rhythm and harmony, employing odd meters and dissonance to create musical counterpoint to the screen action. He was sensitive to the role of music and silence in dramatic and emotional control. His sense of timing and tension control, revealed in his skill at music spotting (placing music in the film), was extremely refined.

Planet of the Apes. Often mistaken for an electronic score, *Planet of the Apes*, one of Goldsmith's most innovative and avant-garde, is all acoustic, save for an Echoplex, a delay device used to feed through pizzicato string tracks. The composer uses unusual sounds and extended techniques.

Chinatown. Goldsmith was hired in 1974 to replace Phillip Lambro's rejected score, and he completed the job in ten days. Regarded as a classic period score, it features an unusual ensemble of solo trumpet, four pianos, four harps, guiro, and strings, a key aspect in defining the film's film noir aspect.

The Omen. The haunting score to the 1976 thriller won an Academy Award for its creator. Goldsmith composed a daring contemporary score, using extended vocal techniques in the choir, unusual percussion and string techniques, and mounting ostinatos.

Islands in the Stream. Goldsmith's favorite, *Islands in the Stream*, is based on one of the last works of Ernest Hemingway. The composer's score is extremely lush and impressionistic, built around a web of haunting themes, one on solo French horn and supplemented by another playful theme using similar intervallic identity in a diminutive form. Most prominent is the introduction of a central whole-tone rising-and-falling motif for the sea.

Star Trek: The Motion Picture. Probably Goldsmith's best-known score, *Star Trek* (1979) was inventive in its instrumentation and use of massive orchestral forces. It was intended to be as dramatic as John Williams's score for *Star Wars*, yet not derivative of it.

Musical Legacy

Goldsmith thought of himself not as a film composer but as a composer who writes for film. He cited Igor Stravinsky and Béla Bartók as his influences, placing himself within the context of twentieth century serious music. Goldsmith credited his work in live television as his training ground for learning how to score films. What set him apart from other film composers and the source of his long-lasting career was his ability to adapt and evolve musically. His scores are models for younger generations of composers.

Yiorgos Vassilandonakis

Further Reading

Burt, George. *The Art of Film Music*. Boston: Northeastern University Press, 1995. An academic look at film music, including analyses, aesthetics, and philosophical issues. Goldsmith is mentioned prominently, and his score to *Tora! Tora! Tora!* is analyzed.

Cordes, Cynthia Ann, et al. *On the Track: A Guide to Contemporary Film Scoring*. New York: Routledge, 2004. A comprehensive technical guide to film scoring, this book includes quotes and score excerpts by Goldsmith.

Darby, William, and Jack Du Bois. *American Film Music: Major Composers, Techniques, Trends, 1915-1990*. Jefferson, N.C.: McFarland, 1999. History and development of film music, focused on the careers of prominent composers, including Goldsmith. Several film scores are considered, and there are musical examples and filmographies for each composer.

Morgan, David. *Knowing the Score: Film Composers Talk About the Art, Craft, Blood, Sweat, and Tears of Writing for Cinema*. New York: HarperCollins, 2000. A collection of interviews with and essays by film composers. Goldsmith offers insight on choosing projects, orchestration, working with directors, using electronics, finding the sound of a film, and more.

Prendergast, Roy M. *Film Music: A Neglected Art— A Critical Study of Music in Films*. New York: W. W. Norton, 1992. Academic look into film scores, including essays on Goldsmith's music style as well as some of his classic scores.

Thomas, Tony. *Music for the Movies*. Los Angeles: Silman-James Press, 1997. A survey of film-scoring styles and composers for the general reader, with a chapter dedicated to Goldsmith.

See also: Bartók, Béla; Newman, Alfred; Rózsa, Miklós; Steiner, Max; Stravinsky, Igor.

Osvaldo Golijov
Argentine classical composer

In his compositions, Golijov utilizes diverse influences, from the ethnic styles of Argentine tango, Ashkenazic and Sephardic Jewish music, and Arabic music of the golden age to the instruments from the Silk Road and Gypsy bands.

Born: December 5, 1960; La Plata, Argentina

Principal works

CHAMBER WORKS: *Yiddish ruakh*, 1990; *There Is Wind and There Are Ashes in the Wind*, 1991; *Yiddishbbuk*, 1992; *Third World*, 1993; *Av horachamin*, 1994; *Ballad of the Drowned Solitude*, 1994; *K'vakarat*, 1994; *November*, 1994; *Last Round*, 1996; *Din*, 1998; *Fish Tale*, 1998; *Rocketekya*, 1998; *Doina*, 1999; *Mariel*, 1999; *How Slow the Wind*, 2001; *Luce*, 2001; *Lullaby and Doina*, 2001; *K'in sventa ch'ul me'tik Kwadalupe*, 2002; *Tenebrae*, 2002; *Ayre*, 2004; *Tekyah*, 2005.

CHORAL WORKS: *Oceana*, 1996; *La pasión según San Marcos*, 2000.
FILM SCORE: *Youth Without Youth*, 2007.
OPERA: *Ainadamar*, 2003.
ORCHESTRAL WORKS: *Crónicas*, 1990; *Amor americano*, 1991; *Death of the Angels*, 1996; *Last Round*, 1996; *How Slow the Wind*, 2002; *Lúa descolorida*, 2002; *Night of the Flying Horses*, 2002; *Rumba Mariana*, 2003; *The Dreams and Prayers of Isaac the Blind*, 2005.

The Life

Osvaldo Golijov (ahz-VAWL-doh GOH-liks-of) was born in Argentina to Jewish parents of Eastern European background. His mother was a pianist whose family had emigrated from Romania, and his father was a physician from the Ukraine. As a child, Golijov studied piano, and he sang in the synagogue choir. He studied at the Rubin Academy in Jerusalem, with George Crumb at the University of Pennsylvania (where Golijov earned a Ph.D.), and with Oliver Knussen at Tanglewood. Beginning in the 1990's, he composed many works on commission from such performers as Dawn Upshaw, the Kronos Quartet, the St. Lawrence Quartet, the Boston Symphony Orchestra, the Silk Road Ensemble, and the Chicago Symphony Orchestra, which appointed him a composer-in-residence in 2006.

Golijov moved with his wife and children to Boston, and he began teaching at the Boston Conservatory and at the College of the Holy Cross. His music has been featured at such venues as Chicago's Ravinia Festival, New York City's Lincoln Center, and the European Music Festival.

The Music

Golijov was exposed to many musical influences while growing up in Argentina. Attending the local opera house, he became familiar with operatic style, which influenced his vocal works. In other venues, he heard the tango style of Astor Piazzolla, which influenced his instrumental music. Guided by his pianist mother, he became familiar with a range of keyboard literature, from Johann Sebastian Bach to the Russian nationalists (Modest Mussorgsky, Nikolay Rimsky-Korsakov) to the twentieth century neoclassicists (Dmitri Shostakovich, Igor Stravinsky, Aaron Copland). Possibly the strongest influence on his work was the Jewish music with which he grew up and in which he was educated. Golijov has written works in every major form, including orchestral, keyboard, chamber, film, choral, and opera and other vocal music. He has shown a tendency to revise works in different versions and instrumentation, influenced by Bach and Gustav Mahler, among others.

The Dreams and Prayers of Isaac the Blind. This five-movement work for klezmer clarinet and string quartet, based on mystical writings of a great Kabbalist rabbi of the thirteenth century, features styles ranging from synagogue music to klezmer. The use of a purely instrumental medium for music based on prose prayers may be founded on models as diverse as Ludwig van Beethoven and Copland, although the fourth movement is a reworking of *K'vakarat*, in which the part written for the clarinet (a frequent instrument among klezmorim) had been composed for a cantorial soloist.

La pasión según San Marcos. This ambitious work for chorus and orchestra is one of four settings of the Passion of Christ in the Gospels commissioned in 2000 by Helmuth Rilling, artistic director of the Internationale Bachakademie Stuttgart, to commemorate the 250 years since Bach's death. The irony of choosing a Jew to follow in the footsteps of Bach in this work was not lost on Golijov, who chose a text in Spanish but included Jewish influences, for example, the Kaddish (a Hebrew prayer for the dead) at the Crucifixion.

Ainadamar. Golijov's opera, was composed in 2003 and revised in 2005. It is based on the story of the relationship between the actress Margarita Xirgu and the poet Federico García Lorca, who was murdered in the Spanish Civil War. The story is portrayed by historical characters, including García Lorca, a role sung by a female singer (perhaps harking back to the trouser roles, in which women dressed in pants sang men's parts, seen in works by Wolfgang Amadeus Mozart and Richard Strauss). Much of this music is folk-based, following the examples of Béla Bartók and the Russian nationalists. Golijov incorporated his earlier setting of the Mexican song "K'in Sventa Ch'ul Me'tik Kwadalupe" (2002) for string quartet, marimba, and tape into this work, adding a chorus.

Youth Without Youth. Golijov had only limited experience with film composition when director Francis Ford Coppola commissioned him to com-

Osvaldo Golijov. (AP/Wide World Photos)

pose the score for this 2007 film, which tells the story of a fugitive in the Europe of the 1930's. It is based on the work of the Romanian writer Mircea Eliade. Working with musicians in Romania (a homecoming to the country from which his mother's family had emigrated), Golijov found his time in Bucharest a learning experience. The story of the fugitive passing through many countries allowed diverse indigenous musical styles, from Gypsy to the Silk Road, to permeate his kaleidoscopic score.

Ayre. This is a group of ten songs and one instrumental composition, composed in 2004 for soprano Dawn Upshaw. The texts are in Ladino (the language of the Jews expelled from Spain in 1492), Spanish, Sardinian, Arabic, and Hebrew. Not a song cycle in the usual sense, this combination evokes the coexistence of Catholics, Jews, and Muslims in southern Spain during the centuries leading up to the Reconquista, and the message of this esoteric grouping is relevant to the political divisions of the present day, a lesson that Golijov probably learned during his studies in Israel, where Jews, Muslims, and Christians must live together. The scoring of the chamber ensemble that accompanies the soloist is reminiscent of the works of early twentieth century composers (including the Second Viennese School, Stravinsky, and Paul Hindemith) in its modest size, probably a reaction to the size of major works of the post-Romantic period.

Musical Legacy

Golijov has said that his work is grounded in his musical education and his ethnic background. The combination of influences of composers from Bach to Hindemith and Stravinsky, of folk music, and of Jewish religiosity is unique without including modernism. While Golijov is a world composer in terms of content and style, his use of form is often neoclassical.

Susan M. Filler

Further Reading

Berger, Kevin. "Golijov's World." *Salon* (January 20, 2006). Written in anticipation of "The Passion of Osvaldo Golijov" at Lincoln Center, New York, it provides an introduction to the composer's life and background.

Eichler, Jeremy. "Standing the Whole World on Its Ear." *The New York Times*, January 22, 2006. Speaks directly to the composer's polyglot musical background as an influence on his music, especially the Jewish aspect.

Ross, Alex. "Deep Song." *The New Yorker* (September 1, 2003). Primarily concerned with the opera *Ainadamar* as an expression of Spanish-Argentine influence on Golijov's music.

Yearwood, Pauline Dubkin. "Making Beautiful Music: From Tango to Klezmer, Osvaldo Golijov Brings a Fresh Sound to Orchestra Hall." *Chicago Jewish News*, February 9-15, 2007, pp. 18-19. An enlightening interview, emphasizing the composer's cosmopolitan views of his life and his work as a facet of his Jewish background.

See also: Crumb, George; Gubaidulina, Sofia; Hindemith, Paul; Ma, Yo-Yo; Piazzolla, Astor; Stravinsky, Igor; Tan Dun.

Benny Goodman

American jazz clarinet player and composer

A virtuoso clarinetist and a bandleader, Goodman was nicknamed the King of Swing for his orchestra and chamber groups that dominated the swing jazz scene in the late 1930's and beyond.

Born: May 30, 1909; Chicago, Illinois
Died: June 13, 1986; New York, New York
Also known as: Benjamin David Goodman (full name); King of Swing

Principal recordings

ALBUMS: *A Jazz Holiday*, 1928; *B. G. and Big Tea in NYC*, 1929 (with Jack Teagarden); *Benny Goodman and the Giants of Jazz*, 1929 (with Teagarden); *Swinging '34, Vol. 1*, 1934; *Swinging '34, Vol. 2*, 1934; *The Birth of Swing*, 1935; *Air Play*, 1936; *Roll 'Em, Vol. 1*, 1937; *Roll 'Em, Vol. 2*, 1937; *From Spirituals to Swing*, 1938; *Mozart Clarinet Quintet*, 1938; *Featuring Charlie Christian*, 1939 (with Charlie Christian); *Eddie Saunter Arrangements*, 1940; *Swing into Spring*, 1941; *Undercurrent Blues*, 1947; *The Benny Goodman Session*, 1949; *Let's Hear the Melody*, 1950; *Session for Six*, 1950; *Sextet*, 1950; *Benny Goodman*, 1951; *The Benny Goodman Trio Plays*, 1951; *Goodman and Teagarden*, 1951 (with Teagarden); *The Benny Goodman Trio*, 1952; *Easy Does It*, 1952; *The Benny Goodman Band*, 1953; *The Benny Goodman Touch*, 1953; *B. G. in Hi-Fi*, 1954; *For the Fletcher Henderson Fund*, 1954; *The New Benny Goodman Sextet*, 1954; *The Benny Goodman Story*, 1955; *With Charlie Christian*, 1955 (with Christian); *Benny Goodman Combos*, 1956; *The Benny Goodman Six*, 1956; *Date with the King*, 1956 (with Rosemary Clooney); *The Great Benny Goodman*, 1956; *Mostly Sextets*, 1956; *Mozart Clarinet Concerto*, 1956 (with the Boston Symphony Orchestra); *Trio Quartet Quintet*, 1956; *The Vintage Benny Goodman*, 1956; *Peggy Lee Sings with Benny Goodman*, 1957 (with Peggy Lee); *Benny Goodman Plays World Favorites in High Fidelity*, 1958; *Benny Rides Again*, 1958; *Happy Session*, 1958; *The Benny Goodman Treasure Chest*, 1959; *Benny in Brussels*, 1959; *In Stockholm 1959*, 1959; *The Sound of Music*, 1959; *Kingdom of Swing*, 1960; *Together Again!*, 1963 (with others); *Hello, Benny*, 1964; *Made in Japan*, 1964; *Meeting at the Summit*, 1966; *Listen to the Magic*, 1967; *Let's Dance Again*, 1969; *London Date*, 1969; *The King Swings*, 1973; *Seven Comes Eleven*, 1975.

SINGLES: "He's Not Worth Your Tears," 1931 (with Scrappy Lambert); "Ain't Cha Glad?," 1934 (with Jack Teagarden); "King Porter Stomp," 1935; "Let's Dance," 1935; "The Glory of Love," 1936; "Goody-Goody," 1936; "It's Been So Long," 1936; "These Foolish Things (Remind Me of You)," 1936; "Don't Be That Way," 1937; "I Let a Song Go out of My Heart," 1937 (with Martha Tilton); "Sing, Sing, Sing (With a Swing)," 1937; "This Year's Kisses," 1937 (with Margaret McCrae); "And the Angels Sing," 1939 (with Tilton); "Memories of You," 1939; "There'll Be Some Changes Made," 1941 (with Louise Tobin); "Somebody Else Is Taking My Place," 1942 (with Peggy Lee); "Taking a Chance on Love," 1943 (with Helen Forrest); "Gotta Be This or That," 1945; "Symphony," 1946 (with Liza Morrow); "Swedish Pastry," 1948 (with Stan Hasselgard).

The Life

Benjamin David Goodman was the ninth of twelve children born to David Goodman and Dora Rezinsky, Jewish immigrants from Eastern Europe. They met in Baltimore, Maryland, in 1894, they married, and they moved in 1902 to Chicago, where Goodman was born in 1909. His father, a tailor, had to take extra jobs to support his large family. Goodman's first music lessons were at a synagogue; later, he and two of his brothers joined the band at Hull House, a settlement house established by Jane Addams. He also received lessons from Franz Schoepp, an excellent teacher who charged modest rates.

Brimming with jazz musicians, Chicago was a propitous place for Goodman to grow up. By the age of thirteen, he was a professional clarinetist, and in addition he had acquired skill on the alto saxophone. He played with a variety of bands, and, at the age of sixteen, he joined Ben Pollack's band for an engagement at the Venice Ballroom in Los

Angeles. By the early 1930's Goodman had migrated to New York and recorded with the well-known bands of Red Nichols, Ben Selvin, Ted Lewis, and Paul Whiteman. By 1934 Goodman was ready to form his own band; its residency at the Palomar Ballroom in Los Angeles the next year made it famous. At the same time he organized his first chamber group, a trio that included pianist Teddy Wilson and drummer Gene Krupa. Later, the trio expanded to a quartet with the addition of vibraphonist Lionel Hampton. The band's most productive years were 1937 and 1938, when its lead trumpeter was Harry James. On January 16, 1938, Goodman's orchestra played a concert at Carnegie Hall in New York, previously the exclusive home of classical music.

Although a number of Goodman's performers had departed to form their own orchestras by 1939, he continued to lead both large and small groups, with his quartet sometimes expanded to six or seven performers, for decades thereafter. The roster of singers with the band included, at various times, Helen Ward, Helen Forrest, Martha Tilton, and Peggy Lee. After World War II Goodman's orchestra made a number of tours in many European, Asian, and South American countries.

In 1942 he married Alice Hammond Duckworth, the sister of John Hammond, a great jazz promoter in the 1930's. They had two daughters, and the marriage ended with her death in 1978. Goodman continued to perform in his sixties and seventies, his last concert coming only days before his death from cardiac arrest in 1986.

The Music

Goodman was an enormously talented and extraordinarily hard-working clarinetist and orchestra leader. He did succeed in classical music, but his great love was the swing music of the late 1930's. Swing was characterized by a steady beat, the harmonic structures of popular songs and the blues, and improvisions for soloists. Goodman was a difficult taskmaster, sometimes seeming to forget that the musicians in his orchestra could not attain his own standards. His bands delighted audiences for more than fifty years.

"Let's Dance." In the 1930's and 1940's radio programs featuring popular orchestras attained popularity. One was *Let's Dance*, with the Goodman

orchestra in 1934 and 1935. A song with this title was published, and it was recorded by Goodman, becoming his theme song throughout his career. The song was heard in a number of films, including *The Benny Goodman Story* in 1956, a film loosely based on Goodman's life.

"King Porter Stomp." Most of Goodman's most popular recordings were made in the 1930's. "King Porter Stomp," recorded in 1935, is an excellent representative of Goodman's swing style. Like a number of his other recordings, it was arranged by Fletcher Henderson, an outstanding black bandleader and arranger. The saxophone, not a particularly popular instrument in classical music since its invention in 1840, became popular in the era of jazz music, and Goodman's saxophone quartets influenced many other orchestras at the time. In this recording the players were unified, and they worked smoothly with the brass section, at that time featuring trumpeter Bunny Berigan. The rhythm section, not always outstanding in Goodman's bands, here

Benny Goodman. (Library of Congress)

gave an effective 4/4 beat, which in this era replaced the 2/4 rhythm that had characterized bands in earlier jazz. Henderson's arrangement provided innovative dynamic contrasts. To this arrangement Goodman added a clarinet solo, with trombones playing softly behind it. This exciting arrangement was demanded repeatedly by dancers who listened to the band on the radio and in ballrooms.

Benny Goodman and His Swing Orchestra. Under this title the Goodman orchestra performed at Carnegie Hall on January 16, 1938. This debut of jazz in a renowned home of classical music was promoted by impresario Sol Hurok. A section of the program called "Twenty Years of Jazz" included "Sensation Rag," as played by the Dixieland Jazz Band (usually considered the first recording jazz band) in 1917; "I'm Coming Virginia," in the style of the great cornetist Bix Beiderbecke; and imitations of works associated with Ted Lewis, Louis Armstrong, and Duke Ellington. Compositions by the leading composers of the day—George Gershwin, Irving Berlin, Richard Rodgers, and Jerome Kern—were heard. The work from this production that became most famous was "Sing, Sing, Sing (With a Swing)," the basic tune composed by Louis Prima and complemented by solos from some of Goodman's best musicians and strains from other works. This number lasted twelve minutes and thirteen seconds. The concert was recorded in a rather primitive fashion: It was temporarily lost, and it was not issued as a recording for twelve years.

"Memories of You." Written by two black performers, Andy Razaf and Eubie Blake, in 1930, this song was recorded several times by Goodman, and it became one of the regular offerings at his concerts. The 1939 version, performed by Goodman's sextet, is particularly interesting. Two members of the original trio had left Goodman, so this recording includes the great jazz guitarist Charlie Christian, whose career was cut short three years later by tuberculosis when he was only twenty-five. Hampton, the vibraphonist who made Goodman's trio into a quartet in 1936, also played in this sextet, as did Goodman's favorite arranger, pianist Henderson. Although white and black musicians had sometimes played together informally in the early days of jazz, Goodman took an important initiative in using black performers as regular members of his musical organizations. Artists such as Wilson, Hampton, and Henderson gained wider acceptance because of Goodman's efforts at racial integration, a policy he regarded as a way of making the best music.

Mozart Clarinet Concerto. Primarily a jazz and popular artist, Goodman also performed classical music brilliantly. In 1956 he joined with the Boston Symphony Orchestra, conducted by Charles Munch, at Tanglewood, Massachusetts, in a performance of Wolfgang Amadeus Mozart's Concerto for Clarinet and Orchestra in A Major (1791). Highly praised by critics, the performance was recorded by RCA Victor, on the album *Mozart Clarinet Concerto.*

Goodman in Moscow. In 1962 the U.S. State Department arranged for American performers to tour the Soviet Union. On May 30, Goodman's orchestra performed at the Soviet Army Sports Palace before forty-six hundred people, including Premier Nikita Khrushchev. The initial number was "Let's Dance." Next the orchestra played "Mission to Moscow," a number composed by Mel Powell. This arrangement, featuring dance syncopations that were Balkan rather than Russian, may have sounded more familiar to the audience. While disavowing any knowledge of American dances, Khrushchev remarked that he enjoyed the concert.

Goodman's orchestra played music from their usual jazz repertoire in Moscow and in other cities during several weeks in the Soviet Union. Public reaction to this tour was mixed, but introducing people in the Soviet sphere to American jazz and popular music was an attempt to break down the cultural divide between the Soviet Union and the United States.

Musical Legacy

Goodman was a superb clarinetist whose work was recognized by jazz, popular, and classical audiences. He made a great contribution in bringing the artistic medium of jazz to the attention of both the American public and the classical audiences. Until Goodman's orchestra appeared in Carnegie Hall in 1938, it was strictly a venue for classical works and audiences. Although Goodman could ably perform the works of such composers as Mozart and Paul Hindemith, his program on that occasion featured jazz and popular music. Later his tours to Europe, Asia, and South America brought American jazz to audiences beyond the relatively few Western European countries where it had been already recognized.

Goodman's career was unusually long and productive. Widely recognized as a great clarinetist even in his early twenties, he continued to perform into his seventy-eighth year. As soon as he became a conductor, his orchestra and chamber groups became springboards for talented performers, many of them black musicians who now could find work in musical organizations previously dominated by white performers playing for white audiences. The success of his small groups inspired other jazz musicians to give new emphasis to a form of jazz endeavor that the larger bands of the 1930's had been neglecting. Recordings made by his groups ranging from three to seven players have remained among his most popular performances.

Goodman received many awards. He was the second jazz performer to be honored at the Kennedy Center for the Performing Arts in Washington, D.C., in 1982, the first having been Count Basie the previous year. His academic awards included a doctor of music degree from Columbia University a few weeks before his death.

Robert P. Ellis

Further Reading

Collier, James Lincoln. *Benny Goodman and the Swing Era*. New York: Oxford University Press, 1989. This biography traces Goodman's life, and the author attempts to analyze the personality of a musician he found enigmatic.

Connor, D. Russell. *Benny Goodman: Wrappin' It Up*. Lanham, Md.: Scarecrow Press, 1996. Connor collects information about Goodman's performances and recordings that had eluded previous biographers.

Giddins, Gary. *Visions of Jazz: The First Century*. New York: Oxford University Press, 1998. Chapter 17 of this book argues that Goodman's death signified that "an age had passed, and not just a musical one."

Goodman, Benny. *Benny, King of Swing: A Pictorial Biography Based on Benny Goodman's Personal Archives*. New York: William Morrow, 1979. This book is primarily a pictorial, with 212 illustrations, but it also contains a fifty-seven-page in-troduction by Stanley Baron that reviews Goodman's career.

Goodman, Benny, and Irving Kolodin. *The Kingdom of Swing*. New York: Stackpole Sons, 1939. Kolodin was one of the first distinguished music critics to acknowledge Goodman's contribution to the musical world.

Schuller, Gunther. *The Swing Era: The Development of Jazz, 1930-1945*. New York: Oxford University Press, 1989. Although Schuller is more critical of Goodman than are other jazz historians, he significantly begins this book with a forty-three-page chapter on the clarinetist. He sees Goodman as a rare example of a true bond between popular taste and creative music.

See also: Barretto, Ray; Beiderbecke, Bix; Carter, Benny; Christian, Charlie; Fitzgerald, Ella; Getz, Stan; Hampton, Lionel; Henderson, Fletcher; Hindemith, Paul; Holiday, Billie; Jones, Elvin; Jones, Hank; Lee, Peggy; McPartland, Marian; Mancini, Henry; Mercer, Johnny; Miller, Glenn; Navarro, Fats; Nichols, Red; Puente, Tito; Shaw, Artie; Smith, Bessie; Szigeti, Joseph; Tormé, Mel; Whiteman, Paul; Williams, Mary Lou; Young, Lester.

Dexter Gordon

American jazz saxophonist and composer

An important link between the swing era and modern bebop, Gordon was noted for his assertive yet sensitive tenor tone, his penchant for quoting, and his incomparable ballad playing.

Born: February 27, 1923; Los Angeles, California
Died: April 25, 1990; Philadelphia, Pennsylvania
Also known as: Dexter Keith Gordon (full name)

Principal recordings

ALBUMS: *Dexter Rides Again*, 1945; *Long Tall Dexter*, 1945; *The Chase*, 1947 (with Wardell Gray); *Dexter Gordon Quintet*, 1947; *The Duel*, 1947 (with Teddy Edwards); *The Hunt*, 1947; *The Daddy Plays the Horn*, 1955; *Dexter Blows Hot and Cool*, 1955; *The Resurgence of Dexter Gordon*, 1960; *Dexter Calling*, 1961; *Dexter Gordon*, 1961; *Doin' Allright*, 1961; *Landslide*, 1961; *Cry Me a River*, 1962; *Go!*, 1962; *A Swingin' Affair*, 1962; *Our Man in Paris*, 1963; *One Flight Up*, 1964; *Clubhouse*, 1965; *Gettin' Around*, 1965; *Body and Soul*, 1967; *Both Sides of Midnight*, 1967; *Take the "A" Train*, 1967; *Day in Copenhagen*, 1969 (with Slide Hampton); *More Power!*, 1969; *Power!*, 1969; *The Tower of Power*, 1969; *Jumpin' Blues*, 1970; *The Panther!*, 1970; *The Shadow of Your Smile*, 1971; *Ca'Purange*, 1972; *Generation*, 1972; *Tangerine*, 1972; *Blues à la Suisse*, 1973; *Dexter Gordon-Sonny Grey with the Georges Arvanitas Trio*, 1973; *The Apartment*, 1974; *Revelation*, 1974; *Bouncin' with Dex*, 1975; *More than You Know*, 1975; *Something Different*, 1975; *Stable Mable*, 1975; *Biting the Apple*, 1976; *Featuring Joe Newman*, 1976 (with Joe Newman); *Homecoming*, 1976; *Lullaby for a Monster*, 1976; *Strings and Things*, 1976; *True Blue*, 1976 (with Al Cohn); *Midnight Dream*, 1977; *Sophisticated Giant*, 1977; *Great Encounters*, 1978; *Manhattan Symphonie*, 1978; *Gotham City*, 1980; *Jive Fernando*, 1981; *The Other Side of 'Round Midnight*, 1985; *'Round Midnight*, 1985.

The Life

Dexter Keith Gordon was born on February 27, 1923, in Los Angeles, California, son of Frank Gordon, one of the first African American doctors in Los Angeles, and Gwendolyn Baker. While still in high school, Gordon was recruited to join Lionel Hampton's band, with which he toured extensively and made his first recordings. He spent the majority of the 1940's touring with some of America's top big bands, most notably with Louis Armstrong and Billy Eckstine.

The 1950's were largely a period of inactivity for Gordon, who was in and out of prison for drug-related offenses. By 1960, however, Gordon had the first of two major resurgences in his career: He signed a contract with Blue Note Records, and he recorded some of his most revered sessions as a leader. In 1962 Gordon relocated to Europe, and he spent the next fourteen years living and recording in Paris and Copenhagen, one of many prominent American jazz musicians who found Europe in the 1960's better suited their musical lives.

Gordon permanently relocated to the United States in 1976, with a special return engagement at the Village Vanguard. That event received such praise that it resulted in the second major revitalization of his career. In the 1980's Gordon's playing began to decrease, and he launched a second career as an actor. He was nominated for an Academy Award for his portrayal of an expatriate jazz musician in *'Round Midnight* (1986), and he had a minor role in *Awakenings* (1991), which was released after his death. When he died of kidney failure on April 25, 1990, Gordon was survived by his widow, Maxine, and his five children, Robin, Dierdre, Mikael, Benjamin, and Woody.

The Music

In the 1940's Gordon first appears on recordings with the Lionel Hampton Big Band (where he shared tenor saxophone duties with Illinois Jacquet). In 1943 he led his first session (released as "I've Found a New Baby"), featuring Nat King Cole on piano. Gordon then went on to perform and to record with many of the top big bands of the era, from Fletcher Henderson to Armstrong to Eckstine. It was his time in Eckstine's band that led to his development as a bebop player, sharing the bandstand on any given evening with fellow swing-to-bop pioneers Fats Navarro, Sonny Stitt, Dizzy Gillespie, Art Blakey, and Sarah Vaughan.

Early Works. As early as 1945, Gordon recorded bebop sides in a quintet led by Gillespie (released as *In the Beginning*), and soon he began increasing the frequency of his releases as a leader. With various quartets and quintets in 1945 and 1946, Gordon released his trademark self-titled compositions, from "Long Tall Dexter," to "Dexter Digs In," to "Blow Mr. Dexter" (ironically, the "Dexter" titles, so closely tied to his career as a leader, were not contributed by Gordon). Many of these tracks can be found on *Long Tall Dexter*, released on Savoy Records in 1945. In 1947 Gordon teamed up with fellow tenor saxophonist Wardell Gray and released *The Chase*, a famous bebop recording featuring extended duels between the two tenors. Later in 1947, Gordon recorded with trumpeter Navarro and pianist-arranger Tadd Dameron on famous bebop sessions for Savoy Records.

Doin' Allright. With a few exceptions (Los Angeles session dates in 1955 under the titles *Dexter*

Dexter Gordon. (AP/Wide World Photos)

Tower of Power, *The Panther!*, *Jumpin' Blues*, *Tangerine*, and *Generation*. Upon permanent relocation to the United States in 1976, Gordon's return engagement to the Village Vanguard was released as *Homecoming* on the Columbia Records label. Throughout the late 1970's and occasionally in the 1980's, Gordon made recordings on various labels (Columbia, Blue Note), and he collaborated with Hampton, Hancock, and Woody Shaw.

Musical Legacy

For much of his career, Gordon did not garner the praise that some of his fellow tenor saxophonists did. Perhaps this was because he was not strictly a swing-era star such as Lester Young or a bebop avant-garde pioneer such as John Coltrane. However, after he returned to live in the United States in 1976, adulation for Gordon and his music grew. Jazz aficionados recognized him as a musician who was influenced by the swing players and who at the same time had a significant influence on the bebop players. Additionally, his style of combining swing and bebop influences with his powerful tone, harmonic inventiveness, and lyrical ballad playing has been emulated by following generations of tenor saxophonists. Gordon was elected to the *Down Beat* Hall of Fame in 1980, and he was nominated for an Academy Award (as Best Actor in *'Round Midnight*) in 1986.

Eric Novod

Blows Hot and Cool and *The Daddy Plays the Horn*), the 1950's saw little recording from Gordon because of his imprisonment on drug charges. Upon his release, Gordon was recruited by Blue Note Records, and he released some of his most critically acclaimed and beloved recordings. The Blue Note period featured *Doin' Allright* (with trumpeter Freddie Hubbard), *Dexter Calling*, *Go!*, *A Swingin' Affair*, *Our Man in Paris*, *One Flight Up*, *Clubhouse*, and *Gettin' Around*. Gordon was also a sideman on Herbie Hancock's legendary first record, *Takin' Off*, in 1962.

Homecoming. Living in Paris and Copenhagen from 1962 to 1976 (returning occasionally to record sessions for Blue Note and to visit his family), Gordon also recorded sessions for the European labels Steeplechase and Black Lion. A series of legendary concerts at Copenhagen's Montmartre Club led to the release of multiple recordings in 1967, including *Body and Soul* and *Both Sides of Midnight*. While still living in Europe, Gordon released American recordings for the Prestige Label, including *The*

Further Reading

Britt, Sam. *Dexter Gordon: A Musical Biography*. New York: Da Capo Press, 1989. Contains biographical information on Gordon with a focus on his career in music. Includes discography.

Gioia, Ted. *West Coast Jazz: Modern Jazz in California, 1945-1960*. Berkeley: University of California Press, 1998. This work includes many references to Gordon's influence on the West Coast jazz scene in the late 1940's.

Outhwaite, Tony. "Back in the U.S.A." *National Review* 29, no. 38 (September 30, 1977). An article that focuses on the excitement surrounding the return of Gordon to the United States after fourteen years of living in Europe.

Panken, Ted. "Jackie McLean on Dexter Gordon." *Down Beat* 71, no. 7 (July, 2004): 32. Famous jazz alto saxophonist McLean discusses the significance of Gordon's tenor saxophone playing and his importance place in jazz history.

Taylor, Arthur. *Notes and Tones: Musician to Musician Interviews*. New York: Da Capo Press, 1993. This expanded edition contains a dialogue between Taylor and Gordon, and they discuss jazz's musical and racial history.

See also: Cole, Nat King; Coltrane, John; Hampton, Lionel; Navarro, Fats; Powell, Bud; Rollins, Sonny; Young, Lester.

Glenn Gould

Canadian classical pianist, composer, and conductor

A prodigiously gifted pianist and multimedia communicator, Gould revived interest in long-neglected composers and advanced aesthetic and philosophical theories that, while initially dismissed as eccentric, have come to be seen as prophetic of the potential for technology to enhance the performance of serious music.

Born: September 25, 1932; Toronto, Ontario, Canada
Died: October 4, 1982; Toronto, Ontario, Canada
Also known as: Glenn Herbert Gould (full name)

Principal works

CHAMBER WORKS: Sonata for Bassoon and Piano, 1950; *Prelude, Cantilena, and Gigue*, 1951 (for clarinet and bassoon); String Quartet, Op. 1, 1956.

CHORAL WORKS: *Lieberson Madrigal*, 1964 (for four solo voices or mixed chorus and piano); *So You Want to Write a Fugue?*, 1964 (for chorus and piano or string quartet).

PIANO WORKS: *A Merry Thought*, 1941; Rondo in D Major, 1948; Sonata for Piano, 1950; *Five Short Piano Pieces*, 1951; *Two Pieces*, 1952.

Principal recordings

ALBUMS (as conductor): *Siegfried Idyll*, 1982 (by Richard Wagner).

ALBUMS (as pianist): *Goldberg Variations*, 1956 (by Johann Sebastian Bach); *Sonata No. 30 in E Major, Op. 109*, 1956 (by Ludwig Van Beethoven); *Sonata No. 3, Op. 92, No. 4*, 1959 (by Ernst Krenek); *Sonata, Op. 1*, 1959 (by Alban Berg); *Three Piano Pieces, Op. 11*, 1959 (by Arnold Schoenberg); *Intermezzi*, 1961 (by Johannes Brahms); *Bach: The Art of the Fugue*, 1962; *Bach: The Well-Tempered Clavier*, 1962-1971 (six volumes); *Brahms: Piano Concerto No. 1 in D Minor, Op. 15*, 1962; *Beethoven: Concerto No. 5 in E-flat Major, Op. 73*, 1966; *Brahms: Piano Concerto No. 1 in D Minor, Op. 15*, 1962; *A Consort of Musicke Bye William Byrde and Orlando Gibbons*, 1971; *Handel: Suites for Harpsichord Nos. 1-4*, 1972; *Schoenberg: Complete Songs for Voice and Piano, Vol. 2*, 1972; *Hindemith: Das Marienleben*, 1978.

RADIO SCORE: *The Solitude Trilogy*, 1967-1977 (includes *The Idea of North*, 1967; *The Latecomers*, 1969; *The Quiet in the Land*, 1977).

The Life

Glenn Herbert Gould (gewld) was born in 1932 to Russell and Florence Gold, their only child. The family changed Gold to Gould probably to avoid being mistaken for Jews during a time of heightened anti-Semitism; the Golds were Scottish. His mother was a piano teacher who traced her lineage to the Romantic Norwegian composer Edvard Grieg. Her early efforts at acquainting her son with the piano revealed his photographic memory, superior digital dexterity, and perfect pitch.

At the age of seven Gould won a competition sponsored by the Toronto Conservatory. By the age of ten he was studying with the Chilean pianist and conductor Alberto Guerrero and rapidly mastering a large body of compositions from the Baroque, classical, and Romantic repertoires. Three years later he performed as a featured soloist with the Toronto Symphony Orchestra.

In the decade that followed, his combination of talent and odd performance mannerisms (humming loudly while he performed, conducting himself, adopting odd performance postures) made him a musical celebrity in Canada. However, it was his January 11, 1955, concert at Town Hall in New York City that earned him a contract with Columbia Records.

Gould's Columbia debut, a recording of Johann Sebastian Bach's *Goldberg Variations*, was an immediate best seller and launched him on a grueling, worldwide performance tour. Nine years and more than 250 concerts later, he stunned his audience by abandoning the concert stage and devoting himself to perfecting his art in the recording studio, where, he insisted, he could achieve ideal performances by splicing together the best of multiple takes.

Contrary to conventional wisdom, Gould's retreat from the stage did not negatively affect his record sales, in part because he used his newly acquired free time to embark upon a career in radio, television, and journalism that kept him in the public eye. From 1967 to 1975 he recorded three celebrated and influential contrapuntal radio documentaries that have come to be known collectively as *The Solitude Trilogy*.

Such extracurricular projects notwithstanding, Gould continued to record music at an exhausting pace, slowing down only during the mid-1970's to combat mysterious illnesses that hindered his playing. A lifelong hypochondriac, Gould relied on a heavy regimen of prescription drugs that, along with his punishing work ethic, most likely contributed to the stroke that he suffered on September 27, 1982, and from which he died one week later, nine days after his fiftieth birthday.

The Music

Although Gould's musical career was by no means limited to his recordings and performances, he was most well known for his charisma as a pianist. He was nearly as infamous for his eccentricities and iconoclastic approach to venerated composers (particularly Wolfgang Amadeus Mozart and Ludwig van Beethoven) as he was for his prolific and excellent musicianship. Best known for his recordings of Bach and Arnold Schoenberg (the two composers whose intellectually rigorous and un-Romantic sensibilities, although separated by

Glenn Gould. (AP/Wide World Photos)

two hundred years, best reflected his own), Gould also recorded music from the repertoires of Franz Joseph Haydn, Alban Berg, Johannes Brahms, Richard Strauss, Sergei Prokofiev, Grieg, William Byrd, George Frideric Handel, Georges Bizet, Richard Wagner, Paul Hindemith, Robert Schumann, Jean Sibelius, Aleksandr Scriabin, Ernst Krenek, Jan Pieterszoon Sweelinck, and Barbara Pentland. Somewhat surprisingly, given how little he recorded of his music, Gould claimed that his favorite composer was the Tudor-era Orlando Gibbons. Gould also recorded on the organ (the instrument on which he first played in public at the age of twelve) and the harpsichord.

Long credited with discovering and perfecting a meticulously tactile approach to the piano, Gould actually adapted techniques that he had absorbed from the recordings of the pianists Artur Schnabel and Rosalyn Tureck and from his years as a student of Guerrero. That he remained frustrated in his often-stated intention to become a great composer and conductor was apparently of consequence only to himself.

Goldberg Variations. Gould's debut, recorded in 1955 and released in 1956, caused an instant sensation and rapidly became a best seller. Perpetually in print, it was rereleased several times by Sony Classical in the years following Gould's death, both alone and paired with his 1981 rerecording. In 2006 it became the template for the first of the Zenph Studios' "re-creations" when, before an audience of Gould's friends and colleagues, a specially prepared Yamaha piano "performed" the piece in response to a computerized encoding of Gould's original performance.

Intermezzi. For all of his deeply rooted anti-Romanticism, Gould was surprisingly receptive to these pieces by Brahms, which he recorded in 1959 and 1960 with a sensitivity born of a genuine and intimate affection.

Piano Concerto No. 1 in D Minor, Op. 15. On April 5, 1962, Gould performed this staple of the Romantic repertoire with the New York Philharmonic under the direction of Leonard Bernstein. Gould's radically un-Romantic reinterpretations of Brahms's well-known tempi, although hesitantly agreed to by Bernstein (who admired Gould's intelligence and respected his instincts), provoked considerable turmoil among critics and audience members alike and became for years the most cited example of Gould's audacity.

String Quartet, Op. 1. The first of what Gould hoped would be many of his original compositions turned out to be his last. Recorded in 1960 with the Symphonia String Quartet, it elicited kind, if generally unenthusiastic, reviews. The most common complaint was that its multitude of musical ideas was ultimately unfocused.

The Art of Fugue, Vol. 1, Contrapunctus 1-9. Gould made the majority of this recording in 1962 on a Casavant organ housed in Toronto's All Saints' Church. Like the twelve piano recordings that preceded it, his sole organ recording emphasized both the precision of his playing and his objection to the typical organ record's reverberant sonorities. In part because the Casavant, whose Baroque-sensitive registration he loved, was destroyed in a fire, he never recorded *The Art of the Fugue, Vol. 2*.

The Well-Tempered Clavier. Gould recorded both books of Bach's monumentally influential keyboard work in six volumes between 1962 and 1971. Together with his two recordings of the *Goldberg Variations*, they represent the fullest musical articulation of Gould's deeply rooted appreciation for the composer whose compositions he recorded more than any other.

Concerto No. 5 in E-flat Major ("Emperor"). This 1966 recording would prove to be unique in Gould's oeuvre for two main reasons. First, it found

him giving an eccentricity-free performance of a well-known composition. Second, it would be his only performance with an orchestra under the baton of his hero, the conductor Leopold Stokowski.

A Consort of Musicke Bye William Byrde and Orlando Gibbons. This Tudor-music album, recorded in 1967, 1968, and 1971, represents Gould's only documented excursion into the music of his favorite composer, Gibbons.

Complete Songs for Voice and Piano. Together with his recording of Hindemith's *Das Marienleben* with Roxolana Roslak, these performances, recorded between 1964 and 1971, capture not only Gould's love of Schoenberg but also his capacity for providing sympathetic accompaniment (in this case to the singers Helen Vanni, soprano; Cornelius Opthof, baritone; and Donald Gramm, bass-baritone).

Suites, Nos. 1-4. For someone who loved the harpsichord so much that he insisted his pianos be tuned to replicate the harpsichord's dry precision as closely as possible (a demand that drove Steinway's, and later Yamaha's, tuners to great frustration), Gould recorded very little on the instrument. He also recorded very little Handel, a fact that makes this 1972 recording doubly valuable.

Das Marienleben. Gould's 1976-1977 recording of the original 1923 version of Hindemith's song cycle based on the life of Mary was released in 1978 and featured not only the exquisite soprano singing of Roslak but also Gould's extensive and critically acute liner notes, which concluded with his declaration that *Das Marienleben* was the finest song cycle ever composed.

Posthumous Releases. Sony Classical (formerly Columbia, later CBS, Masterworks) went to great lengths to keep Gould's recordings in circulation after his death, repackaging them mainly in the *Glenn Gould Edition* and the *Glenn Gould Anniversary Edition* series. The most conceptually original and consistent compilation was 2003's *Glenn Gould . . . and Serenity*, which brought together the most serene recordings from the entire spectrum of Gould's discography.

Musical Legacy

It has been said that Gould was more popular after his death than he was while he lived. Unlike many artists of whom such a statement has been made, however, Gould also enjoyed immense popularity during his lifetime. Indeed, the escalating sales of his many posthumously repackaged recordings were merely a continuation of a long-established trend among lovers of Gould's music.

Gould's notoriously reclusive tendencies notwithstanding, he was open to collaborations with other musicians (the Juilliard Quartet, the Philadelphia Brass Ensemble, violinists Yehudi Menuhin and Israel Baker, cellist Leonard Rose), singers (operatic sopranos Vanni and Roslak), and conductors (Bernstein, Vladimir Golschmann) who shared, or at least tolerated, his often unorthodox interpretations. Gould demonstrated his generosity in other ways as well, notably and endearingly in his championing of Stokowski as the greatest conductor of the twentieth century and one of its most visionary musical geniuses.

In the years after his death, Gould became the subject not only of several well-written biographies but also of video documentaries and the impressionistic biopic *Thirty Two Short Films About Glenn Gould* (the segments of which were structured along the lines of the thirty-two *Goldberg Variations*). In 1988 the National Library of Canada mounted "Glenn Gould 1988," a major exhibition made possible by the library's staggeringly vast amount of Gould memorabilia, which it acquired in 1983. Like every other presentation having to do with Gould's life and music, it attracted a large, enthusiastic, and diverse audience. Since his death, Gould's recordings and his determination to bring the works of neglected or misunderstood composers to his audience (which was the broadest of any classical solo instrumentalist) have emerged as his greatest legacy.

Arsenio Orteza

Further Reading

Angilette, Elizabeth. *Philosopher at the Keyboard: Glenn Gould*. Lanham, Md.: Rowman & Littlefield, 2001. A fascinating attempt to construct a coherent philosophy of art and life from Gould's many writings and documented statements.

Bazzana, Kevin. *Wondrous Strange: The Life and Art of Glenn Gould*. Oxford, England: Oxford University Press, 2006. Authoritative Gould biography, benefitting from the author's scholarly understanding of Gould's repertoire and the subtleties of the pianist's interpretations and from his access to people and documents heretofore inaccessible or underexplored. Thoroughly examines Gould's public accomplishments and what is known of his private life, fairly assessing his strengths and weaknesses. Concludes that the more sensationalized aspects of Gould's life have been exaggerated to the detriment of a sober appreciation of his work, its importance, and its enduring popularity.

Cott, Jonathan, and Glenn Gould. *Conversations with Glenn Gould*. Chicago: University of Chicago Press, 2005. Of value both for the incisiveness of Cott's questions and for the fact that, unlike many of Gould's other widely circulated interviews, Cott's were not ghost-scripted in advance by Gould. Includes photographs and detailed listings of Gould's recordings and radio and television projects.

Friedrich, Otto. *Glenn Gould: A Life and Variations*. New York: Vintage, 1989. Full-scale Gould biography valuable for the accuracy and detail of its interview-enriched narrative and painstakingly documented listings of Gould's concert, studio, radio, and television performances.

McGreevy, John, ed. *Variations: Glenn Gould by Himself and His Friends*. Garden City, N.Y.: Doubleday, 1983. Handsome and skillfully edited combination of career-spanning photographs and essays, combining the best of Gould's writings ("Glenn Gould Interviews Glenn Gould About Glenn Gould," "Stokowski in Six Scenes," "Toronto") with eloquent, humorous, and touching reminiscences written by Gould's closest friends and colleagues (Bernstein, Menuhin, Bruno Monsaingeon).

Payzant, Geoffrey. *Glenn Gould, Music and Mind*. Toronto, Ont.: Key Porter, 2005. Gould-approved exploration of the aesthetic and philosophical ramifications of his abandonment of the concert stage for the studio and his utilization of "creative cheating" to construct the best musical performances possible in an era of increasing technological sophistication.

See also: Berg, Alban; Bernstein, Leonard; Hindemith, Paul; Prokofiev, Sergei; Schoenberg, Arnold; Scriabin, Aleksandr; Stokowski, Leopold; Strauss, Richard; Takemitsu, Tōru; Tan Dun; Watts, André.

Percy Aldridge Grainger

Australian American classical pianist and composer

A virtuoso pianist and an orchestral composer and conductor, Grainger was particularly significant for his preservation of British folk songs and his promotion of band music as a serious art form.

Born: July 8, 1882; Melbourne, Victoria, Australia
Died: February 20, 1961; White Plains, New York
Also known as: George Percy Aldridge Grainger (full name)

Principal works

CHAMBER WORKS: *My Robin Is to the Greenwood Gone*, 1912 (for flute, English horn, and six strings); *Youthful Rapture*, 1929.

CHORAL WORKS: *The Lads of Wamphray*, 1907 (for male chorus and two pianos or orchestra; later arranged for wind band); *Kipling Jungle Book Cycle*, 1947 (for mixed chorus and chamber orchestra).

ORCHESTRAL WORKS: *Fisher's Boarding House*, 1899; *We Were Dreamers*, 1899; *Green Bushes*, 1906 (passacaglia on an English folk song); *Mock Morris*, 1911 (for six solo strings or string orchestra); *Handel in the Strand*, 1912 (for piano and string orchestra); *In a Nutshell*, 1916 (suite for orchestra, piano, and percussion); *The Warriors*, 1916 (music for an imaginary ballet; for three pianos and orchestra); *Blithe Bells*, 1931; *The Immovable "Do" (The Cyphering "C")*, 1939; *Danish Folk Music Suite*, 1941; *Dreamery*, 1943; *The Power of Rome and the Christian Heart*, 1943 (for wind instruments and organ); *Youthful Suite*, 1945; *Faeroe Island Dance*, 1946 (for concert band).

PIANO WORKS: *Klavierstuck in A Minor*, 1897 (for solo piano); *Klavierstuck in E Major*, 1897 (for solo piano); *Klavierstuck in D Major*, 1898 (for solo piano); *Hill Songs Nos. 1 and 2*, 1907 (for solo piano); *English Dance*, 1909 (for two pianos and six hands); *Shepherd's Hey!*, 1913 (folk song for piano); *Spoon River*, 1922 (for solo piano).

VOCAL WORKS: *The Secret of the Sea*, 1898 (for male voice and piano); *The Men of the Sea*, 1899 (for voice and piano); *Merciful Town*, 1899 (for voice and piano); *Northern Ballad*, 1899 (for voice and piano); *Ride with an Idle Whip*, 1899 (for voice and piano); *There Were Three Friends*, 1899; *Songs of the North*, 1900 (fourteen folk songs for voice and piano); *Sailor's Chanty*, 1901 (for male voice and piano); *Ye Banks and Braes o' Bonnie Doon*, 1901; *Irish Tune from County Derry*, 1902; *Zanzibar Boat Song*, 1902; *Colleen Dhas (The Valley Lay Smiling)*, 1904; *Sir Eglamore*, 1904; *The Sea Wife*, 1905; *Walking Tune*, 1905 (for symphonic wind choir); *I'm Seventeen Come Sunday*, 1906; *Bold William Taylor*, 1908 (folk song for solo voice and piano); *Soldier, Soldier*, 1908 (for voice and piano); *Shallow Brown*, 1910 (chanty for one or two voices and piano); *Colonial Song*, 1911 (for voices and piano); *The "Gum-Suckers" March*, 1911; *King Solomon's Espousals*, 1911; *Love Verses from "The Song of Solomon,"* 1911; *Scotch Strathspey and Reel*, 1911; *The Sussex Mummers' Christmas Carol*, 1911; *Willow Willow*, 1911 (for voice and piano); *Six Dukes Went a-Fishin'*, 1912 (folk song for voice and piano); *At Twilight*, 1913; *Molly on the Shore*, 1914 (folk song for orchestra); *The Merry Wedding*, 1915; *Arrival Platform Humlet*, 1916; *Gay but Wistful*, 1916; *Pastoral*, 1916; *Children's March: Over the Hills and Far Away*, 1918 (for voices and band); *Country Gardens*, 1918 (for voice and orchestra); *The Brisk Young Sailor (Who Returned to Wed His True Love)*, 1919; *British Waterside (The Jolly Sailor)*, 1920 (folk song for voice and piano); *The Pretty Maid Milkin' Her Cow*, 1920 (folk song for voice and piano); *Creepin' Jane*, 1921 (folk song for voice and piano); *To a Nordic Princess (Bridal Song)*, 1928; *Lisbon (Dublin Bay)*, 1931; *Tribute to Foster*, 1931; *Harvest Hymn (Harvest Time in Sweden)*, 1932 (for voices and orchestra); *Lincolnshire Posy*, 1937 (folk song suite for wind band); *Lord Melbourne (War Song)*, 1937; *The Lost Lady Found*, 1937 (folk song for voice and piano); *Rufford Park Poachers*, 1937; *The "Duke of Marlborough" Fanfare*, 1939 (for voice and brass band); *The Merry King*, 1939; *Early One Morning*, 1940; *The Beaches of Lukannon*, 1941 (for voice and piano); *Hard-Hearted Barb'ra (H)ellen*, 1946 (folk song for voice and piano); *Marching Song of Democracy*, 1948 (for mixed chorus, organ, and orchestra).

The Life

George Percy Aldridge Grainger (GRAYN-jur) was the only child of John Grainger and Rose Aldridge, a domineering woman who gave her son his first piano lessons. In 1895 Rose took Grainger (whose father had left in 1890) to Europe to further his musical education.

Grainger studied piano and composition in Frankfurt, Germany, forging lifelong friendships with outstanding student musicians. In 1901 the Graingers moved to London, where Percy became a common fixture at recitals and society performances. He also studied in Berlin with Ferruccio Busoni and toured Australia with Ada Crossley. Grainger was one of the first musicians (in 1905) to use a phonograph to collect folk songs. His career as a pianist flourished, exceeding one hundred performances yearly. With encouragement from Edvard Grieg and Frederick Delius, Grainger began to publish his compositions, using the name Percy Aldridge Grainger.

At the outbreak of World War I, Rose and Grainger fled to the United States, where Grainger toured in support of the Red Cross. In 1917 he joined the U.S. military as a band man; he became a U.S. citizen in 1918. At war's end, Grainger continued to tour, perform, compose, and record. In 1922, plagued by health problems and mental deterioration, Rose committed suicide. Grainger temporarily abandoned performing, but by 1923 he had resumed his strenuous regimen of concertizing and touring throughout the world. On one such tour, in 1926, he met a fascinating Swedish woman, Ella Ström.

Ström proved to be a kindred spirit and they became engaged. The wedding was set for August, 1928, coinciding with conducting appearances by Grainger at the Hollywood Bowl. The promoters persuaded Grainger to schedule the ceremony at one of the concerts. Unaware of the enormity of the venue, Ella acquiesced. The Graingers were wed in front of twenty-two thousand audience members.

The 1930's saw the Graingers undertake the establishment of a Grainger Museum at the University of Melbourne. When the United States entered World War II, Grainger again performed in support of the Red Cross. By 1953 prostate cancer forced him to slow down. Despite ongoing treatment, metastatic cancer spread throughout his body and brain, and in February, 1961, he succumbed. Grainger's body was laid to rest in Adelaide, Australia, in the vault of his mother's family, the Aldridges.

The Music

Grainger completed more than twelve hundred compositions, spanning many different genres. Much of his reputation results from his settings of folk songs for piano and for orchestra and from his band music. Grainger's publications were unique, utilizing vernacular words for musical descriptions, "blue-eyed English," rather than the traditional Italian terminology.

"Country Gardens." Grainger's first major success was an uncomplicated arrangement of a folk song. Although much of Grainger's compositional output was substantially more complex, experimental, and cerebral, it is this simpler work that established Grainger's compositional reputation. "Country Gardens" appears in several versions, including solo piano (1918), full orchestra (1949), and

Percy Aldridge Grainger. (Library of Congress)

529

band (completed 1953, published 1990). An earlier version (perhaps 1908) for "two whistlers and a few instruments" remains unpublished.

Lincolnshire Posy. Grainger's six-movement masterpiece for winds demonstrates his innovative nature. This 1937 composition sets folk tunes he had collected decades earlier the way a jeweler sets a gem: the careful, tasteful setting enhances the natural beauty of these musical wildflowers without obscuring their inherent characteristics.

Techniques utilized in *Lincolnshire Posy* are representative of Grainger's style and have influenced subsequent wind composers. To represent different interpretive shadings a folksinger might apply to the verses of a song, Grainger uses continuous variation, with differing rhythmic, harmonic, and orchestrational structures. Exotic harmonies that might have been more at home in the music of Duke Ellington (whom Grainger considered the greatest living composer) bring a richness to the setting. Dynamic effects are meticulously planned, including Grainger's characteristic cross-fade, where one voice increases volume while another fades.

The rhythmic freedom of a folksinger is depicted several different ways. The most basic way is through the use of rhythmic variation. A second method emphasizes the irregularity of the singer by employing continually changing mixed meters. Another technique achieves rhythmic freedom by the temporary banishment of barlines.

Lincolnshire Posy also demonstrates Grainger's concept of tuneful percussion, expanding the mallet percussion choices beyond the simple xylophone and bells favored by so many composers of that era.

Grainger's innovative use of constantly changing and unusual combinations of instruments creates a wide palette of tone colors. This feature might just be the most influential aspect of *Lincolnshire Posy*. Not only did the varying rich timbres demonstrate Grainger's unique abilities as a composer for winds, they also served to demonstrate to other composers the wide range of possibilities inherent in a large collection of wind and percussion instruments. *Lincolnshire Posy* thus accelerated the recognition of the wind band as a serious compositional medium.

Grainger sought rhythmic and melodic freedom echoing the complexities and irregularities of nature but exceeding the capabilities of instruments and musicians. Some of his emphasis on rapidly changing mixed meter caused his most serious compositions to suffer from neglect. The third movement of *Lincolnshire Posy*, for example, is often deleted from performances of the work, even to this day, just as it was at its premiere performance, because of the perception of its rhythmic difficulty.

Experimental Music. Grainger desired to build a machine that would allow him complete freedom of choice in both pitch and rhythm. In the 1920's he began to manipulate piano rolls to create free music, publishing an article about his efforts in 1924. A 1935 Australian radio broadcast employed a string quartet to demonstrate pitch freedom that exceeded the traditional twelve fixed tones of the chromatic scale. Grainger composed for the siren-like electronic musical instrument, the Theremin, and failed in an attempt to induce inventor Léon Theremin to create a device that would achieve Grainger's goals. Grainger experimented with using a phonograph to layer recordings of his voice, a technique which predated later experiments in multitracking by those who manipulated magnetic tape. Grainger eventually turned to the use of electronic media, moving from vacuum tubes to transistors. While his experiments paralleled many similar efforts by composers of electronic music, his efforts remained largely unknown.

Musical Legacy

Grainger's musical legacy consists primarily of his heartfelt settings of folk music. Among his best known works are the *Irish Tune from County Derry*, which is performed by solo pianists, choirs, bands, and orchestras; *Country Gardens*, which is performed in the piano, orchestral, and band versions; and his important series of wind works, including *Lincolnshire Posy*, *Molly on the Shore*, *Children's March*, *Colonial Song*, the *Hill Songs*, and *Ye Banks and Braes o' Bonnie Doon*. Grainger's careful attention to the wind band helped secure its role as a serious musical medium.

William S. Carson

Further Reading

Bird, John. *Percy Grainger*. New York: Oxford University Press, 1999. A definitive depiction of the life and works of Grainger, updated from the

1976 version. Illustrations, list of published compositions, discography, bibliography.

Dorum, Eileen. *Percy Grainger: The Man Behind the Music*. Hawthorn, Vic.: IC & EE Dorum, 1986. An Australian viewpoint informs this biography. Illustrations, bibliography.

Slattery, Thomas C. *Percy Grainger: The Inveterate Innovator*. Evanston, Ill.: Instrumentalist, 1974. This depiction of Grainger's life emphasizes his music. Illustrations, catalog of compositions, discography, selected writings, bibliography.

See also: Busoni, Ferruccio; Ellington, Duke; Theremin, Léon.

Grandmaster Flash

American rap vocalist and songwriter

One of the first deejays in hip-hop, Grandmaster Flash was instrumental in bringing the South Bronx subculture to larger audiences. He introduced a number of important techniques to the repertoire of deejay skills, including scratching, backspin, and punch phrasing.

Born: January 1, 1958; Bridgetown, Barbados
Also known as: Joseph Saddler (birth name); Biggie Grand
Member of: The Furious Five

Principal recordings

ALBUMS (solo): *They Said It Couldn't Be Done*, 1985; *The Source*, 1986; *Ba-Dop-Boom-Bang*, 1987; *Salsoul Jam 2000*, 1997; *Flash Is Back*, 1999; *The Official Adventures of Grandmaster Flash*, 2002.

ALBUMS (with the Furious Five): *The Message*, 1982; *On the Strength*, 1988.

The Life

Grandmaster Flash was born Joseph Saddler in Barbados, and he grew up in the South Bronx. As a child, he expressed great curiosity about his father's jazz record collection. He attended a vocational high school, where he trained to become an electronics technician. Following high school, he adopted the moniker Grandmaster Flash, and he quickly gained a loyal following as a deejay in the local party scene. He soon added a team of five MCs (rappers)—the Furious Five—to his performances, including Cowboy (Keith Wiggins), Melle Mel (Melvin Glover), Rahiem (Guy Williams), Kidd Creole (Nathaniel Glover), and Scorpio (Eddie Morris).

Prompted by this success of the Sugar Hill Gang's "Rapper's Delight," Grandmaster Flash and the Furious Five signed with Enjoy Records to release their first twelve-inch single, "Superappin'," in 1979. The following year, the group signed with Sugar Hill Records. In 1981 and 1982 they won critical and popular acclaim with two revolutionary singles, "The Adventures of Grandmaster Flash on the Wheels of Steel" and "The Message." This success, however, was short-lived. Tension over the popularity of "The Message" grew until the group ruptured, and Grandmaster Flash left Sugar Hill Records. They reunited for a number of concerts and albums throughout the 1980's, but they never achieved the same level of acclaim. Grandmaster Flash remains active as a performer, a radio host, and a hip-hop producer.

The Music

As a teenager, Grandmaster Flash began to experiment with deejay gear (turntables and a mixer) in his bedroom. While he assiduously studied the styles of his forebears, particularly Kool DJ Herc and Pete DJ Jones, he sought to improve what he perceived as their weaknesses. Grandmaster Flash aspired to create a distinctive music and party experience. In his hands, records contained not only the music of other artists but also the possibility of creative manipulation. The pursuit of this goal led him to three technical innovations that are standard deejay practices today.

Grandmaster Flash realized that many songs contain short drum breaks. Seeking to isolate these parts and extend them for long durations to accompany dancing, he developed the backspin technique, or quick-mix theory. Using duplicate copies of the same record, he learned to play the break on one record while searching the other copy on his headphones for the same moment of music. When the break finished on one turntable, he used the mixer to quickly switch to the other. Using this technique, he could repeat the same ten seconds of music indefinitely.

The development of punch phrasing, or clock theory, involved isolating short blasts of sound (typically horn-section hits) and rhythmically interpolating them into the sound matrix. While a beat played on one record, he located horn hits on the other turntable, and then he quickly turned up the volume to punch a new sound over the groove. Far from the earlier deejay model of passively pressing play on a turntable, Grandmaster Flash's new technique was performance.

Finally, Grandmaster Flash perfected the technique of scratching, which involves dragging the record backward and forward under the needle, creating a novel rhythmic sound. Like punch phrasing, scratching allowed the deejay to create new music from old records.

Early Singles. The group's early recordings share a common aesthetic characterized by the instrumental accompaniment of a live band. "Superappin'" (1979) served as an inauguration of this particular sound, with carefully choreographed ensemble rapping and boasts. However, despite lyrical references to the deejay, Grandmaster Flash does not perform on the song. The group's two urban hits from 1980, "Freedom" and "The Birthday Party," share a similar sound: instrumental grooves and party-oriented rapping predominate, while the namesake deejay is conspicuously absent.

"The Adventures of Grandmaster Flash on the Wheels of Steel." In 1981 the group released a radically different single. "The Adventures of Grandmaster Flash on the Wheels of Steel" is a masterful showcase performance of the deejay's technical virtuosity in the form of a playfully polymorphic sonic collage. It was the first record to be composed purely of other records, launching a revolution in deejay technique and hip-hop beat craft. The seven-minute single seamlessly weaves together elements from Chic's "Good Times," Blondie's "Rapture," Queen's "Another One Bites the Dust," the group's own "Freedom," and a host of other recorded material. A purely solo project by Grandmaster Flash, "The Adventures of Grandmaster Flash on the Wheels of Steel" was recorded live in a single take.

"The Message." In 1982 Grandmaster Flash and the Furious Five released the biggest commercial success of their career, "The Message." Utilizing nascent electronic instruments for the beat, the song features only two MCs, Melle Mel and Duke Bootee, a Sugar Hill percussionist. Again, Grandmaster Flash is not included. The most original element of "The Message" is the lyrical subject matter; unlike the party rapping found in earlier hits, "The Message" makes a tragic journey through poverty, drug abuse, violence, and other unfortunate facets of inner-city life. "The Message" was the first socially conscious single in hip-hop. It was also a commercial triumph, entering the *Billboard* Hot 100 and later earning gold-record status.

Musical Legacy

Grandmaster Flash's contributions to hip-hop and dance music are significant. As the inventor of three important deejay techniques, he directly influenced the craft of all modern deejays. He is responsible for the standard deejay gear set-up, consisting of two turntables, headphones, and a mixer. Moreover, Grandmaster Flash is considered by many to be the conceptual father of modern deejaying: Before his refinements, a deejay simply pressed play and listened. His innovations introduced a renaissance of creativ-

Grandmaster Flash. (AP/Wide World Photos)

ity and individuality in the deejay world, showing that records could be musical instruments, not just passive containers for music. Using recorded material as the basis for beats initiated the record-based aesthetic common in hip-hop. In 2007 Grandmaster Flash was inducted into the Rock and Roll Hall of Fame, the first hip-hop musician to be given this honor.

Zachary Wallmark

Further Reading

Chang, Jeff. *Can't Stop Won't Stop: A History of the Hip-Hop Generation.* New York: Picador, 2005. Chang offers a comprehensive social history, showing the origins of Grandmaster Flash's early career. Includes bibliography.

Fricke, Jim, and Charlie Ahearn. *Yes Yes Y'all: The Experience Music Project Oral History of Hip-Hop's First Decade.* Cambridge, Mass.: Da Capo Press, 2002. This insightful publication is a compilation of interviews and conversations with the luminaries of early hip-hop, including frequent appearances by Grandmaster Flash. Includes photographs.

Ogg, Alex, and David Upshal. *The Hip-Hop Years: A History of Rap.* New York: Fromm, 2001. A well-researched, thorough introduction to the history of hip-hop, with extensive references to Grandmaster Flash.

Rose, Tricia. *Black Noise: Rap Music and Black Culture in Contemporary America.* Hanover, N.H.: Wesleyan University Press/New England, 1994. In this seminal text in hip-hop studies, a leading scholar examines the sociological dimensions of the genre, presenting a detailed analysis of Grandmaster Flash's achievements. Includes bibliography.

Toop, David. *Rap Attack: African Jive to New York Hip-Hop.* New York: Serpent's Tail, 1991. Toop was one of the first writers to address the history and culture of early hip-hop, and his book is an excellent resource. Includes photographs.

See also: Combs, Sean; D. M. C.; Ice Cube; Ice-T; Jay-Z; Kool DJ Herc; LL Cool J; Notorious B.I.G.; Simmons, Joseph "Run"; Snoop Dogg.

Amy Grant
American gospel singer and songwriter

A singer-songwriter, Grant was among the first artists from the contemporary Christian market to make a significant impact on mainstream music.

Born: November 25, 1960; Augusta, Georgia
Also known as: Amy Lee Grant (full name)

Principal recordings

ALBUMS: *Amy Grant*, 1977; *My Father's Eyes*, 1979; *Never Alone*, 1980; *Age to Age*, 1982; *A Christmas Album*, 1983; *Straight Ahead*, 1984; *Unguarded*, 1985; *Lead Me On*, 1988; *A Moment in Time*, 1989; *Heart in Motion*, 1991; *Home for Christmas*, 1992; *Creation*, 1993; *The Gingham Dog and the Calico Cat*, 1993; *House of Love*, 1994; *Behind the Eyes*, 1997; *Takes a Little Time*, 1997; *A Christmas to Remember*, 1999; *A Special Wish*, 2001; *Legacy . . . Hymns and Faith*, 2002; *Simple Things*, 2003; *Rock of Ages . . . Hymns and Faith*, 2005; *Hymns for the Journey*, 2006.

The Life

Amy Lee Grant was born in Augusta, Georgia, but she grew up in Nashville, Tennessee, in an affluent household. The youngest of four daughters, she began writing songs when she was fifteen years old, and she was offered her first record contract with Word Records in 1976. Her first album was released in 1977, selling fifty thousand copies in the first year. After graduating from high school, Grant majored in English first at Furman University and then at Vanderbilt University, before dropping out to concentrate on her music career.

In 1982 Grant married singer-songwriter Gary Chapman, and she released her breakthrough album, *Age to Age*, which became the first recording by a solo gospel artist to sell more than one million copies and be certified platinum. Grant's 1985 release, *Unguarded*, was her introduction to the mainstream. The first single from the album, "Find a Way," reached number twenty-nine on the *Billboard* Hot 100 and number nine on the adult contemporary chart. A year later, Grant had her first number-one hit with "The Next Time I Fall in

Love," a duet with Chicago vocalist Peter Cetera. *Lead Me On*, released in 1988, was the first album by a gospel artist to sell more than five hundred thousand copies before it was released.

In 1999 Grant and Chapman separated and then divorced. The couple had three children: Matt, Millie, and Sarah (named after family friend and comedian Minnie Pearl, whose real name was Sarah Cannon). Grant married country singer-songwriter Vince Gill in 2000. Their daughter, Corrina, was born in 2001.

With the exception of her 2003 release, *Simple Things*, Grant remained true to her gospel roots, releasing two collections of hymns, one in 2002 and one in 2005. Grant entered the realm of reality television in 2005 when she hosted the NBC show *Three Wishes*. The show was popular, but high production costs forced its cancellation after only one season. In 2007, Grant's thirtieth year in music, she was inducted into the Gospel Music Hall of Fame, and she released a book entitled *Mosaic: Pieces of My Life So Far*, which she described as a collection of memories rather than as an autobiography.

Amy Grant. (AP/Wide World Photos)

The Music

Grant has explored a variety of musical styles over the course of her career. Many of her early albums draw on the soft rock-folk rock of the 1970's, with a hint of country and Southern gospel. Beginning with 1984's *Straight Ahead*, Grant's music began to mature into a more radio-friendly variety of soft rock. *Heart in Motion* is pure pop, with catchy hooks and bouncy, memorable melodies. Her 1994 release, *House of Love*, exhibits more of a pop-country sound, and the 1997 follow-up, *Behind the Eyes*, is mostly acoustic soft rock. Her hymn collections from 2002 and 2005 feature a blend of gospel, country, bluegrass, and modern worship pop.

"El Shaddai." Grant's first breakthrough album, *Age to Age*, contained many songs that would become a standard part of Christian hymnody. "El Shaddai," written by Michael Card, is one of those songs. The chorus uses Hebrew terms of adoration

and worship while the verses recount biblical accounts of God's greatness and provision, culminating in the sacrifice of Jesus on the cross. The simple piano, drums, and string accompaniment provide a foundation for the lyrics.

"Sing Your Praise to the Lord." Rich Mullins' "Sing Your Praise to the Lord" is another contribution to modern hymnals from the *Age to Age* album. Like "Shaddai," the simplicity of the song is its greatest strength. The song begins with a piano introduction derived from Fugue No. 2 in C Minor from Johann Sebastian Bach's *The Well-Tempered Clavier* (1722) before building to an upbeat rock song to accompany the exuberant exhortation to sing praise to God.

"Thy Word." *Straight Ahead* also contained a song that has become a part of modern hymnody. "Thy Word," a collaboration with singer-songwriter Michael W. Smith, is based on Psalm 119:105: "Thy word is a lamp unto my feet and a light unto my path." (KJV) It is a song of hope and assurance that no matter what circumstances she may face, she is confident that God will lead her through. The simplicity of the lyric is matched by simple piano and strings accompaniment.

"The Next Time I Fall in Love." Grant's first number-one hit outside the Christian music industry was "The Next Time I Fall in Love," a duet with ex-Chicago frontman Peter Cetera. It is a standard pop ballad, with Cetera and Grant splitting verses and coming together to harmonize on the chorus. This song and its accompanying video displeased some of Grant's Christian audience, who believed it was wrong for her to be singing a love song to a man who was not her husband. Many of these fans accused Grant of choosing pop stardom over her Christian faith. Grant faced this charge for much of the rest of her career.

"Baby, Baby." The first single from *Heart in Motion* was marketed as a romantic love song, but it was inspired by a different kind of love. Grant wrote the song six weeks after the birth of her second child, Millie. The lyrics of total devotion to her "baby" along with the infectious keyboard hook made "Baby, Baby" Grant's second number-one hit and her first number-one solo hit.

"I Will Remember You." Perhaps the most artistic track on *Heart in Motion*, "I Will Remember You" is a song of longing and remembrance. It was revived ten years later, when it was used by a number of radio stations in montages commemorating the events of September 11, 2001.

Musical Legacy

Grant started her career as a teenage girl writing songs for her parents, and she ended up a success in both the gospel and the pop markets. Although she was frequently accused of diluting the Christian message, her songs remained honest expressions of her life and faith. Like so many others, Grant does not believe that the wall between gospel music and popular music needs to exist, and her career is testament to that belief.

Eric S. Strother

Further Reading

Grant, Amy. *Mosaic: Pieces of My Life So Far*. New York: Doubleday, 2007. Reflecting its title, this book offers bits and pieces of Grant's life, vignettes that are interspersed with appropriate lyrics from her songs. She recounts her successes, her struggles, and her efforts to remain positive and hopeful through it all.

Keith, Evan. *Amy Grant*. New York: Dell, 1992. A short biography looks at Grant's life, her faith, and her career in music.

Millard, Bob. *Amy Grant: The Life of a Pop Star*. New York: St. Martin's Griffin Press, 1996. A recounting of Grant's life, with emphasis on the challenges she faces in straddling the secular and the religious in her music and in her personal life.

See also: Cleveland, James; King, Carole; Smith, Michael W.; Staples, Pops.

Stéphane Grappelli

French jazz composer and violinist

A pioneer in jazz violin, Grappelli stands out as a responsive, humorous, and melodic improvisator of exceptional tone, clarity, and creativity.

Born: January 26, 1908; Paris, France
Died: December 1, 1997; Paris, France
Member of: Quintet of the Hot Club of France

Principal recordings

ALBUMS (solo): *Unique Piano Sessions*, 1955 (with Stuff Smith); *Violins No End*, 1957; *Improvisations*, 1958; *Feeling + Finesse = Jazz*, 1962; *Two of a Kind*, 1965 (with Svend Asmussen); *I Remember Django*, 1969; *In Paris*, 1969; *Limehouse Blues*, 1969 (with Barney Kessel); *Stéphane Grappelli Meets Barney Kessel*, 1969 (with Kessel); *Venupelli Blues*, 1969 (with Joe Venuti); *I Hear Music*, 1970; *Afternoon in Paris*, 1971; *Homage to Django*, 1972; *Jalousie: Music of the 30's*, 1972 (with Yehudi Menuhin); *Satin Doll*, 1972; *Parisian Thoroughfare*, 1973; *Stardust*, 1973; *Stéphane Grappelli*, 1973; *Stéphane Grappelli/Bill Coleman*, 1973 (with Bill Coleman); *Stéphane Grappelli Meets the Rhythm Section*, 1973; *Talk of the Town*, 1973; *The Giants*, 1974 (with Jean-Luc Ponty); *Les Valseuses*, 1974 (with Georges Delerue); *Stéphane Grappelli Meets Earl Hines*, 1974 (with Earl Hines); *Les Calmos*, 1975 (with Delerue); *Violinspiration*,

1975; *Paris Encounter*, 1976; *The Reunion, with George Shearing*, 1976 (with George Shearing); *Tea for Two*, 1977 (with Menuhin); *London Meeting*, 1978; *Uptown Dance*, 1978; *Stéphane Grappelli and Hank Jones: A Two-fer!*, 1979 (with Hank Jones); *Young Django*, 1979; *At the Winery*, 1980; *Happy Reunion*, 1980 (with Martial Solal); *Vintage 1981*, 1981; *Stephanova*, 1983; *Bringing It Together*, 1984 (with Toots Thielemans); *Together at Last*, 1985 (with Vassar Clements); *Grappelli Plays Jerome Kern*, 1987; *Stéphane Grappelli: Who's Who in Jazz*, 1987; *How Can You Miss?*, 1989; *My Other Love*, 1990; *One on One with McCoy Tyner*, 1990; *Shades of Django*, 1990; *Something Old, Something New*, 1990 (with the Franciscan Chamber Players); *Tivoli Gardens*, 1990 (with Joe Pass); *Anything Goes*, 1992; *Conversations*, 1992; *Stéphane Grappelli and Michel Legrand*, 1992 (with Michel Legrand); *So Easy to Remember*, 1993; *It's Only a Paper Moon*, 1994; *Flamingo*, 1995 (with Michel Petruccian); *Aquarius*, 1996; *It Might As Well Be Swing*, 1996; *Le Sur Le Toit de Paris*, 1996 (recorded 1969).

SINGLES (with Quintet of the Hot Club of France): "Sweet Sue, Just You," 1935; "Ultrafox," 1935; "Georgia on My Mind," 1936; "Swing Guitars," 1936; "Ain't Misbehavin'," 1937; "Tears," 1937; "Black and White," 1938; "Daphne," 1938; "Honeysuckle Rose," 1938; "My Sweet," 1938; "Souvenirs," 1938; "H.C.Q.," 1939; "I Wonder Where My Baby Is Tonight," 1939; "Japanese Sandman," 1939; "Jeepers Creepers," 1939.

The Life

Stéphane Grappelli (grah-PEHL-lee) was the only child of a French mother and an Italian father. When he was four years old, his mother died of cancer. Brief study with Isadora Duncan at the unconventional American expatriate's dance studio exposed Grappelli to the music of Claude Debussy, Maurice Ravel, and Richard Wagner.

Grappelli spent most of World War I under abysmal conditions in the Catholic orphanage system because of his father's compulsory conscription into the Italian army. After the war, Grappelli reunited briefly with his father under penurious circumstances. Encouraged by his father, Grappelli began to study piano and violin, guided by music books from Le Bibliothèque Nacionale de France.

Largely self-taught, Grappelli attended the Paris Conservatory beginning in 1920 for three years, his only formal musical training. Fully professional and living on his own by fifteen, Grappelli performed violin publicly in courtyards and cinema houses. His early repertory consisted primarily of small pieces by composers such as Gabriel Fauré, Robert Schumann, Enrico Toselli, and Wolfgang Amadeus Mozart. Grappelli supported himself through most of the 1920's playing piano in a style akin to Bix Biederbecke's. As part of a jazzy band called Gregor and the Gregorians, Grappelli again picked up the violin, and by the end of the decade he played that instrument almost exclusively.

In the early 1930's, Grappelli and Django Reinhardt formed the Hot Club Quintet, comprising the unusual combination of three guitars, violin, and double bass. Comparable to and inspired by the style of Joe Venuti and guitarist Eddie Lang from Paul Whiteman's Orchestra, the group attained transatlantic fame with virtuosic performances and recordings of American standards by jazz icons such as George Gershwin, Fats Waller, and Irving Berlin, along with original tunes, before disbanding at the start of World War II. Grappelli joined with pianist George Shearing during the 1940's and reunited with Reinhardt briefly before settling into a steady gig at the Paris Hilton.

From the 1960's until the end of his life, Grappelli embarked on multiple recording and performance projects in myriad venues around the world with a wide array of respected artists such as Duke Ellington, Oscar Peterson, Lakshminarayanan Subramaniam, Jean-Luc Ponty, Paul Simon, Earl Hines, Manhattan Transfer, McCoy Tyner, Yo-Yo Ma, and Yehudi Menuhin. Grappelli died in 1997 after complications from surgery, and he was buried in Paris in Pére Lachaise Cemetery.

The Music

Grappelli's music epitomizes the hot jazz movement of the 1930's. His improvisations spring from the melodies to explore the gamut of emotions. Known best for covering jazz standards by composers in a lively swing fashion, Grappelli has also covered an impressive multiplicity of works, ranging from Johann Sebastian Bach's Concerto for Two Violins in D Minor (1731) to the Beatles' "Hey Jude." Although Grappelli has written a modest

Stéphane Grappelli. (AP/Wide World Photos)

number of works, which he keenly conveyed with animation, they have been overshadowed by his renditions of more popular melodies.

"H.C.Q. Strut." Coauthored by Grappelli and Reinhardt, the aptly titled work served as a theme for the Hot Club Quintet. The recording opens with a lively introductory interplay between violin and guitar, which features harmonics and typifies the short lively tunes with steady guitar-driven rhythms and virtuosic improvisation featured in the quintet's repertory during the 1930's. The singing melody provides a vehicle for Grappelli's spirited performance.

"Honeysuckle Rose." This jazz standard by Waller and Andy Razaf, again marked by an introductory duet by Grappelli and Reinhardt, serves as a prime example of the quintet's characteristic approach to familiar melodies. Grappelli answers Reinhardt's stunningly fluid two-fingered solo passages with his archetypal creativity, complete with rapidly bowed arpeggios, swinging scalar runs, and slides.

"Jalousie." Penned by Jacob Gade, this work warrants attention as the first televised collaboration between classical violinist Menuhin and Grappelli on the British Broadcasting Corporation. Despite Menuhin's skills as an interpreter of classic works, he does not improvise, and his part had to be arranged and memorized. Conversely, Grappelli's performances in rehearsals varied each time, earning deep respect from Menuhin for their deftly responsive enthusiasm. The performance plays like a dialogue between two intimate friends, testifying to Grappelli's ability to respond dynamically to the music as it evolves. The unusual partnership helped bridge gaps between the classical and jazz realms, and it further legitimized Grappelli's standing as a world-class violinist.

"Stéphane's Blues for Abby." In 1990 Grappelli composed this blues tune as one of three original pieces for an album of solo piano playing entitled *My Other Love.* Revered for his prowess on violin, Grappelli provides a rare glimpse into his formidable talents as a pianist, and this work represents a fine example of his skills at transforming melodies.

Musical Legacy

Grappelli facilitated the acceptance of violin in all forms of jazz and of jazz violin as a medium for interpreting works from all genres. In his autobiography, Menuhin paid homage to Grappelli, declaring that the artist could off the cuff "use any theme to express any nuance—wistfulness, brilliance, aggression, scorn—with a speed and accuracy that stretch credulity." In 1997 the National Academy of Recording Arts and Sciences honored Grappelli with a Grammy Award for Lifetime Achievement.

Gary Galván

Further Reading

Balmer, Paul. *Stéphane Grappelli: With and Without Django.* London: Sanctuary, 2003. A musician, multimedia director, and British Broadcasting Corporation broadcaster, Balmer constructs this authorized biography from several interviews, including one with Grappelli's only daughter. Includes illustrations.

Glaser, Matt, and Stéphane Grappelli. *Jazz Violin.* New York: Oak, 1981. An instructional guide, this work includes transcriptions of and tips on improvisation from key figures, including Grappelli, Venuti, and Jean-Luc Ponty.

Smith, Geoffrey. *Stéphane Grappelli.* London: Pavilion, Michael Joseph, 1987. Smith capitalizes on exclusive interviews with Grappelli and the violinist's contemporaries to provide a contextualized biography. Includes illustrations and discography.

See also: Beiderbecke, Bix; Berlin, Irving; Debussy, Claude; Ellington, Duke; Legrand, Michel; Ma, Yo-Yo; Menuhin, Sir Yehudi; Reinhardt, Django; Simon, Paul; Tyner, McCoy; Waller, Fats.

Adolph Green and Betty Comden

American musical-theater composers and lyricists

One of Broadway's most prolific and long-lasting lyricist-librettist teams, Comden and Green wrote sophisticated, witty screenplays, and they collaborated with such accomplished composers as Leonard Bernstein, Jule Styne, Cy Coleman, André Previn, and Morton Gould.

Adolph Green
Born: December 2, 1914; Bronx, New York
Died: October 23, 2002; New York, New York

Betty Comden
Born: May 3, 1917; Brooklyn, New York
Died: November 23, 2006; New York, New York
Also known as: Basya Cohen (birth name); Betty Kyle

Principal works

MUSICAL THEATER (lyrics and libretto): *On the Town*, 1944 (music by Leonard Bernstein); *Billion Dollar Baby*, 1945 (music by Morton Gould); *Two on the Aisle*, 1951 (music by Jule Styne); *Wonderful Town*, 1953 (music by Leonard Bernstein; libretto by Joseph Fields and Jerome Chodorov); *Peter Pan*, 1954 (with Carolyn Green; music by Styne, Mark Charlap, Elmer Bernstein, and Trude Rittman; based on the play by James M. Barrie); *Bells Are Ringing*, 1956 (music by Styne); *A Party with Betty Comden and Adolph Green*, 1958 (music by

Leonard Bernstein and Styne); *Say, Darling*, 1958 (music by Styne; libretto by Abe Burrows, Marian Bissell, and Richard Bissell); *Do Re Mi*, 1960 (music by Styne; libretto by Garson Kanin); *Subways Are for Sleeping*, 1961 (music by Styne); *Fade Out—Fade In*, 1964 (music by Styne); *Hallelujah, Baby!*, 1967 (music by Styne; libretto by Arthur Laurents); *Applause*, 1970 (music by Charles Strouse; lyrics by Lee Adams); *Lorelei*, 1974 (music by Styne; libretto by Kenny Solms and Gail Parent); *On the Twentieth Century*, 1978 (music by Cy Coleman); *A Doll's Life*, 1979 (music by Larry Grossman); *Singin' in the Rain*, 1985 (music by Nacio Herb Brown; lyrics by Arthur Freed); *The Will Rogers Follies*, 1991 (music by Coleman; libretto by Peter Stone).

The Lives
Betty Comden was born Basya Cohen in Brooklyn in 1917 to Russian immigrants. Her father, Leonard, was a lawyer, and her mother, Rebecca, was a teacher. Comden credits her interest in music to her father, who encouraged her to take piano lessons, and to her Uncle Ezra and Aunt Celia, who took her to opera productions at the Brooklyn Academy of Music.

Adolph Green was born in the Bronx in 1914 to Hungarian immigrants, Daniel and Helen Green. From an early age, he had an interest in acting and writing, and he had a keen ear for music. As a young man, he infamously whistled symphonies and concerti everywhere he went.

The two first met in 1938 through mutual friends. At the time, Green was working as a Wall Street runner and trying to break into the theater. Comden was studying drama at New York University, although she eventually graduated with a degree in nursing. The two formed an acting troupe with John Frank, Alvin Hammer, and Judy Holliday called the Revuers. The troupe was frequently joined by a young pianist and composer, Leonard Bernstein. Comden and Green wrote not only their own lyrics but also frequently their own music for the Revuers.

Based on the troupe's performances, Comden and Green got an invitation to go to California and to take bit parts in the film *Greenwich Village* (1944), which starred Carmen Miranda and Don Ameche. When that failed to lead to anything more substantial, Comden and Green returned to New York, where Bernstein asked them to transfer choreographer Jerome Robbins's ballet *Fancy Free* into a Broadway show, *On the Town*, which opened in 1944. After the failure of their second Broadway effort, *Billion Dollar Baby*, they began a successful career on the West Coast, writing for Hollywood.

The two enjoyed a six-decade friendship on and off the stage. Although often mistaken for a husband-and-wife team, they were never married to each other. Comden married designer and businessman Stephen Kyle in 1942, and they had two children, Susannah and Alan. Kyle died in 1979, and Comden never remarried. Her son Alan died in 1990 after a long struggle with drug addiction and with AIDS. Adolph Green had two brief, unsuccessful marriages before marrying actress Phyllis Newman in 1960. They had two children, Adam and Amanda. Following Green's death of natural causes in 2002, Comden appeared at a memorial where she interrupted her eulogy to say, "It's lonely up here." Comden died of heart failure in 2006.

The Music

The lyrics and screenplays of Comden and Green are among the wittiest ever penned. Their career spanned six decades, and while they worked with a number of different composers and performers, they never worked separately. Much of their work revolves around New York City or Hollywood and the glamorous spotlit lives of the characters who populated their shows. They frequently incorporated contemporary pop cultural references into their quick-rhyming lyrics.

On the Town. Their first venture, *On the Town*, was one of their most successful and memorable. Expanded from the ballet *Fancy Free*, with choreography by Robbins and a score by Bernstein, the show tells the tale of three sailors on a twenty-four-hour leave in New York City. The show produced several hit songs, from the rousing opening "New York, New York" and jazzy "Come Up to My Place" to the melancholy "Lonely Town" and the closing number, "Some Other Time." Comden and Green contributed not only their writing skills but also their vocal and performing talents. Green appeared as Ozzie, one of the sailors, who pairs up with Comden's man-hungry anthropologist Claire de Loone.

Comden and Green were also hired to retool the show for the screen, a film directed by Stanley Donen and Gene Kelly and starring Kelly and Frank Sinatra. For this, they crafted not only the screenplay but also new lyrics to go with Roger Edens's new music (Bernstein's score was thought by producer Arthur Freed to be too classical). While they kept Bernstein's "New York, New York" and "Come Up to My Place," they revised the lyrics. The former was bowdlerized, changing "New York, New York, a hell of a town" to "New York, New York, a wonderful town," while the latter was more extensively rewritten to update some of the New York City references.

Singin' in the Rain. Following their successful collaboration with Kelly and Donen for *On the Town*, Comden and Green rejoined them three years later for another Metro-Goldwyn-Mayer musical, *Singin' in the Rain*. Initially viewed as a mediocre trifle, the film eventually garnered great acclaim, and it is considered one of the greatest film musicals ever made. In it, Kelly and Jean Hagen are silent-film stars Don Lockwood and Lena Lamont transitioning to "talkies." Among the problems they face are technical difficulties, Lamont's tinny voice, and a romantic triangle among the stars and Debbie Reynolds' golden-voiced chorus girl Kathy Selden. The screenplay is peppered with some of the snappiest one-liners ever assembled. The film mostly uses preexisting tunes, although Comden and Green did contribute the tongue-twisting lyrics to the comic number "Moses Supposes." In 1985 the film was adapted for Broadway, with Comden and Green again as librettists, and it included more interpolated songs.

Wonderful Town. Following a string of successful films, the duo returned to New York, reteaming with Bernstein for another romance set in New York City. *Wonderful Town*, which opened on Broadway in 1953 and starred Rosalind Russell, is an adaptation of several short stories by Ruth McKinney, dramatized later as the play *My Sister Eileen* by Joseph Fields and Jerome Chodorov, who also wrote the libretto for *Wonderful Town*. The story revolves around two sisters, Ruth and Eileen Sherwood, who move from Ohio to New York to pursue careers in journalism and acting respectively. Bernstein's score ranges from an Irish jig sung by the policemen to a conga sung by Brazilian sailors, and Comden and Green's lyrics easily match the diversity of the score. Among the memorable songs are "The Wrong Note Rag," "A Little Bit in Love," and Ruth's comic lament, "One Hundred Easy Ways (To Lose a Man)." Recent archival work by Carol Oja uncovered earlier drafts of songs that display a direct confrontation with McCarthy-era politics, involving Communist witch hunts, although the final drafts are considerably less political.

Peter Pan. The following year was the beginning of Comden and Green's long association with composer Jule Styne, which spanned two decades, from *Peter Pan* in 1954 to *Lorelei* in 1974. The adaptation of J. M. Barrie's classic children's tale of the boy who never grew up was largely conceived as a vehicle for Mary Martin to return to Broadway. While the show closed its Broadway run early, it did so to become a television musical special (for which Martin won an Emmy Award in addition to her Tony Award). Some songs in *Peter Pan* were contributed by lyricist Carolyn Leigh and composer Mark Charlap. Comden and Green supplied the rest to Styne's music; their big number was Peter Pan's anthem, "Never Never Land."

Bells Are Ringing. Comden and Green's second musical with Styne reunited them with longtime friend Holliday, who starred as Ella Peterson, an operator at a telephone answering service who falls in love with the voice of one of her clients. The sparkling score includes some of Comden and Green's best-known songs, including "The Party's Over," "I'm Going Back," and "Just in Time." Styne had composed the music to "Just in Time" earlier, and Comden and Green refused to give up the tune, eventually finding lyrics to match it. *Bells Are Ringing* also marked their first full Broadway libretto in more than a decade.

The two were hired to update the show for director Vincente Minnelli's film treatment of the show, in which Holliday reprised her role, starring opposite Dean Martin. While Comden and Green did not have to write new songs (as for *On the Town*), they did update the lyrics to some songs, including "Drop That Name," which initially featured director Minnelli's name.

On the Twentieth Century. Cy Coleman was the third composer to collaborate with Comden and Green on multiple projects. *On the Twentieth Century* details the backstage battles between a star

and a producer trying to woo her back while riding a luxury train. Coleman's score and Comden and Green's lyrics create an operetta-style pastiche, and although it received strong reviews and multiple awards, the show's run was short-lived, and it remains somewhat in obscurity.

The Will Rogers Follies. If their first musical, *On the Town*, was their most memorable, then their last was their longest running. Opening in 1991, *The Will Rogers Follies* enjoyed a two-and-a-half year run. The score and lyrics sampled many genres, going from country-style cowboy songs to ragtime-era chorus numbers, and Comden and Green make ample and clever use of Rogers's own witticisms, most notably, "I never met a man I didn't like."

Musical Legacy

Creating some of Broadway's best-loved songs, Comden and Green took their place among musical theater's most important lyricists and writers. They are most known for their prolific output, both in terms of numbers of shows and in their versatility in writing lyrics and librettos. Many of the projects they worked on showcased their talent to write for specific singers, from Russell's plain-spoken, jokey delivery in *Wonderful Town* to John Collum's operatic grandeur in *On the Twentieth Century*. They had their share of flops (most notably *A Doll's Life*, a musical sequel to Henrik Ibsen's 1879 play, *A Doll's House*, which ran for only five performances), but success never seemed to be far away. Their collective oeuvre earned them five Tony Awards, four for their lyrical contributions (*The Will Rogers Follies*, *On the Twentieth Century*, *Hallelujah, Baby!*, and *Wonderful Town*) and one for their book for *On the Twentieth Century*. The pair was also awarded Kennedy Center Honors in 1991.

In addition to a prolific career writing for the stage, they were influential in Hollywood. They penned a number of popular musicals, some adapted from the stage and others original. Among them were *The Barkleys of Broadway* (1949), starring Fred Astaire and Ginger Rogers, and *Auntie Mame* (1958), their only nonmusical film. They earned Academy Award nominations for their screenplays for *The Band Wagon* (1953) and *It's Always Fair Weather* (1955). The Writers Guild of America honored them for their work on *On the Town*, *Singin' in the Rain*, and *Bells Are Ringing*, and in 2001 it presented them the Laurel Award for Screen Writing Achievement.

Finally, Comden and Green should not be forgotten for what they began as: performers. They appeared sporadically onstage over the years: in a 1985 concert version of Stephen Sondheim's *Follies* (1971) and in the revue *A Party with Betty Comden and Adolph Green*, which they created and presented in 1958 and later performed in 1977. They also recorded a number of songs they wrote, some of which were cut from shows on which they had worked.

Dan Blim

Further Reading

Bryer, Jackson R., and Richard A. Davison. *The Art of the American Musical: Conversations with the Creators*. New Brunswick, N.J.: Rutgers University Press, 2005. Includes an insightful interview with Comden and Green, focusing on their output and observations on songwriting and also mining their collective memory for reactions to shows.

Comden, Betty. *Off Stage*. New York: Simon & Schuster, 1995. Comden's autobiography brims with witty and touching anecdotes of her childhood and marriage, and it also contains accounts of her personal relationships with several luminaries, including Green, Bernstein, and Lauren Bacall.

Hischak, Thomas A. *Boy Loses Girl: Broadway's Librettists*. Lanham, Md.: Scarecrow Press, 2002. Includes a chapter devoted to Comden and Green, with a broad if not deep introduction to their collected work.

McGillan, Patrick. *Backstory 2: Interviews with Screenwriters of the 1940's and 1950's*. Berkeley: University of California Press, 1991. A rare glimpse at Comden and Green's work for Hollywood, with insight into the differences and similarities between films and musicals.

Robinson, Alice M. *Betty Comden and Adolph Green: A Bio-Bibliography*. Westport, Conn.: Greenwood Press, 1994. Extremely comprehensive and detailed account of the lives and work of Comden and Green. Unrivaled in its scope and informative quality.

See also: Bernstein, Leonard; Previn, Sir André; Sondheim, Stephen; Styne, Jule.

Al Green

American rhythm-and-blues singer and songwriter

Green introduced a smooth and mellow jazzlike vocal style to the soul music of the early 1970's, a lighter approach to the soul shouting that preceded it.

Born: April 13, 1946; Forrest City, Arkansas
Also known as: Albert Greene (birth name); Reverend Al Green
Member of: The Soul Mates

Principal recordings

ALBUMS: *Back up Train*, 1967; *Green Is Blue*, 1970; *Gets Next to You*, 1971; *Let's Stay Together*, 1972; *I'm Still in Love with You*, 1972; *Call Me*, 1973; *Livin' for You*, 1973; *Al Green Explores Your Mind*, 1974; *Al Green Is Love*, 1975; *Full of Fire*, 1976; *Have a Good Time*, 1976; *The Belle Album*, 1977; *Truth 'n' Time*, 1978; *The Lord Will Make a Way*, 1980; *Higher Plane*, 1981; *Highway to Heaven*, 1981; *Precious Lord*, 1982; *I'll Rise Again*, 1983; *The Christmas Album*, 1983; *He Is the Light*, 1985; *Trust in God*, 1986; *White Christmas*, 1986; *Soul Survivor*, 1987; *I Get Joy*, 1989; *From My Soul*, 1990; *Al Green Presents the Full Gospel Tabernacle Choir*, 1990 (with the Full Gospel Tabernacle Choir); *Sings Gospel*, 1992; *Love Is Reality*, 1992; *Don't Look Back*, 1993; *Gospel Soul*, 1993; *Your Heart's in Good Hands*, 1995; *Cover Me Green*, 1995; *Feels Like Christmas*, 2001; *I Can't Stop*, 2003; *Everything's OK*, 2005; *What Makes the World Go Round*, 2008.

SINGLES: "Let's Stay Together," 1971; "Tired of Being Alone," 1971; "I'm Still in Love with You," 1972; "Look What You Done for Me," 1972; "You Ought to Be with Me," 1972; "Sha-La-La (Make Me Happy)," 1974; "Put a Little Love in Your Heart," 1988.

The Life

Al Green was born into a sharecropping family with ten children in the rural Arkansas delta. His family joined the great migration north in search of better economic and social opportunities, relocating to Grand Rapids, Michigan, in the fall of 1955. When his carefree Arkansas childhood was replaced by the frustrations of inner-city living in the industrial North, Greene struggled socially and academically. Eventually, tensions with his strict father over Greene's love of secular music led to Greene leaving home. He spent a couple of hardscrabble years on the ghetto streets of Grand Rapids.

In the early 1970's, Green dropped the final "e" on his surname, and he moved to Memphis, Tennessee, where he met producer Willie Mitchell. With Mitchell's guidance, Green reached great popular success and sold tens of millions of albums. Green experienced a spiritual reawakening in 1973, and in 1974 he was hospitalized after being scalded by a suicidal fan. These incidents led to the singer's departure from pop music and to a break with Mitchell. In 1979 an onstage accident in Cincinnati, Ohio, caused Green to focus his work

Al Green. (Bill Greenblatt/UPI/Landov)

increasingly on gospel music, and he became the pastor of the Full Gospel Tabernacle in the White-haven section of Memphis.

The Music

Green's vocal range modulates from a baritone to a high, heartbreaking falsetto, and his improvisations are often startling. Mitchell's ingenious arranging at Royal Studios layered Green's sweet voice over a rich tapestry of softened drumbeats, string embellishments, and the call-and-response of the celebrated Hi Rhythm and Hi Horn sections (Hi Records' backing band).

Early Works. Green began his musical career touring with the family gospel troupe the Greene Brothers. However, he was soon attracted to the work of such rhythm-and-blues radio stars as Jackie Wilson and Sam Cooke. At the age of eighteen, he had surreptitiously formed a rhythm-and-blues group with high school friends in Grand Rapids, and they frequently performed at the El Grotto Club in Battle Creek, Michigan, playing alongside legendary rhythm-and-blues performers Junior Walker and the All-Stars. In 1967 this group, christened Al Greene and the Soul Mates, self-produced the album *Back up Train*, the title track of which was a rhythm-and-blues hit. Its popularity led to the group's appearance at the Apollo Theater in Harlem in March, 1968, where they performed nine encores. By late fall of 1969, however, the Soul Mates had disbanded. Green, now a solo act, could not re-create the success of "Back up Train," and his music career stalled.

Green met Mitchell by chance at a seedy night-club in Midland, Texas, and they shared a van trip back to Memphis. By the time they arrived, the two men had decided to work together.

"Tired of Being Alone." Green's first major *Billboard* pop hit for Hi Records reached number eleven on the U.S. charts in 1971. He had written the song a year earlier, when he was on the road in the rural Michigan countryside. Green awoke from a dream with the lyrics echoing in his ears. As he observed the dawn creeping over the landscape outside his motel, and as he listened to a lonely rooster call and a solitary dog respond, he was enveloped by a quiet peace. Half an hour later, the song was finished.

"Let's Stay Together." Mitchell and Al Jackson, the drummer for Booker T. and the MGs, had to persuade Green to record this composition, for which Green said that he reluctantly wrote the primary lyrics in less than ten minutes. This was one of Green's many collaborative efforts with Jackson, before the drummer's brutal murder in 1975. During the recording, Mitchell instructed Green to soften his vocals and emphasize his falsetto. Within ten days of the record's pressing, it became a number-one song, and it remained so for nine weeks.

"Love and Happiness." Originally on the album *I'm Still in Love with You,* this song also appeared on *Al Green's Greatest Hits* in 1975. It captures the spirit of Green and his collaborators at Hi Records during their heyday. Primarily written by guitarist Teenie Hodges, this song features Green's heartfelt, mellow singing juxtaposed with the gritty sound of the Hi Rhythm and Hi Horn sections. At its finest, Mitchell's arranging produced a "silky on the top, rough on the bottom" sound that the crew at Royal Studios originated and perfected for Green. The song features a memorable guitar riff by Hodges, as well as some lush organ work, which contributes to the song's gospel feel. Although it starts off as a series of metaphorical vignettes of "Love and Happiness," by its middle, Green has crossed over into the role of a secular witness. As the tempo slowly rises, Green preaches to the lovers' choir, as he calls and responds to Hodge's guitar work, the backup singers, and the blatting staccato of the Hi Horn section.

Musical Legacy

Green's smooth, soft approach opened the door for the velvet soul music of such crooners as Barry White and Luther Vandross. Nevertheless, Green never left his beloved gospel music behind, even at the height of his popular success. He answered his call to preach, but he occasionally returns to secular music. He has collaborated with a wide range of musicians, including Annie Lennox and Lyle Lovett, and has reunited with Mitchell.

Don Allan Mitchell

Further Reading

Awkward, Michael. *Soul Covers: Rhythm and Blues Remakes and the Struggle for Artistic Identity (Aretha Franklin, Al Green, Phoebe Snow).* Durham, N.C.: Duke University Press, 2007. Focusing on Green's *Call Me* album, the book describes the singer's struggles with the sacred and profane in his music.

George, Nelson. *The Death of Rhythm and Blues.* New York: Penguin, 2003. By examining the corporatization and assimilation of black music, the book provides an economic context to understanding how American music becomes popular.

Green, Al, and David Seay. *Take Me to the River.* New York: HarperEntertainment, 2000. A thorough biography, this book traces Green's life from his childhood to his breakthrough to superstardom.

Guralnick, Peter. *Sweet Soul Music: Rhythm and Blues and the Southern Dream of Freedom.* New York: Back Bay Books, 1999. Necessary reading on the rise and fall of Memphis soul, written by a scholar of African American music.

Ward, Brian. *Just My Soul Responding: Rhythm and Blues, Black Consciousness, and Race Relations.* Berkeley: University of California Press, 1998. Firmly locates rhythm-and-blues music in the political foment of the Civil Rights movement and the struggle for African American identity.

See also: Brown, Roy; Cooke, Sam; Gibb, Barry, Maurice, and Robin; Lovett, Lyle; Pickett, Wilson; Raitt, Bonnie; Turner, Tina; Wilson, Jackie.

Dave Grusin

American jazz composer, keyboardist, pianist, and film-score composer

By using electronic components to complement acoustic music, Grusin became a leader in the fusion jazz movement. Unlike many who compose for different fields, Grusin uses the same instruments (and even musicians) in both his jazz recordings and his film scores.

Born: June 26, 1934; Littleton, Colorado

Principal works

FILM SCORES: *Divorce American Style,* 1967; *A Man Called Gannon,* 1968; *The Heart Is a Lonely*

Hunter, 1968; *Generation*, 1969; *Adam at Six o'Clock*, 1970; *The Pursuit of Happiness*, 1971; *Shoot Out*, 1971; *Fuzz*, 1972; *The Great Northfield Minnesota Raid*, 1972; *The Friends of Eddie Coyle*, 1973; *The Midnight Man*, 1974; *Three Days of the Condor*, 1975; *The Yakuza*, 1975; *The Front*, 1976; *Murder by Death*, 1976; *Bobby Deerfield*, 1977; *The Goodbye Girl*, 1977; *Heaven Can Wait*, 1978; *The Champ*, 1979; *Absence of Malice*, 1981; *On Golden Pond*, 1981; *Author! Author!*, 1982; *Tootsie*, 1982; *Falling in Love*, 1984; *The Little Drummer Girl*, 1984; *Racing with the Moon*, 1984; *The Goonies*, 1985; *Lucas*, 1986; *Ishtar*, 1987; *Clara's Heart*, 1988; *The Milagro Beanfield War*, 1988; *Tequila Sunrise*, 1988; *The Fabulous Baker Boys*, 1989; *The Bonfire of the Vanities*, 1990; *Havana*, 1990; *The Firm*, 1993; *The Cure*, 1995; *Selena*, 1997; *Hope Floats*, 1998; *Random Hearts*, 1999.

Principal recordings

ALBUMS: *Subways Are for Sleeping*, 1961; *The Many Moods of Dave Grusin*, 1962; *Kaleidoscope*, 1964; *Discovered Again*, 1977; *One of a Kind*, 1977; *Mountain Dance*, 1979; *Out of the Shadows*, 1982; *Night Lines*, 1983; *Dave Grusin and the N.Y.-L.A. Dream Band*, 1984 (with the N.Y.-L.A. Dream Band); *Harlequin*, 1985 (with Lee Ritenour); *Cinemagic*, 1987; *Little Big Horn*, 1988 (with Gerry Mulligan); *Sticks and Stones*, 1988 (with Don Grusin); *Zephyr*, 1988; *Migration*, 1989; *The Gershwin Connection*, 1991; *Homage to Duke*, 1993; *The Orchestral Album*, 1994; *Two for the Road: The Music of Henry Mancini*, 1996; *West Side Story*, 1997; *Two Worlds*, 2000 (with Ritenour and Renée Fleming); *Discovered Again Plus*, 2004; *Now Playing: Movie Themes, Solo Piano*, 2004; *Amparo*, 2008 (with Ritenour).

The Life

David Grusin (GREW-sihn) was born June 26, 1934, in Littleton, Colorado. Grusin grew up with a classical-music background: His father, Henri, was a professional violinist, and his mother, Rosabelle, began giving Grusin piano lessons when he was four. Grusin continued his piano studies at the University of Colorado under Storm Bull, the grandnephew of Edvard Grieg and a former pupil of Béla Bartók, graduating in 1956.

Dave Grusin. (AP/Wide World Photos)

After serving in the U.S. Navy, Grusin planned to continue his studies at the Manhattan School of Music only to be hired as the accompanist for Andy Williams in 1959. He played piano on the singer's recordings and eventually served as leader of the Dave Grusin Orchestra on the televised *The Andy Williams Show* from 1962 to 1965. In addition to acting as arranger, conductor, producer, and musician on many jazz and pop recordings, Grusin recorded three jazz piano albums during the 1960's.

Grusin became interested in a new challenge after being hired by his friend Quincy Jones to play on the sound track of director Sydney Pollack's *The Slender Thread* (1965). He began composing for the television series *Gidget* in 1965-1966 and for *The Girl from U.N.C.L.E.* the following season. This work led to Grusin's first film score, *Divorce American Style*.

Grusin continued working on film scores, television music, and jazz recordings. He and producer-engineer Larry Rosen, once Grusin's drummer, formed Grusin Rosen Productions to create albums by young jazz artists for such labels as Blue Note. In 1982 they founded GRP Records, a pioneer in digital recording, releasing some of the first jazz albums in the new medium of compact discs.

His most significant film relationship began in 1975 with *The Yakuza*, the first of his nine scores for Pollack. Two of these earned Academy Award nominations: *Havana* and *The Firm*. He was also nominated for an Academy Award for Best Score for *Heaven Can Wait*, *The Champ*, *On Golden Pond*, and *The Fabulous Baker Boys*, in which he also performs the piano pieces played by Jeff Bridges's character. Grusin won an Academy Award for scoring Robert Redford's *The Milagro Beanfield War*. He was nominated for best song, along with lyricists Alan and Marilyn Bergman, for "It Might Be You" from *Tootsie*.

Grusin won Grammy Awards for his work on *The Fabulous Baker Boys*, *The Milagro Beanfield War*, *The Gershwin Connection*, *Homage to Duke*, and *The Orchestral Album* and another for his arrangement of "Mean Old Man" for James Taylor's album *October Road* (2002). He has received honorary doctorates from the Berklee College of Music and the University of Colorado and a Golden Score from the American Society of Musicians, Composers, and Arrangers.

The Music

Fusion Jazz. Grusin became a leader in the fusion jazz movement, melding electronic and acoustic music, and he often uses the same instruments and the same musicians for his jazz recordings and for his film scores. He even includes a piece from his jazz fusion album *Mountain Dance* in his score for *Falling in Love*. While his jazz compositions are generally upbeat, his film scores are more contemplative. Exceptions to the latter include the frisky "New Hampshire Hornpipe" segment from the family drama *On Golden Pond* and the title music for *Tootsie*, which emphasizes the hopeful optimism of the main character, a struggling actor.

Diverse Film Scores. While many film composers specialize in certain genres, often employing variations of the same themes and motifs from film to film, Grusin has been remarkably diverse. He has done Westerns such as *The Great Northfield Minnesota Raid*, crime dramas such as *The Friends of Eddie*

Coyle, Neil Simon comedies such as *The Goodbye Girl*, political films such as *The Front*, and romances about the pain of young love, *Racing with the Moon*, and about adulterous love, *Falling in Love*.

For each type of film, Grusin does not impose his jazz-accented style but finds ways of combining his usual approach with the conventions of the genre. For *On Golden Pond*, Grusin creates a simple, haunting score emphasizing the film's melancholy nature without resorting to sentimentality. This mutedly forlorn sense of loss can also be heard in *Havana*, which resists the musical clichés of a film set in Latin America. For *The Little Drummer Girl*, he adds Middle Eastern drums, pipes, and stringed instruments to reflect the setting, yet he uses them in a jazzy blend to emphasize how the title character is torn between two cultures.

Grusin has probably done his best work for longtime collaborator Pollack. For the thriller *Three Days of the Condor*, his jazz score uses strong percussive beats and dissonance to underscore the paranoia of the spy played by Redford. This film also displays Grusin's skill in counterpoint. The theme carries an almost carefree tone because the protagonist marked for death does not anticipate the horrors awaiting him. Grusin creates a softer, reflective piece for the photographer played by Faye Dunaway to match the mood of her somber black-and-white pictures, yet he mixes it with the theme to show how she is torn between conflicting emotions. For another Pollack paranoia thriller, *The Firm*, Grusin uses a solo acoustic piano, alternating between repetitive and melodic sounds to underscore the uncertainties of the young lawyer played by Tom Cruise.

Because the title characters in *The Fabulous Baker Boys* play well-worn pop tunes in their nightclub act, the initial music is an amalgam of Broadway conventionality. Because the character portrayed by Bridges hates this music and longs to be a jazz pianist, the score gradually shifts, becoming jazzier, more improvisational and introspective, aligning itself with the character's need for freedom.

Jazz Compositions and Performance. Grusin balanced his film and television work with his output as jazz pianist and composer. In addition to *Mountain Dance*, his best-known nonfilm work, his jazz fusion albums include *Out of the Shadows, Dave Grusin and the N.Y.-L.A. Dream Band, Harlequin* (with frequent collaborator guitarist-composer Lee Ritenour), *Little Big Horn* (with saxophonist Gerry Mulligan), *Sticks and Bones* (with his brother Don, also a keyboardist), *Migration*, and *Two Worlds* (with Ritenour and soprano Renée Fleming). *Two Worlds* explores the composer's interests in classical and folk music in addition to jazz.

In the 1990's Grusin returned to acoustic piano and the work of other composers, issuing tribute albums to George Gershwin, Duke Ellington, Elmer Bernstein, Henry Mancini, and *West Side Story* (1957). In 2004 he released *Now Playing: Movie Themes, Solo Piano*, a collection of his film themes transcribed for solo piano.

Musical Legacy

A man of many talents, Grusin has shown aspiring musicians that they can enjoy producing a diverse range of musical styles while working in a variety of positions. By working as soloist, accompanist, sideman, arranger, conductor, and composer in several fields, Grusin has proved that musicians can thrive by meeting numerous challenges. As a recording executive, he helped the careers of young performers while preserving the past accomplishments of jazz greats and film composers. His cofounding of the National Foundation for Jazz Education demonstrates his commitment to encouraging new talent. Grusin's greatest achievement has been his many film and television scores, demonstrating his ability to adapt his style to the needs of the individual projects.

Michael Adams

Further Reading

Kalbacher, Gene. "Film Scoring: An Inside Look." *Down Beat* 52 (March, 1985): 59, 61. Grusin discusses decisions made while composing a score and the work of such composers as Georges Delerue and Jerry Goldsmith.

Pulliam, Becca. "Maintaining Standards: Keith Jarrett and Dave Grusin." *Down Beat* 59 (May, 1992): 19-22. Grusin talks about his love for the Tin Pan Alley tradition.

Yanow, Scott. "Dave Grusin: Scoring It Big." *Down Beat* 56 (July, 1989): 24-26. This article describes Grusin's jazz career.

Zych, David. "Dave Grusin: Inside Story." *Jazz Times* 28 (February, 1998): 48-51. This piece dis-

cusses Grusin's arrangements of songs from *West Side Story*.

See also: Bergman, Alan; Bernstein, Elmer; Ellington, Duke; Gershwin, George; Jones, Quincy; Mancini, Henry; Taylor, James.

Sofia Gubaidulina
Russian classical composer

Gubaidulina's vocal, orchestral, and chamber-music compositions are characterized by emotional strength, an expansive line of development, and a fine sense of sound expressiveness in timbre and performance method. Her works synthesize Eastern and Western traditions into a spiritual whole.

Born: October 24, 1931; Chistopol, Tatar Autonomous Soviet Socialist Republic, Soviet Union (now in Tatarstan)

Also known as: Sofia Asgatovna Gubaidulina (full name)

Principal works

CHAMBER WORKS: Five Études, 1965; Quintet, 1957 (for piano, two violins, viola, and violoncello); *Allegro Rustico: Klänge des Waldes*, 1963 (*Sound of the Forest*; for flute and piano); *Concordanza*, 1971; String Quartet No. 1, 1971; *Detto II*, 1972 (for cello and chamber ensemble); *Dots, Lines, and Zigzag*, 1976 (for bass clarinet and piano); *Trio*, 1976 (for three trumpets); *Duo*, 1977 (sonata for two bassoons); *Lamento*, 1977 (for tuba and piano); *On Tatar Folk Themes*, 1977 (for bass dombra and piano); *Detto I*, 1978 (sonata for organ and percussion); *Introitus*, 1978 (concerto for piano and chamber orchestra); *In Croce*, 1979 (for cello and organ); *Jubilatio*, 1979 (for four percussionists); *Descensio*, 1981 (for three trombones, three percussionists, harp, harpsichord, and piano); *Rejoice!*, 1981 (sonata for violin and cello); *Sieben Worte*, 1982 (*Seven Words*; for cello, bayan, and strings); *Quasi Hoquetus*, 1984 (for viola, bassoon, and piano); String Quartet No. 2, 1987; String Quartet No. 3, 1987; *Der Seiltänzer*, 1993 (*Dancer on a Tightrope*; for violin and string piano); *Early in* the Morning, Right Before Waking, 1993; String Quartet No. 4, 1993; *In Erwartung*, 1994 (for saxophone quartet and six percussionists); *Music*, 1994 (for flute, strings, and percussion); *Quaternion*, 1996 (for four cellos); *In the Shadow of the Tree*, 1998 (for koto and bass koto).

CHORAL WORKS: *Night in Memphis*, 1968 (for mezzo-soprano, men's chorus, and orchestra); *Stufen*, 1972 (for speaking chorus and orchestra); *Hommage à Marina Tsvetayeva*, 1984; *Jauchzt vor Gott*, 1989 (for mixed choir and organ); *Alleluia*, 1990 (for mixed chorus, boy soprano, organ, and large orchestra); *Aus dem Stundenbuch*, 1991 (for cello, orchestra, male chorus, and female speaker); *Jetzt immer Schnee*, 1993 (*Now Always Snow*; for chamber chorus and chamber ensemble); *Sonnensang*, 1997 (*The Canticle of the Sun*; concerto for cello, chamber chorus, and percussion orchestra; based on a poem by Gennadi Aigi); *St. John Passion*, 2000 (for soloists, two choruses, and orchestra).

ELECTRONIC WORK: *Vivente-Non Vivente*, 1970 (for synthesizer and tape recorder).

INSTRUMENTAL WORKS: *Ten Preludes*, 1974 (for solo cello); *Light and Darkness*, 1976 (for organ); Flute Sonatina, 1978.

ORCHESTRAL WORKS: Concerto, 1975 (for bassoon and low strings); *Offertorium*, 1981 (for violin and orchestra); *Stimmen . . . Verstummen*, 1986; *Antwort ohne Frage*, 1989 (*The Unasked Answer*; collage for three orchestras); *The Feast Is in Full Procession*, 1993 (for viola and orchestra); Concerto for Viola and Orchestra, 1996; *Two Paths*, 1998 (for two violas and orchestra).

PIANO WORKS: *Chaconne*, 1962; Piano Sonata, 1965; *Musical Toys*, 1969 (fourteen piano pieces for children).

VOCAL WORKS: *Hour of the Soul*, 1974 (poem for mezzo-soprano and orchestra; based on a poem by Marina Tsvetayeva); *Perception*, 1981 (for soprano and baritone speaking voices and seven string instruments); *Hommage à T. S. Eliot*, 1987 (for soprano and eight instruments); *Witty Waltzing in the Style of Johann Strauss*, 1987 (for soprano and octet); *Galgenlieder à 3*, 1995 (fifteen pieces for voice, percussion, and double bass); *Galgenlieder à 5*, 1996 (fourteen pieces for mezzo-soprano, flute, percussion, bayan, and double bass).

The Life

Sofia Asgatovna Gubaidulina (gew-bi-doo-LEE-nuh) was born on October 24, 1931, in Chistopol, Tatar Autonomous Soviet Socialist Republic. She received her initial musical training at the Kazan Music Academy, and in 1949 she entered the Kazan Conservatory, studying piano with Grigory Kagan and composition with Al'bert Leman. In 1954 she began graduate studies in composition with Nikolai Peiko at the Moscow Conservatory and postgraduate work with Vissarion Shebalin.

Upon completion of her studies, she rejected the prosperity of a pedagogical career to become a freelance composer, encouraged by a first prize for *Sound of the Forest*, a work for flute and piano, awarded to her at the All-Union composition competition, as well as by publication of her works Quintet, *Chaconne*, and Piano Sonata.

The year 1965 was a turning point for Gubaidulina's works. In the early stages of her mature style (1965-1977), chamber music held precedence (around twenty-five works), while orchestral and vocal works took a backseat. Her developing individual style is reflected in Five Études for harp, bass, and percussion, as she began to open up to the world of unusual, rarely used timbres and methods of sound production. Such instruments as the dombra (long-necked string instrument), bayan (Russian button accordion), bassoon, and bass were increasingly used in her works. A purely electronic composition for synthesizer and tape recorder, *Vivente-Non Vivente*, was created in 1970 at an experimental studio in Moscow.

Always interested in ethnic music and instruments of various cultures, Gubaidulina in 1975 formed an improvisational group with Vyacheslav Artyomov and Viktor Suslin called Astrea that researched sounds created by folk instruments from Asia and the Caucasus region. From 1978 to 1991, Gubaidulina began to give more attention to the expressiveness of the vocal line and spiritual subjects. Her musical language was enriched by rhythmic searches and methods of expressing time. She also unexpectedly resorted to light and color, which she organized rhythmically. In one of her largest compositions, *Alleluia*, for mixed chorus, boy soprano, organ, and large orchestra, the composer utilized color projectors with an arrangement of colors—from yellow to purple—specific to the work.

In instrumental works of this time period—*Offertorium* and *Seven Words*—the methods of playing instruments were invested with symbolism: For example, playing above the bridge of a stringed instrument suggests heaven and, below the bridge, earth.

In 1990 a festival of Gubaidulina's works was presented at the Sverdlovsk Philharmonic in Russia. In 1991, an anniversary year for the composer, she was widely celebrated both in Russia and abroad. Also that year Gubaidulina moved to Germany, near Hamburg, where she would be at the center of musical events, accepting worldwide accolades for her works. She undertook many commissions for famous artists and groups. The cycle *Now Always Snow*, on a poem of Gennadi Aigi, was composed for Amsterdam's Schönberg Ensemble and chorus. After meeting with Kazue Sawai, a Japanese instrumentalist who performs on the folk instrument koto, Gubaidulina composed *Early in the*

Sofia Gubaidulina. (Sergei Savostyanov/Itar-Tass/Landov)

Morning, Right Before Waking for seven kotos. Others include the String Quartet No. 4 for the Kronos Quartet; Impromptu for flute, violin, and strings for Gidon Kremer (in honor of the two hundredth anniversary of Franz Schubert's birth); Concerto for Viola and Orchestra for Yuri Bashmet; *The Canticle of the Sun* for cello, chamber choir, and percussion, commissioned by Radio France and first performed in Frankfurt with Mstislav Rostropovich as soloist; and *St. John Passion* for the European Music Festival in Stuttgart.

Gubaidulina has been a recipient of many awards, among them the Koussevitzky Prize, the Russian State Prize, Prize of the International Festival of Women Composers in Heidelberg, and the Léonie Sonning Music Prize in Copenhagen. In 2004 she was elected a foreign honorary member of the American Academy of Arts and Letters.

The Music

In Gubaidulina's compositions, musical numeric progressions of sound and color cross. The progressions are measures of information, chosen arbitrarily, without an organic dependence on sound or other material.

Early Works. Quintet, *Chaconne*, and Piano Sonata, composed during her graduate and postgraduate studies, are tonal compositions. They possess characteristics that presage her later works: polyphony and acute rhythms.

Hour of the Soul. This work on the poem of Marina Tsvetayeva (originally subtitled "Poem for a Large Band with Insertion of Female Voice in the Finale") has undergone a few transformations. The most radical one was in 1976 when it was turned into a concerto for symphony orchestra, multiple percussion, and a female soloist and titled *Percussio di Pekarski* (for Mark Pekarsky, the composer's friend, a percussionist who collects percussion instruments from all over the world). In the new rendition the orchestra was surrounded by six groups of percussion instruments, and the soloist-percussionist went from one to another. The Chinese sheng, a mouth instrument, was used as a ritornello (recurring refrain), accompanying the vocalist singing Tsvetayeva's poem.

Offertorium. In 1980, after meeting violinist Kremer, Gubaidulina composed this violin concerto. A friend suggested that she include in it the royal theme from Johann Sebastian Bach's *Musical Offering*. Here Gubaidulina builds the music on consecutive omission of the end notes on both sides of the theme. At first the theme seems on the brink of destruction, but its gradual restoration brings the work to a beautiful conclusion. Kremer premiered *Offertorium* on May 30, 1981, although Gubaidulina was not able to be present because her visa was denied. It was with Kremer's help that Gubaidulina became known in international circles. This piece, now performed all over the world, merges the contrasting characteristics of the composer: strict calculation and intuition, formal mastery and spiritual awakening.

Seven Words. In this composition for cello, bayan, and fifteen strings, Gubaidulina turns to a religious theme, although it is interpreted subjectively. Compositions of Heinrich Schütz and Joseph Haydn (bearing the same title) served as prototypes, and Haydn's chromatic motif appears in all seven of the sections in her work. Gubaidulina personifies the instruments: bayan is the Father; cello is the Son; strings are the Holy Spirit. There is also harmonic symbolism: chromaticism and microtones are spheres of earthly suffering (depicted in the timbres of bayan and cello), while the diatonic language, reflecting the heavenly sphere, is given to the strings. The intersection of these two systems in unison and octaves make up the shape of a cross.

Stimmen . . . Verstummen. In this symphony, the mystery of the spirit unfolds. The twelve sections are characterized by opposing lines: The odd sections portray the eternal heavenly world; the even represent the chaotic earthly one. In the eighth, and most expanded, section, the theme recreates the universal catastrophe of Judgment Day as revealed in the biblical Apocalypse. The ninth section is the culmination of the piece, in which the orchestra becomes silent and the conductor beats out a rhythm noted in the score (according to the Fibonacci series of 1-2-3, 2-3-5, 3-5-8). This unique solo symbolizes the aftermath of the catastrophe.

String Quartet No. 4. This work, commissioned by the Kronos Quartet, juxtaposes three aspects: a live performance of music; prerecorded music that runs on two separate tracks tuned a quarter-tone apart; and visual effects using light and darkness. String Quartet No. 4 begins in complete dark-

ness with the prerecorded material—rubber balls bouncing on strings. This is followed by color and light effects, and finally the performers begin to play in dialogue with the tracks. The instruments eventually take on the language of the tracks by playing with the same rubber balls. This quiet, calm piece presents a conflict-free conversation between the real and unreal entities.

St. John Passion. In 2000 Gubaidulina was one of four composers commissioned by Helmuth Rilling, artistic director of the Internationale Bachakademie Stuttgart, to compose a Passion in commemoration of the 250 years since Bach's death. Sung in Russian, *St. John Passion*, for soloists, two choruses, and orchestra, demonstrates the composer's deep Russian Orthodox faith.

The oratorio comprises eleven episodes in two sections (1-7 and 8-11). Gubaidulina uses two texts—the Gospel account of Christ's Passion and the narrative of St. John on the Last Judgment—to show an intersection between events on earth (Passion, Nos. 1, 6, 9, and 11) and those in heaven (Apocalypse, Nos. 2-5, 7, and 10). This intersection is supported by the orchestra—glissandi of some instruments cut through the sustained notes of others. In this work, the composer discloses God's Word, showing that his flesh in the Passion and his spirit in the Last Judgment at last come together in perfect balance. The work was recorded on September 1, 2000, by the Orchestra of Mariinsky Theatre, St. Petersburg, conducted by Valery Gergiev at Konzert- und Kongresszentrum Liederhalle, Stuttgart.

Musical Legacy

Her enormous talent coupled with her artistic independence have made Gubaidulina one of the most interesting composers of the twentieth century. Despite the complexity of Gubaidulina's musical language, her aesthetic and spiritual views are becoming more and more accessible to the general public, who are drawn to her intellectual mastery, inventive use of sound, and deep spiritual motivation.

Karina Bruk

Further Reading

Griffiths, Paul. *Modern Music and After: Directions Since 1945.* New York: Oxford University Press, 1995. Includes a short commentary on the composer's style with a brief comparison to other composers in regard to her treatment of various devices such as color, light, and metric values. Cites specific compositions.

Kurtz, Michael. *Sofia Gubaidulina: A Biography.* Edited by Christoph K. Lohmann and Malcom Hamrich Brown. Bloomington: Indiana University Press, 2007. Based on interviews taken with her, her colleagues, and her family, as well as her papers. Discusses the evolution of her work in the context of the culture and politics of the post-Stalin Soviet Union. List of works has been updated for this revised and expanded edition.

Pendle, Karin, and Robert Zieroff. "Composers of Modern Europe, Israel, Australia, and New Zealand." In *Women and Music: A History*, edited by Karin Pendle. 2d ed. Bloomington: Indiana University Press, 2000. Multicultural history of women in music that briefly addresses Gubaidulina's life and includes a discussion of a few of her works: *In Croce, Seven Words, Alleluia.*

Polin, Clair. "Conversations in Leningrad." *Tempo* 168 (March, 1989): 19-20. Gubaidulina speaks of her work *Hour of the Soul* in an interview given at the Soviet Union's Third International Festival of Contemporary Composers held in Leningrad, 1988.

Redepenning, Dorothea. "Sofia Gubaidulina: An Interview with Dorothea Redepenning." In *Contemporary Composers on Contemporary Music*, edited by Elliott Schwartz and Barney Childs. New York: Da Capo Press, 1998. Gubaidulina answers questions regarding the reception of her (and other composers') works in Russia. She discusses her usage of musical quotations and her concept of musical time. Preceded by a brief biographical note.

See also: Nono, Luigi; Pärt, Arvo; Rostropovich, Mstislav; Schnittke, Alfred.

Arlo Guthrie

American folksinger, guitarist, and songwriter

Although identified with the counterculture of the 1960's, Guthrie composed, recorded, and performed into the twenty first century, increasingly using his popularity as a musician to attract attention to his work on behalf of various charitable social causes.

Born: July 10, 1947; Coney Island, New York
Also known as: Arlo Davy Guthrie (full name)
Member of: Shenandoah

Principal recordings

ALBUMS: *Alice's Restaurant,* 1967; *Running down the Road,* 1969; *Washington County,* 1970; *Hobo's Lullaby,* 1972; *The Last of the Brooklyn Cowboys,* 1973; *Arlo Guthrie,* 1974; *Amigo,* 1976; *A Tribute to Leadbelly,* 1977; *Arlo Guthrie with Shenandoah,* 1978; *One Night,* 1978; *Outlasting the Blues,* 1979; *Power of Love,* 1981; *Precious Friend,* 1981 (with Pete Seeger); *Hard Travelin',* 1986 (with Woody Guthrie and others); *Someday,* 1986; *Baby's Storytime,* 1990; *All over the World,* 1991; *Son of the Wind,* 1992; *Woody's Twenty Grow Big Songs,* 1992 (with Woody Guthrie and the Guthrie Family); *Mystic Journey,* 1996; *BanjoMan: A Tribute to Derroll Adams,* 2002.

The Life

Arlo Davy Guthrie (GUH-three) was born into an artistic family. His mother, Marjorie Mazia Guthrie, was a former professional dancer with the Martha Graham Company and taught dance throughout his childhood. His father, Woody Guthrie, was one of America's most prolific and best-known folk-protest singers and the composer of innumerable songs, including "This Land Is Your Land."

Guthrie made an indelible mark in 1967 with "Alice's Restaurant Massacree," an eighteen-minute ballad that told a shaggy-dog story loosely patterned after his father's talking-blues style. An instant counterculture favorite, the real-life events described in the song served as the basis for the

1969 film *Alice's Restaurant*, in which Guthrie starred as himself. Although he continued to record major-label albums through 1981, his only other radio hit was his 1972 recording of Steve Goodman's "City of New Orleans."

After 1991 Guthrie occupied himself increasingly with the Guthrie Center, a nonprofit interfaith church foundation dedicated to various forms of social activism, such as caring for AIDS patients and raising awareness about Huntington's disease, the degenerative disorder from which his father died. A practicing Catholic during much of the 1970's, Guthrie eventually became a follower of the Kali Natha Yoga master Ma Jaya Sati Bhagavati.

The Music

Given his status as the eldest son of Woody Guthrie, Arlo Guthrie could have carved out a comfortable musical niche simply by covering his father's songs or by composing in his father's well-known folk-protest style. Instead—with his instantly recognizable nasal voice, his charming and quirky sense of humor, his ear for catchy melodies, and his intimate familiarity with folk songs from many traditions—he established himself from the outset as a singer-songwriter. Besides covering Woody's "Oklahoma Hills" on *Running down the Road*, "1913 Massacre" on *Hobo's Lullaby*, and "Ramblin' Round" on *The Last of the Brooklyn Cowboys*, Guthrie also wrote protest songs that, similar in spirit to his father's Dust Bowl classics, were clearly a response to the specific sociopolitical crises of the 1960's and 1970's.

Alice's Restaurant. With "Alice's Restaurant Massacree" comprising all of side one, this 1967 album made Guthrie an instant counterculture celebrity. Its length aside, what distinguished Guthrie's eighteen-minute story-song from the rest of the antiwar-music pack was his comic timing.

The Best of Arlo Guthrie. Released ten years after Guthrie's debut, this compilation suffered from the restrictions of the twelve-inch vinyl long-playing record. That "Alice's Restaurant Massacree" would make the cut was obvious, as was the inclusion of "The Motorcycle Song" (in its six-minute version) and Guthrie's 1972 hit "City of New Orleans." The challenge was to condense the best of the rest of Guthrie's first eight albums into the remaining twenty minutes. Predictably, the result was spotty, with two songs from *The Last of the Brooklyn Cowboys* and one apiece from *Running down the Road*, *Washington County*, *Arlo Guthrie*, and *Amigo*.

Outlasting the Blues. When this album appeared in the fall of 1979, it was frequently discussed in conjunction with Bob Dylan's *Slow Train Coming* (1979) and Van Morrison's *Into the Music* (1979), albums that, like this album's first side, drew on biblical imagery. The specific reason for Guthrie's religious focus was that he was on the verge of learning whether he, like his father, would succumb to Huntington's disease. (The eventual diagnosis was that he would not.) Understandably, his own mortality was on his mind, and, rather than indulging in morbid self-pity, he composed a suite of songs that examined his life and its significance and included references to his 1960's status as a protest hero, his Jewish roots, his conversion to Catholicism, and his marriage. Side two, although less thematically coherent, consisted of songs of equally high quality, making the album one of Guthrie's strongest.

Power of Love. Compared to the serious tone of *Outlasting the Blues*, this 1981 follow-up, Guthrie's last album for Warner Bros., struck many as especially lightweight. At least one song, however, the T-Bone Burnett-composed title cut, continued Guthrie's recording of music with Christian themes.

Someday. This was in many ways a typical Arlo Guthrie album, replete with humor, political protest, and catchy melodies. By 1986, however, the Guthrie formula was considered passé, and Warner Bros. refused to release the album, leaving it to Guthrie to release it himself on his own Rising Son label in the early 1990's.

All Over the World. In 1991, ten years after his last Warner Bros. album, Guthrie had finally acquired the rights to enough of his catalog to assemble this thirteen-song compilation, which, except for its reinclusion of "City of New Orleans," made an ideal complement to *The Best of Arlo Guthrie*.

Musical Legacy

Since Guthrie emerged as a solo performer in 1967, two phrases have always appeared in discussions of his music: "Woody Guthrie's son" and "Alice's Restaurant." The former has given even the slightest of Guthrie's recordings an aura of folkloric authenticity, of being connected to the centuries-old troubadour tradition in which Woody Guthrie himself was a link. The latter serves as a reminder of the role that storytelling, wit, and cheering for society's underdogs has played in Guthrie's most enduring music.

Whether that music will live on in the repertoires of subsequent folksingers remains to be seen. Even the perennially popular "Alice's Restaurant Massacree" and "The Motorcycle Song" are so autobiographical that it is difficult to imagine anyone besides Guthrie performing them. As long as there are pretensions, however, there will be songwriters who want to puncture them so effectively that they never reinflate, inspired by the example of Guthrie's preference for the satirical slice over the sledgehammer blow.

Arsenio Orteza

Further Reading

Guthrie, Arlo. *This Is the Arlo Guthrie Book.* New York: Amsco, 1969. The words and music to twenty early Guthrie songs, illustrated with photographs of Guthrie's family and memorabilia.

Lee, Laura. *Arlo, Alice, and Anglicans: The Lives of a New England Church.* Woodstock, Vt.: The Countryman Press, 2000. A history of the Trinity Church, the setting of "Alice's Restaurant Massacree" and the current home of the interfaith Guthrie Center.

Orteza, Arsenio. "Arlo and Ma." *The Christian Century,* May 5, 1993. An examination of Guthrie's spiritual journey from Catholicism to Ma Jaya Sati Bhagavati.

Simon, John. "The Youth Film." In *Movies into Film: Film Criticism, 1967-1970.* New York: Delta, 1971. Contains a review of the film *Alice's Restaurant.*

Unterberger, Richie. *Turn! Turn! Turn! The Sixties Folk-Rock Revolution.* San Francisco: Backbeat Books, 2002. Traces the role of folk music in the evolution of rock and roll with Guthrie among the interviewed musicians.

See also: Dylan, Bob; Guthrie, Woody; Seeger, Pete.

Woody Guthrie
American folksinger, guitarist, and songwriter

The composer of "This Land Is Your Land," Guthrie is perhaps the most influential of modern folk musicians. He wrote thousands of songs, popularized folk music as a medium of populism and protest, and inspired such musicians as Pete Seeger and Bob Dylan.

Born: July 14, 1912; Okemah, Oklahoma
Died: October 3, 1967; Queens, New York
Also known as: Woodrow Wilson Guthrie (full name)
Member of: The Almanac Singers

Principal recordings

ALBUMS (solo): *Bound for Glory,* 1958; *Nursery Days,* 1958; *Woody Guthrie Sings Folk Songs, Vol. 1,* 1962; *Dust Bowl Ballads,* 1964; *One of a Kind,* 1964; *Woody Guthrie Sings Folk Songs, Vol. 2,* 1964; *This Land Is Your Land,* 1967; *Struggle,* 1976; *Poor Boy,* 1981; *Songs to Grow on for Mother and Child,* 1991; *Worried Man Blues,* 1991; *Ballads of Sacco and Vanzetti,* 1996.

ALBUMS (with the Almanac Singers): *Deep Sea Chanteys and Whaling Ballads,* 1941; *Sod Buster Ballads,* 1941; *Songs for John Doe,* 1941; *Talking Union,* 1941; *Dear Mr. President,* 1942.

WRITINGS OF INTEREST: *Bound for Glory,* 1943 (autobiography).

The Life

Woodrow Wilson Guthrie (GUH-three) was born in 1912 in Oklahoma hill country; he was named for the Democratic presidential candidate, Woodrow Wilson. His father, Charles Guthrie, was a town official and businessman; his mother, Nora Belle Tanner, was musically inclined and sang ballads to Woody and his siblings Clara, Roy, George, and Mary Josephine. When Woody was thirteen he heard an African American boy, George, playing blues music on his harmonica. Woody saved up to buy his own harmonica and was soon playing with George. When Woody was sixteen his mother was committed to an insane asylum for suspicion of setting her husband on fire. (Clara had also died from a fire.) Shortly afterward, the family moved to Texas. Already accomplished on the harmonica, Guthrie spent hours practicing the guitar.

At eighteen, Guthrie abandoned high school. With the nation falling into the Great Depression, Guthrie began a life of wandering, hitchhiking, working at odd jobs, playing in bands, and singing on radio shows. On October 28, 1933, Guthrie married seventeen-year-old Mary Jennings. Their daughter Gwendolyn was born two years later, followed by Sue in 1937, and Will in 1939. In 1937 Guthrie joined the scores of Dust Bowl migrants moving to California to find work.

Guthrie launched the *Oklahoma and Woody Show* radio program with his cousin Jack Guthrie on the Los Angeles's station KFVD. Soon Jack was replaced by Maxine Crissman, nicknamed "Lefty Lou" by Guthrie. After a popular two-year run of the *Woody and Lefty Lou Show*, Guthrie resumed his rambling. Dismayed by the impoverished conditions he witnessed in migrant workers' camps, he began attending meetings of the Communist Party of America, which touted a pro-labor platform. Traveling to New York City in 1940, Guthrie was inspired to write his most famous song, "This Land Is Your Land." He also recorded his first commercial songs in 1940 before setting off on a cross-country ramble with young folksinger Pete Seeger.

In 1942 Guthrie returned to New York City to settle, adored as an authentic Oklahoma singer by the city's progressive folk community. He lived a bohemian lifestyle in concert with the Almanac Singers folk collective. Guthrie was sexually unrestrained; in 1943 he and Mary were divorced. He published his autobiography, *Bound for Glory*, befriended blues musician Huddie "Leadbelly" Ledbetter, and toured with the duo of Sonny Terry and Brownie McGhee.

During World War II, Guthrie served in the U.S. Merchant Marine and U.S. Army. After the war he moved with his new wife, Marjorie Greenblatt Mazia, to Coney Island in Brooklyn, New York. They had four children, Cathy in 1943, Arlo in 1947, Joady in 1948, and Nora in 1950. (In 1947, Cathy would die in a house fire.) Guthrie wrote and performed hundreds of songs and ballads, many of which have become classics, as well as writing a stream of columns, poems, essays, and incipient novels. Folk musicians from throughout the country visited Guthrie to learn from him and pay him homage. However, Guthrie's behavior became increasingly erratic and uncontrollable; he drank and philandered. In 1952, he was diagnosed with the hereditary disorder Huntington's chorea, which was almost certainly the cause of his mother's insanity. He and Marjorie divorced in 1953. He married Anneke Van Kirk the

Woody Guthrie. (AP/Wide World Photos)

same year; they had a child, Lorina, in 1954. A campfire accident burned Guthrie's arm, making it impossible for him to play the guitar, and shortly thereafter he and Anneke were divorced.

Guthrie's second wife, Marjorie, became his caregiver during his later years, as his disease began to render him increasingly unable to control his movements. He spent the last decade of his life in various hospitals, including Greystone Park Psychiatric Hospital (1956-1961), Brooklyn State Hospital (1966), and Creedmoor State Hospital in Queens, where he died in 1967. Marjorie would go on to found the Committee to Combat Huntington's Disease, which became the Huntington's Disease Society of America.

The Music

Guthrie's music and lyrics were rooted in the ballads he heard from his mother, African American blues, Oklahoma migrant songs, the Texan yodeler Jimmie Rodgers, and the many hours he spent reading in the library. He was especially influenced by the superb gospel and country recordings of the Carter Family: A. P. Carter, his wife Sara, and her cousin Maybelle. Although elfin and scrawny in person, with a droning voice, Guthrie on stage had a charismatic presence that gripped the attention of his audience. Dressed in work clothes, with a weather-beaten hat, thin and wiry, he seemed hardly removed from his days hitchhiking across the Dust Bowl. His voice was nasal, with a strong Oklahoma twang. His lyrics were wily, rambling, comic, and always in favor of the workingman; his simple guitar playing accented his performance.

Dust Bowl Ballads. Over the course of three days in March, 1940, the American folklorist Alan Lomax recorded Guthrie talking, singing, and playing guitar for his Library of Congress archives. The following month, Lomax arranged for Guthrie to make his first commercial releases for the RCA label. Titled *Dust Bowl Ballads*, eleven songs were issued in July on two 78-rpm records. Although the records sold only a few thousand copies, they include such hard-hitting songs about the plight of farmworkers as "Talking Dust Bowl" and "Do Re Mi."

"This Land Is Your Land." The two twentieth century songs that can be characterized as Amer-

ica's unofficial anthems are linked in origin. Kate Smith popularized Irving Berlin's "God Bless America" in a 1938 recording. Guthrie was annoyed by its patriotic fervor and overheated pitch. On February 23, 1940, in Time Square's Hanover House hotel, he composed six stanzas of "God Blessed America for Me" in response. He set the verses to a melody that may have been derived from the Carter family tune "Little Darling, Pal of Mine," which in turn had been adopted from the gospel hymn "Oh, My Loving Brother." By the time Guthrie recorded the song, he had changed the title and refrain to reflect his attachment to the land he had wandered. The lyrics celebrated the natural wonders of the American landscape and proclaimed, "This land is your land, this land is my land . . . This land was made for you and me."

"This Land Is Your Land" was one of the first of Guthrie's hundreds of songs recorded with Folkways Records under the supervision of Moses Asch in April, 1944. The melody stays within one octave and is easy to sing. Guthrie's guitar accompaniment consists of simple chords, and he sings with an engaging midwestern twang (for example, singing "waters" with a pinched trill).

"Car Song." Also from the first Asch/Folkway recording session is the delightful "Car Song," also known as "Riding in My Car." Free of political content, "Car Song" illustrates Guthrie's talent for children's music. He paints a charming portrait of a family on an automobile outing, playfully singing the "brrrm brm" of the engine, the "click clack" of the door, and the "oorah oogah" of the horn.

"Springfield Mountain." Guthrie's Folkway recording of the traditional American folk ballad "Springfield Mountain" is arresting. He is accompanied by his best friend, Gilbert "Cisco" Houston, on guitar, Sonny Terry on harmonica and Betty Hawes. (Leadbelly accompanies him on other recordings from these sessions.) Guthrie sputters and stutters the tale of a snake-bitten young man.

"Pass Away." Guthrie wrote prolifically throughout his life—his "Woody Sez" columns for the *People's World*, essays, novels, poems, and thousands of songs. He considered his lyrics as important as his music, which he often derived from existing tunes. Many of his verses remained unrecorded, to be mined by later generations of musicians. One example is his 1955 lyric for "Pass Away," which reflects Guthrie's simple religious faith. "Pass Away" was scored and recorded in a moving 2006 version by the band the Klezmatics.

"Talking Subway Blues." "Talking Subway Blues" is a ballad composed by Guthrie upon first arriving in New York City. It illustrates his distinctive form of "talking blues," with its mix of spoken lyric and singing guitar, irregular meters and rhymes, and free commentary. If Guthrie did not invent the style of "talking blues," he certainly popularized it. In homespun language, Guthrie humorously relates his first encounter with the subway and of the mass of New Yorkers "all a-runnin' down that hole in the ground." Although the song remains lighthearted, Guthrie suggests the subway as a metaphor for the plight of workers, too oppressed to emerge from their holes in the ground. He concludes with a plea to join the union, fight fascists, and contribute to victory in World War II. "Talking Subway Blues" is the direct inspiration for Bob Dylan's brilliantly comedic "Talking New York," recorded in 1962.

Musical Legacy

Woody Guthrie's music combined simple, traditional folk tunes with stirring populist and political lyrics. Folk music refers to the spontaneous, informal musical traditions of local communities. In twentieth century America, what had been local or regional folk music was rendered accessible for the first time on a national level. Nineteenth century composers such as Stephen Foster had made famous their own folk-derived songs and melodies; however, it was only with the rise of the recording industry, mass mobility, and national movements that the United States can be said to have attained an "American" folk music.

If Guthrie was not the creator of this national folk music, he was its embodiment. "This Land Is Your Land" is sung by schoolchildren throughout the United States and can be described as America's national folk anthem.

Guthrie was received by folk audiences as if he had sprung directly from the dust bowls of Oklahoma, but he shaped his music not only from the folk ballads his mother had sung to him as a child and from tunes he had picked up around campfires but also from diverse cultures, including blues performers, the gospel music of the Carter family,

country songs, his incessant reading, and the anguished protests of the dispossessed.

Guthrie presaged the youth culture of the 1960's both in his life and music, and for that generation he became an icon. His identification with Oklahoma migrants, his wandering life in Texas and California, and his bohemian life in New York City represented a restless searching that was romanticized in the 1960's. His childlike perspectives, his flirtations with left-wing radicalism, and his casual attitude toward marriage and sex were equally mythologized and celebrated. Most of all, Guthrie's unique form of folk music—autobiographical, tuneful, comedic, working-class, with biting social commentary—was the precursor to both the folk revival and the protest songs of the Vietnam generation. Guthrie believed that popular music could be a powerful force against oppression. "This Machine Kills Fascists" was emblazoned on his guitar. While claiming the role of a down-home country singer, he was also a brilliant innovator whose novel forms were developed by such modern folksingers as Pete Seeger, Ramblin' Jack Elliott, Phil Ochs, Joan Baez, Bob Dylan, and Guthrie's own son, Arlo. There may be no more succinct tribute to Guthrie's personal and musical legacy than Dylan's celebrated 1962 recording, "Song to Woody."

Howard Bromberg

Further Reading

Crawford, Richard. *America's Musical Life: A History*. New York: W. W. Norton, 2001. An engaging, lively survey of America's musical history, situating Guthrie in the context of the folk revival of the 1950's and 1960's.

Cray, Ed. *Ramblin' Man: The Life and Times of Woody Guthrie*. Foreword by Studs Terkel. New York: W. W. Norton, 2004. With a foreword of personal reminiscences by journalist and social commentator Terkel, this is a complete, absorbing biography.

Guthrie, Woody. *Bound for Glory*. 1943. Reprint. Foreword by Pete Seeger. New York: Plume, 1983. Guthrie's acclaimed autobiography is novelistic in tone, with a title taken from a gospel song Guthrie popularized, "This Train Is Bound for Glory." A 1976 movie of the same name was based on this book. Includes illustrations by Guthrie.

Hampton, Wade. *Guerrilla Minstrels*. Knoxville: University of Tennessee Press, 1986. An academic study of the culture of protest and radicalism surrounding singer-songwriters Guthrie, John Lennon, Joe Hill, and Bob Dylan. Notes Dylan's enormous debt to Guthrie.

Jackson, Mark. *Prophet Singer: The Voice and Vision of Woody Guthrie*. Jackson: University Press of Mississippi, 2007. A volume in the American Made Music series that examines Guthrie's lyrics for social content and populist protests.

Klein, Joe. *Woody Guthrie: A Life*. New York: Delta, 1999. A sympathetic biography with striking photographs and illustrations.

Longhi, Jim. *Woody, Cisco, and Me: Seamen Three in the Merchant Marine*. Urbana: University of Illinois Press, 1997. Part of the series Music in American Life, a firsthand account by a shipmate of Guthrie and his friend Cisco Houston in the Merchant Marine. The insightful anecdotes about Guthrie include an inspiring story of Guthrie racially integrating his concert in the ship's hold.

Marsh, Davie, and Harold Leventhal, eds. *Pastures of Plenty: A Self Portrait*. New York: HarperPerennial, 1992. Named for one of Guthrie's most famous Dust Bowl songs, a chronological sampling of his unpublished writings. Edited with a foreword by the executor of Guthrie's estate.

Santelli, Robert, and Emily Davidson. *Hard Travelin': The Life and Legacy of Woody Guthrie*. Hanover, N.H.: University Press of New England, 1999. Commemorating the American Music Masters' salute to Guthrie, a collection of essays on Guthrie by scholars and critics.

See also: Dylan, Bob; Guthrie, Arlo; Leadbelly; Lomax, Alan; Odetta; Paxton, Tom; Ritchie, Jean; Rodgers, Jimmie; Rush, Tom; Seeger, Pete; Terry, Sonny; Travis, Merle; Tweedy, Jeff; Waits, Tom.

Buddy Guy

American blues singer, songwriter, and guitarist

Guy provided the bridge between the electric Chicago blues sound of the late 1950's and the guitar-driven rock music of the late 1960's.

Born: July 30, 1936; Lettsworth, Louisiana
Also known as: George Guy (full name)

Principal recordings

ALBUMS: *I Left My Blues in San Francisco*, 1967; *Blues Today*, 1968; *A Man and the Blues*, 1968; *Buddy and the Juniors*, 1970 (with Junior Wells and Junior Mance); *Buddy Guy and Junior Wells Play the Blues*, 1972 (with Wells); *Hold That Plane*, 1972; *Buddy and Phil Guy*, 1979 (with Phil Guy); *Got to Use Your Head*, 1979; *Pleading the Blues*, 1979 (with Wells); *The Dollar Done Fell*, 1980; *Stone Crazy!*, 1981; *D. J. Play My Blues*, 1982; *Buddy Guy*, 1983; *Ten Blue Fingers*, 1985; *Chess Masters*, 1987; *Breaking Out*, 1988; *I Ain't Got No Money*, 1989; *Alone and Acoustic*, 1991 (with Wells); *Damn Right, I've Got the Blues*, 1991; *My Time After Awhile*, 1992; *Feels Like Rain*, 1993; *Slippin' In*, 1994; *I Cry*, 1995; *The Treasure Untold*, 1997; *Try to Quit You Baby*, 1997; *Heavy Love*, 1998; *The Real Blues*, 1999 (with Wells); *Sweet Tea*, 2001; *Blue on Blues*, 2002 (with Otis Rush); *Everything Gonna Be Alright*, 2002; *Blues Singer*, 2003; *Bring 'Em In*, 2005; *Everyday We Have the Blues*, 2006; *Going Back to Acoustic*, 2006; *Messin' with the Kids*, 2006 (with Wells); *Skin Deep*, 2008.

The Life

George "Buddy" Guy was born to a family of sharecroppers in rural Louisiana. When he was not in school, he worked on the farm, plowing with a mule or picking cotton. He began playing guitar at roadhouses with local bands in his teens, and he decided to move to Chicago, at that time the center of blues music, in 1957. Guy created showcases for live music in Chicago, when in 1972 he bought a blues bar called the Checkerboard, which remained open until 1985. In 1989 he opened Buddy Guy's Legends, a premier venue for live blues music in downtown Chicago.

He had six children with his first wife, Joanne, and two more with his second wife, Jennifer. Guy has won five Grammy Awards, more than thirty W. C. Handy Awards for blues music, and he was inducted into the Rock and Roll Hall of Fame in 2005 by Eric Clapton and B. B. King.

The Music

Guy's life might stand as a model for the development of blues music in America: He began playing the blues in the rural South, he perfected his craft in Chicago, and he found belated recognition when he was "discovered" by rock musicians and introduced by them to a mainstream popular audience.

Early Works. Guy had recorded a demo at a Baton Rouge, Louisiana, radio station before coming to Chicago, and he produced a handful of singles for Cobra Records (released by Artistic Records) after winning a battle of the bands. However, he made his early reputation with Chess Records. Although Guy recorded forty-seven songs under his own name while under contract to Chess Records from 1960 to 1967, the label showed no interest in releasing an album, perceiving him primarily as a versatile session guitarist who could play behind its more established stars, such as Muddy Waters and Howlin' Wolf. Even when Guy was allowed to record his own music, Leonard Chess, a founder of Chess Records, insisted that Guy play traditional blues rather than the sort of unrestrained "noise" on guitar that was the trademark of his explosive live shows. An innovative guitarist, Guy was also a flamboyant showman, playing the guitar behind his back and with his teeth (techniques borrowed by Jimi Hendrix), hanging from rafters by his knees, and using long guitar cords that allowed him to walk out into the crowd as he played. When bands such as Cream, the Jimi Hendrix Experience, and Led Zeppelin began selling millions of albums featuring extended feedback-drenched guitar solos, Chess reportedly went to Guy, bent over, and said, "Kick me!" Chess offered to let Guy record his own style of music, but too late—Guy had just signed a contract with Vanguard Records that offered him artistic control, though none of the al-

bums he recorded with Vanguard were completely successful.

While his recorded output remained frustratingly uneven, Guy made his reputation with his live performances, touring as a solo artist and with harmonica player Junior Wells (recording with Wells as Friendly Chap on the classic *Hoodoo Man Blues* [1965] to avoid contractual conflicts), as a lead-in act with the Rolling Stones, and in appearances with such famous disciples as Clapton and Stevie Ray Vaughan.

Stone Crazy! The first full-length recording that accurately represented Guy's style was *Stone Crazy!*, recorded in one session while he was on a tour of France and released in America in 1981 by Alligator Records. (Remarkably, he had recorded a full album backing up Junior Wells, *Pleading the Blues* [1979], on the same day.) The opening track of *Stone Crazy!*, Guy's "I Smell a Rat," exemplified the freedom he had always needed: The song ran more than nine minutes, and it opened with a guitar solo extending more than two minutes before the first lyrics were sung, an approach that would never have been allowed by traditional blues labels, which had always followed the Chess formula of three-minute songs suitable for radio play.

Damn Right, I've Got the Blues. Guy signed with Silvertone Records in 1990, and he finally achieved his first unalloyed successes with both critics and fans, resurrecting his career and earning him his first Grammy Award for Best Contemporary Blues Album. Now well into his fifties, he had finally begun the richest and most productive period of his career, and he would win the same Grammy Award in 1993, for *Feels Like Rain*, and in 1995, for *Slippin' In*. Guy would collect additional Grammy Awards for Best Rock Instrumental Performance (1996, for the Stevie Ray Vaughan tribute "SRV Shuffle") and for Best Traditional Blues Album (2003, for *Blues Singer*).

Can't Quit the Blues. This definitive career-spanning three-album boxed set, which surveys the first fifty years of Guy's music, beginning with his 1957 demo for Ace Records, was released to coincide with his seventieth birthday. Guy's sporadic and inconsistent recording history, mostly with small record companies, had made it extraordinarily difficult for fans to obtain his earlier works, and these compact discs address that need.

Musical Legacy

Guy unleashed the full potential of the electric guitar, establishing it as the distinctive lead instrument for most rock and blues music. He was twenty years younger than bluesmen such as Muddy Waters and Howlin' Wolf, from whom he had learned his craft, and he became an elder statesman for the rock musicians who would follow him. Guy found himself in the unusual position of being both a living symbol of the classic blues tradition and a restless innovator whose interests extended that tradition. He broadened the range and appeal of the blues while remaining true to its fundamental sound and emotional resonance. Among the notable guitarists who have acknowledged Guy's influence are Hendrix, Clapton, Vaughan, Jeff Beck, Jimmy Page, Robert Cray, and John Mayer.

William Nelles

Further Reading

Dicaire, David. *Blues Singers: Biographies of Fifty Legendary Artists of the Early Twentieth Century*. Jefferson, N.C.: McFarland, 1999. This resource includes a biographical sketch of Guy and partial discography of his works.

Gill, Chris. *Guitar Legends*. New York: HarperCollins, 1995. This book analyzes Guy's guitar techniques, equipment choices, and characteristic guitar licks.

Obrecht, Jas. *Blues Guitar: The Men Who Made the Music*. San Francisco: GPI Books, 1990. A wide-ranging interview covers Guy's life, his influences, and his guitar techniques.

Waterman, Dick. *Between Midnight and Day: The Last Unpublished Blues Archive*. New York: Thunder's Mouth Press, 2003. One of his former managers offers anecdotes about Guy's work in the 1960's.

Wilcock, Donald E., with Buddy Guy. *Damn Right I've Got the Blues: Buddy Guy and the Blues Roots of Rock and Roll*. San Francisco: Woodford Press, 1993. A full-length biography of Guy, presented in the form of an oral history, with extensive interview material from family members and fellow musicians.

See also: Beck, Jeff; Clapton, Eric; Handy, W. C.; Hendrix, Jimi; Howlin' Wolf; King, B. B.; Rush, Otis; Vaughan, Stevie Ray; Waters, Muddy; Williamson, Sonny Boy, II.

H

Merle Haggard
American country singer, guitarist, and songwriter

The gritty realism and emotional rawness of Haggard's lyrics and vocal performances transformed country music into a major commercial art form. Many of Haggard's songs are undisputed country classics that, with simplicity and sincerity, echo the aspirations, values, and concerns of mainstream America.

Born: April 6, 1937; Bakersfield, California
Also known as: Merle Ronald Haggard (full name)
Member of: The Strangers

Principal recordings

ALBUMS: *Strangers*, 1965; *Just Between the Two of Us*, 1966 (with Bonnie Owens); *Swinging Doors*, 1966; *Branded Man*, 1967; *I'm a Lonesome Fugitive*, 1967; *The Legend of Bonnie and Clyde*, 1968; *Mama Tried*, 1968; *Sing Me Back Home*, 1968; *A Portrait of Merle Haggard*, 1969; *Pride in What I Am*, 1969; *Same Train, a Different Time*, 1969; *Introducing My Friends, the Strangers*, 1970; *A Tribute to the Best Damn Fiddle Player in the World*, 1970; *It's Not Love (but It's Not Bad)*, 1972; *Let Me Tell You About a Song*, 1972; *Totally Instrumental . . . with One Exception*, 1973; *If We Make It Through December*, 1974; *Merle Haggard Presents His Thirtieth Album*, 1974; *It's All in the Movies*, 1975; *Keep Movin' On*, 1975; *My Love Affair with Trains*, 1976; *The Roots of My Raising*, 1976; *My Farewell to Elvis*, 1977; *Ramblin' Fever*, 1977; *A Working Man Can't Get Nowhere Today*, 1977; *Goin' Home for Christmas*, 1978; *I'm Always on a Mountain When I Fall*, 1978; *The Way It Was in '51*, 1978; *Serving 190 Proof*, 1979; *Back to the Barrooms*, 1980; *The Way I Am*, 1980; *Big City*, 1981; *Songs for the Mama That Tried*, 1981; *Going Where the Lonely Go*, 1982; *A Taste of Yesterday's Wine*, 1982 (with George Jones); *Heart to Heart*, 1983; *Pancho and Lefty*, 1983 (with Willie Nelson); *That's the Way Love Goes*, 1983; *It's All in the Game*, 1984; *Amber Waves of Grain*, 1985; *Kern River*, 1985; *A Friend in California*, 1986; *Out Among the Stars*, 1986; *Chill Factor*, 1987; *Seashores of Old Mexico*, 1987 (with Nelson); *Walking the Line*, 1987 (with Nelson and Jones); *5:01 Blues*, 1989; *Blue Jungle*, 1990; *1994*, 1994; *1996*, 1996; *If I Could Only Fly*, 2000; *Cabin in the Hills*, 2001; *Two Old Friends*, 2001 (with Albert E. Brumley, Jr.); *Like Never Before*, 2003; *I Wish I Was Santa Claus*, 2004; *Unforgettable*, 2004; *Chicago Wind*, 2005; *The Bluegrass Sessions*, 2007; *Hag's Christmas*, 2007.

WRITINGS OF INTEREST: *Sing Me Back Home*, 1981 (autobiography); *My House of Memories*, 2002 (autobiography).

The Life

The son of Oklahoma farmers Flossie Mae Harp and James Francis Haggard, who migrated to California during the Dust Bowl of the mid-1930's, Merle Ronald Haggard (HA-gurd) grew up in and around Bakersfield, California, a town overflowing with economic refugees from the Midwest. Times were difficult, and when Haggard's father died of a brain tumor, the boy, only age nine, began to rebel against his mother's authority. She sent him to a number of juvenile detention camps, but Haggard remained incorrigible. By age fourteen he was hopping freight trains around the Southwest, and by his late teens had been in and out of a string of reformatories for petty crimes and car theft. Eventually Haggard was arrested for burglary and served a three-year sentence in San Quentin.

Haggard had mastered the guitar while still a teenager, developing a strong love for the country music of such traditionalists as Hank Williams and Lefty Frizzell and the Western swing styles of such legends as Bob Wills and Tex Ritter. Paroled from prison in 1960, he spent the next two years digging ditches by day and paying dues in local country bands by night. Determined to make music his career, Haggard then moved to Las Vegas and began singing backup for local favorite Wynn Stewart. By 1963 he was recording as a solo artist for regional label Tally Records, scoring a number nineteen *Billboard* country single with "Sing a Sad Song." In 1965 he had a Top 10 hit, "(All My Friends Are Gonna Be) Strangers," and promptly signed with Capitol Records.

Shortly thereafter Haggard formed his band, the Strangers, and released a string of successful singles and albums for Capitol Records. Throughout the next two decades his remarkably expressive vocal delivery and poignant lyrics about poverty, despair, and the wayward lives of America's lowest social classes established Haggard as one of country's most celebrated artists. In 1972 California governor Ronald Reagan acknowledged Haggard's significant contributions to American culture by expunging his criminal record and granting him a full pardon for his past offenses.

Haggard's unique ability to write emotionally raw yet commercially viable hits merited him unprecedented commercial success during the 1970's and 1980's. Touring relentlessly throughout the United States and abroad, he also became one of country's most popular live acts. "The Hag," as most of his fans call him, continued to record and perform well into his seventies, a true legend of modern country music.

The Music

Haggard was an accomplished singer and guitarist even in his teens. However, it was not until he was released from San Quentin in 1960 that he began seriously considering music as a career. At first he worked as a musician in any local band that would let him fill in. His raw and distinctive voice and sparkling guitar licks eventually garnered him some regional attention, and his perseverance paid off in 1963, when he began recording singles for Tally Records. Within two years he had earned a pair of hits on the national country charts and had been signed by Capitol Records—a major country and pop label with the necessary resources to bring Haggard's music the broad exposure it demanded. In 1965 Haggard formed his backing band, the Strangers, and embarked upon a professional, and later personal, relationship with country star Buck Owens's ex-wife Bonnie, an accomplished musical talent in her own right. With Bonnie he recorded

the breakthrough 1966 duet album *Just Between the Two of Us*. The duo recorded a string of hits over the next decade. In addition, Haggard cut several hit singles with the Strangers, many of which became country classics. In 1966 the band had two Top 5 hits, "Swinging Doors" and "The Bottle Let Me Down," and their first number one with "The Fugitive." Over the next two decades Haggard released more than a hundred charting country singles and had at least one Top 5 hit single each year within that period—an unprecedented feat for a country artist.

"Hungry Eyes." This highly autobiographical early song portrays the desolation of life during the Great Depression through the eyes of a child whose parents struggle to make ends meet in a labor camp for refugees during the Dust Bowl. Haggard grew up in similar circumstances in Bakersfield in the 1930's, a detail that adds dramatic poignancy to this emotionally wrenching ballad.

"Okie from Muskogee." Several of Haggard's songs, particularly those released at the height of the Vietnam War, were viewed by many listeners as a direct response to the counterculture protest songs so popular in that era. "Okie from Muskogee" is perhaps the most widely known. A diatribe against antiwar protesters, hippies, and other outspoken critics of the American establishment, the song was such a popular hit in 1969 that it penetrated the national consciousness and was regarded as the anthem of the so-called silent majority of patriotic Americans identified in president Richard Nixon's speeches.

"The Fightin' Side of Me." Another noteworthy anticounterculture Haggard hit, "The Fightin' Side of Me" forcefully—if not violently—accuses Vietnam War protesters of being cowardly, shortsighted, and unpatriotic. Its anthemic lyrics boldly advocate an unquestioning devotion to one's country—even to the point of fighting and dying for it—and strongly criticizes those unwilling to do so.

"Today I Started Loving You Again." Because of its simple, engaging chorus and heartbreaking subject matter, "Today I Started Loving You Again" remains one of Haggard's most recognizable and appreciated classics. Like Patsy Cline's "Crazy" and Williams's "I'm So Lonesome I Could Cry," it is one of the most widely known and frequently covered country songs ever written. Hag-

Merle Haggard. (AP/Wide World Photos)

gard's version is generally revered as the finest rendition, and his vocal performance on the song ranks as one of his most heartfelt and outstanding.

"If We Make It Through December." Not all of Haggard's social commentaries concern war and patriotism. "If We Make It Through December," a crossover pop hit in 1973, was especially timely because of its release at the height of a major economic recession in the United States. That year's Middle Eastern oil embargo resulted in record inflation and unemployment. The lyrics tell the story of a father breaking the news to his young daughter that he cannot afford Christmas presents because he has been laid off from his factory job—a scenario that resonated strongly with radio audiences that year.

"Are the Good Times Really Over for Good." It had been nearly a decade since Haggard had charted a socially relevant single, but the Reagan-era "Are the Good Times Really Over for Good" helped him once again win distinction as a spokesman for a new generation. The song directly questions the idea that in the mid-1980's the United States remained the most prosperous—and perhaps most well-intended—nation in the world.

Down Every Road. A lavishly packaged and impressively thorough compilation, *Down Every Road*, released by Capitol Records in 1996, provides the most complete homage to Haggard's career and legacy as a performer. It contains most of his hits, including many of his earliest singles, and several cuts that were not released as singles but typify Haggard's style and themes just as accurately as any of his major chart hits. Rare but quintessential gems such as "I Can't Hold Myself in Line" and "I'm Looking for My Mind" are standout tracks.

"No Time to Cry." The feature track on Haggard's strong but overlooked album *1996*, this mournful ballad laments the loss of a father. Written from the often-neglected point of view of the middle aged, the song addresses the difficulties of finding time to grieve the loss of a parent when besieged with seemingly overwhelming responsibilities. Its profound message, combined with Haggard's unforgettable vocal delivery, make "No Time to Cry" one of the most memorable performances of his later career.

Musical Legacy

At his concerts, Haggard is often introduced as "the poet of the common man," an epithet bestowed on him in the 1970's as his songs began to weave themselves into the fabric of the American social conscience. The name, much deserved, remains with him. His sparse but incisive lyrics chronicle the struggles of the economically as well as the emotionally downtrodden, with a poignancy and musicality that has attracted fans across several genres. Because of their broad appeal and unflinching directness, several of Haggard's songs have become country standards that are performed just as often today as they were in any of the previous decades. Many modern musical artists, country and otherwise, cite him as a key influence on their careers. Haggard has received a string of gold and platinum albums and a number of Grammy Awards for recording excellence. His visibility as one of country's most popular performers has merited him acting roles on television shows and in movies, and he has even performed at the White House. There is scarcely a country band, amateur or professional, that does not perform at least a few of his songs. His timeless and undeniably genuine lyrics assure that listeners will still be enjoying his songs for decades to come.

Gregory D. Horn

Further Reading

Bogdanov, Vladimir, Chris Woodstra, and Stephen Thomas Erlewine. *All Music Guide to Country: The Definitive Guide to Country Music.* San Francisco: Backbeat Books, 2003. Definitive reference work on contemporary country music. Contains extensive biographical information on Haggard's life and career.

Haggard, Merle. *Merle Haggard: The Lyrics.* Milwaukee, Wis.: Hal Leonard, 2002. A true testament to Haggard's reputation as a songwriter, this book is devoted solely to his lyrics.

Haggard, Merle, and Tom Carter. *Merle Haggard's My House of Memories: For the Record.* New York: HarperCollins, 2002. Determined to correct what he saw as several misperceptions about his life and career, Haggard collaborated with Carter on this book. It focuses primarily on his personal life, although it does contain some insight into his creative process as well.

LaChapelle, Peter. "Fightin' Sides: 'Okie from Muskogee,' Conservative Populism, and the Uses of Migrant Identity." In *Proud to Be an Okie: Cultural Politics, Country Music, and Migration to Southern California.* Los Angeles: University of California Press, 2007. Insightful academic study of the Depression-era migration of thousands of Oklahoma farmers to the San Joaquin Valley of California. Because Haggard's music focuses heavily on this migration, of which his parents were a part, the book devotes a great deal of attention to how his lyrics capture the spirit of the era.

Willman, Chris. *Rednecks and Bluenecks: The Politics of Country Music.* New York: The New Press, 2005. Explores how Haggard's lyrics have influenced the populist and conservative ideology of many contemporary country artists, particularly Toby Keith.

See also: Buffett, Jimmy; Cash, Johnny; Cline, Patsy; Frizzell, Lefty; Jones, George; Nelson, Willie; Nono, Luigi; Ritter, Tex; Strait, George; Tubb, Ernest; Van Zandt, Townes; Williams, Hank.

Bill Haley

American rock singer, songwriter, and guitarist

Haley melded country music with rhythm and blues, leading to rock and roll. His signature song, "Rock Around the Clock," was an enthusiastic anthem to the new music genre.

Born: July 6, 1925; Highland Park, Michigan
Died: February 9, 1981; Harlingen, Texas
Also known as: William John Clifton Haley (full name)
Member of: The Downhomers; the Four Aces of Western Swing; the Saddlemen; Bill Haley and His Comets

Principal recordings

ALBUMS (with Bill Haley and His Comets): *He Digs Rock 'n' Roll*, 1955; *Shake, Rattle and Roll*, 1955; *Music for the Boyfriend*, 1956; *Rock Around the Clock*, 1956; *Rock 'n' Roll Stage Show*, 1956; *Rock the Joint!*, 1957; *Rockin' the Oldies*, 1957; *Rockin' Around the World*, 1958; *Chicks*, 1959; *Strictly Instrumental*, 1960; *Bill Haley's Jukebox*, 1961; *Twisting Knights*, 1962; *Rock Around the Clock King*, 1964; *Rip It Up*, 1968; *Mister Rock 'n' Roll*, 1973; *Rock 'n' Roll*, 1975; *Rock Around the Clock*, 1976; *Armchair Rock 'n' Roll*, 1978; *Rock 'n' Roll Forever*, 1981; *Rock 'n' Roll Revival*, 1981.

SINGLES: "She Taught Me to Yodel," 1946 (with the Downhomers); "Too Many Parties and Too Many Pals," 1948 (with the Four Aces of Western Swing); "Candy Kisses," 1949 (with the Four Aces of Western Swing); "Tennessee Border," 1949 (with the Four Aces of Western Swing); "Rocket 88," 1951 (with the Saddlemen); "Rock the Joint," 1952 (with the Saddlemen); "Crazy Man, Crazy," 1953 (with Bill Haley and His Comets); "Rock Around the Clock," 1954 (with Bill Haley and His Comets); "Shake, Rattle and Roll," 1954; "Florida Twist," 1961.

The Life

William John Clifton Haley was born in Highland Park, Michigan, and he grew up in Booth's

Corner, Pennsylvania. During his childhood, he had an operation that left him blind in his left eye. He is said to have cultivated his spit-curl hairstyle to distract from the blind eye, and admirers in the 1950's imitated the style without knowing the reason behind it. Haley joined a Pennsylvania-based Western swing band in 1946, and he made his first professional recordings with it. After that, he formed several Western-themed groups of his own.

Haley began to change his musical style in the early 1950's to a combination of country and rhythm and blues. He renamed his group as the Comets, and his 1953 recording of "Crazy Man, Crazy," which he cowrote, became the first rock-and-roll record to land on American charts.

In 1954 Bill Haley and His Comets recorded "Rock Around the Clock." This song found a huge audience, and it paved the way for the success of

later performers such as Elvis Presley, whose popularity would eclipse Haley's in the United States. Nevertheless, Haley found renewed popularity in Latin America, Mexico, and Europe during the 1960's. Despite a battle with alcoholism, Haley continued as an international star (he gave a command performance in Great Britain for Queen Elizabeth II in 1979). His last performances came in 1980 in South Africa, a year before his death.

The Music

Although he is most famous for launching the music known as rock and roll, Haley began as a country-music artist. Haley also performed in other musical genres for which he is remembered much less.

"Rocket 88." This song marked Haley's change in musical styles. It was originally produced by

Bill Haley (seated) and the Comets. (AP/Wide World Photos)

Jackie Brenston and His Delta Cats, and Haley's rendition was the first time a white country singer performed a traditionally black rhythm-and-blues tune in this manner. Its reception encouraged Haley, a year later, to record "Rock the Joint," previously recorded by other bands. Both records sold almost one hundred thousand copies in the Northeast, persuading Haley that this musical style had great potential.

"Crazy Man, Crazy." Written by Haley and his bass player, Marshall Lytle, this song was the first rock-and-roll song to place significantly on American popularity charts. Soon after its release, the band's name was changed to Bill Haley and His Comets.

"Rock Around the Clock." This was released by Bill Haley and His Comets in 1954 to modest success. It had been written specifically for Haley the previous year. However, when the song was sung behind the opening credits of *Blackboard Jungle* (1955), a film based on Evan Hunter's novel about violence at an inner-city school that was nominated for four Academy Awards, the song's popularity soared. A year later, a film with the song title was released, a light story about young people's enthusiasm about rock and roll, a celebration of the newly popular music style. It featured Haley and other artists playing themselves. The motion picture and song were instrumental in launching a musical revolution.

"Shake, Rattle and Roll." This was Haley's follow-up to "Rock Around the Clock." It had already been a hit for Joe Turner, but that version had more of a blues approach, while Haley's was straightforward rock and roll. It was the first rock-and-roll recording to sell more than a million copies.

"Florida Twist." When Haley's popularity in rock and roll began to be surpassed by other artists, he and his bands toured outside the United States. For a time, he made Mexico his home, and he tried to learn Spanish. In 1961 he made his first recording in Spanish, "Florida Twist." It went to the top of the popularity charts, becoming the biggest-selling single record in Mexico.

Musical Legacy

Rock and roll, as performed by Bill Haley and His Comets, caught on with the younger generation with an enthusiasm that still affects commercial music. Their songs were featured in major entertainment venues, such as popular motion pictures, and Haley appeared in some films. Younger artists such as Presley, Jerry Lee Lewis, and Little Richard followed in Haley's wake, and they eventually eclipsed his fame. However, Haley is remembered for being first. He even received recognition in outer space: In 2006, to mark the twenty-fifth anniversary of Haley's death, the International Astronomical Union named an asteroid in his honor.

Paul Dellinger

Further Reading

Dawson, Jim. *Rock Around the Clock: The Record That Started the Rock Revolution!* San Francisco: Backbeat Books, 2005. This books covers the origin of the song "Rock Around the Clock," and it traces Haley's early years as a professional musician.

DeCurtis, Anthony, ed. *Present Tense: Rock and Roll and Culture*. Durham, N.C.: Duke University Press, 1992. Contributors from a variety of fields look at the rock-and-roll phenomenon from different points of view, covering its creation and its audience.

Haley, John W., and John von Hoëlle. *Sound and Glory: The Incredible Story of Bill Haley, the Father of Rock 'n' Roll and the Music That Shook the World*. Wilmington, Del.: Dyne-American, 1990. Coauthored by one of his sons, the book offers extensive background on Haley, his career, and his influence on rock and roll.

Stuessy, Clarence, and Scott Lipscomb. *Rock and Roll: Its History and Stylistic Development*. Upper Saddle River, N.J.: Prentice-Hall, 2008. Covers the history of rock and roll from its roots to the present, with insights into the music industry and into the key figures in the evolution of this musical style.

Swenson, John. *Bill Haley: The Daddy of Rock and Roll*. Briarcliff Manor, N.Y.: Stein and Day, 1983. The book concentrates on Haley's entire career, from its initial success to the reasons for its decline.

See also: Domino, Fats; John, Sir Elton; Lewis, Jerry Lee; Little Richard; Presley, Elvis; Turner, Big Joe.

Marvin Hamlisch

American musical-theater songwriter and lyricist and film-score composer

Hamlisch's compositions for film and musical theater have influenced a new generation of composers in creating dramatically important songs. His work on A Chorus Line *ushered in the concept, or frame story, musical.*

Born: June 2, 1944; New York, New York
Also known as: Marvin Frederick Hamlisch (full name)

Principal works

FILM SCORES: *The Swimmer*, 1968; *Take the Money and Run*, 1969; *Bananas*, 1971; *The Way We Were*, 1973; *The Spy Who Loved Me*, 1977; *Ice Castles*, 1978; *Starting Over*, 1979; *Ordinary People*, 1980; *Pennies from Heaven*, 1981; *Sophie's Choice*, 1982; *D.A.R.Y.L.*, 1985; *Three Men and a Baby*, 1987; *Little Nikita*, 1988; *Frankie and Johnny*, 1991; *The Mirror Has Two Faces*, 1996.

MUSICAL THEATER (music): *A Chorus Line*, 1975 (lyrics by Edward Kleban; libretto by James Kirkwood and Nicholas Dante); *They're Playing Our Song*, 1979 (lyrics by Carole Bayer Sager; libretto by Neil Simon); *Smile*, 1986 (lyrics and libretto by Howard Ashman); *The Goodbye Girl*, 1993 (lyrics by David Zippel; libretto by Neil Simon); *Imaginary Friends*, 2002 (lyrics by Carnelia; libretto by Nora Ephron); *Sweet Smell of Success*, 2002 (lyrics by Craig Carnelis; libretto by John Guare).

The Life

Marvin Frederick Hamlisch (HAM-lihsh) was born in 1944 to immigrant Viennese Jewish parents, Max and Lily Schachter Hamlisch, in New York City. His father, an accordionist and bandleader, wanted him to study classical music. A child prodigy, Hamlisch began playing the piano at age five, and by age seven he was accepted into the precollege division of Juilliard, where he studied for fourteen years. Lured by the excitement of the theater and popular music, however, Hamlisch pursued a career in the entertainment industry. He began working as a rehearsal pianist and songwriter,

and he graduated from Queens College with a bachelor of arts in music in 1968. He collaborated with his longtime girlfriend, lyricist Carole Bayer Sager, on many works, but when their relationship ended, he entered a period of introspection in which he recognized the emptiness of his life. In 1989 he married independent television producer Terre Blair, whom he credits with changing his life and his priorities in a positive direction. The couple resides in their hometown, New York City.

The Music

Hamlisch began his career in show business as a rehearsal pianist for *Funny Girl* (1964), starring Barbra Streisand, but in 1965 he enjoyed his first big hit at the age of twenty-one with a song, "Sunshine, Lollipops, and Rainbows," sung by Lesley Gore. He went on to work as vocal arranger for television's *Bell Telephone Hour*, and after graduating from college, he moved to Hollywood to work in films. He composed music for several motion pictures, but he made a name for himself by collaborating with Johnny Mercer on the sound track of *Kotch* (1971), for which he received his first Academy Award nomination. He continued to enjoy a successful career in film music, and later he created memorable shows for Broadway. He also composed a symphony, *Anatomy of Peace*. He served as arranger and musical director for Barbra Streisand's concert tour and television special, and he guest-conducted pop concerts for American orchestras, being appointed to the post of pops conductor for the National Symphony in 2000. In 2007 he was inducted into the Long Island Music Hall of Fame.

The Sting *and* The Way We Were. Hamlisch made history in 1974 by winning three Academy Awards in one evening for the motion pictures *The Sting* and *The Way We Were*. These two films exhibit the extent of Hamlisch's range as a composer. The score for *The Sting* contains instrumental adaptation (and, some argue, exploitation) of the early twentieth century piano rag music by Scott Joplin. The theme, "The Entertainer," made number three on the *Billboard* Hot 100 music chart, and it brought modern attention to Joplin's music. In contrast, Hamlisch's romantic music and title song for the Streisand-Robert Redford film *The Way We Were* demonstrates his ability to write memorable songs with a pop sensibility. Although his critics diminish the artistry of his songwriting talent, his music has enjoyed great popular appeal. He has composed original scores for more than forty films, including *Sophie's Choice*, *Ordinary People*, *Ice Castles*, and *Bananas*.

A Chorus Line. In 1975 director-choreographer Michael Bennett gathered a group of Broadway gypsies (the nickname given to dancers who move from one show to another), and he asked them to talk about their lives, their experiences, and why they became dancers. He gave the taped recordings of their answers to James Kirkwood and Nicholas Dante to write the book for a new musical, *A Chorus Line*. With Hamlisch as composer and Edward Kleban as lyricist, the resulting show was the longest-running musical in Broadway history (until *Cats* surpassed it in 1997), and it was nominated for twelve Tony Awards, winning nine. It also received the 1976 Pulitzer Prize for Drama, the *London Evening Standard*'s Best Musical award, and five L.A. Drama Critics' Awards.

Two aspects of *A Chorus Line* made it outstanding: its format and its theme. *A Chorus Line* was a landmark, a groundbreaking concept, or frame story, musical. Stephen Sondheim's *Company* (1970) opened the door, but *A Chorus Line* brought the form to fruition. The concept musical presents a series of scenes, or episodes, centered around a theme. Although this is a common type of plot for plays (called episodic), it had not been used successfully in musicals. For *A Chorus Line*, the theme is individuality versus group conformity, explored through, ironically, the dancers who present, in their anonymity, the great chorus numbers of musical theater. The fact that the audience gets to know and care about each dancer as an individual greatly contrasts with the final glitzy number, "One," in which the dancers become anonymous automatons, dressed alike and moving in unison. Hamlisch and Kleban's songs received both praise and criticism for their role in moving the drama along and in creating a miniature biography for each character. *A Chorus Line*'s most popular song, "What I Did for Love," has been sharply criticized for not belonging in the show, and even Hamlisch concedes it does not fit as well as the other songs. Critic Joseph Swain commented that the song does not fit the musical's form or premise, explaining that the show is not about dancing but about people who happen to be dancers.

Musical Legacy

Although he has suffered some show-business failures, Hamlisch was one of only two people (the other being Richard Rodgers) who has won all four major entertainment awards (Academy, Grammy, Emmy, and Tony) as well as the Pulitzer Prize. Hamlisch's work has earned him three Academy Awards, four Grammy Awards, four Emmy Awards, a Tony Award, three Golden Globes, and numerous other awards, including the Pulitzer Prize. In 2006 the American Society of Composers, Authors, and Publishers (ASCAP) awarded him the Richard Rodgers Award for lifetime achievement in musical theater.

Jill Stapleton-Bergeron

Further Reading

Hamlisch, Marvin, and Gerald C. Gardner. *The Way I Was*. New York: Simon & Schuster, 1992. Hamlisch's autobiography details his career and includes humorous anecdotes about his work and experiences.

Laufe, Abe. *Broadway's Greatest Musicals*. Rev. ed. New York: Funk & Wagnalls, 1977. An indispensable survey of musical theater from its beginnings through most of the 1970's. The appendix outlines the authors, producers, casts, and songs for long-running musicals.

Mordden, Ethan. *The Happiest Corpse I've Ever Seen*. New York: Palgrave MacMillan, 2004. Mordden traces the development of the American musical from 1978 to 2003, and he covers Hamlisch's work in musical theater beyond *A Chorus Line*.

Swain, Joseph. "Frame Story as Musical." In *The Broadway Musical: A Critical and Musical Survey*. 2d ed. Lanham, Md.: Scarecrow Press, 2002. Swain's award-winning book examines musical drama in terms of how plot, character, and conflict are developed through the music.

Viagas, Robert, Baayork Lee, and Thommie Walsh. *On the Line: The Creation of "A Chorus Line."* New York: William Morrow, 1990. Written by three of the original cast members, this book is a memoir of their personal experiences in creating the landmark musical *A Chorus Line*.

See also: Bergman, Alan; Joplin, Scott; Mercer, Johnny; Rodgers, Richard; Simon, Carly; Streisand, Barbra.

M. C. Hammer

American rapper

Hammer was the face of pop rap in the late 1980's and early 1990's, known for his catchy hooks, his catch phrases, and his trademark "Hammer pants."

Born: March 30, 1962; Oakland, California
Also known as: Stanley Kirk Burrell (birth name); Hammer

Principal recordings

ALBUMS: *Feel My Power*, 1987; *Let's Get It Started*, 1988; *Please Hammer, Don't Hurt 'Em*, 1990; *Too Legit to Quit*, 1991; *The Funky Headhunter*, 1994; *Inside Out*, 1995; *Family Affair*, 1998; *Active Duty*, 2001.

The Life

Stanley Kirk Burrell was born March 30, 1962, in Oakland, California. He was given the nickname Hammer by baseball player Reggie Jackson, who thought Burrell resembled "Hammerin'" Hank Aaron. Hammer joined the Navy after graduating from high school, and when he was discharged, he turned to music. His debut album, *Feel My Power*, was released on his label, Oaktown Records, and rereleased by Capitol Records in 1988 as *Let's Get It Started*.

Hammer's 1990 release, *Please Hammer, Don't Hurt 'Em*, brought him to the attention of mainstream music audiences. On the strength of singles "U Can't Touch This," "Have You Seen Her," and "Pray," it became the first hip-hop album to reach diamond certification. In 1991 Hammer dropped the M. C. and released *Too Legit to Quit*, which, although it sold more than three million copies, was considered a failure by Capitol Records.

For his fourth album, *The Funky Headhunter*, Hammer turned to gangsta rap. He also faced the first of two copyright-infringement lawsuits in the early 1990's. He signed a contract with Death Row Records in 1995, and he left the label after rapper Tupac Shakur's death in 1996. In April, 1996, Hammer filled for bankruptcy.

Although he continued to record throughout the 1990's and early 2000's, Hammer never reached the level of success of his early career. In 1997 he began ministerial training and hosting a show on the Trinity Broadcasting Network. He also appeared in the first season of VH1's televised *The Surreal Life*.

The Music

Hammer's music was considered pop rap, because it was sounded more like pop than hip-hop. His big hits relied heavily on sampling of other songs, an aspect of his music that drew criticism from other hip-hop artists, including LL Cool J and Ice Cube.

"U Can't Touch This." The first hit from Hammer's *Please Hammer, Don't Hurt 'Em* album was "U Can't Touch This," based on a sample from the Rick James song "Superfreak." The lyrics are typical rap boasting, indicating that no one can rap (or dance) as well as Hammer. "U Can't Touch This" became Hammer's musical signature, and it has been the source of numerous parodies over the years. It also introduced the catch phrase "Stop, Hammer time," which, along with the parachute pants (often referred to as "Hammer pants"), became a part of popular fashion. The song peaked at number eight on record charts, and it was Hammer's first significant hit.

"Too Legit to Quit." The title track from Hammer's album *Too Legit to Quit* was his response to the criticism leveled at the rapper following the success of *Please Hammer, Don't Hurt 'Em*. The lyrics continue the standard boasting while mixing in defiance directed at his critics. The verses use a sparse accompaniment, primarily a drum machine, synthesizer bass, and muted electric guitar fills. The chorus adds a sampled horn section, multiple male voices repeating "Too legit, too legit to quit," synthesizer punches, and a female voice intoning "hey" and "too legit" over the rest. "Too Legit to Quit" reached number six on the charts. The video also featured appearances by numerous professional athletes (including José Canseco, Jerry Rice, Ronnie Lott, Roger Craig) and the Dallas Cowboy Cheerleaders.

"Addams Groove." "Addams Groove" appeared on Hammer's album *Too Legit to Quit* and on the sound track for the motion picture *The Addams Family* (1991). The song features Hammer rapping a story about interacting with the characters from the

M. C. Hammer. (Hulton Archive/Getty Images)

the song. The first version was banned from MTV because of footage of the rapper in tight swimwear that was deemed obscene by the censors. The second version covers up the rapper almost entirely (long pants, long-sleeved shirts, boots, and a hat) and includes cameo appearances by Deion Sanders making arrangements with various women to appear in the video. The song, like the album, did not fare as well as his previous hits, and it reached only number twenty-six on the charts.

Musical Legacy

While Hammer's rise to fame in the late 1980's and early 1990's and its accompanying wealth led many hip-hop artists to pursue the wider popular music market, his rapid fall was a reminder that the popular music industry can be fickle. Perhaps his most lasting influence on hip-hop is expanding the use and role of sampling. He was one of the first to use larger, more recognizable samples rather than simply mixing rhythm tracks from early funk and soul records. This trend was followed by rappers such as Eminem and Sean Combs. Hammer was also a pop culture icon in the early 1990's. In addition to his influence on music and fashions, Hammer had a cartoon series called *Hammerman*.

Eric S. Strother

film as his neighbors. The subtle message continues one of the themes of the *Too Legit to Quit* album, which is expressing individuality in the face of criticism. He says that even though the members of the Addams Family are unconventional, he respects them for not bowing to the pressure to conform. The musical accompaniment features a drum machine, synthesizer punches, and a sampled horn section. "Addams Groove" peaked at number seven on the charts, and it was Hammer's fifth Top 10 hit.

"Pumps and a Bump." The first single from Hammer's gangsta rap album *The Funky Headhunter* marked a change in lyrical direction. While most of his previous hits were either bragging dance songs or pop ballads, "Pumps and a Bump" was a highly sexual song about women with large backsides. There are at least two recorded versions of the song released by Hammer, the edited radio release and the nonedited version with more explicit language. There were also two videos shot for

Further Reading

George, Nelson. *Hip-Hop America*. New York: Penguin, 2005. This book discusses the role of hip-hop in American society as an expression of African American youth.

Light, Alan. *The Vibe History of Hip-Hop*. Medford, N.J.: Plexus, 1999. This collection of essays traces the development of the hip-hop genre.

Ogbar, Jeffrey O. G. *Hip-Hop Revolution: The Culture and Politics of Rap*. Lawrence: University Press of Kansas. 2007. In this cultural history, the author explores negative perceptions and stereotypes of hip-hop.

Reeves, Marcus. *Somebody Scream! Rap Music's Rise to Prominence in the Aftershock of Black Power*. New York: Faber & Faber, 2008. Examines rap's rise to prominence during the 1980's and 1990's by placing significant artists within a larger social and political context.

See also: Eminem; Ice Cube; LL Cool J.

Oscar Hammerstein II

American musical-theater lyricist and librettist

As a librettist and lyricist, Hammerstein made the words of the song a natural part of the plot.

Born: July 12, 1895; New York, New York
Died: August 23, 1960; Doylestown, Pennsylvania
Also known as: Oscar Greeley Clendenning Hammerstein II (full name)

Principal works

MUSICAL THEATER (lyrics and libretto unless otherwise stated): *Jimmie*, 1920 (music by Herbert P. Stothart; lyrics with Otto Harbach; libretto with Harbach and Frank Mandel); *Tickle Me*, 1920 (music by Stothart; lyrics and libretto with Harbach and Mandel); *Always You*, 1921 (music by Stothart); *Daffy Dill*, 1922 (music by Stothart; libretto with Guy Bolton); *Queen o' Hearts*, 1922 (music by Lewis E. Gensler and Dudley Wilkinson; lyrics with Sydney Mitchell; libretto with Mandel); *Mary Jane McKane*, 1923 (music by Vincent Youmans and Stothart; libretto by William Carey Duncan); *Wildflower*, 1923 (music by Youmans and Stothart; lyrics and libretto with Harbach); *Rose Marie*, 1924 (music by Rudolf Friml and Stothart; lyrics and libretto with Harbach); *Song of the Flame*, 1925 (music by George Gershwin and Stothart; lyrics and libretto with Harbach); *Sunny*, 1925 (music by Jerome Kern; lyrics and libretto with Harbach); *The Desert Song*, 1926 (music by Sigmund Romberg; lyrics and libretto with Harbach and Mandel); *The Wild Rose*, 1926 (music by Friml; lyrics and libretto with Harbach); *Golden Dawn*, 1927 (music by Emmerich Kálmán and Stothart; lyrics and libretto with Harbach); *Show Boat*, 1927 (music by Kern; based on Edna Ferber's novel); *Good Boy*, 1928 (music by Stothart; lyrics by Bert Kalmar and Harry Ruby; libretto with Harbach and Henry Myers); *The New Moon*, 1928 (music by Romberg; lyrics and libretto with Mandel and Laurence Schwab); *Rainbow*, 1928 (music by Youmans; libretto by Laurence Stallings); *Sweet Adeline*, 1929 (music by Kern); *East Wind*, 1931 (music by Romberg; libretto with Mandel); *Free for All*, 1931 (music by Richard A. Whiting; libretto with Schwab); *The Gang's All Here*, 1931 (music by Gensler; lyrics by Owen Murphy and Robert A. Simon; libretto with Morrie Ryskind and Russel Crouse); *Music in the Air*, 1932 (music by Kern); *Ball at the Savoy*, 1933 (music by Paul Abraham; based on Alfred Grünwald and Fritz Löhner-Beda's novel); *Three Sisters*, 1934 (music by Kern); *May Wine*, 1935 (music by Romberg; libretto by Mandel); *Gentlemen Unafraid*, 1938 (music by Kern; lyrics and libretto with Harbach); *Very Warm for May*, 1939 (music by Kern); *Sunny River*, 1941 (music by Romberg); *Carmen Jones*, 1943 (based on Georges Bizet's opera); *Oklahoma!*, 1943 (music by Richard Rodgers; libretto by Hammerstein; based on Lynn Riggs's play *Green Grow the Lilacs*); *Carousel*, 1945 (music by Rodgers; based on Ferenc Molnár's play *Liliom*); *Allegro*, 1947 (music by Rodgers); *South Pacific*, 1949 (music by Rodgers; libretto with Joshua Logan; based on James A. Michener's novel *Tales of the South Pacific*); *The King and I*, 1951 (music by Rodgers; libretto by Hammerstein); *Me and Juliet*, 1953 (music by Rodgers; libretto by Hammerstein); *Pipe Dream*, 1955 (music by Rodgers; libretto by Hammerstein); *Cinderella*, 1957 (music by Rodgers); *Flower Drum Song*, 1958 (music by Rodgers; libretto with Joseph Fields; based on C. Y. Lee's novel); *The Sound of Music*, 1959 (music by Rodgers; libretto by Howard Lindsay and Crouse); *A Grand Night for Singing*, 1993 (music by Rodgers).

SONGS (lyrics): "The Last Time I Saw Paris," 1941 (music by Kern; from the film *Lady Be Good*); "It Might as Well Be Spring," 1945 (music by Rodgers; from the film *State Fair*).

The Life

Oscar Greeley Clendenning Hammerstein (HAHM-mur-stin) II was born into a theatrical family. His father, William Hammerstein, managed the Victoria, the leading vaudeville house in New York City; his mother was Alice Nemo. His grandfather, Oscar Hammerstein, was an opera impresario who built theaters; Arthur Hammerstein, an uncle, was a Broadway producer. Hammerstein was first taken to the theater when he was four, and the lights, the colors, the music, and the actors made a lasting impression. He wrote his first story, "The Adventures of a Penny," when he was twelve. At age seventeen Hammerstein entered Columbia University, where he excelled in his English classes and was encouraged to become a writer. In 1915 Hammerstein became involved in Columbia's annual Varsity Show, as an actor playing a poet. The following year, he helped write a few routines for the libretto, in addition to playing a black-faced comedian. Bowing to pressure from his father, who did not want his son involved in the theater, Hammerstein enrolled in Columbia Law School; however, he retained his enthusiasm for the Varsity Show. While a law student, he wrote for the Varsity Show *Home, James* (1917) with Herman Axelrod.

During his second year at law school, Hammerstein took a job at a law firm, hoping practical experience would initiate enthusiasm for a law career. He left his job and law school in 1917, and he persuaded Uncle Arthur to give him a job as a stagehand. Soon convinced of his nephew's ability, Arthur elevated Hammerstein to production stage manager, a permanent position on the staff. Hammerstein married Myra Finn on August 22, 1917. They had two children and divorced in 1928. Hammerstein married Dorothy Blanchard Johnson on May 13, 1929; they had one child.

Hammerstein's first professional work was a song for the musical *Furs and Frills* (1917). Although his first play, *The Light* (1919), ran only five performances, his first musical, *Always You*, for which he wrote the libretto and lyrics, with music by Herbert Stothart, was well received by the critics. This success led to *Tickle Me*, with Hammerstein writing the book and lyrics with Otto Harbach, the first of Hammerstein's collaborators. Through the 1920's and 1930's, Hammerstein collaborated with composers Vincent Youmans, Sigmund Romberg, and Jerome Kern, writing operettas and musical shows.

Hammerstein's career had its ups and downs. It was at a low point when he first teamed with Richard Rodgers to turn Lynn Rigg's play *Green Grow the Lilacs* (1931) into the hit musical *Oklahoma!* Their collaboration lasted sixteen years and resulted in nine Broadway musicals, some becoming classics of the American theater. While working on *The Sound of Music*, Hammerstein was diagnosed with cancer. He died at his Highland Farm, Hammerstein's favorite place to work, in Doylestown, Pennsylvania. In tribute to Hammerstein, the lights of Broadway were shut off for three minutes.

The Music

Although Hammerstein was not a musician, he did play the piano and, according to Rodgers, had a "superb sense of form." Hammerstein knew about the architecture of a song and what worked musically with his words. Through the libretto, Hammerstein created a cohesive plot and believable characters. The lyrics for the songs reflected the emotions of his characters.

Early Works. When Hammerstein's first full-length play, *The Light* (1919), flopped, he turned to musicals. In *Always You*, the lyrics were good, but the libretto was weak. Hammerstein realized that all the beautiful songs, talented casts, jokes, and expensive production details depended for success solely on a well-constructed plot. He then teamed up with Harbach, a librettist, and with him Hammerstein enjoyed a series of successful shows. In the process, Hammerstein learned how to write. Hammerstein often said that he was born into the theatrical world with two gold spoons in his mouth: one was his family connections, the other was Harbach. Harbach taught Hammerstein to think a long time, rather than rush to get words down on paper. Harbach had two rules: the story must have interest, and all the elements must be integrated in the show. Songs, jokes, and dialogue had to be germane to the plot. With Harbach Hammerstein wrote *Wildflower*, with music by Vincent Youmans, and *Rose Marie*, with music by Rudolf Friml. However, Hammerstein was beginning to break away from the formula of what a musical should be. *Rose Marie* was a decided departure from the standard musical comedy formula of boy meets girl, complications ensue, boy gets girl, *Rose Marie* had a murder, and it ended with just two people on stage, rather than the full cast and chorus. Another distinction was that the musical numbers, as noted in the program, were "such an integral part of the action" that they were not listed separately.

The Desert Song. This 1926 show marked the beginning of an association with composer Romberg. With its exotic setting, its dashing hero, and its romance, *The Desert Song* was in the tradition of the European operetta, yet it was based on the historical uprising of the Riffs in Morocco. Hammerstein and Romberg later wrote *The New Moon*, generally considered the last of the great American operettas and noted for its memorable love songs.

Show Boat. Based on Edna Ferber's novel, *Show Boat* is considered the first modern American musical play. Although Ferber believed that it was a bad idea to attempt to turn her novel into a stage musical, Hammerstein did just that. He eliminated characters and scenes, developed other characters, and handled the racial aspects subtly and effectively. The dramatic conflict was strong enough to stand as a play without the music, but the music enhanced the story and gave it deeper meaning. As a musical play, the songs grew out of the plot. Six of the songs are regarded as standards. The song "Can't Help Lovin' Dat Man" integrates elements of the plot. It is first sung in an upbeat fashion; later, the character of Julie sings it as a lament of lifelong love. The song carries the plot forward as Julie recognizes the significance of Nola, another character, singing it. Working with the novel, Hammerstein recognized that Ferber had used the Mississippi River to unify the plot. He did the same with his song "Ol' Man River." When Ferber heard the song, she said that "my hair stood on end, tears came to my eyes."

Following *Show Boat*, Hammerstein had other hits, but it seemed his style of musical was becoming passé. Many believed Hammerstein's career was finished, but that was only until he began collaborating with Rodgers.

Oklahoma! This show, with its fusion of story, song, and dance, is a landmark in the history of American musical theater. Initially, Hammerstein and Rodgers had problems selling the show to backers because it was so different. Previous ideas of what a musical should be were changed the moment the curtain went up on a stage with one old woman. Working from the original play, a folk comedy, Hammerstein gave the libretto more of a plot, and he added the character of Will Parker to create a comic subplot. As with other musicals with Rodgers, Hammerstein wrote the lyrics first, often agonizing over the words and images. When Hammerstein wrote, his lyrics had "dummy" melodies that he sang in a minor key. All listeners agreed the

tunes were terrible, but the words were lovely. "Oh What a Beautiful Mornin'" took three weeks to write, yet the lyric, with its simplicity and imagery, drawn from the natural setting of the play, was described by Rodgers as "so right." The songs expressed the moods and situations of the play, using vocabulary appropriate to everyday speech. Hammerstein also solved the problem of how to write a fresh, new love song by having the singers describe what not to do, lest "People Will Say We're in Love." With its honesty, resolve, and enthusiasm for the future, *Oklahoma!* was particularly welcome during the dark days of World War II.

South Pacific. The genesis of *South Pacific* was two short stories by James Michener, "Our Heroine" and "Fo' Dollah," in his *Tales of the South Pacific* (1947). Hammerstein used characters from both stories to create the libretto. In the main plot, the developing love between the French plantation owner, Emile de Becque, and the naïve nurse, Nellie Forbush, is complicated by her prejudice over his biracial children. This complements the secondary plot of Lieutenant Cable and his love for Liat, a beautiful island girl. In Hammerstein's lyric

Oscar Hammerstein II. (Library of Congress)

"You've Got to Be Carefully Taught," Cable expresses how racial bigotry is ingrained in children. The song caused some problems in Southern cities of the United States, but Hammerstein and Rodgers refused to take it out of the show. *South Pacific* was awarded the Pulitzer Prize for Drama in 1950.

Carousel *and* The King and I. Hammerstein had other successful shows with Rodgers, including *Carousel*, for which he took the dark play *Liliom* (1909) by Ferenc Molnár, relocated the action from Budapest to Maine, and provided a hopeful ending. In *Allegro*, Hammerstein attempted to write an Everyman musical, following the life of the main character. It was Hammerstein's first original book for his partnership with Rodgers. As a modern morality play, it shows the negative effects of a fast-moving, increasingly superficial society on personal integrity. Critically applauded, it was not an audience favorite. Later, however, *The King and I* was. Hammerstein was never as good at writing an original script as he was at adaptations, such as with Margaret Landon's book *Anna and the King of Siam* (1944). Although he followed Landon's plot, he developed the characters, particularly the king, allowing the audience to see a conflicted man behind the regal exterior.

Other Works. "The Last Time I Saw Paris" expresses Hammerstein's sadness at the German occupation of Paris in 1940 during World War II, and it won an Academy Award. In addition, "It Might as Well Be Spring," from *State Fair* (1945), won the Academy Award. *Carmen Jones* was set to Georges Bizet's music for *Carmen* (1875) and used the same characters, but Hammerstein's libretto and lyrics had an American flavor, and they demonstrated Hammerstein's sensitivity to racial issues. He eliminated the operatic recitatives and focused on the major arias, creating songs of poetry and power. The location was changed from Spain to the South and the characters shifted from Gypsies to blacks.

Musical Legacy

Hammerstein did not set out consciously to break conventions; rather, he wrote a play simply because he liked the subject matter or the characters. Nevertheless, Hammerstein, with his collaborators, created a new type of musical play. Although he had written successful operettas, he worked toward changing the traditional audience expectations of lively dancing, skimpy plot, and formulaic songs. Hammerstein introduced uncomfortable topics in musicals: murder in *Rose Marie*, racism in *Show Boat*, wife abuse in *Carousel*, prejudice in *South Pacific*. His musical plays were more than entertainments; they had a point to convey. Never "preachy," his shows often emphasized the importance of people of different races understanding and tolerating each other. The shows were uplifting, showing how good people experience life's hardships and eventually triumph over them.

The song "You'll Never Walk Alone" is used in *Carousel* initially to comfort the character of Julie and later to inspire her daughter, showing that hope and love are part of her life. Irving Berlin believed it was the greatest song Hammerstein ever wrote. With its inspirational words, the song is often sung at weddings, funerals, and graduations. It has even become the rallying cry of European Football Clubs, as thousands who might never have heard of Hammerstein sing his words at the top of their voices.

Marcia B. Dinneen

Further Reading

Citron, Stephen. *The Wordsmiths: Oscar Hammerstein 2nd and Alan Jay Lerner*. New York: Oxford University Press, 1995. An examination of Hammerstein, with an emphasis on his work with Harbach and Kern.

Fordin, Hugh. *Getting to Know Him: A Biography of Oscar Hammerstein II*. New York: Random House, 1977. With an introduction by Stephen Sondheim, the biography includes background information on the creation of Hammerstein's lyrics and librettos.

Hammerstein, Oscar. *Lyrics*. New York: Simon & Schuster, 1949. In addition to the text of songs, the author includes a special section on writing lyrics.

Hischak, Thomas S. *Boy Loses Girl: Broadway's Librettists*. Lanham, Md.: Scarecrow Press, 2002. Chapter three shows how Hammerstein "led the American musical into maturity."

Mordden, Ethan. *Beautiful Mornin': The Broadway Musical in the 1940's*. New York: Oxford University Press, 1999. Includes interesting material on the creation and presentation of *Oklahoma!*, *Carousel*, and *Allegro*.

Taylor, Deems. *Some Enchanted Evenings: The Story of Rodgers and Hammerstein.* New York: Harper and Brothers, 1953. A renowned music critic provides background as well as inside information on Hammerstein and his collaborators, particularly Rodgers.

See also: Andrews, Dame Julie; Cohan, George M.; Coward, Sir Noël; Fiedler, Arthur; Gershwin, George; Hart, Lorenz; Horne, Lena; Kern, Jerome; Loewe, Frederick; Robeson, Paul; Rodgers, Richard; Romberg, Sigmund; Sondheim, Stephen.

Lionel Hampton

American jazz composer, singer, vibraphonist, drummer, and pianist

One of the first jazz vibraphonists, Hampton was prominently featured in Benny Goodman's quartet, one of the first mainstream musical groups to be racially integrated. He also led a long-lived and popular post-swing-era big band.

Born: April 20, 1908; Louisville, Kentucky
Died: August 31, 2002; New York, New York
Also known as: Lionel Leo Hampton (full name)

Principal recordings

ALBUMS: *The Original Stardust*, 1947; *Moonglow*, 1950; *The Blues Ain't News to Me*, 1951; *Crazy Hamp*, 1953; *Hamp!*, 1953; *Hamp in Paris*, 1953; *Jazztime Paris*, 1953; *The King of the Vibes*, 1953; *Lionel Hampton in Paris*, 1953; *The Lionel Hampton Quartet*, 1953; *Rockin' and Groovin'*, 1953; *Flyin' Home*, 1954; *Hallelujah Hamp*, 1954; *Hamp's Big Four*, 1954; *The High and the Mighty*, 1954; *Hot Mallets*, 1954; *Lionel Hampton*, 1954; *Lionel Hampton Plays Love Songs*, 1954; *The One and Only Lionel Hampton*, 1954; *Swingin' with Hamp*, 1954; *Crazy Rhythm*, 1955; *G. Krupa—L. Hampton—T. Wilson*, 1955 (with Gene Krupa and Teddy Wilson); *The Genius of Lionel Hampton*, 1955; *Hamp and Getz*, 1955 (with Stan Getz); *Hamp Roars Again*, 1955; *The Hampton-Tatum-Rich Trio*, 1955 (with Art Tatum and Buddy Rich); *Jam Session in Paris*, 1955; *Jazz in Paris: Lionel Hampton and His New French Sound*, 1955; *Lionel Hampton and His Giants*, 1955; *Lionel Hampton Big Band*, 1955; *Tatum-Hampton-Rich . . . Again*, 1955 (with Tatum and Rich); *Travelin' Band*, 1955; *Hamp in Hi Fi*, 1956; *Jazz Flamenco*, 1956; *Lionel Hampton Swings*, 1956; *Lionel Hampton's Jazz Giants*, 1956; *Look!*, 1956; *Paris Session 1956*, 1956; *Golden Vibes*, 1958; *Lionel . . . Plays Drums, Vibes, Piano*, 1958; *The Many Sides of Lionel Hampton*, 1958; *Hamp's Big Band*, 1959; *Silver Vibes*, 1960; *All That Twistin' Jazz*, 1961; *The Exciting Hamp in Europe*, 1961; *Soft Vibes, Soaring Strings*, 1961; *Many Splendored Vibes*, 1962; *Bossa Nova Jazz*, 1963; *The Great Hamp and Little T*, 1963 (with Charlie Teagarden); *Lionel Hampton in Japan*, 1963; *A Taste of Hamp*, 1964; *You Better Know It*, 1964; *Hamp Stamps*, 1967; *Newport Uproar*, 1967; *Steppin' Out, Vol. 1*, 1969; *Where Could I Be?*, 1971; *Please Sunrise*, 1973; *Stop! I Don't Need No Sympathy*, 1974; *Transition*, 1974; *Blackout*, 1977; *Blues in Toulouse*, 1977; *Giants of Jazz, Vol. 1*, 1977; *Jazzmaster*, 1977; *Lionel Hampton and His Jazz Giants '77*, 1977; *Lionel Hampton Presents Buddy Rich*, 1977 (with Rich); *Lionel Hampton Presents Gerry Mulligan*, 1977 (with Gerry Mulligan); *Who's Who in Jazz Presents Lionel Hampton*, 1977; *Alive and Jumping*, 1978; *As Time Goes By*, 1978; *Hamp in Haarlem*, 1979; *Made in Japan*, 1982; *Air Mail Special*, 1983; *Sentimental Journey*, 1985; *Cookin' in the Kitchen*, 1988; *Mostly Blues*, 1988; *Mostly Ballads*, 1989; *For the Love of Music*, 1994; *Lionel Hampton and His Jazz Giants*, 1994; *My Man*, 1994; *Rhythm Rhythm*, 1994; *Fun*, 1995; *Hamp's Boogie Woogie*, 1995; *Old Fashioned Swing*, 1995; *All Star Jazz Sessions, Vol. 2*, 1996; *Lionel Hampton and His Orchestra in Europe*, 1996; *Just One of Those Things*, 1999; *Jazz Gallery: Lionel Hampton, Vol. 2*, 2000; *Lionel Hampton Jazz Showcase*, 2000; *Open House: All-Star Session, Vol. 1*, 2000; *Outrageous*, 2000; *Ring Dem Vibes*, 2001.

SINGLES: "Drum Stomp," 1937; "Down Home Jump," 1938; "Flying Home," 1942; "Hamp's Boogie Woogie," 1944; "Midnight Sun," 1947; "Mingus Fingers," 1947; "I Only Have Eyes for You," 1953; "Real Crazy," 1953.

WRITINGS OF INTEREST: *Method for Vibraharp, Xylophone, and Marimba* (1967); *The New Lionel Hampton Vibraphone Method* (1981); *Hamp: An Autobiography* (1989).

The Life

Lionel Leo Hampton was born in Louisville, Kentucky, and he was raised in Chicago by his mother after his father disappeared in World War I. As a youth, he played drums in the *Chicago Defender* Boys' Band, a band organized by the black newspaper that carried many jazz features. In 1928, after graduating from high school, Hampton moved to Los Angeles, where he played with several West Coast bands, including Les Hite's group. This group was hired as a backing band for Louis Armstrong's recordings in 1930 at NBC Studios. During one of these recording dates, Armstrong encouraged Hampton to take up the vibraphone, a relatively new instrument and one scarcely heard in the jazz world at that point.

Hampton took Armstrong's recommendation seriously, and he began performing on the vibraphone during those same recording sessions. Although he had some limited piano training, including a few lessons from Jelly Roll Morton, Hampton transferred easily to the vibraphone.

Hampton continued to perform in California through the mid-1930's, taking time to study music at the University of Southern California. He formed a nine-piece combo that played at the Paradise Club in Los Angeles, and it was this group that Columbia Records producer John Hammond heard one evening in 1936. The following night, Hammond returned with Benny Goodman, who was so impressed by Hampton's playing that he jumped on stage to play along. The next morning, Goodman brought Hampton to a recording studio, and along with Gene Krupa and Teddy Wilson, they recorded several pieces. Three weeks later, Goodman invited Hampton to join his band.

Hampton played with the Goodman band from 1936 to 1940. He was the second African American to join the group (the pianist Teddy Wilson was the first), though both he and Wilson performed exclusively in the small groups with Goodman and Krupa. Goodman encouraged Hampton to make his own recordings, and the vibraphonist organized a series of recordings with various sidemen

for Victor between 1937 and 1940. Hampton participated in Goodman's landmark Carnegie Hall concert of 1938, performing several pieces with the quartet. The quartet performances were widely regarded as highlights of the concert. Shortly after this performance, several of Goodman's stars departed, including Krupa. Hampton briefly replaced Krupa on drums, becoming the first musician to break the color barrier in big band jazz.

In 1940 Goodman briefly dissolved his group, and Hampton took the opportunity to form his own band. He began with several musicians that had recorded with him at his last Victor session, including Marshal Royal, Karl George, Ray Perry (on saxophone and violin), and Irving Ashby. He also hired several jazz stars, such as Dexter Gordon on tenor and Milt Buckner on piano, who is credited with inventing the locked-hands (block chord) style that became popular during the bebop era. At first, Hampton and his band were not successful, especially since the first tour took them through the South. Once they reached New York, however, audiences were more receptive. Few other big bands enjoyed the remarkable success Hampton's band did when the swing era ended. Part of his success came from Hampton's embracing of musical styles other than swing, ranging from early rhythm and blues and boogie-woogie to bebop and modern jazz. Even though the band was long-lived, lasting in various forms through the 1990's, Hampton had only a single hit: 1942's "Flying Home."

The Lionel Hampton Orchestra performed at many important events, including the inaugural balls of two presidents (Harry Truman's ball in 1949 and Dwight Eisenhower's ball in 1953). By 1953 Hampton had earned nearly one million dollars, and he played more than two hundred engagements a year, including a tour of Europe. He accomplished this success in spite of the fact that the band never held a long-term engagement (such as a hotel residency, the usual mark of success for a band) and had only one hit. In the 1970's, while continuing to lead his big band, Hampton formed a smaller band called Jazz Inner Circle. He toured with his groups into the 1990's. He authored several books, including *Method for Vibraharp, Xylophone, and Marimba*, *The New Lionel Hampton Vibraphone Method*, and an autobiography called *Hamp: An Autobiography*.

In his private life, Hampton was quiet and contemplative. He met Gladys Neal, a dressmaker, in 1929, and he married her in 1936. Their marriage lasted until Gladys's death thirty-four years later. The couple was active in politics, in the Civil Rights movement, and in supporting humanitarian causes. Hampton was a devout Christian, and he composed a religious piece called *King David Suite* based on his experiences traveling in Israel in 1956. He died of heart failure in 2002.

The Music

Hampton's appeal stemmed from his rambunctious energy, and many of his solos, which often lasted many choruses, were accented with his enthusiastic grunting. This energy had a strong effect on the musicians around him. Even after swing fell out of favor, Hampton and his band members stayed successful because they were masterful entertainers. Hampton was a technical master at the vibraphone, though his energy sometimes clouded his musical ideas. Harmonically, he generally stayed within the confines of standard swing-era progressions.

Hampton also made recordings, to varying degrees of success, that featured his piano playing, his drumming, and his voice. After he picked up the vibraphone, his piano playing was done in a two-fingered percussive style. He achieves remarkable effects, using only his index fingers, though this style is essentially limited. Hampton's drumming is characterized by his trademark exuberance, which sometimes disguises technical issues. He greatly enjoyed singing, and he modeled his performances after Armstrong's.

Early Works. Hampton first recorded in 1924 on drums. He performed the first recorded vibraphone solo in 1930, during Armstrong's recording "Memories of You." He also participated in radio broadcasts from the Cotton Club in California (with Armstrong).

Victor Recordings. Hampton's recordings for Victor comprised twenty-three sessions cut between 1937 and 1940. Hampton used varying sidemen in his groups, which were almost always called Lionel Hampton and His Orchestra. His sidemen included members from the groups of Goodman, Duke Ellington, and Count Basie. Hampton's Victor recordings were intended to compete with the Teddy Wilson-Billie Holiday recordings made for Brunswick Records (begun in 1935). However, the Hampton sessions were less successful than Wilson's.

Many of the inspired moments on these recordings come from Hampton's sidemen. Ziggy Elman, section trumpeter for Goodman, is featured on many pieces, and he contributes several excellent solos. Cootie Williams and Johnny Hodges, members of Ellington's orchestra, add a distinctive sound to "The Sun Will Shine Tonight" from the January 18, 1938, session. September 11, 1939, is widely regarded as one of the best sessions, and it features a young Gillespie playing with Coleman Hawkins and Charlie Christian (on his first recording), among others.

In addition to his vibraphone solos, which are plentiful, Hampton is showcased in several other ways on these recordings. He plays in his two-fingered piano style on several pieces ("China Stomp" is one of the best examples). He sings several times, including on "After You've Gone" and "In the Mood That I'm In." He also performs on drums on

Lionel Hampton. (AP/Wide World Photos)

"Drum Stomp." Hampton had the opportunity to play some original pieces during these recordings, including "Rock Hill Special," "Down Home Jump," and "Fiddle Diddle."

"Flying Home." This piece, a Hampton original, received its first treatment in 1939 with the Goodman Sextet. Hampton and his sidemen also recorded it during the February 26 small group session for Victor. These first two versions are relaxed, almost listless, hardly foreshadowing the raucous big band rendition that would make the charts. In 1942 the pianist for Hampton's big band, Milt Buckner, arranged the piece, and the Hampton band recorded it that same year. This version features a trumpet solo by Ernie Royal that echoes the explosive power of Hampton and a tenor solo by Illinois Jacquet that was emulated by countless rhythm-and-blues and rock-and-roll tenor players in the following years. This recording, Hampton's first and only hit, was rehashed many times on records and in performances throughout the band's lifespan, sometimes under different guises (such as 1949's "Wee Albert"). The song was also popular among other big bands, and it was recorded by several bands in the years following 1940.

"Mingus Fingers." This 1947 piece represented Hampton's short foray into bebop. The piece, written by the bassist Charles Mingus when he was only twenty-five, was more complex and unorthodox music than the Hampton band was accustomed to playing. Though Mingus, who played with Hampton's band from 1947 to 1948, would move on to a fruitful career as a jazz composer, "Mingus Fingers" was a fragmented piece ill-suited for the Hampton band. It was the reaction of the band and the public to this piece that turned Hampton back toward more popular styles, including rhythm and blues and boogie-woogie.

Musical Legacy

Hampton was essentially the first and only important vibraphone player until Milt Jackson, a bop player. Though Red Norvo had experimented with the instrument in the 1920's, it was Hampton who transformed the instrument from a novelty into an exciting medium for improvisation. Hampton left behind a staggering number of recordings. His best

are those with the Benny Goodman groups, in which he exhibits a fine technical command over his instrument and cohesive musical ideas.

He received numerous honorary doctorates, including his first in 1953 from Allen University in Columbia, South Carolina. In 1983, the music school at the University of Idaho in Moscow, Idaho, was renamed the Lionel Hampton School of Music in honor of the jazz musician. The school also renamed its international jazz festival for Hampton.

Sarah Caissie Provost

Further Reading

Condon, Eddie. _Eddie Condon's Treasury of Jazz_. Westport, Conn.: Greenwood Press, 1956. A chapter on Hampton gives biographical details and offers an assessment of his music.

Dance, Stanley. _The World of Swing_. New York: Da Capo Press, 1979. In an interview, Hampton recalls his life in jazz until 1972. Includes illustrations.

Hampton, Lionel, with James Haskins. _Hamp: An Autobiography_. New York: Amistad, 1989. Hampton recounts his life and musical escapades in this engaging autobiography. Includes a discography and illustrations.

Oliphant, Dave. "Other Black Bands." In _The Early Swing Era, 1930 to 1941_. Westport, Conn.: Greenwood Press, 2002. Details on the music and the musicians who recorded on Hampton's sessions for Victor. Includes illustrations.

Schuller, Gunther. "The Great Black Bands." In _The Swing Era: The Development of Jazz, 1930-1945_. New York: Oxford University Press, 1968. The author offers a somewhat critical, although fair, analysis of Hampton's improvisations and his work as a bandleader. Includes discography.

See also: Armstrong, Louis; Basie, Count; Brown, Clifford; Burton, Gary; Carter, Benny; Christian, Charlie; Cole, Nat King; Dorsey, Thomas A.; Ellington, Duke; Getz, Stan; Goodman, Benny; Gordon, Dexter; Hawkins, Coleman; Holiday, Billie; Jones, Quincy; Mingus, Charles; Montgomery, Wes; Navarro, Fats; Peterson, Oscar; Puente, Tito; Smith, Bessie; Washington, Dinah.

Herbie Hancock

American jazz pianist, keyboardist, synthesizer player, guitarist, and songwriter, and film-score composer

Hancock incorporates into his personal modern jazz piano style elements from blues, rhythm-and-blues, rock and roll, world, and classical music. As a composer, he wrote several significant standards for the jazz repertoire.

Born: April 12, 1940; Chicago, Illinois

Also known as: Herbert Jeffrey Hancock (full name)

Member of: The Donald Byrd-Pepper Adams Quintet; the Miles Davis Quintet; the Herbie Hancock Trio; the Herbie Hancock Quartet; V.S.O.P.

Principal works

FILM SCORES: *Blow-Up*, 1966; *The Spook Who Sat by the Door*, 1973; *Death Wish*, 1974; *A Soldier's Story*, 1984; *Jo Jo Dancer, Your Life Is Calling*, 1986; *'Round Midnight*, 1986; *Colors*, 1988; *Action Jackson*, 1988; *Harlem Nights*, 1989; *Livin' Large*, 1991; *Pioneers for Peace: American Kosen Rufu*, 2007.

Principal recordings

ALBUMS (solo): *Takin' Off*, 1962; *Inventions and Dimensions*, 1963; *My Point of View*, 1963; *Empyrean Isles*, 1964; *Succotash*, 1964 (with Willie Bobo); *Maiden Voyage*, 1965; *Hear O Israel*, 1968; *The Prisoner*, 1968; *Speak Like a Child*, 1968; *Fat Albert Rotunda*, 1969; *Mwandishi*, 1970; *Crossings*, 1971; *Sextant*, 1972; *Head Hunters*, 1973; *Death Wish*, 1974; *Dedication*, 1974; *Thrust*, 1974; *Love Me by Name*, 1975; *Man-Child*, 1975; *Kawaida*, 1976; *Secrets*, 1976; *The Herbie Hancock Trio*, 1977 (with the Herbie Hancock Trio); *Sunlight*, 1977; *Corea/Hancock*, 1978 (with Chick Corea); *Directstep*, 1978; *An Evening With Herbie Hancock and Chick Corea: In Concert*, 1978 (with Corea); *The Piano*, 1978; *Feets Don't Fail Me Now*, 1979; *Monster*, 1980; *Mr. Hands*, 1980; *Herbie Hancock Trio*, 1981 (with the Herbie Hancock Trio); *Magic Windows*, 1981; *Quartet*, 1981 (with the Herbie Hancock Quartet); *Lite Me Up*, 1982; *Future Shock*, 1983; *Sound System*, 1984; *Village Life*, 1985 (with Foday Musa Suso); *Jazzvisions: Jazz Africa*, 1986 (with Foday Musa Suso); *Third Plane*, 1986 (with others); *Perfect Machine*, 1988; *Songs for My Father*, 1988; *Dis Is Da Drum*, 1995; *The Originals*, 1995; *The New Standard*, 1996; *1 + 1*, 1997 (with Wayne Shorter); *Gershwin's World*, 1998; *Directions in Music: Celebrating Miles Davis and John Coltrane*, 2002 (with Roy Hargrove and Michael Brecker); *Future 2 Future*, 2001; *Possibilities*, 2005; *Baraka*, 2006 (with Albert "Tootie" Heath and Don Cherry); *Piano Fiesta*, 2006 (with Corea); *River: The Joni Letters*, 2007.

ALBUMS (with the Miles Davis Quintet): *Seven Steps to Heaven*, 1963; *E.S.P.*, 1965; *Miles Smiles*, 1966; *Nefertiti*, 1967; *Sorcerer*, 1967; *Water Babies*, 1967; *Filles de Kilimanjaro*, 1968; *Miles in the Sky*, 1968; *Big Fun*, 1969; *Bitches Brew*, 1969; *In a Silent Way*, 1969; *Live-Evil*, 1970; *A Tribute to Jack Johnson*, 1970; *Get Up with It*, 1972; *On the Corner*, 1972.

ALBUMS (with V.S.O.P.): *The Quintet*, 1976; *V.S.O.P.*, 1977; *Live Under the Sky*, 1979; *Live Under the Sky, No. 2*, 2002; *Five Stars*, 2007.

The Life

Herbert Jeffrey Hancock began studying piano at the age of seven. Four years later, he performed the first movement of Wolfgang Amadeus Mozart's Piano Concerto in D Major (1788) with the Chicago Symphony Orchestra. During his years at Hyde Park High School, Hancock became interested in jazz, and he formed a jazz ensemble. At Grinnell College in Iowa, where Hancock studied electrical engineering and composition from 1956 to 1960, he founded a seventeen-piece big band, he performed his works, and he had the opportunity to play with touring artists such as Coleman Hawkins and Donald Byrd.

After his return to Chicago, Hancock replaced Duke Pearson in the Donald Byrd-Pepper Adams Quintet, with which he had his first professional recording date in 1961. In the same year, at the urging of Byrd, Hancock moved to New York City, where the young pianist worked—next to Byrd and Adams—with Phil Woods and Oliver Nelson. Around

Herbie Hancock. (AP/Wide World Photos)

Bitches Brew sessions resulted in one of the first jazz rock albums, the immensely successful *Head Hunters*. In the same year, Hancock formed *V.S.O.P.*, a reunion band of the Miles Davis Quartet, with Freddie Hubbard substituting for Davis.

In 1983 the collaboration between Bill Laswell and Hancock began, bearing fruit with the platinum album *Future Shock*. The second album, *Sound System*, contained the Grammy Award-winning tune "Rockit." Laswell and Hancock reunited in 2001 for the hip-hop-influenced album *Future 2 Future*.

Through the 1990's, Hancock continued his explorations of electronic funk projects with *Dis Is Da Drum*. A testimonial to Hancock's increasing interest in fusing jazz with rock began with his album *The New Standard*, and it was reaffirmed with his tribute album to Joni Mitchell, *River: The Joni Letters*. Hancock's examination of the possibilities of stylistic crossovers among rock, African, and classical music was equally evident in the 1998 album *Gershwin's World*, which was the recipient of three Grammy Awards.

The Music

Musical Influences. Hancock became interested in jazz improvisation at the age of thirteen. Primarily self-taught in jazz, he acquired impressive knowledge of different jazz styles by transcribing solos from records. His major influences were Erroll Garner, Oscar Peterson, George Shearing, Dave Brubeck, Horace Silver, Davis, and Art Blakey and His Jazz Messengers. Hancock was captivated by the rich harmonic language of Bill Evans, by the unusual arrangements of Clare Fisher for the vocal ensemble Hi Lo, and the novel orchestra arrangements of Robert Farnon. After his move to New York, Hancock, while enrolled as a continuing student at Manhattan School of Music, discovered the music of European composers Maurice Ravel, Igor Stravinsky, Olivier Messiaen, Edgard Varèse, Karlheinz Stockhausen, and Krysztof Penderecki.

Hancock started his professional jazz career in the middle of the hard-bop movement, which was the major trademark of the Blue Note Records la-

the same time he signed a contract with Blue Note Records, resulting in his debut album *Takin' Off*.

In the summer of 1963, after having been contacted by Miles Davis for a test rehearsal, he was invited to join the trumpeter's quintet with Wayne Shorter, Ron Carter, and Tony Williams, and he stayed with the group until 1968. Independent of his engagement with Davis, Hancock led an active career as a leader on Blue Note Records and as a sideman on several labels under leaders such as Lee Morgan, Woody Shaw, Charles Tolliver, Sonny Rollins, Jackie McLean, Shorter, Sam Rivers, and Bobby Hutcherson. Hancock signed a contract with Warner Bros. Records, for which he recorded three albums between 1969 and 1971 with his sextet, expanding the jazz vocabulary with influences from rock, African, and Indian music.

In 1972 Hancock moved to Los Angeles, where he became increasingly interested in Buddhism. His growing involvement with electronic instruments and his participation in Davis's legendary bel. Consequently, Hancock used Byrd's funky rhythm-and-blues compositions such as "Pentecostal Feelings" from the Blue Note album *Free Form*, on which Hancock was a sideman, as the model for two early compositions of his own, "Watermelon Man" and "Driftin'" (both on his debut album *Takin' Off*). "Watermelon Man" became a hit in a cover version by Mongo Santamaria a year later, and subsequently it has been recorded by more than two hundred artists.

Hancock, however, would not limit himself to the funky rhythm-and-blues style. He explored modal jazz in his "Maiden Voyage," postbop in "Dolphin Dance" and "The Eye of the Hurricane," arranged ensemble jazz in "I Have a Dream," free forms in "Succotash" and "The Egg," and free jazz in "The Omen" (on Bobby Hutcherson's *Happenings* in 1963). During his Blue Note years, Hancock explored the possibilities of creating a concept album (*Maiden Voyage* on the topic of the sea and *Speak Like a Child* on the topic of childhood), a preoccupation to which he returned frequently from the 1990's onward.

Warner Bros. and Columbia. The strong influence that Davis had on the members of his quintet and the participants in his *Bitches Brew* project manifested itself in Hancock's output of the late 1960's and early 1970's. Hancock experimented with free forms and extensive improvisational tune structures based on ostinatos, for example, in "Ostinato (Suite for Angela)." He began to incorporate electronic instruments into his music. For his solo albums, he first used the Fender Rhodes piano (with altered sound, such as distortion and wah-wah) on *Fat Albert Rotunda*, *Mwandishi*, and *Crossings*, and he introduced the use of synthesizers, sequencers, Vocoder, Mellotron, and Hohner Clavinet on the first Columbia Records album, *Head Hunters*. A top-selling album, *Head Hunters* marked the beginning of Hancock's emergence into the jazz-rock movement of the 1970's, which led to a series of successful albums. Hancock produced eleven albums, which all made the charts, an unprecedented occurrence for a jazz musician.

During his success with his commercially oriented jazz-rock albums, Hancock also dedicated his efforts to acoustic jazz projects, such as the V.S.O.P. quintet and several piano-duo tours with Chick Corea (1976-1979). The former can be heard on the

live recordings of an open-air concert that V.S.O.P. gave in Tokyo in 1977, and the latter on the two albums *Corea/Hancock* and *An Evening With Herbie Hancock and Chick Corea*, both recorded live in February of 1978.

Crossover. In 1983 Hancock began his collaboration with producer and bassist Laswell. Their extremely successful albums, *Future Shock* and *Sound System*, are continuations of Hancock's funk- and rhythm-and-blues-influenced jazz-rock projects of the 1970's, and they anticipate the development of popular music of the 1980's and 1990's. "Rockit" (on *Sound System*) produced a video that received five MTV Awards, and it has been regarded as one of the earliest examples of hip-hop and turntablism.

After *Perfect Machine*, Hancock and Laswell worked together again on *Future 2 Future*, an album that contains backbeat loops of the early 2000's and world music samples. This album can be regarded as Hancock's answer to the European electronica and nu jazz movement of the 1990's. Artists such as the British hip-hop group US3 remixed and recomposed Hancock's "Cantaloupe Island" and released it in a hip-hop, electronica version under the title "Cantaloop" in 1994. Likewise, the frequent use of the Fender Rhodes piano and analogue synthesizers in the 1990's and 2000's (for instance by the Norwegian pianist Bugge Wesseltoft) demonstrate the influence of Hancock's 1970's jazz-rock style.

Beginning in the 1990's, Hancock became increasingly interested in rock music, releasing such albums as *The New Standard* (interpreting rock tunes by the Beatles, Prince, Simon and Garfunkel, and Steely Dan in a jazz idiom), *Possibilities* (a crossover project with Carlos Santana, Angelique Kidjo, Christina Aguilera, Paul Simon, Annie Lennox and Sting), and *River: The Joni Letters* (a tribute album to Mitchell).

Gershwin's World marked Hancock's return to classical music. On this album, which is dedicated to Gershwin and won three Grammy Awards, Hancock improvises in a jazz style through large sections of the second movement of Maurice Ravel's Concerto for Piano in G Major.

Parallel to these crossover projects, Hancock participated in pure jazz projects, such as with his longtime collaborator Shorter (*1 + 1*) and in a quintet with trumpeter Roy Hargrove and saxophonist Michael Brecker (*Directions in Music: Celebrating Miles Davis and John Coltrane*).

Musical Legacy

Hancock—whose early piano style was influenced by funky rhythm-and-blues patterns, Bill Evans and Shearing, and the advanced functional harmonies of Claude Debussy and Ravel—explored all relevant jazz idioms during the 1960's. His duties as a sideman gave him broad stylistic experience. Of particular importance was Hancock's time with Davis. In Davis's quintet, Hancock played a major role in the rhythm group, developing a sensitive interaction with bassist Ron Carter and drummer Tony Williams. From the 1970's onward, he extended his musical interests into rock, soul, rhythm-and-blues, hip-hop, world, and classical music, demonstrating that the creation of remarkable music could be achieved through the crossbreeding of different musical styles and traditions.

The versatile talents of Hancock extend into his compositional activities. Many of his jazz tunes of the 1960's have become standards. As a film composer, he wrote two influential sound tracks, for Michelangelo Antonioni's *Blow-Up* (1966) and for Bertrand Tavernier's depiction of a jazz musician in Paris in the late 1950's, *'Round Midnight* (1986), which won Hancock an Academy Award for Best Original Music Score.

Michael Baumgartner

Further Reading

Baker, David N., Lida M. Belt, and Herman C. Hudson, eds. "Herbert Jeffrey Hancock." In *The Black Composer Speaks.* Metuchen, N.J.: Scarecrow Press, 1978. This resource provides interviews with fifteen black composers, who talk about the black musical experience. In the chapter on Hancock, the artist discusses his compositional style and aethetics. Includes a list of compositions.

Lyons, Len. "Herbie Hancock." In *The Great Jazz Pianists: Speaking of Their Lives and Music.* New York: Da Capo Press, 1983. In this book, which provides a history of jazz piano and covers the lives and careers of twenty-seven jazz pianists, Hancock outlines his musical goals and influences.

Pond, Steven F. *Head Hunters: The Making of Jazz's*

First Platinum Album. Ann Arbor: University of Michigan Press, 2005. A chronicle of the making of Hancock's influential and controversial *Head Hunters.* It was unprecedented for its fusion of jazz and rock and for its large sales, the first jazz album to go platinum.

See also: Blakey, Art; Corea, Chick; Davis, Miles; Debussy, Claude; Evans, Bill; Gordon, Dexter; Hawkins, Coleman; Jones, Quincy; McFerrin, Bobby; Metheny, Pat; Mingus, Charles; Mitchell, Joni; Nascimento, Milton; Peterson, Oscar; Ravel, Maurice; Rollins, Sonny; Shorter, Wayne.

W. C. Handy
American cornetist and songwriter

Handy's compositional work established the twelve-bar blues form and the altered notes used in blues performance.

Born: November 16, 1873; Florence, Alabama
Died: March 28, 1958; New York, New York
Also known as: William Christopher Handy (full name); Father of the Blues

Principal works

SONGS (music and lyrics by Handy unless otherwise stated): "Jogo Blues," 1913 (for piano); "Memphis Blues," 1913 (lyrics by George A. Norton); "Saint Louis Blues," 1914; "Yellow Dog Blues," 1914; "Hesitating Blues," 1915; "Joe Turner Blues," 1915; "Beale Street Blues," 1917; "The Kaiser's Got the Blues," 1918 (lyrics by Dorner C. Browne); "Aunt Hagar's Children Blues," 1920 (lyrics by J. Tim Brymn); "Long Gone John (from Bowling Green)," 1920 (lyrics by Chris Smith); "Loveless Love," 1921; "John Henry Blues," 1922; "Darktown Reveille," 1923 (music with Smith; lyrics by Walter Hirsch); "Harlem Blues," 1923; "Atlanta Blues (Make Me One Pallet on Your Floor)," 1924 (lyrics by Dave Elman); "Friendless Blues," 1926 (lyrics by Mercedes Gilbert); "Golden Brown Blues,"

1927 (lyrics by Langston Hughes); "Chantez Les Bas," 1931 ("Sing 'Em Low"); "Opportunity," 1932 (lyrics by Walter Malone).
WRITINGS OF INTEREST: *Blues: An Anthology*, 1926; *Negro Authors and Composers of the United States*, 1935; *Book of Negro Spirituals*, 1938; *Father of the Blues*, 1941 (autobiography); *Negro Music and Musicians*, 1944.

The Life

William Christopher Handy was born to former slaves Charles B. Handy and Elizabeth Brewer in the rural town of Florence, Alabama. As a minister, his father had high moral standards of behavior for his children, and he was horrified when young Handy brought home a guitar he had bought with his own money. After making him exchange the instrument for a dictionary, Handy's father relented and allowed his son to take organ and voice lessons from a local teacher, with the idea that he would eventually perform religious music.

Handy was still young when he heard a cornet player accompanying a gospel choir, and he vowed to learn to play, which he did after surreptitiously buying an instrument. In spite of his parents' objections, he applied his musical training to find work playing cornet in local dance bands and singing in minstrel shows and church choirs. By his late teens, Handy was traveling outside the Florence area and experiencing the life of a touring musician, which he embraced for thirty years.

By 1892 Handy was forming and directing his own groups. He relocated to Bessemer, where he was engaged as a teacher. Finding the salary insufficient, he got a job in an ironworks while he dreamed of attending Wilberforce University. When that plan failed, he took a job singing with the Lauzetta Quartet in 1893, and he spent the next several years traveling as far as St. Louis and Chicago (for the Columbian Exposition in 1893). During this period, Handy experienced bouts of financial desperation and homelessness, which provided material for his later compositions.

The mid-1890's found him in Evansville, Indiana, where he worked as a manual laborer while playing cornet in local groups. In 1896 he moved to Henderson, Kentucky, where he made his living outside of music, while performing on evenings and weekends. At this time, Handy was introduced to European choral music, courtesy of a German musical society directed by Professor Bach, who gave him some informal instruction. In addition, he courted and married Elizabeth Price, with whom he had six children.

Shortly after his marriage, Handy was engaged to perform with (and ultimately direct) Mahara's Minstrels, a road company of black performers, with which he toured from 1896 to 1900. This experience was crucial in forming Handy's musical outlook: It exposed him to numerous regional African American genres, and it introduced him to an active form of show business. After traveling throughout the South (including a short tour to Cuba), he left the road in 1900 to teach music at the Alabama Agricultural and Mechanical School in Normal, where he remained for two years.

After a brief return to Mahara's Minstrels in 1902, Handy was engaged to direct a Knights of Pythias band in Clarksdale, Mississippi, where he was first exposed to traditional blues. While not initially impressed with its musical validity, he was quick to grasp the popularity of the genre as well as its rhythmic vitality, and he began arranging some of the folk melodies for his band. By 1909 he had settled in Memphis, Tennessee, where he led a band for municipal and private functions, and he actively composed and arranged music, with his first attempt at a blues composition, "Memphis Blues," dating from this period.

From that point, Handy had a string of successes with his band, largely because of his growing catalog of compositions. In 1914 he formed Pace and Handy with his friend, banker Harry Pace, in order to publish his works as well as those of other black composers. The publicity surrounding his songs generated interest from other bands, and Handy found a reliable source of income from royalties from recordings of his work. In 1917 his band was invited to New York to make recordings, although many in his regular group did not make the trip, and he was forced to use numerous substitutes. Nevertheless, these successes encouraged him to relocate himself and the offices of Pace and Handy to New York in 1918.

After some initial success, Pace and Handy (one of the first African American publishing companies) dissolved in 1920, when Pace left to found Black Swan Records. Handy attempted to continue publishing, but the strain became too much, and he suffered a breakdown, which included temporary blindness. Friends (including Bill "Bojangles" Robinson and Clarence Williams) came to his aid, saving him from bankruptcy.

In 1926 Handy wrote *Blues: An Anthology*, which was the first attempt to make a cultural presentation of the blues and to contextualize his contributions. Handy was a driving force in producing a 1928 Carnegie Hall concert celebrating the evolution of black music, and in 1929 he cowrote a treatment for a short film that became *St. Louis Blues*, starring Bessie Smith. In 1931 the city of Memphis named a municipal park after him.

For the rest of his life, Handy continued to be celebrated for his pioneering work. He occasionally appeared in variety shows and even on television. Handy published his autobiography in 1941, and he was recorded speaking about his life and playing his works by the Library of Congress (1938) and the Audio Archives (1952). Late in life, when Handy went completely blind and was confined to a wheelchair, he was active in starting the Foundation for the Blind in 1951. He married again in 1954 (his first wife having died in 1937), and he oversaw a 1958 film made about his life (called *St. Louis Blues* and starring Nat King Cole), which was released shortly after his death.

The Music

"**Memphis Blues.**" One of Handy's popular publications and one of the first published blues, this was originally composed in 1909 as "Mr. Crump," for a mayoral candidate in Memphis. Crump commissioned Handy to write a tune to be played at rallies, although some of his detractors changed the lyrics to poke fun at the reform candidate. In 1912 Handy self-published a more fully realized version of the piece, including two blues strains and one sixteen-bar strain. Its multistrain organization, with its introduction, transition, and internal key change, align it with a modified ragtime form, but the frequent use of lowered thirds and sevenths suggest the blues idiom discovered by Handy during his travels through the South. Handy claimed he was cheated out of royalties from "Memphis Blues" by an unscrupulous white publisher, although he was never denied composer credit.

"**Saint Louis Blues.**" Originally published in 1914, this tune is similar to "Memphis Blues" in that it consists of two blues strains separated by a sixteen-bar section. In this case, the middle section is in the parallel minor, and it is built on a tango rhythmic device that Handy had heard during his tours in the South. The last strain is adapted from his 1913 piece, "Jogo Blues," which had been published as an instrumental. Since its publication, "Saint Louis Blues" has become perhaps the best known piece of its kind, and it is often cited as the most frequently recorded song in history.

"**Yellow Dog Blues.**" This 1914 composition was inspired by a lyrical strain about a railroad crossing in Mississippi overheard by Handy in 1903. Ironically, it was originally titled "Yellow Dog Rag," although this tune is perhaps the least ragtime-like of any of Handy's early works, containing only two twelve-bar strains. Although the sheet music has both strains in D major, performers generally modulate to G for the second.

"**Loveless Love.**" This 1921 composition is an illustration of Handy's process of adapting existing material. By his own account (in *Blues: An Anthology*), Handy said that this was a "series of arrangements" of the folk tune "Careless Love," "prefaced by an original Handy blues." Indeed, the verse is a twelve-bar blues moving to the subdominant for two thirty-two-bar choruses based on the earlier tune.

Musical Legacy

Handy's musical legacy rests largely on his compositions from before 1920, although several from the 1920's (including "Loveless Love" and "Aunt Hagar's Children Blues") are ranked among his best work. His first published works, such as "Memphis Blues," "Saint Louis Blues," "Yellow Dog Blues" (originally called "Yellow Dog Rag"), and "Beale Street Blues" became standards, first in the repertoire of contemporary popular music, with numerous recordings being made by leading musicians, then in the canon of jazz and blues. Extensive sheet music sales also aided with the dissemination of Handy's music and the enhancement of his reputation.

In his publications, Handy drew on decades of experience touring through the South with minstrel shows and bands. He had witnessed a wide cross section of African American music-making, and, guided by his own training in Western musical methodology, he was able to notate what was until that time largely an oral tradition. While not the first to publish blues, Handy was among the earliest, and the consistency and quality of his work made the elements of the country blues (such as the lowered third and seventh scale degrees, the *aab* structure of the poetry, and the call-and-response between the singer and accompaniment) comprehensible to those not familiar with the tradition.

Recordings by bands and singers from the pre-jazz era are close stylistically to what Handy had in mind when he originally published his compositions, but subsequent versions by jazz and blues performers are today considered more definitive regarding the original style. "Saint Louis Blues," for example, was recorded dozens of times during the 1920's, but the most famous versions are probably those done by Bessie Smith and Louis Armstrong (together in 1925, Smith alone in the 1929 film *St. Louis Blues*, and Armstrong in 1930). These versions, while different, established stylistic and interpretive traits copied to this day.

John L. Clark, Jr.

Further Reading

Brooks, Tim, and Dick Spottswood. *Lost Sounds: Blacks and the Birth of the Recording Industry, 1890-1919*. Urbana: University of Illinois Press, 2004. This encyclopedic book of early recordings contains a chapter on Handy. The biographical information is taken largely from Handy's autobiography, but the later material is useful. Includes a discography of recordings of his music by other artists.

Handy, W. C. *Father of the Blues: An Autobiography*. New York: Macmillan, 1941. This wide-ranging account of his life is often vague about dates and chronology. Nevertheless, this book is well written and contains a wealth of information about black show business in the late 1800's and early 1900's. The work list compiled by the composer is a valuable resource.

Handy, W. C., with Abbe Niles, eds. *Blues: An Anthology*. New York: Albert and Charles Boni, 1926. This was the first large-scale attempt to present an historical overview of the blues. Handy provided sheet music for some of his best-known work as well as piano arrangements of folk material. The introductory essay by Niles on the history of the blues was based on interviews done with Handy.

See also: Armstrong, Louis; Cole, Nat King; Dorsey, Thomas A.; Guy, Buddy; Hooker, John Lee; Hunter, Alberta; Jackson, Mahalia; Joplin, Scott; Roach, Max; Rodgers, Jimmie; Smith, Bessie; Still, William Grant; Tatum, Art.

Nikolaus Harnoncourt
Austrian classical conductor, cellist, and viol player

A brilliant and versatile conductor, Harnoncourt is widely recognized for his interpretations of Renaissance and Baroque music, the classical and Romantic repertoire, and works from the twentieth century. In addition, he has been instrumental in the revival of early music.

Born: December 6, 1929; Berlin, Germany
Also known as: Nikolaus de la Fontaine und d'Harnoncourt (full name)

Principal recordings

ALBUMS: *Bach: Brandenburg Concertos*, 1964; *Bach: St. John Passion*, 1965; *Bach: Four Orchestral Suites*, 1966; *Bach: Mass in B Minor*, 1968; *Bach: St. Matthew Passion*, 1970; *J. S. Bach: The Complete Sacred Cantatas*, 1971-1988 (with Gustav Leonhardt); *Bach: Christmas Oratorio*, 1972; *Monteverdi: Il ritorno d'Ulisse in Patria*, 1975; *Monteverdi: L'Incoronazione di poppea*, 1975; *Monteverdi: L'Orfeo*, 1975; *Beethoven: Symphonies Nos. 1-9*, 1991; *Telemann: Der tag des gerichts*, 1993; *Bach: Sacred Cantatas*, 1994; *Purcell: Dido and Aeneas*, 1994; *Haydn: Symphonies 30, 34, and 73*, 1995; *Handel: Water Music*, 1996; *Schumann: Genoveva*, 1997; *Johann Strauss in Berlin*, 2000.

WRITINGS OF INTEREST: *Zur Geschichte der Streichinstrumente und ihres Klanges*, 1961; *Das Musizieren mit alren Instrumenten: Einflüsse der Spieltechnik auf die Interpretation*, 1967; *Das quasi Wort-ton-verhältnis in der Instrumentalen*

Barockmusik, 1969 (*Baroque Music Today: Music as Speech—Ways to a New Understanding of Music*, 1988); *Probleme der Wiedergabe von Bachs Chor-orchester-werken*, 1969; *Notenschrift und Wektreue*, 1971; *Musik als Klangrede: Wege zu einem Neuen Musikverständnis*, 1982; *Monteverdi, Bach, und Mozart*, 1984 (*The Musical Dialogue: Thoughts on Monteverdi, Bach, and Mozart*, 2003); *Was ist Wahrheit?*, 1995.

The Life

Austrian conductor Nikolaus de la Fontaine und d'Harnoncourt (NIH-koh-lows HAHR-nuhn-koort) was born to Eberhard de la Fontaine, Count of Harnoncourt-Unverzagt, and Ladislaja, Countess of Meran and Baroness of Brandhofen. Brought up in Graz, he studied cello with Hans Kortschak and Paul Grümmer. In 1952, upon completion of his studies at the Vienna Academy of Music with Emanuel Brabec, he joined the Vienna Symphony Orchestra as a cellist, and he held his position until 1969.

Harnoncourt's work on early music began in 1949 when he founded the Vienna Viola da Gamba Quartet. In 1953, with his wife Alice and fellow musicians, he founded the Concentus Musicus Wien ensemble, devoted to performances of Renaissance and Baroque music on period instruments. After four years of research and rehearsals, the ensemble made its debut in May, 1957. They began touring in 1960; in the same year, one of the first of their many recordings, *Heinrich Ignaz Franz Biber: Georg Muffat*, was released by Amadeo.

Since the 1980's, Harnoncourt has increasingly performed classical and Romantic repertoire with modern instrumental ensembles, including the Chamber Orchestra of Europe, the Concertgebouw Orchestra, and the Vienna and Berlin Philharmonic Orchestras. From 1973 to 1993, he was a professor at the Mozarteum University of Music and Dramatic Arts in Salzburg, where he became an artist in residence in 2006.

The Music

Founded in 1953, the Concentus Musicus Wien is one of the first major ensembles devoted to the performance of Renaissance and Baroque music on period instruments. Conducted by Harnoncourt from his cello or viola da gamba, the ensemble has

performed and recorded the major works of Claudio Monteverdi, Georg Philipp Telemann, Georg Frideric Handel, and Johann Sebastian Bach. After his debut at the conductor's rostrum with Monteverdi's *Il ritorno d'Ulisse in patria* at the Piccola Scala in Milan in 1972, Harnoncourt conducted the acclaimed Monteverdi and Mozart cycles at the Zurich Opera House, from 1975 to 1987, in collaboration with Jean-Pierre Ponnelle. He has conducted at the Vienna State Opera, at the Amsterdam Opera House, at the Zurich Opera House, and at other venues, performing a wide range of works by Handel, Wolfgang Amadeus Mozart, Ludwig van Beethoven, Franz Schubert, Carl Maria von Weber, Johann Strauss, and others.

In 1985 Harnoncourt became involved in the annual Styriarte Festival in his hometown of Graz, performing cycles of works by Joseph Haydn, Beethoven, Schubert, Robert Schumann, and Felix Mendelssohn with the Chamber Orchestra of Europe. He has appeared regularly with the Concertgebouw Orchestra since 1975 and the Berlin Philharmonic Orchestra since 1991, and he conducted the New Year's Concert of the Vienna Philharmonic Orchestra in 2001 and 2003.

J. S. Bach: The Complete Sacred Cantatas. In 1971, in collaboration with musician Gustav Leonhardt, Harnoncourt began his pioneering recordings of Bach's complete cantatas. Besides the soloists, a number of instrumental and vocal groups took part in this groundbreaking project, including the Concentus Musicus Wien and the Leonhardt Consort playing on period instruments, the Vienna Boys' Choir, the Chorus Viennensis, the Tölz Boys' Choir, the King's College Choir Cambridge, the Hanover Boys' Choir, and the Collegium Vocale Gent. By the time the project was completed, almost two hundred sacred cantatas had been recorded, and a total of ninety albums in forty-five volumes had been issued. *J. S. Bach: The Complete Sacred Cantatas* was awarded the Gramophone Special Achievement Award in 1990.

Beethoven: Symphonies Nos. 1-9. Under Harnoncourt's direction, the complete cycle of Beethoven's nine symphonies played by the Chamber Orchestra of Europe was recorded at the Styriarte Festival in 1990 and 1991. For the recordings, Harnoncourt employs a mid-size orchestra, similar to those during Beethoven's time, and he mixes modern instruments played in period style with period trumpets. The five-disc recording received critical acclaim, and it was awarded the German Record Critics' Award in 1991, as well as the Emmy Award, the Gramophone Record of the Year, the Stella d'Oro, the Grand Prix du Disque, and the Belgian Caecilia Prize in 1992.

Schumann: Genoveva. *Genoveva* is the only complete opera by Schumann with a libretto by the composer. Harnoncourt conducted the rarely performed work at the Styriarte Festival in 1996, featuring Ruth Ziesak, Marjana Lipovsek, Deon van der Walt, Rodney Gilfry, Thomas Quasthoff, and Oliver Widmer, together with the Arnold Schoenberg Choir and the Chamber Orchestra of Europe. On two compact discs, the live recording for Teldec was awarded the BBC Music Magazine Best of 1997, the Caecilia Prize, and the Independent 50 Best of the Year CDs in 1998.

Johann Strauss in Berlin. Recorded in 1998 and 1999 on Teldec DVD-audio, *Johann Strauss in Berlin* contains a collection of polkas, waltzes, and marches performed by the Berlin Philharmonic Orchestra under the direction of Harnoncourt. A selection of works by Strauss in connection to his time in Berlin is featured, including the "Pigeons of St. Mark's," the "Tritsch-Tratsch Polka," and the "Emperor Waltz." The recording was given the Edison Award in 2000.

Musical Legacy

Harnoncourt has an extensive discography of almost five hundred recordings, many of which have been awarded international prizes. In 2006 he won the Echo Klassik 2006 for his recording of Handel's *Messiah* with the Concentus Musicus Wien and with the Arnold Schoenberg Choir. His views on music are documented in several acclaimed books, including *The Musical Dialogue: Thoughts on Monteverdi, Bach and Mozart* and *Töne sind höhere Worte: Gespräche zur Interpretation romantischer Musik* (2007, notes are superior words: conversations on the interpretation of Romantic music).

In recognition of his lifetime achievements, Harnoncourt has received numerous international awards, including the Polar Music Prize (1994), the Ernst von Siemens Music Prize (2002), and the Kyoto Prize (2005). He became an honorary member of the Vienna Concert House Society in 1989, of

the Vienna Society of the Friends of Music in 1992, and of the Viennese Philharmonic Orchestra in 2004. He received an honorary doctorate from the University of Edinburgh in 1987, and he became an honorary member of the universities of music in Graz and Vienna.

Sonia Lee

Further Reading

Elste, Martin. "Nikolaus Harnoncourt: A Profile." *Fanfare* 13, no. 3 (January/February, 1990): 449-452. This article discusses Harnoncourt's career and the changes in his performance style over the years.

Harnoncourt, Nikolaus. *Baroque Music Today: Music as Speech—Ways to a New Understanding of Music.* Translated by Mary O'Neill. Edited by Reinhard G. Pauly. Portland, Oreg.: Amadeus Press, 1988. This is a collection of essays written by Harnoncourt that summarize his views on Baroque performance practice.

_____. *The Musical Dialogue: Thoughts on Monteverdi, Bach, and Mozart.* Translated by Mary O'Neill. Edited by Reinhard G. Pauly. Portland, Oreg.: Amadeus Press, 1988. This book by Harnoncourt contains a collection of essays, lectures, and talks relating to the music of Monteverdi, Bach, and Mozart.

See also: Casadesus, Henri; Hogwood, Christopher; Karajan, Herbert von; Leonhardt, Gustav.

Emmylou Harris
American country/rock singer, guitarist, and songwriter

A multiple Grammy Award recipient, Harris is one of the most successful female performers in modern country-music history. She has also received wide recognition for her contributions to country-rock, folk music, the bluegrass revival, and the Americana movement since the 1980's.

Born: April 2, 1947; Birmingham, Alabama
Member of: The Angel Band; the Hot Band; the Nash Ramblers

Principal recordings

ALBUMS: *Gliding Bird*, 1968; *GP*, 1973 (with Gram Parsons); *Grievous Angel*, 1974 (with Parsons); *Elite Hotel*, 1975; *Pieces of the Sky*, 1975; *Luxury Liner*, 1977; *Quarter Moon in a Ten-Cent Town*, 1978; *Light of the Stable*, 1979; *Blue Kentucky Girl*, 1980; *Roses in the Snow*, 1980; *Cimarron*, 1981; *Evangeline*, 1981; *Last Date*, 1982; *White Shoes*, 1983; *The Ballad of Sally Rose*, 1985; *Thirteen*, 1986; *Angel Band*, 1987; *Trio*, 1987 (with Dolly Parton and Linda Ronstadt); *Bluebird*, 1989; *Brand New Dance*, 1990; *At the Ryman*, 1992 (with the Nash Ramblers); *Cowgirl's Prayer*, 1993; *Songs of the West*, 1994; *Wrecking Ball*, 1995; *Spyboy*, 1998; *Trio II*, 1999 (with Parton and Ronstadt); *Western Wall: The Tuscon Sessions*, 1999 (with Ronstadt); *Red Dirt Girl*, 2000; *Nobody's Darling but Mine*, 2002; *Stumble into Grace*, 2003; *All the Roadrunning*, 2006 (with Mark Knopfler); *All I Intended to Be*, 2008.

The Life

The younger of two children, Emmylou Harris was born to Eugenia Murchison Harris and Walter Rutland "Bucky" Harris, a Marine Corps pilot who was reported missing in action in Korea in 1952 and spent ten months as a prisoner of war. Her early childhood was spent in North Carolina and later in Woodbridge, Virginia, where she won the Miss Woodbridge beauty pageant as a teenager and graduated from Garfield Senior High School as class valedictorian in 1965. She received a scholarship to study drama at the University of North Carolina in Greensboro, where she formed a folk duo with classmate Mike Williams, performing at a local club.

Harris moved to New York City before finishing college. She performed folk songs in Greenwich Village coffeehouses and became a regular at Gerde's Folk City, where she met fellow performers Jerry Jeff Walker, David Bromberg, and Paul Siebel. In 1970, not long after the release of her debut album, *Gliding Bird*, her label Jubilee Records filed for bankruptcy. Her short marriage with songwriter Tom Slocum also ended. Together with her newborn daughter Hallie, Harris moved back in with her parents in the Maryland suburbs outside Washington, D.C.

In 1971, while performing as part of a trio at Clyde's in Georgetown, Harris was discovered by members of the Flying Burrito Brothers and was recommended to country-rock pioneer Gram Parsons by former Byrds member Chris Hillman. Subsequently, she toured with Parsons's band, the Fallen Angels, and sang on his two highly acclaimed solo albums, *GP* (1973) and *Grievous Angel* (1974, posthumously).

After Parsons's death from a drug overdose in 1973, Harris formed her backup groups, the Angel Band and the Hot Band, and released her major label debut album, *Pieces of the Sky*, in 1975 on Reprise Records. From 1977 to 1984, she was married to Canadian producer Brian Ahern, with whom she has her second daughter, Meghann. Her third marriage (1985-1993) was to English songwriter Paul Kennerley, who became her producer in 1985.

Harris relocated to Nashville, Tennessee, in the early 1980's. Besides working on her solo releases, she collaborated with Dolly Parton and Linda Ronstadt for the Grammy Award-winning album *Trio*. In 1991, soon after the dissolution of the legendary Hot Band, she formed the new acoustic Nash Ramblers, with whom she recorded a live album at the Ryman Auditorium in Nashville. Two of her later albums, *Red Dirt Girl* and *Stumble into Grace*, showcase her talent as a songwriter.

The Music

Harris's repertoire embraces a wide spectrum of styles, including country, rock, contemporary folk, and bluegrass. In a career spanning more than three decades, she has melded elements of different styles to create her own sound. Not only is she well known for her interpretation of other songwriters' works; she has also established herself as a singer-songwriter. She has performed in a wide range of venues, from colleges and universities to Carnegie Hall, and from the Bonnaroo Music Festival to bluegrass events. She has toured throughout the United States, Canada, Europe, Australia, and New Zealand.

Early Works. As seen in her first solo album, *Gliding Bird*, Harris's early repertoire was mainly folk music with some subtle country undertones. Through Parsons, not only did she learn about country music, but she was also introduced to artists such as the Louvin brothers. She toured with Parsons's Fallen Angels and sang vocals on his solo recordings. In 1975, she released her first country album, *Pieces of the Sky*, which included a number of cover songs, including her first hit single, "If I Could Only Win Your Love," by the Louvin Brothers.

Elite Hotel. Harris's second successful album, *Elite Hotel*, was released the same year as the highly acclaimed *Pieces of the Sky*. The album showcased her then newly formed backup group, the Hot Band, with Elvis Presley's guitarist James Burton, as well as Rodney Crowell and Glen D. Hardin. Her first album to hit number one on *Billboard*'s top country albums chart, *Elite Hotel* features songs by Hank Williams, the Beatles, Gram Parsons, Buck Owens, and others. Two of the tracks, "Together Again" and "Sweet Dreams," became number-one country hits. The album earned Harris her first Grammy Award for Best Female Country Vocal Performance in 1976.

The Ballad of Sally Rose. Released by Warner Bros. in 1985, *The Ballad of Sally Rose* comprises songs written by Harris and her husband-producer Kennerley. It is a semiautobiographical conceptual work loosely based on her relationship with Parsons, telling the story of a young singer named Sally Rose whose lover and mentor is tragically killed on the road in a traffic accident. Described by Harris as a "country opera," the album follow one song with another without pauses. The album received mixed reviews and did not enjoy commercial success.

Trio. Released in 1987 by Warner Bros., *Trio* features Harris and two longtime friends, Parton and Ronstadt. The three vocalists first started the recording project in 1977 but, because of scheduling conflicts, did not complete the work until the mid-1980's. Produced by George Massenburg, *Trio* became one of Harris's best-selling albums. Several of the tracks, including "To Know Him Is to Love Him," "Telling Me Lies," and "Those Memories of You," were Top 10 country hits; the album also reached number one

on the top country albums chart. *Trio* won the 1987 Grammy Award for Best Country Performance by a Duo or Group with Vocal. The three musicians reunited in the studio in the 1990's and released their *Trio II* in 1999.

At the Ryman. Harris's *At the Ryman* is a live recording with her then newly formed acoustic backup band, the Nash Ramblers (Larry Atamanuik, Roy Huskey, Jr., Sam Bush, Al Perkins, and John Randall Stewart). Recorded in 1991 from a series of concerts at the legendary Ryman Auditorium, the original home of the Grand Ole Opry, the album brought renewed attention to the then hundred-year-old building and led to a complete restoration of the facility into a concert venue. The album won the Grammy Award for Best Country Performance by a Duo or Group with Vocal in 1992.

Wrecking Ball. Released in 1995 on the Elektra label, *Wrecking Ball* marks a radical departure from Harris's previous albums. Highly praised by critics, the hypnotic album features songs and guest performances by Steve Earle ("Goodbye"), Daniel Lanois ("Where Will I Be?), Anna McGarrigle ("Goin' Back to Harlan"), Lucinda Williams ("Sweet Old World"), and Neil Young, who wrote the title track. Best known for his work with U2, Peter Gabriel, and Bob Dylan, producer Lanois invited guest rock musicians to perform on the album, in-

Emmylou Harris. (AP/Wide World Photos)

cluding Tony Hall from the Neville Brothers and Larry Mullen, Jr., from U2. The recording won the 1995 Grammy Award for Best Contemporary Folk Album.

Red Dirt Girl. Harris's *Red Dirt Girl* from 2000 showcases her remarkable talent as a songwriter; she wrote or cowrote eleven of the twelve tracks in this Nonesuch Records debut. Featuring guest appearances from Patty Griffin, Julie Miller, Dave Matthews, Kate McGarrigle, Patti Scialfa, and Bruce Springsteen, the album delivers a variety of sounds from rock and world music to traditional country and folk. The album reached number five on the top country albums chart and won the 2000 Grammy Award for Best Contemporary Folk Album. She continued to emphasize her songwriting in her next album, *Stumble into Grace*.

Musical Legacy

Harris has recorded more than twenty-five albums on such labels as Reprise/Warner Bros., Elektra, and Nonesuch, and she has made guest appearances on numerous recordings by a diverse pool of artists, including Gram Parsons, Linda Ronstadt, Neil Young, Bob Dylan, Buck Owens, Charlie Louvin, John Denver, Roy Orbison, Johnny Cash, and Mark Knopfler. She has appeared in several documentary videos and films, including *The Last Waltz* (1978), *Live at the Ryman* (1992), *In the Hank Williams Tradition* (1995), *Emmylou Harris: Spyboy—Live from the Legendary Exit* (1999), *Down from the Mountain* (2000), *Neil Young: Heart of Gold* (2006), and *Real Live Roadrunning* (2006).

Harris is a recipient of many Grammy Awards, including four for Best Female Country Performance (1976, 1979, 1984, 2005), two for Best Contemporary Folk Album (1995 for *Wrecking Ball* and 2000 for *Red Dirt Girl*), and two for Best Country Performance by a Duo or Group with Vocal (1987 with Dolly Parton and Linda Ronstadt, and 1992 with the Nash Ramblers). She also received three Country Music Association Awards, including Female Vocalist of the Year (1980), Vocal Event of the Year (1988 for *Trio*), and Album of the Year (for *O Brother, Where Art Thou?*, 2000), as well as the *Billboard* Century Award (1999). A past president of the Country Music Foundation, she served on the board of the Country Music Hall of Fame and Museum for many years, eventually becoming a

trustee emerita. She became a member of the Grand Ole Opry in 1992 and was inducted into the Country Music Hall of Fame in 2008.

Sonia Lee

Further Reading

Brown, Jim. *Emmylou Harris: Angel in Disguise.* Kingston, Ont.: Fox Music Books, 2004. An informative biography of Harris, covering her life, career, and music. Contains excerpts from some of her interviews.

Bufwack, Mary A., and Robert K. Oermann. "Back to Country: Emmylou Harris and the Country-Rock Fusion." In *Finding Her Voice: Women in Country Music, 1800-2000*. Nashville, Tenn.: The Country Music Foundation Press and Vanderbilt University Press, 2003. This book chapter discusses the blending of country and rock music by Emmylou Harris and several other women performers in the 1960's, 1970's, and 1980's.

Clark, Rick. "Recording Notes: Emmylou Harris and Brian Ahern, Together Again." *Mix* 32, no. 5 (May, 2008): 104, 108-110, 112. This article focuses on Harris's latest release, *All I Intended to Be* (2008), which features some of her favorite songs as well as her talent as a songwriter. Also discusses her working relationship with her producer/ex-husband Ahern since the production of *White Shoes* (1983).

Geisel, Ellen. "Emmylou Harris: Taking Chances & Soothing Souls." *Dirty Linen* 63 (April/May, 1996): 44-47, 49. This article reports a phone interview in which Harris speaks about her then-latest release, *Wrecking Ball* (1995), as well as her collaboration with Lanois and others for the album.

Nixon-John, Gloria. "Getting the Word Out: The Country of Bronwen Wallace and Emmylou Harris." In *The Women of Country Music: A Reader*, edited by Charles K. Wolfe and James E. Akenson. Lexington: University Press of Kentucky, 2003. Inspired by "Burn That Candle" from Harris's *Quarter Moon in a Ten Cent Town* (1978), the late Canadian poet and short story writer Bronwen Wallace wrote a collection of poems prior to her death in 1989 and dedicated the work to Harris. This book article centers on the country connection between Wallace's *Keep That*

Candle Burning Bright & Other Poems: Poems for Emmylou Harris (1991, posthumously) and Harris's music.

Sandall, Robert. "The Ballad of Emmylou Harris." *Sunday Times Magazine,* June 1, 2008, 16. A *Times Magazine* writer reports an interview in which Harris reveals her struggles after Parsons's death.

Thompson, Dave. "Emmylou Harris: Thirty Years On." *Goldmine* 32, no. 14 (July 7, 2006): 14-18. Celebrating the release of Harris's 23d album *All The Roadrunning* (2006), this article looks back on Harris's career of over 30 years and discusses some of her musical influences, including Parsons, Ahern, Ronstadt, the Louvin Brothers, Lanois, and Mark Knopfler.

See also: Baez, Joan; Burke, Solomon; Earle, Steve; Nelson, Willie; Orbison, Roy; Parsons, Gram; Parton, Dolly; Ritchie, Jean; Ronstadt, Linda; Van Zandt, Townes; Williams, Lucinda.

George Harrison

English rock guitarist, singer, and songwriter

As a member of the Beatles and as a solo artist, Harrison produced popular songs of distinction, and he experimented with a variety of non-Western musical sources.

Born: February 25, 1943; Liverpool, England
Died: November 29, 2001; Los Angeles, California
Also known as: George Harold Harrison (full name)
Member of: The Beatles; the Traveling Wilburys

Principal recordings

ALBUMS (solo): *Wonderwall Music,* 1968; *Electronic Sound,* 1969; *All Things Must Pass,* 1970; *Living in the Material World,* 1973; *Dark Horse,* 1974; *Extra Texture,* 1975; *Thirty Three and One Third,* 1976; *George Harrison,* 1979; *Somewhere in England,* 1981; *Gone Troppo,* 1982; *Cloud Nine,* 1987; *Chant and Be Happy: Indian Devotional Songs,* 1991; *Brainwashed,* 2002.

ALBUMS (with the Beatles): *Please Please Me,* 1963; *With the Beatles,* 1963; *Beatles for Sale,* 1964; *The Beatles' Second Album,* 1964; *Beatles '65,* 1964; *The Beatles' Story,* 1964; *A Hard Day's Night,* 1964; *Introducing the Beatles,* 1964; *Meet the Beatles,* 1964; *Something New,* 1964; *Beatles VI,* 1965; *Help!,* 1965; *Rubber Soul,* 1965; *Revolver,* 1966; *Yesterday . . . and Today,* 1966; *Magical Mystery Tour,* 1967; *Sgt. Pepper's Lonely Hearts Club Band,* 1967; *The Beatles,* 1968 (*The White Album*); *Abbey Road,* 1969; *Yellow Submarine,* 1969; *Let It Be,* 1970.

ALBUMS (with the Traveling Wilburys): *Traveling Wilburys, Vol. 1,* 1988; *Traveling Wilburys, Vol. 3,* 1990.

The Life

George Harold Harrison was born in Liverpool, England, on February 25, 1943. At an early age, he exhibited a keen interest in popular music, and soon he began to study guitar. At the Liverpool Institute for Boys, he met Paul McCartney, a student who shared his passionate interest in rock and roll. At McCartney's insistence, Harrison was invited to join the Quarrymen, a musical group led by John Lennon. This group later evolved into the Beatles, and it achieved global success in the 1960's. In the group, Harrison was lead guitarist and occasional vocalist. Soon he developed a distinctive compositional style informed by his burgeoning interest in the music of India. He later collaborated with diverse artists such as Delaney and Bonnie, the Band, and Bob Dylan, and he also experimented with electronic music. By the time the Beatles disbanded in 1970, Harrison was widely recognized as a composer and musician of the first rank.

Harrison flourished in the wake of the Beatles' breakup. Although he had only been allotted one or two tracks on the group's albums, he had been steadily composing for seven years, and he had a selection of songs from which to choose for his solo debut. The album, *All Things Must Pass,* was a three-record set that featured the hit singles "What Is Life?" and "My Sweet Lord." In August, 1971, Harrison organized an all-star benefit concert at New York's Madison Square Garden that brought attention to the plight of refugees in Bangladesh. A recording of this event, *The Concert for Bangladesh,* became a million-seller, with all proceeds going

George Harrison. (AP/Wide World Photos)

again from the limelight. He returned in 1987 with *Cloud Nine*, a remarkable tour de force that successfully highlighted his strengths as a singer, songwriter, and guitarist. He next teamed with veteran rockers Jeff Lynne, Tom Petty, Roy Orbison, and Bob Dylan to form the Traveling Wilburys.

In the 1990's, Harrison worked sporadically, but he was heavily involved in *The Beatles Anthology* project with former bandmates Ringo Starr and Paul McCartney. He also prepared tracks for a new solo album. In 1999, he was assaulted by an intruder in his home, and he suffered multiple stab wounds. He recovered from this attack, but he succumbed to cancer on November 29, 2001.

to charity. His solo success continued in 1973 with *Living in the Material World*, an album that featured the songs "Give Me Love" and "Sue Me, Sue You Blues."

Personal turmoil surfaced in 1974, when Harrison became estranged from his wife of eight years, Patti Boyd. Their breakup soured the mood of *Dark Horse*, an album further hindered by the poor condition of the singer's vocal cords. His troubles continued on a North American solo tour, which demonstrated that he was losing touch with the mainstream audience. He received another setback in 1976 when he lost a copyright-infringement suit brought against him regarding the song "My Sweet Lord." During a three-year hiatus from recording, Harrison married Olivia Arias and celebrated the birth of a son, Dhani. He also began a career as a film producer. His company, Handmade Films, financed the hit comedy *Monty Python's Life of Brian*, and it went on to produce many successful films throughout the 1980's.

He returned in 1979 with *George Harrison*, an album that initiated a period in which the singer worked increasingly from his home studio. This was quickly followed by *Somewhere in England*, which featured the hit single "All Those Years Ago." The lackluster response to his next album, *Gone Troppo*, caused Harrison to withdraw once

The Music

As the junior composer in the Beatles, Harrison labored in the shadow of Lennon and McCartney. Gradually, he developed a distinctive compositional style characterized by a fascination with unusual modal structures. He also explored exotic instrumentation as a result of his interest in the music of India. His lyrics tended to address the spiritual aspirations that lay at the heart of the counterculture, though in a forthright fashion. He continued to develop these elements during his solo career, and he also began to incorporate harmonic structures derived from American jazz.

The Beatles. During his time with the Beatles, Harrison composed works with remarkably exotic harmonic structures. "Don't Bother Me" employs a Dorian progression that provides an appropriate setting for the song's dour lyrical content. This quality was also evident on his contributions to the albums *Help!* and *Rubber Soul*. For *Revolver*, Harrison incorporated gestures derived from Indian music ("Love You To," "Taxman"), and on *Sgt. Pepper's Lonely Hearts Club Band*, he successfully integrated Eastern and Western styles in "Within You, Without You," a song that features an authentic Indian ensemble (sitar, dilruba, tabla, swarmandal, and tambura), combined with Western classical instruments (violin, cello). On *The Beatles*, Harrison returned to a more traditional rock-and-roll approach ("Savoy Truffle," "While My Guitar Gently Weeps"), but the Indian influence was still evident on "Long, Long, Long." Harrison finally came into his own on the Beatles' swan song, *Abbey Road*, which featured "Here Comes the Sun" and the hit single "Something."

Solo Work. The backlog of songs Harrison had accrued while a member of the Beatles formed the basis of his first solo release, *All Things Must Pass*, a sprawling three-record set that featured the hits "What Is Life" and "My Sweet Lord." In 1973 he recorded *Living in the Material World*, an album that continued to explore the wall-of-sound textures of *All Things Must Pass*, but with an increased focus on spiritual themes. It also showcased his newly developed slide guitar technique. The breakup of his marriage to Patti dominated *Dark Horse*, which nonetheless contained such interesting musical hybrids as "Maya Love," and "It Is 'He' (Jai Sri Krishna)." On his next two releases, *Extra Texture* and *Thirty Three and One Third*, Harrison rebounded from his personal troubles, although with diminishing commercial success.

Later Works. The new songs from *George Harrison* exhibited a more relaxed approach than shown on the singer's earlier albums. In 1981 he released *Somewhere in England*, which contained the hit single "All Those Years Ago," an exploration of Harrison's feelings regarding the death of former bandmate Lennon. *Gone Troppo* was a commercial and critical disappointment, but Harrison rebounded in 1987 with *Cloud Nine*, an album that yielded the hits "When We Was Fab" and "Got My Mind Set on You." He subsequently joined forces with Lynne, Petty, Orbison, and Dylan to record as the Traveling Wilburys. During the 1990's, Harrison continued to record and tour sporadically. His final album, *Brainwashed*, was released posthumously in 2002.

Musical Legacy

As solo artists, each member of the Beatles struggled to live up to the group's early success. However, Harrison's time with the group can be viewed as an apprenticeship during which he developed his diverse influences into a highly original musical style. His songs, which once seemed exotic to Western ears, now sound increasingly like world music. In that sense, Harrison's works may have presaged the cross-cultural influences that would characterize the music that followed.

Thomas MacFarlane

Further Reading

Giuliano, Geoffrey. *Dark Horse: The Life and Art of George Harrison*. New York: Da Capo Press, 1997. This work provides an overview of Harrison's career.

Harrison, George. *I Me Mine*. New York: Simon & Schuster, 1980. This personal memoir provides valuable insights into the creation of Harrison's works with the Beatles and his development as a solo artist.

Leng, Simon. *While My Guitar Gently Weeps: The Music of George Harrison*. Milwaukee, Wis.: Hal Leonard, 2006. This work presents a remarkably detailed analysis of Harrison's entire catalog.

Lewisohn, Mark. *The Beatles Recording Sessions*. New York: Harmony Books, 1988. This seminal work provides detailed descriptions of all the Beatles' recorded works.

_____. *The Complete Beatles Chronicle*. New York: Harmony Books, 1992. This work expands on *The Beatles Recording Sessions* by including detailed descriptions for all of the group's documented activities between 1957 and 1970.

See also: Clapton, Eric; Dylan, Bob; Eddy, Duane; Lennon, John; McCartney, Sir Paul; Martin, Sir George; Notorious B.I.G.; Orbison, Roy; Perkins, Carl; Petty, Tom; Robinson, Smokey; Shankar, Ravi; Simone, Nina; Spector, Phil.

Lou Harrison

American classical and film-score composer and pianist

Harrison created large- and small-scale musical compositions in a variety of modernist classical idioms and with elements of Asian musical practices. He was an early advocate of the study and the use of the Indonesian gamelan.

Born: May 14, 1917; Portland, Oregon
Died: February 2, 2003; Lafayette, Indiana
Also known as: Lou Silver Harrison (full name)

Principal works

BALLETS: *Green Mansions*, 1939 (scenario and choreography by C. Beals); *In Praise of Johnny Appleseed*, 1942 (for flute and percussion; scenario and choreography by Beals); *Solstice*, 1949 (scenario and choreography by Jean Erdman).

CHAMBER WORKS: *The Winter's Tale*, 1937; *Electra*, 1938 (for chamber orchestra; incidental music for Euripides' play); *The Beautiful People*, 1941 (for trumpet and piano); *Alleluia*, 1945; *Western Dance (The Open Road)*, 1947; *The Perilous Chapel*, 1948; *Seven Pastorales*, 1952 (for flute, oboe, bassoon, harp, and strings); *The Only Jealousy of Emer*, 1957 (for piano, flute, cello, bass, and percussion); *Elegy to the Memory of Calvin Simmons*, 1982 (for oboe, vibraphone, harp, and strings); *New Moon*, 1986 (for flute, clarinet, brass, strings, and percussion); *Ariadne*, 1987 (for flute and percussion).

CHORAL WORKS: *Political Primer*, 1951 (for solo voice, chorus, and orchestra); *Mass to Saint Anthony*, 1952 (for chorus, trumpet, harp, and strings); *Four Strict Songs*, 1955 (for chorus and orchestra); *Nak Yang chun*, 1961 (*Spring in Nak Yang*; for chorus and chamber orchestra); *Easter Cantata*, 1966 (for chorus and chamber orchestra); *Haiku*, 1968 (for chorus, Chinese flute, harp, and percussion); *Peace Piece One*, 1968 (for chorus and chamber orchestra); *Orpheus*, 1969 (for chorus and percussion); *La Koro Sutro*, 1972 (for chorus, organ, harp, and gamelan); *Scenes from Cavafy*, 1980 (for chorus, harp, and gamelan); *Faust*, 1985 (for solo voices, chorus, orchestra, harp, and gamelan); *Three Songs*, 1985 (for chorus, piano, and strings); *Homage to Pacifica*, 1991 (for chorus, bassoon, harp, percussion, and gamelan); *White Ashes*, 1992 (for chorus and keyboard).

FILM SCORES: *Nuptiae*, 1968 (for two voices, chorus, and kulintang); *Beyond the Far Blue Mountains*, 1982 (for gamelan); *Devotions*, 1983 (for gamelan).

OPERAS (music): *Rapunzel*, 1952 (for voice and chamber orchestra; libretto by William Morris); *Young Caeser*, 1971 (libretto by Robert Gordon).

ORCHESTRAL WORKS: *Suite for Symphonic Strings*, 1936; *Suite No. 1*, 1947 (for strings); *Suite No. 2*, 1948 (for strings); *The Marriage at the Eiffel Tower*, 1949 (for orchestral suite; incidental music for Jean Cocteau's play *Les Mariés de la Tour Eiffel*); *Suite for Cello and Harp*, 1949; *Nocturne*, 1951; *Praises for Hummingbirds and Hawks*, 1951 (for small orchestra); *Suite for Violin, Piano, and Small Orchestra*, 1951; *Symphony on G*, 1952; *At the Tomb of Charles Ives*, 1963 (for trombone, psalteries, dulcimers, harps, tam-tam, and strings); *Suite for Violin and American Gamelan*, 1973; *Elegiac Symphony*, 1975; *Praise for the Beauty of Hummingbirds*, 1975 (for two violins, flute, and percussion); *Bubaran Robert*, 1976 (for gamelan); *Third Symphony*, 1982; *Fourth Symphony*, 1990; *Suite for Four Haisho with Percussion*, 1993; *New First Suite*, 1995 (for strings); *A Parade for M.T.T.*, 1995; *Suite for Cello and Piano*, 1995.

PIANO WORKS: *The Trojan Women*, 1939 (incidental music for Euripides' play); *Gigue and Musette*, 1941 (for solo piano); *Suite for Piano*, 1943; *Cinna*, 1957 (incidental music for Pierre Corneille's play); Piano Concerto, 1985; *Tandy's Tango*, 1992 (for solo piano).

VOCAL WORKS: *Sanctus*, 1940 (for voice and piano); *King David's Lament*, 1941 (for voice and piano); *May Rain*, 1941 (for voice, piano, and percussion); *Pied Beauty*, 1941 (for voice, trombone or cello, flute, and percussion); *Fragment from Calamus*, 1946 (for voices and piano); *Alma Redemptoris Mater*, 1951 (for voice, violin, trombone, and piano); *Peace Piece Three*, 1953 (for voice, harp, and strings); *Holly and Ivy*, 1962 (for voice, harp, and strings); *Joyous Procession and Solemn Procession*, 1962 (for two voices, brass, and percussion; *Peace Piece Two*, 1968 (for voice and chamber orchestra); *Io and Prometheus*, 1973 (for voices and piano); *Ketawang Wellington*, 1983 (for voice and gamelan); *The Foreman's Song Tune (Coyote Stories)*, 1987 (for voice and gamelan); *A Soedjatmoko Set*, 1989 (for voices and gamelan).

The Life

Lou Silver Harrison was born on May 14, 1917, in Portland, Oregon. His father, Clarence, was the son of an immigrant, Thomas Nëjsa, who had adopted the name Harrison because his Norwegian name was so often mispronounced. A second son, Arthur, was born to Clarence and his wife, Callie, in 1920.

In 1911, when Callie received an inheritance from the estate of a Midwestern relative, she had a handsome apartment building constructed in Portland. The family lived comfortably, and Callie was able to acquire Asian art and furnishings for her home as well as pay for music lessons for her older son. In 1926 the family moved to Woodland, California, and then to a succession of other cities and towns in the region, settling finally in Burlingame, where Harrison completed high school in 1934.

His early musical experiences included instrument-building and lessons in piano, violin, and voice. Harrison's first compositions date from as early as his tenth year, and he was given private lessons in composition during high school. While attending San Francisco State College for three semesters in 1935 and 1936, he continued to study and to perform instrumental and vocal music, and he had pivotal exposure to aspects of modern music, including the works of the American composer Henry Cowell, who became a lifelong friend and teacher.

In 1942 Harrison moved to Los Angeles, where he taught a form of dance notation at the University of California, and he had an opportunity to study for six months with the legendary composer Arnold Schoenberg. The following year Harrison moved to New York City to further his musical career. However, the ten years he spent there brought creative and professional growth as well as personal distress. Obliged to take on part-time work to meet his living expenses and deeply unsettled by the noise of the city, he suffered a nervous breakdown that led to his hospitalization for a period of months.

Realizing that he needed to live in a rural environment, Harrison ended his East Coast sojourn in 1953 to move back to California, settling permanently in Aptos, a small community in the hills above Santa Cruz. In 1961 Harrison made his first trip to Japan; this was soon followed by periods of study in other Asian countries that deepened his relationship to Oriental musical traditions.

In 1967 Harrison met William Colvig, an electrician and amateur musician with whom he collaborated on acoustical and musical matters over the next three decades. Colvig and Harrison were life

companions until Colvig's death in March, 2000. Harrison died suddenly of heart failure at age eighty-five while en route to a music festival in his honor at the University of Ohio.

The Music

Harrison's musical career began in young adulthood in San Francisco during the mid-1930's, when he participated in vocal and in instrumental performances while studying composition and world music. Before his twentieth birthday, he had found work as a composer and an accompanist for dance groups, and in 1937 and 1938 he taught at Mills College in Oakland, California. Many of his early works were composed for the theater, and he achieved early critical notice for his percussion ensemble work. *Third Symphony*, begun in 1937, was not completed until 1982; Harrison had a well-known penchant for reconsidering early work in the light of subsequent musical explorations, and

Lou Harrison. (© Christopher Felver/CORBIS)

the chronology of his creative work is unusually complex.

Musical Influences. The composer's moves to Los Angeles and then to New York were undertaken to enlarge his musical horizons. His education had from the beginning been unconventional. An early, intense involvement with the music of Charles Ives and a thorough engagement with the twelve-tone practices of Schoenberg placed Harrison solidly on the side of advanced modernism in the mid- and late 1940's. In 1946 Harrison conducted the premiere of Ives's Symphony No. 3 to critical acclaim, thus demonstrating both versatile musicianship and critical acumen, as he had been instrumental in preparing the work's score for performance.

Music Reviews. A notable aspect of Harrison's New York years is his work as a music reviewer. He was hired by the composer and critic Virgil Thomson to cover a range of musical events for the *New York Herald Tribune*, sometimes attending several performances in a single weekend. Thomson helped shape Harrison's understanding of how to address a broad audience in his critical and his analytical writing, and Harrison remained a confident, eloquent writer on music and other cultural matters throughout his career.

Mass to Saint Anthony. In these years, Harrison's compositions included a number of ballets and works for small instrumental ensembles. Work continued on a *Mass to Saint Anthony* that he had begun in 1939 in response to the beginning of World War II. Completed in 1952, it is a harbinger of subsequent works in which Harrison gives outspoken expression to political and social views. *A Political Primer*, for solo voice with chorus and orchestra, was begun in the early 1950's, but it remained unfinished.

Rapunzel. Harrison's opera *Rapunzel*, based on a retelling of the German fairy tale by the English writer William Morris, dates from 1952. An air from this work won a prize in Rome in 1954, when it was sung by Leontyne Price. Despite such artistic successes, the composer's financial situation required that he sometimes take on everyday employment to make ends meet. Newly resettled in California in a small house that his parents had purchased for him, Harrison worked in an animal hospital and as a firefighter. He never regretted these circumstances,

later stating that composing and performing music were pleasures that he was happy to pay for by such means.

Gamelan Music. In 1960 Harrison received a grant to study in Japan, China, and Korea. His decisive turn in the following years toward Asian musical culture accorded with his long-standing interests and with the Pacific Rim orientation of his West Coast milieu. Harrison had heard gamelan recordings as early as 1935, and he was captivated by live performances of Balinese gamelan at an international exposition in San Francisco in 1939. The gamelan, a kind of percussion orchestra, offered the composer both beauty of sound and complexity of rhythm, and its status as a popular social institution in Indonesia reinforced his belief in the connection between musical performance and everyday life.

Musical Acoustics. Related to Harrison's involvement in Asian music was his growing attention to musical acoustics, in particular to the concepts of tuning and intonation. In 1949 he read *Genesis of a Music*, by fellow California composer Harry Partch. Partch advanced the idea of dividing the musical octave into forty-three steps. Beginning in the 1920's, Partch had forged a musical language using novel, homemade instruments to perform in this unorthodox intonation. In sympathy with Partch's notion that European-based musical language was tonally exhausted, Harrison advocated the use of tuning systems of varied historical and geographical origins. He especially promoted just intonation, a tuning that ensures that instruments produce pure, harmonic tones rather than intervals adjusted to the system of equal temperament that has for centuries been the mainstay of Western instrumental music.

La Koro Sutro. From the 1960's, Harrison produced dozens of compositions employing his alternative tuning ideas. Over the years Harrison and Colvig built several gamelans that successfully adapted basic Indonesian concepts to contemporary materials; these are heard in numerous recordings of Harrison's compositions. Among these, of particular note is *La Koro Sutro*; the text of this majestic composition is the Buddhist "Heart Sutra" translated into the modern, invented language called Esperanto. In some cases only gamelan influences, rather than the instruments themselves, are heard in Harrison's compositions: an acclaimed and popular Piano Concerto, composed in 1985 for the pianist-composer Keith Jarrett, blends elements of nonstandard instrument tuning and large-scale orchestral idiom with the spirit of the gamelan ensemble.

Musical Legacy

Harrison's motto, "Cherish, conserve, consider, create," illuminates the scope of his contribution to music as well as his impact on the social and cultural climate of his times. His embrace of elements of Asian music was a facet of Harrison's respectful attention to cultural traditions outside his own, and he is recognized as a pioneer in the fusion of Western music with what is known as world music. Though he was not the earliest American advocate of the gamelan, he was perhaps its most articulate and creatively persuasive modern one.

For Harrison, the commitment to "conserve" and "consider" applied equally to Western as to world traditions, and it caused him to resist the musical partisanship that characterized aspects of the twentieth century classical music scene, notwithstanding his early mastery of the twelve-tone idiom descending from Schoenberg. If his music was inherently eclectic in its sources and inspiration, it was never conceived to occupy an aesthetic middle ground, and his compositions are noted for sonorities and structures that are highly personal. Much of Harrison's work embraces a simplification and purification of musical materials that have directly influenced late twentieth century minimalism.

Harrison was as concerned with the totality of his musical life and its ethical consequences as he was with the production of a definitive body of compositions. Nonetheless, these number in the hundreds. The relatively limited number of his works that are regularly performed is balanced by a widespread appreciation for the range of his creative work and the lifetime of study that underlay it.

Clyde S. McConnell

Further Reading

Garland, Peter, ed. *A Lou Harrison Reader*. Santa Fe, N.Mex.: Soundings Press, 1987. A volume issued in celebration of Harrison's seventieth birthday, this book includes essays, photographs, drawings, poems, correspondence, examples of Harrison's excellent calligraphic writing, and other memorabilia.

Kostelanetz, Richard, with Lou Harrison. "A Conversation, in Eleven-Minus-One-Parts, with Lou Harrison about Music/Theater." *The Musical Quarterly* 76, no. 3 (Autumn, 1992): 383-409. This vivid, informal interview of Harrison by a noted poet and critic provides an indispensable view of Harrison both as a composer and as a personality. The transcription contains a few minor and inconsequential errors.

Miller, Leta E., and Fredric Lieberman. *Lou Harrison*. Urbana: University of Illinois Press, 2006. The first in a series of short, readable books in the *American Composers* series, this volume recapitulates the material in the authors' 1998 book, adding some important biographical details while consolidating much technical material for the general reader. It does not supersede the earlier study and is better integrated. A compact disc of musical examples is included.

_____. *Lou Harrison: Composing a World*. New York: Oxford University Press, 1998. Published five years before the composer's death, this book documents and celebrates Harrison's life while selectively exploring the range and quality of his work. Based in part on Harrison's conversations with the authors over a period of years, it presents a well-written, integrated view of Harrison's personal and professional experiences. A compact disc with selections of representative works by Harrison is included.

Perlman, Marc. "American Gamelan in the Garden of Eden: Intonation in a Cross-Cultural Encounter." *The Musical Quarterly* 78, no. 3 (Autumn, 1994): 510-555. This wide-ranging scholarly article provides a cross-cultural and historical background to Harrison's investigation and use of intonation and the gamelan, with substantial attention to his predecessors and contemporaries.

Von Gunden, Heidi. *The Music of Lou Harrison*. Metuchen, N.J.: Scarecrow Press, 1995. The author is a musicologist with an interest in just intonation, and she pursues technical matters to a degree that will satisfy a specialist reader. Like Miller and Lieberman, she demonstrates a keen grasp of the broader cultural and issues at work in Harrison's complex body of work. While this study is parallel to Miller and Lieberman's

595

slightly later work, its scholarly emphasis makes it equally valuable.

See also: Adams, John; Cowell, Henry; Ives, Charles; Jarrett, Keith; Partch, Harry; Price, Leontyne; Schoenberg, Arnold; Thomson, Virgil.

Deborah Harry

American rock singer and songwriter

The iconic lead singer for Blondie, a popular band on the New York punk scene in the 1970's, Harry was known for her witty lyrics, distinctive velvety voice, streetwise wardrobe, and sex appeal.

Born: July 1, 1945; Miami, Florida
Also known as: Deborah Ann Harry (full name); Debbie Harry
Member of: The Wind in the Willows; Blondie; the Jazz Passengers

Principal recordings

ALBUMS (solo): *KooKoo*, 1981; *Rockbird*, 1986; *Def, Dumb and Blonde*, 1989; *Debravation*, 1993; *Necessary Evil*, 2007.

ALBUMS (with Blondie): *Blondie*, 1976; *Plastic Letters*, 1977; *Parallel Lines*, 1978; *Eat to the Beat*, 1979; *Autoamerican*, 1980; *The Hunter*, 1982; *No Exit*, 1999; *The Curse of Blondie*, 2004.

ALBUMS (with the Jazz Passengers): *In Love*, 1994; *Individually Twisted*, 1996.

ALBUM (with Wind in the Willows): *Wind in the Willows*, 1968.

SINGLE (with Blondie): "Call Me," 1980.

The Life

Deborah Ann Harry was born in Miami, Florida, and raised by adoptive parents Catherine and Richard Harry in suburban Hawthorne, New Jersey. Initially hoping to pursue an art career, Harry moved to New York City at the age of twenty, and she supported herself with various jobs. Her first recording experience was singing with the folk-rock band the Wind in the Willows in the late 1960's, after which she left the city for a few years.

Harry eased back into the New York City scene in the early 1970's with a stint in the girl group the Stillettoes, where she met guitarist Chris Stein, her longtime boyfriend and cofounder of Blondie. Drummer Clement Burke and keyboardist James Destri were also part of the initial band that formed in the mid-1970's and went on to achieve international fame.

At the height of Blondie's commercial success in the late 1970's and early 1980's, public attention focused on the photogenic lead singer so intensely that Harry's name became synonymous with Blondie, causing significant tension within the group. Blondie disbanded after Stein collapsed on tour in 1982, and he was diagnosed with the life-threatening autoimmune disease pemphigus vulgaris. Despite being at the height of her popularity, Harry stayed with Stein constantly over the next few years while he recovered his health. Their romantic relationship dissolved in the mid-1980's, although they remained friends. After Stein's recovery, in addition to her solo career, Harry pursued acting, with numerous motion-picture roles to her credit. She also performed and recorded with the Jazz Passengers in the 1990's, before Blondie regrouped to record and to tour again.

The Music

In the band's early years, Blondie built up a cult following by performing regularly in New York clubs such as CBGB. After a poorly selling self-titled debut album in 1976, the band attracted enough attention with *Plastic Letters* to move to Chrysalis Records, and it finally achieved mainstream success with *Parallel Lines*. At that time, punk and new wave music were considered too inaccessible to sell, but with the band's youthful energy and eclectic mix of styles—including more familiar pop genres—Blondie broke through the stereotype. At the pinnacle of Blondie's success, following *Eat to the Beat* and *Autoamerican*, Harry started branching out into a solo career, remaking her image for the album *Koo Koo* before a return to Blondie for the coolly received album *The Hunter*, the band's last before breaking up. Harry continued her solo career with the albums *Rockbird*, *Def, Dumb and Blonde*, and *Debravation*, which sold moderately at best. It would seem listeners preferred Harry and Blondie together, as verified by the success of the hit single "Maria" from the album *No Exit*, recorded by a reunited Blondie and a fifty-three-year-old Harry. Blondie released yet another album, *The Curse of Blondie*, which met with good reviews but poor sales. On her own, Harry released the pop-oriented *Necessary Evil*.

Parallel Lines. Blondie's third album, *Parallel Lines*, launched the band into superstardom, and it is a definitive album of the late 1970's. The punk-meets-disco song "Heart of Glass" was Blondie's first U.S. hit single, albeit a controversial one. "Heart of Glass" had been recorded earlier with the title "Once I Had a Love," but producer Mike Chapman brought out the disco feel that made it famous. Blondie had always experimented with various popular styles, but many accused the group of pandering to mainstream taste, which is what their fellow punk musicians were struggling against. The album's most enduring singles demonstrate Harry's range of vocal qualities, from breathy in "Heart of Glass," to tough girl with a Jersey accent in the band's cover of "Hanging on the Telephone," to aggressive and even downright funny in the relentless "One Way or Another," which Harry has said is about an ex-boyfriend who turned to stalking.

"Call Me." "Call Me," the theme song from the film *American Gigolo* (1980) starring Richard Gere, was the top-selling single in both the United States and England in 1980, as well as Blondie's best-selling U.S. single overall. The song represents the band's collaborative effort with producer Giorgio Moroder. Moroder provided an instrumental track that he had dubbed "Man Machine," and Harry wrote the lyrics to capture the essence of the film. The driving beat, with Harry's smooth vocals on the bold minor-key melody and the compelling chorus, helped make "Call Me" one of pop culture's most enduring songs.

Autoamerican. Blondie's fifth album, released in 1980, explored a wide variety of genres, and it produced two hit singles. A reggae-inspired cover of "The Tide Is High" charted at number one in both the United States and England. "Rapture" was the first number-one pop hit to incorporate rap-style music, and it was many listeners' first exposure to the genre. Although perhaps obvious today, the title is a clever play on words, reflecting the name of the emerging rap-music genre as well as a condi-

tion brought to mind by the song's bizarre lyrics. Perhaps what is most appealing about "Rapture" is the stark musical contrast within the song: The verses feature an ultra-smooth melody sung in Harry's most sensual voice, making her funky rap all the more unexpected.

Musical Legacy

Blondie had tremendous influence on popular music in the 1980's, and Harry played an essential role in the band's success: Her offbeat lyrics and her distinctive voice defined their sound. Equal significant to her direct musical influence was her image: Her trademark bleached-blonde hair with dark roots and streetwise style brought Hollywood glamour to rock music, coupled with an audacious punk sensibility. Certainly the band's striking visual image was to its advantage when music videos came into play. In many ways, Harry garnered a respect for women in music that paved the way for Madonna's groundbreaking success, as Madonna has often acknowledged.

Gretchen Rowe Clements

Further Reading

Bayley, Roberta. *Blondie: Unseen, 1976-1980*. London: Plexus, 2007. A candid and striking photographic chronicle of Blondie's rise to superstardom.

Che, Cathay. *Deborah Harry: Platinum Blonde*. London: André Deutsch, 2005. Authorized biography featuring interviews with Harry and Stein and a discussion of Harry's impact on popular culture.

Harry, Deborah, Chris Stein, and Victor Bockris. *Making Tracks: The Rise of Blondie*. New York: Da Capo Press, 1998. Fascinating look at Blondie through Harry's voice, with unique candid photographs by Stein.

Metz, Allan. *Blondie, from Punk to the Present: A Pictorial History*. Springfield, Mo.: Musical Legacy, 2002. Thoroughly detailed chronology for the serious Blondie fan. Includes a prologue by Stein.

Rock, Mick. *Picture This: Debbie Harry and Blondie*. A collection of previously unpublished photographs focusing on Harry at the pinnacle of Blondie's success.

See also: Madonna; Nicks, Stevie; Summer, Donna.

Lorenz Hart

American popular music and musical-theater composer and lyricist

Hart brought wit, sophistication, and complex emotions to the lyrics of popular songs in the 1920's and of musical theater in the 1930's and 1940's.

Born: May 2, 1895; New York, New York
Died: November 22, 1943; New York, New York
Also known as: Lorenz Milton Hart (full name); Larry Hart

Principal works

MUSICAL THEATER (lyrics): *A Lonely Romeo*, 1919 (libretto by Harry B. Smith and Lew M. Fields; music by Malvin M. Franklin and Robert Hood Bowers; lyrics with Robert B. Smith); *Poor Little Ritz Girl*, 1920 (libretto by Fields and George Campbell; music by Richard Rodgers and Sigmund Romberg; lyrics with Alex Gerber); *Dearest Enemy*, 1925 (libretto by Fields; music by Rodgers); *The Garrick Gaieties*, 1925 (music by Rodgers); *The Girl Friend*, 1926 (libretto by Fields; music by Rodgers); *Peggy-Ann*, 1926 (libretto by Fields; music by Rodgers); *Betsy*, 1926 (libretto by Irving Caesar, David Freedman, and Anthony McGuire; music by Rodgers); *A Connecticut Yankee*, 1927 (libretto by Fields; music by Rodgers); *Chee-Chee*, 1928 (libretto by Fields; music by Rodgers); *Present Arms*, 1928 (libretto by Fields; music by Rodgers); *She's My Baby*, 1928 (libretto by Bert Kalmar and Harry Ruby; music by Rodgers); *Heads Up!*, 1929 (libretto by John McGowan and Paul Gerard Smith; music by Rodgers); *Spring Is Here*, 1929 (libretto by Owen Davis; music by Rodgers); *Simple Simon*, 1930 (libretto by Guy Bolton and Ed Wynn; music by Rodgers); *America's Sweetheart*, 1931 (libretto by Fields; music by Rodgers); *Jumbo*, 1935 (libretto by Ben Hecht and Charles MacArthur; music and lyrics by Rodgers and Hart); *On Your Toes*, 1936 (libretto by Rodgers, George Abbott, and Hart; music by Rodgers); *Babes in Arms*, 1937 (libretto by Rodgers and Hart; music by Rodgers); *I'd Rather Be Right*, 1937 (libretto by George S. Kaufman and Moss Hart; music by Rodgers); *The Boys from Syracuse*, 1938 (libretto by Abbott; based on William Shakespeare's play *The Comedy of Errors*; music by Rodgers); *I Married an Angel*, 1938 (libretto by Rodgers and Hart; based on a play by Johann Vaszary; music by Rodgers); *Too Many Girls*, 1939 (libretto by George Marion, Jr.; music by Rodgers); *Higher and Higher*, 1940 (libretto by Gladys Hurlbut and Joshua Logan; music by Rodgers); *Pal Joey*, 1940 (libretto by John O'Hara; music by Rodgers); *By Jupiter*, 1942 (libretto by Rodgers and Hart; based on Julian F. Thompson's *The Warrior Husband*; music by Rodgers); *Rodgers and Hart*, 1975 (libretto by Richard Lewine and John Fearnley; music by Rodgers).

The Life

Lorenz Milton Hart was born in New York City, the older of two sons of Freida and Max Hart, Jewish immigrants to the United States. Lorenz was a distant descendant of the German poet Heinrich Heine, and he was fluent in German from boyhood. He attended Columbia University, but he dropped out of college to work in the Schubert Theater organization in New York City. Known as Larry from an early age, Hart was a short man with a large head. Although he was quick-witted, articulate, and funny, women did not find him attractive as a romantic companion. As one friend observed, since he could not find love with the opposite sex, he turned to the only other sex there was.

In 1919 Hart met Richard Rodgers, an aspiring songwriter. During the next twenty-five years, they became one of the most popular songwriting teams of the era. For Hart, their professional success came at a personal price. By the early 1940's, Hart's troubles took a toll on his health. Because Hart was drinking heavily and conflicted about his sexuality, he and Rodgers found it more difficult to work together. When Rodgers decided to collaborate with Oscar Hammerstein II on what became *Oklahoma!*, the Rodgers and Hart partnership ended in bitterness. Hart died in November, 1943, from the effects of pneumonia and exposure brought on by excessive drinking.

The Music

Collaborating with Rodgers. When they began their partnership, Rodgers and Hart shared similar ideas about the nature of popular songs. They wanted to avoid conventional rhymes and trite images in order to explore the language of the city. In the beginning, they experienced difficulty in persuading theatrical producers to use their unconventional work. One song, "Any Old Place with You," enjoyed a brief success, but it was not enough.

Success came in 1925, when their song "Manhattan" was the big hit of *The Garrick Gaieties*, an annual revue composed of individual sketches and songs. On opening night, "Manhattan" stopped the show, with the audience demanding repeated renditions. Hart's engaging lyrics about summer journeys to Niagara and the fantasies of boys and girls on the sidewalks of New York captivated listeners. For the next eighteen years, Hart and Rodgers had one hit show after another. They learned that the only sure recipe for failure was to repeat what they had done before.

From Broadway to Hollywood and Back. In this working relationship, Hart proved a frustrating partner. Rodgers wrote melodies with great ease, and then he had to wait for Hart's lyrics. While he could dash off a lyric quickly, Hart often disappeared for days without an explanation. He required the stimulation of a situation within a show or a deadline to do his best work. For the punctual and meticulous Rodgers, these traits proved increasingly difficult to tolerate.

Still, Hart had an uncanny facility for writing both songs and their lyrics. The most noteworthy example occurred when the two men were in Paris, riding in a taxi with several women. A collision took place, and after the crash one of the women observed to her companions, "My heart stood still." From the taxi floor, where he had been thrown by the impact, Hart told Rodgers that the phrase would make a great title for a song, and so it did.

During the second half of the 1920's, they wrote such shows as *Dearest Enemy*, *The Girl Friend*, and *A Connecticut Yankee* with numerous hit songs. During the early 1930's, the team moved to Hollywood and motion pictures. Although they wrote some good songs, such as "Isn't It Romantic" and "Blue Moon," in this period, the two men were not happy with how filmmakers treated them. They returned to New York and Broadway to began their most productive time as songwriters. Hart's lyrics for shows such as *Jumbo*, *On Your Toes*, and *Babes in Arms* displayed his prodigious talent. Perhaps the show that best defined what Hart could accomplish was *Pal Joey*, with such hits as "Bewitched" and "I Could Write a Book."

Musical Legacy

Hart began his career at a time when American popular song lyrics lacked sophistication and wit. He brought a poetic sensibility to his craft, along with a determination to have the words of his songs reflect the language of everyday people. At his best in songs such as "My Romance," "My Funny Valentine," and "The Lady Is a Tramp," Hart combined intricate rhymes with emotional energy and power. He also explored complex emotions, such as the sense of knowing someone even though the

Lorenz Hart (right) with Richard Rodgers. (Library of Congress)

599

couple had just met in "Where or When." Hart captured the rhythms and vernacular of the 1920's and 1930's in enduring songs such as "Thou Swell." The works of Rodgers and Hart demonstrated that popular songs could attain a significant level of artistic excellence.

Although Hart was largely forgotten when Rodgers joined Hammerstein to create such hit musicals such as *The King and I* (1951) and *South Pacific* (1949), his reputation rebounded as singers and musicians revived his songs and recognized what an important influence he had had on popular music.

Lewis L. Gould

Further Reading

Furia, Philip. *The Poets of Tin Pan Alley: A History of America's Great Lyricists.* New York: Oxford University Press, 1990. This resource provides a perceptive and informed chapter on Hart's lyrics.

Hart, Dorothy, and Robert Kimball, eds. *The Complete Lyrics of Lorenz Hart.* New York: Knopf, 1986. This indispensable guide to Hart's career offers a look at the innovative lyrics he provided to musical theater.

Nolan, Frederick W. *Lorenz Hart: A Poet on Broadway.* New York: Oxford University Press, 1994. This well-researched biography of Hart offers a look at the life and career of the lyricist. While Hart helped to revitalize the songs of Broadway, his erratic behavior cost his successful partnership with Rodgers.

Rodgers, Richard. *The Rodgers and Hart Songbook.* New York: Simon & Schuster, 1951. Rodgers provides a fascinating biographical essay about his partner.

Sheed, Wilfred. *The House That George Built.* New York: Random House, 2007. This lively history of American songwriting provides some comments on Hart's influence.

Wilk, Max. *They're Playing Our Song: The Truth Behind the Words and Music of Three Generations.* New York: Moyer and Bell, 1991. This history of songs has an informative and insightful chapter on Hart.

See also: Berlin, Irving; Chevalier, Maurice; Cohan, George M.; Hammerstein, Oscar, II;

Jordan, Louis; Lee, Peggy; McPartland, Marian; Mercer, Johnny; Newman, Alfred; Porter, Cole; Rodgers, Richard; Romberg, Sigmund; Simone, Nina; Tormé, Mel.

Coleman Hawkins
American tenor saxophonist

Hawkins is generally recognized as the first great tenor saxophonist in jazz. He influenced virtually all subsequent players on all types of saxophones in the jazz world.

Born: November 21, 1904; St. Joseph, Missouri
Died: May 19, 1969; New York, New York
Also known as: Coleman Randolph Hawkins (full name); Hawk; Bean

Principal recordings

ALBUMS: *April in Paris, Featuring Body and Soul,* 1936; *The King of the Tenor Sax,* 1943; *Coleman Hawkins/Lester Young,* 1945 (with Lester Young); *Hawk in Flight,* 1947; *The Hawk Returns,* 1954; *The Tenor Sax Album,* 1954; *Cool Groove,* 1955; *The Hawk in Hi Fi,* 1956; *The Hawk in Paris,* 1956; *Coleman Hawkins Encounters Ben Webster,* 1957 (with Ben Webster); *The Genius of Coleman Hawkins,* 1957; *The Hawk Flies High,* 1957; *Standards and Warhorses,* 1957 (with Red Allen); *Coleman Hawkins and His Friends at a Famous Jazz Party,* 1958 (with others); *Coleman Hawkins Meets the Sax Section,* 1958; *High and Mighty Hawk,* 1958; *Soul,* 1958; *Coleman Hawkins with the Red Garland Trio,* 1959 (with the Red Garland Trio); *Hawk Eyes,* 1959; *Stasch,* 1959; *At Ease with Coleman Hawkins,* 1960; *Coleman Hawkins All Stars,* 1960; *In a Mellow Tone,* 1960; *Night Hawk,* 1960 (with Eddie Davis); *Swingville,* 1960 (with Coleman Hawkins All Stars); *The Hawk Relaxes,* 1961; *Jam Session in Swingville,* 1961 (with Pee Wee Russell); *Jazz Reunion,* 1961 (with others); *Alive!,* 1962 (with Roy Eldridge and Johnny Hodges); *Desafinado: Bossa Nova and Jazz Samba,* 1962; *Duke Ellington Meets Coleman Hawkins,* 1962; *Good Old Broadway,* 1962; *No Strings,* 1962; *Plays Make*

Someone Happy, 1962; *Hawk Talk*, 1963; *Sonny Meets Hawk*, 1963; *Today and Now*, 1963; *Wrapped Tight*, 1965; *Sirius*, 1966; *Supreme*, 1966.

The Life

Coleman Randolph Hawkins was born in St. Joseph, Missouri. His parents had one other child, a girl who died one year before Coleman was born. His father was an electrical engineer; his mother taught him to play the piano at the age of five. He also learned to play the cello before taking up the instrument with which he became associated, the saxophone. He attended high school in Chicago and in Topeka, Kansas, where he also studied harmony and composition at Washburn College.

Hawkins was a music professional when only sixteen. In 1921, while playing in a theater orchestra in Kansas City, he was signed by Mamie Smith, a black singer whose Jazz Hounds was one of the first African American jazz groups to be recorded regularly. In 1924 he joined the band of one of the foremost jazz musicians, Fletcher Henderson. In ten years with Henderson, a long stint for a jazz musician at the time, he developed a highly innovative style.

By 1934 many opportunities for black American musicians were developing in Europe. From March, 1934, Hawkins worked in Britain, France, Holland, Switzerland, Belgium, and the Scandinavian countries for more than five years. His associations there included the great British orchestra leader Jack Hylton, who had invited Hawkins to play with his orchestra; Django Reinhardt, the most renowned European guitarist; and another American who was also touring Europe at the time, Benny Carter. Hawkins is credited with raising the level of European jazz to a new height. By 1939, however, he, along with many other Americans abroad, returned from the wartorn European continent as World War II escalated.

At this point, Hawkins's style reached a peak, especially with his highly original yet popular recording of "Body and Soul." For two years he led his own bands and then toured with small bands. He continued to perform with important jazz figures of the 1920's and 1930's but also appeared with bebop organizations that developed in the mid-1940's, playing with Dizzy Gillespie as early as 1943. In his own band in 1944 he employed and

played the compositions of pianist Thelonious Monk and helped raise Monk to prominence.

Among his later successes were a return trip to Europe in 1954, recordings with Duke Ellington in 1962, and many appearances at the Village Vanguard in Manhattan. Although he had a problem with alcohol in his last years, he worked until shortly before his death in 1969. He was survived by his wife, Delores, his son Rene, and his two daughters, Mimi and Colette.

The Music

The saxophone, with few exceptions an unpopular instrument in the performance of classical music, was not used in the ragtime era from the late 1890's until well into the 1910's. A few early jazz musicians played it in the World War I period (1914-1919), but these men did not become important figures, and they employed the tenor saxophone as a rhythmical instrument, not a melodic one. Coleman Hawkins has generally received

Coleman Hawkins. (AP/Wide World Photos)

credit from jazz historians for making the tenor saxophone a staple of jazz music. Influenced by Louis Armstrong, who revolutionized trumpet playing, Hawkins did the same thing with the saxophone. He introduced a smoother and more rhythmical tonguing of his instrument and adopted hard and heavy reeds that his contemporaries did not have the strength to use.

Hawkins was a competitive man with the urge to outdo his contemporaries, but his originality involved a great capacity for listening and learning from other musicians. He could adapt to the tenor saxophone the best musical expressions that he heard on other instruments. By the late 1930's he was able to do what only Armstrong had done: interpret the songs that he played—in effect recompose them—in performances that went far beyond the intentions of the original composer. He was one of the great energizers of European jazz during his five years abroad. His unique style became the standard for almost all saxophonists, especially tenor saxophonists in the field of jazz.

"One Hour." It must be remembered that performances of jazz music, especially in recordings before the time of long-playing (LP) records and later developments such as compact discs (CDs), usually lasted about three minutes, and a new and important stage of a musician's development might be reflected in several recordings made at about the same time. Therefore, it is sometimes difficult to choose one banner performance by Hawkins. In 1929, Hawkins, while a member of the Fletcher Henderson orchestra, on occasion played with other organizations, including McKinney's Cotton Pickers and the Mound City Blue Blowers. Within a week he recorded with both these bands, and in each case the style he had been developing in this decade became obvious.

"One Hour," with the latter group, can be associated with James P. Johnson's song "If I Could Be with You One Hour Tonight," still well known many decades later. Although Johnson's melody is never heard directly, "One Hour" is clearly based on its chords. A six-measure introduction by Hawkins, in which he abandons the conventional staccato rhythm employing short notes that even he had been relying upon and instead offers a legato style with descending figures that would become one of the features of his later playing. This perfor-

mance illustrates the improvisational approach to familiar songs that is taken for granted today but was unknown in jazz at that time. Critic Gary Giddins considers this eighteen-measure solo to be the first "entirely successful tenor solo."

"Body and Soul." Hawkins recorded one of the most famous of all jazz performances on October 11, 1939, in the RCA studio in New York City. The song was "Body and Soul," composed nine years earlier by John Green. The theme of this song is never stated directly, although it is recognizable in the early measures of the recording. Thereafter the performance is all an improvisation, grounded on Hawkins's grasp of the song's melodic and rhythmical possibilities. Today it sounds conventional, but that is because instrumentalists after Hawkins enthusiastically adapted his kind of jazz invention.

Like Armstrong's interpretation of "West End Blues" eleven years earlier, Hawkins "Body and Soul" was recognized as entirely original, both in way he played the tenor saxophone and in his method of recording the song. Although truly original work is often not recognized as such until long afterward, this recording proved to be enormously popular. Hawkins had been developing this style for many years, and thus his interpretation of "Body and Soul" was not a sudden breakthrough into a new style of playing the saxophone but rather a particularly pure example of a style he had been perfecting in his decades with the Fletcher Henderson orchestra.

He was immediately obliged to repeat his performance, which he sometimes did on recordings and sometimes transformed extensively. It is likely that he had performed it many times on the European tour that he had just concluded, but now his fans demanded it, and he would continue to play it throughout his career. He began to play an expanded version of the song that fall of 1939 while fronting a band he had organized. Using the harmonies of the song, he elaborated the possibilities of the earlier three-minute recording, moving from a lower range upward in the second chorus. Despite the tedium of repeating this popular number, Hawkins was able, twenty years later, to perform it with enormous success at the Chicago Playboy Jazz Festival.

"Picasso." In 1948 Norman Granz, who produced a number of important jazz performances, issued "Picasso" on his Clef Record label. Hawkins recorded this work either in that year or perhaps somewhat earlier. It was an unaccompanied saxophone solo, an innovation at the time. Hawkins mingled dramatic passages with free-form excursions in a remarkable display. The title reflects Granz's interest in artist Pablo Picasso, although for Hawkins the Pablo who beguiled him was the great cellist, Pablo Casals. Having played the piano and cello before taking up the saxophone, and continuing to play them for his own satisfaction, Hawkins was able to use his insights into the capacities of the piano and the cello in this solo recording of "Picasso" on the tenor saxophone.

"Mood Indigo." Until 1962, when Hawkins was in his late fifties and Duke Ellington in his early sixties, the two men had never recorded together, probably because Ellington's orchestra had over the years included several outstanding saxophonists, such as Ben Webster, whose style Hawkins had obviously influenced. Now, with Webster on his own, Hawkins joined with Ellington and six members of his orchestra for an album called *Duke Ellington Meets Coleman Hawkins*. It included several Ellington compositions, among them a six-minute version of his already famous "Mood Indigo," which became a highlight of this recording session. This is the only recorded combination of these two powerhouses of jazz late in their careers, but it took place while each was still performing at a high level.

Musical Legacy

Coleman Hawkins was essentially a gifted soloist, the first outstanding tenor saxophonist in jazz. Although he led his own musical groups at times, his temperament did not permit him to guide and discipline other musicians, who for him were essentially accompanists, and his own orchestras were not outstanding. Highly competitive, he enjoyed matching skills with other performers. It has been argued that he influenced virtually all later tenor saxophonists with the exception of Lester Young, the first man recognized as having defeated Hawkins in a jam session.

Hawkins was one of the most influential jazz musicians in style and technique. He moved away from the old "slap-tongue" style to a more powerful, fluent, legato manner of playing and character-istically projected an exciting, driving rhythm. Because he was adept at both piano and cello, Hawkins was able to bring a measure of their polyphonic capacities to a single-note instrument. His style drew adherents throughout the 1930's, and in the following decade Hawkins did what few of his contemporaries, the jazz musicians born before World War I, attempted. He encouraged younger musicians like Thelonious Monk and Miles Davis and performed with Dizzy Gillespie, Max Roach, and Sonny Rollins and other jazzmen of the bebop era, even as he continued his associations with the men who dominated jazz between the two world wars. As late as the 1960's, Hawkins, who had made the tenor saxophone a melodic instrument and performed for more than forty years, remained a major force in jazz music.

Robert P. Ellis

Further Reading

Chilton, John. *The Song of the Hawk.* Ann Arbor: University of Michigan Press, 1990. Hawkins has not been blessed with an outstanding biography, but this work by a significant British jazz historian is the most informative work.

Giddins, Gary. *Visions of Jazz: The First Century.* New York: Oxford University Press, 1998. The chapter on Hawkins is a good short biography, including accounts of the author's personal observations of the saxophonist's late concerts.

Hentoff, Nat. *Jazz Is.* New York: Random House, 1976. Hentoff's short section on Hawkins contains an account of the first time he was beaten in one of the saxophone competitions that were part of the jazz ritual known as the jam session.

Kirchner, Bill, ed. *The Oxford Companion to Jazz.* New York: Oxford University Press, 2000. The Hawkins chapter highlights some of his major performances, especially in the 1940's, when he collaborated with several young musicians who transformed jazz after World War II.

Schuller, Gunther. *The Swing Era: The Development of Jazz, 1930-1945.* New York: Oxford University Press, 1989. Schuller's chapter on Hawkins contains eight reproductions of musical examples transcribed by the author from recordings.

See also: Bechet, Sidney; Carter, Benny; Coltrane, John; Ellington, Duke; Gillespie, Dizzy;

Hampton, Lionel; Hancock, Herbie; Henderson, Fletcher; Holiday, Billie; Jones, Hank; Lewis, John; Monk, Thelonious; Navarro, Fats; Parker, Charlie; Powell, Bud; Roach, Max; Rollins, Sonny; Smith, Bessie; Smith, Mamie; Sun Ra; Webster, Ben; Young, Lester.

Isaac Hayes

American rhythm-and-blues singer, songwriter, pianist, and saxophone player

Hayes excelled in producing the Memphis sound, a style of soul music that blended gospel and blues and that inspired funk, disco, and hip-hop. In addition, he was a noted composer of motion-picture scores.

Born: August 20, 1942; Covington, Tennessee
Died: August 10, 2008; Memphis, Tennessee
Also known as: Isaac Lee Hayes, Jr. (full name); Ike
Member of: The Mar-Keys

Principal works

FILM SCORES: *Maidstone*, 1970; *Shaft*, 1971; *Tough Guys*, 1974; *Truck Turner*, 1974; *Ninth Street*, 1999; *Bui Doi*, 2001.

Principal recordings

ALBUMS (solo): *Presenting Isaac Hayes*, 1967; *Hot Buttered Soul*, 1969; *The Isaac Hayes Movement*, 1970; . . . *To Be Continued*, 1970; *Black Moses*, 1971; *Shaft*, 1971; *In the Beginning*, 1972; *Joy*, 1973; *Tough Guys*, 1974; *Truck Turner*, 1974; *Chocolate Chip*, 1975; *Disco Connection*, 1976; *Groove-a-Thon*, 1976; *Juicy Fruit*, 1976; *A Man and a Woman*, 1977 (with Dionne Warwick); *New Horizon*, 1977; *For the Sake of Love*, 1978; *Hotbed*, 1978; *Don't Let Go*, 1979; *And Once Again*, 1980; *Royal Rappins*, 1980 (with Millie Jackson); *Lifetime Thing*, 1981; *U-Turn*, 1986; *Love Attack*, 1988; *Wonderful*, 1994; *Branded*, 1995; *Raw and Refined*, 1995; *Instrumentals*, 2003.
ALBUM (with the Mar-Keys): *The Great Memphis Sound*, 1966.

The Life

Born into poverty in Covington, Tennessee, Isaac Lee Hayes, Jr., was the second child of sharecroppers Isaac Hayes, Sr., and Eula Hayes. The Hayes children were orphaned early, and they were raised by their grandparents. Hayes picked cotton and performed other menial labor to help make ends meet. Although he dropped out of Manassas High School, he returned at age twenty-one to earn a diploma.

A gospel singer as a child, Hayes learned to play saxophone and piano in his teens, performing with numerous local groups. In the early 1960's, Hayes became a session musician with Stax Records, and he contributed as a songwriter (in collaboration with David Porter), an arranger, and a producer. He produced hits for many artists, especially Sam and Dave, in the process creating what came to be known as the Memphis sound. Later, he earned a reputation in his own right as a performer and a composer. He founded his own record label, Hot Buttered Soul, in 1975, but he was forced to declare bankruptcy before making a comeback later in the decade. Beginning in the mid-1970's, he appeared frequently in films and on television shows, including a long run on the animated series *South Park*.

Well known for his humanitarian work—particularly in support of literacy—and a controversial figure for his association with Scientology, Hayes resided in Memphis, where he hosted a popular radio show and owned two restaurants. The father of twelve children, he lived with his fourth wife, Adjowa, who gave birth to their son Nana in 2006. On August 10, 2008, the sixty-five-year-old Hayes collapsed and died at his home in Memphis.

The Music

Hayes became a driving force in African American music during the height of the civil rights era of the early 1960's. He was a leader in creating what became known as the Memphis sound, a form of soul music that blended the spiritual feel of gospel with the secular subject matter of blues. He borrowed shouts, call-and-response, and vocal harmonic style from gospel, and then he added horns to emphasize and underscore particular vocal phrases, encouraged instrumental improvisation, and stressed strong bass lines and clear-cut rhythm with a hard-hitting backbeat. Hayes's musical production dropped off in the early 1980's as tastes and styles changed. At the same time, he devoted more energy to acting, appearing in television series such as *The Rockford Files*, *The A-Team*, *Miami Vice*. From 1997 to 2006, he was the voice of Chef on the animated series *South Park*. He also appeared in such films as *Escape from New York* (1981), *I'm Gonna Get You Sucka* (1988), and *Johnny Mnemonic* (1995).

Early Works. Though other artists recorded songs composed at Stax Records by the team of Hayes and Porter, it was Sam and Dave (Samuel David Moore and Dave Prater) that had the greatest success. Between 1965 and 1970, Hayes and Porter wrote more than a dozen rhythm-and-blues/soul hits for Sam and Dave that performed well on pop charts in the United States and in England. The best-known songs included "Hold On! I'm Comin'" (1966), "When Something Is Wrong with My Baby" (1967), "Soul Man" (1967), and "I Thank You" (1968).

Hot Buttered Soul. A studio album released in 1969, this represented Hayes's second solo effort, and it was a major departure from typical soul recordings of the day. Instead of the usual series of short songs appropriate for singles, *Hot Buttered Soul* presented just four cuts, from the five-minute-long original about adultery, "One Woman," to an eighteen-minute version of Jimmy Webb's "By the Time I Get to Phoenix," featuring narration and full orchestration complete with horns, strings, and chorus bolstered with delayed reverb.

Shaft. Hayes may be best remembered for this double-disc release that contains highlights from the sound track of the Metro-Goldwyn-Mayer black private-eye film *Shaft* (1971), which Hayes scored. The primarily instrumental album, which reached number one on the *Billboard* black and jazz charts, produced "Theme from Shaft," which reached number one on the *Billboard* Hot 100 list, remaining on the charts for more than a year. *Shaft* garnered three Grammy Awards (Best Instrumental Composition for Motion Picture or Television, Best Engineered Recording, Best Instrumental Arrangement). Hayes—who had a cameo role in the film—also won an Academy Award for Best Original Composition, the first African American to earn an Oscar in a nonacting role.

New Horizon. This 1977 release was Hayes's well-received and critically acclaimed rhythm-and-blues/soul debut with a new label, Polydor. A live

Isaac Hayes. (AP/Wide World Photos)

album, and a comeback of sorts for Hayes, it featured duets with singer Dionne Warwick, and had several tracks that proved popular with listeners, including the hit "Out of the Ghetto"; a ballad, "It's Heaven to Me"; and the erotic dance tune "Moonlight Lovin' (Menage a Trois)."

Branded. A 1995 release on Virgin Records, this album marked another Hayes comeback, after his long hiatus in the late 1980's and early 1990's. A mix of fast-paced, funky jams and slowed-down love ballads showcasing Hayes's distinctive voice, *Branded* is considered a masterpiece of vocal and instrumental arrangements. Outstanding cuts include "Thanks to the Fool," "Soulsville," "Summer in the City," "I'll Do Anything (To Turn You On)," and a reworking of Sting's "Fragile."

Musical Legacy

Hayes built an impressive body of work since he started as a keyboard player in the house band at Stax Records in the early 1960's. With partner Porter, Hayes gained fame as a songwriter and producer, helping pen a string of hits for Sam and Dave. Throughout his Grammy and Academy

Award-winning solo career he broke new ground: blending black and white musical styles, mixing the sacred and the secular, merging funk with unusual orchestrations, and creating extended mini-symphonies of soul that shattered preconceptions of pop music. In the process, he pioneered a fresh, instantly recognizable form that inspired later artists, setting the stage for further expansion of African American music. A leader of innovation by example, Hayes was inducted into the Rock and Roll Hall of Fame in 2002.

Jack Ewing

Further Reading

Bowman, Rob. *Soulsville, U.S.A.: The Story of Stax Records*. Woodbridge, Conn.: Schirmer Trade Books, 2003. This is a history of the influential record label, where Hayes began his career, with interviews and photographs.

Goldman, Vivien. *The Black Chord*. New York: Universe, 1999. An overview of African American music, from ancient roots to the present, this contains an introduction by Hayes and many photographs.

Gordon, Robert. *It Came From Memphis*. New York: Atria, 2001. This book provides unusual insight into the hidden character of the city called the birthplace of rock and roll. Includes references to Hayes and photographs.

Guralick, Peter. *Sweet Soul Music: Rhythm and Blues and the Southern Dream of Freedom*. New York: Back Bay Books, 1999. This book focuses on Stax Records and its involvement in the evolution of contemporary rhythm and blues. Includes profiles of artists, among them Hayes, and criticism.

Hayes, Isaac, and Susan DiSesa. *Cooking with Heart and Soul*. New York: Putnam, 2000. This autobiographical cookbook offers background information on Hayes and recipes for down-home cuisine. Includes photographs.

See also: King, Albert; Pickett, Wilson; Sting; Webb, Jimmy.

Jascha Heifetz

Lithuanian American classical violinist

Heifetz was known for interpretations of violin works that emphasized fast tempi, an intense vibrato, and a powerful tone. Later in life he became a pedagogue, but his principal influence upon the world of music was as an inimitable performer.

Born: February 2, 1901; Vilna, Lithuania, Russian Empire (now in Lithuania)
Died: December 10, 1987; Los Angeles, California
Also known as: Iosef Ruvinovich Heifetz (full name)

Principal recordings

ALBUMS: *Bach: Sonatas and Partitas*, 1952; *Beethoven: Sonatas*, 1952; *Conus: Concerto in E Minor*, 1952; *Spohr: Concerto No. 8*, 1954; *Brahms: Violin Concerto in D Major, Op. 77*, 1955 (with Fritz Reiner and the Chicago Symphony Orchestra); *Beethoven: Concerto*, 1956; *Mozart: Sinfonia Concertante*, 1956; *Tchaikovsky: Concerto for Violin in D Major, Op. 35*, 1957 (with Reiner and the Chicago Symphony Orchestra); *Mendelssohn: Violin Concerto in E Minor, Op. 64*, 1959 (with Charles Munch and the Boston Symphony Orchestra); *Prokofiev: Violin Concerto No. 2 in G Minor, Op. 63*, 1959 (with Munch and the Boston Symphony Orchestra); *Sibelius: Violin Concerto in D Minor, Op. 47*, 1959 (with Walter Hendl and the Chicago Symphony Orchestra); *Bach: Concerto for Two Violins*, 1961 (with Sir Malcolm Sargent and the New Symphony Orchestra of London); *Bruch: Scottish Fantasy in E-flat Major, Op. 46*, 1961 (with Sargent and the New Symphony Orchestra of London); *Glazunov: Concerto for Violin in A Minor, Op. 82*, 1963 (with Hendl and the RCA Victor Symphony Orchestra); *George Gershwin: Three Preludes*, 1965 (with Brooks Smith); *Bach: Chaconne from Partita No. 2 in D Minor*, 1970; *Tchaikovsky: Sérénade Mélancolique for Violin and Orchestra in B Minor, Op. 26*, 1970.

The Life

Following early lessons on a quarter-sized violin with his father, Iosef Ruvinovich "Jascha" Heifetz

(JAH-shah HI-fehts) continued his studies at age five with Ilya Malkin, a student of Leopold Auer (the leading violin professor in Russia at the turn of the twentieth century). Later, Heifetiz studied in St. Petersburg, Russia, with Auer himself. At age ten, Heifetz embarked upon concert tours, leading to debuts around the world, repeat engagements, and recording contracts. His life was so intimately bound with his music that it is nearly impossible to separate the man from the violin. He became a naturalized citizen of the United States in 1925, an act that caused the Soviet Union to label him essentially a traitor and to disparage him in the Russian press. Later in his life, the Russian musical and political establishment worked to humiliate his students (especially Erick Friedman) when they entered the international Tchaikovsky Competition held in Moscow.

Heifetz married a silent film actress named Florence Vidor in 1928, and they had two children, Josefa and Robert. The couple divorced in 1945. He married Frances Spiegelberg in 1947, and the couple had a son named Joseph (who is a photographer in Australia). The couple divorced in 1962.

In 1953 Heifetz suffered minor arm injuries when he was attacked in Jerusalem following a concert on which he had programmed the violin sonata by Richard Strauss, disdaining an Israeli ban at the time that prohibited performances of music by German composers. In the late 1950's, he curtailed his performing career, which had included more than one hundred concerts a year, adding other musical roles, such as recording and teaching, to his life and also spending more time at his home in California, where he enjoyed tennis, Ping-Pong, and sailing. He retired from performing completely following a televised broadcast of his final concert on October 23, 1972. For fifteen more years, he continued to teach, and his teaching studio, which was designed by Frank Lloyd Wright, is preserved in the Colburn School of Music in downtown Los Angeles. Heifetz died at Cedars-Sinai Medical Center in Los Angeles on December 10, 1987.

The Music

At age six, Heifetz performed Felix Mendelssohn's Violin Concerto in E Minor (1845) before an audience of a thousand people. By age eleven, he had logged a debut in St. Petersburg and in Berlin. The teacher who changed Heifetz's life was Auer, who took Heifetz as a student in 1910. Auer imparted to Heifetz the essentials of technique and of interpretation in the Russian tradition that remained with him throughout his career. These characteristics included the high right elbow and the strongly angled bow fingers (since dubbed the Russian bow grip). Another is audible portamenti and shifts between notes (since called Russian or Heifetz shifts), in which a violinist changes position using the finger that will play the note following the shift rather than the finger playing the note prior to the shift (called a French-style shift).

Jascha Heifetz. (Library of Congress)

Early Performances. Heifetz's official debut in St. Petersburg occurred on April 30, 1911, before an audience of about twenty-five thousand, and his European debut occurred on October 28, 1912, when he performed Peter Ilich Tchaikovsky's Violin Concerto (1878) with the Berlin Philharmonic. It appears, however, that it was his New York debut in 1917 (at the age of sixteen) that sparked the sensation that he maintained for more than fifty years.

From 1917, Heifetz performed with every major orchestra in the world, and in recital venues of all levels of prestige. His most frequent accompanists throughout his career were André Benoist, Samuel Chotzinoff, Isidor Achron, Emanuel Bay, and Brooks Smith. Additionally, he collaborated frequently as a chamber musician with cellists Emanuel Feuermann and Gregor Piatigorsky, pianist Artur Rubinstein, and violist William Primrose.

Rock Star Status. Between 1920 and 1940, Heifetz acquired a status that in the twenty-first century has been granted only to rock, pop, and motion picture stars. Would-be concert attendees in the 1920's who could not get tickets to a Heifetz concert exhibited unruly behavior. The violinist required police protection after at least one of his early concerts in Russia because the fervor of his adoring public was so great.

Stories floated around him, including reports that world-famous violinist Fritz Kreisler said, upon hearing Heifetz perform, "Well, now the rest of us can all go and break our violins!" Another story, reputedly at Heifetz's sensational New York debut in 1917, involved the great violinist Mischa Elman. Elman complained to his pianist friend Leopold Godowsky that it was awfully hot in the concert hall, to which Godowsky replied, "Not for pianists!"

Technique and Repertoire. Heifetz's intensity of tone and vibrato, combined with the typically blistering speeds at which he took his tempi, created a style so unique that, though it was inimitable, most violinists who were students while Heifetz was performing attempted to imitate him, hoping for similar careers. Without exception, no one succeeded in this task (though his students Erick Friedman and Eugene Fodor probably came closest), and many students incurred problems with their violin playing for trying.

Heifetz's repertoire was encyclopedic, yet most critics believed that his strength was the repertoire of the Romantic and twentieth century eras. Though he recorded and performed music by Johann Sebastian Bach and the classic composers, his interpretations of this repertoire met with mixed reviews more frequently than his interpretations of the music of Ludwig van Beethoven, Johannes Brahms, Max Bruch, Jean Sibelius, Tchaikovsky, Erich Wolfgang Korngold, Jules Conus, and Sergei Prokofiev, for example.

Violins and Bows. Heifetz played three instruments throughout his life. His early instrument was a 1736 violin fashioned by the Venetian maker Carlo Tononi, which Heifetz used till about 1937. In that year, he acquired on loan (and later purchased in 1951) the 1714 Dolphin Stradivarius. Heifetz's favorite violin was the 1742 Ferdinand David Guarnerius del Gésu (named for its former owner, the concertmaster of the Leipzig Gewandhaus Orchestra, who premiered Felix Mendelssohn's violin concerto). Heifetz habitually strung these violins with gut or wound gut strings and with a gold E string. He collected a variety of bows by famous French makers, but a Nikolaus Kittel bow given to Heifetz by Auer was his prized bow. Heifetz bequeathed his Tononi to his student Sherry Kloss, and his Guarneri to the San Francisco Legion of Honor Museum, from where it is occasionally loaned for use by celebrated violinists (currently San Francisco Symphony concertmaster Alexander Barantschik). The Dolphin Stradivarius was bought by the Nippon Foundation.

The Critics. Critical reactions to Heifetz's performance style ranged across a spectrum of opinion. Positive reviews typically spoke of his "silken tone, technical perfection, and regard for the composer's slightest markings" (Harold Schonberg in *The New York Times*). Others called him "a modern miracle." Not all reviews were completely favorable, and those less positive tended toward descriptors such as "cold," "impersonal," or "austere."

Arrangements. Throughout his career, but principally during the World War II years, Heifetz arranged many short character pieces for his use as encores or for entertainment for the Allied troops in Europe. Most famous among these arrangements were *Hora Staccato* (1906) by Grigoras Dinicu, *The Girl with the Flaxen Hair* (1910) and *Golliwog's Cake-*

walk (1909) by Claude Debussy, *Three Preludes* (1926) by George Gershwin, and *Estrellita* (1912) by Manuel Ponce.

Film Appearances. In 1939 Heifetz made his film debut in *And They Shall Have Music* (1939). Serving largely as a vehicle for Heifetz's performance, this film has a loose story line about a music school that needs his philanthropy to survive. In 1946 Heifetz, using the pseudonym Jim Hoyl, composed a successful popular song entitled *When You Make Love to Me, Don't Make Believe,* which was sung and recorded by Bing Crosby and Margaret Whiting. In 1949 he invented and patented a rubber mute for the violin called the Heifetz Mute, which in its day had an advanced design over the traditional three-pronged wooden mutes because it could be placed, when not in use, between the strings behind the violin bridge.

Hiatuses. On several occasions throughout his career, Heifetz took sabbaticals from concertizing (one of these lasted about twenty months), during which time he rested from his arduous schedule, and he reputedly reconsidered his interpretations. However, several sources indicate that Heifetz's interpretations changed little over the span of his career, especially after he immigrated to America. In many ways, Heifetz embodied the quintessence of musical consistency.

Retirement and After. In 1972, at his final recital, Heifetz chose a program that was similar to programs he had done during his entire life: sonatas by César Franck and Richard Strauss, selections from Bach's Partita No. 3 in E Major (1720), and several encores by Debussy, Ernest Bloch, Kreisler, Sergei Rachmaninoff, and Maurice Ravel.

Following his retirement from the concert stage in 1972, Heifetz taught violin lessons and master classes at the University of California, Los Angeles and the University of Southern California (through 1983), several of which were videotaped and are available for viewing. His most famous students included, in addition to Friedman and Fodor, Yuval Yaron, Sherry Kloss, and Ayke Agus. (Kloss and Agus each wrote a book describing Heifetz as they knew him.) As a teacher, Heifetz produced fewer star protégés than other teachers, probably because of his inimitable style and because of his generally acknowledged impatience with student performances that lacked polish.

Musical Legacy

According to *The New York Times* critic Tim Page, Heifetz refused a request for an interview for a biography of his life. Page concluded that Heifetz was a fiercely private man with few friends, an estranged family (following the two divorces), and a life best documented from the stage and the recording.

Heifetz's legacy rests almost entirely with his performances and with his incredible recordings. An unsurpassed virtuoso, he left behind numerous arrangements of encores, and many important twentieth century violin concerti would have remained in obscurity without his promotion of them. He held himself to the highest standards, which might best be captured in his own words: "If I don't practice one day, I know it; if I miss two days, the critics know it; if I miss three days, the public knows it."

Heifetz received three Grammy Awards for chamber music recordings, he was posthumously awarded the Grammy Lifetime Achievement Award in 1989, and he was inducted into the Grammy Hall of Fame in 1999. He held an honorary doctorate from Northwestern University, and in 1957 he was granted membership in the French Legion of Honor.

Jonathan A. Sturm

Further Reading

Agus, Ayke. *Heifetz as I Knew Him.* New York: Amadeus Press, 2005. A portrait of Heifetz from one of his students and late-in-life violin studio accompanists.

Axelrod, Herbert. *Heifetz.* Neptune City, N.J.: Paganiniana, 1991. A biography of Heifetz by a noted music aficionado and violin collector.

Creighton, J. *Discopaedia of the Violin: 1889-1971.* Toronto, Ont.: University of Toronto Press, 1974. Covering nearly a century, a list of recordings by violinists, including Heifetz.

Flesch, Carl. *Memoirs.* London: Rockliff, 1960. Flesch was one of the great violin pedagogues of the early twentieth century, and his memoirs include mention of Heifetz.

Kloss, Sherry. *Jascha Heifetz Through My Eyes.* Muncie, Ind.: Kloss Classics, 2000. Another useful portrait of Heifetz from the eyes of a student, in this case the one to whom he gave his Tononi violin.

Weschler-Vered, Artur. *Jascha Heifetz*. New York: Music Sales, 1986. A biography of Heifetz that tends toward the adulatory; useful as a supplement, but not endorsed as an authoritative biography.

See also: Busch, Adolf; Crosby, Bing; Debussy, Claude; Korngold, Erich Wolfgang; Kreisler, Fritz; Oistrakh, David; Prokofiev, Sergei; Ravel, Maurice; Rózsa, Miklós; Rubinstein, Artur; Stern, Isaac; Strauss, Richard; Thomson, Virgil; Walton, Sir William.

Fletcher Henderson

American jazz composer, arranger, and pianist

Henderson's orchestra was one of the foremost in jazz throughout the 1920's and early 1930's, and he is credited with increasing the size of the standard big band. He was also a prominent arranger, contributing several of Benny Goodman's most famous arrangements.

Born: December 18, 1897; Cuthbert, Georgia
Died: December 29, 1952; New York, New York
Also known as: Fletcher Hamilton Henderson, Jr. (full name)
Member of: The Fletcher Henderson All Stars; Fletcher Henderson's Sextet

Principal recordings

ALBUMS: *Fletcher Henderson's Sextet*, 1950 (with Fletcher Henderson's Sextet); *The Big Reunion*, 1957 (with Fletcher Henderson's All Stars).

SINGLES (solo): "Charleston Crazy," 1923; "Down South Blues," 1923; "Just Hot," 1923; "Naughty Man," 1924; "Sud Bustin' Blues," 1924; "Florida Stomp," 1925; "Get It Fixed," 1925; "Hey Foot Straw Horse," 1925; "King Porter Stomp," 1925; "Sugar Foot Stomp," 1925; "Dynamite," 1926; "Hard to Get Gertie," 1926; "Hi Diddle Diddle," 1926; "Honeybunch," 1926; "Snag It," 1927; "I'm Feeling Devilish," 1928; "Keep a Song in Your Soul," 1930; "Oh It Looks Like Rain," 1931; "Poor Old Joe," 1932; "Sing Sing Sing," 1932; "Down South Camp Meeting,"

1934; "Happy as the Day Is Long," 1934; "Hocus Pocus," 1934; "Wrappin' It Up," 1934; "Christopher Columbus," 1936 (with Leon Berry); "Knock Knock Who's There," 1936.

The Life

Fletcher Hamilton Henderson, Jr., was raised in a musical household by his father, Fletcher Hamilton Henderson, Sr., and his mother, Ozie, a pianist and music teacher. Henderson began piano lessons at the age of six, and he was trained exclusively in European music with little exposure to the black folk tradition. He attended Atlanta University as a chemistry and mathematics major, and he moved to New York in 1920 to begin a career as a chemist. Opportunities for black chemists were few at the time, and Henderson took work as a musician.

Henderson's first position in New York City was as a song demonstrator for Pace-Handy Music Company, playing new songs on the piano to potential customers. In 1921 Harry Pace left the company and established Black Swan, the first record company owned and operated by blacks and devoted to black artists. Pace took Henderson to Black Swan, where his responsibilities included accompanying singers at the keyboard for their recordings (particularly blues singers, as blues music was growing immensely popular in black communities) and assembling and leading bands to back up the singers.

By 1923 Henderson had established a band that, in addition to accompanying singers for recordings, was performing regularly at dances and cabarets. That year Henderson's band, primarily a dance band, won an audition at Club Alabam. The group held a residency at Roseland, a ballroom club, in 1924. As music from the New Orleans and Chicago Dixieland groups gradually infiltrated New York, Henderson's orchestra began to turn to jazz.

By 1927 Henderson's orchestra was one of the most popular in the field. Henderson frequently sought out the best soloists, employing at various times players such as Louis Armstrong, Coleman Hawkins, and Rex Stewart. He also employed Don Redman, a reed player who arranged many songs for the group. In 1927 Redman left the group to arrange for McKinney's Cotton Pickers, leaving Henderson scrambling for arrangements.

In 1928 Henderson injured his head in a car accident. Prior to the accident, Henderson was known for being timid and ineffective as a leader, and the head injury possibly exacerbated these problems. His band members took advantage of Henderson's condition, showing up late to rehearsals and recording sessions, which resulted in erratic performance quality.

Henderson was too willing to turn over creative control of his group. In 1929 he accepted the firing of many of his players by a white revue conductor, which led to the breakup of the band. Henderson worked on rebuilding the band until 1931, when the group started recording again. Finding himself without an arranger, Henderson was forced to write some arrangements himself, launching a new career.

Henderson's band performed until 1934, when the members, tired of Henderson's lax leadership, turned in their notices all at once. The next year, a financially despondent Henderson sold a group of arrangements to Benny Goodman, who was in need of new music for his radio spot *Let's Dance.* Henderson's superb arrangements were partly responsible for Goodman's rapid rise to fame, and in 1939 Goodman hired Henderson as his arranger.

Henderson repeatedly tried to assemble bands throughout the 1930's and into the 1940's, but none was as successful or as stable as his late 1920's and early 1930's bands. In the 1940's, Henderson toured as the pianist and arranger for Ethel Waters, a singer with whom he worked at Black Swan. In 1950 Henderson suffered a stroke, and he died two years later.

The Music

Although Henderson was often ineffective at motivating his band members to perform to the best of their abilities, he excelled at finding the best soloists for his groups, often launching his band members into lengthy jazz careers. Hawkins was easily Henderson's star soloist, playing in the orchestra for ten years and becoming the most prominent tenor saxophonist in jazz until he was upstaged by Lester Young (who replaced Hawkins in Henderson's orchestra). Henderson hired the young Armstrong, who played in the band for a little more than a year, leaving because he felt he did not get enough solo time on recordings. At various times Henderson employed cornetist Stewart, alto saxophonist

Benny Carter, trombonist Benny Morton, and trumpeter Cootie Williams, among many others.

Henderson's arranging style owes a large debt to Redman, his arranger until 1927. From Redman, Henderson learned to create a balance between scored passages for the band and improvised solo sections. Henderson's arrangements are clean and economical, avoiding the cumbersome complexities of Ferde Grofé's writing for Paul Whiteman's orchestra. Henderson often wrote in unusual keys for jazz, expecting a high level of musicianship from his players.

Early Works. Redman's arrangements allowed soloists unprecedented freedom, particularly compared with the most prolific band of the day, Whiteman's orchestra. Usually doctored stock arrangements, Redman's arrangements were playful, witty renderings of popular songs.

Armstrong made a significant impact on Henderson's orchestra during the early years. Though his stay in the group was brief (from September, 1924, to November, 1925), his hot soloing pushed the group members to play in a more jazzy, New Orleans style, as opposed to the dance style of the band's roots. Redman changed his arranging to accommodate the rising star, though neither he nor Henderson ever thought to put Armstrong in a vocal role, a deciding factor in Armstrong's decision to leave.

"Sugar Foot Stomp." A Redman reworking of King Oliver's "Dippermouth Blues," the Henderson orchestra's first recording showcases Armstrong, who brought the original Oliver manuscript with him from Chicago. One of Henderson's personal favorites, this recording helped to make the Henderson band famous. In the 1930's, Henderson reworked Redman's version, recording it several times. This piece was one of the arrangements that Henderson sold to Goodman in 1935, and it became a staple in Goodman's repertory. "Sugar Foot Stomp" was also recorded by numerous other groups during the swing era.

"King Porter Stomp." This piece showcases the talent of the Henderson orchestra to create head arrangements (pieces composed collectively by a band over a number of rehearsals and performances). "King Porter Stomp" began as a ragtime piece written and recorded by Jelly Roll Morton, and it was released as a stock arrangement in 1924. Henderson's band first recorded it in 1925, when

Armstrong was in the group, but for reasons unknown, that recording was never released. The subsequent 1928 recording, however, was colored by Armstrong's original interpretation, and it was characterized by strings of solos mixed with ensemble riffs. The piece was reworked in 1932 and released as "New King Porter Stomp," featuring a faster tempo and elimination of the two-beat bass style of ragtime in favor of the four-beat style that characterized music of the swing era. The band released another recording in 1933, removing the "new" from the title and making changes in the solo structure. Through these years, the piece remained a head arrangement. It was not written down until Henderson sold it to Goodman for the *Let's Dance* program, and it consequently became one of swing's biggest hits.

"Down South Camp Meeting." Composed and arranged by Henderson in 1934, "Down South Camp Meeting" (with another Henderson original, "Wrappin' It Up") was recorded for Decca Records shortly before the Henderson band broke up. The title refers to a Southern black Pentecostal revival, reflecting Decca's developing interest in "race" records, products aimed at the black audience. This piece is similar to "King Porter Stomp" in that it features the band's sections set against one another in call-and-response figures and in phrase structure (once it leaves a phrase, it does not return to that phrase for the rest of the piece). However, it is not a head arrangement, and it features few solos (in Henderson's recording, only the trumpeter Red Allen solos). This piece was sold to Goodman with only minor changes, though the slower tempo that Goodman preferred removes the lively quality of the Henderson orchestra's original recording.

"Blue Skies." Beginning as a Tin Pan Alley song by Irving Berlin, "Blue Skies" was memorably featured in the first talking picture, *The Jazz Singer* (1927), sung by Al Jolson. While the song was popular, it did not become a jazz standard until Henderson's 1935 arrangement for Goodman. The introduction to this arrangement features an unusual dissonance, picturesquely representing the storm before the blue skies (as described by Henderson in a 1938 radio broadcast). The arrangement features the *aaba* Tin Pan Alley melody prominently, but Henderson expertly mixes the standard format with big band figures such as call-and-response

and improvised solos. This piece was one of Goodman's favorites, and he included it on the 1938 Carnegie Hall concert.

Musical Legacy

Without Henderson, big band jazz may have taken a different turn. Although Whiteman helped establish the saxophone as a standard jazz instrument, it was Henderson and his orchestra that established the saxophone as a solo instrument. Henderson also expanded the big band format to include three trumpets and two trombones, while his former arranger Redman later expanded the saxophone section to include four players.

Henderson's group was one of the most popular in jazz in its time, but Henderson was mostly forgotten by the time of his death. Interest in this key figure has resurged, allowing Henderson the prominence he deserves as a jazz innovator.

Sarah Caissie Provost

Further Reading

Collier, James Lincoln. *The Making of Jazz*. Boston: Houghton Mifflin, 1978. Collier includes a chapter on Henderson's life and his innovative arrangements, connecting his personality with his musical style. Includes illustrations and discography.

Hadlock, Richard. *Jazz Masters of the 1920's*. New York: Da Capo Press, 1972. This book includes a chapter on Henderson and Redman, focusing on Henderson's band members and the contributions of Henderson and Redman to later big band jazz. Includes discography.

Magee, Jeffrey. *The Uncrowned King of Swing: Fletcher Henderson and Big Band Jazz*. New York: Oxford University Press, 2005. Magee's book offers a comprehensive look at Henderson's life and music, delving deeply into his arrangements and the influences on his musical life. Includes illustrations, musical examples, and a catalog of Henderson's arrangements for Goodman.

Oliphant, Dave. *The Early Swing Era, 1930-1941*. Westport, Conn.: Greenwood Press, 2002. Oliphant details the history and the influence of Henderson's bands and his instrumental position in Goodman's orchestra. Includes illustrations.

Schuller, Gunther. *Early Jazz: Its Roots and Musical Development*. New York: Oxford University Press,

1968. Schuller details several of Henderson's arrangements and recordings. Includes discography.

See also: Armstrong, Louis; Bechet, Sidney; Berlin, Irving; Blakey, Art; Carter, Benny; Goodman, Benny; Gordon, Dexter; Hawkins, Coleman; Hunter, Alberta; Jefferson, Blind Lemon; Morton, Jelly Roll; Rainey, Ma; Smith, Bessie; Webster, Ben; Whiteman, Paul; Young, Lester.

Jimi Hendrix

American rock singer, guitarist, and songwriter

Hendrix is generally recognized as the most influential rock guitarist in history. His unique style and unconventional technique, his showmanship in concert, and his innovation in the recording studio are all legendary.

Born: November 27, 1942; Seattle, Washington
Died: September 18, 1970; London, England
Also known as: Johnny Allen Hendrix (full name); James Marshall Hendrix; Jimmy James
Member of: The Jimi Hendrix Experience; Band of Gypsys; Gypsy Sons and Rainbows; Cry of Love

Principal recordings

ALBUMS: *Are You Experienced*, 1967; *Axis: Bold as Love*, 1967; *Electric Ladyland*, 1968; *Band of Gypsys*, 1970; *The Cry of Love*, 1971; *Rainbow Bridge*, 1971; *War Heroes*, 1972; *Crash Landing*, 1975; *Midnight Lightning*, 1975; *Nine to the Universe*, 1980; *Kiss the Sky*, 1985; *Radio One*, 1989; *Stages*, 1992; *The Ultimate Experience*, 1993; *Blues*, 1994; *Voodoo Soup*, 1995; *First Rays of the New Rising Sun*, 1997; *South Saturn Delta*, 1997; *BBC Sessions*, 1998.

The Life

Johnny Allen Hendrix (later changed by his father to James Marshall Hendrix), of African American, Cherokee, and Irish American ancestry, was born in Seattle, Washington, to Lucille Jeter Hendrix, while his father, James Allen ("Al") Hendrix, was serving in the military. Lucille registered the child's name as Johnny Allen Hendrix. Since Lucille could not properly care for her young son, he was reared, in part, by kindly neighbors and relatives. When Al Hendrix was discharged from the Army in 1945, he reclaimed his son, changing his name to James Marshall Hendrix in 1946. Young Jimmy attended school in Seattle, and his parents divorced in 1951, with Al taking custody of Jimmy and his two younger brothers. (Lucille died in 1958.) After finding Jimmy trying to play guitar on a broom, Al bought him a cheap instrument. Jimmy dropped out of high school and played guitar (left-handed, typically playing a right-handed guitar strung upside down) in local bands. In 1961 he enlisted in the 101st Airborne Division of the U.S. Army.

After his discharge in 1962, Hendrix played guitar in bands in and around Nashville, supporting such performing artists as Sam Cooke, Curtis Mayfield, Slim Harpo, and Little Richard. He moved to New York City in 1964, and in 1964-1965 he played with the Isley Brothers, Ike and Tina Turner, King Curtis, and Curtis Knight, among others. In the summer of 1966 Hendrix formed his own band, Jimmy James and the Blue Flames, performing in Greenwich Village in New York City. Animals bassist Chas Chandler discovered him there and made arrangements to take him to London. It was at this time that Jimmy's name became Jimi.

Less than a month after his arrival in London in September, 1966, the Jimi Hendrix Experience was formed, with bassist Noel Redding and drummer John "Mitch" Mitchell, and Hendrix began his first concert tour. With Chandler's managerial acumen, many club dates soon followed. Hendrix's virtuosity attracted the attention of Britain's top music stars, including members of the Beatles and the Rolling Stones.

Hendrix's performance at the Monterey International Pop Festival in California on June 18, 1967, concluding with his setting his guitar aflame, brought him international fame. He toured in the United States and Europe and recorded his first two albums, *Are You Experienced* and *Axis: Bold as Love*. In 1968 the Jimi Hendrix Experience toured extensively and recorded *Electric Ladyland*. In early 1969 the band again toured Europe and the United States; in May Hendrix was arrested in Toronto on drug charges, released on bail, and eventually found not guilty.

The Jimi Hendrix Experience played its final show in June, 1969. Hendrix formed a new but short-lived band, Gypsy Sons and Rainbows, expressly for the Woodstock Festival in August, 1969, where he was the headliner. At the end of 1969 Hendrix formed a new group with bassist Billy Cox and drummer Buddy Miles. A Band of Gypsys recorded a series of high-profile concerts at the Fillmore East auditorium in New York for a live album, *Band of Gypsys*.

In late January, 1970, that group also disbanded. In April, 1970, Hendrix formed his final band, retaining Cox on bass and bringing Mitchell back on drums. Hendrix recorded and toured with this band throughout the spring and summer.

Hendrix was found dead of asphyxiation after inhalation of his vomit in his London flat on September 18, 1970, after taking a large dose of a prescription sleep aid. Hendrix's remains were sent to Seattle, and he was buried in Renton, Washington.

The Music

From 1963 to 1966, before the formation of the Jimi Hendrix Experience, Hendrix made several live and studio recordings as a backing musician for such artists as Don Covay, Little Richard, the Isley Brothers, Lonnie Youngblood, and Curtis Knight. While some of these recordings reveal flashes of the extraordinary work to come, none represents Hendrix's finest work.

After the formation of the Jimi Hendrix Experience, the group worked quickly to release three singles. The first, a cover of "Hey Joe," was a hit, as was the second, a psychedelic original called "Purple Haze," opening with a distinctive tritone interval and featuring a dissonant seventh and ninth chord, often known as the Hendrix chord. Both songs remained part of Hendrix's live repertoire for the remainder of his career. The third single, "The Wind Cries Mary," is a beautiful ballad, showcasing Hendrix's delicate touch and evocative lyrics.

Are You Experienced. The Jimi Hendrix Experience's debut album, released in Britain in May, 1967, took different forms in the United States and

Jimi Hendrix. (AP/Wide World Photos)

Britain. Standout tracks include "Foxey Lady," which begins with gradually swelling feedback and utilizes the Hendrix chord. "Manic Depression" is one of the first rock compositions in waltz meter. An original twelve-bar blues, "Red House," showcases Jimi's lead guitar skills, and "I Don't Live Today" includes an early use of the wah-wah effect. "Fire" features Hendrix's driving, soulful rhythm guitar, along with some wild bends with the tremolo bar. An ambitious science-fiction epic, "Third Stone from the Sun" incorporates speech sounds that are unintelligible unless played back at double-speed, and the title track features guitar tracks played backward (accomplished by flipping the analog tape over in the recording studio). Hendrix's adventurous studio techniques were remarkable in 1967 and remain so today.

Axis: Bold as Love. The second album, released in Britain in October, 1967, opens with a free-form sound painting called "EXP," featuring atonal feedback guitar tracks, drenched with fuzz-box distortion and manipulated with the tremolo bar. Other album highlights include such rockers as "You Got Me Floatin'" and "Spanish Castle Magic" (the latter long retained in Hendrix's stage repertoire) and such gorgeous ballads as "One Rainy Wish" and "Little Wing." Hendrix continued to explore sonic possibilities in the recording studio, experimenting with the wah-wah pedal on "Up from the Skies," the Octavia on "Little Miss Lover," and phase shifting on the title track, "Bold as Love." Hendrix continued to refine his backward-guitar technique, evident on the lovely ballad "Castles Made of Sand," and to experiment with overdubbing multiple guitar tracks on several songs, including "If Six Was Nine." The stereo mix of the album (in which Hendrix had a significant hand) incorporated innovations such as generous amounts of panning from speaker to speaker.

Electric Ladyland. Released in October of 1968, this double album is widely recognized as a masterpiece. Hendrix himself served as producer, and it is the only such album released in his lifetime. It features extensive improvisation and includes several songs breaking the boundaries of the rigid three-minute pop song format. Again, the keynote is variety: Driving rockers such as "Come On (Part One)," "Crosstown Traffic," and "Voodoo Child (Slight Return)" are set against beautiful ballads such as the title track, "Have You Ever Been (to Electric Ladyland)." Hendrix also works in the jazz idiom, playing with horns and organ on "Rainy Day, Dream Away" and "Still Raining, Still Dreaming," and jamming with Steve Winwood on "Voodoo Chile." Hendrix's cover of Bob Dylan's "All Along the Watchtower" is commonly regarded (by Dylan, among others) as the definitive version. Perhaps the most extraordinary piece is "1983 . . . (A Merman I Should Turn to Be)," a fourteen-minute science-fiction soundscape of haunting beauty, utilizing to the fullest the multitracking possibilities of the recording studio.

Later Work. Hendrix did not live to complete another studio album, but many of the songs he was working on in 1969 and 1970 are collected on such posthumous collections as *First Rays of the New Rising Sun*, *South Saturn Delta*, and *Blues*. Standout tracks include rocking classics such as "Freedom,"

"Ezy Rider," "Earth Blues," and "In from the Storm" and delicate ballads such as "Angel" and "Drifting." Three essential studio masterpieces, "Pali Gap," "Hey Baby (Land of the New Rising Sun)," and "Dolly Dagger," were all recorded at a single session in July of 1970.

Musical Legacy

Studio recordings tell only part of the Hendrix story; he also left a remarkable legacy of live recordings. The fine recordings the Jimi Hendrix Experience made for BBC radio on various dates in 1967 are collected on *BBC Sessions*. Professional concert recordings were also made of the Jimi Hendrix Experience at the Monterey Pop Festival in June of 1967, at a series of six shows at the Fillmore auditorium in San Francisco in October of 1968, and at London's Royal Albert Hall in February of 1969. Hendrix's performance at the Woodstock Festival in August of 1969, including his iconic cover of "The Star-Spangled Banner," was captured on tape and film. Four shows with the Band of Gypsys at New York's Fillmore East (December 31, 1969-January 1, 1970) include such extraordinary works as "Message to Love" and "Machine Gun." Hendrix's final band was well recorded in concerts in Berkeley, California (May, 1970), and Maui, Hawaii (July, 1970). Hendrix's performances at the Atlanta (July, 1970) and Isle of Wight (August, 1970) festivals were both recorded; most of these shows were also professionally filmed.

Hendrix's productivity was nothing short of amazing. Though he released only three studio albums in his lifetime (along with a live album and a greatest-hits package), his inexhaustible work in the studio and in performance left behind material for a seemingly endless supply of high-quality posthumous albums. Hendrix's principal legacy is as a virtuoso guitarist: He approached the instrument in a fundamentally new way, producing innovative, inspirational music. Virtually all blues, jazz, funk, and rock guitarists admire his work and cite him as influential; he won a number of top awards in his lifetime, and his songs and albums regularly make it to the top of current polls. However, it is not just as a guitarist that his work endures. His singing and songwriting are celebrated in the innumerable covers of his work that continue to appear, and his innovative work in the studio—

exploring the resources of analog sound effects, multitracking, and stereo panning—have altered the sonic vocabulary of rock.

Joel J. Brattin

Further Reading

Aledort, Andy. *In Deep with Jimi Hendrix: A Complete Exploration of His Innovative Guitar Style.* Milwaukee, Wis.: Hal Leonard, 1995. Valuable analysis of Hendrix's style. Aledort is responsible for many of the transcriptions of Hendrix's guitar work in the excellent series of *Transcribed Scores* books, also published by Hal Leonard.

De Lange, Kees, and Ben Valkhoff. *Plug Your Ears: A Comprehensive Guide to Audio and Video Recordings of Jimi Hendrix.* Nijmegen, The Netherlands: Up from the Skies Unlimited, 1993. Itemizes the principal elements in Hendrix's recorded legacy.

Geldeart, Gary, and Steve Rodham. *From the Benjamin Franklin Studios: A Complete Guide to the Available Recordings of Jimi Hendrix and Complete Bootleg Discography.* 2d ed. Warrington, Cheshire, England: Jimpress, 1998. Useful discography, listing songs alphabetically and identifying multiple versions of each—more than a hundred extant versions of songs such as "Purple Haze" and "Foxey Lady." Rodham publishes *Jimpress*, a Hendrix magazine focusing on discographical matters.

Glebbeek, Caesar, and Harry Shapiro. *Jimi Hendrix: Electric Gypsy.* New York: St. Martin's Press, 1995. Authoritative biography, with discography, time line, and information about equipment. Glebbeek publishes *UniVibes*, a Hendrix magazine focusing on historical matters.

McDermott, John, with Billy Cox and Eddie Kramer. *Jimi Hendrix Sessions: The Complete Studio Recording Sessions, 1963-1970.* Boston: Little, Brown, 1995. Describes most of Hendrix's studio recording sessions, offering valuable technical information.

Mitchell, Mitch, with John Platt. *Jimi Hendrix: Inside the Experience.* New York: Harmony, 1993. Hendrix's main drummer provides stories and photographs.

Murray, Charles Shaar. *Crosstown Traffic: Jimi Hendrix and Post-war Pop.* New York: St. Martin's Press, 2001. Places Hendrix's music in its cultural context, considering the sources on which Hendrix drew, and his prodigious influence on blues, rock, soul, funk, and jazz music.

Shadwick, Keith. *Jimi Hendrix: Musician.* London: San Francisco: Backbeat Books, 2003. An excellent overview of Hendrix's career, focusing on his work rather than his life.

Willix, Mary. *Jimi Hendrix: Voices from Home.* San Diego: Creative Forces, 1995. Good source of biographical information about Hendrix's life in Seattle, in the years before his fame.

See also: Clapton, Eric; Cooke, Sam; Diddley, Bo; Domino, Fats; Eddy, Duane; Fleck, Béla; Guy, Buddy; Jagger, Sir Mick; James, Elmore; King, Albert; Little Richard; Mayfield, Curtis; Nicks, Stevie; Page, Jimmy; Pickett, Wilson; Redding, Otis; Shankar, Ravi; Slick, Grace; Stills, Stephen; Stone, Sly; Townshend, Pete; Van Halen, Eddie; Vaughan, Stevie Ray.

Victor Herbert

American cellist, popular music and musical-theater composer

Herbert composed more than forty operettas, two operas, and many instrumental and vocal works. Although best remembered for his stage productions, Herbert was an accomplished cello soloist, chamber musician, conductor, and advocate for musicians' rights.

Born: February 1, 1859; Dublin, Ireland
Died: May 26, 1924; New York, New York
Also known as: Victor August Herbert (full name)

Principal works

FILM SCORE: *Fall of a Nation*, 1916.

MUSICAL THEATER (music): *The Wizard of the Nile*, 1895 (lyrics and libretto by Harry B. Smith); *The Serenade*, 1897 (lyrics and libretto by Harry B. Smith); *The Fortune Teller*, 1898 (lyrics and libretto by Harry B. Smith); *The Ameer*, 1899 (lyrics and libretto by Kirke La Shelle and Frederic M. Ranken); *Cyrano de Bergerac*, 1899 (lyrics by Harry B. Smith; libretto by Stuart Reed); *The Singing Girl*, 1899 (lyrics by Harry B.

Smith; libretto by Hugh Stanislaus Stange); *The Viceroy*, 1900 (lyrics and libretto by Harry B. Smith); *Babes in Toyland*, 1903 (lyrics and libretto by Glen MacDonough); *Babette*, 1903 (lyrics and libretto by Harry B. Smith); *It Happened in Norland*, 1904 (lyrics and libretto by MacDonough); *Miss Dolly Dollars*, 1905 (lyrics and libretto by Harry B. Smith); *Mlle. Modiste*, 1905 (lyrics and libretto by Henry Blossom); *Wonderland*, 1905 (lyrics and libretto by MacDonough); *Dream City*, 1906 (lyrics and libretto by Edgar Smith); *The Magic Knight*, 1906 (lyrics and libretto by Edgar Smith); *The Tattooed Man*, 1907 (lyrics by Harry B. Smith; libretto by Harry B. Smith and A. N. C. Fowler); *Algeria*, 1908 (lyrics and libretto by MacDonough); *Little Nemo*, 1908 (lyrics and libretto by Harry B. Smith); *The Prima Donna*, 1908 (lyrics and libretto by Blossom); *Old Dutch*, 1909 (lyrics by George V. Hobart; libretto by Edgar Smith); *The Rose of Algeria*, 1909 (lyrics and libretto by MacDonough); *Naughty Marietta*, 1910 (lyrics and libretto by Rida Johnson Young); *The Duchess*, 1911 (lyrics and libretto by Harry B. Smith and Joseph Herbert); *The Enchantress*, 1911 (lyrics by Harry B. Smith; libretto by Harry B. Smith and Fred De Gresac); *When Sweet Sixteen*, 1911 (lyrics and libretto by Hobart); *The Lady of the Slipper*, 1912 (lyrics by James O'Dea; libretto by Anne Caldwell and Lawrence McCarty); *The Madcap Duchess*, 1913 (lyrics and libretto by David Stevens and Justin Huntly McCarthy); *Sweethearts*, 1913 (lyrics by Robert B. Smith; libretto by Harry B. Smith and De Gresac); *The Debutante*, 1914 (lyrics by Robert B. Smith; libretto by Robert B. Smith and Harry B. Smith); *The Only Girl*, 1914 (lyrics and libretto by Blossom); *The Princess Pat*, 1915 (lyrics and libretto by Blossom); *The Century Girl*, 1916 (music with Irving Berlin; lyrics by Berlin and Blossom; libretto by Sydney Rosenfeld); *Eileen*, 1917 (lyrics and libretto by Blossom); *Her Regiment*, 1917 (lyrics and libretto by William Le Baron); *Miss 1917*, 1917 (music with Jerome Kern; lyrics and libretto by Guy Bolton and P. G. Wodehouse); *Angel Face*, 1919 (lyrics by Robert B. Smith; libretto by Harry B. Smith); *The Velvet Lady*, 1919 (lyrics by Blossom;

libretto by Fred Jackson); *The Girl in the Spotlight*, 1920 (lyrics and libretto by Richard Bruce); *My Golden Girl*, 1920 (lyrics and libretto by Frederic Arnold Kummer); *Sally*, 1920 (music with Kern; lyrics by Clifford Grey; libretto by Bolton); *Orange Blossoms*, 1922 (lyrics by B. G. DeSilva; libretto by De Gresac); *The Dream Girl*, 1924 (lyrics by Young; libretto by Young and Harold Atteridge); *The Fortune Teller*, 1929 (lyrics and libretto by Harry B. Smith); *The Red Mill*, 1945 (lyrics and libretto by Blossom); *Gypsy Lady*, 1946 (lyrics by George Forrester and Robert Wright; libretto by Henry Myers).

OPERA: *Natoma*, 1911 (libretto by Joseph D. Redding).

OPERETTA (music): *Prince Ananias*, 1894 (libretto by Francis Neilson).

ORCHESTRAL WORK: *Suite for Cello and Orchestra*, 1883.

The Life

Victor August Herbert was born February 1, 1859, in Dublin Ireland, to Fannie Lover and Edward Herbert. His father died, in circumstances that are unclear, when Herbert was a child. Upon his father's death, Herbert moved with his mother to the home of his maternal grandfather, the poet, painter, and novelist Samuel Lover. After a short courtship, Fannie married Wilhelm Schmid, a German doctor she had met in London. The family moved to Stuttgart, Germany, in the spring of 1866.

As a child, Herbert played piano, flute, and piccolo. Later he decided to pursue the cello and to seek a career in music, studying cello with Bernhard Cossman at the Stuttgart Gymnasium from 1874 to 1876. He then left Stuttgart, touring Europe in several orchestras. In 1879 Herbert joined the orchestra of a Russian baron. After one season with the court orchestra, he moved to Vienna and joined the orchestra of Eduard Strauss, brother of the "waltz king," Johann Strauss.

Herbert returned to Stuttgart, and he joined the Court Orchestra of Stuttgart in 1881. Believing he had focused on performance to the detriment of his musical understanding, Herbert enrolled in the Stuttgart Conservatory, where he studied composition with Max Seifriz. Herbert's first appearance as soloist with the Court Orchestra came in 1881. In

1883 he performed his own Suite for Cello and Orchestra, Op. 3, with the orchestra, and in 1885 he played the premiere of his first (unpublished) cello concerto.

In 1885 Herbert met Therese Forester, the Viennese soprano. He was infatuated with her, establishing a musical relationship (he volunteered to serve as her accompanist) and later a romantic one. In 1886 Forester was offered a position in the Metropolitan Opera Company in New York City, and Herbert was hired to play cello in the orchestra. The two were married in Vienna on August 14, 1886, just prior to sailing for the United States.

In 1889 Herbert joined the faculty of the National Conservatory of Music in New York. His career took an unexpected turn in 1893, when he became director of the Twenty-second Regiment Band. The band had been made famous by its founder, Patrick Gilmore, and it had struggled after his death in 1892. Despite public fears to the contrary, Herbert remained an active cello soloist while focusing on

Victor Herbert. (© Bettmann/CORBIS)

composing and conducting. In 1898 Herbert became the conductor of the Pittsburgh Symphony Orchestra, a post he retained until 1904. In that year, Herbert returned to New York to form the Victor Herbert Orchestra.

Herbert was one of the founding members of the American Society of Composers, Authors, and Publishers (ASCAP), and he served as its vice president and director from 1914 until 1924. In 1917 Herbert was involved in a suit resulting in a Supreme Court ruling that granted composers and other copyright owners the rights to receive royalties from public performances.

In his later years, Herbert was best known as a songwriter and composer of music for the stage. He composed operas, operettas, incidental music, and the score to the 1916 film *Fall of a Nation*, the sequel to D. W. Griffith's *Birth of a Nation* (1915). Herbert's score is one of the earliest full-length orchestral film scores in existence. Herbert was working on music for the Ziegfeld Follies and negotiating the composition of music for a motion picture when he died of a heart attack in his doctor's office on May 26, 1924.

The Music

Herbert began his compositional career writing instrumental music, a path not surprising considering his early renown as an instrumentalist. After moving to the United States, however, Herbert became best known for his vocal works for the stage. Herbert was well regarded for his sensitive orchestration and for his ability to write for the voice. While he excelled in these aspects of composition, he was often hindered by the weakness of the librettos chosen for his works. Herbert's musical stage productions represented the end of an era, as radio, jazz, and motion pictures became prominent forces in American musical culture near the end of his life.

Suite for Cello and Orchestra. Herbert's earliest known large-scale composition, this suite was first performed by the composer in October of 1883, as part of the Stuttgart Orchestra's subscription series. The serenade from this work achieved considerable popularity as an independent concert piece, and the work did much to establish Herbert as both a composer and a performer.

Prince Ananias. Herbert's first extant operetta (an earlier work was never performed and is now lost) premiered in New York in November of 1894.

In a pattern that would continue throughout his career, critics praised Herbert's music while condemning the libretto. *Prince Ananias* is an operetta in two acts, set in France in the sixteenth century. It was originally performed by the Bostonians, a well-regarded touring company.

Babes in Toyland. Early in 1903, producers Fred Hamlin and Julian Mitchell had great success with the musical *The Wizard of Oz*. While the text of *The Wizard of Oz* was highly acclaimed, the music was lacking. Hamlin and Mitchell believed a similar production with better music would eclipse even the great success of *The Wizard of Oz*, and they approached Herbert to compose the music for *Babes in Toyland*. The libretto, written by Glen MacDonough, was largely a vehicle for spectacular scenery and effects. Consisting of a prologue and three acts, *Babes in Toyland* tells the story of orphaned siblings Alan and Jane and their attempts to escape their malevolent Uncle Barnaby. *Babes in Toyland* opened in New York on October 13, 1903, and it ran for 192 performances. It has since been revived and adapted many times, and it remains a popular Christmas spectacle.

Natoma. Herbert's first attempt at full-scale opera, *Natoma*, was born of a collaboration among Herbert, impresario Oscar Hammerstein, and librettist Joseph Redding. Hammerstein approached Herbert in 1907 to compose an opera, offering to pay one thousand dollars for a suitable American libretto. In 1909 Herbert entered into a contract with Redding, a lawyer, playwright, and accomplished composer in his own right, to produce *Natoma*, an opera set in California in the early nineteenth century.

Natoma finally premiered in Philadelphia on February 25, 1911, with Mary Garden singing the title role, and it was staged in New York at the Metropolitan Opera three days later. The critical response to *Natoma* was harsh, and, as for many of Herbert's productions, it was focused on the weakness of the libretto. Though Redding's text was nearly universally derided, Herbert's music was well received. Herbert's musical structure was heavily influenced by German Romantic opera (Herbert was an ardent supporter of Richard Wagner), and it incorporated elements designed to imply Native American and Spanish music, although Herbert admitted that he did not use authentic Native American or Spanish

melodies in the score. Although *Natoma* was neither a critical nor a box office success, the anticipation and critical interest generated by the production did much to further public and critical interest in American opera.

The Fall of a Nation. This sequel to the landmark 1915 film *The Birth of a Nation* was released in 1916. Unlike *The Birth of a Nation*, which had been directed by D. W. Griffith, *The Fall of a Nation* was written and directed by Thomas Dixon, who had written both books. Prior to this film, it was standard practice to accompany motion pictures with familiar pieces from the standard art music repertory. Herbert, however, announced that he would create the first thoroughly original American film score. Herbert composed more than two hours of music for *The Fall of a Nation*, though he was forced to make significant cuts because of extensive editing of the film.

Like many of the projects Herbert chose, *The Fall of a Nation* suffered from an inferior text. Herbert's score was generally admired, but the film was not. It ran for less than two months in New York, and its nationwide release was hampered by the inability of many local theaters to assemble orchestras capable of performing Herbert's score. *The Fall of a Nation* is now considered lost, although the extant pieces of Herbert's score are housed at the Library of Congress, and a recording of fifteen selections from the score has been released.

Musical Legacy

Herbert lived to see many of his own compositions go out of style, and by the end of his career he considered himself a relic of a bygone era. Although he made an effort to adapt to changing popular tastes by writing music for motion pictures and the variety stage, America had largely moved away from the type of musical theater popularized by Herbert and others early in the century. By the 1920's, popular musical tastes were also shifting toward jazz, an idiom to which Herbert was not accustomed.

Although Herbert did not establish an American school of opera, his celebrity generated enough publicity for and discussion of *Natoma* that, despite the opera's lack of success, public and critical attention turned to the idea of American opera. Herbert was also responsible for the resurrection of Gilmore's Band, and his association with the band advanced the wind band as an outlet for art music in America. Though the popularity of his instrumental music was short-lived, Herbert counted many prominent performers and conductors among his friends. Antonín Dvořák cited Herbert's Second Cello Concerto as the inspiration for his own Concerto for Cello and Orchestra in B Minor, Op. 104.

Paige Clark Lush

Further Reading

Kaye, Joseph. *Victor Herbert: The Biography of America's Greatest Composer of Romantic Music.* New York: G. H. Watt, 1931. This biography focuses on the sensational aspects of Herbert's life and musical career. Written in a novel-like fashion, it is similar to the later motion picture *The Great Victor Herbert* (1939).

Purdy, Claire Lee. *Victor Herbert, American Music-Master.* New York: J. Messner, 1945. A biography suitable for juvenile readers and those unfamiliar with Herbert and his work.

Traubner, Richard. *Operetta: A Theatrical History.* Rev. ed. New York: Routledge, 2003. Contains a thorough biography of Herbert, including in-depth discussions of many of his operettas. This volume also addresses Herbert's musical legacy and his posthumous success in new media such as film and radio.

Waters, Edward N. "American Musical History and Victor Herbert." *Notes* 13, no. 1 (1955): 33-40. Waters, author of a definitive biography of Herbert, reflects on his research in this article. The article provides a concise biography of Herbert, and it discusses how a study of the career of a composer such as Herbert can contribute to a heightened understanding of American music and of music historiography.

_____. *Victor Herbert: A Life in Music.* New York: Macmillan, 1955. A thorough and factually accurate Herbert biography, this contains more than five hundred pages of biographical information and musical discussion. It also lists all of Herbert's known compositions and phonograph recordings, and it contains extensive notes on sources used for the book.

See also: Berlin, Irving; Björling, Jussi; Romberg, Sigmund; Whiteman, Paul.

Bernard Herrmann

American classical and film-score composer and conductor

Herrmann composed film music scores that not only enhanced the action on the screen but also conveyed the emotions of the characters. His trendsetting scores ranged from playful to shocking, in some of the best-known pictures of directors such as Orson Welles, Alfred Hitchcock, Ray Harryhausen, and François Truffaut.

Born: June 29, 1911; New York, New York
Died: December 24, 1975; North Hollywood, California

Principal works

CHAMBER WORKS: *Aria for Flute and Harp*, 1932; *Marche Militaire*, 1932; *Echoes*, 1965 (for string quartet); *Souvenirs de voyage*, 1967 (for clarinet and string quartet).

CHORAL WORKS: *Moby Dick*, 1938 (for solo voices, male chorus, and orchestra; based on Herman Melville's novel); *Johnny Appleseed*, 1940 (for solo voices, chorus, and orchestra); *The Fantasticks*, 1942 (song cycle for mixed voices, chorus, and orchestra; lyrics by Nicholas Breton).

FILM SCORES: *Citizen Kane*, 1941; *The Devil and Daniel Webster*, 1941; *The Magnificent Ambersons*, 1942; *Jane Eyre*, 1944; *Hangover Square*, 1945; *Anna and the King of Siam*, 1946; *The Ghost and Mrs. Muir*, 1947; *Portrait of Jennie*, 1948; *The Day the Earth Stood Still*, 1951; *Five Fingers*, 1952; *On Dangerous Ground*, 1952; *The Snows of Kilimanjaro*, 1952; *Beneath the Twelve-Mile Reef*, 1953; *King of the Khyber Rifles*, 1953; *White Witch Doctor*, 1953; *The Egyptian*, 1954; *Garden of Evil*, 1954; *Prince of Players*, 1954; *The Kentuckian*, 1955; *The Trouble with Harry*, 1955; *The Man in the Gray Flannel Suit*, 1956; *The Man Who Knew Too Much*, 1956; *The Wrong Man*, 1956; *A Hatful of Rain*, 1957; *Williamsburg: The Story of a Patriot*, 1957; *The Naked and the Dead*, 1958; *The Seventh Voyage of Sinbad*, 1958; *Vertigo*, 1958; *Blue Denim*, 1959; *Journey to the Center of the Earth*, 1959; *North by Northwest*, 1959; *Psycho*, 1960; *The*

Three Worlds of Gulliver, 1960; *Mysterious Island*, 1961; *Cape Fear*, 1962; *Tender Is the Night*, 1962; *Jason and the Argonauts*, 1963; *Marnie*, 1964; *Joy in the Morning*, 1965; *Fahrenheit 451*, 1966; *The Bride Wore Black*, 1967; *Twisted Nerve*, 1968; *The Battle of Neretva*, 1969; *Endless Night*, 1971; *The Night Digger*, 1971; *Sisters*, 1973; *It's Alive*, 1974; *Obsession*, 1976; *Taxi Driver*, 1976.

ORCHESTRAL WORKS: *Aubade*, 1933; *Prelude to Anathema*, 1933; *Variations on "Deep River" and "Water Boy,"* 1933; *Currier and Ives Suite*, 1935; Nocturne and Scherzo, 1935; Sinfonietta for Strings, 1935; Symphony No. 1, 1940; *For the Fallen*, 1943; *Welles Raises Kane*, 1943 (suite); *Wuthering Heights*, composed 1951, first performed 1965.

The Life

Bernard Herrmann (HUR-muhn) was born in 1911, the son of Russian Jewish immigrants. He developed an early interest in the arts through his father, Abraham, an optometrist, who took Herrmann to opera and symphony performances, exposed him to symphonic music on records, and supplied him with musical instruments. In addition, Herrmann was drawn to writers who were passionate about their craft. At age twelve, he won a prize for a song he composed. At thirteen, Herrmann read an 1844 treatise on orchestration by French composer Hector Berlioz, which he later said pointed him to his own musical career.

Herrmann began studying music formally in 1927 as a student at DeWitt Clinton High School. He audited composition classes at New York University and the Juilliard School, and in 1929 he enrolled in New York University, where he studied composition and conducting. Within four years, he was conducting performances of his own work and that of others by the New Chamber Orchestra, and he was hired in 1934 to be an assistant to Johnny Green, CBS Radio's music director. He also started composing a number of concert pieces.

He started composing and conducting for CBS's Columbia Workshop radio series in 1937, and a year later he was providing music for Orson Welles's *Mercury Theatre on the Air*, including its updated adaptation of H. G. Wells's 1898 novel *The War of the Worlds*, which convinced a number of listeners that an invasion from Mars was under way.

The association with Welles led to Herrmann's first film score, for *Citizen Kane*. Their association came to an end after their next collaboration, *The Magnificent Ambersons*, when the studio altered Herrmann's original score, foreshadowing future times when Herrmann would challenge those who would change his work. In between, he won his only Academy Award, for *The Devil and Daniel Webster*.

Herrmann returned to the CBS Symphony, remaining there until 1951, when it was disbanded. He scored other films at Twentieth Century-Fox through the 1940's, including *Jane Eyre, Hangover Square, Anna and the King of Siam*, and *The Ghost and Mrs. Muir*. In the 1950's, he scored seven of the most popular of director Alfred Hitchcock's films: *The Trouble with Harry, The Man Who Knew Too Much, The Wrong Man, Vertigo, North by Northwest, Psycho*, and *Marnie*. He supervised the electronic sound effects for *The Birds*, which had no music, and he wrote a score for *Torn Curtain*, which differed from the pop score Hitchcock had ordered. Hitchcock abandoned Herrmann's score, a bitter end to their collaborations.

Herrmann moved to England, and he scored films by other directors. On December 23, 1975, despite not feeling well, Herrmann finished recording music he composed for *Taxi Driver* to meet the deadline. He died in his sleep just past midnight the next day.

The Music

Herrmann's musical contributions to more than forty films evoked psychological nuances that differed with each production. His work ranged from the romantic (*The Ghost and Mrs. Muir* and *Obsession*) and the fantastic (*The Day the Earth Stood Still, Fahrenheit 451*, and *Jason and the Argonauts*) to the folk (*The Devil and Daniel Webster*) and the frightening (*Psycho*).

Although he won only one Academy Award, for scoring a dramatic picture (*The Devil and Daniel Webster*), his music received nominations for original score in 1976 (*Taxi Driver*), best musical scoring of a drama or comedy in 1946 (*Anna and the King of Siam*), and best dramatic score for 1941 (*Citizen Kane*).

A demanding and often argumentative perfectionist, Herrmann had no hesitancy about ignoring instructions from directors. He ignored Hitchcock's request for a jazz score for a *Psycho* scene, and Hitchcock ended up agreeing with him. The opposite, however, occurred with *Torn Curtain*.

Citizen Kane. Welles brought actors from his radio show to Hollywood in 1941, for a film about the rise and fall of a newspaper magnate, based loosely on the career of publisher William Randolph Hearst. He also invited Herrmann, who had scored music for the radio program, to compose and conduct music for the motion picture. This first film for both Welles and Herrmann introduced groundbreaking techniques at all levels (Herrmann, for example, found it more effective to have music for key scenes rather than to follow the then-current practice of nonstop music throughout the picture).

Herrmann chose somewhat eerie music for the opening, segued into a livelier score to underlie the growth of Kane's newspaper ventures, and concluded on a somber note, using the tuba, bass clarinets, and low trombones to achieve a dark tone (the technique has been imitated to the present day).

The Welles-Herrmann collaboration might have continued to greater success, but it ended after Welles's second picture (as director). The studio became nervous about Welles's approach to *The Magnificent Ambersons* and took over production, recutting and reshooting parts of it. As a result, Herrmann's music was chopped up and additional music added without his consent. Herrmann, who had a volatile temper, had his name removed from the credits. He did score another film in which Welles acted, *Jane Eyre*, but he never scored another Welles project.

The Day the Earth Stood Still. Hitchcock sought Herrmann to score *Spellbound*, which used a theremin to provide high-pitched, ethereal music. (The picture ended up being scored by Miklós Rósza.) In 1951 Herrmann made extensive use of two of the instruments for director Robert Wise's science-fiction classic about an alien emissary bringing a warning about the consequences of the planet's warlike ways. The instrument afterward became widely used, and almost a trademark, for science-fiction films of the 1950's. Herrmann also made effective use of electrical violins, pianos, and harps.

Herrmann would later score other science-fiction films, such as François Truffaut's *Fahrenheit 451*, based on a Ray Bradbury novel, and *Journey to the Center of the Earth* and *Mysterious Island*, based on Jules Verne's novels.

The Man Who Knew Too Much. Although Hitchcock had done this film in 1934, he directed a new version in 1956. It involves a vacationing couple who become aware of an assassination plot and have their young son kidnapped to keep them quiet. They race against time to stop the murder, which is to take place at a symphony performance. Hitchcock used Arthur Benjamin's *Storm Clouds Cantata* (1934) from the original film, with its clash of cymbals to hide the gunshot.

Not all the music was by Herrmann. The song "Que Sera, Sera," sung by Doris Day, who appeared in the film, and the cantata are by other composers. Herrmann appeared in a cameo in the film, as the symphony conductor in the assassination scene.

The Seventh Voyage of Sinbad. Producer Charles Schneer hired Herrmann to orchestrate a series of fantasy films, using stop-motion animation by Ray Harryhausen to create the fantasy creatures and the effects. The result was some of Herrmann's most sweeping and adventurous scores, in which he would use different instrument combinations to characterize each of Harryhausen's creatures.

The Seventh Voyage of Sinbad was the first of these in 1958. Herrmann went on to score two similar Harryhausen fantasies, *The Three Worlds of Gulliver*—each "world" having its own musical theme—and *Jason and the Argonauts*, and also the science-fiction thriller *Mysterious Island*.

Vertigo. Hitchcock used minimal dialogue in this 1958 film about a former policeman who falls for the woman he is hired to shadow, and, following her apparent death, becomes obsessed with shaping another woman in her image. The director, instead, allowed Herrmann's music to dominate the action, and as a result the film has more music than speech.

In 1976 Herrmann orchestrated Brian De Palma's *Obsession*, inspired by *Vertigo*. The music was nominated for an Academy Award in 1977 for Best Original Score.

Psycho. In Hitchcock's 1960 horror film about murders at a remote motel, Herrmann used only a string orchestra and jarring violins to jangle the nerves of viewers. For the shower scene of the first shocking murder, Hitchcock wanted no music whatever. Herrmann disagreed, and he wrote a screeching-violins score for it anyway. After hearing it, the director changed his mind and included it. It became one of the most recognizable film-music pieces in cinematic history.

Six years later, when the short-tempered Herrmann tried to overrule Hitchcock on a musical decision for *Torn Curtain*, things turned out differently. Hitchcock fired Herrmann in an acrimonious conflict that ended their film collaborations forever. Hitchcock hired a different composer, and much later Herrmann's never-used score was released on a recording that drew favorable responses.

Taxi Driver. Herrmann's brooding jazz score for director Martin Scorsese's *Taxi Driver* proved to be his last work. It differed from most of his earlier music, and it was, for Herrmann, an experiment in another musical style. Scorsese described the score as "New York Gothic." The motion picture's last credit reads: "Our gratitude and respect, Bernard Herrmann, June 29, 1911-December 24, 1975."

Musical Legacy

Herrmann won an Academy Award and other accolades for his film and television work. He may be best known for his work on Hitchcock films, but he also composed scores for fantasies by Harryhausen and, following his relocation to England, for such directors as Truffaut, De Palma, Scorsese, and Larry Cohen. Early in his career, as chief conductor of the CBS Symphony, he introduced radio listeners to composers whose work had gotten little exposure His television work included such series as *The Twilight Zone*, *The Alfred Hitchcock Hour*, *The Virginian*, and *Have Gun Will Travel*.

Even when some of the films for which he composed were remade, some portion of his music for the originals remained. Composer Danny Elfman adapted Herrmann's music for the original *Psycho* for director Gus Van Sant's 1998 remake. Elmer Bernstein, who said he first thought of a career writing film music after hearing Herrmann's score for *The Devil and Daniel Webster*, adapted and arranged Herrmann's original score for *Cape Fear* for the 1991

remake. Bernstein adapted and rerecorded Herrmann's score for a new version of *The Ghost and Mrs. Muir* (1975).

Quentin Tarantino used part of Herrmann's score for *Twisted Nerve* in *Kill Bill* (2003). Utopia, a progressive rock group, recorded in 1977 a segment of Herrmann's sound track for the film *Journey to the Center of the Earth*.

Paul Dellinger

Further Reading

Bruce, Graham. *Bernard Herrmann: Film Music Narrative*. Ann Arbor, Mich.: UMI Research, 1985. This resource emphasizes the musicology of Herrmann's works.

Burt, George. *The Art of Film Music*. Boston: Northeastern University Press, 1995. This book focuses on case studies of professionals composing motion picture scores, including references to Herrmann.

Davis, Richard. *Complete Guide to Film Scoring*. Boston: Berklee Press, 2000. Davis offers interviews with nineteen composers, including Herrmann, on their film work.

Morgan, David. *Knowing the Score: Film Composers Talk About the Art, Craft, Blood, Sweat, and Tears of Writing for Cinema*. New York: Harper Paperbacks, 2000. Several film composers, including Herrmann, talk about their process of composing for pictures.

Prendergast, Roy M. *Film Music, a Neglected Art: A Critical Study of Music in Films*. New York: W. W. Norton, 1992. The author discusses the technology and the aesthetics of film music, and he includes some of Herrmann's work.

Smith, Steven C. *A Heart at Fire's Center: The Life and Music of Bernard Herrmann*. Los Angeles: University of California Press, 1991. This is a well-researched biography of Herrmann, showing the relationship between his music and his often-turbulent personal life.

See also: Bernstein, Elmer; Elfman, Danny; Mancini, Henry; Martin, Sir George; Newman, Alfred; Rózsa, Miklós; Williams, John.

Paul Hindemith

German classical composer

A composer, teacher, and performing musician, Hindemith composed music with the aim of making it pedagogically useful to amateur musicians or practically useful to performing ensembles. Such Gebrauchsmusik, or music for use, demonstrated Hindemith's influential view that people should make music, not just passively hear it.

Born: November 16, 1895; Hanau, Germany
Died: December 28, 1963; Frankfurt, West
Germany (now in Germany)

Principal works

BALLETS (music): *Nobilissima visione*, 1938 (libretto by Hindemith); *Theme with Four Variations*, 1940 (libretto by Hindemith); *Hérodiade*, 1946 (libretto by Paul Millet and Henri Grémont).

CHAMBER WORKS: *Sonate für Bratscheallein*, Op. 11, No. 5, 1918; Sonata for Viola Solo, Op. 11, No. 5, 1919; String Quartet No. 2 in F Minor, Op. 10, 1918; Chamber Music No. 1, 1922 (for twelve solo instruments); Chamber Music No. 2, 1924 (for piano); Chamber Music No. 3, 1925 (for cello); Chamber Music No. 4, 1925 (for violin); Chamber Music No. 5, 1927 (for viola); Chamber Music No. 6, 1928 (for viola); Chamber Music No. 7, 1928 (for organ); *Konzert für Klavier, Blechbläser, und Harfen*, 1930; *Triosatz für drei Gitarren*, 1930; *Konzert für Streichorchester, und Blechbläser*, 1931; *Trio für Geige, Bratsche, und Cello*, 1933.

CHORAL WORKS: *Das Marienleben*, 1922 (*The Life of Mary*; based Rainer Maria Rilke's poetry); *Das Unaufhörliche*, 1931; *Twelve Madrigals*, 1958.

OPERAS (music): *Das Nusch-nuschi*, 1920 (libretto by Franz Blei); *Mörder, Hoffnung der Frauen*, 1921 (*Murder, Hope of Women*; libretto by Oskar Kokoschka); *Die Junge Magd*, 1922 (*The Young Maid*; libretto by Hindemith; based on Georg Trakl's poetry); *Sancta Susanna*, 1922 (libretto by August Stramm); *Cardillac*, 1926, revised 1952 (libretto by Ferdinand Lion); *Lehrstück*, 1929 (*Lesson*; libretto by Bertolt Brecht); *Neues vom Tage*, 1929, revised 1954 (*News of the Day*;

libretto by Hindemith); *Mathis der Maler*, 1938 (*Matthias the Painter*; libretto by Hindemith); *Die Harmonie der Welt*, 1957 (*Harmony of the World*; libretto by Hindemith); *The Long Christmas Dinner*, 1961 (libretto by Hindemith).

ORCHESTRAL WORKS: Sonata for Viola Solo, Op. 11, No. 5, 1919; String Quartet, 1921; Concert Music for Brass Orchestra, 1926; Concert Music for Viola and Large Chamber Orchestra, 1930; *Sabinchen*, 1930; *Wir bauen eine Stadt*, 1930; Philharmonic Concerto, 1932; *Symphonie Mathis der Maler*, 1934; *Der Schwanendreher*, 1935; *Trauermusik*, 1936; *Symphonische Tänze*, 1937; Violin Concerto, 1939; Cello Concerto, 1940; Concerto for Violin and Orchestra, 1940; Concerto for Cello and Orchestra, 1941; Symphonie in E, 1941; *Amor und Psyche*, 1943; *Symphonic Metamorphosis After Themes by Carl Maria von Weber*, 1944; *Symphonia serena*, 1947; Concerto for Woodwinds, Harp, and Orchestra, 1949; Concerto for Clarinet in A, 1950; Concerto for Horn and Orchestra, 1950; Sinfonietta in E, 1950; Symphony in B-flat for Concert Band, 1951; Concerto for Trumpet, Bassoon, and String Orchestra, 1952; *Pittsburgh Symphony*, 1959; *Marsch für Orchester über den alten "Schweizerton,"* 1960; *Der mainzer Unzug*, 1962 (*The Mainz Procession*); Concerto for Organ and Orchestra, 1963; *Messe*, 1963; Concerto for Piano and Orchestra, 1974.

PIANO WORK: *Ludus Tonalis*, 1942.

WRITINGS OF INTEREST: *Unterweisung im Tonsatz, I: Theoretischer Teil*, 1937 (*The Craft of Musical Composition, Part 1: Theory*, 1942); *Unterweisung im Tonsatz, II: Übungsbuch für den zweistimmigen Satz*, 1939 (*The Craft of Musical Composition, Part 2: Exercises in Two-Part Writing*, 1941); *A Concentrated Course in Traditional Harmony, Vol. I*, 1943; *A Concentrated Course in Traditional Harmony, Vol. II*, 1943; *Elementary Training for Musicians*, 1946; *A Composer's World*, 1952; *Johann Sebastian Bach: Heritage and Obligation*, 1952; *Unterweisung im Tonsatz, III: Übungsbuch für den dreistimmigen Satz*, 1970.

The Life

Paul Hindemith (HIHN-deh-mihth) was born to Robert Rudolph Hindemith, a house painter of limited financial means, and Marie Sophie Warneke.

An amateur musician and avid music lover, his father encouraged his children in musical pursuits, never allowing the family's poverty to interfere with the children's musical education. Aided by a scholarship and by income earned playing in local taverns, Hindemith enrolled in Frankfurt's Hoch Conservatorium when he was thirteen. In 1912 he began studying composition with Arnold Mendelssohn and eventually with Bernhard Sekles.

Hindemith secured an appointment as a first violinist in the orchestra of the Frankfurt Opera in 1915, and he also began playing with the Rebner Quartet. When Hindemith was drafted into the German army in 1917, he played bass drum in the military band, and he was first violin in a string quartet whose performances were intended to provide a momentary escape from the chaos of World War I for the regiment's commanding officer. The musical nature of Hindemith's military service still allowed him time to compose.

Following his discharge from the army in 1919, Hindemith returned to his position as concertmaster with the Frankfurt Opera. The composer organized a concert of his own works, which was so successful that Schott and Sons offered him a contract to publish his music. By 1923 Hindemith had renegotiated the contract, winning a regular monthly salary, which allowed him to resign from the Frankfurt Opera orchestra.

The success, recognition, and happiness Hindemith experienced in the 1920's—including his new contract with Schott and Sons, the founding of the well-known Amar Quartet, his marriage to Gertrud Rottenberg in 1924, and his prestigious appointments to the directorial committee of the Festival for New Music in Donaueschingen in 1923 and to the composition faculty of Berlin's Hochschule für Musik in 1927—gave way to the difficulties he encountered in the 1930's. When the National Socialist Party took control of the German government in 1933, a large amount of Hindemith's music was banned for exhibiting so-called "cultural Bolshevism." The Nazi Party also took a negative view of his continued association with Jewish musicians and of his marriage to a half-Jewish woman. The triumphant premiere of his *Symphonie Mathis der Maler* in 1934 only led to a ban of its further performance in Germany and to renewed attacks of Hindemith in the press. In 1935 all of Hindemith's works were banned from public performance.

During the official ban of his music, Hindemith was unable to perform or teach, leaving him time to develop a compositional theory, published in his *Unterweisung im Tonsatz* (1937; *The Craft of Musical Composition, Part 1: Theory*, 1942). By 1938 Hindemith's conciliatory gestures toward the Nazi regime, including his mission to establish a school of music in Turkey and the oath of allegiance he signed to Adolf Hitler, could not prevent his scores from being featured in an exhibit of degenerate music. Four months following the opening of the exhibit, Hindemith moved with his wife to Switzerland. The deteriorating situation in Europe led Hindemith to emigrate in 1940 to the United States, undertaking a variety of part-time positions before becoming a professor of music theory at Yale University. In addition to teaching composition and music theory, Hindemith founded Yale's Collegium Musicum, dedicated to the performance of early music.

Despite offers of employment by schools and orchestras in Germany, Hindemith remained in the

Paul Hindemith. (Library of Congress)

United States until he received an offer from the University of Zurich to join its faculty as professor of musicology in 1949. Although he returned to Germany for performances and concert tours, Hindemith was never again resident of his homeland. Scarcely a month after he conducted the premiere of his *Messe*, for a cappella mixed choir, Hindemith died unexpectedly of a heart attack in December, 1963.

The Music

Hindemith became noticed as a composer with his embrace of the New Objectivity in the 1920's. In their art, exponents of the New Objectivity moved away from disturbing psychological insights of Expressionism, instead seeking to appeal to broad audiences by using familiar subjects and styles. Rather than focusing on the experience of isolated individuals, Hindemith, along with composers such as Kurt Weill and Ernst Krenek as well as the playwright Bertolt Bretcht, hoped to create art that was socially useful. Often associated with Hindemith, the term Gebrauchsmusik, or music for use, indicates that such compositions were intended to teach or to serve another social function instead of being passively heard in a concert hall. Hindemith's compositions often feature linear counterpoint reminiscent of Johann Sebastian Bach combined with an advanced harmonic language that never wholly abandons tonality.

Early Works. In his earliest compositions, Hindemith demonstrates the clear influence of a variety of composers and styles. The chromatic counterpoint of the String Quartet in F Minor, Op. 10 has an affinity with the music of the late-Romantic composer Max Reger, while the Opus 11 sonatas show evidence of the harmonic language of composers such as Richard Wagner, Claude Debussy, and Richard Strauss. Two of Hindemith's earliest operas—*Murder, Hope of Women* and *Sancta Susanna*—were based on expressionist plays by Oskar Kokoschka and August Stramm, respectively. The scandalous nature of the operas' subject matter and Hindemith's use of an advanced harmonic language earned the composer a reputation as a member of the avant-garde.

Chamber Music No. 1. Throughout the 1920's, Hindemith composed pieces for small chamber ensembles, entitled Chamber Music. Although six of the seven feature solo instruments, the four-movement Chamber Music No. 1 functions more like a concerto for chamber orchestra. In addition to relatively standard instruments—a string quintet, flute, clarinet, bassoon, trumpet, and piano—Hindemith included nontraditional instruments such as an accordion and a siren. Chamber Music No. 1 manifests the composer's turn to the New Objectivity in its contrapuntal style and its use of popular elements, such as the quotation of a popular foxtrot in the raucous finale and the use of instruments commonly associated with jazz.

Mathis der Maler. In 1933, shortly after the National Socialist Party came to power, Hindemith began work on an opera about the sixteenth century painter Matthias Grünewald, who had painted the famous Isenheim Altarpiece depicting the temptation of Saint Anthony and his interview with Saint Paul. Through the story of Grünewald's brief abandonment of art to participate in an uprising of serfs in the 1520's, Hindemith explored the role of the artist in a time of political upheaval. In the end, Hindemith's Mathis realizes that his deepest obligation is to create art. Although Hindemith finished work on the opera by 1935, it did not premiere until 1938 in Zurich—the Nazi government would not allow it to be performed in Germany—where, however, it met with instant critical acclaim.

Ludus Tonalis. Hindemith's *Ludus Tonalis*, or play of tones, consists of twelve three-part fugues, one for each chromatic pitch, separated by eleven interludes. The entire set is bracketed by a prelude and a postlude. The order of the fugues is based on a series of pitches found in *The Craft of Musical Composition*; according to Hindemith, the series becomes gradually more distantly related to the first pitch. The interludes connect the fugues harmonically, but they also have varying expressive characters, including a waltz and a march. Hindemith's musical wit becomes fully clear with the postlude, which looks like the prelude turned upside down and played from end to beginning.

Symphonic Metamorphosis After Themes by Carl Maria von Weber. Following their successful collaboration on the ballet *Nobilissima visione*, the choreographer Léonide Massine requested that Hindemith orchestrate piano pieces by Weber for a new project. When he saw sketches, Massine criticized Hindemith for reinterpreting the music rather than merely orchestrating it. Abandoning the collaboration, Hindemith instead reused the sketches as the basis for his well-known orchestral piece, the four-movement *Symphonic Metamorphosis After Themes by Carl Maria von Weber*. In a masterful stroke, Hindemith uses a single brief phrase from Weber's overture for *Turandot* (1809) to create the entire second movement, clothing it in jazzy syncopations in the process.

Die Harmonie der Welt. Hindemith had been considering composing an opera based on the life of the astronomer Johannes Kepler since 1939. After completing the *Harmonie der Welt Symphony* in 1951 and the libretto in 1956, Hindemith began working on the opera in earnest in 1957. Kepler's search for universal harmony in the opera reflects in many ways Hindemith's own quest for a tonal system in *The Craft of Musical Composition*. In the final scene, Hindemith presents a vision in which each of the characters is associated with a planet in Kepler's heliocentric system. Although the opera was only mildly successful at its premiere in Munich in 1957 and has since fallen out of the repertory, *Die Harmonie der Welt* powerfully summarizes Hindemith's philosophy and his compositional method.

Twelve Madrigals. With his collection of twelve madrigals for five unaccompanied voices, Hindemith sought to encourage ensemble singing, which he thought was an integral part of musical culture and a practice that had unfortunately fallen into decline. The texts by Josef Weinheber chosen by Hindemith are consistently pessimistic, and the musical style with which he set them is harmonically strident and rhythmically complex. Reflecting his belief that music should be useful to its performers, Hindemith indicates in the foreword to the collection that ensembles should feel free to sing the pieces individually or to reorder them.

Musical Legacy

Hindemith's musical theories had a far smaller impact than those of Arnold Schoenberg, and he also failed to establish a school of composition to the extent that Schoenberg did with his students Alban Berg and Anton von Webern. However, the same conservative strand in Hindemith's musical thinking that prevented him from opening revolutionary new paths to his successors allowed him to draw attention to neglected facets of composition and musical life.

In his theoretical writings and with his music, Hindemith consistently advocated a harmonic language that included a significant amount of dissonance but never completely lost its sense of a tonal center. Hindemith demonstrated that because the tonal system could be manipulated without destroying it, new and original music could still be composed using its materials.

Such general ways of thinking about musical composition are Hindemith's most significant contribution to his successors, primarily because he encouraged his composition students to avoid imitating him and instead to find their own voice. Although they did not result in a school of composition, Hindemith's theoretical texts are still used around the world in college-level music theory classes.

Perhaps the most visible legacy left by Hindemith was his belief that music should be made and not merely consumed. By composing a large series of sonatas within the capabilities of skilled amateurs for nearly every conceivable instrument—including even double bass and tuba—he made modern music accessible to more than a professional elite. Hindemith's sonatas, like Béla Bartók's compositions for piano, expose many young musicians to modern music for the first time, and they encourage similar outreach by new composers and performing ensembles to broader audiences.

Ryan R. Kangas

Further Reading

Bruhn, Siglind. *The Musical Order of the World: Kepler, Hesse, Hindemith.* Hillsdale, N.Y.: Pendragon Press, 2005. An interdisciplinary study of the concept of universal harmony, this work explores the relationship of Hindemith's *Die Harmonie der Welt* and Herman Hesse's nearly contemporary *Glass Bead Game* (1943) to the ideas of Kepler.

Hindemith, Paul. *A Composer's World: Horizons and Limitations.* Cambridge, Mass.: Harvard University Press, 1952. Hindemith collected in this book the six Norton lectures—in which he discusses his philosophy and aesthetics—that he gave at Harvard. This work is suitable for the lay reader.

Kater, Michael H. "Paul Hindemith: The Reluctant

Emigré." In *Composers of the Nazi Era: Eight Portraits*. New York: Oxford University Press, 2000. Provides an account of Hindemith's relationship with the Nazi regime and with Germany following his emigration to Switzerland and the United States.

Neumeyer, David. *The Music of Paul Hindemith.* New Haven, Conn.: Yale University Press, 1986. Neumeyer discusses Hindemith's compositional theory, and he develops an analytical method from it. Through technically complex analyses, Neumeyer demonstrates the connection between Hindemith's theory and his compositional practice.

Skelton, Geoffrey. *Paul Hindemith: The Man Behind the Music.* London: Victor Gollancz, 1975. An authoritative account of Hindemith's life that includes images and a chronological list of works.

See also: Anderson, Marian; Barretto, Ray; Berg, Alban; Carter, Elliott; Chávez, Carlos; Debussy, Claude; Fischer-Dieskau, Dietrich; Golijov, Osvaldo; Goodman, Benny; Gould, Glenn; Klemperer, Otto; Martin, Frank; Oistrakh, David; Perlman, Itzhak; Schoenberg, Arnold; Schreker, Franz; Serkin, Rudolf; Stern, Isaac; Strauss, Richard; Weill, Kurt.

Christopher Hogwood

English classical conductor and pianist

As the founder of the Academy of Ancient Music, a period instrument orchestra, Hogwood helped bring early music into the mainstream.

Born: September 10, 1941; Nottingham, England
Also known as: Christopher Jarvis Haley Hogwood (full name)
Member of: The Early Music Consort; the Academy of Ancient Music

Principal recordings

ALBUMS (as conductor): *Mozart: Symphony No. 38 "Prague"; Symphony No. 39,* 1984; *Bach: Brandenburg Concertos Nos. 1-6,* 1990; *Mozart: Clarinet Concerto; Oboe Concerto,* 1990; *Mozart:*

Requiem, 1990; *Music from Pachelbel, Handel, Vivaldi, and Gluck,* 1990; *Vivaldi: Four Seasons,* 1990; *Handel: Messiah,* 1991; *Handel: Orlando,* 1991; *Mozart: La Clemenza di Tito,* 1995; *Bach: Brandenburg Concertos,* 1997; *Bach: Eight Symphonies; Three Quartets,* 1997; *Beethoven: Symphonies,* 1997; *Handel: Water Music; Music for the Royal Fireworks,* 1997; *Haydn: Orfeo ed Euridice,* 1997; *Mozart: The Symphonies,* 1997; *Mozart: Violin Concertos,* 1997; *Vivaldi: Concerto for Two Mandolins,* 1997; *Bach: Orchestral Suites,* 1998; *Emma Kirkby Sings Handel, Arne, Haydn, and Mozart,* 1998; *Vivaldi: L'Estro Armonico,* 1998; *Albinoni: Twelve Concertos, Op. 9,* 1999; *Mozart: Great Mass in C Minor,* 1999; *Mozart: Wind Concertos,* 1999; *Handel: Rinaldo,* 2000; *Haydn: Symphonies Vol. 10, 1779-1781,* 2000; *Mozart: Piano Concertos Nos. 5, 14, and 16,* 2000; *Vivaldi: Violin Concertos, Op. 6,* 2000; *Fairest Isle,* 2001; *The Baroque Experience,* 2002; *Vivaldi: Stabat Mater,* 2003; *Purcell: Theatre Music,* 2004; *Handel: Oratorios,* 2005; *Beethoven: Five Piano Concertos; Three Popular Sonatas,* 2006; *Vivaldi: Concertos,* 2006.

WRITINGS OF INTEREST: *Music at Court,* 1977; *The Trio Sonata,* 1979; *Haydn's Visits to England,* 1980; *Music in Eighteenth-Century England,* 1983; *Handel,* 1984.

The Life

Christopher Jarvis Haley Hogwood was born in Nottingham, England, in 1941. In addition to studying music and classics at Pembroke College, Cambridge, Hogwood studied harpsichord with Gustav Leonhardt and Rafael Puyana. He studied conducting under Raymond Leppard and Thurston Dart, the latter a harpsichordist and a specialist in Johann Sebastian Bach.

From 1946 to 1965, the British Broadcasting Corporation produced a radio show called *Third Programme.* It offered significant broadcasts of early music, and it is considered seminal in the early-music revival. Coming of age in England during these years, Hogwood was exposed to performances by Dart on the British Broadcasting Corporation, and he began his career primarily as a harpsichordist. In that capacity, he cofounded the Early Music Consort with woodwind player David Munrow in 1973. Among the most musically accomplished of its time, this ensemble set a new standard in performance practice, and it made a somewhat radical move by commissioning new music for early instruments.

The Academy of Ancient Music was founded with a mission to perform seventeenth and eighteenth century music. The ensemble took its name from the original Academy of Ancient Music, an eighteenth century London group created to explore works from the sixteenth and seventeenth centuries. The repertoire of Hogwood's ensemble ranges from Henry Purcell to Igor Stravinsky. In addition, Hogwood has been a prolific conductor of live and recorded music, and he was the first conductor to record the complete symphonies of Wolfgang Amadeus Mozart and Ludwig van Beethoven on period instruments.

Hogwood has been active as an opera conductor, a scholar, and a writer. In addition to his work as a conductor of early music, he was the music director of the St. Paul Chamber Orchestra from 1987 to 1992.

The Music

Hogwood's work in music reflects his talents as conductor, writer, and editor. As a conductor, some of his most significant achievements have been the recordings of the Mozart and Beethoven symphonies, as well as the recordings of the Mozart piano concerti with fortepianist Robert Levin. Hogwood's combined talents have made him a significant part of the early-music revival, and his paleographic and editorial abilities have raised standards for historically informed performance around the world. Hogwood has continually broadened his own repertoire, and he is an expert conductor of Stravinsky (in particular the neoclassical works) as well as of earlier music. Hogwood has championed and recorded Bohuslav Martinů's music, in addition to presenting works by the so-called Entartete (degenerate) composers, whose music was banned by the Nazi Party in the 1930's. In addition to his work with twentieth century music, Hogwood has commissioned and premiered new works for period instruments. In concert programming, Hogwood often juxtaposes new and old works.

Conductor. Hogwood recorded and released Mozart's symphonies between 1978 and 1985, and

these recordings were lauded for their accuracy of performance practice and for their accuracy and clarity. In addition, they were notable for adhering to the score, devoid of the interpretive elements that were common in recordings of standard repertoire. While other early-music performers and audiences expected this stylistic approach, it took the mainstream classical audience by surprise. Well-reviewed and with good sales, the recordings set a standard for orchestral performance in the early music community.

Opera. Hogwood made his opera debut in 1983 with a production of Mozart's *Don Giovanni* (1787) in St. Louis. Since then, he has conducted around the world, becoming a particular proponent of George Frideric Handel operas. He was the music director for Boston's Handel and Haydn Society for many years.

Writer. Hogwood has written extensively on music. His output includes a significant monograph on Handel, a book on the trio sonata form, and a Cambridge Music Handbook on Handel's *The Music for Royal Fireworks* (1749) and *Water Music* (1717). His books are notable for their fluid writing and for their combination of musicological insight and practical concerns of a performer. Hogwood has contributed articles to books on music of eighteenth century England, on the classical period, and on many other topics. In addition, he has written a significant number of liner notes for a wide variety of recordings.

Editor. Hogwood's skills as an editor have contributed to the performance and interpretation of early music. He has prepared editions of keyboard music, including the complete keyboard works of Purcell. Other projects encompass the preparation of new editions of many of Felix Mendelssohn's works, which include many of the sketches and alternative endings left by the composer. Hogwood has also edited twentieth century works, including a new edition of Edward Elgar's *Enigma Variations* (1899), and he sits on the board of the Martinů Complete Edition.

Musical Legacy

Hogwood's musical legacy is significant. As a conductor, he has made hundreds of recordings and performed with numerous ensembles. His recordings are seminal in the field, and many of the earlier recordings with the Academy of Ancient Music are being rereleased. His work as an impresario created two period instrument ensembles; while the Early Music Consort disbanded in the 1970's, the Academy of Ancient Music continues to tour internationally. Hogwood's topics as a writer span hundreds of years, offering insight into both the source materials and the process of bringing the music to life. In addition to being a conductor, writer, and editor, Hogwood has held several teaching positions, and he was appointed international professor of early-music performance at the Royal Academy of Music in 1992. As a pedagogue, he influences young musicians, and he continues to develop the practice of historically informed performance. He was appointed a Commander of the British Empire in 1989.

Andrea Moore

Further Reading

Haskell, Harry. "Early Music." *The New Grove Dictionary of Music and Musicians*. Edited by Stanley Sadie. New York: Grove's Dictionaries, 2000. A valuable overview of the early-music movement, especially since World War II, that places Hogwood's work in historical context.

Hogwood, Christopher. *Handel*. Thames & Hudson, 2007. A significant biography of Handel, with a valuable chapter on the oratorios.

Pratt, George. "Christopher Hogwood." *The New Grove Dictionary of Music and Musicians*. Edited by Stanley Sadie. New York: Grove's Dictionaries, 2000. A brief biography of Hogwood, with a list of his writings.

Van Tassel, Eric. "Mozart Symphonies." *Early Music* 12, no. 1 (February, 1984): 125-129. A review of Hogwood's recordings of the Mozart symphonies from the early-music perspective.

See also: Casadesus, Henri; Elgar, Sir Edward; Leonhardt, Gustav; Martinů, Bohuslav; Stravinsky, Igor.

Billie Holiday
American jazz singer

A great jazz singer, Holiday developed a unique style that avoided athletic vocal techniques in favor of subtlety and dramatic irony. While eloquently expressing a full emotional range from personal despair to triumph, she was one of the first jazz artists to address social concerns and racial injustice.

Born: April 7, 1915; Philadelphia, Pennsylvania
Died: July 17, 1959; New York, New York
Also known as: Eleanora Fagan (birth name); Lady Day

Principal recordings

ALBUMS: *Billie Holiday Sings*, 1950; *Billie Holiday, Vol. 1*, 1950; *Billie Holiday, Vol. 2*, 1950; *An Evening with Billie Holiday*, 1953; *Billie Holiday, Vol. 3*, 1954; *Lady Sings the Blues*, 1954; *Music for Torching*, 1955; *Jazz Recital*, 1956; *A Recital by Billie Holiday*, 1956; *Velvet Moods*, 1956; *Body and Soul*, 1957; *Songs for Distingué Lovers*, 1957; *Blues Are Brewin'*, 1958; *Lady in Satin*, 1958; *Billie Holiday*, 1959; *Stay with Me*, 1959.

SINGLES: "Miss Brown to You," 1935; "What a Little Moonlight Can Do," 1935; "Billie's Blues," 1936; "Did I Remember?," 1936; "No Regrets," 1936; "He's Funny That Way," 1937; "Me, Myself and I," 1937; "Mean to Me," 1937; "Fine and Mellow," 1939; "Strange Fruit," 1939; "Gloomy Sunday," 1941; "God Bless the Child," 1941; "Loveless Love," 1941; "Lover Man," 1944.

WRITINGS OF INTEREST: *Lady Sings the Blues*, 1956 (with William Dufty).

The Life

Although born in Philadelphia, Pennsylvania, Billie Holiday grew up in Baltimore, Maryland, raised by her mother, Sadie Fagan (Harris), and her aunt, Eva Miller. She had only occasional contact with her father, Clarence Holiday, a jazz guitarist and banjo player. Her impoverished environment provided little hope for a life beyond menial labor, but she loved music. She frequented after-hours clubs to sing with Baltimore's best jazz musicians, and she sang along with recordings by her favorites, Louis Armstrong and Bessie Smith.

Soon after moving to New York in 1929, she sang for tips in jazz clubs and attended jam sessions. In 1930 she discarded her birth name, Eleanora Fagan, and took her father's last name and the actor Billie Dove's first name to create her stage name. In 1933, after record producer John Hammond heard her sing in Harlem, he arranged for Holiday to record with Benny Goodman, and she started performing and recording with other famous jazz musicians. In 1935 she recorded "What a Little Moonlight Can Do" and "Miss Brown to You." These became so popular that she was able to perform and record under her own name. She went on the road with two big bands: Count Basie's in 1937 and Artie Shaw's in 1938. While working with Shaw, she bravely met the challenge of being one of the first African American women to tour with a white orchestra. However, she was angered by the segregation she encountered as they traveled.

She returned to New York, and in 1939 she began singing at the Café Society, an integrated club, where she introduced many of her most famous songs in a generally supportive environment. She recorded on the Columbia Records label until 1942, and later she recorded for Decca Records. In 1947 Holiday appeared with Armstrong and Kid Ory in the film *New Orleans*. An arrest for a narcotics charge interfered with her New York career, but she continued to record and to perform at other locations, including a European tour in 1954. From 1952 to 1959, she recorded with Verve Records. On May 25, 1959, Holiday gave her final public concert at the Phoenix Theatre in New York. She died from liver disease at New York's Metropolitan Hospital on July 17, 1959.

The Music

Holiday's music can be divided into three style periods. The early years through 1938 can be characterized as energetic and playful, with faster tempi, light rhythms, and often humorous material with commercial appeal. During the middle period, from 1939 through the 1940's, Holiday utilized slower tempi to introduce an unprecedented level of dramatic, poetic expression and understatement to jazz song, while retaining rhythmic and melodic flexibility. Finally, in the 1950's, with a voice deteri-

Billie Holiday. (Library of Congress)

orated and raspy, partly because of health problems and drug addiction, she was at the peak of her mature artistic expression, giving profound meaning to every note and word.

Early Works. The recordings Holiday made before 1939 could be characterized as energetic and playful. These pieces included "He's Funny That Way," "Me, Myself, and I," "Mean to Me," and many others. Pianist Teddy Wilson arranged and performed on most of these recordings. Among the talented instrumentalists who worked with Holiday during this period was Lester Young, who became one of her dearest friends. He dubbed her Lady Day, and she in turned named him Pres (for president).

Like many of the jazz artists of her time, Holiday was self-taught and did not learn standard music notation. Instead, she relied on her incredible ear and musical memory. One of Holiday's most important vocal influences was Armstrong. Although she did not use the scat singing (improvisational use of nonlexical syllables) that Armstrong had popularized, she did utilize a similar approach to phrasing, with subtle pitch inflections and placing notes a bit behind or ahead of the beat and then resolving them rhythmically. The success of this depended on Holiday's high level of metronomic precision, which rivaled that of the great musicians of her time. Another important influence was Smith, who primarily sang blues. Holiday did not have Smith's dynamic range, but she deeply appreciated the older singer's emotional honesty and courage. Vocally, Holiday developed the ability to enhance, redirect, or even subvert a song's lyrics, adding an element of ambiguity and mystery to even the most commonplace pieces.

"Strange Fruit." Ironically, it was a song protesting racial injustice that broadened Holiday's audience beyond the jazz community. Her earlier collaborations with white musicians, such as Goodman and Shaw, did not generate the same level of interest as her recording in 1939 of "Strange Fruit" on the Commodore label. This song described the aftermath of a lynching of two black men. Lynching was all too frequent in the 1930's, but it was not a common topic in commercial music. Based on a poem written by schoolteacher Abel Meeropol, under the pen name Lewis Allan, "Strange Fruit" was the first recorded protest song to be widely heard. While most popular songs of the day were sentimental love ballads or humorous novelty tunes, this piece contained vividly gruesome imagery introduced with a bitter sense of ironic contrast. For instance, the song described a pastoral setting with the "strange fruit" of hanging bodies and blood everywhere. The sweet fragrance of magnolias competed with the smell of burning flesh. Holiday's singing turned Meeropol's poem into an indictment of an entire society.

"God Bless the Child." Arthur Herzog, Jr., wrote the music and Holiday wrote the lyrics for another of her famous songs, "God Bless the Child," based on a proverb. The song's message of self-reliance and strength in the face of adversity followed in the tradition of Smith's rendition of "Nobody Knows You When You're Down and Out" (1929). It is believed that Holiday wrote "God Bless the Child" after she and her mother had argued about money. Holiday first performed this masterpiece in 1939 and recorded it in 1941. Other artists who recorded or performed the song include Aretha Franklin, Stevie Wonder, Sonny Rollins,

and Blood, Sweat, and Tears. Diana Ross performed it in *Lady Sings the Blues*, the 1972 movie based on Holiday's life. In 2004 a picture book titled "God Bless the Child" was published, listing Holiday and Herzog as the authors, and it was illustrated by artist Jerry Pinkney, who graphically interpreted the song with images of a family moving to the North during the Great Migration of the 1930's. The song was an overwhelmingly popular choice for many contestants on television's *American Idol*.

"Fine and Mellow." Although not primarily thought of as a blues singer, Holiday sang "Fine and Mellow" for CBS television's *The Sound of Jazz*, the classic hour-length program, in 1957. One of her last recordings, this revealed her complete mastery of the blues form. Using her own composition (first recorded in 1939) as a starting point, she alternated her verses with improvised solos by the great musicians assembled for the session, including Coleman Hawkins, Mal Waldron, Ben Webster, Gerry Mulligan, Roy Eldridge, Doc Cheatham, Vic Dickenson, Danny Barker, and Milt Hinton. This was also a beautiful musical reunion of Lady Day and Pres after many years. The recording exemplified her later style, in which her athletic skills had diminished, but her ability to achieve emotional transformation of syllables through nuances of inflection had increased.

Musical Legacy

A legendary singer who struggled against personal and social obstacles, Holiday had a profound impact on both her contemporaries and future generations of musicians. Stylistically, Holiday's practice of recomposition, in which she freely altered the melodic shapes of songs, was a form of improvisation that differed from the practice of instrumental improvisers, who did not have to contend with lyrics and therefore could utilize varied rhythmic patterns in their solos. Instead, Holiday often added rhythmic tension, by anticipating or delaying a note, adding further pitch inflections, and increasing emotional intensity. This had a significant impact on instrumentalists and singers alike. Instrumentalists noted that she listened to and understood what they played, and then she related her virtuoso improvisations to their musical statements. Such renowned vocalists such as Frank Sinatra and Carmen McRae acknowledged Holiday as a great inspiration.

Holiday also expanded the social dimension of music. Her friendship with a select group of musicians was matched by her toughness and willingness to confront the hostility of the outside world, as she challenged gender as well as ethnic stereotypes. Along with other prominent jazz musicians of the late 1930's, Holiday helped to end the practice of segregation, long before sports, education, and the military services became integrated.

Posthumous honors showed her lasting influence. In 1959 poet Frank O'Hara wrote a tribute, "The Day Lady Died." In 1987 Holiday was awarded the Grammy Lifetime Achievement Award, and in 1988 the rock band U2 released the tribute song "Angel of Harlem." In 1994 the U.S. Postal Service introduced a Holiday postage stamp, and in 2000 Holiday was inducted into the Rock and Roll Hall of Fame.

Alice Myers

Further Reading

Blackburn, Julia. *With Billie*. New York: Pantheon Books, 2005. Personal stories from and interviews with people who knew the singer well: childhood friends, musicians, dancers, comedians, drug dealers, narcotics agents, lovers, and others. Bibliography and index.

Chilton, John. *Billie's Blues: The Billie Holiday Story, 1933-1959*. New York: Stein & Day, 1975. Written by a jazz historian, this was the first significant book about Holiday's career and recordings. Illustrated, with bibliography, discography, and index.

Clarke, Donald. *Wishing on the Moon: The Life and Times of Billie Holiday*. New York: Viking, 1994. Comprehensive biography based on interviews and extensive research of archival materials. Twenty-four pages of photographs. Index.

Davis, Angela. *Blues Legacies and Black Feminism: Gertrude "Ma" Rainey, Bessie Smith, and Billie Holiday*. New York: Pantheon Books, 1998. The chapter "When a Woman Loves a Man" discusses the social implications of Holiday's love

songs. The chapter "Strange Fruit" examines music and social consciousness. Illustrated, with index and extensive bibliography.

Gourse, Leslie. *The Billie Holiday Companion: Seven Decades of Commentary*. New York: Schirmer Books, 1997. An essential resource, including essays, news stories, reviews, and interviews with Holiday and Hammond. Index and discography.

Griffin, Farah Jasmine. *If You Can't Be Free, Be a Mystery: In Search of Billie Holiday*. New York: Free Press, 2001. Dispelling the myths and stereotypes surrounding Holiday, the author reveals the singer to be a true musical genius. Illustrated, with bibliography, chronology, and index.

Holiday, Billie. *Billie Holiday Anthology: "Lady Day" Had a Right to Sing the Blues*. Ojai, Calif.: Creative Concepts, 2000. Includes biographical information and musical scores for forty-three songs, including "The Birth of the Blues," "I Can't Give You Anything but Love," "St. Louis Blues," and "Stormy Weather." Illustrated.

Holiday, Billie, and William Dufty. *Lady Sings the Blues*. New York: Harlem Moon, 2006. Fiftieth-anniversary edition of Holiday's candid and revealing autobiography, which inspired the motion picture starring Ross. Illustrated, with index, discography, and sound disc.

Margolick, David. *"Strange Fruit": The Biography of a Song*. New York: Ecco Press, 2001. Well-researched and insightful account of one of the most significant songs in history. Illustrated, with discography.

O'Meally, Robert. *Lady Day: The Many Faces of Billie Holiday*. New York: Arcade, 1991. A biography beautifully illustrated with photographs. Includes discography and bibliography.

See also: Armstrong, Louis; Basie, Count; Cooke, Sam; Dorsey, Thomas A.; Fitzgerald, Ella; Goodman, Benny; Hampton, Lionel; James, Etta; Legrand, Michel; Robinson, Smokey; Rollins, Sonny; Ross, Diana; Shaw, Artie; Simone, Nina; Smith, Bessie; Vaughan, Sarah; Young, Lester.

Eddie and Brian Holland

American rhythm-and-blues songwriters

During the 1960's, Brian Holland, Lamont Dozier, and Eddie Holland (better known as Holland-Dozier-Holland, or H-D-H) formed a songwriting and production partnership that went on to produce some of the most memorable "Motown sound" hits in the history of popular music.

Eddie Holland

Born: October 30, 1939; Detroit, Michigan
Also known as: Edward Holland, Jr. (full name)

Brian Holland

Born: February 15, 1941; Detroit, Michigan

Members of: Holland-Dozier-Holland (H-D-H)

Principal works

SONG (with Georgia Dobbins, William Garrett, Robert Bateman, and Freddie Gorman): "Please, Mr. Postman," 1961 (performed by the Marvellettes).

SONGS (with Lamont Dozier): "Can I Get a Witness," 1963 (performed by Marvin Gaye); "Come and Get These Memories," 1963 (performed by Martha and the Vandellas); "Heat Wave," 1963 (performed by Martha and the Vandellas); "Mickey's Monkey," 1963 (performed by the Miracles); "Quicksand," 1963 (performed by Martha and the Vandellas); "Baby I Need Your Loving," 1964 (performed by the Four Tops); "Baby Love," 1964 (performed by the Supremes); "Come See About Me," 1964 (performed by the Supremes); "How Sweet It Is (to Be Loved by You)," 1964 (performed by Gaye); "Locking Up My Heart," 1964 (performed by the Marvelletes); "When the Lovelight Starts Shining in His Eyes," 1964 (performed by the Supremes); "Where Did Our Love Go?," 1964 (performed by the Supremes); "Back in My Arms Again," 1965 (performed by the Supremes); "I Can't Help Myself (Sugar Pie, Honey Bunch)," 1965 (performed by the Four Tops); "(It's the) Same Old Song," 1965 (performed by the Four Tops); "Nowhere to Run," 1965 (performed by Martha and the Vandellas); "Stop! In the Name of Love," 1965 (performed by the Supremes); "Take Me in Your Arms (Rock Me a Little While)," 1965 (performed by Kim Weston); "I'm Ready for Love," 1966 (performed by Martha and the Vandellas); "Little Darling (I Need You)," 1966 (performed by Gaye); "Reach Out I'll Be There," 1966 (performed by the Four Tops); "This Old Heart of Mine (Is Weak for You)," 1966 (performed by the Isley Brothers); "You Can't Hurry Love," 1966 (performed by the Supremes); "You Keep Me Hangin' On," 1966 (performed by the Supremes); "Bernadette," 1967 (performed by the Four Tops); "The Happening," 1967 (performed by the Supremes); "Jimmy Mack," 1967 (performed by Martha and the Vandellas); "Love Is Here and Now You're Gone," 1967 (performed by the Supremes); "Reflections," 1967 (performed by Diana Ross and the Supremes); "Give Me Just a Little More Time," 1970 (performed by Chairmen of the Board).

The Lives

Edward Holland, Jr., was born on October 30, 1939, in Detroit, Michigan. His younger brother, Brian Holland, was born on February 15, 1941, also in Detroit. Their future songwriting partner, Lamont Dozier, also was born in Detroit. Growing up in an urban environment, the Holland brothers learned to appreciate the music that surrounded them. As children, they attended church on a regular basis. Their grandmother was a strong force in both their lives. She refused to let the young brothers listen to any other kind of music in the home except gospel music and classical music. The brothers attended local Detroit schools, including Davison Elementary School, Cleveland Intermediate School, and Wilbur Wright High School. While popular music was banned from the home, they would get a chance to hear secular music when they were out with their friends at local skating rinks, clubs, or ballrooms. Music became a strong force in their lives.

Eddie met the future founder of Motown Records, Berry Gordy, Jr., in 1958. Out of the relationship established between the two, Eddie dropped out of college in order to work for Gordy. With

Gordy as his producer, Eddie released several singles as a solo artist between 1958 and 1960, including "You" for Mercury, "Because I Love Her" for United Artists, and "The Last Laugh," also for United Artists. In the fall of 1961, Eddie released the single "Jamie" for Motown. By the next year, it had reached number thirty on the *Billboard* pop singles chart and number six on the rhythm-and-blues singles chart. Although Eddie would release several more singles for Motown, none of them would be as successful as "Jamie."

While Eddie was busily establishing himself in the music business, Brian also was working as a vocalist. In 1958, he released his first solo single under the name Briant Holland. Eventually, he became the lead vocalist for the group the Satintones. In 1960, Brian worked as the piano player for Barrett Strong. Out of this relationship, he would join Motown Records in 1961. After joining Motown, Brian would co-write the Marvelettes' hit single "Please, Mr. Postman." In 1962, Brian began working with Freddy Gorman and Dozier. This arrangement would last only until 1963, when older brother Eddie replaced Gorman. The legendary team of Holland-Dozier-Holland was now established, and they soon would be making music history, producing a string of hits for Motown engines such as Martha and the Vandellas, Diana Ross and the Supremes, the Four Tops, and Marvin Gaye.

By the early 1970's, the Holland-Dozier-Holland partnership was becoming somewhat frayed around the edges. Dozier decided that it was time to go back to being a solo artist and began releasing solo albums. Although the Holland brothers did not remain as active in the music business as Dozier after their dissolution, the partnership was revived in 1984, when the three revived Music Merchant Records in order to take control of their back catalog and to groom new artists.

The Music

During their collaboration, H-D-H believed that they were inventing the way songs should be written. There was no precedent for their form of songwriting. While Brian and Dozier concentrated on the melody and production of a song, Eddie was the primary lyricist of the team, and, more times than not, the music inspired his lyrics. During many recording sessions, they would experiment with what could be considered unorthodox chords, in the end finding the perfect combination. They established an effective way to communicate with one another that allowed for flexibility and the free flow of ideas. It could happen that at the opening stages of putting a song together they would imagine one particular vocalist singing it, but by the end of the process they would realize that the octave needed to be changed and that another vocalist would do a better job with the finished song. In their prime, Holland-Dozier-Holland knew how to keep their ideas flowing and how to keep their options open. Since none of the team could write music, it was necessary for them to call in someone to right down the chords. Ideas for songs often came from real-life experiences, or at least there was a real-life experience that got the song started. Since each member brought a diversity of musical experience to the process, it was possible for each to focus on one particular aspect during a recording session. On most occasions, Dozier would work with the rhythm section and the background vocals, Eddie would concentrate on coaching the lead vocal, and Brian would function as the team's sound engineer.

Motown Hits. Beginning in 1963, Holland-Dozier-Holland began having fantastic success writing songs for Berry Gordy's Motown Records. During this memorable year, they wrote such classic songs as "Come and Get These Memories," "Heat Wave," and "Quicksand" for Martha and the Vandellas; "Locking Up My Heart" for the Marvelettes; "Mickey's Monkey" for the Miracles; and "Can I Get a Witness" for Marvin Gaye. All of these vibrant and upbeat singles charted on the *Billboard* pop charts. "Heat Wave" would rise to number four, and "Quicksand" to number eight. Because of the creative efforts of Holland-Dozier-Holland, Martha and the Vandellas would have several more hit singles during the mid-1960's, including the single "Nowhere to Run," which went to number eight on the pop singles chart in 1965; the single "I'm Ready for Love," which went to number nine in 1966; and the single "Jimmy Mack," which went to number ten in 1967. During this same period, H-D-H wrote the 1964 number six hit "How Sweet It Is (to Be Loved by You)" for Gaye and the 1966 number-twelve hit "This Old Heart of Mine (Is Weak for You)" for the Isley Brothers. With upbeat melodies and catchy lyrics, these hit songs firmly established Holland-Dozier-Holland as one of the premier songwriting partnerships in America.

The Supremes. H-D-H produced an amazing string of hits for the Supremes and the Four Tops. Although the first single they wrote for the Supremes, "When the Lovelight Starts Shining Through His Eyes," was something of a disappointment since it rose only to number twenty-three on the pop singles chart, many of the songs to come would make music history. The Supremes had three number-one H-D-H hits in 1964 with "Where Did Our Love Go?," "Baby Love," and "Come See About Me." From 1965 to 1967, the Supremes would have seven number-one H-D-H singles, including such remarkable songs as "Stop! In the Name of Love," "Back in My Arms Again," "You Can't Hurry Love," "You Keep Me Hangin' On," and "The Happening." Through the brilliance of Holland-Dozier-Holland, Diana Ross and the Supremes became superstars.

The Four Tops. During this time period, Holland-Dozier-Holland also wrote spectacular hits for the Four Tops, including the single "Baby I Need Your Loving," which went to number eleven; the single "(It's the) Same Old Song," which went to number one; the single "Reach Out I'll Be There," which also went to number one; the single "Standing in the Shadows of Love," which went to number six; and the single "Bernadette," which went to number four.

End of the Motown Years. By 1968, the working relationship between Gordy and Holland-Dozier-Holland had become extremely difficult. They were dissatisfied with their royalty agreement with Motown, and since no quick resolution was forthcoming, they decided that it was time to leave Motown. After cutting their ties with Gordy's label, they started Hot Wax and Invictus Records. Because of legal entanglements with Gordy, however, they were unable to release any recordings under their new labels until 1970. From 1970 to 1971, they released hits by such recording artists as Chairmen of the Board, Freda Payne, and Honey Cone. They also started Music Merchant Records in 1972, but it folded in 1973.

Musical Legacy

During the 1960's, the Motown songwriting and production partnership of Holland-Dozier-Holland produced an amazing number of hit sin-gles for such legendary recording artists as the Supremes, the Four Tops, the Marvelettes, the Miracles, Martha and the Vandellas, and Marvin Gaye. From 1963 to 1967, they wrote twenty-five Top 10 hits. Remarkably, twelve of these songs went to number one on the pop singles chart. They also charted songs on the rhythm-and-blues singles charts, several of which rose to the Top 10.

Because of their ability to write songs that combined the best elements of pop, soul, country, and rhythm and blues, they were able to appeal to a large cross-section of Americans. Their songs became synonymous with the "Motown sound" and entered the American songbook as all-time classics. In 1988, Lamont Dozier, Brian Holland, and Eddie Holland were inducted into the Songwriters Hall of Fame. They were inducted into the Rock and Roll Hall of Fame in 1990.

Jeffry Jensen

Further Reading

Abbott, Kingsley, ed. *Calling Out Around the World: A Motown Reader*. London: Helter Skelter, 2001. An extraordinary collection of essays that delves into the many sides of Motown.

Bianco, David. *Heat Wave: The Motown Fact Book*. Ann Arbor, Mich.: Pieran Press, 1988. A fascinating portrait of Motown Records, including perceptive insights into how Holland-Dozier-Holland worked with the Motown recording artists.

Egan, Sean. *The Guys Who Wrote 'Em: Songwriting Geniuses of Rock and Pop*. London: Askill, 2004. Includes a fine tribute to Holland-Dozier-Holland.

George, Nelson. *Where Did Our Love Go? The Rise and Fall of the Motown Sound*. Rev. ed. New York: St. Martin's Press, 2007. A hard-hitting chronicle of the rise and fall of Motown Records.

Posner, Gerald. *Motown: Music, Money, Sex, and Power*. New York: Random House, 2002. This is a powerful study of what Motown achieved and how power, sex, and money tore at its very foundation. What Holland-Dozier-Holland were able to achieve during their tenure at Motown represents one of the company's most remarkable positive legacies.

Smith, Suzanne E. *Dancing in the Street: Motown and the Cultural Politics of Detroit*. Cambridge, Mass.: Harvard University Press, 1999. An extraordinary portrait of the crucial role Motown played in the socially charged African American community.

Waller, Don. *The Motown Story*. New York: Charles Scribner's Sons, 1985. Gives the reader a behind-the-scenes look at how Motown produced such extraordinarily popular music.

See also: Cooke, Sam; Costello, Elvis; Dozier, Lamont; Fogerty, John; Gabriel, Peter; Gaye, Marvin; Jackson, Janet; Jackson, Michael; Jamerson, James; Latifah, Queen; Odetta; Pickett, Wilson; Plant, Robert; Robinson, Smokey; Ross, Diana; Seger, Bob; Taylor, James; Van Halen, Eddie; Webb, Jimmy; Wilson, Jackie; Wonder, Stevie.

Buddy Holly

American singer, guitarist, and songwriter

A talented innovator and one of the originators of rock and roll, Holly excelled as a musician, composer, performer, and arranger. The makeup of his band—lead guitar, rhythm guitar, bass, and drums—became the standard in the 1960's and is emulated by groups to this day.

Born: September 7, 1936; Lubbock, Texas
Died: February 3, 1959; Near Clear Lake, Iowa
Also known as: Charles Hardin Holley (birth name)
Member of: Buddy Holly and the Crickets; Buddy Holly and the Three Tunes

Principal recordings

ALBUMS: *The "Chirping" Crickets*, 1957 (with the Crickets); *Buddy Holly*, 1958; *That'll Be the Day*, 1958 (with the Three Tunes); *The Buddy Holly Story*, 1959; *The Buddy Holly Story, Vol. 2*, 1960; *Reminiscing*, 1963; *Showcase*, 1964; *Holly in the Hills*, 1965; *Giant*, 1969.

The Life

Buddy Holly was born in the west Texas town of Lubbock in 1936, the fourth and final child of Lawrence and Ella Holley. Buddy was gifted in music and won a talent show at the age of five. By the end of his teenage years he had largely taught himself to play a variety of instruments, including the violin, guitar, piano, and drums. While still in junior high school, he formed his first music group with a friend named Bob Montgomery, and they played locally wherever a willing audience could be found. Holly's musical tastes were eclectic, but he was particularly a fan of country singer Hank Williams and bluegrass and gospel music.

Holly saw Elvis Presley perform live at Lubbock twice in 1955, and they shared a friendly conversation backstage. Presley was impressed with the young Texan and gave Holly the chance to open for him during his second Lubbock concert, an opportunity Holly immediately seized. He now knew that being a professional musician would be his life's work.

Holly (who by then had dropped the "e" in his surname) formed a new band which he named the Crickets. Other members of the band were Jerry Allison (drums), Joe Mauldin (bass), and Niki Sullivan (rhythm guitar). After an unsatisfactory recording session in Nashville, Holly and the Crickets recorded a series of hits at producer Norman Petty's studio in nearby Clovis, New Mexico. After a string of successes, Buddy hit a dry spell and his newer recordings did poorly on the charts. His relationship with Petty ended in an acrimonious dispute over royalties. By late 1958 Sullivan had quit the group, but Allison and Mauldin remained loyal to Petty. In August, 1958, Buddy married Maria Elena Santiago, a woman he met in New York, and they settled in Greenwich Village, where Holly hoped to restart his stalled career. By the following year the newlyweds were strapped for money because Holly's earnings were tied up with Petty in New Mexico. He reluctantly agreed to leave the pregnant Maria and tour with a show called the Winter Dance Party. While on the tour, Holly and fellow performers Ritchie Valens and the Big Bopper were tragically killed in a plane crash.

The Music

"That'll Be the Day." This song's title was lifted from a phrase in a John Wayne movie and hit the number-one spot on the record charts in September, 1957. Earlier recordings of this song in Nashville had failed to excite anyone, but when it was

Buddy Holly. (AP/Wide World Photos)

rerecorded at Petty's studio, Holly sang in a different octave and changed the tempo, producing an all-time classic song.

"Peggy Sue." Originally "Cindy Lou," the title was changed to honor drummer Allison's girlfriend. This song features Holly's unique lyrical styling, extensive studio experimentation, and a driving beat. Released in the fall of 1957, this song topped out at number three on the charts.

"Not Fade Away." Although significant, this song did not enjoy the commercial success of other Holly tunes. A cover version by the Rolling Stones would be that group's first release in the United States. The song demonstrated again Holly's penchant for improvisation, as he had drummer Allison beat on an empty cardboard box rather than his drums.

"Everyday." Underappreciated at the time, this tune, recorded in 1957, displayed the artist's creativity by featuring a celesta, an instrument similar to a harpsichord. Allison, not originally scheduled to be on the recording, can be heard keeping rhythm by slapping his hands on his legs, a sound Holly liked and kept in the record.

"Maybe Baby." Holly's mother helped write this song, suggesting the title and a few lyrics. It was recorded at Tinker Air Force Base in Oklahoma City and is a great example of 1950's rock and roll.

"It's So Easy." This jubilant song about the power and ease of falling in love was one of Holly's most successful commercially. It has been rerecorded by many artists since its 1958 composition.

"True Love Ways." Recorded in 1958, this song indicates Buddy's musical curiosity was alive and well. He had been in something of a sales slump and wanted to experiment with strings, so this original composition was recorded using an orchestra. Beautiful and haunting, this love song has maintained its appeal for more than five decades.

"It Doesn't Matter Anymore." This song was recorded at the same session that produced "True Love Ways" and also features the backing orchestra. It was written by Paul Anka with Holly in mind. Although the song is generally upbeat, its title seemed sadly prophetic when Holly was killed shortly after its release.

Musical Legacy

Holly had a tremendous influence on popular music, with his creative talents as a singer, musician, composer, and arranger. He was one of the first pop singers to record his own compositions, and his masterful playing helped popularize the Fender Stratocaster guitar. The instrumental makeup of his group the Crickets became the standard for countless future groups. Holly sang in various vocal styles, and his recordings appealed to fans across musical genre lines. He defied the musical customs of his time by experimenting with different instruments and sounds, yet his songs were instantly recognizable. Both the Beatles and the Rolling Stones acknowledged a debt to Holly, and his songs have been recorded by artists as diverse as Chad and Jeremy, Waylon Jennings, and Linda Ronstadt. Although he died a half century ago, his musical impact shows no indication of fading away.

Thomas W. Buchanan

Further Reading

Amburn, Ellis. *Buddy Holly*. New York: St. Martin's Press, 1995. Thorough source, covering Holly's life from cradle to grave. Well researched and containing many interviews of those who knew him best, Amburn's work provides encyclopedic information.

Brown, Pete, and H. P. Newquist. *Legends of Rock Guitar: The Essential Reference of Rock's Greatest Guitarists*. Milwaukee, Wis.: Hal Leonard, 1997. An outstanding reference, this book covers hundreds of guitar players from the beginning of the rock era. There is an informative section about Holly's technical ability, stressing his open chord playing and reliance on powerful downstrokes.

Goldrosen, John. *The Buddy Holly Story*. New York: Quick Fox, 1979. Satisfactory telling of the main events in the artist's life, covering in some detail the historical inaccuracies found in the 1978 motion picture starring Gary Busey as Holly. It also provides the history of every Holly recording session.

Lehmer, Larry. *The Day the Music Died*. New York: Schirmer Books, 1997. The tragic 1959 Winter Dance Party is the focus, with voluminous information about the stars, the itinerary, and the plane crash.

Norman, Philip. *Rave On: The Biography of Buddy Holly*. New York: Simon & Schuster, 1996. Another comprehensive biography with an insightful look at Holly's family history and his widow, Maria Elena.

See also: Dylan, Bob; Jagger, Sir Mick; Jennings, Waylon; Nelson, Ricky; Orbison, Roy; Presley, Elvis; Valens, Ritchie; Vincent, Gene; Williams, Hank.

Gustav Holst

English classical composer, ethnomusicologist

Holst was a prolific composer, best known for his seven-movement orchestral suite The Planets. *He also was significant for preserving British folk music and composing serious music for bands.*

Born: September 21, 1874; Cheltenham, England
Died: May 25, 1934; London, England

Also known as: Gustavus Theodore von Holst (full name)

Principal works

BALLETS (music): *The Lure*, 1921; *The Golden Goose*, Op. 45, No. 1, 1926 (choral ballet; scenario by Jane Marian Joseph); *The Morning of the Year*, Op. 45, No. 2, 1927 (choral ballet).

CHAMBER WORKS: String Trio in G Minor, composed 1894, first performed 1984; *Fantasiestücke*, Op. 2, 1896 (for oboe and string quartet); Quintet in A Minor, Op. 3, 1896 (for piano and wind instruments); Wind Quintet in A-Flat, Op. 14, composed 1903, first performed 1982; *Two Songs Without Words*, Op. 22, 1906; *Seven Scottish Airs*, 1907 (for strings and piano); *Terzetto*, 1926 (for flute, oboe, and viola); *Lyric Movement*, 1934 (for viola and chamber orchestra); *Fantasia on Hampshire Folksongs*, 1970 (for string orchestra; arranged by Imogen Holst; based on Gustav Holst's *Phantasy*).

CHORAL WORKS: *Short Partsongs*, 1896 (for female chorus); *Clear and Cool*, Op. 5, 1897; *Autumn Song*, 1899 (for female chorus); *Five Partsongs*, Op. 9a, 1900; *Ave Maria*, Op. 9b, 1901 (for female chorus); *Five Partsongs*, Op. 12, 1903; *King Estmere*, Op. 17, 1903; *Thou Didst Delight My Eyes*, 1904; *Home They Brought Her Warrior Dead*, 1905 (for female chorus); *Songs from "The Princess,"* Op. 20a, 1905 (for female chorus; based on Alfred, Lord Tennyson's poem); *Four Old English Carols*, Op. 20b, 1907 (for chorus and piano); *In Youth Is Pleasure*, 1908 (based on Robert Wever's poem); *Pastoral*, 1908 (for female chorus); *A Welcome Song*, 1908 (for chorus, oboe, and cello); *O England My Country*, 1909; *The Cloud Messenger*, Op. 30, 1910; *Four Partsongs*, 1910 (for female chorus and piano; lyrics by John Greenleaf Whittier); *Hecuba's Lament*, Op. 31, No. 1, 1911; *Incidental Music to a London Pageant*, 1911 (for military band and chorus); *Two Eastern Pictures*, 1911 (for female chorus and harp); *Two Psalms*, 1912 (for chorus, strings, and organ); *The Homecoming*, 1913 (for male chorus; lyrics by Thomas Hardy); *Hymn to Dionysus*, Op. 31, No. 2, 1913; *The Swallow Leaves Her Nest*, 1913; *Choral Hymns from the Rig Veda*, Op. 26, 1914; *Nunc dimittis*, 1915 (for chorus and eight voices); *Bring Us in Good Ale*, Op. 34, No. 4, 1916; *Lullay My Liking*, Op. 34, No. 2, 1916 (for soprano and chorus); *Of One That Is So Fair*, Op. 34, No. 3, 1916 (for chorus and four voices); *Terly Terlow*, 1916 (for chorus, oboe, and cello); *This Have I Done for My True Love*, Op. 34, No. 1, 1916; *Three Festival Choruses*, Op. 36a, 1916; *Two Carols*, 1916 (for chorus, oboe, and cello); *Diverus and Lazarus*, 1917; *A Dream of Christmas*, 1917 (for female chorus and strings or piano); *The Hymn of Jesus*, Op. 37, 1917 (for two choruses, female semichorus, and orchestra); *Two Partsongs*, 1917 (for female chorus, two voices, and piano; lyrics by Whittier); *Ode to Death*, Op. 38, 1919; *Short Festival Te Deum*, 1919; *Seven Choruses from Alcestis*, 1920 (for chorus, harp, and three flutes; based on Euripides' play); First Choral Symphony, Op. 41, 1924; *The Evening-Watch*, Op. 43, No. 1, 1925 (lyrics by Henry Vaughan); *Sing Me the Men*, Op. 43, No. 2, 1925 (lyrics by Digby Mackworth Dolben); *Two Motets*, Op. 43, 1925; *Seven Partsongs*, Op. 44, 1926; *Two Anthems*, 1927 (for chorus, organ, and bells); *Twelve Songs*, Op. 48, 1929 (for chorus and piano); *A Choral Fantasia*, Op. 51, 1930; *Wassail Song*, 1930; *Eight Canons*, 1931 (for chorus and piano); *Twelve Welsh Folk Songs*, 1931.

OPERAS (music): *The Revoke*, 1895 (libretto by Fritz B. Hart); *The Idea*, 1898 (children's operetta; libretto by Hart); *The Youth's Choice*, 1902 (libretto by Holst); *Sita*, Op. 23, 1906 (based on the poem "The Rāmāyaṇa"); *The Vision of Dame Christian*, Op. 27a, 1909 (masque); *Savitri*, Op. 25, 1916 (based on the epic *The Mahabharata*); *The Perfect Fool*, Op. 39, 1923; *At the Boar's Head*, Op. 42, 1925 (based on William Shakespeare's play *Henry IV*); *The Wandering Scholar*, Op. 50, 1934 (libretto by Clifford Bax).

ORCHESTRAL WORKS: *A Winter Idyll*, composed 1897, first performed 1983; *Walt Whitman Overture*, Op. 7, composed 1899, first performed 1982; Symphony in F Major, Op. 8, 1900 (*The Cotswolds*); *Indra*, Op. 13, 1903 (symphonic poem); *A Song of the Night*, Op. 19, No. 1, composed 1905, first performed 1984; *Songs of the West*, Op. 21, No. 1, 1907; *Stepney Children's Pageant*, Op. 27b, 1909; Suite in E-flat Major, Op. 28, No. 1, 1909 (for military band);

A Somerset Rhapsody, Op. 21, No. 2, 1910; *Invocation*, Op. 19, No. 2, 1911 (for cello and orchestra); Suite in F Major, Op. 28, No. 2, composed 1911, first performed 1922 (for military band); *Beni Mora*, Op. 29, No. 1, 1912 (oriental suite); *Saint Paul's Suite*, Op. 29, No. 2, 1913 (for strings); *Japanese Suite*, Op. 33, 1916; *The Planets*, Op. 32, 1918; *A Fugal Concerto*, Op. 40, No. 2, 1923 (for flute, oboe, and strings); *A Fugal Overture*, Op. 40, No. 1, 1923; *Egdon Heath*, Op. 47, 1928; *Fugue à la Gigue*, 1928 (for brass band); *A Moorside Suite*, 1928 (for brass band); *Hammersmith*, 1930 (for brass band); Double Concerto, Op. 49, 1930 (for two violins and orchestra); *Brook Green Suite*, 1934 (for strings); *Scherzo*, 1935.

PIANO WORKS: Toccata, 1924; *Chrissemas Day in the Morning*, Op. 46, No. 1, 1926 (for solo piano); *Two Folk Song Fragments*, Op. 46, No. 2, 1927; Nocturne, 1930; *Jig*, 1932.

VOCAL WORKS: *Örnulf's Drapa*, Op. 6, 1898 (for baritone and orchestra); *The Mystic Trumpeter*, Op. 18, 1905 (scena for soprano and orchestra; based on Walt Whitman's poem *From Noon to Starry Night*); *The Heart Worships*, 1907 (song for voice and piano); *Hymns from the Rig Veda*, Op. 24, 1908 (for voice and piano); Four Songs, Op. 35, 1917 (for soprano or tenor and violin).

The Life

Gustavus Theodore von Holst (GEW-stahv holst) was the first of two children born to Adolph von Holst, a music teacher, and his wife Clara, an amateur musician who died when Holst was eight years old. Holst suffered from neuritis, a nerve inflammation that hampered his studies of violin and piano. He began to compose while in grammar school and eventually studied at Oxford and the Royal College of Music.

In 1895 Holst met Ralph Vaughan Williams, another Royal College of Music student, who became his closest musical friend and ally. The two composers developed a lifelong tradition of playing their new scores for each other and providing earnest feedback. Still suffering from crippling neuritis, Holst switched to trombone, which he played professionally for a short time.

Holst failed in his first attempts to make a living as a composer, so he turned to teaching. In 1905 he became musical director at St. Paul's Girls' School, in Hammersmith, a post he retained for the remainder of his career, while also teaching at Morley College in London, University College, Reading, and the Royal College of Music.

Holst's compositions became better known, eliciting conducting engagements, including 1911 performances at Queen's Hall in London. As World War I began and it became popular to support British composers, Holst was completing his masterpiece, the large orchestral suite *The Planets*. At the same time, in response to anti-German sentiment, Holst dropped the "von" that had been spuriously added to the family name only two generations earlier. His career flourished in the second half of the decade.

In 1923 a fall from a conductor's podium weakened Holst's fragile constitution. In 1932, despite his poor health, Holst accepted an invitation to lecture at Harvard University, and he never recovered from his exhausting schedule in the United States. In 1934, just short of his sixtieth birthday, Holst, weakened by ulcer surgery, died of a heart attack. His ashes rest at the cathedral in Chichester.

The Music

Holst was a prolific composer, though few of his works remain in the repertoire. His operas, for example, are rarely revisited, except for a ballet suite from *The Perfect Fool*. While his early works were influenced by the music of Maurice Ravel, Richard Strauss, and Richard Wagner, Holst gradually developed a more individual style as he became increasingly interested in setting folk melodies and incorporating folk modality. His harmonic language and asymmetrical meters, while not as challenging as those of Igor Stravinsky or Anton von Webern, were bold for a British composer, and he often found resistance in domestic audiences.

Early Works. Several of Holst's student compositions won prizes, and when he was seventeen, his father arranged for three of his works to receive public performances. In 1905 Holst completed *The Mystic Trumpeter* for soprano and orchestra, mostly Wagnerian in its chromaticism, with hints of the polytonality that Holst would employ more extensively in later works. His interest in folk songs brought the use of modes into his composing, and

his awareness of current trends on the Continent brought him additional compositional resources. Holst had studied Sanskrit in London, and several of his early works reflected the influence of Hindu philosophy and religion, in particular the series of *Choral Hymns from the Rig Veda* that he set between 1907 and 1912.

Saint Paul's Suite. Holst composed the four-movement *Saint Paul's Suite* to fit the abilities of the young string players in St. Paul's school. The work evinces the influence of folk melody on his music of this period. Holst would later produce other educational works, including *Brook Green Suite*, composed for the school orchestra in 1933.

Band Music. In 1909 Holst composed his Suite in E-flat Major for military band. This three-movement suite, based on a single theme, gave the band its first serious composition that was not an opera or orchestral transcription, beginning a lifelong relationship between Holst and band musicians. The Suite in F Major that followed two years later challenged the musicians with mixed-meter syncopation. Two more band works entered the repertoire in 1928: *A Moorside Suite* and *Fugue à la Gigue*. In 1930 the BBC Military Band commissioned Holst to write *Hammersmith*, which, like his other band works, is still in the standard repertoire of bands around the world.

The Planets. Always interested in astrology, Holst began in 1914 to compose his seven-movement astrological suite, *The Planets*. What is considered Holst's masterpiece reflects the influence of the important and controversial composers of the time, Stravinsky and Arnold Schoenberg. Familiar sections of *The Planets* range from the relentless militaristic march of "Mars, Bringer of War," with its asymmetrical five-beat meter, to the famous hymn from "Jupiter, Bringer of Jollity." The huge orchestration of *The Planets* (even requiring double timpanists) was capped by the use of an offstage wordless chorus fade-out at the end of "Neptune, the Mystic." As famous as *The Planets* has become, however, it was never Holst's favorite.

Egdon Heath. In May, 1927, Holst received a commission from the New York Symphony Orchestra, and he chose to dedicate the new piece to the author Thomas Hardy. After visiting Hardy, Holst was inspired to write what he considered his best composition. At the time, audience and critical opinion of the tone poem did not match Holst's high opinion, and the piece languished.

Musical Legacy

While Holst's musical legacy is perpetuated primarily by the quality of his compositions, he was also significant for preserving British folk song and composing serious band music. He also helped perpetuate the memory of earlier great British composers, arranging, in 1911, for the first performance since 1697 of Henry Purcell's *The Fairy Queen* (1692). Holst's work as a music educator affected generations of young students of all abilities, notably American composer Elliott Carter, with whom he worked at Harvard University. Holst was awarded the Gold Medal of the Royal Philharmonic Society and was a fellow of the Royal College of Music. Along with these honors and accomplishments, Holst is remembered for his most famous orchestral composition, *The Planets*.

William S. Carson

Further Reading

Holmes, Paul. *Illustrated Lives of the Great Composers—Holst: His Life and Times*. London: Omnibus Press, 1997. Holmes's volume includes portions of Imogen Holst's biography of her father, as well as materials from Michael Short's Holst biography. Illustrations, bibliography, discography.

Holst, Imogen. *Gustav Holst: A Biography*. Oxford, England: Oxford University Press, 1988. Holst's only child, Imogen, was also a composer and conductor. She served as Benjamin Britten's assistant before retiring to devote her time to cataloging her father's music.

Short, Michael. *Gustav Holst: The Man and His Music*. London: Oxford University Press, 1990. Short studied Holst's diaries and letters and worked with his daughter Imogen to create a definitive picture of her father. Analysis, references.

See also: Carter, Elliott; Debussy, Claude; Ravel, Maurice; Strauss, Richard; Vaughan Williams, Ralph.

Arthur Honegger
French classical composer

Honegger composed more than two hundred works in a variety of genres, including music for the theater, concert hall, and cinema. His unique approach to form and his integration of French and German musical traditions are hallmarks of his innovative style.

Born: March 10, 1892; Le Havre, France
Died: November 27, 1955; Paris, France
Also known as: Oscar Arthur Honegger (full name)

Principal works

BALLETS (music): *Le Dit des jeux du monde*, 1918 (libretto by Paul Méral); *Vérité? Mensonge?*, 1920 (*Truth? Lies?*; libretto by André Hellé); *Danse de la chévre*, 1921 (*Dance of the Goat*; libretto by Sacha Derek); *La Noce massacrée*, 1921 (*The Ruined Wedding*; libretto by Jean Cocteau); *Skating Rink*, 1922 (libretto by Ricciotto Canudo); *Sous-marine*, 1925 (libretto by Carina Ari); *Horace victorieux*, 1928 (libretto by Guy-Pierre Fauconnet; based on Titus Livius's poem); *Les Noces d'Amour et de Psyché*, 1928 (*The Wedding of Cupid and Psyche*; libretto by Ida Rubenstein); *Roses de métal*, 1928 (libretto by Elisabeth de Gramont); *Amphion*, 1931 (libretto by Paul Valéry); *Sémiramis*, 1934 (libretto by Valéry); *Icare*, 1935 (libretto by Serge Lifar); *Un Oiseau blanc s'est envolé*, 1937 (libretto by Sacha Guitry); *Le Cantique des cantiques*, 1938 (*The Song of Songs*; libretto by Gabriel Boissy and Lifar); *Le Mangeur de rêves*, 1941 (*The Dream Eater*; libretto by Henri-René Lenormand); *L'Appel de la montagne*, 1945 (*The Call of the Mountain*; libretto by Robert Favre le Bret); *Chota roustaveli*, 1946 (libretto by Nicolas Evreinoff and Lifar); *La Naissance des couleurs*, 1949 (*The Birth of Colors*; libretto by Ernest Klausz and René Morax).

CHORAL WORKS: *Le Roi David, psaume symphonique*, 1921, revised 1923; *Jeanne d'Arc au bûcher*, 1938 (libretto by Paul Claudel); *Une Cantate de Noël*, 1953.

FILM SCORES: *La Roue*, 1923; *Napoléon*, 1927; *La Fin du monde*, 1931; *L'Idée*, 1932; *Cessez le feu*, 1934; *Der Dämon der berge*, 1934; *Les Misérables*, 1934; *Rapt*, 1934; *Crime et châtiment*, 1935; *L'Équipage*, 1935; *Les Mutinés de l'elseneur*, 1936; *Mademoiselle Docteur*, 1937; *Miarka, la fille à l'ourse*, 1937; *Passeurs d'hommes*, 1937; *Regain*, 1937; *The Woman I Love*, 1937; *Pygmalion*, 1938; *Cavalcade d'amour*, 1940; *Le Captaine Fracasse*, 1943; *Les Démons de l'aube*, 1946; *Un Ami viendra ce soir*, 1946; *Un Revenant*, 1946; *Storm over Tibet*, 1952; *Giovanna d'Arco al rogo*, 1954.

OPERAS: *Judith*, 1926 (libretto by René Morax); *Antigone*, 1927 (libretto by Jean Cocteau; based Sophocles' play); *Les Aventures du roi pausole*, 1930 (*The Adventures of King Pausole*; libretto by Albert Willemetz; based on Pierre Louÿs's novel); *La Belle de moudon*, 1931 (libretto by Morax); *L'Aiglon*, 1937 (libretto by Henri Cain; based on a play by Edmond Rostand); *Les Petites Cardinal*, 1938 (libretto by Willemetz and Paul Brach; based on Ludovic Halévy's novel).

ORCHESTRAL WORKS: *Le Chant de Nigamon*, 1917; Mouvement Symphonique No. 1, 1924 (*Pacific 231*); Symphonic Poem for Chamber Orchestra, 1924 (*Pastorale d'été*); Mouvement Symphonique No. 2, 1929 (*Rugby, Tone Poem*); Symphony No. 2 in D Major, 1942 (for strings and trumpet); Symphony No. 3, 1946 (*Liturgique*); Symphony No. 4, 1946; Symphony No. 5 in D Major, 1951 (*Di Tre Re*).

The Life

Oscar Arthur Honegger (HOH-nehg-gur) was born to Swiss parents in Le Havre, France, where he spent his youth. After two years at the Zurich Conservatory, Honegger enrolled at the prestigious Paris Conservatory, where he studied from 1911 to 1918. In 1920 he became a member of Les Six, the collective of six young Parisian composers whose fashionable, lighthearted style and audacious stage works epitomized the French avant-garde's obsession with youth and novelty following World War I.

Honegger came to international prominence with his 1921 *Le Roi David, psaume symphonique*, and the same year saw an increase in activity by Les Six, including their only collaborative stage work, *Les Mariés de la Tour Eiffel*. His increasing fame led to further collaborations with Jean Cocteau, René Morax, Paul Claudel, and Paul Valéry. In 1926 Honegger married the talented pianist Andrée Vaurabourg, with whom he spent the rest of his life.

During the 1930's Honegger composed a great amount of music for radio, film, and the theater, geared to both public audiences and musical sophisticates. Throughout his career he maintained close ties with Switzerland, notably through conductor Paul Sacher, who premiered many of Honegger's most substantial works, including *Jeanne d'Arc au bûcher*; Symphony No. 2 in D Major; Symphony No. 4; and his last work, *Une Cantate de Noël*.

During the occupation of Paris, Honegger taught at the École Normale de Musique. In 1947 he suffered a heart attack, and his declining health diminished his compositional activity. His autobiography, *I Am a Composer* (1966), conveys a pessimistic view of the future of music. Honegger, who made Paris his lifelong home, became Grand Officer of the Legion of Honor in 1954, and he died in his home on November 27, 1955.

The Music

Honegger's early appreciation of Ludwig van Beethoven, Richard Strauss, and Richard Wagner instilled in the composer a commitment to ideals of musical beauty based on thematic unity and formal structure. His studies in Paris led him to pursue the contrapuntal techniques, expanded harmonic idiom, and emphasis on classical form espoused by the Paris Conservatory. Honegger's adherence to these principles is evident from his lighthearted works of the 1920's through his mature symphonic works of the 1940's and 1950's, and it lends his music an aesthetic of high seriousness. His idiosyncratic approach to tonality, based more on pitch-centricity than common practice harmony, manifests itself as patterns of tension and release, corresponding to relative harmonic dissonance and consonance. Honegger's music often uses driving rhythms, coloristic harmonies, and extremes in melodic amplitude and timbre. His lyric and colorful passages point to the influences of Debussy, Gabriel Fauré, and Jules Massenet. Honegger's five symphonies, written at a time when the genre was under relative neglect, are testaments to the composer's alliance with tradition.

Early Works. Honegger's earliest compositions were chamber music, small works for orchestra, and music for the stage and ballet. His student works show experimentation with different aspects of his voice, at turns immensely complex and lyrically elegant. *Le Chant de Nigamon*, a symphonic poem, is based on a morbid tale of an Iroquois chief who is burned at the stake, and it utilizes authentic American Indian melodies which compete in a sonata form. *Le Dit des jeux du monde* caused a riotous scandal at its premiere because of Honegger's agitated, highly dissonant music and radical stage effects. His 1920 Symphonic Poem for Chamber Orchestra, *Pastorale d'été*, shows a light, relaxed, and Romantic style that is also evident in his chamber pieces and operettas.

Le Roi David. In 1921 Honegger accepted a commission to write the incidental music for René Morax's biblical drama *Le Roi David*. Written in two months, the music was originally scored for three vocal soloists with choir and a small pit band. After its initial towering success, Honegger, who became known as "le roi Arthur," reworked the piece for large orchestra, the form heard most often today. The piece presents a series of short scenes from the life of the biblical king David, linked by tonal and thematic correspondences to the dramatic action. Drawing on styles reminiscent of Igor Stravinsky, Massenet, Maurice Ravel, and Honegger's idol, Johann Sebastian Bach, the extreme eclecticism of the music reveals Honegger's Expressionist style, juxtaposing and blending a great variety of musical idioms. Honegger contrasts simplicity and complexity through his use of austere chorale tunes and lyrical melodies placed against massively wrought passages and abrupt tonal shifts. The music is exciting, majestic, and at times grotesque, and it played a major role in solidifying Honegger's status as one of the most innovative and serious composers of his generation.

Mouvement Symphonique No. 1. Honegger's passion for trains inspired him to write the short Mouvement Symphonique No. 1, also known as *Pacific 231*, named after the powerful steam locomotive. The work has been viewed as a musical depiction of a train, although Honegger insisted the title was an afterthought. Using the form of an extended chorale, Honegger sought to portray the visual and experiential qualities of trains with a novel, conceptual treatment of rhythm, pitting tempo and rhythmic momentum against one another, creating the effect of rhythmically speeding up while the tempo gradually slows down.

Jeanne d'Arc au bûcher. Honegger had great success with his dramatic oratorio *Jeanne d'Arc au bûcher*. Paul Claudel's masterful libretto presents Joan of Arc as she is burned at the stake, telling her story through a series of flashbacks. The music draws on realistic pictorialisms, through the use of folk music, trumpet calls, psalmody, hymns, laments, and chiming bells, interspersed with passages conveying the mystical ecstasy associated with the French saint. The innovative orchestration includes parts for saxophone, tempered piano, and ondes Martenot (an electronic musical instrument). Honegger's trademark style of French prosody, in which the first syllable of text begins on the downbeat as opposed to the conventional anacrusis, lends an air of dignity and power to the vocal setting.

Musical Legacy

For composers of the subsequent generation, Honegger was regarded as a monumental figure who composed innovative, novel music while engaging with the traditions of the past, contributing some of the most important dramatic and symphonic works of the first half of the twentieth century. Pierre Boulez, Olivier Messaien, Hans Werner Henze, and Luigi Dallapiccola memorialized Honegger after his death, pointing to his critical influence on contemporary music. Honegger's music stands apart for its craftsmanlike rigor and ingenuity without abandoning the tonal system or relying on contemporary technical models. He is notable for his prolific work in film, his interest in recording his music for a wide public audience, and his professed desire to write accessible music appealing to both the average musical listener and the connoisseur.

Jonathan W. Boschetto

Further Reading

Halbreich, Harry. *Arthur Honegger*. Translated by Roger Nichols. Portland, Oreg.: Amadeus Press, 1999. This authoritative biography provides a meticulously detailed account of Honegger's life and works, and it includes a series of topical essays on the composer.

Honegger, Arthur. *I Am a Composer*. Translated by Wilson O. Clough and Allan Arthur Willman. New York: St. Martin's Press, 1966. An exposition of the composer's life, music, and philosophy in his own words, offering a provocative, if deeply pessimistic, view of the future of music, art, and civilization.

Spratt, Geoffrey K. *The Music of Arthur Honegger*. Cork, Ireland: Cork University Press, 1987. An exhaustive study of Honegger's music, focusing primarily on major dramatic works and the development of his musical language.

Waters, Keith. *Rhythmic and Contrapuntal Structures in the Music of Arthur Honegger*. Aldershot, England: Ashgate Publishing, 2002. This concise volume offers a heavily analytical look at rhythm and counterpoint in Honegger's music.

See also: Boulez, Pierre; Debussy, Claude; Kodály, Zoltán; Koussevitzky, Serge; Messiaen, Olivier; Milhaud, Darius; Poulenc, Francis; Ravel, Maurice; Rózsa, Miklós; Strauss, Richard; Stravinsky, Igor; Szigeti, Joseph; Tiomkin, Dimitri; Xenakis, Iannis.

John Lee Hooker

American blues singer, guitarist, and songwriter

Covering traditional blues songs as well as writing distinctive songs with memorable diction, Hooker used his husky baritone voice, stomping foot, and repetitive chords on an open-tuned guitar to define the blues in twentieth century America.

Born: August 22, 1917; Clarksdale, Mississippi
Died: June 21, 2001; Los Altos, California
Also known as: Delta John; John Lee Booker; John Lee Cooker; Johnny Lee; Birmingham Sam; Boogie Man; Texas Slim

Principal recordings

ALBUMS: *Everybody's Blues*, 1950; *The Folk Blues of John Lee Hooker*, 1959; *How Long Blues*, 1959; *I'm John Lee Hooker*, 1959; *The Blues*, 1960; *Blues Man*, 1960; *The Country Blues of John Lee Hooker*, 1959; *House of the Blues*, 1960; *That's My Story*, 1960; *Travelin'*, 1960; *The Folk Lore of John Lee Hooker*, 1961; *John Lee Hooker Plays and Sings the Blues*, 1961; *John Lee Hooker Sings the Blues*, 1961; *Burnin'*, 1962; *Drifting thru the Blues*, 1962; *Tupelo Blues*, 1962; *Don't Turn Me from Your Door: John Lee Hooker Sings His Blues*, 1963; *John Lee Hooker*, 1963; *Living with the Blues*, 1963; *The Big Soul of John Lee Hooker*, 1964; *Burning Hell*, 1964; *Great Blues Sounds*, 1964; *The Great John Lee Hooker*, 1964; *I Want to Shout the Blues*, 1964; *. . . and Seven Nights*, 1965; *Hooker and the Hogs*, 1965; *It Serves You Right to Suffer*, 1966; *The Real Folk Blues*, 1966; *Urban Blues*, 1967; *Hooked on Blues*, 1968; *Big Maceo Merriweather and John Lee Hooker*, 1969; *Big Red Blues*, 1969; *Get Back Home*, 1969; *Highway of Blues*, 1969; *In the Mood*, 1969; *Simply the Truth*, 1969; *That's Where It's At*, 1969; *Endless Boogie*, 1970; *If You Miss 'Im I Got 'Im*, 1970; *John Lee Hooker on the Waterfront*, 1970; *Moanin' and Stompin' Blues*, 1970; *No Friend Around*, 1970; *Coast to Coast Blues Band*, 1971; *Goin' down Highway 51*, 1971; *Guitar Loving Man*, 1971; *Half a Stranger*, 1971; *Hooker 'n' Heat*, 1971 (with Canned Heat); *I Feel Good*, 1971; *Boogie Chillun*, 1972; *Detroit Special*, 1972; *Never Get out of These Blues Alive*, 1972; *Born in Mississippi, Raised Up in Tennessee*, 1973; *Free Beer and Chicken*, 1974; *Mad Man Blues*, 1974; *Black R and B*, 1975; *In Person*, 1976; *Black Snake*, 1977; *Dimples*, 1977; *Dusty Road*, 1977; *The Cream*, 1978; *King of Folk Blues*, 1978; *Sad and Lonesome*, 1979; *Slims Stomp*, 1979; *Everybody Rockin'*, 1980; *Sittin' Here Thinkin'*, 1980; *This Is Hip*, 1980; *World's Greatest Blues Singer*, 1980; *Tantalizing the Blues*, 1982; *Hookered on Blues*, 1983; *Blues Before Sunrise*, 1984; *Do the Boogie*, 1984; *Solid Sender*, 1984; *Detroit Blues*, 1987; *House Rent Boogie*, 1987; *Jealous*, 1987; *The Blueway Sessions*, 1988; *Want Ad Blues*, 1988; *The Healer*, 1989; *Let's Make It*, 1989; *Trouble Blues*, 1989; *Don't You Remember Me*, 1990; *Hobo Blues*, 1990; *More Real Folk Blues*, 1991; *Mr. Lucky*, 1991; *Walking the Blues*, 1991; *Boom Boom*, 1992; *Graveyard Blues*, 1992; *Turn Up the Heat!*, 1992; *Nothing but the Blues*, 1993; *King of the Boogie*, 1994; *Blues for My Baby*, 1995; *Chill Out*, 1995; *Helpless Blues*, 1995; *Electric*, 1996; *Don't Look Back*, 1997; *The Best of Friends*, 1998; *Black Man*

Blues, 1998; *Anywhere, Anytime, Anyplace*, 2000; *Down at the Landing*, 2000; *Lonesome Road*, 2000; *On Campus*, 2000; *Boogie Man*, 2001; *I'm Ready*, 2002; *Shake, Holler, and Run*, 2002; *Too Much Boogie*, 2002.

The Life

Born in Clarksdale, Mississippi, on August 22, 1917, John Lee Hooker was the youngest of eleven children of William Hooker and Minnie Ramsey. Since William Hooker was a Baptist minister as well as a sharecropper, his children were allowed to sing only religious songs. The Reverend Hooker died when John Lee was six, and Minnie married Will Moore, a blues singer who taught John Lee his distinctive way of playing guitar. During the 1920's, blues legends Blind Lemon Jefferson, Blind Blake, and Charley Patton stayed at the Moore-Hooker residence, providing a musical education for the boy.

John Lee Hooker. (© Michael Ochs Archives/CORBIS)

Hooker left home to live with an aunt in Memphis, Tennessee, in 1932, where he worked as an usher at the W. C. Handy Theatre, played at house parties, and occasionally attended school, completing only the fifth grade. Hooker moved farther north to Cincinnati, Ohio, in 1936, living with another aunt, until World War II started, and the lure of a regular factory job took him to wartime Detroit in 1943. Hooker worked at several factory jobs over the next two decades; his longest stint was as a janitor at the Ford Motor Company Rouge Factory complex. In postwar Detroit Hooker quickly became known on Hastings Street in Paradise Valley on the near east side, playing at the Rainbow Lounge, the Congo Club, and the Apex Bar, among other venues, with such local blues legends as Willie D. Warren, Detroit Piano Fats, and Harmonica Shah. One evening at the Apex Bar, Hooker was discovered by Bernie Besman, who wanted to record Hooker's tribute to a favored aunt, "Sally Mae." For the flip side of the record Besman asked Hooker to riff out an extemporaneous blues number, and the result was "Boogie Chillun." The disc sold more than a million copies for Modern Records, climbing to number one on the rhythm-and-blues charts in 1949.

Over the next decade, Hooker developed a reputation in the ghetto blues bars of the Lower Great Lakes—Detroit, Toledo, Cleveland, Buffalo, Chicago—but his crossover to a wider national and international audience occurred with his first appearance at Rhode Island's Newport Folk Festival in 1960. After that Hooker began to play East Coast nightclubs and college campuses and started to tour Europe. For the next four decades, he maintained a consistent touring schedule, usually with a four-piece group (second guitar, bass, drums, piano) backing him up.

Hooker's popularity and influence not only in the blues but also in the rock and folk-rock arenas can be seen in his collaborations with Canned Heat, John Mayall, Ten Years After, and the Rolling Stones. *The Healer* remains the best-selling blues album in recording history and includes Hooker collaborations with Carlos Santana, Bonnie Raitt, and Robert Cray. With homage to one of his earliest hit records, Hooker opened the Boom Boom Room in San Francisco in 1997. He continued to perform until four days before his death in 2001.

The Music

What some critics have termed the harmonic simplicity of Hooker's style can be attributed to his preference to open-tune his six-string guitar, usually to open-G (DGDGBD). Add to that Hooker's large foot stomping the floor and his Mississippi baritone voice growling out memorable lines such as the opening of the song "I'm Bad, Like Jesse James."

Hooker 'n' Heat. This is one of the best examples of matching a blues musician with a rock band. Canned Heat performed seamlessly as Hooker's backup in the 1971 album, with the band's Bob Hite selflessly deferring to Hooker on vocals. There are some remarkable musical exchanges between harp (harmonica) player Alan Wilson and Hooker, made all the more memorable because of Wilson's untimely death soon after the release of the album.

The Healer. Hooker jump-started his career with this critically acclaimed and commercially successful album. The title track is a tight duet with Santana, and the duet with Raitt, "I'm in the Mood," remains one of the most popular songs in the Hooker corpus. The album justifiably earned a Grammy Award.

Mr. Lucky. Continuing the model of blues singer paired with crossover rock, folk, and other blues musicians, this release was nominated for a Grammy Award and includes Cray on the title track; a memorable vocal duet with Van Morrison, "I Cover the Waterfront"; another collaboration with Santana, "Stripped Me Naked"; a new arrangement of "This Is Hip" with Ry Cooder; and a duet with Albert Collins, "Backstabbers" (elsewhere titled "Backbiters and Syndicators").

Musical Legacy

Hooker's collaborations with notable artists from other musical categories often produced work that gave value to both traditions, though fans and music critics generally seem to prefer Hooker solo onstage. His improvisations were often too eclectic and unpredictable for backup bands that expected an even, measured beat. In addition to his prolific and lengthy recording career, Hooker pioneered a tradition of performing under a series of aliases that allowed him to do backup and foreground work for different record labels without explicitly violating the terms of a record contract. In 1980 Hooker was inducted into the Blues Hall of Fame; in 1991 he was inducted into the Rock and Roll Hall of Fame; he received a star on the Hollywood Walk of Fame in 1997; and he received a Grammy Lifetime Achievement Award in 2000.

Richard Sax

Further Reading

Cohn, Lawrence, ed. *Nothing but the Blues: The Music and the Musicians*. New York: Abbeville Press, 1993. With more than four hundred pages, more than three hundred black-and-white photographs, and an extensive discography and bibliography, this is a comprehensive written and pictorial history of the blues.

Kennedy, Timothy. *Midnight Sun: A Tribute to John Lee Hooker*. Tampa, Fla.: University of Tampa Press, 2006. Museum-quality photographs taken by the author during a summer-solstice performance by Hooker in Alaska in the 1970's.

Murray, Charles Shaar. *Boogie Man: The Adventures of John Lee Hooker in the American Twentieth Century*. New York: St. Martin's Press, 2002. Drawing on interviews with Hooker's contemporaries, Murray places Hooker's career and achievements within relevant cultural and sociological contexts.

Obrecht, James. "John Lee Hooker." *Guitar Player* (November, 1989): 50ff. Review article on Hooker as a guitar player, specifically his two-finger picking.

Russell, Tony. *The Blues: From Robert Johnson to Robert Cray*. New York: Schirmer Books, 1997. Russell provides profiles of twenty-four blues legends and summarizes the blues in twentieth century America through nine chronological stages. Includes more than a hundred color and black-and-white photographs.

See also: Diddley, Bo; Hopkins, Lightnin'; James, Etta; Jefferson, Blind Lemon; Morrison, Van; Patton, Charley; Raitt, Bonnie; Reed, Jimmy; Santana, Carlos; Williamson, Sonny Boy, I.

Lightnin' Hopkins

American blues songwriter and guitarist

Hopkins played guitar with the "Texas pinch," a right-hand thumb-and-forefinger interaction characteristic of country blues-based Texas guitarists.

Born: March 15, 1912; Centerville, Texas
Died: January 30, 1982; Houston, Texas
Also known as: Sam Hopkins (full name)

Principal recordings

ALBUMS: *Lightnin' Hopkins,* 1959; *Autobiography in Blues,* 1960; *Country Blues,* 1960; *Lightnin' and the Blues,* 1960; *Last Night Blues,* 1961; *Lightnin',* 1961; *Walkin' This Road by Myself,* 1961; *How Many More Years I Got,* 1962; *Lightnin' Hopkins and the Blues,* 1962; *Lightnin' Strikes,* 1962; *Mojo Hand,* 1962; *Blues in My Bottle,* 1963; *Goin' Away,* 1963; *Lightnin' and Co.,* 1963; *Smokes Like Lightnin',* 1963; *Down Home Blues,* 1964; *Hopkins Brothers: Lightnin', Joel, and John Henry,* 1964 (with the Hopkins Brothers); *Swarthmore Concert,* 1964; *Blue Lightnin',* 1965; *First Meeting,* 1965; *Hootin' the Blues,* 1965; *My Life in the Blues,* 1965; *The Roots of Lightnin' Hopkins,* 1966; *Soul Blues,* 1966; *Gotta Move Your Baby,* 1968; *The Great Electric Show and Dance,* 1968; *California Mudslide,* 1969; *Texas Blues Man,* 1969; *Blues Is My Business,* 1971; *Double Blues,* 1973; *Low Down Dirty Blues,* 1975; *Lightnin' Strikes Back,* 1981.

SINGLES: "Going Home Blues," 1946; "Katie Mae Blues," 1946; "Grosebeck Blues," 1947; "Tim Moore's Farm," 1949.

The Life

Sam "Lightnin'" Hopkins was playing guitar by age eight, when he reportedly received encouragement from the legendary Blind Lemon Jefferson. After becoming confident enough to play for dances in his community, Hopkins left home to travel across Texas, where in Dallas he again encountered Jefferson. Another primary influence was his reputed cousin, Alger "Texas" Alexander, who played no instrument but whose powerful voice sang topical verses in the style of the work

songs that predated blues. Hopkins often accompanied Alexander, and this apprenticeship helped him develop his strengths as a lyrical improviser.

In the late 1930's, Hopkins served time on a Houston County prison farm, an experience he would later recall in such songs as "Prison Farm Blues." By 1946 he was back accompanying Alexander on Houston's Dowling Street, where a talent scout heard him and hired him to accompany a pianist, "Thunder" Smith, at a recording session in Los Angeles. The record company thought "Thunder and Lightnin'" would look good on a label, so Hopkins acquired a nickname and made his first recordings. His "Katie Mae Blues" became a hit.

For the better part of a decade, Hopkins recorded prolifically for a variety of labels, but by the mid-1950's recording offers dried up. After a few lean years in Houston, the appearance of Hopkins's first album on the Folkways label ended his recording slump and introduced him to a new audience.

A 1960 trip to New York was a watershed: Hopkins appeared on CBS television's *A Pattern of Words and Music,* he recorded fifty songs for four labels (among them Nat Hentoff's Candid), and he even performed at Carnegie Hall on a folk bill with Pete Seeger and Joan Baez.

In 1962 Hopkins won the *Down Beat* International Jazz Critics Poll as New Star, Male Singer. Two years later, he traveled to Europe and to England as part of the American Folk Blues Festival Tour. With little change in his style, Hopkins continued to tour and record until he died of cancer in 1982.

The Music

Hopkins epitomized the lone blues singer with guitar, his songs at once deeply personal and expressive of universal emotions. Thanks to his mentors Jefferson and Alexander, he drew on deep wells of tradition, yet nothing he sang or played was merely derivative of those who came before him. He created his own musical world, alternately harsh and poetic, and he had a rare knack for drawing listeners into it. For all his music's intimacy, Hopkins was an expert performer who understood musical dynamics and getting an audience on his side. Whether that audience was one person listening to a record or a packed festival crowd, Hopkins knew how to connect. He did it with his expressive guitar, which was a voice all its own. He did it with his lyrics, more tightly focused than the often rambling verses strung together by many blues singers. He did it with a raw voice that adeptly conveyed the rough pleasures and sorrows of his life.

"Katie Mae Blues." Hopkins's 1946 recording debut shows his musical talent fully formed. The lyrics praise a woman with some humorous blues poetry, comparing her to various makes of cars, while the guitar playing is assured and speaks of long experience. The success of this recording launched a brief renaissance of so-called country blues recorded for black audiences, at a time when rhythm and blues was moving in a more urbane direction.

"Short Haired Woman." Hopkins's 1947 hit, with its rueful dismissal of its subject and picturesque references to hairpieces called "rats," made a deep impression on black audiences of its time. B. B. King, who worked as a deejay before his success as performer, admired the song for its topical reference to a then-popular hairstyle. He must have also noticed Hopkins's stinging, now-electrified guitar lines as well.

"Tim Moore's Farm." The harsh lot of the sharecropper is vividly depicted in this song, supposedly about a plantation overseer named Tim Moore who earned a bad reputation for his rough treatment of black workers. Hopkins reputedly cobbled this together from sundry local songs on the topic, but his cohesive result shows his knack for sharply focused storytelling. This is a rare example of a blues that plainly criticizes racial and economic conditions.

"Going Home Blues." This autobiographical song (also known as "Going Back and Talk to Mama") opens with Hopkins's birth date. It is the sort of tune that came effortlessly to Hopkins, who could yearn for his mother and his birthplace, the usual turf of hillbilly singers, but without sounding maudlin.

"Grosebeck Blues." Hopkins reported learning this from Alexander, though Hopkins follows a straight narrative thread, which was not typical of Alexander. The song does have a chantlike pre-blues freedom, and structurally it is not blues. It is a prison work song, representing the oldest strain of tradition in Hopkins's recorded repertoire. His guitar work is likewise noteworthy, especially for the way the guitar traces the complex vocal melodic line.

Musical Legacy

Hopkins made more than six hundred recordings; he was the subject of a documentary by Les Blank, *The Blues According to Lightnin' Hopkins* (1969); and he inspired Jane Phillips's novel *Mojo Hand* (1966). Although he enjoyed international celebrity, Hopkins was happiest in Houston, where he became something of a hero in its Third Ward. His music has lost none of its capacity to move as it depicts the world of Texas sharecroppers. Hopkins's first recordings led to other country blues singers and guitarists being recorded in the late 1940's and the early 1950's, a time when their music might otherwise have faded into obscurity. Without the success of Hopkins, we might never have heard of John Lee Hooker or Muddy Waters.

Mark Humphrey

Further Reading

Charters, Samuel B. *The Country Blues*. New York: Rinehart, 1959. Charters's groundbreaking book closes with a chapter on Hopkins, presenting him as the last great country blues singer.

Obrecht, Jas, ed. *Rollin' and Tumblin': The Postwar Blues Guitarists*. San Francsico: Miller Freeman Books, 2000. Obrecht offers a fine chapter on Hopkins's life, music, and impact on the white blues-rock guitarists who admired him.

Waterman, Dick. *Between Midnight and Day: The Last Unpublished Blues Archive*. New York: Thunder's Mouth Press, 2003. Waterman offers some funny and insightful recollections of Hopkins, along with stunning photographs.

See also: Baez, Joan; Jefferson, Blind Lemon; Seeger, Pete; Terry, Sonny; Van Zandt, Townes; Waters, Muddy.

Lena Horne
American pop and jazz singer

A prominent African American pop singer, Horne is noted for her cool, elegant beauty and her sultry renditions of popular standards.

Born: June 30, 1917; New York, New York

Also known as: Lena Mary Calhoun Horne (full name)

Principal recordings

ALBUMS: *It's Love*, 1955; *Lena and Ivie*, 1957 (with Ivie Anderson); *Lena Horne at the Waldorf Astoria*, 1957; *Stormy Weather*, 1957; *Give the Lady What She Wants*, 1958; *Porgy and Bess*, 1959; *The Songs by Burke and Van Heusen*, 1959; *Lena on the Blue Side*, 1962; *Lena Goes Latin*, 1963; *Lena Horne Sings Your Requests*, 1963; *Lovely and Alive*, 1963; *Here's Lena Now!*, 1964; *Feelin' Good*, 1965; *Lena in Hollywood*, 1966; *Merry from Lena*, 1966; *Soul*, 1966; *Lena and Gabor*, 1969 (with Gabor Szabo); *Watch What Happens*, 1969; *Nature's Baby*, 1971; *Lena and Michel*, 1975 (with Michel Legrand); *Lena, A New Album*, 1976; *The Exciting . . . Lena*, 1977; *The Men in My Life*, 1981 (with Joe Williams and Sammy Davis, Jr.); *We'll Be Together Again*, 1994; *Lena Horne: The Lady and Her Music*, 1994; *Being Myself*, 1998.

WRITINGS OF INTEREST: *In Person: Lena Horne as Told to Helen Arstein and Carlton Moss*, 1950; *Lena*, 1965.

The Life

The family of Lena Mary Calhoun Horne was a distinguished one—her grandmother was a civil rights activist and her uncle was an adviser to Franklin Delano Roosevelt. Horne sang as a teenager at the legendary Cotton Club in Harlem, but in 1937 she left show business to marry politician Louis Jordan Jones, with whom she had two children. They divorced in 1944. During this time, Horne began singing with swing bands, but her big career break came in 1943's film *Stormy Weather*. A glamorous woman, Horne became the first black actor to be awarded a long-term film contract, becoming the most highly paid black actor in the country.

Throughout her career Horne advanced the causes of racial integration and civil rights, participating in many rallies, marches, and fund-raising events. When entertaining American troops in Europe, she refused to sing for segregated audiences, and she would not take film parts that stereotyped black women. In 1947 she challenged social convention when she married the Jewish American ar-

ranger and conductor Lennie Hayton, who became her manager, a position he held until his death in 1971.

Horne's social activism led to her being blacklisted from television and film during the 1950's, although she continued to perform on Broadway and in nightclubs. In the wake of the deaths of her husband, son, and father in quick succession, Horne abandoned her career in the early 1970's. In 1981 she returned to show business in an acclaimed one-woman show, continuing to perform throughout the world until officially retiring in 2000 at the age of eighty-three.

The Music

Although Horne's first success as a singer was with the all-black Noble Sissle Society Orchestra, she soon joined Charlie Barnet's swing band, becoming the first African American to tour with an all-white band. Eventually Horne was known for her association with music notables both black and white, including Artie Shaw, Nelson Riddle, Billy Strayhorn, and Duke Ellington.

"Stormy Weather." The song "Stormy Weather" is a touchstone of Horne's musical career. Sung by Horne in the all-black film musical *Stormy Weather* (1943), this Ted Koehler-Harold Arlen song is one with which she became deeply identified. Her silky rendition of this bluesy song is also number twenty-six on the Songs of the Century list compiled by the Recording Industry Association of America. Her performance of this song brought her a racially integrated fan base, allowing her not only to cross between the black and white music worlds but also to further a musical culture enjoyed by Americans of either race. This song also identifies her with the sophisticated music that dominated American popular culture from the 1920's to 1960, and which in subsequent years became cabaret and jazz standards.

Lena Horne at the Waldorf Astoria. By the 1950's, Horne's powerful voice, with its signature mellow drawl and open-vowel enunciation, became the foundation for an even more electric singing style. In 1957 she reached a career high point with her triumphant engagement at the Waldorf Astoria nightclub, during which she delivered creative and vocally impressive interpretations of standards by such classic American songwriters as

Lena Horne. (AP/Wide World Photos)

Cole Porter, Jule Styne, Richard Rodgers, Oscar Hammerstein II, Yip Harburg, and Ellington. Her repertoire for this engagement demonstrated how Horne was at home with popular songs written by composers associated with Broadway, Hollywood, and Tin Pan Alley. Her experience as a singer with the big swing bands, as well as her own distinctive song stylings, also consolidated her credentials as a jazz artist. Recorded live, *Lena Horne at the Waldorf Astoria* is one of her most highly regarded albums, capturing the inspired quality of her nightclub performances.

Lena Horne: The Lady and Her Music. Horne's withdrawal from the music business in the 1970's led her to reconsider her identity as an African American singer. She returned to music about a decade later, free of the cultural and musical inhibitions she felt had been imposed on her in earlier decades. Taking advantage of the greater expressivity allowed by popular musical artists at that time, and feeling less restricted by a decorum expected by her white audiences, Horne enthusiastically embraced a franker and more ferocious performance and singing style. This transformation in Horne's music was powerfully demonstrated in 1981 when she presented her autobiographical one-woman show on Broadway, *Lena Horne: The Lady and Her Music*, which chronicled Horne's early life and many years

in show business. At sixty-three, Horne still boasted her powerful voice, but she performed with greater abandon and with a new, more audacious emotional range. Horne acknowledged her personal transformation by singing her signature song, "Stormy Weather," twice—first done in the genteel style of the 1940's, and later with the melismatic runs and the earthy emotional power associated with gospel music, reinventing the song as a revelatory cry of pain. Horne was given a special Tony Award for this show, and the show's album won a Grammy Award for Best Pop Vocal Performance and another for Best Cast Show Album. Having successfully become her own woman as an artist, Horne continued to perform until the year 2000, when she retired.

Musical Legacy

An exceptional interpretive musical artist who found tremendous popularity with both black and white audiences, Horne used her successful career to accelerate changes in attitudes about race in America. Her example and her social activism played a major role in the integration of black musicians and singers into the mainstream of American performing arts. As a musical artist, Horne won three Grammy Awards, including a Lifetime Achievement Award in 1989, and she has been the recipient of numerous awards, including the Kennedy Center Honors and the American Society of Composers, Authors, and Publishers (ASCAP) Pied Piper Award, given to entertainers who have made significant contributions to words and music. Her distinctive song stylings and her legendary performances had a major impact on female jazz and pop singers of her generation as well as on singers of succeeding generations, such as Dionne Warwick, Diana Ross, Nancy Wilson, Liza Minnelli, Julie London, Dee Dee Bridgewater, Keely Smith, and Annie Ross.

Margaret Boe Birns

Further Reading

Bloom, Ken. *The American Songbook: The Singers, Songwriters, and the Songs.* New York: Black Dog & Leventhal, 2005. This reference includes Horne in an examination of more than two hundred prominent American singers of the twentieth century.

Bogle, Donald. *Brown Sugar: Over One Hundred Years of America's Black Female Superstars.* New York: Continuum, 2007. This resource includes Horne in an examination of black female superstars from Ma Rainey to Beyoncé.

Buckley, Gail Lumet. *The Hornes: An American Family.* New York: Applause Books, 2002. This study of six generations of the Horne family by Horne's daughter discusses her mother's struggles with race prejudice.

Vogel, Shane. "Performing 'Stormy Weather': Ethel Waters, Lena Horne, and Katherine Dunham." *South Central Review* (Spring, 2008). This article examines "Stormy Weather" as interpreted by three African American artists: singers Waters and Horne and dancer Dunham.

Williams, Megan E. "The Crisis Cover Girl: Lena Horne, the NAACP, and Representations of African American Femininity, 1941-1945." *American Periodicals: A Journal of History, Criticism, and Bibliography* 16, no. 2 (2006): 200-218. This article examines the efforts of the National Association for the Advancement of Colored People to utilize Horne's image to empower African American women.

See also: Arlen, Harold; Burke, Johnny; Carter, Benny; Ellington, Duke; Fitzgerald, Ella; Hammerstein, Oscar, II; Jones, Quincy; Kern, Jerome; Legrand, Michel; Porter, Cole; Rodgers, Richard; Ross, Diana; Serkin, Rudolf; Shaw, Artie; Strayhorn, Billy; Waller, Fats.

James Horner
American film-score composer

A prolific scorer for motion pictures and television, Horner began his career composing for low-budget science-fiction films. He went on to write scores for films in every genre, adding to his sound tracks new approaches, such as utilizing choirs and solo voices and mixing voices with synthesizers.

Born: August 14, 1953; Los Angeles, California

Principal works

FILM SCORES: *The Watchers,* 1978; *The Lady in Red,* 1979; *Battle Beyond the Stars,* 1980; *Humanoids from the Deep,* 1980; *The Hand,* 1981; *Wolfen,* 1981; *Forty-eight Hours,* 1982; *Krull,* 1982; *Star Trek: The Wrath of Khan,* 1982; *Space Invaders,* 1983; *Star Trek III: The Search for Spock,* 1984; *Cocoon,* 1985; *Commando,* 1985; *Heaven Help Us,* 1985; *Aliens,* 1986; *An American Tail,* 1986; *Batteries Not Included,* 1987; *Project X,* 1987; *Cocoon: The Return,* 1988; *The Land Before Time,* 1988; *Red Heat,* 1988; *Willow,* 1988; *Field of Dreams,* 1989; *Glory,* 1989; *Honey, I Shrunk the Kids,* 1989; *Another Forty-eight Hours,* 1990; *I Love You to Death,* 1990; *An American Tail: Fievel Goes West,* 1991; *The Rocketeer,* 1991; *Patriot Games,* 1992; *Unlawful Entry,* 1992; *The Man Without a Face,* 1993; *The Pelican Brief,* 1993; *Swing Kids,* 1993; *Clear and Present Danger,* 1994; *Legends of the Fall,* 1994; *Braveheart,* 1995; *Casper,* 1995; *Jumanji,* 1995; *Ransom,* 1996; *The Spitfire Grill,* 1996; *Titanic,* 1997; *Deep Impact,* 1998; *The Mask of Zorro,* 1998; *Bringing Down the House,* 1999; *How the Grinch Stole Christmas,* 2000; *The Perfect Storm,* 2000; *A Beautiful Mind,* 2001; *House of Sand and Fog,* 2003; *Bobby Jones: Stroke of Genius,* 2004; *The Forgotten,* 2004; *Troy,* 2004; *The Chumscrubber,* 2005; *Flightplan,* 2005; *The Legend of Zorro,* 2005; *Apocalypto,* 2006; *The Spiderwick Chronicles,* 2008.

ORCHESTRAL WORK: *Spectral Shimmers,* 1978.

The Life

Born in Los Angeles, James Horner is the son of Hollywood set designer and art director Harry

Horner. He began studying piano at age five. The family moved to London when James was ten, and he studied at the Royal College of Music. Returning to Los Angeles in the 1970's, he earned a degree in composition from the University of Southern California. He later earned a master's degree and a doctorate in musical composition and theory at the University of California, Los Angeles, and he taught music theory there for several years.

Horner composed a classical concert piece, *Spectral Shimmers*, which was performed by the Indianapolis Symphony Orchestra. He began scoring student films for the American Film Institute, which brought him into contact with low-budget film producer Roger Corman. Horner scored some of Corman's films, which gave him enough exposure to land jobs on bigger-budget productions.

Horner rose in Hollywood's music echelons, scoring nearly one hundred motion pictures and becoming a composer who has to turn down more assignments than he accepts. He developed relationships with directors ranging from James Cameron to Ron Howard, and he is noted for his continued innovations in his scores, such as mixing voices and synthesizers.

The Music

Horner had his first successes with science-fiction films, with both large and low budgets, and he went on to score in nearly every motion-picture genre: cop and buddy films (*Forty-eight Hours*; *Another Forty-eight Hours*), swashbucklers (*The Mask of Zorro*; *The Legend of Zorro*), biopics (*A Beautiful Mind*; *Bobby Jones: Stroke of Genius*), children's films (*How the Grinch Stole Christmas*), and many more.

Battle Beyond the Stars. Horner scored two 1980 films for Corman (the other was *Humanoids from the Deep*), who was known as an innovative but low-budget producer of unusual films, many science fiction or horror. With *Battle Beyond the Stars*, an outer-space version of *The Magnificent Seven* (1960), Corman was trying for a bigger-budget look and sound, more in line with the *Star Trek* and *Star Wars* films, and Horner gave it to him.

Star Trek: The Wrath of Khan. The recognition from his work on the Corman films helped Horner get the assignment for the second *Star Trek* motion picture, the first having been a disappointment. Horner developed a rousing score for this 1982 se-

quel, emphasizing the kind of action and interplay among the characters that had made the *Star Trek* television series so popular. (Horner is seen briefly on screen in a cameo as one of the starship's crew.) He was called back to score the next film in the series, *Star Trek III: The Search for Spock*, two years later.

Aliens. This 1986 film, a sequel to the popular *Alien* (1979), marked the first teaming of Horner with director James Cameron. This sequel emphasized space-marines-style action over the horror mood of the first one. It was also Cameron's first big film, and the director agonized over every frame. For the composer, however, it was a rush job; Horner had only ten days to come up with the score. Although friction developed between the composer and director, the job got done on time, and the score received an Academy Award nomination.

Braveheart. Even critics of Mel Gibson's 1995 blockbuster about a hero from Scottish history gave its musical score credit for emphasizing the action and the background of Scotland. Another Horner-Gibson collaboration followed a year later with *Ransom*.

Titanic. Horner and Cameron patched up their differences after working on *Aliens*, and they got together again for what would prove a huge success for Horner. The 1997 film about the tragic sinking of the passenger ship *Titanic* in 1912, surrounded by a fictional love story dramatized through a flashback, prompted Horner to generate a score ranging from a full orchestra to a solo voice for "My Heart Will Go On," sung by Céline Dion. The sound track from the motion picture stayed at the top of the *Billboard* chart for sixteen weeks. The thirty million-plus copies it sold make it one of the best-selling sound tracks in motion-picture history. It won two Academy Awards, for Original Song (in collaboration with lyricist Will Jennings) and for Best Original Music, along with three Grammy Awards and two Golden Globe Awards.

The Legend of Zorro. Horner scored *The Mask of Zorro* in 1998, and seven years later he got the assignment to provide the music for an even more lavish take on the pulp-magazine character dating back nearly a century. Thanks to special effects, this version of the character is even more extravagant than his previous cinema incarnations. As Horner had done to achieve the Scottish flavor of *Brave-*

heart, the composer worked up a Spanish-style sound track for the *Zorro* features, punching up the action scenes throughout the picture and using an almost laid-back musical sequence for the final twelve-minute climax of the picture.

Musical Legacy

Horner has won two Academy Awards, plus thirty-two other awards and thirty-three nominations. His music is heard almost every evening on television: He composed the theme for the *CBS Evening News*, which debuted when Katie Couric began anchoring the program on September 5, 2006. It is now used by other CBS News programs. His music can be heard in motion pictures he has not even scored. For example, his end-title music for *Battle Beyond the Stars* and for *Glory* are often heard in film trailers.

Paul Dellinger

Further Reading

Burlingame, Jon. *Sound and Vision: Sixty Years of Motion Picture Sound Tracks*. New York: Watson-Guptill, 2000. Covers notable sound track composers and offers a history of film sound tracks. Specifically, it recounts the Cameron-Horner dissension over *Aliens*, and how they smoothed over their differences to make the award-winning *Titanic*.

Hickman, Roger. *Reel Music: Exploring One Hundred Years of Film Music*. New York: W. W. Norton, 2005. A historical survey of the role of music in film, outlining its development over the past century. Includes profiles of composers, including Horner.

McArthur, Colin. *Brigadoon, Braveheart, and the Scots: Distortions of Scotland in Hollywood Cinema*. New York: I. B. Tauris, 2003. Critiques these film depictions of Scotland, and discusses Horner's score and its contribution to the emotional impact of *Braveheart*.

Morgan, David. *Knowing the Score: Film Composers Talk About the Art, Craft, Blood, Sweat, and Tears of Writing Music for Cinema*. New York: Harper Paperbacks, 2000. A collection of interviews with some of the top composers in Hollywood, covering how they got their start, how they developed their musical styles, and how they collaborate with their directors.

See also: Bernstein, Elmer; Morricone, Ennio; Newman, Alfred; Newman, Randy; Rota, Nino; Rózsa, Miklós; Tiomkin, Dimitri; Williams, John; Zimmer, Hans.

Vladimir Horowitz
Russian classical pianist

Horowitz's recordings embrace more than two hundred different works that include definitive performances of his own and other composers' works, all rendered with his astounding technique and unique vocal approach to piano playing.

Born: October 1, 1903; Kiev, Russia (now in Ukraine)
Died: November 5, 1989; New York, New York
Also known as: Vladimir Samoylovich Horowitz

Principal recordings

ALBUMS: *Moment Exotique*, 1921 (for piano); *Variations on a Theme for Bizet's "Carmen,"* 1926 (for piano); *Rachmaninoff: Piano Concerto No. 3*, 1930 (with London Symphony Orchestra); *Liszt: Sonata in B Minor*, 1932; *Brahms: Piano Concerto No. 2*, 1940 (with the NBC Symphony Orchestra); *Danse macabre*, 1941 (for piano); *Tchaikovsky Piano Concerto No. 1*, 1941 (with the NBC Symphony Orchestra); *By the Water*, 1947 (for piano); *Toccata for Piano in C Major, Op. 11*, 1947; *Mussorgsky: Pictures at an Exhibition*, 1951; *Beethoven Moonlight and Waldstein Sonatas: Vladimir Horowitz*, 1956; *Hungarian Rhapsody, No. 19*, 1962 (for piano); *Horowtiz Plays Scarlatti*, 1964; *Horowitz on Television*, 1968; *Vladimir Horowitz: A Concert at Carnegie Hall*, 1968; *Schumann: Kreisleriana*, 1969; *Great Romantic Piano Favorites*, 1972; *Rachmaninoff Concerto No. 3 in D Minor, Op. 30*, 1978; *Mozart: Piano Concerto No. 23*, 1987; *Horowitz at Home*, 1989; *Horowitz Plays Clementi*, 1989; *Horowitz Plays Schumann*, 1989; *Horowitz Plays Scriabin*, 1989; *Horowitz: The Last Recording*, 1990; *Horowitz Plays Prokofiev, Barber, and Kabalevsky Sonatas*, 1990; *Horowitz Plays Chopin*, 2003.

The Life

Vladimir Samoylovich Horowitz (HOHR-oh-vihtz) was raised in a prosperous Jewish family in Kiev, Russia. His father, Simeon, was an electrical engineer, and his mother, Sophie Bodick, was a former piano student at the Royal Conservatory. He had two brothers, Jacob and George, and a sister, Regina, who was a fine chamber pianist. Horowitz studied piano with his mother until age nine, and then he enrolled at the Kiev Conservatory to study with Vladimir Puchalsky. During this period, Aleksandr Scriabin recognized the boy's talent. Horowitz learned much of his future concert repertoire while studying with Sergei Tarnowsky, and he attributed his astounding piano technique to his work with Felix Blumenfeld.

When the Bolsheviks took over Kiev, his family lost everything, and Horowitz quickly finished his studies to graduate in May, 1920, in order to help out with family finances. Appearing throughout Russia with violinist Nathan Milstein, Horowitz gave twenty-three concerts in one year that included more than one hundred different works. Dissatisfied with the economic and social situation in Russia, he left in 1925.

In 1926 Horowitz got a career boost when he successfully substituted at the last minute for another concerto soloist in Hamburg, Germany. Over the next two years, he gave more than 150 European performances, and he gained notoriety in America after his virtuoso technique astonished everyone in a New York performance of the Tchaikovsky Concerto No. 1.

Horowitz married Wanda Toscanini (daughter of conductor Arturo Toscanini) in January, 1934. Their daughter, Sonya, was born the following year. In 1935 he gave seventy-five concerts, but medical and family problems resulted in his first retirement from the stage. In 1942 Horowtiz became a U.S. citizen, and the following year he performed with Arturo Toscanini in a war bond concert to raise money for the U.S. effort in World War II, collecting more than ten million dollars.

In 1953 the silver-anniversary concert of Horowitz's first U.S. appearance was a huge success. Nevertheless, the pianist, exhausted from years of continuous travel, decided to retire from the stage again. Carnegie Hall was filled with musical luminaries at his historic return twelve years later on May 9, 1965. Horowitz appeared in a nationally broadcast television recital (later released as *Horowitz on Television*), but he retired again in 1969. Therapy successfully improved a nervous condition, and he continued to concertize. A televised interview on *Sixty Minutes* was followed by a White House performance for President Jimmy Carter in early 1978.

Horowitz appeared in Europe and Japan in the mid-1980's, but his return to Russia in 1986, after a sixty-one-year absence, was symbolically important for relations between the Soviet Union and the United States. President Ronald Reagan presented him with the Presidential Medal of Freedom. Horowitz died of a heart attack three years later, and he was buried in the Toscanini family mausoleum in the Cimitero Monumentale, Milan, Italy.

Vladimir Horowitz. (Library of Congress)

The Music

Horowitz's performances fall into three categories: performances of his own compositions, arrangements and transcriptions of other composer's works, and performances of other composers' works. Horowitz's original

655

compositions include early works such as the Étude-Fantaisie, Op. 4 (*Les Vagues*), dedicated to his teacher Tarnowsky; the Waltz in F Minor; *Dance eccentrique*; and his lifelong concert trademark, *Variations on a Theme for Bizet's "Carmen."* He made numerous arrangements and transcriptions of other composers' works, including Franz Liszt's Hungarian Rhapsodies Nos. 2, 15, and 19 and *Danse macabre*. He also arranged Felix Mendelssohn's "Wedding March" (1842), John Philip Sousa's "The Stars and Stripes Forever" (1897), and Modest Mussorgsky's *Pictures at an Exhibition* (1874). Horowitz made hundreds of recordings and public performances of other composers' works.

Original Composition. *Variations on a Theme from Bizet's "Carmen"* is an original, unpublished composition by Horowitz that he first recorded for Welte in 1926 and again for RCA and Duo Art in 1928. He recorded new versions every ten years, and it became a trademark composition of his programs. Each variation explores technically difficult patterns, such as chromatic double thirds and sixths in one hand and big leaps and fast, repeated chromatic alternating octaves between the hands. In the six different recorded versions of the work, Horowitz shows his skill not only at flawlessly navigating the complex textures at an incredible tempo but also by composing interesting new patterns for each rendition.

The variations are based upon the opening figure from Bizet's opera overture, and each variation adds to the progress of the work until the arrival of the bravura ending. Because Horowitz composed new music for this composition over the decades, there is no fixed version of this work. He believed that it would be impossible to notate the piece accurately because of the complicated hand-over-hand technique and fast, dense passage work. However, a musical score of the 1928 piano roll version is available from the Vladimir and Wanda (Toscanini) Horowitz Collection of papers in the Irving S. Gilmore Library at Yale University as transcribed by this author. Horowitz's performances of *Variations on a Theme from Bizet's "Carmen"* after his 1953 retirement abandon speed in favor of compositional originality and sonority.

Arrangement. Mussorgsky's *Pictures at an Exhibition* was considered ineffective until the stunning performance by Sviatoslav Richter in 1956. Horo-

witz made a brilliant arrangement of the work in the 1940's to correct what he perceived as idiomatic weaknesses in the piano writing. Retaining Mussorgsky's original music, Horowitz added new passage work and counterpoint to *Gnomus, Bydlo, Ballet of the Unhatched Chicks, Two Jews, Market Place, Catacombs, Hut of Baba Yaga*, and *Great Gate of Kiev*. His changes to *Gnomus* consist mainly of octave doublings and of a redistribution of a trill figure across several octaves. He superimposes a large dynamic curve over *Bydlo* to create the effect of an approaching ox cart that passes by and then disappears into the distance. Simple trills are replaced by decorative alternating double thirds in the middle section of the *Ballet of the Unhatched Chicks*, and *The Rich Jew* (from *Two Jews*) is amplified with octave doublings to increase its declamatory effect. A surprising alteration occurs in *Market Place*, in which Horowitz distributes Mussorgsky's repeated notes across the entire range of the piano; he does a similar thing with the repeated notes of *Catacombs*. The *Hut of Baba Yaga* is, once again, dramatized with octave doublings. Perhaps the greatest changes come at the end of the *Great Gate of Kiev*, in which Horowitz adds a triplet figure in octaves borrowed from *Boris Godonov*. Leaping back and forth from Mussorgsky's original chords in the mid-range to Horowitz's octaves in the extremes of the instrument, this is one of the most powerful and effective codas in piano music.

Performance. Horowitz became famous as a miniaturist toward the end of his career when he performed short works, such as the Scarlatti sonatas. He had always played Scarlatti, even in his early school years, but he was motivated to place his stamp upon the entire repertory after his wife obtained a complete Alessandro Longo edition of the works. Baroque keyboard specialist Ralph Kirkpatrick listened to Horowitz play, discussed performance problems with him, and loaned him microfilms of the original manuscripts so that Horowtiz could avoid mistakes in the Longo edition. Horowitz's principal contribution to the genre was the application of classical piano touch and nineteenth century pedaling to these harpsichord pieces. His recording of Scarlatti's sonatas consists of seventeen works organized primarily on the basis of tempo (slow and fast groups) and not on the more conventional historical chronology or key relations. Sonatas in the major mode are located mainly at the beginning of the album, and those in the minor mode predominate toward the end. Horowitz effectively brings out implied effects of drums, strumming guitars, and other Spanish and Gypsy sounds wherever they are found in the music. The clarity of his scales is unmatchable, and since Horowitz said that he applied a range of about three dozen dynamic levels to his playing, his Scarlatti performances seem more colorful than those of any other pianist.

Musical Legacy

Horowitz recorded hundreds of works, covering a wide range of styles and composers, from the 1920's to the 1980's. In addition to his renderings of the works of Liszt, Mendelssohn, Bizet, Mussorgsky, and Scarlatti, he is known for recordings of the works of Franz Schubert, Robert Schumann, Frédéric Chopin (especially the "Wind over the Grave" finale of the Sonata No. 2 in B-flat Minor, Op. 35), and Scriabin (Sonata No. 9, also known as the "Black Mass," and *Vers la flamme, poème*). He premiered Sergei Prokofiev's Sonatas Nos. 6, 7, and 8 in America, and he produced a stunning performance of the last movement of Sonata No. 7 during his silver-anniversary concert. Horowitz's recording of Prokofiev's Toccata for Piano in C Major, Op. 11 has never been duplicated in terms of its sonority and characteristic cross accents. His recording of Samuel Barber's Sonata for Piano remains without peer, and his collaboration on the last movement illustrates the esteem with which he was held by the composer. Horowitz performed concerti by Wolfgang Amadeus Mozart, Ludwig van Beethoven, Liszt, and Johannes Brahms, and he was recognized as the one of the greatest interpreters of the Tchaikovsky Concerto No. 1 and the Rachmaninoff Concerto No. 3. His recordings span the development of technology throughout the twentieth century, and they clearly demonstrate what people heard at his live performances: that he was one of the greatest piano virtuosos of the twentieth century.

Stephen Husarik

Further Reading

Dubal, David. *Remembering Horowitz: 125 Pianists Recall a Legend*. New York: Schirmer Books, 1993.

These essays describe other pianists' reactions to Horowitz, with details on personal encounters. The volume contains some photographs of Horowitz with other musicians and a few of his programs.

Plaskin, Glenn. *Horowitz: A Biography of Vladimir Horowitz*. New York: William Morrow, 1983. The first authoritative account of Horowitz's life in English recounts the pianist's difficulties in launching a musical career in Bolshevik Russia, and it describes the tragic consequences of leaving his country, the loss of his parents, his life with Wanda, and other personal details. An appendix includes Robert McAlear's thorough discography of the Horowitz recordings made in the United States and the United Kingdom.

Schonberg, Harold C. *Horowitz: His Life and Music*. New York: Simon & Schuster, 1992. Schonberg interviewed Horowitz, and in this book the author provides an authoritative account of the pianist's private and professional life. Notable in this account is the complete story of the sad death of Sonya, Horowitz's daughter. There is a four-part overview of the recordings, but the list excludes Horowitz's private recordings and piano rolls.

See also: Barber, Samuel; Busch, Adolf; Rachmaninoff, Sergei; Scriabin, Aleksandr; Sousa, John Philip; Stern, Isaac; Toscanini, Arturo.

Son House

American blues singer-songwriter and guitarist

House was an innovative and influential early Delta blues singer, songwriter, and guitarist. His music style was accentuated by a highly rhythmic guitar and vocal style, influenced by black gospel and spiritual music, and frequently utilized slide guitar. Ultimately, House's musical contributions heavily informed the sound of the Delta blues and therefore the blues tradition as a whole.

Born: March 21, 1902; Riverton, Mississippi
Died: October 19, 1988; Detroit, Michigan

Also known as: Eddie James House, Jr. (full name); Eugene House

Principal recordings

ALBUMS: *Son House and J. D. Short: Blues from the Mississippi Delta*, 1963; *Father of the Delta Blues: The Complete 1965 Sessions*, 1965; *The Legendary Son House: Father of Folk Blues*, 1965; *Son House and Blind Lemon Jefferson*, 1972; *Son House: The Legendary 1941-1942 Recordings in Chronological Sequence*, 1972; *Son House: The Real Delta Blues*, 1974; *Delta Blues: The Original Library of Congress Sessions from Field Recordings, 1941-1942*, 1991; *Son House at Home: The Legendary 1969 Rochester Sessions*, 1992.

SINGLES: "Clarksdale Moan," 1930; "Dry Spell Blues, Parts I and II," 1930; "Mississippi County Farm Blues," 1930; "My Black Mama, Parts I and II," 1930; "Preachin' the Blues, Parts I and II," 1930; "Walkin' Blues," 1930; "Shetland Pony Blues," 1941; "American Defense," 1942; "John the Revelator," 1965.

The Life

Eddie James "Son" House, Jr., was born in Riverton, Mississippi, near Clarksdale. Upon his parents' divorce, when he was about seven or eight years old, he moved with his mother to Tallulah, Louisiana, and became a preacher by fifteen. Church music, and the church's position on music, greatly influenced House in that he originally despised blues music and guitar playing. Instead, House was a self-proclaimed rambler who held several jobs (as a tree-moss gatherer, cotton-field hand, and steel-plant worker) in a variety of locations (Louisiana, Tennessee, Arkansas, Mississippi, and Missouri) until his mid-twenties. Then, in 1927, House was instantly inspired when he saw bluesman Willie Wilson playing guitar with a small medicine bottle on his finger, which he used as a slide. Only a few of these details regarding House's life were known until his "rediscovery" by Phil Spiro, Nick Perls, and Dick Waterman in 1964.

In 1943, House moved to Rochester, New York, to work for the rail system and gave up playing music altogether not long afterward. Two decades later—with the folk revival in full swing in the mid-1960's—Son House became an epic name and ultimately was sought out. After relearning his craft,

House played the Newport Folk Festival (1964-1966), toured Britain with the American Folk Blues Festival in 1967 (when he appeared on the BBC2's *Late Night Line-Up*), and also enjoyed time on the coffeehouse circuit throughout the United States.

House's health declined in the early 1970's. Diagnosed with both Alzheimer's and Parkinson's disease, he gave up playing in 1976. He eventually moved to live with his family in Detroit, where he died in his sleep on October 19, 1988. His music was featured in the 2007 film *Black Snake Moan*.

The Music

Willie Wilson was Son House's first teacher. Initially House learned familiar tunes in "Spanish" tuning, but he soon began experimenting with other tuning systems and composing original works. In 1930, he met Willie Brown and Charley Patton, and eventually the three began playing at old plantation balls and similar events. It was at such an engagement that House met the young, eager Robert Johnson. That same year, Patton brought House to the attention of Paramount Records through his manager, Arthur Laibly, and the three bluesmen traveled to Grafton, Wisconsin, to record their respective albums. House was also recorded in Lake Cormorant, Mississippi, by ethnomusicologist Alan Lomax for the Library of Congress in 1941-1942.

After House moved to Rochester, New York, he quit playing music once "All [his] boys [were] gone." Regrettably, Patton (1934), Johnson (1938), and Brown (1952) had died prior to the folk revival.

"Shetland Pony Blues." Recorded in 1941 (and again in 1942 under the title "Pony Blues"), the basic song is borrowed from Charley Patton. House, however, crafted his own arrangement, complete with original verses and his distinctive style of playing bottleneck guitar. Open D-tuning in the guitar accompanies House's wailing but strong voice. Characteristically, he aggressively snaps his low strings and employs heavy vibrato in both his playing and singing. House uses the pony theme as a pretense to expresses advances toward a woman. The 1941 Library of Congress recording took place at Klack's Store in Lake Cormorant, Mississippi, to utilize the store's essential supply of electricity. For this reason, one version includes the background railway noise of a passing train.

Son House. (Hulton Archive/Getty Images)

"Walkin' Blues." An ideal example of the "standard" twelve-bar blues, the 1941 recording includes Brown on guitar, Fiddlin' Joe Martin on mandolin, and Leroy Williams on harmonica. Therefore, this recording archives the sound that Brown and House created together at their numerous plantation ball performances. House sings and shouts his lyrics while forcefully strumming his famous steel-bodied National guitar. His musicians contribute by providing brief instrumental interludes, lively commentary, and other vocalizations. In a 1942 interview with Lomax, House claimed "Walkin' Blues" to be the precursor to his composition "My Black Mama."

"American Defense." In stark contrast to most of his music, "American Defense" uses a waltz tempo while maintaining House's typical Delta blues style. House paints himself as a patriot with lines such as "There won't be enough Japs to shoot a little game of craps." However, in every chorus he warns "This war may last you for years."

"John the Revelator." House's arrangement of the traditional song is one the most frequently cited of House's recordings, and it links him to his religious background. Lyrically, the biblical subject matter is a clear connection to gospel. Musically, House abandons the use of guitar in favor of nothing but hand claps and foot stomping to accompany himself. The call-and-response chorus alternates between "Who's that writin'?" and "John the Revelator," evoking church choir undertones, both lyrically and melodically. House makes use of falsetto, near-shouting, and near-speaking vocal techniques as well as substantial melismata to complete the connection with the gospel tradition.

"Preachin' the Blues." Like many of House's songs, this selection begins at a moderate tempo, slowly escalates in intensity, and ends with a three-note, stepwise motion leading to, but not actually ending on, the tonic. His guitar accompaniment is very simple, placing emphasis on the lyrics. "Preachin' the Blues" reflects House's personal purgatory, his inability to commit completely to either the sacred or the profane. "I can't hold God in one hand and the Devil [the blues] in the other one," he laments. This dichotomy is illustrated by his curious lyrical juxtaposition of becoming a Baptist preacher to his love for women and corn liquor. House first recorded "Preachin' the Blues," an original composition, for Paramount Records.

Musical Legacy

The musical legacy of Son House resides primarily in his voice, guitar, slide techniques, and repertoire. While few recordings exist from his early, and arguably prime, period, the raw intensity, percussive and bottleneck slide guitar practice, and religious subject matter made a profound impression on many prevailing blues musicians. Notably, Robert Johnson and Muddy Waters fortuitously had personal interactions with House. Waters has been quoted as saying, "it was Son House who influenced me to play" and, in reference to bottleneck playing, that he "picked that up from Son House." Johnson observed House perform at several plantation balls as a youth. Subsequently, House's influence reached most of the blues movement and helped establish rock and roll. As late as 1999, the alternative rock band the White Stripes credited House as a major inspiration and dedicated their their first album to him. In 1980, Son House was inducted into Blues Foundation's Hall of Fame.

Janine Tiffe

Further Reading

Charters, Samuel. *The Bluesmen: The Story and the Music of the Men Who Made the Blues*. New York: Oak, 1967. A collection of chapters devoted to several bluesmen, including Son House, which features an interview transcription and song lyrics.

Cohn, Lawrence. "Son House." *Sounds and Fury* 3 (1965): 18-21. After House's "rediscovery," several articles were published devoted to his personal history. This article also includes a short discography.

Cowley, John. "Really the 'Walking Blues': Son House, Muddy Waters, Robert Johnson, and the Development of a Traditional Blues." *Popular Music* 1 (1981): 57-72. This article provides an in-depth analysis and discussion of House, Waters, Johnson, and the composition "Walkin' Blues."

Koda, Cub. "Son House." In *All Music Guide to the Blues*, edited by Michael Erlewine, Vladimir Bogdanov, Chris Woodstra, and Cub Koda. San Francisco: Miller Freeman Books, 1999. This encyclopedic guide to the blues contains entries on bands and musicians, including biographies and albums.

Oliver, Paul. "House, Son." In *The New Grove Dictionary of Music and Musicians*, edited by Stanley Sadie. New York: Macmillan, 2001. A substantial entry in this definitive multivolume dictionary dedicated to all styles of music and musicians. Provides a concise biography of House.

See also: Howlin' Wolf; Jefferson, Blind Lemon; Johnson, Robert; Patton, Charley; Raitt, Bonnie; Waters, Muddy.

Howlin' Wolf

American blues singer, guitarist, harmonica player, and songwriter

Wolf was one of the most exciting performers in the postwar electric Chicago blues scene. Wolf's towering body—reportedly six feet, three inches and weighing 275 pounds—and low, guttural voice contributed to his dynamic performing style.

Born: June 10, 1910; West Point, Mississippi
Died: January 10, 1976; Hines, Illinois
Also known as: Chester Arthur Burnett (birth name)

Principal recordings

ALBUMS: *Moanin' in the Moonlight*, 1959; *Howlin' Wolf*, 1962; *Howlin' Wolf Sings the Blues*, 1962; *Poor Boy*, 1965; *Big City Blues*, 1966; *Evil*, 1967; *The Original Folk Blues*, 1967; *The Super Super Blues Band*, 1968 (with Muddy Waters and Bo Diddley); *The Howlin' Wolf Album*, 1969; *Goin' Back Home*, 1970; *The London Howlin' Wolf Sessions*, 1971; *Message to the Young*, 1971; *The Back Door Wolf*, 1973; *Howlin' Wolf A.K.A. Chester Burnett*, 1974; *London Revisited*, 1974; *Cadillac Daddy: Memphis Recordings, 1952*, 1987.

The Life

Born Chester Arthur Burnett in West Point, Mississippi, Howlin' Wolf grew up in the midst of the Delta blues culture. Wolf's nickname and his performing persona originated in the roaming wolf character in the tale of Little Red Riding Hood that was etched into his mind by his grandfather. While helping to farm on the plantation of Sam Young and Will Morrow near Ruleville, Mississippi, he met legendary blues performer Charley Patton, who lived on the nearby Dockery's farm, an important base for blues performers. Although Wolf did not learn much from Patton's subtle guitar style, he was certainly influenced by Patton's low voice and clownish performing style. Patton also taught Wolf the blues repertoire that he played throughout his career.

In 1933 the Burnett family moved to Arkansas, where Wolf met another of his main influences, Sonny Boy Williamson, who was married for a while to Wolf's sister. Williamson taught Wolf harmonica techniques, and they teamed up for street performances, which Robert Johnson, Johnny Shines, and Floyd Jones sometimes joined. Other musicians with whom Wolf played when he was an amateur musician include Son House and Willie Brown.

As soon as Wolf was discharged from his military service in 1943, he focused on public performance. In 1948 he formed his first band, the House Rockers. Although band membership was still unstable, some of the important musicians who played included guitarists Willie Johnson, Matt Murphy, and Pat Hare and harmonica players Little Junior Parker and James Cotton, all of whom were teenagers then (Wolf was almost forty years old). In the same year, Wolf started his radio show on KWEM in West Memphis, Arkansas.

In 1951 Wolf signed a recording contract with Sam Phillips, the owner of the Memphis Recording Service. Phillips leased some of Wolf's masters to Chess Records and others to RPM Records. Phillips esteemed Wolf's performance more highly than that of anyone he recorded in his lifetime, including Elvis Presley, Johnny Cash, and Jerry Lee Lewis. In 1953 the Chess brothers, Leonard and Phil, owners of Chess Records, bought Wolf's exclusive contract. Subsequently, Wolf moved his base to Chicago.

During his Memphis era, Wolf was famous for his unique performing style. His low, loud, cracking voice emanating from his huge body, he howled, moaned, growled, and shouted. Although he liked to sit on a stool while performing, he would spend a good part of his show walking, crawling, and rolling around on the stage. He had a chilling smile and often rolled his eyes while he was playing.

Until the mid-1960's Wolf's performing venues were mostly African American clubs, though his performances for a blues package tour in Europe—the American Folk Blues Festival—helped increase his popularity, especially in England. He influenced British rock artists whose musical style was based on blues. When the Rolling Stones were invited to perform for ABC's music show *Shindig* in 1965, the condition for their appearance was to share the bill with Wolf as a special guest. Following Brian Jones's respectful introduction, Wolf performed for more than a million viewers.

In the early 1970's Wolf's health declined drastically; he had several heart attacks and was on dialysis treatment because his kidneys had been de-

Howlin' Wolf. (Hulton Archive/Getty Images)

stroyed in a car accident. In spite of his ailments, he continued to perform in Chicago clubs and make albums for Chess. Wolf's last major performance was for a blues package show at the Chicago Amphitheater in November, 1975. He died two months later.

The Music

"Moanin' at Midnight." In many ways this song represents all of Howlin' Wolf's recordings. The opening—a lower-range spine-chilling moan rising to a falsetto with the hypnotic repetition of a one-chord riff by guitar and harmonica—exemplifies the singer's violent performing persona. This recording also shows Wolf's musical roots, with guitar riffs based on Delta blues performer Tommy Johnson's "Cool Drink of Water Blues" and vocal style influenced by Wolf's mentor Patton. Throughout his career Wolf offered variations on the musical device heard in "Moanin' at Midnight": repetitive riffs on a single chord. This song, coupled with "How Many More Years," was a double-sided hit record in 1951.

"Smokestack Lightning." Another of Wolf's representative recordings is "Smokestack Lightning." Abstract and surreal, the lyrics are built around images of a train and a crying man, sung over a stripped-down one-chord riff derived from "Moanin' at Midnight." These songs are analogous to field hollers, African American songs before the Civil War, in which different images are juxtaposed and sung over one chord. The flavor of the Delta's anachronistic provincialism is an important and attractive feature of Wolf's music.

Compositions by Willie Dixon. Like his compositions for other artists on Chess Records, such as "Hoochie Coochie Man" for Muddy Waters and "My Babe" for Little Walter, house songwriter Willie Dixon's compositions for Howlin' Wolf—"Back Door Man," "Spoonful," "Little Red Rooster," and "Tail Dragger"—were important in his repertoire. While Dixon was skilled at creating songs for Wolf, Waters, and Koko Taylor that portrayed the singers as powerful figures, he also gave them didactic songs in the tradition of preaching blues. "Back Door Man," which is about stealing someone else's wife and its consequence, emphasizes Wolf's ominous character. Its musical structure rests on one chord, and the simplified riff derives from "Moanin' at Midnight." On the other hand, "Spoonful" is a sermon—about how a tiny amount of a thing can be significant for either good or bad. The musical structure of "Spoonful" is also built on a stripped-down one-chord riff. "Little Red Rooster"—adopted from Patton's "Banty Rooster Blues" and Memphis Minnie's "If You See My Rooster (Please Run Him Home)"—is a didactic song with a rustic flavor; the wisdom presented in the song is that the value of a thing is not recognized until it is lost. In "Tail Dragger" Dixon amalgamates melodramatic music and blues to personify a feral beast, and the lyrics about a wolf stealing chicks are reminiscent of Little Red Riding Hood, which was the basis for Wolf's stage name. The riff played by the horn section, sounding like music for a mobster movie, is a shortened version of the "Smokestack Lightning" riff. In all of these recordings Wolf demonstrates a soulful vocal performance, but his guitarist partner, Hubert Sumlin, is important in supporting him. Dixon compositions rise to an exciting level with the interaction between Sumlin's exquisite guitar and Wolf's voice.

"Killing Floor." Another Wolf classic, "Killing Floor," was perhaps inspired by the early Delta blues songs "Dry Spell Blues" by House and "Hard Time Killin' Floor Blues" by Skip James. Reportedly

Wolf sang of his own experience. According to his biography, Wolf spent some time in the Parchman Farm Mississippi State Penitentiary for splitting open someone's head with a hoe in a fight to protect a girl who had been abused by the man. In this song Wolf's powerful vocal is supported by Sumlin's guitar with a sharp driving beat, while Buddy Guy plays the second guitar.

The Howlin' Wolf Album. In the early 1960's young white audiences began to discover the blues. To capitalize on the increasing popularity of the blues in the white community, Chess Records made efforts to sell blues records to a new audience, catering to musical trends. In 1968, in response to the psychedelic music movement, Chess Records produced *Electric Mud* with Waters, Wolf's chief rival. Although this was controversial, the record was Waters's first album to rank on *Billboard* and *Cash Box* charts. Following this trend, Chess Records produced another psychedelic record featuring Wolf, a project he hated. This album lacks musical dynamism, and there is no lively interaction between Wolf and the other musicians. However, "Moanin' at Midnight," in which Wolf's voice and harmonica with two electric guitars sound like ambient music, turned out to be a somewhat interesting musical experiment.

The Back Door Wolf. This was Wolf's last album, released in 1973. While he and his band successfully re-create the good old sound of Chicago blues in the 1960's, some of the lyrics have topical content that reflect the early 1970's. As the title shows, "Watergate Blues" is about the political scandal, and in "Coon on the Moon" Wolf looks back at the history and social progress of African Americans. Sumlin is still an important partner for Wolf.

Musical Legacy

Wolf was influential on the British rock scene, his songs forming an important part of the repertoire for many groups in the British invasion: "Little Red Rooster" for the Rolling Stones, "Spoonful" for Cream, "I Ain't Superstitious" for the Jeff Beck Group (with Rod Stewart), and "The Lemon Song" (adaptation of "Killing Floor") for Led Zeppelin. The album *The London Howlin' Wolf Sessions* captures moments of his collaboration with British rock musicians Eric Clapton, Steve Winwood,

Charlie Watts and Bill Wyman of the Rolling Stones, and Ringo Starr. The album includes the rehearsal scene of Wolf teaching the band how to play "Little Red Rooster." Because Wolf was not in good shape during the sessions, the album lacks his usual power, but it was his best-selling album.

Wolf's unique performing style had some followers: Little Wolf, The Highway Man, and Tail Dragger. His vocal style was an inspiration for vocalist Tom Waits and radio disc jockey Wolfman Jack. Wolf's achievements were honored with his induction into the Rock and Roll Hall of Fame in 1991.

Mitsutoshi Inaba

Further Reading

Escott, Colin, with Martin Hawkins. *Good Rockin' Tonight: Sun Records and the Birth of Rock 'n' Roll.* New York: St. Martin's Press, 1991. The book features a description Wolf's Memphis recording with Sam Phillips.

Guralnick, Peter. *Feel Like Going Home: Portraits in Blues and Rock 'n' Roll.* New York: Harper & Row, 1989. A chapter on Wolf has a detailed description of one of his performances.

Segrest, James, and Mark Hoffman. *Moanin' at Midnight: The Life and Times of Howlin' Wolf.* New York: Pantheon Books, 2004. Highly recommended biography based on the authors' long-term research and interviews with Wolf's family members and musicians who played with him. A documentary DVD based on this book is available.

See also: Berry, Chuck; Butterfield, Paul; Clapton, Eric; Cotton, James; Dixon, Willie; Guy, Buddy; House, Son; Jagger, Sir Mick; Morrison, Jim; Patton, Charley; Raitt, Bonnie; Waters, Muddy; Williamson, Sonny Boy, I; Williamson, Sonny Boy, II; Zappa, Frank.

Alberta Hunter
American jazz/blues singer and songwriter

With a career spanning seven decades, Hunter was a blues pioneer in the 1920's and an American jazz expatriate in Europe in the 1930's and 1940's, onstage and in cabarets. She made a remarkable comeback at the age of eighty-two, with nightly performances at New York City's famous nightclub the Cookery and recordings that harked back to the days of Bessie Smith and Josephine Baker.

Born: April 1, 1895; Memphis, Tennessee
Died: October 17, 1984; New York, New York
Also known as: Alberta Prime; Josephine Beatty; May Alix

Principal recordings

ALBUMS: *Alberta Hunter with Lovie Austin and Her Blues Serenaders*, 1961; *Songs We Taught Your Mother*, 1961 (with Lucille Hegamin and Victoria Spivey); *Remember My Name*, 1977; *Amtrak Blues*, 1978; *The Glory of Alberta Hunter*, 1981; *Look for the Silver Lining*, 1982; *The Legendary Alberta Hunter: The London Sessions, 1934*, 1989.

SINGLES: "Downhearted Blues," 1922; "Jazzin' Baby Blues," 1922; "Stingaree Blues," 1923; "Texas Moaner Blues," 1924; "Your Jelly Roll Is Good," 1925; "Beale Street Blues," 1927; "Sugar," 1927.

The Life

Alberta Hunter was born in Memphis in 1895 to Charles and Laura Hunter. Charles, a sleeping car porter, abandoned Laura and her two children soon after Alberta's birth. When she was sixteen, Hunter moved to Chicago and got her first job as a singer at Dago Frank's, a cabaret and bordello. On January 27, 1919, she married Willard Townsend, and they were separated within weeks and divorced a few years later. Meanwhile, her popularity as a singer netted her the headlining act at the famous Dreamland Café and recordings with top jazz names. In 1924 she became a star of Broadway and vaudeville and moved to Harlem. In 1927 she traveled to Europe, where African American entertainers such as Josephine Baker were the rage. Hunter became a stage hit in Paris and starred in the London production of *Show Boat* (1927) with Paul Robeson. With the expiration of her passport in 1940, she returned to New York. During World War II, she performed for the United Services Organization (USO). With her theatrical career waning, she received a nurse's license in 1957, working for the next twenty years at Goldwater Hospital on Welfare (now Roosevelt) Island.

In 1977 she was rediscovered and began a remarkable new career singing at the Cookery restaurant near Greenwich Village. A nationwide sensation, Hunter performed at the White House, at Carnegie Hall, at the Smithsonian (where she was captured on videotape), and on ABC's *Good Morning America*. She toured Europe and Brazil and recorded three albums. In ill health, Hunter retired in 1983 and died the following year.

The Music

Hunter grew up in the midst of Memphis's flourishing blues culture, centered on Beale Street. She sang in church choirs from an early age, and she was only a teenager when she moved to Chicago and her musical career began in earnest.

Alberta Hunter. (AP/Wide World Photos)

Chicago Blues. Hunter established her reputation singing in the bordellos and honky-tonks of Chicago. In the 1910's and 1920's, Chicago had an exciting mix of Southern blues and New Orleans jazz amalgamating in its nightclubs. As a blues singer, Hunter lacked the raw power and emotion of Bessie Smith, the Empress of the Blues, but Hunter was renowned for her smooth vocalizations, sophisticated diction, and world-weary ballads, and for the frank sensuality of her lyrics. Hunter sang with Joe "King" Oliver's band and recorded songs accompanied by such famous jazz musicians as Fletcher Henderson, Fats Waller, Eubie Blake, Sidney Bechet, and Louis Armstrong. She was the first to sing "Sweet Georgia Brown" for its composer Maceo Pinkard, and she showcased "St. Louis Blues" and "Beale Street Blues" for their composer W. C. Handy. A prolific songwriter, Hunter saw her composition "Downhearted Blues" become a classic when sung by Smith.

"My Castle's Rockin'." With her gift for physical expression and a more entertaining than powerful voice, Hunter gravitated to musical theater. In 1920 she sang a blues number in the revue *Canary Cottage*, and she performed in numerous shows in the following years. In 1924 she formed her own vaudeville troupe, and in 1925 she popularized, if not invented, the flapper dance known as the Black Bottom. Following in the footsteps of Baker, Hunter moved to Europe in 1927 and performed over the next two decades in shows in Paris, London, and Amsterdam. With Chicago blues in decline, her songs became more personal, upbeat, and showy, as reflected in her 1940 composition "My Castle's Rockin'," which would become her theme song. It was shortly after this, however, that Hunter returned to the United States and her career declined.

Cookin' at the Cookery. Incredibly, in 1977, at age eighty-two, Hunter emerged from a twenty-year hiatus to be the headline singer at the Cookery restaurant in Manhattan. For enthusiastic audiences, it was a glimpse of 1920's Chicago and 1930's Paris, as Hunter belted out classic blues numbers and sophisticated ballads, described by one critic as "joyous, sly, sensual as well as sad." Her voice, richer and more assured, had ripened with age. With her entertaining mannerisms and theatricality born of decades onstage, she formed an instant rapport with her audiences. Her trademark renditions of "Nobody Knows You When You're Down and Out," "You Can't Tell the Difference After Dark," and "I Got a Mind to Ramble" combined a blues style with an upbeat theatrical patter. Her blatant double entendres are humorously evident in the song "My Man Is Such a Handy Man," and her *joie de vivre* shines through in "I'm Having a Good Time."

Building on her newfound popularity, she recorded several award-winning albums for Columbia Records and the sound track for the 1978 Robert Altman film *Remember My Name*, and she appeared on numerous television talk shows. *My Castle's Rockin'*—a 1988 video documentary—captured her performances at the Cookery with all of their charm and verve. The musical *Cookin' at the Cookery: The Music and Times of Alberta Hunter*, written by Marion Caffey in 2003, is still popular.

Musical Legacy

Alberta Hunter was a pioneer of urban blues in 1920's Chicago and much celebrated at the time. Although she was an original and enthralling blues singer, her recordings lack the intensity and strength that characterize other great female blues singers of that era, such as Smith and Ma Rainey. In the succeeding decades, she was a success on the stages of New York and Europe but by and large in ephemeral musical numbers.

Perhaps her greatest legacy stems from her years at the Cookery. Live and in recordings, she transported new generations back to the early years of Chicago blues and swinging jazz. Her sassy and sophisticated vocal style, enhanced by a lifetime of stage performance, left a charming and indelible memory with her audiences.

Howard Bromberg

Further Reading

Harrison, Daphne Duval. *Black Pearls: Blues Queens of the 1920's*. New Brunswick, N.J.: Rutgers University Press, 1990. Assesses Hunter in the context of the social and cultural phenomenon of black female blues pioneers.

Santelli, Robert. *Big Book of Blues*. New York: Penguin, 2001. Comprehensive reference work with more than six hundred biographical entries on individual blues musicians, including Hunter.

Shipton, Alyn. *New History of Jazz*. New York: Continuum International Publishing Group, 2007. Notes Hunter's theatrical style of diction and presentation.

Taylor, Frank, with Gerald Cook. *Alberta Hunter: A Celebration in Blues*. New York: McGraw-Hill, 1987. Based on extensive interviews with Hunter and her friends, this conversational biography, cowritten with her Cookery pianist, includes a discography and videography.

Ward, Geoffrey, and Ken Burns. *Jazz: A History of America's Music*. New York: Alfred Knopf, 2000. Based on Burns's award-winning documentary film, includes a historic 1923 photograph of Hunter from the days when she sang with Louis Armstrong.

See also: Armstrong, Louis; Robeson, Paul; Smith, Bessie; Waller, Fats.

Mississippi John Hurt

American blues singer, songwriter, and guitarist

Storytelling balladry and touches of ragtime were strong elements in Hurt's music, which was deeply rooted in traditions that predated the blues.

Born: March 8, 1893; Teoc, Mississippi
Died: November 2, 1966; Grenada, Mississippi
Also known as: John Smith Hurt (full name)

Principal recordings

ALBUMS: *Avalon Blues*, 1963; *Folk Songs and Blues*, 1963; *Worried Blues*, 1963; *Last Session, 1966*, 1966; *Today!*, 1966; *The Immortal*, 1967; *Avalon Blues: The Complete 1928 OKEH Recordings*, 1996 (individual songs recorded 1928); *The Candy Man*, 1980.

The Life

Born John Smith Hurt, Mississippi John Hurt spent most of his life in Carroll County, in Mississippi hill country. Geographically and culturally removed from the Mississippi Delta, it was an area where white and black stringband musicians interacted fairly freely and where the harder edges of the Delta's blues softened. Inspired by a guitar-playing schoolteacher, William H. Carson, Hurt got his first guitar at age nine, and he claimed to be self-taught. During his teens, he entertained locally at dances as a solo singer-guitarist and as a performer in stringbands, some of which were probably racially mixed. That would account for white fiddler Willie Narmour, a neighbor of Hurt in the town of Avalon and half of the popular Narmour and Smith duo, recommending him to record producer Tommy Rockwell of the Okeh label.

Hurt made his first recordings in Memphis, Tennessee, in February of 1928, and he was summoned to New York City for further recordings in December of that year. A half dozen 78-rpm discs by Hurt were issued by Okeh Records, but none sold spectacularly. The economic strains of the Great Depression slowed record sales in general, and Hurt would not record again for thirty-five years.

In 1952 Hurt's 1928 recording of "Frankie" appeared on Harry Smith's influential reissue, *The Anthology of American Folk Music*. This spurred interest in Hurt's music among both record collectors and aspiring folk guitarists. In 1963 one of these enthusiasts, Tom Hoskins, followed a clue Hurt had left regarding his whereabouts in one of his 1928 recordings, "Avalon Blues." Hurt was still there, herding cattle. He was persuaded to relocate to Washington, D.C., and over the next three years he enjoyed extraordinary popularity on the folk scene, making triumphant appearances at the Newport and Philadelphia folk festivals and at New York City's Carnegie Hall. Hurt would record extensively and appear on television's popular *The Tonight Show* and in the pages of such publications as *Time* before succumbing to a heart attack some twenty miles from his Mississippi birthplace.

The Music

Had the Okeh label not pinned the "Mississippi" moniker onto Hurt's name for his initial releases, there's a good chance listeners might have sur-

mised he was from elsewhere, probably from the Southeast. Hurt's light touch on the guitar, sure pitch, clear diction, and relaxed, conversational singing style are all at odds with the stereotype of the intense Mississippi bluesman. Little of Hurt's music, however, was blues in the conventional sense. The term "songster" has been applied to African American artists such as Hurt, whose style and repertoire were broader than the blues and included elements of ballad traditions. Nevertheless, Hurt put an individualistic stamp on any tradition that touched him. Songs entirely his own, such as "Avalon Blues," are no less compelling than traditional ones, such as "Frankie," which were arranged to sound original. Hurt's evident isolation from his musical contemporaries was, if anything, a boon to his creating a unique musical world. The gentle good humor in his voice and the buoyancy of his guitar accompaniments provide a somewhat ironic frame for his lyrics, rife with sagas of murder and other dark doings.

"Frankie." Variously known as "Frankie and Albert" or "Frankie and Johnny," this tale of jealousy and murder was once one of the best-known American folk songs. Hurt's version, which is driven by his gently relentless guitar and the eloquent economy of his lyrics, is entirely sympathetic to the killer.

"Avalon Blues." Hurt wrote and recorded this song that, like a message in a bottle, washed ashore decades after its release and led to his rediscovery. Likely prompted by his feelings of homesickness, this tune, a response to the culture shock the New York City of 1928 dealt to Hurt, vividly shows that his talent as a songwriter was fully equal to his talent for reworking traditional material.

"Stack O'Lee." Hurt turned again to a traditional murder ballad, this one about a cold-blooded killer who valued his hat over a man's life. There are other recordings of the song from this era and later reworkings well into the time of rock and roll, yet Hurt's version emits a quietly assured authority.

"Candy Man Blues." Double-entendre songs were a staple in most blues singers' repertoires. Despite its title, the risqué "Candy Man Blues" is not structurally a blues, and while ragtime embellishments sparkle throughout Hurt's guitar accompaniment, his most complex, the song springs from a deeper well of tradition: through minstrelsy and all the way back to Africa. Whatever its arcane origins, the song is one Hurt delighted audiences with after his rediscovery.

"Spike Driver Blues." This is not a blues at all, but a work song of the sort that predated blues. There is only one chord in the entire song, a fact easily overlooked because of Hurt's bobbing, melodic guitar work, which aids Hurt's storytelling. Again, he has taken the traditional—in this case, the folk song "John Henry"—and made of it something individual and essentially archetypal.

Musical Legacy

When Hurt was rediscovered in 1963, he was revealed as a true folksinger, the genuine article, with a formidable résumé, thanks to his 1928 recordings. Despite being labeled a blues artist, as much for his race as for his repertoire, Hurt was far more accessible to young folk enthusiasts than other rediscovered bluesmen, on whom age and drink had often taken a serious toll. Hurt recorded and performed extensively during the brief years of his celebrity. Such disparate folk-based singer-guitarists as Dave Van Ronk and Doc Watson heard Hurt, and they adopted both his songs and his guitar style into their repertoire.

Mark Humphrey

Further Reading

Erlewine, Michael, et al., eds. *All Music Guide to the Blues.* San Francsico: Miller Freeman Books, 1999. This guide to the recorded blues world features a good entry on Hurt, along with listening recommendations.

Rucker, Leland, ed. *Music Hound Blues: The Essential Album Guide.* Detroit, Mich.: Visible Ink Press, 1998. Though albums go in and out of print, this listening guide has a worthwhile entry on Hurt by Bryan Powell.

Waterman, Dick. *Between Midnight and Day: The Last Unpublished Blues Archive.* New York: Thunder's Mouth Press, 2003. As manager and friend, Waterman was close to a number of rediscovered bluesmen of the 1960's. Hearing Hurt was Waterman's personal gateway to their world, and his exquisite photographs illuminate touching recollections of Hurt and others.

See also: Beck; Van Ronk, Dave; Watson, Doc.

Chrissie Hynde
American rock singer, songwriter, and guitarist

With her gritty, intelligent songs and swaggering performance style, Hynde led her band the Pretenders to great success.

Born: September 7, 1951; Akron, Ohio
Also known as: Christine Ellen Hynde (full name)
Member of: The Pretenders

Principal recordings

ALBUMS: *Pretenders*, 1980; *Pretenders II*, 1981; *Learning to Crawl*, 1984; *Get Close*, 1986; *Packed!*, 1990; *Last of the Independents*, 1994; *Viva el Amor*, 1999; *Loose Screw*, 2002; *Pirate Radio*, 2006; *Break Up the Concrete*, 2008.

The Life

Christine Ellen Hynde was born on September 7, 1951, to Bud and Delores ("Dee") Hynde. She was the second of two children. Her father worked for Ohio Bell Telephone Company, and her mother was a part-time secretary. Hynde was a restless child, with little interest in formal education. By the time she was attending high school, she had become totally disillusioned with what school had to offer.

At that time, Hynde was a huge fan of the British Invasion bands, such as the Beatles, the Rolling Stones, and the Kinks. After graduating from high school, Hynde attended Kent State University, majoring in fine arts. She dropped out of college in 1971, and she supported herself by working as a waitress. As a vegetarian, however, she was upset that she had to serve meat dishes to the customers.

Frustrated with American life, Hynde moved to London in 1973. She worked at various jobs, including for a short time as a rock critic for the music newspaper *New Musical Express*. Hynde became friends with several struggling musicians, including Mick Jones of the Clash and Sid Vicious of the Sex Pistols. After several attempts to form a band, Hynde finally found the right combination of musicians for her band in 1978. Her vision and patience resulted in the Pretenders.

In 1980 Hynde began a relationship with one of her rock heroes, Ray Davies of the Kinks. While their tempestuous relationship did not last, it did produce a daughter, Natalie Rae, who was born in 1983. Hynde married Jim Kerr, the lead singer and songwriter of the band Simple Minds, in 1984. Their daughter, Yasmin, was born in 1985, and they divorced in 1990.

During the 1990's, Hynde became a strong supporter of the group People for the Ethical Treatment of Animals (PETA). In 1997 she married the Colombian artist Lucho Brieva, and they separated in 2002. In 2007 Hynde opened a vegetarian restaurant in her hometown of Akron, Ohio.

The Music

As the rhythm guitarist, lead singer, and primary songwriter of the Pretenders, Hynde established herself as a distinctive female persona in rock music. Taking inspiration from her heroes of 1960's rock music and the punk scene of the 1970's, Hynde carved out a significant position for the Pretenders in the new wave movement.

Early Success. In 1978 Hynde formed the Pretenders in London. In addition to Hynde as vocalist and rhythm guitarist, the original members were Pete Farndon on bass, James Honeyman-Scott on lead guitar, and Martin Chambers on drums. The Pretenders' first single was a cover version of the Kinks' "Stop Your Sobbing." The single was a solid hit in England, and it received some airplay in the United States. In January, 1980, the Pretenders' self-titled album was released to critical acclaim, an auspicious beginning for the band. The album was a blend of punk aggression, a new wave pop sensibility, and a Rolling Stones' earthiness. With such provocative original songs as "Brass in Pocket," "Precious," "Up the Neck," "Tattooed Love Boys," "Kid," and "Mystery Achievement," Hynde established herself as a tough yet vulnerable singer-songwriter. With its bold sexual swagger, the song "Brass in Pocket" became a number-one hit in England. The album also became number one in England, and it rose to number nine on the American music charts.

Learning to Crawl. Through a combination of strong melodies and literate, blistering lyrics, the Pretenders established themselves as a band with almost unlimited potential. While their first album was nominated for three Grammy Awards, *Pretenders II* was not as universally praised. Nevertheless, it included several poignant and striking topical songs, including "The Adultress," "Message of Love," "I Go to Sleep," and "Talk of the Town." Some music critics characterized the second album as a misstep, unfocused and derivative. While a misstep could be corrected, the problems within the band would prove to be a greater challenge. In 1982 Hynde asked Farndon to leave the group because of his serious drug problem. Tragically, within days of Farndon being asked to leave, Honeyman-Scott died of heart failure, from an overdose of cocaine, on June 16, 1982. With the help of new musicians, Hynde recorded a touching tribute to her friend and bandmate Honeyman-Scott in the song "Back on the Chain Gang." By March of 1983, "Back on the Chain Gang" had reached number five on the American singles charts. In another shocking incident, on April 14, 1983, Farndon was found dead from a heroin overdose.

Hynde had no intention of allowing the Pretenders to collapse, so she recruited new members for the band and went into the recording studio to work on the next album. Against all the odds, the refurbished Pretenders produced a remarkable third album in 1984 with *Learning to Crawl*. In addition to "Back on the Chain Gang," the album includes such powerful Hynde songs as "Middle of the Road," "Thumbelina," "My City Was Gone," and "2000 Miles."

The Pretenders, in various forms, have continued to record and perform, the only constant being Hynde. In 1994 the single "I'll Stand by You" became a successful pop hit for the band. In addition to her work with the Pretenders, Hynde has worked on various outside projects. A Pretenders box set, *Pirate Radio*, was released in 2006. It included eighty-one tracks on four compact discs and a DVD with nineteen videos of performances.

Musical Legacy

In 2005 the Pretenders were inducted into the Rock and Roll Hall of Fame. As the driving force of one of the most important bands of their era, Hynde stands as an inspiration to all women rock musicians, and she influenced Courtney Love, Liz Phair, and P J Harvey. In several surveys, Hynde is listed as one of the most important rock musicians. In

2002 she (as a member of the Pretenders) was ranked by *Rolling Stone* as number twelve on the list of fifty essential "women in rock" for the group's debut album.

Jeffry Jensen

Further Reading

Gaar, Gillian G. *She's a Rebel: The History of Women in Rock and Roll*. 2d ed. New York: Seal Press, 1992. A penetrating and positive exploration of women in rock music, including an incisive portrait of Hynde's place in the pantheon of women rockers.

Juno, Andrea. *Angry Women of Rock*. New York: Juno Books, 1996. This resource includes a thoughtful interview with Hynde.

Rees, Dafydd, and Luke Crampton. *Encyclopedia of Rock Stars*. New York: DK, 1996. This reference includes an excellent chronology of the Pretenders.

Salewicz, Chris. *Pretenders*. London: Proteus, 1982. A solid introduction to the band's early years.

See also: Blackwell, Otis; Davies, Ray; Harry, Deborah; Jett, Joan; Madonna; Mitchell, Joni; Slick, Grace.

I

Ice Cube

American rapper

A seminal figure in West Coast gangsta rap, Ice Cube is a founding member of the influential group N. W. A. He is noted for the frank and controversial opinions found in his songs.

Born: June 15, 1969; Los Angeles, California
Also known as: O'Shea Jackson (birth name)
Member of: Westside Connection; N. W. A.

Principal recordings

ALBUMS (solo): *AmeriKKKa's Most Wanted*, 1990 (with Da Lench Mob); *Death Certificate*, 1991; *The Predator*, 1992; *Lethal Injection*, 1993; *War and Peace, Vol. 1 (the War Disc)*, 1998; *War and Peace, Vol. 2 (the Peace Disc)*, 2000; *Laugh Now, Cry Later*, 2006.

ALBUMS (with N. W. A.): *N. W. A. and the Posse*, 1987; *Straight Outta Compton*, 1989; *Niggaz4life*, 1991.

ALBUMS (with Westside Connection): *Bow Down*, 1996; *Terrorist Threats*, 2003.

The Life

Ice Cube was born O'Shea Jackson in South Central Los Angeles to Doris and Andrew Jackson. In 1987 Jackson started a hip-hop group called the C. I. A. He also contributed the song "Boyz-n-the-Hood" to the debut album for the newly formed N. W. A. (Niggaz with Attitude), which included himself, Easy-E, and Dr. Dre. Their second album, *Straight Outta Compton*, was the group's landmark recording and the last one Ice Cube would record with the group because of disagreements over financial matters.

Ice Cube released his first solo album, *AmeriKKKa's Most Wanted*, in 1990 with his new group Da Lench Mob. The album was a hit despite (or because of) the controversy surrounding the expressions of anti-white racism and misogyny in the lyrics. These themes were extended to include what was perceived as anti-Semitic and anti-immigrant

lyrics on his 1991 follow-up, *Death Certificate*. It was also around this time that Ice Cube converted to Islam and became loosely associated with the Nation of Islam.

His most successful album, *The Predator*, was released in 1992, and in 1994 he formed the group Westside Connection with rappers Mack 10 and WC. The primary purpose of the group's debut album, *Bow Down*, was to engage in the growing bicoastal rap feud. Following the completion of this album, Ice Cube took a hiatus from recording to focus on other projects.

Ice Cube launched his acting career in the John Singleton-directed film *Boyz N the Hood* (1991). He later went on to appear in films such as *Anaconda* (1997), *Three Kings* (1999), and *Barbershop* (2002). He also wrote and starred in the trilogy *Friday* (1995), *Next Friday* (1997), and *Friday After Next* (2002) along with Chris Tucker. In 2005 he collaborated on the television documentary series *Black, White*. In 2005 he appeared in the family film *Are We There Yet?*, then in its sequel, *Are We Done Yet?*, in 2007.

The Music

Ice Cube's music is closely connected with African American popular music from the 1960's and 1970's. Many of the music tracks for his songs sample the songs of James Brown, George Clinton and Parliament, Sly and the Family Stone, Kool and the Gang, and other soul and funk superstars.

Ice Cube's early lyrics contain some of the themes that became staples of gangsta rap, including drug use, violence, sex, cars, and neighborhood pride. In his early career, he was criticized for promoting anti-white, anti-woman, anti-Semitic, and anti-immigrant sentiments in his songs. Though his lyrics have changed little, the controversy around them has waned over the years as similar themes have become an accepted part of the gangsta image.

"Boyz-n-the-Hood." Although the song was performed by Easy-E on N. W. A.'s debut album, *N. W. A. and the Posse*, "Boyz-n-the-Hood" was written by Ice Cube. His lyrics, which sound immature and dated in comparison with his songs from just a year later, reference several gangsta rap themes (drug deals, sex, prison, violence against women). Sounding like a demo recording, the music track is primarily electronic, with synthesized melody and bass, drum machines, scratching, and vocal interjections from other group members. Easy-E's rapping sounds awkward and measured rather than flowing. It also contains a sample from Jean Knight's "Mr. Big Stuff."

"AmeriKKKa's Most Wanted." The title track of Ice Cube's debut album was its only hit, rising to number one on the *Billboard* hot rap singles chart. The title has several meanings: Ice Cube's music being wanted by the whole nation, the criminal connotations, and the KKK (Ku Klux Klan, a secret organization in the South that oppressed and lynched blacks). The lyrics involve a gangsta rap mafioso bragging about crime and how tough Ice Cube is. One of the messages of the song is that Americans do not care about black-on-black crime, that is, violence within the black community. However, if a black commits a crime against a white, the perpetrator becomes America's most wanted. The backing track is compiled from four samples: "Humpin'" by the Bar-Kays, "There It Is" by James Brown, "Let the Music Take Your Mind" by Kool and the Gang, and "Advice" by Sly and the Family Stone. There are also samples inserted from the Fox television series *America's Most Wanted*.

"Bop Gun (One Nation)." The fourth single from the *Lethal Injection* album, "Bop Gun (One Nation)," pays homage to Clinton, who created the bop gun for the 1977 song of the same name to be shot at "funkless people" to fill them with the funk, a source of energy for all life. Rapped over samples of the Parliament funkadelic song "One Nation Under a Groove," the lyrics contain multiple references to Clinton's song and are a gangsta challenge to those who would try to stop people from having a good time. "Bop Gun (One Nation)" is among several Ice Cube songs that draw on the influence of Clinton through direct reference and through sampling.

"It Was a Good Day." One of Ice Cube's best-charting singles is "It Was a Good Day" from *The Predator*. It rose to number one on the *Billboard* hot rap chart, number seven on the rhythm-and-blues chart, and number fifteen on the Hot 100. The song is about a good day in South Central Los Angeles, which includes basketball, sex, drugs, alcohol, and driving around. The backing track consists of multiple samples, including "Footsteps in the Dark" by the Isley Brothers.

Musical Legacy

Ice Cube is one of the key figures in West Coast gangsta rap. From his early work with N. W. A. to his solo albums, his music helped define the genre and has remained a steady force within it. Across his career, Ice Cube has remained largely true to his roots and influences, which has enabled him to maintain his following. While controversy over his early songs has dogged his career, it also has served to keep him and his music in the public consciousness. Along with being a significant contributor to N. W. A., Ice Cube has been instrumental in developing the careers of others, particularly his colleagues from Westside Connection and his cousin Kam.

Eric S. Strother

Further Reading

George, Nelson. *Hip-Hop America*. New York: Penguin, 2005. This book discusses the role of hip-hop in American society. The basic premise is that although hip-hop began as an expression of African American youth, it has become a new form of blaxploitation, which consists of stereotyping.

Light, Alan. *The Vibe History of Hip-Hop*. Medford, N.J.: Plexus, 1999. A collection of essays that trace the development of the genre, although many are commentaries and not historically based.

McIver, Joel. *Ice Cube: Attitude*. London: Sanctuary, 2002. In this biography of Ice Cube, some details seem exaggerated to emphasize his gangsta status.

Ogbar, Jeffrey O. G. *Hip-Hop Revolution: The Culture and Politics of Rap*. Lawrence: University Press of Kansas, 2007. A cultural history of hip-hop in which the author explores negative perceptions and stereotypes.

Quinn, Eithne. *Nuthin' but a "G" Thang: The Culture and Commerce of Gangsta Rap*. New York: Columbia University Press, 2004. This interdisciplinary study explores the development of gangsta rap and its relation to urban culture.

See also: Brown, James; Dr. Dre; Hammer, M. C.; Ice-T; Stone, Sly.

Ice-T

American rapper

A seminal figure in West Coast gangsta rap, Ice-T was a pioneer in fusing rap with hardcore punk and heavy metal.

Born: February 16, 1958; Newark, New Jersey
Also known as: Tracy Lauren Marrow (birth name)
Member of: Body Count

Principal recordings

ALBUMS (solo): *Rhyme Pays*, 1987; *Power*, 1988; *The Iceberg/Freedom of Speech . . . Just Watch What You Say*, 1989; *O. G. Original Gangster*, 1991; *Home Invasion*, 1993; *VI: Return of the Real*, 1996; *Below Utopia: The Lost Score*, 1998; *7th Deadly Sin*, 1999; *Gang Culture*, 2004; *Ice T Presents Westside*, 2004; *Gangsta Rap*, 2006.

ALBUMS (with Body Count): *Body Count*, 1992; *Born Dead*, 1994; *Violent Demise: Last Days*, 1997; *Murder 4 Hire*, 2006.

The Life

Ice-T was born Tracy Lauren Marrow in New Jersey, and as a teenager after the deaths of his parents, he moved to the Crenshaw district of South Central Los Angeles. He graduated from Crenshaw High School, where he became obsessed with rap, and he joined the U.S. Army in 1976. After leaving the Army in 1982, he began recording under his street name, Ice-T. He signed with Sire Records and released his first album, *Rhyme Pays*, in 1987. He formed his own label, Rhyme $yndicate Records, in 1989, and in 1991 he recorded *O. G.: Original Gangster*.

In addition to his raps, *O. G.: Original Gangster* introduced Ice-T's heavy metal band Body Count. Body Count was never as successful as Ice-T the solo artist, but it did provide another musical direction. The original members recorded three albums between 1992 and 1997. A fourth album, *Murder 4 Hire*, was released in 2006 with a new lineup.

While Ice-T also released three solo albums through the 1990's, much of the decade was dedicated to establishing himself as an actor. In addition to film appearances in *New Jack City* (1991), *Johnny Mnemonic* (1995), and *Tank Girl* (1995), Ice-T had a recurring role as a drug dealer in the television series *New York Undercover*. In 2000 Ice-T was added to the cast of *Law and Order: Special Victims Unit* as Detective Fin Tutuola. He has also voiced characters in several video games.

The Music

Ice-T's music was instrumental in the formation of the genre known as gangsta rap. While the songs on his debut album, *Rhyme Pays*, are largely party-oriented, later releases contain more political and social content. Ice-T's views are in many ways radically different from his peers'. For instance, he speaks out against anti-white and anti-immigrant racism and homophobia, which are prevalent in the songs of Ice Cube and other West Coast rappers. He also stands out from these performers by depicting ghetto life as something to escape rather than embrace. More controversial views include his belief that the Central Intelligence Agency and local police forces are involved in drug trafficking and that corporate America profits excessively from building prisons.

Musically, Ice-T mixes influences from hip-hop, soul, funk, rock, punk, and heavy metal in his songs. He believes that all these styles derive from African Americans and that one should limit oneself to only one style of music.

"Cop Killer." The song "Cop Killer" was written in 1990 as a protest song against police brutality, and it was performed live several times before being recorded for Body Count's self-titled release. The song was immediately condemned by law enforcement organizations and politicians as encouraging violence against police officers. After the album was released, Ice-T requested that it be pulled from the shelves and rereleased without "Cop Killer" because he believed the controversy surrounding the song was overshadowing the band and the rest of its music.

The spoken introduction dedicates the song to the Los Angeles Police Department on behalf of everyone who has been a target of profiling and brutality, and the lyrics are sung from the perspective of a person who is fed up with corruption and brutality among police officers and decides to get even. The music is fairly typical of the hardcore punk metal of the time, in which the bass and guitar melodies essentially double each other and a guitar solo appears near the end of the song. The snare drum is used (along with sound effects) to emulate gunshots leading into the refrain.

"6 'n the Mornin'." One of the defining songs of early gangsta rap, "6 'n the Mornin'" was released as a B-side in 1986 and rereleased a year later on *Rhyme Pays*. In first person, the lyrics recount a story filled with sex, crime, violence, and boasting, all of which would become staple images of gangsta rap. The accompaniment, just electronic drumbeats and synthesizer punches, is sparse. The song "Midnight" from *O. G.: Original Gangster* is interpreted by some to be a prequel to "6 'n the Mornin'" because it tells a similar tale that ends at six in the morning with police officers at the door, which is where this song begins.

"Escape from the Killing Fields." "Escape from the Killing Fields," from *O. G.: Original Gangster*, is Ice-T's advice to African Americans to reject the notion that they should embrace poverty and ghetto life, which he characterizes as brainwashing perpetrated by the American government to keep African Americans (and other racial and ethnic minor-

ity groups) under control. He even compares their treatment in modern America to the treatment of the American Indians in early America. The accompaniment is based on samples of James Brown's "Get Up Offa That Thing" and Marva Whitney's "What Do I Have to Do to Prove My Love to You." The upbeat tempo emphasizes the urgency of the message.

Musical Legacy

Although Ice-T is one of the defining figures in the development of gangsta rap, his legacy goes beyond the lyrical gratuitous sex and violence to include an intellectual element. While songs such as "Mic Contract," "6 'n the Mornin'," and "The Tower" show that Ice-T can work within the standard rap themes, songs such as "Escape from the Killing Fields" and the final commentary from *O. G.: Original Gangster*, "You Should Have Killed Me Last Year," which touches on the Gulf War, prison conditions, and the plight of young African Americans, show that he is a thinking revolutionary. Ice-T is also credited with bridging the gap between rock and rap. Through his work with Body Count, merging hip-hop and hardcore genres, he indirectly influenced rap-core and nu-metal bands such as Limp Bizkit and Korn.

Eric S. Strother

Further Reading

George, Nelson. *Hip-Hop America*. New York: Penguin, 2005. This book covers music from the post-soul of the 1980's to rap and its latest innovators.

Light, Alan. *The Vibe History of Hip-Hop*. Medford, N.J.: Plexus, 1999. This chronicle of hip-hop has references to the major players and regional rivalries that contributed to the genre's culture.

Marrow, Tracy, and Heidi Siegmund. *The Ice Opinion: Who Gives a Fuck?* New York: St. Martin's Press, 1994. This collection of essays offers Ice-T's philosophies on a number of subjects.

Ogbar, Jeffrey O. G. *Hip-Hop Revolution: The Culture and Politics of Rap*. Lawrence: University Press of Kansas, 2007. This cultural history refutes many popular perceptions of hip-hop culture.

See also: Brown, James; D. M. C.; Dr. Dre; Ice Cube; Jones, Quincy; Simmons, Joseph "Run"; Stone, Sly.

Ice-T. (AP/Wide World Photos)

Julio Iglesias

Spanish singer and songwriter

An international superstar and symbol of romance, Iglesias sings in a passionate and soothing voice, in many languages, and his seductive stage presence draws overcapacity crowds to his concerts.

Born: September 23, 1943; Madrid, Spain
Also known as: Julio José Iglesias de la Cueva (full name)

Principal recordings

ALBUMS: *Gwendolyne*, 1970; *Julio Iglesias*, 1972; *Un Canto à Galicia*, 1973; *À flor de piel*, 1974; *À México*, 1974; *El amor*, 1975; *À mis 33 años*, 1977; *Yo canto*, 1977; *Sono un pirata, sono un signore*, 1978; *Soy*, 1978; *À vous les femmes*, 1979; *Aimer la vie . . .*, 1979; *America*, 1979; *Emociones*, 1979; *Innamorarsi alla mia eta*, 1979; *Amanti*, 1980; *Hey!*, 1980; *Sentimental*, 1980; *Fidèl*, 1981; *From a Child to a Woman*, 1981; *Amor, Amor, Amor*, 1983; *Et l'amour créa la femme*, 1982; *Momenti*, 1982; *Moments*, 1982; *Julio*, 1983; *Pelo amor de uma mulher*, 1983; *1100 Bel Air Place*, 1984 (with others); *Libra*, 1985; *Tutto l'amore che ti manca*, 1987; *Un hombre solo*, 1987; *Non Stop*, 1988; *Latinamente*, 1989; *Raices*, 1989; *In Italian*, 1990; *Starry Night*, 1990; *Calor*, 1992; *Ein Weinachtsabend mit Julio Iglesias*, 1992; *Schenk mir deine Liebe*, 1992; *Crazy*, 1994; *La carretera*, 1995; *Tango*, 1996; *Noche de cuatro lunas*, 2000; *Ao meu Brasil*, 2001; *Una donna puo cambiar la vita*, 2001; *Divorcio*, 2003; *En français*, 2004; *La vida sigue igual*, 2004; *L'Homme que je suis*, 2005; *Romantic Classics*, 2006; *En directo desde el Olympia*, 2007; *Hautnah: Die Geschichten meiner Stars*, 2007; *Je n'ai pas changé*, 2007; *Quelque chose de France*, 2007.
SINGLES: "To All the Girls I've Loved Before," 1984 (with Willie Nelson); "My Love," 1988 (with Stevie Wonder).

The Life

Julio José Iglesias de la Cueva (HOO-lee-oh ih-GLAY-see-uhs) was born to Julio Iglesias Puga, a prominent physician, and Maria del Rosario de la Cueva y Perign. Although he studied law at Complutense University of Madrid, he enjoyed sports. A goalkeeper for the junior Real Madrid soccer team, Iglesias hoped to become a professional soccer player someday.

However, Iglesias's soccer ambitions ended on September 22, 1963, when he and three friends were involved in a near-fatal auto accident, which left him paralyzed with little hope of ever walking again. However, with intense physical therapy and with the support of his family, Iglesias fought to overcome the severe effects of his accident. During his recuperation, his nurse, Eladio Magdaleno, gave him a guitar, which he learned to play, and he also began singing and writing poems and songs.

Miraculously, in less than two years, Iglesias recovered completely, and he could walk again. He went to England to study English at Ramsgate and then at Bell's Language School in Cambridge. After returning to Spain, he performed his song "La vida sigue igual" (life goes on) at the famous Benidorm Music Festival in Madrid on July 17, 1968. He won first prize, and he signed a contract with Columbia Discos. In 1969 Iglesias recorded his first album at the Decca Studios in London, and he made his first film, *La vida sigue igual*, a biographical drama. In 1970, at the Eurovision Festival, Iglesias sang one of his most famous songs, "Gwendolyne," which was inspired by a girlfriend in Cambridge. Also that year he set a record with his tour of Spain: forty-one concerts in forty-one different cities in thirty days. In 1971 he sold his first million albums.

On January 20, 1971, Iglesias married Isabel Preysler Arrastia, and they had three children: "Chabeli" María Isabel, born in 1971; Julio José, born in 1973; and Enrique Miguel, born in 1975. The couple divorced in 1979.

During the 1970's and 1980's Iglesias performed at sold-out concerts worldwide, and he became an international superstar, with number-one hits in various countries. By 1973 he had sold ten million albums, and in 1980 his album sales surpassed seventy-five million worldwide.

In 1984 he released his first album in English, *1100 Bel Air Place*. In 1987 Iglesias won a Grammy Award for *Un hombre solo*, and he was named goodwill ambassador to the United Nations Children's Fund (UNICEF) in 1989.

In 1990 Iglesias met Dutch model Miranda Rijnsburger, and they later had five children: Miguel Alejandro, born in 1997; Rodrigo, born in 1999; twin daughters Victoria and Cristina, born in 2001; and Guillermo, born in 2007.

By the 1990's Iglesias had established himself as one of the world's top ten best-selling recording artists in any genre. On December 21, 2007, Iglesias received France's Legion of Honor award.

The Music

Iglesias began his career singing in Spanish in 1968; by 1983 he had recorded in many foreign languages: Spanish, German, Japanese, English, Italian, Portuguese, French, and English. Although he started singing some songs in English on *Julio* and on *Amor, Amor, Amor*, Iglesias's successful crossover English album was *1100 Bel Air Place* in 1984. He perfected a unique soulful style of singing popular music that gained fans, especially women, throughout the world. With his brilliant musicianship and low-key, trilling voice, he became known as the singer of romance. He filled concert halls worldwide, he appeared on television and before royalty, and he earned several gold and platinum records.

"To All the Girls I've Loved Before." Cowritten by Hal David and Albert Hammond, "To All the Girls I've Loved Before" was Iglesias's breakthrough song in the English-language market, and particularly in the U.S. market. His Spanish version of Cole Porter's "Begin the Beguine" had reached number one in England, so Columbia Broadcasting System (CBS) International, with whom Iglesias had signed a contract, planned to release English versions. Popular American country singer Willie Nelson heard the song, and he invited Iglesias to sing with him at the Country Music Festival in Nashville.

The incongruous duo—a Latin idol in suit and bow tie singing with an American icon in bandanna and T-shirt—turned out to be a immediate hit. The remarkable combination of their contrasting vocal timbres, reflecting their distinct musical personalities and traditions, underscored the universal and romantic theme of the song. They dedicated the song to all the women who had shared their lives, had helped them grow, and had given them so much pleasure.

Released as a single, "To All the Girls I've Loved Before" soon reached number one on the country-music charts, number five on the *Billboard* Hot 100, and number seventeen on the U.K. singles chart. The song won the Country Music Association Award for Single of the Year in 1984, and it became Iglesias's signature English-language piece.

1100 Bel Air Place. In 1984 Iglesias released *1100 Bel Air Place*, his first English-language album, which was designed to be his breakthrough in the U.S. market. It had been planned for years, and it took about sixteen months to produce. Iglesias was meticulous in every detail during the creation of this record. Named for the Los Angeles address where he stayed during the production, *1100 Bel Air Place* showcased Iglesias's multigenre emphasis and his smooth, emotional vocals.

The album proved that Iglesias could sing with American artists and produce a commercial sound while staying true to his own style. The sophisticated instrumentation and sound were also engi-

Julio Iglesias. (AP/Wide World Photos)

neered within the conventions of mid-1980's soft rock, which helped make it a commercial success. The album included "To All the Girls I've Loved Before," which had already sold more than a million copies, a huge success for both Iglesias and Nelson. Also on the album were "All of You," a duet with superstar Diana Ross, and "The Air that I Breathe," sung with the Beach Boys. Legendary saxophonist Stan Getz played on the track with "When I Fall in Love." Within a week of release, *1100 Bel Air Place* sold more than a million copies in the United States, and it established Iglesias as a successful crossover artist, combining Latin and U.S. music.

Crazy. In 1994 Iglesias released another English-language album, *Crazy*. Like *1100 Bel Air Place*, the recording featured beautiful ballads and celebrated guest artists. "Let It Be Me" included Art Garfunkel, "Fragile" featured Sting, and the "Song of Joy" was recorded with the London Symphony Orchestra and the Ambrosian Singers. "When You Tell Me That You Love Me" was a duet with Dolly Parton. The album quickly sold fifteen million copies in the United States, and it went platinum in England and other countries.

Romantic Classics. In September, 2006, Iglesias released another English-language album. For *Romantic Classics*, he selected eleven popular love songs from the 1960's, 1970's, and 1980's that he believed, with their memorable lyrics and melodies, would become standards or classics. In his sensual voice with soft dynamic range and rapid vibrato, Iglesias reinterpreted songs from pop, rock, and country music that were originally recorded by other artists. He included a range of songs to cover various stages of a romance: infatuation, desire, betrayal, and heartbreak. Tracks include "Everybody's Talking," first recorded by Harry Nilsson; the Bee Gees' song "How Can You Mend a Broken Heart?"; "I Want to Know What Love Is" by the British American rock band Foreigner; "It's Impossible," originally recorded by Perry Como; and Nelson's "Always on My Mind." Saxophonist Dave Koz was the guest artist on George Michael's "Careless Whisper" track, and Grammy Award-winner Chris Botti played trumpet on Herb Alpert's "This Guy's in Love With You." Also remarkable was that the multilingual Iglesias recorded for the first time in Mandarin Chinese, Bahasa Indonesian, and Filipino on an additional track twelve ("Crazy") for the compact-disc editions for distribution in China, Indonesia, and the Philippines.

Musical Legacy

In 1983 the Guinness World Book of Records awarded Iglesias its first Diamond Record Award, for selling more records in more languages than any other musician in history. During the 1970's and 1980's Iglesias reinterpreted traditional romantic ballads and the Latin bolero, and he revitalized the Latin recording industry. By 2007, he had sold more than 250 million records in fourteen languages, released seventy-seven albums, performed in more than five thousand concerts, and earned more than 2,500 gold and platinum records.

In crossing musical and language barriers, Iglesias became a legendary international superstar. He has used this universal voice and his popularity to help raise funds for various charities and humanitarian causes. Named a UNICEF Special Representative for the Performing Arts in 1989, Iglesias has continued through the years to support UNICEF with benefit concerts and personal appearances. In 2001, on behalf of the world's underprivileged children, he gave the first benefit for UNICEF in the former Soviet Union. Iglesias has also performed at fund-raisers for victims of earthquakes, floods, and other disasters. In the United States, he has donated his time to many different causes, including Farm Aid, the Muscular Dystrophy Association, the American Foundation for AIDS Research, and the Grammy Foundation's Grammy in the Schools program.

Beyond his considerable artistic influence on the musical artists with whom he has recorded and performed, and on the popular music industry in general, Iglesias has inspired a new generation of musicians, including his own sons Enrique and Julio, Jr., who have become musical superstars in their own right.

Alice Myers

Further Reading

Daly, Marsha. *Julio Iglesias*. New York: St. Martin's Press, 1986. One of the few biographies in English, this detailed account describes the disappointments and achievements of Iglesias's life. Illustrated with many photographs. Index.

Dews, Charles, and David Everett. "Julio Iglesias, the Forgotten Soccer Star: 2,650 Gold and Platinum Records and Seventy-seven Albums with 260 Million Copies Sold." *Latino Leaders: The National Magazine of the Successful American Latino* (December, 2003): 40. Biographical and career information on Iglesias.

Garcia, Elizabeth. *Julio.* New York: Ballantine Books, 1985. A candid early biography that chronicles Iglesias's personal life and his rise to international stardom. Illustrated. Discography of albums released in English, Spanish, French, Italian, German, and Portuguese.

Gett, Steve. *Julio Iglesias: The New Valentino.* Port Chester, N.Y.: Cherry Lane Books, 1985. A short biography describes the rise of Iglesias's career and his romantic style of music. Illustrated.

Lockyer, Daphne. *Julio: The Unsung Story.* Secaucus, N.J.: Carol, 1997. A comprehensive biography based on extensive archival research and interviews with Iglesias's father, ex-wife Preysler, manager Alfredo Fraile, childhood friends, and others. Illustrated. Index.

McAleer, Dave. *Hit Singles: Top 20 Charts from 1954 to the Present Day.* San Francisco: Backbeat Books, 2004. Rock and pop charts of the United States and England, with artists' information, record labels, and monthly chart entry dates from 1954 through 2003. Includes information on Iglesias's numerous hit songs. Illustrated. Index.

Morales, Ed. *The Latin Beat: The Rhythms and Roots of Latin Music, from Bossa Nova to Salsa and Beyond.* Cambridge, Mass.: Da Capo Press, 2003. Includes analyses of Iglesias's significance to the Latin recording industry and of his use of and reinterpretation of traditional Spanish and Latin American styles of music, such as the bolero and flamenco. Bibliography and index.

Whitburn, Joel, ed. *The Billboard Book of Top 40 Country Hits.* New York: Watson-Guptill Billboard Books, 2006. The official guide and complete history of Top 40 country hits since 1942. Includes information on Iglesias and Nelson's extraordinarily successful song, "To All the Girls I've Loved Before." Illustrated.

See also: Alpert, Herb; David, Hal; Garfunkel, Art; Getz, Stan; Nelson, Willie; Parton, Dolly; Piaf, Édith; Ross, Diana; Sting.

Burl Ives
American folksinger

A distinguished folksinger called America's favorite balladeer, Ives worked to keep historical folk music a permanent part of American culture, bringing folk music to the pop charts.

Born: June 14, 1909; Hunt, Illinois
Died: April 14, 1995; Anacortes, Washington
Also known as: Buele Icle Ivanhow "Burl" Ives (full name)

Principal recordings

ALBUMS: *Burl Ives*, 1949; *More Folksongs by Burl Ives*, 1949; *Ballads and Folk Songs, Vol. 1*, 1950; *Ballads and Folk Songs, Vol. 2*, 1950; *Ballads, Folk, and Country Songs*, 1950; *The Lonesome Train: A Musical Legend About Abraham Lincoln*, 1950; *Christmas Day in the Morning*, 1952; *Folk Songs Dramatic and Dangerous*, 1953; *Women: Folk Songs About the Fair*, 1954; *Burl Ives Sings for Fun*, 1956; *Down to the Sea in Ships*, 1956; *In the Quiet of Night*, 1956; *Men*, 1956; *Women*, 1956; *Christmas Eve with Burl Ives*, 1957; *Australian Folk Songs*, 1958; *Captain Burl Ives' Ark*, 1958; *Songs of Ireland*, 1958; *Ballads with Guitar*, 1959; *The Wayfaring Stranger*, 1959; *It's Just My Funny Way of Laughin'*, 1962; *The Versatile Burl Ives*, 1962; *Scouting Along with Burl Ives*, 1963; *Chim Chim Cheree and Other Children's Choices*, 1964; *Have a Holly Jolly Christmas*, 1964; *Sings the Great Country Hits*, 1968; *Songbook*, 1973; *Santa Claus Is Coming to Town*, 1987; *Burl Ives Sings*, 1995; *How Great Thou Art*, 2001; *Songs I Sang in Sunday School*, 2001.

WRITINGS OF INTEREST: *Wayfaring Stranger*, 1948.

The Life

Buele Icle Ivanhow "Burl" Ives (ivz) was one of seven children born to Levi and Cordelia White Ives. His musical talent was noticed by his uncle while Ives was a young boy. After playing football in high school, he attended Eastern Illinois State Teachers College from 1927 to 1930, where he studied history, with the goal of becoming a teacher. Convinced that his music would provide a better direction for his life, he left college and traveled the country, singing his favorite songs and collecting stories and other songs for his performances.

In 1937 Ives moved to New York City to receive formal voice instruction and to break into show business. From 1940 to 1942 he hosted his own radio show, *The Wayfaring Stranger*, and popularized folksinging. In 1946 he made his first film appearance, as a singing cowboy, in *Smoky*. Ives was identified as an entertainer with supposed Communist Party ties in 1950, but he was later removed from the list. His most notable Broadway performance was as Big Daddy in *Cat on a Hot Tin Roof* (1955), which ran from 1955 to 1956. He also played the same role in the motion-picture version in 1958. Ives won an Academy Award for Best Supporting Actor for his performance in *The Big Country* in 1958.

In 1962 he recorded three country hits, "A Little Bitty Tear," "Call Me Mr. In-Between," and "Funny Way of Laughin'." For the last song, he won a Grammy Award for Best Country-Western Recording. All three songs reached the Top 10 on the pop charts.

Ives and his first wife, Helen Peck Ehrlich, had one child, and they divorced in 1971. He married Dorothy Koster Paul later that same year. They had three children. He retired in 1989 and died of mouth cancer in 1995.

The Music

Ives promoted the traditional songs sung on the front porch or in the living room by ordinary people for their own pleasure. He brought authentic folk music into the mainstream of popular music, keeping that part of American heritage alive. His heartfelt music was a celebration of the American people and their way of life. His easy, casual style and his smooth-flowing tunes evoked warm memories. His finely honed, deep folk voice delivered a soothing, moving sound. For most of his songs, Ives was content to accompany himself with a guitar, not relying on other musical support. His songs appealed to children and adults of all ages.

The Wayfaring Stranger. This album, recorded in 1959, set the standard for folk-music albums. The classic folk songs are mostly performed by Ives and his acoustic guitar. The songs are short, simple, and arranged in folk tradition. Using his deep, folksy voice, Ives allows listeners to savor the music, as if he were performing just for them.

Songs from the Big Rock Candy Mountain. This collection, released in 2007, contains more than thirty of Ives's greatest folk songs that span his career from the late 1930's to the late 1970's. The songs are delivered by Ives with his customary comfortable, easy approach, and his joyful voice takes the rough edges off many ragged folk melodies. Songs such as "Big Rock Candy Mountain," "Blue Tail Fly" (with the Andrews Sisters), "Call Me Mr. In-Between," and "Lavender Blue" generate fond memories for listeners.

Burl Ives's Greatest Hits. In this compilation most of the songs are pop versions of the ones that made Ives an American legend. Some of his great renditions include "A Little Bitty Tear," "Funny Way of Laughin'," "True Love Goes On and On," "Pearly Shells," and "On Top of Old Smoky" performed with the Percy Faith Orchestra. His pleasing tunes are meant to be enjoyed by people of all ages.

Very Best of Burl Ives Christmas. This 1999 album contains fifteen Christmas standards, ranging from Ives's trademark Christmas song "A Holly Jolly Christmas" to "Silver Bells" and "What Child Is This?" His deep, warm voice and Santa Claus countenance are perfectly suited to the merriment of the season. In some of the carols, Ives is accompanied by backup vocalists and instruments, including strings, harp, bass, and flute, in unison with Ives's acoustic guitar. The way he playfully delivers the songs, in his sweet voice, cements his place in the genre of Christmas music.

Musical Legacy

Ives recorded more than seventy albums and performed on radio throughout the 1940's and 1950's. He was lauded for telling stories, in a grandfatherly croon, through American folk songs. His recordings and anthologies of folk songs kept folk music vital in the American tradition. His Christmas classic "A Holly Jolly Christmas" was a radio staple during the Christmas season. He was the voice of Sam the Snowman on the television special *Rudolph, the Red-Nosed Reindeer* (1964). A long-running holiday special, it featured some of Ives's most popular Christmas tunes.

Alvin K. Benson

Further Reading

Ives, Burl. *The Burl Ives Sing-Along Song Book: A Treasury of American Folk Songs and Ballads.* New York: Franklin Watts, 1963. Ives discusses America's musical heritage, presenting the background and lyrics to important folk songs and ballads.

Ives, Burl. *Wayfaring Stranger.* Whitefish, Mont.: Kessinger, 2007. Ives recounts his travels across America in pursuit of success as a singer, and he discusses some of the folk songs and stories that he collected along the way.

Parish, James Robert. *Hollywood Songsters: Singers Who Act and Actors Who Sing.* London: Routledge, 2003. Contains a biographical sketch of Ives that recounts his success as a singer, actor, and author.

See also: Baez, Joan; Belafonte, Harry; Denver, John; Guthrie, Woody; Leadbelly; Lomax, Alan; Paxton, Tom.

Charles Ives

American classical composer

An original voice in American classical music, Ives composed complex and innovative works that earned him an international reputation.

Born: October 20, 1874; Danbury, Connecticut
Died: May 19, 1954; New York, New York
Also known as: Charles Edward Ives (full name)

Principal works

CHAMBER WORKS: *From the Steeples and the Mountains*, 1901 (for one or two trumpets, trombone, bells, and two pianos); String Quartet No. 1, composed 1909, first performed 1943 (*From the Salvation Army*); String Quartet No. 2, composed 1915, first performed 1954; Sonata No. 4 for Violin and Piano, composed 1916, first performed 1940 (*Children's Day at the Camp Meet*); Sonata No. 1 for Violin and Piano, composed 1917, first performed 1953; Sonata No. 2 for Violin and Piano, composed 1917, first performed 1924; Sonata No. 3 for Violin and Piano, 1917.

ORCHESTRAL WORKS: Symphony No. 1 in D Minor, composed 1901, first performed 1953; *Central Park in the Dark*, 1907; *The Unanswered Question*, composed 1908, first performed 1946 (for trumpet, winds, and string orchestra); Symphony No. 2, composed 1909, first performed 1951; Symphony No. 3, composed 1911, first performed 1946 (*The Camp Meeting*); *Robert Browning Overture*, 1912; *Three Places in New England*, 1914; Symphony No. 4, composed 1918, first performed 1965; *New England Holidays*, composed 1919, first performed 1954; Prelude No. 1, 1923; Prelude No. 2, 1927; *Universe Symphony*, composed 1928, first performed 1993.

ORGAN WORK: Variations on "America," 1891.

PIANO WORKS: Piano Sonata No. 1, 1916; Piano Sonata No. 2, 1920 (*Concord, Massachusetts, 1840-1860*).

VOCAL WORKS: "General William Booth Enters into Heaven," 1914 (music; poem of Vachel Lindsay); "The Things Our Fathers Loved," 1917; *114 Songs*, 1922.

The Life

Charles Edward Ives (ivz) was born into a civic-minded New England family. His father, George Edward Ives, had a successful career as a musician—trained in harmony, counterpoint, and several instruments—in the Union Army during the Civil War and later as the director of bands and choirs in and around Danbury, Connecticut. As a result of his father's musical activities, as well as an openness to new musical ideas in the household, Ives was raised in an environment that profoundly influenced him as a composer.

During his youth, Ives studied piano and organ; he was exposed to American vernacular music, Protestant church music, and European art music. His first success as a composer came in his early teens, followed by professional success as a church organist. Ives received instrumental lessons from various teachers, although his most significant musical training came in the form of harmony, counterpoint, and composition lessons from his father. At the age of twenty, having already established himself as a superb organist, as well as a composer of both popular and church music, Ives entered Yale University, where he studied with composer

Charles Ives. (© Bettmann/CORBIS)

and teacher Horatio Parker. During his university studies with Parker, Ives explored the European art music tradition, and that shifted his compositional focus to American art music.

Despite his successful graduation from Yale with studies in music, Ives did not pursue music as his primary occupation. He chose a career in the insurance profession, and his financial success provided comfortable support for him and his wife. This decision corresponded with his father's belief that a man's interest in music could be freer and stronger if he did not have to rely on it for his living. This philosophy allowed Ives to pursue his increasingly innovative compositional career unimpeded by outside influences. At the same time, however, since he composed largely in isolation, he began to gain musical recognition only after he stopped composing in 1927. Ives spent the last several decades of his life revising earlier works and gaining notoriety as a composer through the efforts of such advocates as Nicolas Slonimsky, Aaron Copland, and Leonard Bernstein. After several decades of

poor health, Ives died of a stroke following surgery in 1954.

The Music

Although not the most popular or best-known American composer, Ives is an innovative figure in twentieth century classical music. Immediately striking is his confident use of such advanced compositional techniques as free dissonance, quarter tones, tone clusters, polytonality, and polyrhythm at a time when the late Romanticism of Gustav Mahler and Richard Strauss was in vogue and before the radical musical developments of Arnold Schoenberg, Igor Stravinsky, and Béla Bartók. As important as his avant-garde musical language is Ives's seminal position as a composer of nationalistic American works. In addition to writing pieces based on American subject matter, especially relating to his native New England, Ives frequently incorporated—in a fragmentary or collage-like manner—vernacular, patriotic, and Protestant-hymn tunes and ragtime elements into his compositions. Notable to Ives's style is a focus on the Transcendental philosophies (known as Transcendentalism) of such American writers as Ralph Waldo Emerson and Henry David Thoreau.

Early Works. Written for organ, Variations on "America" may be considered Ives's first major composition. Its significance lies not in its traditional formal structure but in its virtuosic demands and notable, though sparing, bitonality. Although Ives had written and published a number of short works, including a song for William McKinley's 1896 presidential campaign, before graduating from Yale University, his first major orchestral work was Symphony No. 1 in D Minor. This traditional four-movement work was written under Parker's tutelage and reflects Ives's university studies of the late-Romantic symphonies of Johannes Brahms, Antonín Dvořák, and Peter Ilich Tchaikovsky.

The Unanswered Question. Perhaps Ives's most famous composition, *The Unanswered Question*, described by the composer as a "cosmic drama," explores the spiritual question of existence through the use of three individual, though complementary, planes of sound that combine to create extreme dissonance. The first layer, which Ives referred to as "the silences of the Druids, who know, see, and hear nothing," is assigned to the strings. Above this foundation, a recurring trumpet line asks "the perennial question of existence," while the winds furiously, though unsuccessfully, attempt to pose an answer. As a result, the work closes as eerily as it opens, with quiet, slowly shifting harmonies in the strings. Although this work was originally scored for string quartet, woodwind quartet, and solo trumpet, Ives also produced arrangements of the work for chamber orchestra and full orchestra. *The Unanswered Question* is sometimes paired, as Ives originally intended, with the more extroverted orchestral work *Central Park in the Dark* under the title *Two Contemplations*.

Symphony No. 3. Subtitled *The Camp Meeting*, Ives's Symphony No. 3 garnered the Pulitzer Prize for Music in 1947, the year after its premiere performance, because of its folklike character. The three-movement work, scored for chamber orchestra and derived from earlier organ works, is largely programmatic, meant to depict a Protestant revival meeting around the turn of the nineteenth century. Throughout the work's three movements ("Old Folks Gatherin'," "Children's Day," and "Communion"), Ives incorporates a number of hymn tunes, including "What a Friend We Have in Jesus," "O, for a Thousand Tongues to Sing," "There Is a Fountain Filled with Blood," and "Just as I Am." Musically, Symphony No. 3 displays Ives's use of counterpoint, chromaticism, dissonance, altered formal structures, and layering effects in which two or more unrelated melodies are presented simultaneously.

Three Places in New England. As is the case with many of his orchestral scores, Ives's *Three Places in New England* is programmatic in nature. Further, the score exemplifies the composer's interest in the relationship between time and space by placing the listener in three specific musical settings, by layering borrowed tunes and by using extreme dissonances. The first movement, "The 'St. Gaudens' in Boston Common (Col. Shaw and His Colored Regiment)," portrays emotions evoked by a Civil War monument dedicated to the first all-black regiment to serve in the Union Army. The third movement, "The Housatonic at Stockbridge,"

captures the atmosphere of a morning walk along the Housatonic River near Stockbridge, Massachusetts. Central to *Three Places in New England*, both musically and popularly, is the second movement, "Putnam's Camp, Redding, Connecticut." Incorporating quotations from numerous patriotic tunes, most notably "Yankee Doodle" and "Hail, Columbia," the movement depicts the events of a Fourth of July picnic, including a Revolutionary War battle scene, from the perspective of a young boy.

Piano Sonata No. 2. Ives's Piano Sonata No. 2, or *Concord, Massachusetts, 1840-1860*, is the most direct musical statement concerning his interest in Transcendentalism. The four-movement work presents musical impressions of major figures, as well as their literary and philosophical views, connected with the Transcendental movement centered in Concord, Massachusetts, during the mid-nineteenth century. Ives's sonata is cyclical in that all four movements ("Emerson," "Hawthorne," "The Alcotts," and "Thoreau") include multiple quotations of the famous four-note motif from Ludwig van Beethoven's Symphony No. 5. In addition, several other borrowed tunes are incorporated in the work, including the hymn "Martyn," the patriotic song "Columbia, Gem of the Ocean," the Celtic folk song "Loch Lomond," the minstrel song "Massa's in de Cold Ground" by Stephen Foster, and the wedding march from Richard Wagner's *Lohengrin* (1850). Other notable compositional techniques are dense textures, the frequent use of tone clusters (one spanning more than two octaves, requiring the use of a board to depress the necessary piano keys), and the occasional abandonment of key signatures, notated meters, and bar lines.

Musical Legacy

Ives's *The Unanswered Question* and Piano Sonata No. 2 may define the composer as one of the most significant of the twentieth century. In these two works were found a synthesis of his unique and innovative musical language. The fact that so many of the composer's works were published, performed, and recorded demonstrated his monumental importance. His compositions enhanced the repertoire of the American orchestra, the piano literature, and the chamber ensemble. Important in establishing American vocal music are such art songs as "The Circus Band," "General William

Booth Enters into Heaven," "The Things Our Fathers Loved," and "The Housatonic at Stockbridge."

Though isolated as a composer, Ives created a musical language that was strikingly original and at the same time strangely familiar, that was deeply spiritual and at the same time overtly nationalistic. Ives's innovative compositional techniques, his frequent use of musical quotation, and his general lack of concern for musical tradition paved the way for future developments in American and European art music.

Frederick Key Smith

Further Reading

Burkholder, J. Peter, ed. *Charles Ives and His World*. Princeton, N.J.: Princeton University Press, 1996. A collection of essays by leading scholars of Ives's life and music. Includes selected correspondence of the composer, numerous reviews of his music, and profiles by several of his contemporaries.

Crawford, Richard. *America's Musical Life: A History*. New York: W. W. Norton, 2001. An accessible history of all facets of American music. Includes a chapter on Ives, placing him in the context of twentieth century American music.

Ives, Charles. *Essays Before a Sonata: The Majority and Other Writings*. New York: W. W. Norton, 1961. The composer reflects on his politics and musical philosophy.

Lambert, Philip, ed. *Ives Studies*. New York: Cambridge University Press, 1997. A collection of essays by leading scholars of Ives's life and music.

Magee, Gayle Sherwood. *Charles Ives Reconsidered*. Urbana: University of Illinois Press, 2008. Reexamines the life and music of Ives, as well as his influence on modern music.

Perlis, Vivian. *Charles Ives Remembered: An Oral History*. Urbana: University of Illinois Press, 1974. A collection of writings on Ives's life and music by people close to the composer throughout his career.

Ross, Alex. *The Rest Is Noise: Listening to the Twentieth Century*. New York: Farrar, Straus and Giroux, 2007. A narrative view of modern music, including a chapter focused on Ives and his American contemporaries.

Swafford, Jan. *Charles Ives: A Life with Music*. New York: W. W. Norton, 1996. A detailed biography of the composer, focusing on his personality and his musical output. Includes musical examples, extensive notes, and a useful bibliography.

See also: Adams, John; Bernstein, Leonard; Carter, Elliott; Coleman, Ornette; Copland, Aaron; Harrison, Lou; Mahler, Gustav; Mingus, Charles; Nancarrow, Conlon; Schnittke, Alfred; Schreker, Franz; Stokowski, Leopold; Strauss, Richard; Thomas, Michael Tilson; Tippett, Sir Michael.

J

Janet Jackson

American rhythm-and-blues singer and songwriter

As an influential artist in pop, rock, hip-hop, and rhythm and blues, Jackson has influenced her audiences through her music's messages of self-awareness, determination, and success.

Born: May 16, 1966; Gary, Indiana
Also known as: Janet Damita Jo Jackson (full name)

Principal recordings

ALBUMS: *Janet Jackson*, 1982; *Dream Street*, 1984; *Control*, 1986; *Rhythm Nation 1814*, 1989; *janet.*, 1993; *The Velvet Rope*, 1997; *All for You*, 2001; *Damita Jo*, 2004; *20 Y.O.*, 2006; *Discipline*, 2008.

SINGLES: "What Have You Done for Me Lately," 1986; "Control," 1989; "Rhythm Nation," 1989; "The Best Things in Life Are Free," 1992 (with Luther Vandross); "If," 1993; "That's the Way Love Goes," 1993.

The Life

Janet Damita Jo Jackson was born in Gary, Indiana, on May 16, 1966, the youngest of Katherine and Joseph Jackson's nine children. Although the family was lower middle class, the success of her brothers' group, the Jackson Five, allowed Jackson and her family to move to Encino, California, in 1971.

In 1974 Jackson began performing at the MGM Grand in Las Vegas with her older siblings. Jackson's witty impressions of Mae West and Cher caught the attention of CBS producers, and in 1976 the Jackson family hosted a television variety show, *The Jacksons*. After *The Jacksons* ended, Jackson continued her career in television. From 1977 to 1979, Jackson played Penny in the comedy series *Good Times*. In 1982 the producers of *Diff'rent Strokes* cast her as Charlene Dupree. Jackson also made appearances on *Fame*. Despite her rigorous schedule, Jackson attended day school. She attended the Lanai Road Elementary School in Encino, Portola Middle School in Tarzana, and the San Fernando Valley Professional School.

Although Jackson succeeded as an actress, her father wanted his daughter to pursue her music career. Jackson began her career as a serious musician in 1982. In 1984 Jackson married James DeBarge; however, the marriage was annulled in 1985. In 1986 Jackson began to secretly date René Elizondo, Jr. They married in 1991; however, in 1999 Jackson and Elizondo filed for a divorce. He sued Jackson for twenty-five million dollars. In 2003 the divorce was finalized, and Elizondo was granted half his request. After these heartaches, Jackson began dating producer Jermaine Dupri, and they had a caring relationship. Jackson remained with Virgin Records until 2007, when she signed with Island Records. She has continued her film career with parts in *Nutty Professor II: The Klumps* (2000) and *Why Did I Get Married?* (2007).

The Music

Although Jackson was raised on the music of the Jackson Five and other Motown artists, she developed her own style and lyricism. During most of her career, Jackson recorded for two record labels, A&M Records and Virgin Records. Ten number-one singles have appeared on the Hot 100 *Billboard* chart, and sixteen singles have reached the number-one rhythm-and-blues singles *Billboard* chart.

Early Works. Jackson's first recording was with her brother Randy, "Love Song for Kids," in 1978. In 1982, with her father as her manager, she signed a four-album contract with A&M Records. Soon after, she released her debut, self-titled album *Janet Jackson*. Record sales were not successful; *Janet Jackson* sold only three hundred thousand copies. In 1984 Jackson released her second album, *Dream Street*, and it sold about two hundred thousand copies. Her first two albums received a lot of criticism, with many saying that Jackson had used her family's fame to gain a record deal. These early works show Jackson's timidity and youth as an artist, and her music career started on a rocky path.

Control. Released in 1986, *Control* marks the beginning of Jackson's success as a musician. After the poor sales of Jackson's first two albums, A&M Records asked Jimmy Jam and Terry Lewis to work with Jackson on her musical style. She accepted their help, and in effort to gain further independence she released her father as her manager. *Control* proved a great success; it sold more than five million copies, and the single, "When I Think of You," topped the *Billboard* charts.

Jackson's direct involvement in the production of *Control* emphasizes the album's importance in Jackson's career. She played keyboard, coproduced, and wrote several songs on the album. The initiative Jackson took on this album is reflected in the music. She had control of the album's production, and the tentativeness in her voice and lyrics (apparent in previous albums) did not appear in *Control*. *Control* symbolizes Jackson's independence as an artist; in 2007 it was included as one of the Rock and Roll Hall of Fame's 200 Definitive Albums of All Time.

The Velvet Rope. In 1991 Jackson expanded her career internationally by signing with Virgin Records, and in 1996 Jackson renewed her contract with Virgin Records for eighty million dollars. In 1997 Jackson released her second album with Virgin Records, *The Velvet Rope*. Prior to the album's release, Virgin Records released her top singles, including "Together Again," "I Get Lonely," "Go Deep," "Got 'Til It's Gone," and "Every Time." During her U.S. tour to promote *The Velvet Rope*, Jackson taped an HBO special in Madison Square Garden.

The Velvet Rope demonstrates how Jackson uses her music as a vehicle for social commentary. Prior to this album, Jackson reportedly suffered from clinical depression, and *The Velvet Rope* was a response to her personal struggles. Many of the songs consider issues of self-esteem, loneliness, and relationships. In her willingness to address her audience in a candid manner, Jackson shows her maturity as an artist. "Together Again," a song from the album in commemoration of a friend Jackson lost to AIDS, topped the *Billboard* charts.

Musical Legacy

Throughout her career Jackson has asserted herself as an individual, becoming more than the youngest Jackson. In a 1990 interview she stated, "I wanted to do this; I chose to because there is a responsibility I feel as a young entertainer. I started to realize that I had become a role model for young people." Her socially conscious music in *Control* and *The Velvet Rope* educated her audiences about self-worth, relationships, and success by revealing Jackson's inner thoughts.

Jackson has proved influential in the recording industry through her business choices. She never left a record label at a low point in her career. Jackson's substantial career has gained her fame and fortune. In 2007 Forbes magazine announced that Jackson was the seventh richest woman in the entertainment business (amassing more than 150 million dollars). Her discipline as an artist and as an entrepreneur has allowed Jackson to place on the *Billboard* Top 100 charts for more than two decades.

Joy M. Doan

Further Reading

Andrews, Bart. *Out of the Madness: The Strictly Unauthorized Biography of Janet Jackson.* New York: HarperCollins, 1994. This biography focuses on Jackson's early career, along with personal information on the singer and the Jackson family.

Cornwall, Jane. *Janet Jackson.* London: Carlton Books, 2002. A biographical study, this work covers Jackson's career in its early days and in its subsequent successes. Particular attention is given to her personal life. Includes photographs from throughout her career.

Jackson, Janet. *Too Many Miles, Not Enough Love.* Philadelphia: Xlibris, 2005. The singer describes in her own words her personal struggles, and she details the important events of her career.

McMillan, Constance Van Brunt. *Randy and Janet Jackson: Ready and Right!* St. Paul, Minn.: EMC, 1977. This biography chronicles the lives and musical careers of the two youngest Jackson children.

Nathan, David. *The Soulful Divas.* New York: Billboard Books, 2002. Nathan presents a biographical outlook on the maturation of Jackson's music as it relates to other musical divas of the 1980's and 1990's.

See also: Alpert, Herb; Carey, Mariah; Elliott, Missy; Jackson, Michael; Turner, Tina.

Mahalia Jackson

American gospel singer

The Queen of Gospel, Jackson developed a style that originated in Baptist church choirs and incorporated elements of blues and jazz. The combined effect was deeply spiritual, yet sensual music.

Born: October 26, 1911; New Orleans, Louisiana
Died: January 27, 1972; Evergreen Park, Illinois

Principal recordings

ALBUMS: *Silent Night, Holy Night*, 1950; *Bless This House*, 1956; *Just as I Am*, 1960; *The Power and the Glory*, 1960; *Sweet Little Jesus Boy*, 1961; *Mahalia*, 1965; *A Mighty Fortress*, 1968; *Mahalia Jackson Sings the Best-Loved Hymns of Dr. M. L. King*, 1968; *How I Got Over*, 1976.

SINGLES: "God's Gonna Separate the Wheat from the Tares," 1934; "Move on up a Little Higher," 1948; "He's Got the Whole World in His Hands," 1958.

The Life

A granddaughter of slaves, Mahalia Jackson (mah-HAYL-yah JAK-suhn) was born in New Orleans, Louisiana, into poverty and into a society divided by racial segregation. Jackson, nicknamed Halie, was the third of six children born to John Jackson, a stevedore, minister, and barber, and Charity Clark, a domestic servant. By age four, Jackson had memorized Negro spirituals, and she soon joined the Mount Moriah Baptist Church Choir. Not long after Mahalia's baptism in the Mississippi River, her mother, at the age of twenty-five, died of undetermined causes. Jackson's father sent her and her older brother Peter to live with their mother's sister, Aunt Duke Paul.

Aunt Duke was a stern disciplinarian and ruthless taskmaster; Mahalia worked long hours doing household and yard chores. Though her aunt was keenly aware of Jackson's singing talent, she wanted the child to acquire the domestic skills needed to make a living in the segregated South, where most blacks worked at menial jobs serving whites. Each evening, though, was reserved for attending prayer services. Listening to the music

coming out of the homes as she walked to church, Jackson heard songs by successful black artists such as Bessie Smith, Ma Rainey, and W. C. Handy. Though Jackson had no plans to sing secular music, she did admire and imitate the soulful styles and rhythmic beat of the blues and jazz songs she heard on the way to church.

Because money was scarce, when Jackson was seven, she added employment as a domestic to her schedule of schooling and church services. She cleaned, did laundry, and took care of children for a white family, receiving as compensation two dollars a week, leftover food, and hand-me-down clothing. In spite of many obligations at such a young age, Jackson did well in school, and her goal was to become a nurse. She quit school after eighth grade, however, in order to earn more money.

In 1927, at age sixteen, Jackson left Louisiana for Chicago, Illinois, to live with another aunt, Hannah, who had persuaded her that the North provided a better life for blacks. At first, Jackson worked as a domestic, but she soon found employment as a gospel soloist for churches, funerals, and other religious events. She joined forces with a Chicago-based professional gospel group, the Johnson Gospel Singers, and later she met composer Thomas Dorsey. Jackson toured the country, including the Deep South, with Dorsey and his musicians. Their collaboration endured for several years, and it gave Jackson the widespread exposure that in later years would form the base of her devoted audience. Jackson, Dorsey, and their musicians frequently traveled with their own food, gas, and oil, because they were often denied entrance to restaurants, restrooms, and service stations that did not serve blacks.

Jackson married in 1936 at age twenty-five. Her husband, Isaac Hockenhull, an educated and engaging older man, pushed Jackson to earn big money by performing secular music, which she adamantly refused to do. The friction culminated in divorce in 1941.

Jackson's goals expanded from singing to include business entrepreneurship. Though she never became a nurse, she attended beauty school, eventually opening both a beauty shop and a flower shop, and buying real estate. With these financially successful ventures, Jackson assured herself of the income she needed to continue to sing gospel with-

Mahalia Jackson. (Library of Congress)

was nationally televised. Jackson engaged a supporting cast that performed a more secular style, pleasing mainstream white audiences but disappointing gospel purists.

Jackson continued an escalating rise to popularity and wealth. She appeared in a few big-screen motion pictures, and she sang at the inauguration of President John F. Kennedy in 1961. During this politically and racially dynamic era, Jackson also made many fund-raising appearances and gave financial support to the efforts of Dr. Martin Luther King, Jr., in the hope of eradicating segregation and racial violence in the United States, and particularly in her homeland of the Deep South. After the assassinations of Kennedy and King, however, Jackson became so discouraged that she withdrew from political activism. Because of her heavy touring schedule and another unpleasant marriage and divorce, Jackson developed heart problems, becoming intermittently ill. In the meantime, she was a worldwide musical and financial success, performing in many important and glamorous venues, including at a much-acclaimed performance at Carnegie Hall in New York City. Jackson died of a heart attack at age sixty on January 27, 1972, in Chicago, where she had lived and become successful over the course of forty-five years. She was buried in her birthplace of New Orleans.

The Music

Jackson's style of gospel singing radicalized the concept of religious music throughout the United States and the world. From childhood, Jackson wanted to sing only gospel music, eschewing secular songs. She was, however, greatly influenced by the jazz and blues singers to whom she was exposed during her early years and throughout her life.

Jackson was considered the Queen of Gospel, and she helped make religious music internationally popular during the mid-twentieth century. Combining Negro spirituals sung with naked emotion and the sensual elements displayed in jazz and blues, Jackson created a volatile and rhythmic gospel sound. Her habit of swaying to the musical beat while singing deeply spiritual songs added greatly to her appeal to the general public.

Early Works. Jackson's earliest works were Christian spirituals performed as a soloist in church

out resorting to the more lucrative but secular jazz and blues.

In 1937 Jackson made her first studio recording for Decca Records, "God's Gonna Separate the Wheat from the Tares." The song did not sell well, and Jackson did not receive another recording contract for a decade. Her career, however, continued to blossom as she received invitations for live performances in various churches and religious venues across the country.

For Apollo Records, Jackson recorded "Move on up a Little Higher," which was released in 1948. It became a best-selling gospel record, making Jackson the first gospel superstar. In the early 1950's, Jackson recorded and released more vastly popular gospel songs, and she was catapulted onto the world stage. This degree of demand and popularity for a gospel singer was unprecedented, and Jackson's style became a prototype for those aspiring to sing gospel.

In 1954 Jackson hosted a television show, marking the first time in musical history that pure gospel choirs. Raised in one of the most musically diverse cities in the country, New Orleans, Jackson focused on gospel, but she was surrounded and influenced by the emerging trends of jazz and blues. As a result, the preteen Jackson developed an innovative style that integrated sensuality of voice and physical movement with exceedingly devout fervor and overtly genuine and spiritually moving pleas to her Lord.

"God's Gonna Separate the Wheat from the Tares." Recorded on the Decca Records label in 1934, this song was not a critical or a financial success. Jackson recorded a few other songs on the same label, but she was dropped when none of the recordings made money. Lyrics of the song came from the Bible, and they reflected the need of a farmer to harvest weeds (tares) to get to the harvesting of his wheat crop. Considered a "race" record, or music aimed to sell to blacks, "God's Gonna Separate the Wheat from the Tares" was a simple and soulful spiritual classic made stirring by Jackson's powerful voice and sensual delivery.

"Move on up a Little Higher." Written by William Herbert Brewster and recorded on the Apollo label in 1947, this song sold one hundred thousand copies overnight, and it soon sold more than a million. Gospel music catapulted from the preference of a few to the many, becoming a huge business in the process. Fans told Jackson that the song inspired them to try harder to succeed in the white world, and it eventually became an anthem for the Civil Rights movement in the 1950's and 1960's. This recording eventually sold more than two million copies, and it made Jackson a critical, financial, and popular success. It was the demand for Jackson's records and public appearances following "Move on up a Little Higher" which led Jackson to be called Queen of Gospel.

"He's Got the Whole World in His Hands." Released by Columbia Records in 1958, this song entered *Billboard*'s Top 100 singles chart, an unusual achievement for a gospel song. Also recorded separately by male singer Laurie London, the song was a welcome antidote to widespread dissatisfaction with race riots in the American Deep South and with general social unrest around the world.

"I Been 'Buked and I Been Scorned." At the peak of her success, Jackson sang "I Been 'Buked and I Been Scorned" as a prelude to King's March

on Washington on August 28, 1963. The date was the centennial of the Emancipation Proclamation by President Abraham Lincoln in 1863, marking the end of slavery. The March on Washington and King's speech attracted 250,000 supporters. Jackson faced the huge crowd and the radio and television audiences, singing softly, and then her voice lifted into a full, deep contralto. She swayed and clapped her hands along with the huge crowd, and the whole assemblage began to resemble an evangelical revival meeting. Jackson's song was followed by King's famous "I have a dream" speech.

Musical Legacy

Jackson was a musical pioneer, integrating the soulfulness of blues and the rhythm of jazz into her gospel songs. Her groundbreaking style generated mass interest in the concept of soul singing, inspiring many new artists to follow her example.

Jackson's stirring renditions and unusual performing style spawned a new way of interpreting and performing gospel music. Her rich, grainy voice, fervent delivery, and rhythmic movements inspired a new generation of gospel, jazz, and blues singers. Her influence was not limited to those genres, however. Youthful imitators of her free-spirited, passionate style of performing caused Jackson to remark that "rock and roll [music] was stolen from the sanctified church." Jackson mentored young artists such as Aretha Franklin, Della Reese, and Billy Preston, all of whom started in gospel and went on to succeed variously as "crossover" artists of blues, jazz, soul, and rock-and-roll music.

There was a sensuality and personal expression to Jackson's gospel renditions previously unheard in religious music. Jackson was the first gospel superstar at a time when it was extremely difficult for African Americans to cross the racial divide into mainstream success in any field.

Twyla R. Wells

Further Reading

Goreau, Laurraine. *Just Mahalia, Baby: The Mahalia Jackson Story*. Los Angeles: Pelican, 1985. The biographer, a personal friend of Jackson, chronicles the gospel singer's rise from poverty to international success.

Harris, Michael W. *The Rise of Gospel Blues: The Mu-*

sic of Thomas Andrew Dorsey in the Urban Church. New York: Oxford University Press, 1994. A comprehensive look at the evolution of gospel music through the life of a master gospel composer, Dorsey, one of Jackson's collaborators. Dorsey went from composing risqué songs to some of the great modern gospel masterpieces.

Jackson, Jesse. *Make a Joyful Noise unto the Lord.* New York: Thomas Y. Crowell, 1974. For young readers, this is a simple biographical sketch of Jackson.

McNeil, W. K. *Encyclopedia of American Gospel Music.* New York: Routledge, 2005. A reference on gospel origins that lists hundreds of gospel artists and biographical information, including an entry on Jackson. This is an excellent source for lay readers as well as musical history scholars.

Reagon, Bernice Johnson, ed. *We'll Understand It Better By and By: Pioneering African American Gospel Composers.* Washington, D.C.: Smithsonian Institution Press, 1992. A Smithsonian curator presents essays by gospel performers and gospel producers that discuss major figures in African American gospel music. Included is an essay from Dorsey, with whom Jackson performed for many years.

See also: Blackwell, Otis; Blakey, Art; Dorsey, Thomas A.; Franklin, Aretha; Handy, W. C.; Little Richard; Morrison, Van; Rainey, Ma; Smith, Bessie; Ward, Clara.

Michael Jackson

American pop/soul singer and songwriter

A multifaceted artist, Jackson redefined the worlds of pop, soul, rock, and dance.

Born: August 29, 1958; Gary, Indiana
Also known as: Michael Joseph Jackson (full name); King of Pop
Member of: The Jackson Five; the Jacksons

Principal recordings

ALBUMS (solo): *Ben*, 1972; *Got to Be There*, 1972; *Music and Me*, 1973; *Forever, Michael*, 1975; *Off the Wall*, 1979; *Thriller*, 1982; *Ain't No Sunshine*, 1984; *Bad*, 1987; *Dangerous*, 1991; *HIStory: Past, Present and Future—Book I*, 1995; *Blood on the Dance Floor: HIStory in the Mix*, 1997; *Invincible*, 2001.

ALBUMS (with the Jackson Five): *Diana Ross Presents the Jackson Five*, 1969; *ABC*, 1970; *The Jackson Five Christmas Album*, 1970; *Third Album*, 1970; *Goin' Back to Indiana*, 1971; *Maybe Tomorrow*, 1971; *Lookin' Through the Windows*, 1972; *Get It Together*, 1973; *Skywriter*, 1973; *Dancing Machine*, 1974; *Moving Violation*, 1975.

ALBUMS (with the Jacksons): *The Jacksons*, 1976; *Goin' Places*, 1977; *Destiny*, 1978; *Triumph*, 1980; *Victory*, 1984; *2300 Jackson Street*, 1989.

The Life

Michael Joseph Jackson was the born the eighth of ten children to Joseph and Katherine Jackson. Jackson's mother was a Jehovah's Witness, and she raised her children under the tenets of that religion. The family's home in Gary, Indiana, was filled with music, and Jackson's father, in addition working in the steel industry to support his family, had a role in a local musical group called the Falcons. Jackson's father encouraged music in his sons, training them to sing, perform, and dance in a group originally called the Jackson Brothers and eventually renamed the Jackson Five. Jackson, though still a boy, was subject to the strict practice sessions and firm discipline of his father.

Jackson became one of the group's lead vocalists, and he fronted the group with dance movements he mimicked from watching videotapes of James Brown. In 1968 the Jackson Five, comprising Jackson and his brothers Jackie, Tito, Jermaine, and Marlon, signed with Motown Records. The Jackson Five remained in the public eye well into the 1970's, though Jackson frequently recorded solo albums, finding his first success with *Off the Wall*. In the 1980's, the group maintained its popularity, and Jackson had large sales for his solo recordings, especially *Thriller*. In the late 1980's, Jackson earned notoriety for his repeated plastic surgeries and for his increasingly reclusive and eccentric lifestyle.

In 1993 Jackson was accused of child molestation, though he settled out of court, claiming innocence. The following year he married Lisa Marie

Michael Jackson. (AP/Wide World Photos)

Presley, the daughter of Elvis Presley. After they divorced, he married Deborah Jeanne Rowe, his dermatologist's nurse, and they had two children, Michael Joseph Jackson, Jr. (called Prince) and Paris Michael Katherine Jackson. They divorced in 1999. Jackson had a third child in 2002, named Prince Michael Jackson II, though the mother was never publicly identified.

In late 2003, the entertainer was charged again with child molestation, and this time the case went to trial. The court proceedings lasted the first half of 2005, ending with a not-guilty verdict. Jackson put his recording career on hold, in the wake of the trial and the financial problems involved with his Neverland Ranch in Los Olivos, California, which has been threatened with foreclosure.

The Music

The Jackson Five. The Jackson Five provided the stage for Jackson to exhibit his talents as a vocalist, a songwriter, and a dancer. The group toured actively and was prolific in the studio during its early stages, starting with *Diana Ross Presents the Jackson Five* in 1969 (after the group performed with her group, the Supremes). The lead single, "I Want You Back," showcased the group's harmonies. Soon, the Jackson Five had its own identity, releasing *ABC*, known for its title cut and "The Love You Save."

The group was productive throughout the first half of the 1970's, at the same time allowing Jackson to record albums and singles on his own, including the smashes "Got to Be There" and "Ben." As the

689

1970's ended, the group was struggling, trying a funk style on *Dancing Machine* and a pre-disco style on *Moving Violation*. The group left Motown to debut on Epic Records in 1976.

With the new record deal, the group shortened its name to the Jacksons, and it embraced the disco style in *Destiny*, which launched the club favorites "Blame It on the Boogie" and "Shake Your Body (Down to the Ground)." At that time, Jackson reunited with Ross to star in the film *The Wiz* (1978).

Off the Wall. Jackson's solo breakthrough came with *Off the Wall*, which sold twenty million albums. The project was noted for its effective fusing of soul, rhythm and blues, pop, and disco, ranging from the dance tunes "Don't Stop 'Til You Get Enough" and "Rock with You" to the ballad "She's out of My Life." The album also scored Jackson a 1980 Grammy Award for Best Male Rhythm and Blues Vocal Performance.

Thriller. Jackson balanced his work with the Jacksons with studio work for *Triumph* (featuring "Can You Feel It" and "This Place Hotel"), followed by a tour. When he returned, Jackson went back to the studio to record *Thriller*, which sold an astounding 104 million albums and which earned a spot in the *The Guinness Book of Records* as the biggest-selling album in history. The album received eight Grammy Awards, and it made Jackson an MTV sensation, with a video of the title cut becoming a critically acclaimed short film. "Beat It" featured unconventional choreography, and "Billie Jean," when performed on the *Motown Twenty-five: Yesterday, Today, Forever* television special, featured Jackson's signature moonwalk dance move and his single sequined glove.

Jackson returned to the group for the *Victory* album and tour, setting records for ticket sales and incorporating state-of-the-art production elements onstage. In 1985 Jackson cowrote "We Are the World" with Lionel Richie (and performed it with a celebrity choir) to benefit African famine relief. In addition, he purchased shares in ATV Music Publishing (which owned several of the Beatles' most famous songs), outraging his friend and duet partner, Beatle Paul McCartney.

Bad. In 1988 Jackson presented his long-awaited follow-up to *Thriller*, *Bad*, which sold thirty-two million copies, although it produced an unprecedented five chart-topping singles. In order to tour

in support of the project, Jackson mostly sat out of the Jacksons' 1989 sessions for *2300 Jackson Street*. *Dangerous* bowed in 1991 to great fanfare, and it produced nine hit singles and an extensive world tour, which was chronicled on the video *Live in Bucharest: The Dangerous Tour* (2005).

HIStory. In 1995 Jackson made *HIStory: Past, Present and Future—Book I*. The double-disc project comprised fifteen of Jackson's solo hits and fifteen new songs (including "Scream," a duet with his sister Janet Jackson). Two years later, Jackson was inducted into the Rock and Roll Hall of Fame as a member of the Jackson Five, and he released the remix record *Blood on the Dance Floor: HIStory in the Mix*.

Invincible. In 2001 Jackson released *Invincible*, and he was inducted as a solo performer into the Rock and Roll Hall of Fame. There was a concert commemorating his thirtieth anniversary in show business, with performances by the Jacksons, Whitney Houston, Liza Minnelli, and Slash. Nevertheless, *Invincible* was a commercial and critical disappointment. Its release shortly after the September 11, 2001, terrorist attacks on the United States did not help sales, and a bitter feud with the record label fueled by Jackson's claim that *Invicible* was poorly promoted made this album his last recording for Epic Records.

Musical Legacy

Among his many accolades, Jackson was named the Best-Selling Pop Male Artist of the Millennium by the World Music Awards and the Artist of the Century by the American Music Awards. In 2006 *The Guinness Book of World Records* named him the Most Successful Entertainer of All Time. Jackson's innovative music videos, especially the one for *Thriller*, have been emulated by artists and directors, and they have become MTV staples. Known for his artistic diversity, Jackson, whether performing with the Jackson Five or solo, created songs that climbed the pop, soul, and rock charts. He has produced remixes, collaborated with hip-hop artists, and engaged other artists in support of worldwide charitable causes (most notably "We Are the World"). With strong record sales and continued radio play, Jackson reaches new generations of listeners.

Andy Argyrakis

Further Reading

Andersen, Christopher. *Michael Jackson Unauthorized*. New York: Simon & Schuster, 1994. This unauthorized biography, which mixes factual accounts with gossip and tabloid stories, is a compelling, sometimes stilted view of Jackson.

Campbell, Lisa. *Michael Jackson: The King of Pop*. Boston: Branden Books, 1993. Exhaustively researched, this source assesses Jackson's pop milestones, his recordings, and his concert tours.

Diamond, Diane. *Be Careful Who You Love: Inside the Michael Jackson Case*. New York: Atria Books, 2005. The reporter for *Hard Copy* and Court TV provides a somewhat one-sided view of Jackson's various court cases, presenting the entertainer in a mostly negative light.

Jackson, Michael. *Moon Walk*. New York: Doubleday, 1988. This autobiography was written during the height of popularity of Jackson's *Bad* album. Though the text lacks personal details, Jackson presents a good account of the early years of his career.

Jones, Aphrodite. *Michael Jackson Conspiracy*. New York: iUniverse, 2007. After a foreword by Jackson's lead attorney Thomas Mesereau, the text traces conspiracy theories surrounding the singer's second round of sexual allegations.

Jones, Bob, with Stacy Brown. *Michael Jackson: The Man Behind the Mask*. New York: SelectBooks, 2005. With the subtitle "An Insider's Story of the King of Pop," Jones provides details on his experiences at Motown Records and serving as head of Jackson's MJJ Communications.

Taraborrelli, J. Randy. *Michael Jackson: The Magic and the Madness*. New York: Birch Lane Press, 1991. Using interviews with more than one hundred sources close to Jackson, this source offers a thorough look at Jackson's personal and professional life. This exhaustive biography has more than six hundred pages.

See also: Brown, James; Crouch, Andraé; Davis, Sammy, Jr.; Jones, Quincy; McCartney, Sir Paul; Ross, Diana; Van Halen, Eddie; Wilson, Jackie; Wonder, Stevie.

Sir Mick Jagger

English rock singer and songwriter

Jagger is the lead singer for the Rolling Stones, known for his strutting, dancing, and jumping around the stage.

Born: July 26, 1943; Dartford, Kent, England
Also known as: Michael Philip Jagger (full name)
Member of: The Rolling Stones

Principal recordings

ALBUMS (solo): *She's the Boss*, 1985; *Primitive Cool*, 1987; *Wandering Spirit*, 1993; *Goddess in the Doorway*, 2001.

ALBUMS (with the Rolling Stones): *The Rolling Stones (England's Newest Hitmakers)*, 1964; *12 x 5*, 1964; *December's Children (and Everybody's)*, 1965; *Out of Our Heads*, 1965; *The Rolling Stones No. 2*, 1965; *The Rolling Stones Now*, 1965; *Aftermath*, 1966; *Between the Buttons*, 1967; *Flowers*, 1967; *Their Satanic Majesties Request*, 1967; *Beggars Banquet*, 1968; *Let It Bleed*, 1969; *Sticky Fingers*, 1971; *Exile on Main Street*, 1972; *Jamming with Edward*, 1972; *Goats' Head Soup*, 1973; *It's Only Rock 'n' Roll*, 1974; *Black and Blue*, 1976; *Some Girls*, 1978; *Emotional Rescue*, 1980; *Tattoo You*, 1981; *Undercover*, 1983; *Dirty Work*, 1986; *Steel Wheels*, 1989; *Voodoo Lounge*, 1994; *Bridges to Babylon*, 1997; *A Bigger Bang*, 2005.

The Life

Michael Philip Jagger was born July 26, 1943, in Dartford, Kent, England, to Eva and Joe Jagger. His father was a physical education instructor at St. Mary's Training College, now part of the University of Surrey. To his father's chagrin, Jagger grew up loving the blues and rock and roll. After graduating from Dartford Grammar School in 1960, Jagger went to the London School of Economics on a government grant to study accounting. He then met former Dartford acquaintance Keith Richards, a student at Sidcup Art School.

Jagger was playing guitar in the blues band Little Boy Blue and the Blue Boys, which Richards soon joined as a guitarist. A year later they met Brian Jones, a blues guitarist, who asked Jagger, then with Blues, Inc., and Richards to form a new band. In the summer of 1962, with Dick Taylor on guitar, Mick Avory on drums, and Ian Stewart on piano, they performed at the Marquee, a small jazz club, as the Rolling Stones, taking their name from Muddy Waters's 1950 blues tune "Rollin' Stone." Bill Wyman soon replaced Taylor as bass guitarist, and Charlie Watts, from Blues, Inc., became the drummer.

Playing at the Crawdaddy Club in 1963, the band attracted the attention of promoter Andrew Loog Oldham. Because he wanted to promote the musicians as bad boys, Oldham's first act as the group's manager was to fire the straitlaced Stewart. This image led British politicians to decry the group as a corrupter of youth.

The Rolling Stones signed with Decca Records in 1963, releasing a version of Chuck Berry's "Come On" as their first single. The band's first original song, "Tell Me," written by Jagger and Richards, was released in June, 1964. In 1965 "Satisfaction" became their biggest hit to that point.

The band quickly became known for its energetic stage shows. Jagger strummed a guitar or played another instrument, usually the harmonica, and he sang. With his full, pouty lips, Jagger was an overtly sexual performer, thrusting a microphone between his legs, creating a sensation like Elvis Presley during his hip-shaking period. When the group appeared on *The Ed Sullivan Show* in 1967, Jagger was forced to alter the lyrics to "Let's Spend the Night Together," substituting "some time" for "the night." The singer's facial expressions mocked this censorship.

Jagger and Richards were arrested for drug possession in February, 1967, and Jones was arrested three months later. Jagger was initially sentenced to three months in jail for having drugs without a prescription. Because the drugs had been legally purchased in Italy, another judge reduced Jagger's sentence to a year's probation.

Despite its title, *Their Satanic Majesties Request* reflected a brief retreat from the group's bad-boy image, but the trendy psychedelic songs struck many as pretentious and bland. Firing Oldham in 1968, the Rolling Stones returned to their roots with *Beggars Banquet*, which included hard-driving rock, blues, and tongue-in-cheek country music. Resenting the group's dominance by Jagger and Richards, Jones left in 1969; he drowned in the swimming pool at his home a few weeks later. Later that year a spectator was beaten to death by members of the Hell's Angels motorcycle gang, whom the Stones had hired as security for a concert at the Altamont Speedway in California. Some blamed Jagger for inciting the incident with his stage antics. *Gimme Shelter* (1970), a documentary by Albert and David Maysles, captures the concert's chaos.

Around this time, Jagger tried to launch a career as a film actor. He appeared as a legendary Australian outlaw in Tony Richardson's *Ned Kelly* (1970) and as a reclusive former rock star in Donald Cammell and Nicolas Roeg's *Performance* (1970). Neither film did well at the box office, with *Performance* widely condemned as decadent and sadistic (although the film eventually developed a cult status). Jagger's love scenes with Anita Pallenberg reportedly upset Richards, her boyfriend.

Sir Mick Jagger. (AP/Wide World Photos)

Jagger had a daughter with British actress Marsha Hunt, for whom the song "Brown Sugar" was written. In 1971 Jagger married Bianca Pérez-Mora Macias, a socialite from Nicaragua. They had a daughter, Jade.

By 1974 Jagger and Richards had begun to take more control over their music, producing, under the name the Glimmer Twins, their recordings. After the two disagreed over the musical direction of the Rolling Stones, the singer did not tour with the band from 1981 to 1989, even when *Dirty Work* was released. During this period, Jagger released *She's the Boss*, the first of several solo albums, and he toured as a single act. After the Rolling Stones were inducted into the Rock and Roll Hall of Fame in 1989, Jagger and Richard worked out their differences. The Voodoo Lounge tour of 1994 began a hectic concert schedule, with performances featuring enormous video screens and other high technology.

Jagger returned to films with *Running Out of Luck* (1987), as a rock star kidnapped in Brazil. His other acting can be seen in *Freejack* (1992), as a time-traveling bounty hunter; in the Holocaust drama *Bent* (1997), as a transvestite; and in *The Man from Elysian Fields* (2001), as a male prostitute, an affecting performance. Contemplating retirement, his character asks a longtime client, played by Anjelica Huston, to marry him, and he is answered by her laughter. After briefly displaying pained disappointment, Jagger quickly assumes a sly grin as he accepts his lonely fate. Jagger also produced the World War II espionage thriller *Enigma* (2001).

Divorced from Bianca in 1980, the singer married American model Jerry Hall in 1990. The couple had four children before their 1999 divorce. Jagger became a grandfather in 1993 with the birth of Jade's first child, and he became a father for the seventh time in 1999 when Brazilian model Luciana Gimenez gave birth to his son.

For his contributions to music, Jagger was knighted by Queen Elizabeth II in 2002. Richards complained to the press that his friend was becoming part of the establishment at which they once sneered.

Though Jagger once famously said he would rather be dead than still be performing "Satisfaction" when he was forty-five, he has continued performing this song and other Rolling Stones hits into

his sixties. The two-year Bigger Bang tour of 2005-2007 proved that the Rolling Stones could still attract massive audiences all over the world, grossing $558 million.

The Music

Jagger's voice has greater range and expression than most rock performers, and he is adept at high-speed rockers as well as slow-tempo songs. He easily shifts from a screech to a forceful shout to a melancholy whine, sometimes within the same song. He often adopts a Southern twang reminiscent of blues and country-music performers. The twang also accentuates the irony in many songs. As a musician, Jagger is mediocre on the guitar, but he can soar on the harmonica, which he plays, as in "Midnight Rambler," in the honking manner of bluesman Little Walter.

Early Stones. The early Rolling Stones recordings are packed with stylish versions of blues, rock, and rhythm-and-blues songs originally recorded by Berry, Solomon Burke, Sam Cooke, Bo Diddley, Marvin Gaye, Buddy Holly, Howlin' Wolf, Otis Redding, Jimmy Reed, Rufus Thomas, Bobby Womack, and others. Like those of their models, the songs written by Jagger and Richards offered simple lyrics, but the music is complex, with shifting tempi. The best of their early collaborations is 1965's "Satisfaction." Mixing the speaker's need for female attention with disgust at being manipulated by the media, "Satisfaction" quickly became a rock anthem, showing the songwriters' talent for sardonic lyrics.

Aftermath. *Aftermath* was the first album to feature all original Jagger-Richards songs. The songwriters made lyrical social criticism by attacking adults' reliance on prescription drugs in "Mother's Little Helper," showing the influence of Bob Dylan and the Kinks. "Paint It Black," featuring Jones on the sitar, is one of the group's most powerful songs. The singer's relentless anger has led some to call it the first punk song.

"Under My Thumb." Many of the Jagger-Richards songs present misogynistic views. "Under My Thumb" celebrates the singer's ability to control an otherwise unruly woman. In "Stray Cat Blues" (about having sex with a fifteen-year-old runaway) and "Honky Tonk Women," the songwriters capitalized on the new freedom given radio stations beginning in the late 1960's to play more risqué lyrics.

"As Tears Go By." Jagger and Richards were also capable of tender songs, as with the plaintive ballad "As Tears Go By," originally written for Jagger's girlfriend Marianne Faithfull. She also inspired "Wild Horses," often considered the Rolling Stones' best ballad, a haunting account of a pained, tempestuous relationship.

Peak Period. Jagger and Richards were never afraid of experimentation. "You Can't Always Get What You Want" opens with the London Bach Choir before shifting into the rock style of the songwriters' most productive period. Between 1968 and 1978 the pair produced such lasting rock classics as "Street Fightin' Man," "Can't You Hear Me Knocking," "Tumbling Dice," "It's Only Rock 'n' Roll," and "Beast of Burden."

Political Songs. Early in their careers, Jagger and Richards made only tangential references to politics. Beginning in the 1980's, they became more directly political. "Undercover of the Night" opens with a vivid description of political prisoners being tortured in South America. "Highwire" criticizes Western nations that sell weapons to Middle Eastern countries. "Sweet Neo Con" attacks the policies of George W. Bush.

Solo Career. *She's the Boss* sold well, helped by the frequent appearance of its music videos on MTV. "Just Another Night" and "Lucky in Love" were moderate hits, but many considered the dance-inflected rhythms of *She's the Boss* too mainstream and a step backward for Jagger creatively. Jagger's next solo album, *Primitive Cool*, was better received by critics, but only one single, "Let's Work," was a hit.

Wandering Spirit was a successful Jagger solo album, offering a greater diversity of musical styles. "Out of Focus," for example, is a gospel-tinged rocker. While several Rolling Stones songs mock country-music conventions, as with "Dead Flowers," "Evening Gown" is an irony-free, heartfelt ballad. Jagger's fondness for the song can be heard in his duet on Jerry Lee Lewis's *Last Man Standing* (2006). "Wandering Spirit" is a combination of country and gospel influences. "I've Been Lonely for So Long" is a throwback to the blues-influenced rock of Jagger's youth.

Goddess in the Doorway represented a return to the bland mainstream style of *She's the Boss*, and it was poorly received. Jagger succeeded with his contributions to the sound track for *Alfie* (2004), especially the bittersweet "Old Habits Die Hard," and for the project he was nominated for a Golden Globe.

Musical Legacy

When *Rolling Stone* named the five hundred greatest songs of all time in 2004, fourteen Jagger-Richards compositions made the list, with "Satisfaction" placing second after Dylan's "Like a Rolling Stone." The length, quality, and diversity of the band's career, despite several personnel changes, have encouraged thousands of other performers and songwriters. Jagger and the Rolling Stones have influenced such bands as Aerosmith and Bon Jovi.

Michael Adams

Further Reading

Davis, Stephen. *Old Gods Almost Dead: The Forty-Year Odyssey of the Rolling Stones*. New York: Broadway Books, 2001. An authoritative and readable account of the Rolling Stones covers their musical influences, their creative talents, and their excesses of drugs.

Faithfull, Marianne. *Faithfull: An Autobiography*. New York: Cooper Square Press, 2000. The singer offers an often disturbing account of her drug-addicted life and her affair with Jagger.

Greenfield, Robert. *Exile on Main St.: A Season in Hell with the Rolling Stones*. New York: Da Capo, 2006. This is a colorful portrait of the recording of *Exile on Main Street* in 1971, describing personal and professional conflicts between Jagger and Richards.

Jagger, Mick, and others. *According to the Rolling Stones*. San Francisco: Chronicle Books, 2003. Photographic record of the history of the Rolling Stones, with comments by band members and thirteen essays by fans and friends.

Sanford, Christopher. *Mick Jagger: Rebel Knight*. London: Omnibus Press, 2004. This informative biography emphasizes Jagger's love affairs and his discord with the other Rolling Stones.

Wyman, Bill, and Ray Coleman. *Stone Alone: The Story of a Rock 'n' Roll Band*. New York: Viking, 1990. History of the band through Jones's death, combined with an autobiography of Wyman, who left the group in 1993.

See also: Berry, Chuck; Burke, Solomon; Cooke, Sam; Diddley, Bo; Gaye, Marvin; James, Etta; Jennings, Waylon; Lewis, Jerry Lee; Presley, Elvis; Redding, Otis; Richards, Keith; Tosh, Peter; Turner, Tina; Waters, Muddy; Webb, Jimmy.

James Jamerson
American rhythm-and-blues bassist

A longtime member of the Motown house band known as the Funk Brothers, Jamerson was the primary bass player on the majority of Motown's hit records of the 1960's and 1970's. He was noted for making unusual melodic note choices and combining syncopated rhythmic lines.

Born: January 29, 1936; Charleston, South Carolina
Died: August 2, 1983; Los Angeles, California
Member of: The Funk Brothers

Principal recordings
SONGS (bass): "Dancing in the Street," 1964 (by Martha and the Vandellas); "Going to a Go-Go," 1965 (by the Miracles); "My Girl," 1965 (by the Temptations); "Shotgun," 1965 (by Jr. Walker and the All Stars); "Reach out I'll Be There," 1966 (by the Four Tops); "You Can't Hurry Love," 1966 (by the Supremes); "I Heard It Through the Grapevine," 1967 (by Gladys Knight and the Pips); "For Once in My Life," 1968 (by Stevie Wonder); "I Heard It Through the Grapevine," 1968 (by Marvin Gaye); "Rock the Boat," 1974 (by Hues Corporation); "Boogie Fever," 1976 (by the Sylvers); "You Don't Have to Be a Star (To Be in My Show)," 1976 (by Marilyn McCoo and Billy Davis, Jr.).

The Life
James Lee Jamerson was born in Charleston, South Carolina, to James Jamerson, Sr., who worked at the local shipyards, and Elizabeth, a homemaker. His parents divorced when he was young, so Jamerson spent the majority of his time with his aunt and grandmother, who encouraged his early interest in gospel, jazz, and blues music.

At the age of ten, Jamerson was severely injured in a bicycle accident, which kept him wheelchair bound. When he recovered, his mother sent for him, and he relocated with her to Detroit in 1954. There he met Annie Wells, and, though still in their teens, they were married. Jamerson entered Northwestern High School, joined the school orchestra, and chose the acoustic bass as his instrument. Influenced by jazz greats Ray Brown and Paul Chambers, Jamerson was offered the opportunity to study jazz bass at the collegiate level, but he decided to pursue a career as a professional musician. Local sessions and gigs with Jackie Wilson led to his recruitment by Motown founder Berry Gordy to become a member of the Funk Brothers, the legendary Motown house band for which Jamerson recorded on acoustic and electric bass.

After nearly fifteen years with the Funk Brothers in Detroit, Jamerson followed Motown Records to Los Angeles, where he made additional recordings as a freelance bassist. His long-standing struggles with alcoholism caused gradual deterioration of his health, and Jamerson died on August 2, 1983, in Los Angeles.

The Music
Jamerson began constructing influential bass tracks as soon as Motown began producing records in 1959. He appeared on hundreds of popular Motown recordings as the primary bass player in the Funk Brothers, the Motown backing band comprising roughly one hundred musicians who performed on all Motown recordings. Although other prominent, talented bassists worked with Funk Brothers and appeared on Motown tracks (notably Bob Babbitt and Eddie Watkins), the bass player on nearly all of the number-one Motown songs was Jamerson.

The construction and implementation of the Funk Brothers sound allowed Jamerson to turn out distinctive, historic bass grooves. While the general role of the bass player in jazz music is to provide a stable rhythmic pulse, there is always room for each player of a jazz rhythm section to improvise and share rhythmic and harmonic duties. In the Funk

Brothers' formula, however, the drums, guitar, piano, and percussion had fixed, specific rhythmic roles essential to the interlocking Motown grooves. The Funk Brothers' bass player, however, had some musical independence. Jamerson's bass lines, from the earliest Motown grooves, syncopate (or play against) the other rhythm-section players, providing a feeling of musical momentum through the freely moving and shifting bass lines. In Jamerson's skillful hands, this technique was not purely rhythmic in effect. He made interesting melodic note choices, while moving up and down the bass, to provide colorful accents to the chord changes, vocal melodies, and horn lines. In many respects, Jamerson's bass lines were the glue that held the Funk Brothers together and ultimately created the Motown sound.

The Early Motown Recordings. The list of Jamerson's most influential tracks parallels the history of Motown hits. He played on the Miracles' "Shop Around" (1960), which was the first Motown track to reach number one on the rhythm-and-blues charts, and the Marvelettes' "Please Mr. Postman" (1961), which was Motown's first number-one record on the pop charts. Two tracks that reached number one on the rhythm-and-blues charts quickly followed: "Do You Love Me?" (the Contours, 1962) and "(Love Is Like a) Heat Wave" (Martha and the Vandellas, 1963). In 1965 Jamerson recorded one of his most famous and most recognizable grooves, returning to the acoustic bass on Mary Wells's "My Guy," which reached number one on the pop charts.

The Classic Motown Performances. By the mid-1960's, Motown had hit its stride and released an unprecedented series of number-one hits, nearly all of which featured Jamerson with his instantly recognizable bass performances. He performed on tracks by Diana Ross and the Supremes ("Stop in the Name of Love," "You Can't Hurry Love," "Where Did Our Love Go?"), Stevie Wonder ("Uptight," "For Once in My Life," "My Cherie Amour," "Fingertips, Part 2"), Marvin Gaye ("I Heard It Through the Grapevine," "Ain't No Mountain High Enough," "How Sweet It Is," "What's Going On?"), Smokey Robinson and the Miracles ("Ooh Baby Baby," "You've Really Got a Hold on Me," "I Second That Emotion," "Tracks of My Tears"), the Temptations ("My Girl," "The Way You Do the Things You Do," "Ain't Too Proud to Beg," "Beauty Is Only Skin Deep"), and the Four Tops ("Standing in the Shadows of Love," "I Can't Help Myself," "Reach out I'll Be There," "Baby I Need Your Loving"). A few other famous tracks include the famous bass line on the Jackson 5's "I Want You Back," Jr. Walker and the All-Stars' "Shotgun," and the famous non-Motown Jackie Wilson track, "Higher and Higher."

Musical Legacy

The Motown sound was a major influence on the enormously popular hip-hop, rap, neo-soul, and contemporary rhythm-and-blues styles that emerged in the 1980's and 1990's. Jamerson played a vital role in establishing that Motown sound. Additionally, Jamerson influenced bass players and songwriters in the rock-and-roll genre; Paul McCartney cited Jamerson as a major influence. Jamerson's melodic, thoughtful, supportive, and syncopated bass lines influenced bass players who performed popular music after 1960. Jamerson was inducted into the Rock and Roll Hall of Fame in 1990.

Eric Novod

Further Reading

Early, Gerald Lyn. *Motown and American Culture.* Ann Arbor: University of Michigan Press, 2004. A cultural study of the popularization of African American music through Motown. Brief references to Jamerson.

Posner, Gerald. L. *Motown: Music, Money, Sex, and Power.* New York: Random House, 2002. A cultural history of Motown.

Rubin, Dave. *Motown Bass.* Milwaukee, Wis.: Hal Leonard, 2000. An instructional book with recording that highlights Jamerson's work and musical style. Includes full transcriptions of many Jamerson bass tracks.

Slutsky, Allan. *Standing in the Shadows of Motown: The Life and Music of Legendary Bassist James Jamerson.* Milwaukee, Wis.: Hal Leonard, 1989. A thorough biography of Jamerson, with popular bass players discussing their reverence for Jamerson's work. Includes discography.

See also: Costello, Elvis; McCartney, Sir Paul; Wilson, Jackie.

Elmore James

American blues singer-songwriter, bandleader, and guitarist

James is a vital link between the pre-World War II acoustic country blues of the Mississippi Delta and the postwar electric blues of Chicago. A master of the electric slide guitar, he brought the idiom, intensity, and even guitar licks of such Delta blues legends as Robert Johnson into the urban rhythm-and-blues era.

Born: January 27, 1918; Richland, Mississippi
Died: May 24, 1963; Chicago, Illinois
Also known as: Elmore Brooks (birth name)
Member of: The Broomdusters

Principal recordings

ALBUM: *Blues After Hours*, 1961.

SINGLES: "Dust My Broom (I Believe My Time Ain't Long)," 1951; "I Believe," 1952; "Please Find My Baby," 1952; "Country Boogie," 1953; "Early in the Morning," 1953; "Dark and Dreary," 1954; "Hand in Hand," 1954; "Blues Before Sunrise," 1955; "Dust My Blues," 1955; "I Believe My Time Ain't Long," 1955; "Cry for Me Baby," 1957; "It Hurts Me Too," 1957; "Make My Dreams Come True," 1959; "I Can't Hold Out," 1960; "Knocking at Your Door," 1960; "Rockin' and Tumblin'," 1960; "The Sky Is Crying," 1960; "Look on Yonder Wall," 1961; "Everyday I Have the Blues," 1965; "My Bleeding Heart," 1965; "Standing at the Crossroads," 1965; "Shake Your Money Maker," 1966.

The Life

Elmore Brooks was born in the Mississippi Delta in 1918. He was the illegitimate son of fifteen-year-old Leola Brooks and took the surname of his stepfather, Joe Willie "Frost" James. He was raised on a sharecropping farm but early decided to become a musician. Without money and with only a fourth-grade education, he gravitated toward blues music. He constructed a one-string instrument using old broom wire and a lard can (a "diddley bow") and practiced assiduously. By the time he was able to buy his first guitar, he had already become a skilled musician. By the age of fourteen, he was performing in juke joints, in roadhouses, and at catfish suppers, supporting himself during the week as a radio repairman.

Around 1936, James met the legendary bluesman Robert Johnson, who may have taught him the rudiments of slide guitar. James married Minnie Mae around 1942, Georgianna Crump in 1947, and a woman named Janice (her surname is unknown) around 1954. The legal status of his three marriages is uncertain but produced, it is believed, seven children, including musician Elmore James, Jr. From 1943 to 1945, James was in the U.S. Navy, stationed in Guam during World War II and rising to the rank of coxswain. When he returned to the Delta after the war, he adopted the newly popular electric guitar. In 1946 he was diagnosed with a weak heart.

James's career took off with the release of his classic recording of "Dust My Broom." He moved to Memphis and then to Chicago, the center of the burgeoning electric blues music, and formed his band, the Broomdusters, which became one of the top Chicago bands. Although performing regularly, James suffered recurring heart problems that slowed his career. His medical condition was aggravated by heavy drinking and a tempestuous lifestyle. Then, because of unpaid dues and contractual difficulties, he was blacklisted by the Chicago Musicians' Union for three years. In 1963, while James was staying with his older cousin, "Homesick" James Williamson, and preparing to join the American Folk Blues Festival tour in Europe, he died of a heart attack.

The Music

As he was growing up in the Delta, James played in Delta juke joints with such legendary musicians as Sonny Boy Williamson II (Rice Miller), Robert Lockwood, and Arthur "Big Boy" Crudup. It is also possible that he performed with the bluesman most influential on his music, Robert Johnson, before Johnson's untimely death in 1938. Shortly thereafter, James formed a partnership with his stepbrother, guitarist Robert Earl Holston, and began leading his own band, with Holston on second guitar, Precious White on saxophone, Frock O'Dell on drums, and Tutney Moore on trumpet.

By the early 1940's James was already known for

Elmore James. (Hulton Archive/Getty Images)

his electric slide guitar—the most important contribution he would make to modern blues. Delta musicians such as Johnson played acoustic slide or bottleneck guitar, with the neck of a broken bottle or a metal ring gliding across the guitar frets, producing sustained, bended notes. James was one of the first musicians to add electric amplification to the slide guitar. A radio repairman by trade, he experimented with various amplifier hookups, making his guitar not only louder but also capable of tonal distortion and echo effects. Even on his early release "Please Find My Baby" (1952), James can be heard playing a raucous, powerful synthesis of slide guitar and electric amplification.

"Dust My Broom." Perhaps no blues musician is as heavily identified with a single song as James is with "Dust My Broom (I Believe My Time Ain't Long)." The legendary Johnson was the first to release a recording of "I Believe I'll Dust My Broom" in 1937, which he had adapted from various sources. James recorded his own version on August 5, 1951,

on the Trumpet label with O'Dell on drums, Leonard Warren on electric bass, and Sonny Boy Williamson on harmonica. When it was released in early 1952 it hit the Top 10 on *Billboard*'s rhythm-and-blues chart. James sings with a raw quality reminiscent of the Delta holler

> I'm gonna get up in the morning,
>   I believe I'll dust my broom
> I'm gonna get up in the morning,
>   I believe I'll dust my broom
> I'll quit the best gal I'm lovin',
>   now my friends can get my room.

On his 1937 recording of "I Believe I'll Dust My Broom," Johnson had played four sets, and a truncated fifth set, of high-velocity, high-note triplets. Johnson had repeated the triplet figures on "Ramblin' Blues" but with slide guitar. James begins "Dust My Broom" with these high-note triplets over Williamson's blues harp, but now playing electric slide guitar.

This riff has become one of the signature sounds of the electric blues guitar. Thousands of blues guitarists have since played some version of these repeated triplet notes and motifs at the twelfth fret of the guitar. When combined with boogie lines on bass and piano, this sound would become one of the building blocks of rhythm and blues. James's biographer Steve Franz gives his own reason for the prevalence of the "Dust My Broom" riff in modern blues. The blues was based on the call-and-response of both religious music and the field holler. In modern blues, according to Franz, the sung verse serves as a two-measure call and the high-pitch triplet riff represents a one-measure response, echoing the traditional call-and-response.

"I Believe." With the success of "Dust My Broom," James formed his electric blues group the Broomdusters at the end of 1952. The Broomdusters would become one of the best known of the Chicago blues bands, rivaling the groups put together by Muddy Waters. Although the band personnel would vary, the heart of the group consisted of James on lead electric guitar, with his cousin "Homesick" James Williamson on electric bass (and sometimes second lead guitar), Odie Payne, Jr., playing drums, Johnny Jones at the piano, and J. T. Brown on tenor saxophone. One of the Broomdusters' first releases in 1952 was "I Believe."

A James composition, "I Believe" picks up where "Dust My Broom" left off, featuring variations of the high-pitch triplets run: "I believe, I believe, my time ain't long/ Dust my broom this mornin', I know I treat my baby wrong." In early rhythm and blues, the guitar and saxophone competed for the lead, and here Brown's saxophone has replaced Williamson's harmonica in the introduction. The rhythm section follows the introduction with tightly crafted and energetic support. James's singing is raw and energetic. James concludes with a linear, single-note slide solo that soars over the rhythm section.

"Hawaiian Boogie." In 1953, the Broomdusters released "Hawaiian Boogie." This instrumental shows the cohesiveness and precision of the Broomdusters, as well as their versatility. James begins with an explosive guitar lick. Brown's saxophone honkings, Jones's barrelhouse piano, and the insistent bass playing of Ransom Knowling add a jazzlike groove. Both Jones on piano and Brown on saxophone play succinctly and impressively, while James fills the song with intricate guitar runs.

"The Sky Is Crying." "The Sky Is Crying" was James's most popular song in the 1960's. It made the rhythm-and-blues charts and sold 600,000 copies. This slow, haunting blues piece features an evocative title and refrain:

> The sky is cryin', look at the tears roll down the street
> The sky is cryin', look at the tears roll down the street
> I'm wadin' in tears lookin' for my baby,
>   and I wonder where she can be?

James's slide guitar sounds especially lyrical. His singing is dramatic and decorated with glissandi notes.

"Madison Blues." "Madison Blues" was the last recording by the Broomdusters, capping a collaboration of more than seven years. Inspired by a then current dance, "Madison Blues" is a rollicking rhythm-and-blues number. It illustrates how the electric amplification, the boogie bass line of the rhythm section, the lead guitar riffs, and the squawking saxophone transformed the Delta blues sound of the 1930's and 1940's into 1950's and 1960's rhythm and blues.

"Shake Your Money Maker." "Shake Your Money Maker" would be one of James's most popular and most often covered songs. While retaining his intensity on vocals, James leads his band in an up-tempo, danceable rhythm-and-blues number. Except for twanging a few well-placed blue notes, James's slide guitar is submerged into the rhythm section.

Musical Legacy

Elmore James is one of the foremost architects of the electric blues and rhythm-and-blues music emerging from postwar Chicago, and he may well be the most influential electric slide guitarist in blues history. He played with great virtuosity, embellished by his fierce, heartfelt vocals. He was sought after on the blues circuit for his renditions of "Dust My Broom." He was also an accomplished bandleader. His Broomdusters band was perhaps second only to the Muddy Waters bands among Chicago electric blues groups.

Without diminishing his unique contributions, it is fair to note James's place as a transitional figure. He was profoundly influenced by the prewar Delta bluesmen, especially Robert Johnson. When Johnson had fallen into obscurity in the 1940's, James continued to pay homage to such Johnson recordings as "I Believe I'll Dust My Broom," "Crossroad Blues," and "Ramblin' on My Mind." James would make use of Johnson's "turnaround" guitar technique between verses. After a verse, Johnson would often play a dominant seventh rather than resting on a tonic chord like most blues guitarists. This technique added tension and propulsion to the song's movement.

Most notably, James electrified Johnson's slide triplet riffs on lead guitar. James also took the boogie bass lines that Johnson played on the lower strings and assigned them to the piano, drum, and bass guitar rhythm sections. With the bass guitar now driving a one-two beat and the lead guitar playing various riffs, James's electric band helped pioneer the precursors to rhythm and blues. Moreover, when polished and smoothed out, this basic vocabulary would help form both soul music and early rock and roll. James's experiments with guitar amplifications demonstrated not only that electric blues could be loud enough to reach the back of any crowded juke joint or concert hall but also that he could distort and twist the aural sound—effects that would be heard again in psychedelic rock. James's slashing, single-note guitar technique, amplified sounds, and high-intensity vocals influenced Chicago blues guitarists such as B. B. King and Albert King and rock guitarists such as Jimi Hendrix, Frank Zappa, Duane Allman, Eric Clapton, and Johnny Winter. James's influence can also be heard in such blues-rock bands as the Butterfield Blues Band, Canned Heat, and Fleetwood Mac.

Howard Bromberg

Further Reading

Dixon, Willie, and Don Snowden. *I Am the Blues: The Willie Dixon Story*. London: Quartet Books, 1989. The Chicago blues leader's autobiography.

Franz, Steve. *The Amazing Secret History of Elmore James*. Saint Louis, Mo.: BlueSource, 2003. The definitive biography of James, with an exhaustive discography, bibliography, and musical references. An entire chapter is devoted to the phenomenon, covers, and musical structure of the song "Dust My Broom" and its signature riff.

George-Warren, Holly, and Patricia Romanowski, eds. *The Rolling Stones Encyclopedia of Rock and Roll*. 3d ed. New York: Fireside, 2005. This A through Z reference work archives James's influence as a precursor to rock and roll.

Kimora, Edward. *The Road to Robert Johnson*. Milwaukee: Hal Leonard, 2007. A musical discussion of Johnson's blues that examines his influence on James's electric guitar.

Palmer, Robert. *Deep Blues: A Musical and Cultural History of the Mississippi Delta*. London: Viking Penguin, 1982. A seminal history of the Delta blues, by the late *New York Times* pop and rock critic. Emphasizes James's transitional role.

Rowe, Michael. *Chicago Breakdown*. London: Eddison Press, 1973. This history of Chicago blues includes firsthand accounts of James's life and death.

Wald, Elijah. *Escaping the Delta: Robert Johnson and the Invention of the Blues*. New York: Amistad, 2005. An excellent musical biography of Robert Johnson, explaining how Johnson's innovative guitar work laid the ground for James and other urban blues and rhythm-and-blues musicians.

See also: Berry, Chuck; Cotton, James; Fuller, Blind Boy; House, Son; Howlin' Wolf; Johnson, Robert; King, Albert; Patton, Charley; Raitt, Bonnie; Rodgers, Jimmie; Turner, Big Joe; Waters, Muddy; Williamson, Sonny Boy, II.

Etta James
American rhythm-and-blues singer and songwriter

For a blues singer, James had a voice of remarkable range. She was adept at shouting the pain of love as well as at crooning tenderly about love's disappointments.

Born: January 25, 1938; Los Angeles, California
Also known as: Jamesetta Hawkins (birth name); Peaches

Principal recordings

ALBUMS: *At Last!*, 1961; *The Second Time Around*, 1961; *Sings for Lovers*, 1962; *Top Ten*, 1963; *The*

Queen of Soul, 1965; *Call My Name*, 1966; *Tell Mama*, 1968; *Funk*, 1970; *Losers Weepers*, 1971; *Peaches*, 1973; *Come a Little Closer*, 1974; *Deep in the Night*, 1978; *Etta Is Betta than Evah*, 1978; *Changes*, 1980; *Chess Masters*, 1981; *Good Rockin' Mama*, 1981; *Tuff Love*, 1983; *R & B Queen*, 1986; *Etta James on Chess*, 1988; *The Sweetest Peaches, Pt. 2*, 1988; *The Gospel Soul of Etta James*, 1989; *Seven Year Itch*, 1989; *Stickin' to My Guns*, 1990; *The Sweetest Peaches, Pt. 1*, 1990; *Tell Mama, Vol. 1*, 1991; *Back in Blues*, 1992; *I'd Rather Go Blind*, 1992; *The Right Time*, 1992; *Mystery Lady: Songs of Billie Holiday*, 1994; *Time After Time*, 1995; *Love's Been Rough on Me*, 1997; *Respect Yourself*, 1997; *Life, Love, and the Blues*, 1998; *Twelve Songs of Christmas*, 1998; *The Heart of a Woman*, 1999; *Matriarch of the Blues*, 2000; *Blue Gardenia*, 2001; *Let's Roll*, 2003; *Blues to the Bone*, 2004; *All the Way*, 2006; *To Go: Stick It in Your Ear*, 2006.

SINGLES: "Good Rockin' Daddy," 1955; "The Wallflower (Dance with Me, Henry)," 1955; "All I Could Do Was Cry," 1960; "If I Can't Have You," 1960 (with Harvey Fuqua); "At Last," 1961; "Something's Got a Hold on Me," 1962; "In the Basement," 1966 (with Sugar Pie De Santo).

Etta James. (AP/Wide World Photos)

The Life

Etta James was born Jamesetta Hawkins in Los Angeles on January 25, 1938, when her mother, Dorothy, was fourteen. James grew up not knowing her father's identity; later, she discovered he was believed to have been Rudolf Wanderone, Jr., the famous pool player known as Minnesota Fats. James did not meet Wanderone until 1987. Because her mother was unable to care for her, James was raised by Dorothy's landlady, Lula Rogers. James began singing in a church choir, and she performed on radio broadcasts when she was five. After Rogers died in 1950, James moved to San Francisco to live with her mother. There James formed the singing group the Creolettes, and in 1954 rhythm-and-blues performer Johnny Otis changed the group's name to the Peaches and the lead singer's name to Etta James.

She and Otis wrote "The Wallflower (Dance with Me, Henry)," recorded by Modern Records as a response to Hank Ballard's popular "Work with Me, Annie," and it reached number two on the rhythm-and-blues charts, with a sanitized version by Georgia Gibbs becoming a number-one pop hit. James soon became a solo act, with such songs as "Good Rockin' Daddy" serving as a prototype for early rock and roll. James extended her range when she moved to Chicago and signed with Chess Records in 1960. Influenced by Billie Holiday, Dinah Washington, and Johnny "Guitar" Watson, James had ten rhythm-and-blues hits during the 1960's, including "At Last," "All I Could Do Was Cry," "I'd Rather Go Blind," and "Tell Mama," songs that would remain in her repertoire during the following decades.

As is documented in her autobiography, James

began using heroin in 1959. When she tried to end the addiction through methadone treatment in the late 1960's, she became addicted to this drug as well. After being arrested for writing bad checks, James began rehabilitation in 1973.

When James resumed recording for Chess Records later that year, she assumed more artistic control, and her voice had become grittier, more soulful. Her first album in this period, *Etta James*, was nominated for a Best Rhythm and Blues Vocal Grammy Award. After Chess Records declared bankruptcy, James began recording for other labels. In 1978 she was the opening act for the Rolling Stones' American tour at the request of Keith Richards, who would later select James to perform in the documentary *Chuck Berry: Hail! Hail! Rock and Roll* (1987). A highlight of director Taylor Hackford's film is the scene of irascible Berry, unable to remember that the teenaged James was one of his backup singers on "Almost Grown" and "Back in the U.S.A.," being astounded floored by her passionate bellowing of Berry's "Rock and Roll Music."

In the 1990's James's sons joined her recording and touring group. Donto James played drums and percussions and sang backup, while Sametto James played bass. James settled in Riverside, California, with her husband, Artis Mills. A longtime problem with obesity led to knee problems, forcing the singer to perform while seated. After gastric bypass surgery in 2003, she lost two hundred pounds.

James won Grammy Awards for Best Jazz Vocal Performance for *Mystery Lady: Songs of Billie Holiday* in 1994, Best Contemporary Blues Album for *Let's Roll* in 2003, and Best Traditional Blues Album for *Blues to the Bone* in 2004. James was inducted into the Rock and Roll Hall of Fame in 1993 and into the Blues Hall of Fame in 2001. She received a National Association for the Advancement of Colored People (NAACP) Image Award in 1990, a Rhythm and Blues Foundation Pioneer Award in 1989, a star on the Hollywood Walk of Fame in 2003, and a Grammy Lifetime Achievement Award in 2004.

The Music

As with many blues performers, the influence of gospel music is evident in James's vibrant singing. She moves easily from blues to rhythm-and-blues, to rock, to jazz, and even to country music.

"At Last." The most famous of James's early songs is "At Last." Written by Mack Gordon and Harry Warren, the song was a hit for big band leader Glenn Miller in 1941, but it never became part of the standards repertoire until James's rousing 1961 rendition, a definitive power ballad. James draws out the lyrics to accentuate the joy of love fulfilled. Her chilling version of "At Last" has frequently appeared in television commercials and films, including *Rain Man* (1988).

Mixing Genres. James began moving more earnestly toward traditional blues with *Seven Year Itch*, nominated for a Best Contemporary Blues Grammy Award. Her commitment to the hard-driving rhythms she described as "gutbucket" continued with *Stickin' to My Guns*, which mixed rock, soul, and funk with the blues, an indication of James's musical curiosity and restlessness, her resistance to being pinned down to a single genre. James asked the legendary music producer Jerry Wexler to leave retirement to produce *The Right Time*, a similar mix of genres, with the highlight being her forceful rendition of Ray Charles's "Nighttime Is the Right Time," making it more sexually suggestive than the original, a quality she has accentuated in her live performances, especially with such songs as "I Want to Ta-Ta You, Baby." She long wanted to do a country album, but after *Love's Been Rough on Me* was remixed to sound jazzier, James disowned it.

Mystery Lady. She made the biggest departure of her career and she had one of her greatest successes with *Mystery Lady: The Songs of Billie Holiday*. Singing such ballads as "Don't Explain" and "Lover Man," James does not imitate Holiday's voice or her phrasing (as a young woman James briefly met Holiday), but she gives the songs a distinctive spin of her own. Her husky, throaty voice on "Body and Soul" erases the thin line between jazz and blues. More standards albums followed, including *Time after Time* and *Blue Gardenia*, in which her mother, a longtime jazz fan, joined her on the title song.

Blues to the Bone. *Blues to the Bone* is a counterpart to her ballad albums, with such blues classics as Jimmy Reed's "Hush Hush," Willie Dixon's "Little Red Rooster," John Lee Hooker's "Crawlin' King Snake," and Robert Johnson's "Dust My Broom." Although such songs present a male perspective on love and sex, James makes them applicable to women as well through the theatricality of her voice, which shifts effortlessly from a roar to a purr.

Musical Legacy

James's powerhouse vocals have influenced numerous performers, particularly Mick Jagger and Janis Joplin (who was thirteen years old when she met James). Singers such as Norah Jones and Joss Stone have also cited James as a model for their singing styles. Since the mid-1950's, James has presented a persistently female perspective in her songs, paving the way for such singer-songwriters as Maria Muldaur, Bonnie Raitt, and Susan Tedeschi. Songs such as "Only Women Bleed" and "Sugar on the Floor" emphasize how women suffer for love.

Michael Adams

Further Reading

Dieckman, Katherine. "Etta James." *Rolling Stone* (November 13, 1997): 152-153. In this article, James discusses the feminist and sexual sides of her music.

James, Etta, and David Ritz. *Rage to Survive: The Etta James Story*. New York: Villard, 1995. James provides an honest and often painful account of her personal and professional life.

Ritz, David. "Etta James, Soul Mama." In *Bluesland: Portraits of Twelve Major American Blues Masters*, edited by Toby Byron. New York: Dutton, 1991. This chapter presents an overview of James's contribution to the development of the modern blues.

Waller, Don. "The *Billboard* Interview: Etta James." *Billboard* 113 (August 11, 2001): 20-22. James discusses her favorite singers and songwriters, and she explains how she selects the songs she records.

See also: Berry, Chuck; Charles, Ray; Dixon, Willie; Jagger, Sir Mick; Jefferson, Blind Lemon; Joplin, Janis; King, B. B.; Otis, Johnny; Pickett, Wilson; Reed, Jimmy; Washington, Dinah.

Leoš Janáček
Czech classical composer

Janáček spent most of his professional life as a teacher and conductor in Moravia. As a composer, he sought inspiration in real motives encountered in nature, particularly the intonations and rhythms of human speech. He contributed to preserving and elaborating on regional folk musics.

Born: July 3, 1854; Hukvaldy, Moravia, Austrian Empire (now in Austria)
Died: August 12, 1928; Ostrava, Czechoslovakia (now in Czech Republic)

Principal works
CHAMBER WORKS: *Pohádka*, 1910, revised 1912 (*Fairy Tale*; for cello and piano); Violin Sonata, 1922; String Quartet No. 27, 1924 (*Kreutzer*); *Mládí*, 1925 (*Youth*); *Capriccio: Vzdor*, 1926 (*Defiance*); Concertino, 1926; String Quartet No. 2, 1928 (*Listy důvěrné; Intimate Letters*).
CHORAL WORKS: *Válečná*, 1873 (*War Song*); *Osud neujdeš*, 1876 (*You Cannot Escape Your Fate*); *Naše píseň*, 1890 (*Our Song*); *Už je slúnko z tej hory ven*, 1894 (*The Sun Has Risen Above That Hill*); *Zápisník zmizelého*, 1921 (*Diary of One Who Disappeared*); *Mša glagolskaja*, 1927 (*Glagolitic Mass*); *Osamělá bez těchy*, 1978 (*Alone Without Comfort*).
OPERAS (music): *Jenůfa*, 1904 (libretto by Janáček; based on Gabriela Preissova's play *Její pastorkyóa*); *Osud*, 1904 (*Fate*; libretto by Janáček and Fedora Bartošová); *Výlety páně Broučkovy*, 1920 (*The Adventures of Mr. Brouček*; libretto by František Sarafínský Procházka; based on Svatopluk Čech's novel); *Kát'a kabanová*, 1921 (libretto by Janáček; based on Alexander Ostrovsky's novel *The Storm*); *Příhody lišky bystroušky*, 1924 (*The Cunning Little Vixen*; libretto by Janáček; based on Ostrovsky's play *The Thunderstorm*); *Věc Makropulos*, 1926 (*The Makropulos Case*; libretto by Janáček; based on Karel Čapek's play); *Z mrtvého domu*, 1930 (*From the House of the Dead*; libretto by Janáček; based on Fyodor Dostoevski's novel).

Leoš Janáček and his wife.

ORCHESTRAL WORKS: Suite for String Orchestra, 1877; *Taras Bulba, Rhapsody*, 1921; Sinfonietta, 1926; *Lašské tance*, 1928 (*Lachian Dances*).

PIANO WORKS: *Zdenči-menuetto*, 1880 (*Zdenka's Minuet*); *Z ulce dne 1. října 1905*, 1906 (*From the Street, October 1, 1905*; piano sonata); *V mlhách*, 1912 (*In the Mists*); *Ej, duby, duby*, 1922 (*O, the Oaks, the Oaks*); *Moravské lidové písně*, 1922 (*Moravian Folksongs*); *Po zarostlém chodníčku*, 1942 (*On the Overgrown Path*).

The Life

Leoš Janáček (LAY-ohsh yah-NAY-chehk *or* YAY-nah-chehk) was born in the village of Hukvaldy in Moravia, then part of the Austrian Empire. His father, a village teacher and musician, brought the eleven-year-old Janáček to an old friend and former pupil, Pavel Křížkovský, who was director of a monastery foundation in Brno. The foundation provided scholarships for promising young stu-

dents in exchange for singing in their choir. Janáček boarded as a chorister at the monastery, and he enrolled in a German-language day school. The contrast between life and culture at the monastery and at the day school was stark. At the day school, he was treated as a second-class individual, which had a major impact on his developing self-identity and on the Czech pride that later emerged in his character. His early interest in psychology, which would prove a strong influence on his ideas and music, also dates from this period.

Expecting to follow the same career as his father (who had died in 1866), Janáček attended the Teachers' Training Institute in Brno from 1869 to 1872. From 1872 to 1874, he served there as a teacher of music, and he became active as a choirmaster. In the fall of 1874, he enrolled at the Organ School in Prague. His enthusiasm and drive led him to compress the normal three-year course into two years. During this time, he began his lifelong friendship with Antonín Dvořák, at the time a relatively unknown musician and composer. By 1874, Janáček was committed to his desire to become a composer. although he spent most of his career employed as a teacher, an administrator, and a conductor. His compositions did not gain widespread notoriety until late in his life, even more so posthumously.

He married Zdenka Schulzová in 1881. They had two children: their son, Vladimir, died in 1890 at the age of two; their daughter, Olga, died at the age of twenty in 1903. These losses, especially the latter, had a deleterious impact on the already shaky relationship between him and his wife.

Janáček left behind a mass of writings, published and private, which are now housed in archives in Brno. He filled the margins of his books with notes, and he carried on numerous lengthy correspondences. His seventy-five notebooks, his essays on speech melodies, his calendars, and his various jottings, spanning nearly fifty years, further enrich the understanding of his thought processes, motivations, and interests.

The Music

Janáček's compositions include solo piano works, chamber music, and orchestral compositions. He is most noted for his vocal works, including many choruses, chamber song cycles, and numerous operas. He was committed to realism in his dramatic works, and he openly reveals strongly held political and social convictions in his choice of texts. In addition to working on original compositions, he spent many years gathering and elaborating on native folk musics.

Lachian Dances. *Lachian Dances* stand as testament to Janáček's friendship with and emulation of Dvořák, a symbol of his dedication to the folk arts. Inspired by Dvořák's *Slavonic Dances* (1878), Janáček produced a series of dances reflective of the culture of his homeland. These works were composed separately beginning in the late 1880's. During this time he had traveled frequently with his friend, the linguist František Bartoš, who was known especially for seminal efforts to describe regional dialects. Together they collected and published many folk songs. It was likely that on these excursions Janáček cultivated an interest not only in the varieties of folk music encountered but also in the melodies and rhythms of dialectic speech and everyday life. Some of his notebooks preserve the impressions of roosters, hens, and other birds and the soundscapes of wind and waves, beehives and cows.

Jenůfa. Completed in early 1903, and premiered on the stage in Brno a year later, *Jenůfa* would not be performed in Prague for another dozen years. Sadly for Janáček, the deciding conductor at the National Theater in Prague was Karel Kovařovic, who apparently had not forgotten a harsh critique of one of his compositions penned by Janáček more than a decade earlier. Kovařovic's biting initial rejection evinced his revenge, though he would eventually relent, allowing a Prague premiere in 1916. Significantly, *Jenůfa* was the first of Janáček's operas to fully incorporate his brand of realism based on what he considered the natural melodies of speech. The composer had been producing transcriptions of speech melodies from as early as 1897. He continued this practice for the rest of his life, eventually filling nearly fifty notebooks with his observations.

From the Street, October 1, 1905. This sparse piano sonata was a personal reaction to a peaceful street protest seeking the establishment of a Czech-language university in Brno in which the composer may have participated. The protest was brutally suppressed by soldiers, culminating in the unfortunate death by bayonet goring of an unarmed young carpenter named František Pavlík. This work portrays a somber and reflective mood, and at times it is angry, stark, and unadorned. It was first performed publicly in January, 1906. The work was originally composed of three movements, but the composer inexplicably destroyed the third movement before the performance, eventually discarding the other two as well. Decades later, the first two movements were recovered, when the performer from the premiere concert produced her copy of the manuscript.

Diary of One Who Disappeared. *The Diary of One Who Disappeared* is difficult to classify as a composition. Its twenty-one sections are set mostly for tenor solo and piano, with two including other voices, and another set for piano alone. The text had appeared as poems published anonymously in the popular newspaper *Lidové noviny*. They tell the story of a boy, with the name of Janáček, who falls in love with a mysterious Romany girl. His affection blossoms, and he finally departs from the world he has known to join his lover and their son. Completing the cycle in 1919, its style shows a remarkable independence of mind. The work presents a ripening of his speech melody technique, short independent motives, and little development in a traditional musical sense. The piano emerges both to support and to comment on the action. The text itself—the illicit love affair and the fantasy of disappearance—clearly spoke to the hidden world of the composer, whose relationship with his wife was strained and his affections for others well known.

Sinfonietta. Janáček's Sinfonietta, dating from 1926, provides a glimpse into the mature and the finally confident composer. The first movement presents an enduring, celebratory, brassy, and percussive fanfare. The second movement has a folksy, dance air, with a continuous melodic weaving similar to his contemporary, Giacomo Puccini. The third movement leads through a dreamy, peaceful nostalgia, toward a Slavic-flavored fanfare, reminiscent of Hector Berlioz's symphonic experiments of the previous generation. The fourth movement, with its simple, driving motivation, evokes the sort of country village portrayed in many of his operas. The fifth movement ties this all together, from a Felix Mendelssohn-like entrance, with a fantasy of wood nymphs, through the triumphalism of his dramatic close. Overall, there is a freedom of rhythmic movement and a continuous flow of melody, at times almost directionless. Janáček's blending of the cutting edge and the traditional speak of his mastery of both new and old in the styles that surrounded him. His relative isolation, his long wait for broader recognition, and his stubborn personality allowed the development of a voice, clearly influenced by the cultures of his milieu and by some of the musical experimentalism of his day, yet unique in its execution.

Musical Legacy

Janáček's legacy is both direct and indirect. Much of his career involved his role as pedagogue. In 1881 he was appointed founding director of the new Brno Organ School (later Conservatory), in whose establishment he had played a prominent role. He taught not only composition but also violin, piano, voice, and theory, having written several texts in these areas. His many students included prominent Czech composers and performers of the subsequent generation: Rudolf Firkušny, Vilém Tauský, and Pavel Haas.

While the incorporation of speech melodies and folk elements in twentieth century compositions has often been linked with work by other composers (Modest Mussorgsky, Béla Bartók), Janáček's contributions went well beyond the curiosity of a musician's sketchbook. His study of sound perception and the emotional content encoded in the prosody of speech remain of interest to scholars decades after his death. Janáček's often sparse and disjunct style of composition; his approach to the role of music and drama in relation to local cultures, especially the sound culture of spoken languages; his exploration of the musical aspects of the environment, predating the musings of John Cage; and his reflections on cultural as well as universal differences mark him as a singular figure in music history. Further study by scholars of Janáček's notebooks and published articles reveals nuances in his sometimes opaque writing, and his musical compositions continue their rise in popularity.

Jonathan G. Secora Pearl

Further Reading

Beckerman, Michael. *Janáček as Theorist.* Stuyvesant, N.Y.: Pendragon Press, 1994. This volume presents a view of Janáček's theoretical output and his sometimes questionable application of his theories within his own compositions. The discussion is placed firmly within historical context, providing evidence and commentary alongside technical considerations.

_____, ed. *Janáček and His World.* Princeton, N.J.: Princeton University Press, 2003. Essays from established and new Janáček scholars, followed by a selection of the composer's own writings, newly translated with commentary. This volume was published in the wake of the Bard Music Festival presentation of the same name, held in preparation for the sesquicentennial of the composer's birth.

Drlíková, Eva, ed. *Leoš Janáček: Chronology of His Life and Work.* Brno, Czechoslovakia: Opus Musicum, 2004. A concise chronology of the composer's life, including major events and works, along with numerous photographs. Edition is in Czech and English.

Tyrrell, John. *Janáček: Years of a Life, Vol. 1 (1854-1914).* London: Faber & Faber, 2006. The first in a two-volume work of nearly eighteen hundred pages represents the culmination of its author's lifetime study of Janáček's life and work.

_____. *Janáček: Years of a Life, Vol. 2 (1914-1928).* London: Faber & Faber, 2007. The second in a two-volume work looks at the latter part of Janáček's life. A thoroughly scholarly edition that is extensively supported by documents, citations, and references.

Wingfield, Paul, ed. *Janáček Studies.* Cambridge, England: Cambridge University Press, 1999. This collection of articles by leading Janáček scholars represented the first major effort to gather and present English-language critical scholarship regarding Janáček's compositional output.

Zemanová, Mirka. *Janáček: A Composer's Life.* Boston: Northeastern University Press, 2002. This is a popular, well-researched biography of the composer's life. By design, the focus is more on the life of the composer than on his compositions.

See also: Bartók, Béla; Cage, John; Klemperer, Otto; Martinů, Bohuslav; Puccini, Giacomo.

Bert Jansch

Scottish folk guitarist, singer, and songwriter

Strongly influenced by folk music during his early years, Jansch evolved into a folk-rock musician, using popular, jazz, and blues elements for his compositions and performances.

Born: November 3, 1943; Glasgow, Scotland
Also known as: Herbert Jansch (full name)
Member of: Pentangle

Principal recordings

ALBUMS (solo): *Bert Jansch*, 1965; *It Don't Bother Me*, 1965; *Bert and John*, 1966 (with John Renbourn); *Jack Orion*, 1966; *Needle of Death*, 1966; *Nicola*, 1967; *Birthday Blues*, 1969; *Lucky Thirteen*, 1969; *Sampler*, 1969; *Stepping Stone*, 1969; *Rosemary Lane*, 1971; *Box of Love*, 1972; *Moonshine*, 1973; *L.A. Turnaround*, 1974; *Santa Barbara Honeymoon*, 1975; *A Rare Conundrum*, 1977; *Avocet*, 1979; *Thirteen Down*, 1980; *Heartbreak*, 1982; *From the Outside*, 1985; *Leather Laundrette*, 1988 (with Rod Clements); *Ornament Tree*, 1990; *Sketches*, 1990; *When the Circus Comes to Town*, 1995; *Conundrum*, 1998; *Toy Balloon*, 1998; *Crimson Moon*, 2000; *Edge of a Dream*, 2002; *River Sessions*, 2004; *The Black Swan*, 2006.

ALBUMS (with Pentangle): *The Pentangle*, 1968; *Sweet Child*, 1968; *Basket of Light*, 1969; *Cruel Sister*, 1970; *Reflection*, 1971; *Solomon's Seal*, 1972; *Pentangling*, 1973; *Open the Door*, 1985; *In the Round*, 1986; *So Early in the Spring*, 1990; *Think of Tomorrow*, 1991; *One More Road*, 1993; *On Air*, 1997; *Passe Avant*, 1999.

The Life

Herbert Jansch (jansh) was born in Glasgow, Scotland, on November 3, 1943, of Austrian-Scottish parentage, but he lived in Edinburgh for most of his childhood. During his mid-teens, Jansch studied the guitar with Jill Doyle, whose stepbrother Davy (later spelled Davey) Graham, in 1961, wrote "Angi," a piece that Jansch recorded in 1965. In the early 1960's he spent time in London, where he became

acquainted with the music of Jackson C. Frank, Bob Dylan, and Paul Simon. He recorded his first album, *Bert Jansch*, under primitive circumstances in the home of Bill Leader, his London-based producer, over several months in 1964 and 1965.

Jansch solicited the talents of his flatmate, guitarist John Renbourn, on his next two albums. In September of 1966, Jansch gave Renbourn equal billing on *Bert and John*. During this fertile period, Jansch and Renbourn were overseeing a London folk club, and they became associated with London-born folksinger Jacqui McShee, percussionist Terry Cox, and bassist Danny Thompson to form the acclaimed folk-rock group Pentangle in 1967. Pentangle reflected Jansch's diverse stylistic creativity until 1973, when the group disbanded. Jansch maintained a steady output of solo albums while he was associated with Pentangle. Later group connections, notably with Conundrum and the Second Pentangle, were short-lived.

The Music

Jansch's premier skill was his guitar playing. The aggressive, percussive approach of his fingerpicking style begged attention, even from the casual listener. Beginning with his first home-produced recording in 1964, Jansch's performing conformed to a high standard of excellence. Jansch's voice presented an untrained but easygoing sound; he reached for his notes and wrapped his voice around the pitch, keeping the listener attentive. His early compositions reflected a debt to Bob Dylan's poetic rendition of original material demonstrated through voice and guitar.

Early Works. Jansch honed his guitar skills in the folk clubs of Edinburgh and London during the early 1960's. His first album, *Bert Jansch*, features Jansch as singer and guitarist. "Needle of Death" is a moving, if brutally honest, eulogy to a friend, who had died of a heroin overdose. The heavily blues-influenced "Strolling Down the Highway" is a masterful showcase for Jansch's mature acoustic guitar skills. Included in a rerelease of these early recordings is an eight-and-a-half-minute piece, "Instrumental Medley 1964." Despite the flaws of recording (interference of a handheld mike, a door creaking, and Jansch humming), the work testifies to Jansch's high level of improvisational skill.

"Jack Orion." The traditional song "Jack Orion" makes two notably different appearances. Its initial manifestation, on the album *Jack Orion* in 1966, with Renbourn on the second guitar, is a nine-and-a-half-minute murder-suicide ballad, constructed on an F minor chord alternating with an E-flat major chord. Jansch uses the higher octave of the tonic note like a recitation tone, eventually falling to the lower octave at the cadence of each quatrain. He includes spontaneous-sounding blues responses on the lead guitar as the song progresses. The 1970 version on Pentangle's *Cruel Sister* lasts eighteen and a half minutes, with Jansch alternating the lead vocal line with McShee. The first seven minutes recall the early Jansch recording style, but then Jansch and Renbourn take recorders in hand (with Thompson on a bowed upright bass) and produce an antiquated stylistic effect for the next four minutes. Then the group turns to a purely jazz style in an instrumental segment, featuring some astonishing guitar solo work, before finishing the story in the recording's opening style.

"The Black Swan." As a composed song from 2006, "The Black Swan," from *The Black Swan*, is a fine example of Jansch's orchestration abilities. His guitar playing provides a stabilizing foundation for cello, percussion, and keyboard to support his singing. The space-age lyrics consider life from a universal perspective. Although the swan of this song bears no musical relation to other musical swans, Orlando Gibbons's "The Silver Swan" (1612) and Camille Saint-Saëns's "The Swan" from *Carnival of Animals* (1886), the finality of life in the Gibbons madrigal text and the lonely elegance of the cello in the Saint-Saëns work do come to mind during the Jansch creation. The guitar part is based primarily on a B minor ninth chord moving to an A major chord, as the voice travels leisurely downward from the ninth (C-sharp) to the notes of the A major chord. After two repetitions of these chord progressions, the motion is echoed in the closing of each stanza with an E major chord moving to a B minor chord. An instrumental coda presents more melodic freedom in the cello part.

Musical Legacy

Although Jansch's music did not earn massive popular recognition, the artist was revered by many musicians and followers, who appreciated

his energetic approach to a fingerpicking guitar style. He experimented with various tunings, which was emulated by many guitarists. In addition to his usual instrument, the six-string acoustic guitar, he occasionally used the twelve-string guitar, the electric guitar, the banjo, the dulcimer, the piano, and the recorder, adding to the colorful variety of music evident in his many albums. He served as an inspiration for Jimmy Page (of Led Zeppelin fame), Neil Young, and fellow Scotsman Donovan.

Dennis E. Ferguson

Further Reading

Harper, Colin. *Dazzling Stranger: Bert Jansch and the British Folk and Blues Revival.* London: Bloomsbury, 2006. Harper, an Irish music journalist, presents a thorough biography of Jansch.

Hodgkinson, Will. *Guitar Man.* London: Bloomsbury, 2006. On a quest to learn how to play the guitar in six months well enough to perform a gig in public, the author seeks the help of several guitarists, including Jansch, who figures most prominently in the chapter "The Cosmic Guitarist."

Stambler, Irwin, and Lyndon Stambler. *Folk and Blues: The Encyclopedia.* New York: St. Martin's Press, 2001. The article on Jansch covers important contacts during his early life and quotes extensively from journal interviews.

See also: Dylan, Bob; Page, Jimmy; Simon, Paul.

Keith Jarrett

American jazz composer, pianist, singer, and keyboard player

A versatile jazz pianist, Jarrett has performed extended solo improvisation concerts around the world, and he has recorded several well-regarded piano works by classical composers.

Born: May 8, 1945; Allentown, Pennsylvania
Also known as: Keith Daniel Jarrett (full name)
Member of: The Charles Lloyd Quartet; the Standards Trio

Principal recordings

ALBUMS (solo): *Life Between the Exit Signs*, 1967; *Restoration Ruin*, 1968; *Somewhere Before*, 1968; *With Gary Burton*, 1968 (with Gary Burton); *Birth*, 1971; *ECM Works*, 1971; *Expectations*, 1971; *Facing You*, 1971; *The Mourning of a Star*, 1971; *Ruta and Daitya*, 1972 (with Jack DeJohnette); *Fort Yawuh*, 1973; *In the Light*, 1973; *Backhand*, 1974; *Belonging*, 1974; *Luminessence*, 1974 (with Jan Garbarek); *Personal Mountains*, 1974; *Treasure Island*, 1974; *Arbour Zena*, 1975; *The Köln Concert*, 1975; *Death and the Flower*, 1975; *Mysteries*, 1975; *Shades*, 1975; *El juicio (The Judgement)*, 1976; *Hymns/ Spheres*, 1976; *Spheres*, 1976; *Staircase*, 1976; *The Survivor's Suite*, 1976; *Bop-Be*, 1977; *Byablue*, 1977; *My Song*, 1977; *Ritual*, 1977; *Silence*, 1977; *Nude Ants*, 1979; *The Celestial Hawk*, 1980; *Sacred Hymns*, 1980; *Invocations/The Moth and the Flame*, 1981; *Changes*, 1983; *Standards, Vol. 1*, 1983; *Standards, Vol. 2*, 1983; *Spirits 1 and 2*, 1985; *The Well-Tempered Clavier: Book 1 (J. S. Bach)*, 1988; *Standards in Norway*, 1989; *Works by Lou Harrison*, 1989; *Bye Bye Blackbird*, 1991; *J. S. Bach: Three Sonatas for Viola da Gamba and Harpsichord*, 1991; *Shostakovich: The Twenty-four Preludes and Fugues, Op. 87*, 1991; *The Well-Tempered Clavier: Book 2 (J. S. Bach)*, 1991; *At the Deer Head Inn*, 1992; *Bridge of Light*, 1993; *Handel: Suites for Keyboard*, 1995; *The Melody at Night with You*, 1999; *Whisper Not*, 2000; *Radiance*, 2005; *The Carnegie Hall Concert*, 2006; *Works*, 2006; *Setting Standards: New York Sessions*, 2007.

ALBUMS (with the Charles Lloyd Quartet): *Dream Weaver*, 1966; *The Flowering*, 1966; *Nirvana*, 1968; *Soundtrack*, 1969.

The Life

Keith Daniel Jarrett (JAHR-reht) was born on May 8, 1945, to Daniel and Irma Jarrett in Allentown, Pennsylvania. A child prodigy, Jarrett was playing melodies on the piano by ear by the age of two. Jarrett began taking piano lessons at the age of three, and at the age of seven he presented an entire solo recital that included classical works as well as his own compositions.

Jarrett's parents separated when he was eleven, leaving his mother to raise him and his four brothers. At age fifteen, he turned to playing jazz and popular music, and he began playing in local jazz bands. Contacts through summer music camps led to scholarships to the Berklee School of Music in Boston, but he attended only one year before moving to New York, where Art Blakey asked him to join his band, the Jazz Messengers, after hearing Jarrett at a jam session at the Village Vanguard.

After the year at the Berklee School of Music, Jarrett married Margot Erney in Boston. Once he became successful, the family moved to a house on several acres of land in New Jersey, where they raised two sons. Jarrett's extensive touring and other disagreements led to their separation in 1979. He later married long-term girlfriend Rose Anne Colavito. In the 1970's he contended with severe back pain while touring, and in 1996 he was forced

Keith Jarrett. (AP/Wide World Photos)

to stop performing for more than two years because of chronic fatigue syndrome. He returned to performing and recording, but on a limited basis.

The Music

Jarrett's eclectic style was forged through the influences of his training in classical piano, listening to jazz artists such as Bill Evans, McCoy Tyner, Ahmad Jamal, and Paul Bley, and performing in his early twenties with such prominent jazz musicians as Miles Davis, Art Blakey, and Charles Lloyd. Many of his recordings (more than one hundred) feature the various jazz trios and quartets with whom he has performed, but he is perhaps best known for recordings of solo concerts in the 1970's, which consisted of extended improvisations that defy categorization by genre. He has also recorded piano works by composers such as Johann Sebastian Bach, Wolfgang Amadeus Mozart, Dmitri Shostakovich, and Lou Harrison.

Early Works. After only a few months performing with Blakey, and still only twenty years old, Jarrett joined a quartet headed by Charles Lloyd in 1965 that toured Europe and the United States extensively. Several live and studio recordings of the group were made in the late 1960's, such as *Forest Flower*, and included several songs composed by Jarrett for the group. Jarrett also performed for two years with Davis's group on several important recordings that highlight Jarrett's talents at piano improvisation.

Expectations. The fusion of styles on this 1971 studio recording highlights the proficiency of Jarrett as a composer, arranger, and improviser. Romantic strings in the title ballad "Expectations" add a richness and glow not typically heard playing with a jazz trio of piano, bass, and drums. Perhaps the most representative and engaging track is "There Is a Road (God's River)," which begins with an improvisational flight of fancy by Jarrett on piano, settles into a gospel groove with funk overtones in the guitar, and effortlessly melts into and out of slow sections, featuring a lush string ensemble that has the reverence of a hymn. The varied styles do not seem out of place, showing an inevitable quality that flows from one to another.

The Köln Concert. Recorded live in Cologne, Germany, in 1975, this may be Jarrett's most popular album, selling more than three million copies. It consists of three improvisatory sections for piano, lasting twenty-six, thirty-four, and seven minutes each. Its popularity can be attributed to its accessibility, with sections of infectious rhythms and repeating, simple harmonies that push the listener forward on a joyful journey. While the repetition can create a hypnotic effect, there is always an internal logic and depth of influence that make this music more substantial and satisfying than works by imitators in the later genre of New Age music.

Standards, Vol. 1. This 1983 recording is the first of what would become an ongoing collaboration of twenty-five years among Jarrett on piano, Gary Peacock on double bass, and Jack DeJohnette on drums. Standards, or well-respected pieces in the jazz repertory, are the mainstay of most jazz improvisation. The quality of playing and the unconventional interpretations on this recording, and the many subsequent recordings by this group, though, make these renditions of standards notable. The final track, "God Bless the Child," starts with a bluesy, gospel feel that smolders for several minutes before solos by all three musicians find new directions to impel the work forward. It then returns to the opening feel and a satisfying fadeout.

Handel: Suites for Keyboard. Issued in 1995, this recording presents a completely different side to Jarrett's abilities as a pianist. He demonstrates the control and precision needed to correctly play this music from the Baroque period, but he gives these groups of dances a lightness of touch that makes his interpretations compelling.

Musical Legacy

The recording *Radiance* from 2005 and *The Carnegie Hall Concert* issued in 2006 demonstrate Jarrett's ability as a solo improviser. He tours with the Standards Trio, playing both traditional and free jazz. Jarrett is often criticized for the vocal grunts, sighs, and partial singing that accompany his jazz and solo improvisations, along with his tendency to thrust and move his body while playing. While these sounds and movements can be a distraction to listeners, they seem to indicate his total immersion into his performance that makes so much of his music engaging. Jarrett has been a strong advocate for the use of acoustic, rather than electronic, musical instruments, and his innovations in improvised and composed music on traditional instruments prove that electronics are not necessary for musicians to find new ways of expression.

R. Todd Rober

Further Reading

Carr, Ian. *Keith Jarrett: The Man and His Music.* London: Grafton Books, 1991. This solid, although at times bland, account of Jarrett's life places his vast number of recordings into perspective.

Moreno, Jairo. "Body 'n' Soul? Voice and Movement in Keith Jarrett's Pianism." *The Musical Quarterly* 83, no. 1 (Spring, 1999): 75-92. A dense, academic justification of Jarrett's vocalizing and body movements.

Ouellette, Dan. "Out of Thin Air." *Down Beat* 72, no. 8 (August, 2005): 36-41. An interview with Jarrett focuses on his return to solo improvisation concerts and the recording *Radiance*.

Strickland, Edward. *American Composers: Dialogues on Contemporary Music.* Bloomington: Indiana University Press, 1991. Jarrett is one of eleven composers interviewed, and he provides insight into the influence of minimalism in his work.

Yamashita, Kimihiko. "Ferociously Harmonizing with Reality." In *Keeping Time: Readings in Jazz History,* edited by Robert Walser. New York: Oxford University Press, 1999. Yamashita's interview focuses on Jarrett's views of playing with Davis.

See also: Blakey, Art; Burton, Gary; Corea, Chick; Davis, Miles; Evans, Bill; Harrison, Lou; Shostakovich, Dmitri.

Jay-Z

American rapper

Jay-Z helped shape hip-hop music in the wake of the East Coast-West Coast gangsta rap rivalry. Through his role as a record executive, both at Roc-A-Fella Records and Def Jam Records, Jay-Z has discovered and fostered a number of successful artists.

Born: December 4, 1969; Brooklyn, New York
Also known as: Shawn Corey Carter (birth name)
Member of: Original Flavor

Principal recordings

ALBUMS (solo): *Reasonable Doubt*, 1996; *In My Lifetime, Vol. 1*, 1997; *Vol. 2: Hard Knock Life*, 1998; *Vol. 3: Life and Times of S. Carter*, 1999; *The Dynasty Roc la Familia*, 2000; *The Blueprint*, 2001; *Unplugged*, 2001; *The Blueprint²: The Gift and the Curse*, 2002; *The Black Album*, 2003; *The Blueprint 2.1*, 2003; *Collision Course*, 2004 (with Linkin Park); *Kingdom Come*, 2006; *American Gangster*, 2007; *Brooklyn Gangster*, 2008 (with Tapemasters Inc.).

ALBUMS (with Original Flavor): *This Is How It Is*, 1992; *Beyond Flavor*, 1993.

The Life

Born and raised in the Marcy projects of Brooklyn, Jay-Z (jay zee) spent the early portion of his career involved with drugs and establishing himself as a rapper in New York. Unable to secure a major label record deal, Jay-Z formed Roc-A-Fella Records with Damon Dash and Kareem "Biggs" Burke. The label initially pressed and sold records on its own, but it teamed with distributor Priority Records for the release of Jay-Z's first album, *Reasonable Doubt*, in 1996. After reaching a new distribution deal with Def Jam, *In My Lifetime, Vol. 1* was released in 1997, followed the next year by Jay-Z's commercially successful album *Vol. 2: Hard Knock Life*. Jay-Z continued to release new studio albums until 2003, when he announced his retirement from recording and performing in order to focus on business ventures. Though retired, Jay-Z continued to work on side projects, such as his 2004 collaboration with rock group Linkin Park, *Collision Course*. In addition, in 2004 Jay-Z was named president and chief executive officer of Def Jam Records, which finalized his split from Dash and Burke. Jay-Z officially ended his retirement in 2005, and he released his next album the following year. In addition to his activities as an artist and record executive, Jay-Z has his own clothing line, Rocawear, which specializes in hip-hop fashion, and he is co-owner of the New Jersey Nets basketball team. In April, 2008, Jay-Z married singer Beyoncé Knowles.

The Music

While his musical style has evolved throughout his career, Jay-Z is generally known for accessible narratives that present his gritty life story to a mainstream audience. His music also contains a great deal of posturing. He frequently sings his own praises in songs and lyrically retaliates against rivals. Jay-Z is also known for his musical collaborations and utilization of numerous guest artists and producers for his albums.

Reasonable Doubt. Jay-Z's first solo album, *Reasonable Doubt*, was moderately successful. However, it was a critical success, and positive reviews drew attention to the emerging rapper. The songs on this album frequently refer to Jay-Z's past criminal lifestyle and utilize samples drawn from soul, funk, and jazz artists. Of the four singles released from this album "Ain't No Nigga" was the most successful. The song features female rapper Foxy Brown, and it details a relationship between Jay-Z and Brown. The album's second most successful single, "Can't Knock the Hustle," features rhythm-and-blues singer Mary J. Blige and samples "Much Too Much" by Marcus Miller and "Fool's Paradise" by Meli'sa Morgan. Lyrically the song addresses Jay-Z's past life on the streets and celebrates his extravagant lifestyle.

Vol. 2: Hard Knock Life. Jay-Z's *Vol. 2: Hard Knock Life* was a huge commercial success, and it propelled him to the forefront of the music industry. The success of the album, which received a Grammy Award for Best Rap Album, rests on its numerous popular singles. The first single, "Can I Get A . . .," helped popularize the rappers Amil and Ja Rule, while the second single, "Hard Knock Life (Ghetto Anthem)," samples the song of the same name from the musical *Annie* (1976). The third single, "Money, Cash, Hoes," features the rapper DMX and heavily utilizes descending synthesizers, and the fourth single, "Nigga What, Nigga Who," features a subdivided beat and quickly delivered lyrics.

The Blueprint. Released in 2001, *The Blueprint* was received well both critically and commercially, and it managed to maintain street credibility while appealing to mainstream audiences, partly because it sampled vintage soul music. Unlike other Jay-Z albums, *The Blueprint* has only one featured guest artist, Eminem, although it features a number of producers, including Kanye West, Timbaland, Just Blaze, and Bink. Included on the album is the song "Takeover," which samples the Doors' "Five to One," and KRS-ONE's "Sound of da Police." Dur-

ing the verses of the song Jay-Z attacks Prodigy of the hip-hop group Mobb Deep and the rapper Nas, which led to a rap battle between Jay-Z and Nas. "Izzo (H.O.V.A.)" was the first, and most successful, single released from the album, and it features a sample of "I Want You Back" by the Jackson Five. The song addresses, among other topics, his struggles with the music industry.

Musical Legacy

By filling the void left in the New York rap world after the death of the Notorious B.I.G. in 1997, Jay-Z helped shape the future direction of rap. He demonstrated how a rap artist could appeal to a mainstream audience while maintaining street credibility, sustaining his core base of fans while appealing to new ones. Jay-Z has also helped propel the careers of numerous artists both through collaborations on his solo albums and through his activities as a record executive. Last, Jay-Z has demonstrated how a rap artist can be a successful entrepreneur and serve as a trend-setter for hip-hop culture and fashion.

Matthew Mihalka

Further Reading

Brown, Jake. *Jay-Z and the Roc-A-Fella Dynasty*. New York: Colossus Books, 2005. This biography of Jay-Z is divided into three parts: his early years before Roc-A-Fella, his life and works from 1996 to 1999, and his work from 2000 to 2005. Includes black-and-white photographs and a timeline that documents the success of his music.

Bryan, Carmen. *It's No Secret: From Nas to Jay-Z, from Seduction to Scandal, a Hip-Hop Helen of Troy Tells All*. New York: VH1 Books, 2006. Written by Nas's ex-girlfriend, this memoir describes her relationships with various hip-hop icons, including Jay-Z.

Clements, Car. "Musical Interchange Between Indian Music and Hip-Hop." In *Critical Minded: New Approaches to Hip-Hop Studies*, edited by Ellie M. Hisama and Ruth Crawford. Brooklyn, N.Y.: Institute for Studies in American Music, 2005. This essay looks at Jay-Z's use of the bhangra song "Mundian to bach ke," by Punjabi MC, in his song, "Beware of the Boys."

Oliver, Richard, and Tim Leffel. *Hip-Hop, Inc.: Success Strategies of the Rap Moguls*. New York: Thunder's Mouth Press, 2006. A chapter in this book focuses on the business ventures of the founders of Roc-A-Fella Records: Damon Dash, Kareem "Biggs" Burke, and Shawn "Jay-Z" Carter.

Wang, Oliver, ed. *Classic Material: The Hip-Hop Album Guide.* Toronto, Ont.: ECW Press, 2003. A chapter in this book investigates three of Jay-Z's albums: *Reasonable Doubt, Vol. 3: Life and Times of S. Carter,* and *The Blueprint.*

See also: Babyface; Blige, Mary J.; Combs, Sean; Dr. Dre; Eminem; 50 Cent; LL Cool J; Morrison, Jim; Notorious B.I.G.; Shakur, Tupac.

Blind Lemon Jefferson

American blues singer and songwriter

Jefferson was the first self-accompanied country-blues musician to be a commercial recording success, transforming an industry that had previously been dominated by large bands fronted by female singers. His brief recording career offers a glimpse into the origins of the blues.

Born: July 11, 1897; Couchman, Texas
Died: December, 1929; Chicago, Illinois
Also known as: Deacon L. J. Bates

Principal recordings

ALBUMS: *Immortal Blind Lemon Jefferson, Vol. 1,* 1961; *The Folk Blues of Blind Lemon Jefferson,* 1967; *One Dime Blues,* 1980; *Immortal Blind Lemon Jefferson, Vol. 2,* 1990.

SINGLES: "Corrina Blues," 1926; "Easy Rider Blues," 1927; "He Arose from the Dead," 1927; "Matchbox Blues," 1927; "Prison Cell Blues," 1928; "See That My Grave Is Kept Clean," 1928; "Big Night Blues," 1929; "Cheater's Spell," 1929; "Pneumonia Blues," 1929; "That Crawling Baby Blues," 1929; "Tin Cup Blues," 1929.

The Life

Lemon Jefferson was born to Alec and Classy Jefferson in Couchman, Texas, a small farming community sixty miles south of Dallas. Born either

blind or visually impaired, Jefferson turned to music in order to make a living. After gaining popularity performing at churches, picnics, parties, and street corners near his rural home, he moved to Dallas, where there was a vibrant music scene. After a few years he was able to support himself and later a wife and son, playing the street corners and bars of Dallas and traveling throughout the South.

In 1925 Sam Price, a local record store employee and pianist, contacted Paramount Records about Jefferson. The label brought him to Chicago to record that same year. His early recordings, released in 1926, sold well not only in the rural South but also in Northern cities. Jefferson returned to Chicago frequently, recording nearly a hundred sides for Paramount Records as well as two sides for Okeh Records.

Four years into his recording career, Jefferson was found dead on the streets of Chicago after a snowstorm. Although many legends surround his death (including that he, like Robert Johnson, was poisoned by a jealous girlfriend), the date and exact circumstances are unclear and no death certificate was issued. Despite his popularity he was buried in an unmarked grave that was neglected until 1967, when the Texas State Historical Association placed a plaque nearby.

The Music

Prior to the release of Jefferson's first records in 1926, blues was primarily recorded by women singers with large ensembles. As a self-accompanied male singer and guitarist, Jefferson was a huge departure from this model. Unlike these female singers, who mostly performed other people's compositions, Jefferson came to the studio with a full repertoire of both traditional and original music. His unexpected success changed the way record companies perceived the blues and opened the doors for a generation of country-blues musicians that followed.

"Corrina Blues." Because Jefferson was a solo artist, he was able to take more improvisational liberties with the blues form than the large ensembles. This flexibility is evident in his treatment of "See See Rider," a song first recorded in 1924 by Ma Rainey. Rainey, backed by an ensemble featuring Louis Armstrong and Fletcher Henderson, sings a standard twelve-bar blues, which consists of three four-bar phrases. (A bar, or measure, is a regularly repeating group of beats, four in this case. This consistent rhythmic structure ensures that the ensemble stays together.)

Jefferson's version, called "Corrina Blues," stretched the form, adding extra measures and beats as he saw fit. He used the guitar as a second voice, responding to each vocal phrase with an intricate run. He often slows the tempo when the guitar breaks away from its accompaniment role, then returns to the original tempo when the vocal comes back in. Jefferson also changed the basic structure of this song from a three-phrase to a four-phrase form by repeating the second phrase. This four-phrase blues structure is not uncommon and can also be heard on his recording of "One Dime Blues."

"Easy Rider Blues." On "Easy Rider Blues," Jefferson uses the twelve-bar blues structure instead of the regular four-bar phrases, and almost every phrase is four and a half measures (a two-bar vocal answered by a two-and-a-half-bar guitar pattern). While these variations on twelve-bar blues were exhibited by many self-accompanied blues artists who would record in the following years, Lemon had a virtuosic guitar style and a rubato vocal approach that made him immediately recognizable.

"He Arose from the Dead." Though Jefferson is most remembered for his blues, he learned many spirituals during his early days in rural Texas. In fact, Jefferson's first recording was a set of gospel numbers recorded under the pseudonym Deacon L. J. Bates, a name he would use again in 1927. Listening to these songs, one can imagine Jefferson leading a congregation. In "He Arose from the Dead" the lyrics are repetitive, the tempo is stable, and Jefferson refrains from adding extra measures or beats except between choruses. He takes fewer liberties with this community-based music than with the more narrative blues form.

"See That My Grave Is Kept Clean." Another number that Jefferson recorded in 1927 was "See That My Grave Is Kept Clean." It sold so well that Jefferson was asked to rerecord it in 1928. When Jefferson sings, "Have you ever heard that church bell toll?" he mimics the sound of a church bell on the bass notes of his guitar.

Blind Lemon Jefferson.

Musical Legacy

As the first commercially successful country-blues artist, Jefferson influenced generations of musicians. He traveled throughout Texas with Huddie Ledbetter, known as Leadbelly, years before Leadbelly was discovered by John and Alan Lomax (musicologists who preserved folk music) and became famous in his own right. Leadbelly recorded at least five tributes to Jefferson and often recalled their travels. Other musicians who knew Jefferson before he began to record include Victoria Spivey, Mance Lipscolm, and T-Bone Walker.

In the 1940's Son House outlined Jefferson's importance to Alan Lomax. A mentor to Robert Johnson and Muddy Waters, House learned the blues from a man in Clarksdale, Mississippi, who had taught himself to play from Jefferson's recordings. To Lomax, the discovery of this lineage was a breakthrough in his search for the origin of the blues. B. B. King cites Jefferson as one of his main inspirations.

Jefferson's influence reached well beyond the blues genre. Carl Perkins recorded a rockabilly version of his hit "Matchbox Blues," which was later covered by the Beatles. Bob Dylan's debut album featured a cover of Jefferson's "See That My Grave Is Kept Clean." Other covers or tributes have been recorded by the White Stripes and Nick Cave. In 1980 Jefferson was inducted into the Blues Foundation's Hall of Fame.

Oran Etkin

Further Reading

Charters, Samuel B. "Blind Lemon." In *The Country Blues*. New York: Da Capo Press, 1975. The strong narrative in this biographical account might appeal to younger audiences.

Evans, David. "Goin' Up the Country: Blues in Texas and the Deep South." In *Nothing but the Blues*, edited by Lawrence Cohn. New York: Abbeville Press, 1993. This chapter places Jefferson among fellow Texas musicians Leadbelly and Texas Alexander.

Govenar, Alan. "Blind Lemon Jefferson, That Black Snake Moan: The Music and Mystery of Blind Lemon Jefferson." In *Bluesland: Portraits of Twelve Major American Blues Masters*, edited by Pete Welding and Toby Byron. New York: Dutton, 1991. This essay features analysis of several songs, with lyrics included.

Santelli, Robert. "Blind Lemon Jefferson." In *The Big Book of the Blues*. New York: Penguin Books, 2001. A concise biography of Jefferson.

Uzzel, Robert L. *Blind Lemon Jefferson: His Life, His Death, and His Legacy*. Waco, Tex.: Eakin Press, 2002. Comprehensive biography on Jefferson.

Wald, Elijah. "Race Records: Blues Queens, Crooners, Street Singers, and Hokum." In *Escaping the Delta: Robert Johnson and the Invention of the Blues*. New York: HarperCollins, 2004. Fresh look at the birth of the blues, challenging many preconceptions.

See also: Armstrong, Louis; Henderson, Fletcher; Hooker, John Lee; Hopkins, Lightnin'; House, Son; King, B. B.; Leadbelly; Rainey, Ma; Walker, T-Bone.

Waylon Jennings
American country singer, guitarist, and songwriter

One of the founders of country music's outlaw movement, Jennings gave voice to the sorrowful side of the genre's lyrical content.

Born: June 15, 1937; Littlefield, Texas
Died: February 13, 2002; Chandler, Arizona
Also known as: Waylon Arnold Jennings (full name)
Member of: The Highwaymen

Principal recordings

ALBUMS: *Waylon Jennings at J. D.'s*, 1964; *Folk Country*, 1966; *Leavin' Town*, 1966; *Nashville Rebel*, 1966; *Love of the Common People*, 1967; *The One and Only Waylon Jennings*, 1967; *Waylon Jennings Sings Ol' Harlan*, 1967; *Hangin' On*, 1968; *Jewels*, 1968; *Only the Greatest*, 1968; *Country-Folk*, 1969 (with the Kimberlys); *Just to Satisfy You*, 1969; *Waylon Jennings*, 1969; *The Country Style of Waylon Jennings*, 1970; *Don't Think Twice*, 1970; *Ned Kelly*, 1970; *Singer of Sad Songs*, 1970; *The Taker*, 1970; *Waylon*, 1970; *Cedartown, Georgia*, 1971; *Good Hearted Woman*, 1972; *Heartaches by the Number*, 1972; *Ladies Love Outlaws*, 1972; *Honky Tonk Heroes*, 1973; *Lonesome, On'ry, and Mean*, 1973; *Ramblin' Man*, 1974; *This Time*, 1974; *Dreaming My Dreams*, 1975; *Are You Ready for the Country?*, 1976; *Mackintosh and T. J.*, 1976; *Wanted! The Outlaws*, 1976 (with Jessi Colter, Willie Nelson, and Tompall Glaser); *Ol' Waylon*, 1977; *I've Always Been Crazy*, 1978; *Waylon and Willie*, 1978 (with Nelson); *White Mansions*, 1978 (with Steve Cash, Colter, and John Dillon); *What Goes Around Comes Around*, 1979; *Music Man*, 1980; *Leather and Lace*, 1981; *Black on Black*, 1982; *WWII*, 1982; *It's Only Rock 'n' Roll*, 1983; *Take It to the Limit*, 1983 (with Nelson); *Waylon and Company*, 1983; *Never Could Toe the Mark*, 1984; *Highwayman*, 1985 (with the Highwaymen); *Turn the Page*, 1985; *A Couple More Years*, 1986; *Heroes*, 1986 (with Johnny Cash); *Sweet Mother Texas*, 1986; *Waylon!*, 1986; *Will the Wolf Survive*,

1986; *Hangin' Tough*, 1987; *A Man Called Hoss*, 1987; *Full Circle*, 1988; *The Eagle*, 1990; *Highwayman 2*, 1990 (with the Highwaymen); *Clean Shirt*, 1991; *Ol' Waylon Sings Ol' Hank*, 1992; *Too Dumb for New York City, Too Ugly for L.A.*, 1992; *Waymore's Blues, Part 2*, 1994; *The Road Goes on Forever*, 1995 (with the Highwaymen); *Right for the Time*, 1996; *Closing in on the Fire*, 1998; *Cowboys, Sisters, Rascals, and Dirt*, 1998; *Old Dogs*, 1998 (with Bobby Bare, Jerry Reed, and Mel Tillis).
WRITINGS OF INTEREST: *Waylon*, 1996.

The Life

Waylon Arnold Jennings was just twelve years old when he began working at a radio station in Littlefield as a country-music deejay. At fourteen, Jennings quit school, spent some time picking cotton, and then settled in Lubbock, about forty miles from his hometown. In 1954 Jennings began deejaying again at KLLL in Lubbock. While working at the radio station, he met up-and-coming artist Buddy Holly, who would go on to become an acclaimed rock singer and guitarist. The two became close friends, and Holly asked the nineteen-year-old Jennings to join his band, the Crickets, as bass player. Jennings later admitted that he had been playing the instrument for only a few weeks when he began touring with Holly.

Waylon Jennings. (AP/Wide World Photos)

During the tour, Holly chartered a plane for his bandmates one night in February, 1959. Jennings gave up his seat to J. P. Richardson, also known as the Big Bopper, who was suffering from a cold. That split-second decision affected the rest of Jennings's life. In what became known as "the day the music died," the plane crashed in Iowa, killing Holly, Richardson, and Ritchie Valens (known for his hit "La Bamba"). Jennings harbored guilt over the accident because he had joked to Holly that he hoped his plane would crash.

After he found little success in Texas and Arizona, Jennings moved to Nashville, Tennessee, in the mid-1960's, and he became roommates with Johnny Cash. The two formed a lifelong friendship, cemented at the time by their substance abuse.

In 1965, with the help of Bobby Bare and Chet Atkins, Jennings signed a contract with RCA Records. Jennings appreciated the artistic freedom his producer Atkins allowed him, as opposed to the demands placed by the rest of the country-music industry to look, act, and sing a certain way.

Jennings also found a friend in Willie Nelson, who, like Jennings, stubbornly asserted artistic control against the Nashville establishment. The two quickly became known as "outlaws."

Jennings had been married three times before he was thirty, but in October, 1969, he married country musician Jessi Colter, in a lasting union. The Cash-Jennings relationship is depicted in the motion picture *Walk the Line* (2005), with Jennings and Colter's son Shooter playing Waylon.

Substance abuse problems, particularly his use of cocaine, plagued Jennings throughout the height of his popularity in the 1970's, and it would take until the mid-1980's until he was free from drugs. By 1989 Jennings, who had dropped out of school in the tenth grade, had received his GED, a high school equivalency diploma. He wanted to finish high school to impress upon his ten-year-old son the importance of education. Jennings died from complications related to diabetes on February 13, 2002, in Chandler, Arizona.

The Music

Early Works. While on Holly's Winter Dance Party Tour, Jennings's star as a bassist began to rise, prompting him to form his own band, Jennings and the Waylors, in Phoenix, Arizona, in late 1960 after Holly's tragic death. Three years later, he moved again, to Los Angeles, signing a contract with Herb Alpert's A&M Records. The label wanted him to make a pop album, which Jennings refused to do. His first single, "Sing the Girl a Song, Bill," and his album were failures.

Folk-Country. With this first album from RCA Records, marking his first attempt at the Nashville sound, Jennings began scoring hits in the world of country music, starting with "Stop the World (And Let Me Off)," which made the Top 40. He continued with this success, releasing several albums that featured such hits as "Walk on out of My Mind," "I Got You," "Only Daddy That'll Walk the Line," and "Yours Love"—all Top 10 hits in 1968. After these successes, Jennings was even more determined to do things his way. He was constantly in conflict with the music establishment in Nashville. When he began working with staff producer Danny Davis, after Atkins, Jennings said that he was being bullied, and he pointed a pistol at Davis in the studio.

Wanted! The Outlaws. Jennings's next big move solidified his reputation as an outlaw and helped him to become a mainstream artist. The album *Wanted! The Outlaws* focused on Jennings but his collaborators were Willie Nelson, Tompall Glaser, and Colter. It became the first country record to be certified platinum, and it peaked at number one on the pop charts. *Wanted! The Outlaws* catapulted Jennings into pop music stardom, and it certainly boosted his career as a country musician. Jennings continued his solo success with *Dreaming My Dreams*, which was the first of his many number-one albums. He was also voted Best Male Vocalist of the Year at the Country Music Awards in 1975, and his work with Nelson on *Wanted! The Outlaws* earned them the Country Music Awards Duo of the Year in 1977.

Waylon and Willie. After the success of *Wanted! The Outlaws*, the duo teamed up for *Waylon and Willie*, an album that would link their names for a generation of country fans. The two worked together on many projects throughout the years, but it all started with the crossover hits "Luckenbach, Texas" and "Mammas Don't Let Your Babies Grow up to Be Cowboys"—which won a 1978 Grammy for Best Country Vocal Performance by a Duo or Group.

The Dukes of Hazzard. Throughout the 1980's, Jennings maintained his musical popularity. He had several number-one singles, such as "Amanda," "I Ain't Living Long Like This," "Lucille (You Won't Do Your Daddy's Will)," and "I've Always Been Crazy." Jennings was also a large part of the television comedy *The Dukes of Hazzard*. Jennings wrote and sang the show's theme song, and he did the off-screen narration, which introduced his voice to millions of viewers.

Highwayman. In 1985 Jennings teamed up with friends Nelson, Cash, and Kris Kristofferson to record *Highwayman*. The Columbia Records album went gold, and the title track was a number-one single and a huge hit for all four artists. At the same time, Jennings's solo career underwent a change when he left RCA in 1986 and signed a contract with MCA Nashville Records, in an effort to revitalize his career after kicking his addiction. He had a few number-one singles with MCA, including "Rose in Paradise." Jennings switched labels again in 1990 to Epic Records, where he scored two more Top 40 hits with "Wrong" and "The Eagle."

Closing in on the Fire. Although Jennings continued to work throughout the 1990's, most of his solo work and compilations—including more work with the Highwaymen and Nelson—did not reach the success he had experienced in the 1970's and the 1980's. Jennings was an accomplished performer, and his tours drew huge crowds. In 1996 Jennings released his autobiography, *Waylon*. Throughout the late 1990's, Jennings's work slowed down as his health deteriorated because of heart disease and diabetes. Jennings stopped touring in 1997, but the following year he released the well-received album *Closing in on the Fire*, which featured Travis Tritt, Sting, Sheryl Crow, Mick Jagger, and Colter. This was Jennings's last studio album.

Musical Legacy

A stunningly prolific artist, Jennings released seventy-two albums throughout his career, all while battling the conservative tendencies of the Nashville music establishment. A rebel to the end, Jennings refused to attend the ceremony when he was inducted into the Country Music Hall of Fame in 2001, believing that artists should not compete against each other. In spite of his aversion to awards ceremonies, he received two Grammy Awards, for Best Country Performance by a Duo, and four Country Music Awards, for Album of the Year, Single of the Year, Vocal Duo of the Year, and Male Vocalist of the Year.

Louis R. Carlozo, Laura Burns, and LeeAnn Maton

Further Reading

Allen, Bob. *Waylon and Willie*. New York: Quick Fox, 1979. Allen describes the Jennings-Nelson collaborations and the personalities behind the music.

Denisoff, R. Serge. *Waylon: A Biography*. Knoxville: University of Tennessee Press, 1983. This biography relates Jennings's story from his career beginnings through the peak of his success in the 1980's. Includes rare photographs and a full discography.

Jennings, Waylon, and Lenny Kaye. *Waylon*. New York: Warner Books, 1996. The singer retraces his hardscrabble life and musical career in typical uncompromising fashion.

Mansfield, Brian. "Waylon Jennings Marched to His Own Outlaw Beat." *USA Today*, February 14, 2002. An informative news story on Jennings's death, including a career overview, statistics, and a partial discography.

Smith, John L. *The Waylon Jennings Discography*. Westport, Conn.: Greenwood Press, 1995. This volume covers the singer-songwriter's career in detail, including Jennings's six hundred songs and 850 studio sessions.

See also: Atkins, Chet; Buffett, Jimmy; Cahn, Sammy; Cash, Johnny; Eddy, Duane; Holly, Buddy; Jagger, Sir Mick; Kristofferson, Kris; Nelson, Willie; Sting; Valens, Ritchie.

Joan Jett
American rock singer, songwriter, and guitarist

Jett was a founding member of the Runaways, one of the first all-female rock-and-roll bands. She specialized in combining glam-rock beats, bubblegum hooks, and loud guitars with emotionally naked lyrics sung in a raw, feral voice.

Born: September 22, 1958; Ardmore, Pennsylvania
Also known as: Joan Marie Larkin (birth name)
Member of: The Runaways; Joan Jett and the Blackhearts

Principal recordings

ALBUMS (solo): *Joan Jett*, 1980 (reissued as *Bad Reputation*, 1981); *I Love Playing with Fire*, 1982; *The Hit List*, 1990; *Notorious*, 1991.

ALBUMS (with Joan Jett and the Blackhearts): *I Love Rock 'n' Roll*, 1981; *Album*, 1983; *Glorious Results of a Misspent Youth*, 1984; *Good Music*, 1986; *Up Your Alley*, 1988; *Pure and Simple*, 1994; *Naked*, 2004; *Sinner*, 2006.

ALBUMS (with the Runaways): *The Runaways*, 1976; *Queens of Noise*, 1977; *Waitin' for the Night*, 1977; *And Now . . . the Runaways*, 1978; *Mama Weer All Crazee Now*, 1978.

The Life

While most girls her age were completing high school and entering college, Joan Jett was touring the world and recording for Mercury Records as the rhythm guitarist and occasional lead singer of the

Runaways. Neither she nor the band achieved more than cult status, but the experience prepared her for the solo career that she began in 1980. Jett's first solo album (released in England in 1980 and in the United States in 1981) went largely unnoticed. However, the follow-up, *I Love Rock 'n' Roll* (credited, like Jett's subsequent albums, to Joan Jett and the Blackhearts), sold more than a million copies on the strength of its immensely popular title anthem. While none of the other recordings that Jett released throughout the 1980's generated as much enthusiasm, she and the Blackhearts remained a regular presence on MTV and a popular attraction on the arena touring circuit. In 1987 Jett starred with Michael J. Fox and Gena Rowlands in the film *Light of Day*. During the 1990's, Jett recorded sporadically, focusing more on touring and promoting People for the Ethical Treatment of Animals (PETA), the 2004 presidential candidacy of Howard Dean, the Women's National Basketball Association, abortion rights, and vegetarianism.

The Music

From her teenage beginnings as a member of the Runaways, Jett enjoyed solo success as a hard-rocking woman in rock and roll. Although she wrote or cowrote much of her material, Jett's biggest hits were renditions of songs first recorded by the Arrows ("I Love Rock 'n' Roll"), Tommy James and the Shondells ("Crimson and Clover"), Sly and the Family Stone ("Everyday People"), and Gary Glitter ("Do You Wanna Touch Me?").

Early Works. Jett honed her guitar-playing and singing style on the five albums that she released with the Runaways. Although stylistically limited by the band's youth and inexperience and their manager Kim Fowley's insistence on exploiting their image as leather-clad rebels, the albums helped launch the solo careers of Jett and Lita Ford.

Bad Reputation. Released in England in 1980 as *Joan Jett* and retitled upon its release in the United States one year later, *Bad Reputation* was overshad-

owed at the time of its appearance by the immense popularity of its follow-up, *I Love Rock 'n' Roll*. In retrospect, however, it established the part-originals, part-covers pattern that Jett would follow on her subsequent recordings, and it did so with an enthusiastic and refreshingly defiant indifference to trends that has allowed it to age well. The title song, in particular, has had a long life as a soundtrack staple and an advertising jingle.

I Love Rock 'n' Roll. This best-selling and high-charting album rose to number two on the *Billboard* album chart in 1982, propelled by the instant popularity of its title track. Written and originally recorded by the British band the Arrows, "I Love Rock 'n' Roll" spent seven weeks at number one, and it was the subject of one of Weird Al Yankovic's earliest hit parodies ("I Love Rocky Road"). In the

Joan Jett. (AP/Wide World Photos)

follow-up single, "Crimson and Clover" (another cover), Jett introduced the lesbianism that would become a recurring theme in her music by not changing the object of the singer's affection from "her" to "him."

Up Your Alley. Released in 1988, this million-selling album capitalized on Jett's renewed popularity in the wake of her appearance in the 1987 film *Light of Day*. Although its contents did not differ from what had by then become Jett's formula (the covers: Chuck Berry's "Tulane" and the Stooges' "I Wanna Be Your Dog"), it contained "I Hate Myself for Loving You," another Top 10 hit that in 2007 joined "Bad Reputation" in Jett's catalog of soundtrack appearances when it was rewritten as the theme song for NBC television's *Sunday Night Football* and performed by Faith Hill.

Compilations. *Flashback* (1993), *Fit to Be Tied: Great Hits by Joan Jett and the Blackhearts* (1997), and *Fetish* (1999) comprised the highlights of Jett's discography. *Flashback* included "Light of Day" and live versions of "Bad Reputation" and the Runaways' "Cherry Bomb," but otherwise it consisted of lesser-known material that emphasized Jett's connection to the "riot grrrl" movement. *Fit to Be Tied* contained Jett's best-known singles: a previously unreleased version of her cover of the Modern Lovers' "Roadrunner" and a hard-rocking rendition of *The Mary Tyler Moore Show* theme song that became an anthem of the Women's National Basketball Association, "Love Is All Around." *Fetish* emphasized Jett's raunchier material, earning it an explicit-lyrics warning sticker.

Musical Legacy

When Jett could not persuade record companies to release her first solo album in 1980, she founded Blackheart Records, thus becoming the first woman to start her own record company and establishing herself as an icon of independence. Even when under contract to CBS (in the 1980's) and Warner Bros.

(in the 1990's), her albums bore the Blackheart Records imprint. (The cycle began again in 2006 when major labels passed on Jett's album *Sinner*, making it her first album of new material in twenty-five years to be released exclusively on Blackheart.) Her music both as a Runaway and as a solo artist was frequently cited as an influence and as an inspiration by all-female rock-and-roll bands such as the Go-Go's, the Bangles, and the Donnas and the all-female grunge bands such as L7. Jett's open espousal of various liberal sociopolitical causes made her a heroine to a generation of feminist activists.

Arsenio Orteza

Further Reading

Christgau, Robert. *Christgau's Consumer Guide: Albums of the Nineties*. New York: St. Martin's Griffin, 2000. This guide contains assessments of the compilations *Flashback* and *Fit to Be Tied: Great Hits by Joan Jett and the Blackhearts*.

_____. *Christgau's Record Guide: The Eighties*. New York: Pantheon, 1990. Contains critiques of Jett's 1980's' albums.

Spitz, Mark, and Brendan Mullen. *We Got the Neutron Bomb: The Untold Story of L.A. Punk*. New York: Three Rivers Press, 2001. Includes information on the Runaways' place in the West Coast punk movement.

Stieven-Taylor, Alison. "The Prodigal Daughter." In *Rock Chicks: The Hottest Female Rockers from the 1960's to Now*. Sydney, N.S.W.: Rockpool, 2007. A discussion of Jett in the context of other rock-and-roll women.

Young, Jon. "Joan Jett." *The Rock Yearbook 1983*, edited by Al Clark. New York: St. Martin's Press, 1982. A detailed summary of Jett's career from the Runaways through *I Love Rock 'n' Roll*.

See also: Lang, K. D.; Simmons, Joseph "Run"; Simon, Carly; Slick, Grace.